AS LAW FOR AQA

The Elliott & Quinn Series
for the best start in law

This renowned author team draw on their extensive experience to bring an unbeatable selection of texts that provide total clarity on the core areas of law.

ISBN: 9781405859417

ISBN: 9781405858717

ISBN: 9781405846714

ISBN: 9781405846721

Sourcebooks of carefully selected cases, commentary and articles are also available to accompany books in the series.

The Elliott & Quinn Series is supported by extended companion websites that include regular updates to the law and a range of resources from interactive questions, exam advice and weblinks, for students to use throughout their course.

For further information or to order these books, please visit:
www.pearsoned.co.uk/law

PEARSON
Longman

AS LAW FOR AQA

Catherine Elliott and
Frances Quinn

PEARSON
Longman

Harlow, England • London • New York • Boston • San Francisco • Toronto
Sydney • Tokyo • Singapore • Hong Kong • Seoul • Taipei • New Delhi
Cape Town • Madrid • Mexico City • Amsterdam • Munich • Paris • Milan

Pearson Education Limited

Edinburgh Gate
Harlow
Essex CM20 2JE
England

and Associated Companies throughout the world

Visit us on the World Wide Web at:
www.pearsoned.co.uk

First published 2008

ISBN 978-1-4058-5886-1

British Library Cataloguing-in-Publication Data
A catalogue record for this book is available from the British Library

Library of Congress Cataloging-in-Publication Data
Elliott, Catherine, 1966–
  AS law for AQA / Catherine Elliott and Frances Quinn.
      p. cm.
  Includes bibliographical references and index.
  ISBN-13: 978-1-4058-5886-1 (pbk.)
  1. Justice, Administration of–Great Britain–Problems, exercises, etc. 2. Law–Great
Britain–Sources–Problems, exercises, etc. 3. Law–Great Britain–Examinations–Study guides.
I. Quinn, Frances. II. Title.
  KD663.E447 2008
  347.410076–dc22

                                                    2008014438

10 9 8 7 6 5 4 3 2 1
12 11 10 09 08

Typeset in 9.5/12.5pt Stone Serif by 35
Printed and bound by Ashford Colour Press Ltd. in Gosport

The publisher's policy is to use paper manufactured from sustainable forests.

Brief contents

Unit 1
Law-making and the legal system

Unit 2
The concept of liability

Brief contents

Detailed contents

Unit 2
The concept of liability

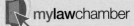

Visit the *AS Law for AQA* mylawchamber site at **www.mylawchamber.co.uk/elliottaqa** to access valuable learning material.

FOR STUDENTS

Do you want to give yourself a head start come exam time?

Companion Website support
- Use the multiple choice questions, quizzes and activities to test yourself on each topic throughout the course
- Use our live weblinks and further reading suggestions to help you read more widely around the subject, and really impress your lecturers.

For more information please contact your local Pearson Education sales representative or visit **www.mylawchamber.co.uk/elliottaqa**

List of figures and tables

Figures

Tables

Guided tour

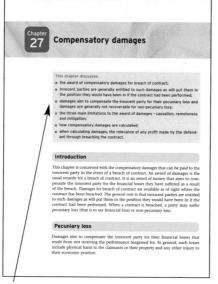

Chapter outlines at the start of each chapter introduce the content of each chapter.

Task boxes provide activities that can be carried out to help you to explore the subject.

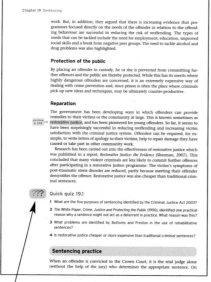

Quick quizzes allow you to test your knowledge and understanding of the law.

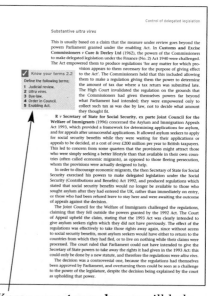

Know your terms boxes will help you to understand and remember technical legal terms.

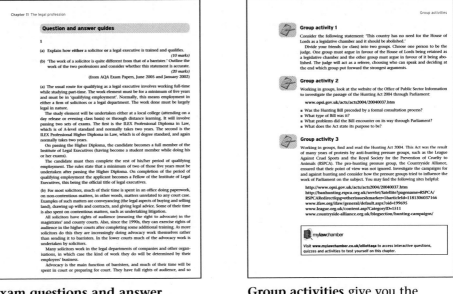

Exam questions and answer guides placed at the end of each chapter aid your exam preparations and provide useful advice on answering exam questions.

Group activities give you the opportunity to compare notes with your fellow students on key issues.

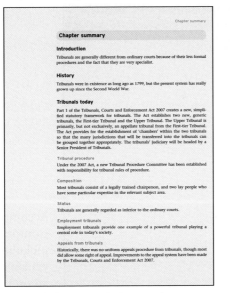

Chapter summaries provide you with an outline of the main topic areas covered in the chapter to ensure that you have covered all the essential points.

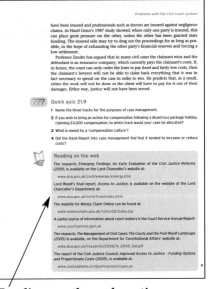

Reading on the web sections direct you to interesting further reading which is available on the internet.

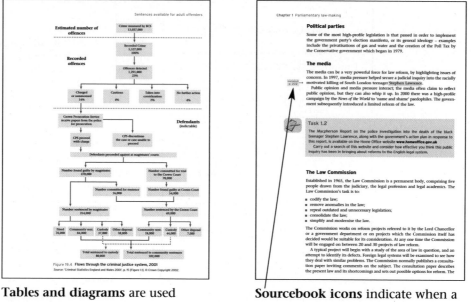

Tables and diagrams are used to highlight complicated legal processes.

Sourcebook icons indicate when a case or document is included in *the English Legal System Sourcebook*, and direct you to the relevant page.

Accompanied by a **Companion Website**, including links to valuable web resources, an online glossary to explain key terms and extra quizzes and exercises.

Preface

This book aims to be both interesting and enjoyable to read while at the same time providing excellent preparation for the AS examinations. It follows very closely the new AS specifications for the AQA examination board, so that students can rely on this book to help them to be fully prepared for their AS assessments. In every subject there is sufficient depth of coverage followed by AQA exam questions (or where these are not available, AQA style exam questions) and answer guidelines to help students get top grades in their examinations. The book builds on the strengths of previous books written by the authors by offering a clear explanation of the law in plain English. It includes certain features to provide extra help and stimulation for the student, including:

- **Chapter outlines** at the start of each chapter, introducing the student to the content of each chapter.
- **Know your terms** boxes to help students understand and remember some of the technical legal vocabulary that they need to know. There is also a detailed glossary at the back of the book.
- **Tasks** providing possible activities that can be carried out easily to help the student explore the subject further.
- **Quick quizzes** at key stages in each chapter, to give students an opportunity to test their knowledge and understanding of the law.
- **Reading on the web** sections at the end of each chapter. These provide references to interesting material that has been referred to in the chapter and which is available free on the internet.
- **Exam questions and answer guidelines** at the end of each chapter to assist students in preparing for their assessments.
- **Chapter summaries** at the end of each chapter providing a quick and easy outline of the material covered.

All the chapters are structured so that the material is in a systematic order for the purposes of both learning and revision, and clear subheadings make specific points easy to locate. There is also an appendix at the end of the book which gives useful general advice on answering exam questions in law.

We would like to thank Peter Blood and Elaine Williams for their invaluable assistance in the preparation of the group exercises and exam question and answers in this book. Peter Blood is a barrister and part-time tutor. He has extensive experience of teaching law and is a regular contributor to student law journals. Elaine Williams is a law lecturer with considerable experience in teaching and examining law.

This book is part of a series that has been written by the same authors. The other books in the series which will be of use to students when they progress to A2 level law and the study of law at university are *Criminal Law*, *Contract Law* and *Tort Law*.

We have endeavoured to state the law as at 1 January 2008.

Catherine Elliott
Frances Quinn
London, 2008

Key skills communication portfolio table

Group Activity	Communication: level 3 – key skill			
	C3.1a	C3.1b	C3.2	C3.3
Chapter 1 Parliamentary law-making	Y	Y	N	N
Chapter 2 Delegated legislation	Y	N	N	N
Chapter 3 Statutory interpretation	Y	N	N	N
Chapter 4 Judicial precedent	Y	N	N	N
Chapter 5 The civil courts	Y	N	N	N
Chapter 6 Tribunals	Y	N	N	N
Chapter 7 Alternative methods of dispute resolution	Y	N	N	N
Chapter 8 Criminal courts	Y	N	N	N
Chapter 9 Magistrates	Y	N	N	N
Chapter 10 The jury	Y	N	N	Y
Chapter 11 The legal profession	Y	N	N	N
Chapter 12 Paying for legal services	Y	N	N	N
Chapter 13 The judges	Y	N	Y	N
Chapter 14 Elements of a crime – *actus reus*	Y	N	Y	Y
Chapter 15 Elements of a crime – *mens rea*	Y	N	N	Y
Chapter 16 Non-fatal offences against the person	Y	N	Y	N
Chapter 17 Strict liability in criminal law	Y	N	Y	N
Chapter 18 Criminal procedure	Y	N	N	N
Chapter 19 Sentencing	Y	N	N	N
Chapter 20 Negligence	Y	N	Y	N
Chapter 21 Civil procedure	Y	N	N	N

Acknowledgements

We are grateful to the following for permission to reproduce copyright material:

Figure 1.1: Front page from *News of the World*, 23 July 2000. Copyright © News Group Newspapers Ltd. Reproduced with permission from NI Syndication; Figure 1.2: Home Office (2001) Criminal Defence Service Act 2001. Crown Copyright © 2001. Crown copyright material is reproduced with the permission of the Controller of Her Majesty's Stationery Office (HMSO) under terms of the click-use; Figure 1.3: Copyright © Brand X Pictures; Figure 1.4: Copyright © Tony Harris / PA Photos; Figure 6.1: Department for Constitutional Affairs (2006) *Judicial Statistics Annual Report 2005*, p. 106. Crown Copyright © 2006. Crown copyright material is reproduced with the permission of the Controller of Her Majesty's Stationery Office (HMSO) under terms of the click-use licence; Figure 8.2: Crown Prosecution Service (2005) *Crown Prosecution Service Annual Report 2004–2005*, p. 38. Crown Copyright © 2005. Crown copyright material is reproduced with the permission of the Controller of Her Majesty's Stationery Office (HMSO) under terms of the click-use licence; Figure 8.3: Home Office (2002) Criminal Statistics England and Wales 2001, p. 16, Figure 1.2. Crown Copyright © 2002. Crown copyright material is reproduced with the permission of the Controller of Her Majesty's Stationery Office (HMSO) under terms of the click-use licence; Figure 8.4: Roy Peters / Roy Peters Photography; Figure 8.5: Department for Constitutional Affairs (2005) *Judicial Statistics Annual Report 2004*, p. 6. Crown Copyright © 2005. Crown copyright material is reproduced with the permission of the Controller of Her Majesty's Stationery Office (HMSO) under terms of the click-use licence; Figure 8.6: Department for Constitutional Affairs (2005) *Judicial Statistics Annual Report 2004*, p. 3. Crown Copyright © 2005. Crown copyright material is reproduced with the permission of the Controller of Her Majesty's Stationery Office (HMSO) under terms of the click-use licence; Figure 9.1: Department for Constitutional Affairs (2005) *Judicial Statistics Annual Report 2004*, p. 128. Crown Copyright © 2005. Crown copyright material is reproduced with the permission of the Controller of Her Majesty's Stationery Office (HMSO) under terms of the click-use licence; Figure 9.3: Crown Prosecution Service (2006) *Crown Prosecution Service Annual Report 2005–2006*, p. 80. Crown Copyright © 2006. Crown copyright material is reproduced with the permission of the Controller of Her Majesty's Stationery Office (HMSO) under terms of the click-use licence; Tables 9.1 and 9.2: Morgan, R. and Russell, N. (2000) The Judiciary in the Magistrates' Courts, Home Office RDS Occasional Paper No. 66. Crown Copyright © 2000. Crown copyright material is reproduced with the permission of the Controller of Her Majesty's Stationery Office (HMSO) under terms of the click-use licence; Figure 10.1: PA Photos; Figure 10.2: PA Photos; Figure 11.1: The Law Society, Fact Sheet 2: Women in the profession (www.lawsociety.org.uk). Reproduced with permission from The Law Society; Figure 11.2: The Honourable Society of Gray's Inn; Figure 11.3:

The Law Society, Fact Sheet 3: Solicitors from minority ethnic groups (www.law-society.org.uk). Reproduced with permission from The Law Society; Figure 11.4: The Law Society of England and Wales. Reproduced with permission from The Law Society; Figure 13.1: Department for Constitutional Affairs (2005) *Judicial Statistics Annual Report 2004*, p. 131. Crown Copyright © 2005. Crown copyright material is reproduced with the permission of the Controller of Her Majesty's Stationery Office (HMSO) under terms of the click-use licence; Figure 16.1: Nicholas, S., Povey, D., Walker, A. and Kershaw, C. (2005) *Crime in England and Wales 2004/2005*, p. 73, Figure 5.1. Home Office. Crown Copyright © 2005. Crown copyright material is reproduced with the permission of the Controller of Her Majesty's Stationery Office (HMSO) under terms of the click-use licence; Table 16.1 and Figure 16.3: Flood-Page, C. and Taylor, J. (eds.) (2003) *Crime in England and Wales 2001/2002: Supplementary Volume*, p. 57, Table 3g, Figure 3.8. Crown Copyright © 2003. Crown copyright material is reproduced with the permission of the Controller of Her Majesty's Stationery Office (HMSO) under terms of the click-use licence; Figure 16.5: Nicholas, S., Povey, D., Walker, A. and Kershaw, C. (2005) 'Adults most at risk of violence', 2004/05 British Crime Survey Interviews, *Crime in England and Wales 2004/2005*, p. 84, Figure 5.7. Crown Copyright © 2005. Crown copyright material is reproduced with the permission of the Controller of Her Majesty's Stationery Office (HMSO) under terms of the click-use licence; Figure 19.1: PA Photos; Figure 19.2: Home Office (2002) *Criminal Statistics England and Wales 2001*, p. 18, Figure 1.3. Crown Copyright © 2002. Crown copyright material is reproduced with the permission of the Controller of Her Majesty's Stationery Office (HMSO) under terms of the click-use licence; Figure 19.3: Home Office (2002) Criminal Statistics England and Wales 2001, p. 81, Figure 7.4. Crown Copyright © 2002. Crown copyright material is reproduced with the permission of the Controller of Her Majesty's Stationery Office (HMSO) under terms of the click-use licence; Figure 19.4: Home Office (2002) *Criminal Statistics England and Wales 2001*, p. 15, Figure 1.1. Crown Copyright © 2002. Crown copyright material is reproduced with the permission of the Controller of Her Majesty's Stationery Office (HMSO) under terms of the click-use licence; Figure 21.1: Department for Constitutional Affairs (2006) *Judicial Statistics Annual Report 2005*, p. 44. Crown Copyright © 2006. Crown copyright material is reproduced with the permission of the Controller of Her Majesty's Stationery Office (HMSO) under terms of the click-use licence; Figure 21.2 © Crown Copyright; Figures 21.3, 21.4, 21.5, 21.6 and 21.7: Department for Constitutional Affairs (2002) Further Findings: a continuing evaluation of the Civil Justice Reforms, August 2002, Figure 12, Figure 1, Figure 2, Figure 6 and Figure 10. Crown Copyright © 2002. Crown copyright material is reproduced with the permission of the Controller of Her Majesty's Stationery Office (HMSO) under terms of the click-use licence.

We would also like to thank The Assessment and Qualification Alliance for the use of AQA examination questions. Note: Where worked solutions to, and/or commentaries on AQA questions or possible answers are provided it is the author of this title who is responsible for them; they (a) have neither been provided or approved by AQA and (b) do not necessarily constitute the only possible solutions.

In some instances we have been unable to trace the owners of copyright material, and we would appreciate any information that would enable us to do so.

Table of cases

Table of legislation

Table of statutory instruments

Unit 1

LAW-MAKING AND THE LEGAL SYSTEM

Note that for Unit 1 the exam paper contains eight questions and you have to answer three. Each question is divided into three parts a, b and c and you have to answer all three parts to each question. The exam specifications have grouped topics together which are reflected in the eight parts in this book for this Unit. It is likely that the exam questions will reflect the way the specifications have grouped topics together. For example, the specifications group together the legal profession and funding of legal advice (Part 7 of this book). Therefore, if you revise the legal professions, you would be sensible to also revise legal funding as parts a and b of a question might be on the legal profession but part c might be on funding. If you have only revised the legal profession and not funding then you will not be able to answer the whole question.

The questions for Unit 2 do not appear to be grouped in the same way, so the division into parts is not so important for Unit 2.

Section A
LAW-MAKING

English law stems from three main sources, though these vary a great deal in importance. The basis of our law today is case law, a mass of judge-made decisions which lay down rules to be followed in future court cases. For many centuries it was the main form of law and it is still very important today. However, the most important source of law, in the sense that it prevails over most of the others, are Acts of Parliament. Delegated legislation is made by the administration rather than the legislature, and tends to lay down detailed rules to implement the broader provisions of Acts of Parliament. In addition, the judges sometimes have to interpret this legislation to determine its application to cases before the court. Thus this section looks at:

- parliamentary law-making;
- delegated legislation;
- statutory interpretation; and
- judicial precedent.

Part 1
PARLIAMENTARY LAW-MAKING

Parliamentary law-making

This chapter discusses:

● the influences on Parliament;

● making an Act of Parliament;

● the supremacy of Parliament;

● the advantages and disadvantages of parliamentary law-making.

Introduction

The most important laws in the UK are made by Parliament. These laws are known as Acts of Parliament or statutes. Parliament is the democratically elected governing body for the nation. It consists of the House of Commons, the House of Lords and the monarch (currently Queen Elizabeth). A lengthy process of informal and formal debate needs to be carried out before an Act of Parliament becomes law. The informal process starts outside Parliament, when different organisations and people try to influence the government to decide what new laws are needed in the country to tackle a particular problem. For example, a newspaper might publish headlines suggesting that new offences should be created to tackle the problem of drug abuse. The government might accept this and commence a formal legislative process through Parliament to pass an Act of Parliament creating new drug offences. Thus, this chapter will start by looking at the external influences on Parliament which help to decide which new laws are made by Parliament. We will then go on to look at the formal process of making an Act of Parliament. We will consider the doctrine of the supremacy of Parliament, which is the principle that Parliament is supreme and can therefore make or unmake any law it chooses. The chapter concludes with a review of the advantages and disadvantages of the parliamentary law-making process.

Influences on Parliament

An effective legal system cannot stand still. Both legal procedures and the law itself must adapt to social change if they are to retain the respect of at least most of society, without which they cannot survive. Different organisations and people try to influence Parliament to make changes to the law. These include:

- pressure groups;
- political parties;
- the media; and
- the Law Commission.

Each of these will be considered in turn.

Pressure groups

Groups concerned with particular subjects may press for law reform in those areas – examples include charities such as Shelter, Help the Aged and the Child Poverty Action Group; professional organisations such as the Law Society and the British Medical Association; business representatives such as the Confederation of British Industry. Justice is a pressure group specifically concerned with promoting law reform in general.

Task 1.1

The following organisations are examples of influential pressure groups:

The Campaign for Nuclear Disarmament: www.cnduk.org/

Greenpeace: www.greenpeace.org/international/

Shelter: www.shelter.org.uk/

Select the website of one of them and consider the ways in which they are trying to influence Parliament in this country.

Pressure groups use a variety of tactics, including lobbying MPs, gaining as much publicity as possible for their cause, organising petitions and encouraging people to write to their own MP and/or relevant ministers. Some groups are more effective than others: size obviously helps, but sheer persistence and a knack for grabbing headlines can be just as productive – the anti-porn campaigner Mary Whitehouse almost single-handedly pressurised the government into creating the Protection of Children Act 1978, which sought to prevent child pornography. The amount of power wielded by the members of a pressure group is also extremely important – organisations involved with big business tend to be particularly effective in influencing legislation, and there is a growing industry set up purely to help them lobby effectively, for a price. At the same time, pressure groups made up of ordinary individuals can be very successful, particularly if the issue on which they are campaigning is one which stirs up strong emotion in the general public. An example is the Snowdrop Petition, organised after the shooting of 16 young children and their teacher in Dunblane, Scotland. Despite enormous opposition from shooting clubs, it managed to persuade the previous government to ban most types of handguns.

Political parties

Some of the most high-profile legislation is that passed in order to implement the government party's election manifesto, or its general ideology – examples include the privatisations of gas and water and the creation of the Poll Tax by the Conservative government which began in 1979.

The media

The media can be a very powerful force for law reform, by highlighting issues of concern. In 1997, media pressure helped secure a judicial inquiry into the racially motivated killing of South London teenager Stephen Lawrence.

sourcebook p. 202 →

Public opinion and media pressure interact; the media often claim to reflect public opinion, but they can also whip it up. In 2000 there was a high-profile campaign by the *News of the World* to 'name and shame' paedophiles. The government subsequently introduced a limited reform of the law.

Task 1.2

The Macpherson Report on the police investigation into the death of the black teenager Stephen Lawrence, along with the government's action plan in response to this report, is available on the Home Office website **www.homeoffice.gov.uk**

Carry out a search of this website and consider how effective you think this public inquiry has been in bringing about reforms to the English legal system.

The Law Commission

Established in 1965, the Law Commission is a permanent body, comprising five people drawn from the judiciary, the legal profession and legal academics. The Law Commission's task is to:

- codify the law;
- remove anomalies in the law;
- repeal outdated and unnecessary legislation;
- consolidate the law;
- simplify and modernise the law.

The Commission works on reform projects referred to it by the Lord Chancellor or a government department or on projects which the Commission itself has decided would be suitable for its consideration. At any one time the Commission will be engaged on between 20 and 30 projects of law reform.

A typical project will begin with a study of the area of law in question, and an attempt to identify its defects. Foreign legal systems will be examined to see how they deal with similar problems. The Commission normally publishes a consultation paper inviting comments on the subject. The consultation paper describes the present law and its shortcomings and sets out possible options for reform. The

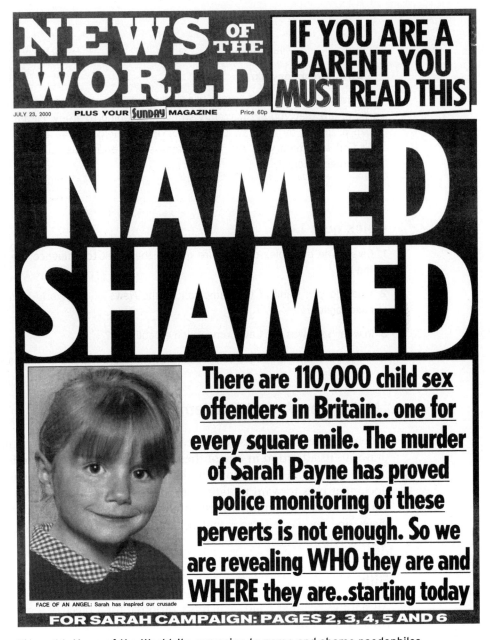

Figure 1.1 *News of the World*: its campaign to name and shame paedophiles

Source: Front page from *News of the World*, London, 23 July 2000. Copyright © News Group Newspapers Ltd. Reproduced with permission from NI Syndication.

Commission's final recommendations are set out in a report which contains a draft Bill where legislation is proposed. It is then essentially for the government to decide whether it accepts the recommendations and to introduce any necessary Bill in Parliament.

Task 1.3

Visit the Law Commission's website at:

www.lawcom.gov.uk/

The work it undertakes is grouped together according to the area of law. Choose an area of law that you are currently studying or going to study. Find a report that has been prepared by the Law Commission in this field. At the end of the report you will find a summary of the Law Commission's proposals. Summarise three of its recommendations.

Quick quiz 1.4

1 Give three examples of pressure groups that seek to influence the development of the law.

2 What do you think of the campaign by the *News* of the *World* to name and shame paedophiles?

3 In what year was the Law Commission established?

4 Is the government obliged to pass legislation recommended by the Law Commission?

Making an Act of Parliament

When a government has identified a policy objective, which may have been drawn to its attention in one of the ways described above, then it may choose to include this in an official consultation document, known as a Green Paper. This document puts forward tentative proposals for reform, often through the use of parliamentary legislation, which interested parties may consider and give their views on. The Green Paper will be followed by a White Paper containing the specific reform plans.

Bills

All statutes begin as a Bill, which is a proposal for a piece of legislation. There are three types of Bill:

1 **Public Bills.** These are presented to Parliament by government ministers and change the general law of the whole country. They are written by lawyers known as parliamentary counsel, who specialise in drafting legislation.

2 **Private members' Bills.** These are prepared by an individual backbench MP (someone who is not a member of the Cabinet). MPs wanting to put forward a Bill have to enter a ballot to win the right to do so, and then persuade the government to allow enough parliamentary time for the Bill to go through. Consequently, very few such Bills become Acts, and they tend to function more as a way of drawing attention to particular issues. Some, however, have made

ELIZABETH II   c. 4

Criminal Defence Service (Advice and Assistance) Act 2001

2001 CHAPTER 4

An Act to clarify the extent of the duty of the Legal Services Commission under section 13(1) of the Access to Justice Act 1999.   [10th April 2001]

B E IT ENACTED by the Queen's most Excellent Majesty, by and with the advice and consent of the Lords Spiritual and Temporal, and Commons, in this present Parliament assembled, and by the authority of the same, as follows:—

1   Extent of duty to fund advice and assistance

   (1) Subsection (1) of section 13 of the Access to Justice Act 1999 (c. 22) (duty of Legal Services Commission to fund advice and assistance as part of Criminal Defence Service) shall be treated as having been enacted with the substitution of the following for paragraph (b) and the words after it—

        "(b) in prescribed circumstances, for individuals who—

           (i) are not within paragraph (a) but are involved in investigations which may lead to criminal proceedings,

          (ii) are before a court or other body in such proceedings, or

         (iii) have been the subject of such proceedings;

      and the assistance which the Commission may consider appropriate includes assistance in the form of advocacy."

   (2) Regulations under subsection (1) of section 13 (as amended above) may include provision treating them as having come into force at the same time as that subsection.

2   Short title

      This Act may be cited as the Criminal Defence Service (Advice and Assistance) Act 2001.

© Crown copyright 2001

Printed in the UK by The Stationery Office Limited
under the authority and superintendence of Carol Tullo, Controller of
Her Majesty's Stationery Office and Queen's Printer of Acts of Parliament

Figure 1.2 **Criminal Defence Service (Advice and Assistance) Act 2001**
Source: The Stationery Office. © Crown Copyright 2001.

important contributions to legislation, an example being the Abortion Act 1967, which stemmed from a private member's Bill put forward by David Steel.

3 **Private Bills.** These are usually proposed by a local authority, public corporation or large public company, and normally affect only that sponsor. An example might be a local authority seeking the right to build a bridge or road.

The actual preparation of Bills is done by expert draftsmen known as Parliamentary Counsel.

Task 1.5

Public Bills that are currently being considered by Parliament are available at:

www.parliament.the-stationery-office.co.uk/pa/pabills.htm

Visit this website and find a public Bill that is before Parliament.

First reading

The title of the prepared Bill is read to the House of Commons. This is called the first reading, and acts as a notification of the proposed measure.

Second reading

At the second reading, the proposals are debated fully, and may be amended, and members vote on whether the legislation should proceed. In practice, the whip system (party officials whose job is to make sure MPs vote with their party) means that a government with a reasonable majority can almost always get its legislation through at this and subsequent stages.

Committee stage

The Bill is then referred to a committee of the House of Commons for detailed examination, bearing in mind the points made during the debate. At this point, further amendments to the Bill may be made.

Report stage

The committee then reports back to the House, and any proposed amendments are debated and voted upon.

Third reading

The Bill is re-presented to the House. There may be a short debate, and a vote on whether to accept or reject the legislation as it stands.

House of Lords

The Bill then goes to the House of Lords, where it goes through a similar process of three readings. If the House of Lords alters anything, the Bill returns to the Commons for further consideration. The Commons then responds with agreement, reasons for disagreement, or proposals for alternative changes.

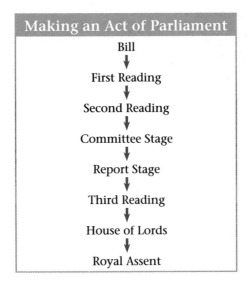

At one time, legislation could not be passed without the agreement of both Houses, which meant that the unelected House of Lords could block legislation put forward by the elected House of Commons. The Parliament Acts of 1911 and 1949 lay down special procedures by which proposed legislation can go for Royal Assent without the approval of the House of Lords after specified periods of time. These procedures are only rarely used, because the House of Lords usually drops objections that are resisted by the Commons, though their use has increased in recent years. Only four Acts of Parliament have been passed to date relying on the Parliament Act 1949. It is of particular note that the procedures were used to pass the controversial Hunting Act 2004. This Act bans hunting wild animals with dogs and a form of hunting known as hare coursing. It was passed despite the House of Lords' opposition, by using the Parliament Act 1949.

Task 1.6

Recent legislation is published on The Stationery Office website. Visit this site at:

www.opsi.gov.uk/acts.htm

Find s. 46 of the Criminal Justice and Court Services Act 2000. What is the definition of an exclusion order?

Explanatory notes provide guidance as to the implications of new legislation. These are available at:

www.opsi.gov.uk/legislation/uk-expa.htm

Find the explanatory notes that accompany the Criminal Justice and Court Services Act 2000. What guidance is given in relation to s. 46?

Royal Assent

In the vast majority of cases, agreement between the Lords and Commons is reached, and the Bill is then presented for Royal Assent. Technically, the Queen must give her consent to all legislation before it can become law, but in practice that consent is never refused.

The Bill is then an Act of Parliament, and becomes law, though most do not take effect from the moment the Queen gives her consent, but on a specified date in the near future or when a commencement order has been issued by a government minister. Acts of Parliament are referred to by their short title and the year in which they were passed, for example, the Police and Criminal Evidence Act 1984.

Quick quiz 1.7

Put the following events into chronological order for the ordinary process of passing a public Bill:

- Second reading in the House of Commons
- Royal Assent
- House of Lords considers the Public Bill
- Public Bill drafted
- First reading in the House of Commons
- Report stage
- Green Paper
- Committee stage in the House of Commons
- Third reading.

The supremacy of Parliament

✓ Know your terms 1.8

Define the following terms:

1 Hereditary peer.
2 Royal Assent.
3 Public Bill.

The supremacy of Parliament (also known as the 'sovereignty of Parliament') is a fundamental principle of our constitution. This means that Parliament is the highest source of English law; so long as a law has been passed according to the rules of parliamentary procedure, it must be applied by the courts. So if, for example, Parliament had passed a law stating that all newborn boys had to be killed, or that all dog owners had to keep a cat as well, there might well be an enormous public outcry, but the laws would still be valid and the courts would, in theory at least, be obliged to uphold them. The reasoning behind this approach is that Parliament, unlike the judiciary, is democratically elected, and therefore ought to have the upper hand when making the laws that every citizen has to live by.

This approach is unusual in democratic countries. Most comparable nations have what is known as a Bill of Rights. This is a statement of the basic rights which citizens can expect to have protected from state interference and takes precedence over other laws. The courts are able to refuse to apply legislation which infringes any of the rights protected by it.

Britain does not have a Bill of Rights but, under the Human Rights Act 1998, the European Convention on Human Rights has been incorporated into domestic law. The Act does not give the Convention superiority over English law, however.

Figure 1.3 **Houses of Parliament**
Source: Copyright © Brand X Pictures

It requires that, wherever possible, legislation should be interpreted in line with the principles of the Convention, but it does not allow the courts to override statutes that are incompatible with it, nor does it prevent Parliament from making laws that are in conflict with it.

Section 19 of the Act requires that when new legislation is made, a government minister must make a statement before the second reading of the Bill in either House of Parliament, saying either that in their view the provisions of the Bill are compatible with the Convention, or that even if they are not, the government wishes to proceed with the Bill anyway. Although the implication is obviously that, in most cases, ministers will be able to say that a Bill conforms with the Convention, the Act's provision for the alternative statement confirms that parliamentary supremacy is not intended to be overridden. The Act does make one impact on parliamentary supremacy, though a small one: s. 10 allows a minister of the Crown to amend by order any Act which has been found by the courts to be incompatible with the Convention, whereas normally an Act of Parliament could only be changed by another Act. However, there is no obligation to do this and a piece of legislation which has been found to be incompatible with the Convention would remain valid if the government chose not to amend it.

By contrast, a definite erosion of parliamentary supremacy has been brought about by Britain's membership of the European Union. The EU can only make laws concerning particular subject areas, but in those areas, its law must take precedence over laws made by Parliament, and in this respect Parliament is no longer strictly speaking the supreme source of law in the UK. In areas of law not covered by the EU, however, Parliament remains supreme.

In 1998 some important constitutional changes were made, which passed some of the powers of the Westminster Parliament to new bodies in Scotland and Northern Ireland. The new Scottish Parliament, created by the Scotland Act 1998, can make laws affecting Scotland only, in many important areas, including health, education, local government, criminal justice, food standards and agriculture, though legislation on foreign affairs, defence, national security, trade and industry and a number of other areas will still be made for the whole of the UK by the Westminster Parliament. The Northern Ireland Act 1998 similarly gives the Northern Ireland Assembly power to make legislation for Northern Ireland in some areas, though again, foreign policy, defence and certain other areas are still to be covered by Westminster.

In the same year, the Government of Wales Act established a new body for Wales, the Welsh Assembly, but unlike the other two bodies, the Welsh Assembly does not have the power to make primary legislation; legislation made in Westminster will continue to cover Wales. However, the Welsh Assembly is able to make what is called delegated legislation (discussed in Chapter 2).

Advantages of parliamentary law-making

Democratic process

A key advantage of the parliamentary process is that the House of Commons has been democratically elected and therefore the legislation that it issues should reflect the will of the majority of the general public.

Open debate

The legislative process takes place in public and there is an opportunity through the consultative processes for the public to directly influence the content of the legislation.

Disadvantages of parliamentary law-making

The House of Lords

Membership of the House of Lords is currently in transition. Historically, this body has not been elected and therefore has not been democratic. The Labour government has reduced the role of people who sat in the House of Lords simply because of who their parents were (known as hereditary peers) and in the future the intention is that at least some of its members will be elected.

Figure 1.4 **Scene outside the Lawrence Inquiry, Elephant and Castle, London**
Source: Photograph © Tony Harris/PA Photos.

Limited time

The parliamentary process is relatively slow and sometimes people would accept that law reform is necessary but no time is available for Parliament to pass the legislation. This has been particularly frustrating for the Law Commission, which has produced lengthy and well-argued documents arguing for a specific law reform and while the government accepts that such a reform is necessary, no parliamentary time is made available to push through this reform.

Task 1.9

Read the following article and then answer the questions that follow:

Many of the measures announced by Tony Blair to tackle terrorism in the wake of the London suicide bombings could and should have been taken long ago. Announcing plans for new legislation and more extensive use of existing powers to deport those who advocate terrorism, the Prime Minister twice said 'the rules of the game' are changing. By this, he seemed to mean the 'rules' within international human rights law and the Human Rights Act needed changing. That impression was strengthened when the Lord Chancellor, Lord Falconer, warned that British judges might have to be instructed by Act of Parliament on how to interpret and apply Article 3 of the European Convention on Human Rights (prohibiting torture) more restrictively than the European Court of Human Rights.

   Our courts need no instruction from government or parliament about how to interpret and apply the Human Rights Act. Contrary to the intemperate and ignorant attacks on the judiciary by Michael Howard, they have not been guilty of 'aggressive ▶

judicial activism', 'thwarting the will of parliament'. Our courts are in a weaker position than those of the rest of Europe and the common-law world. In deference to parliamentary sovereignty, they cannot strike down Acts of Parliament, but can only give declarations of incompatibility, leaving it to ministers and parliament to decide what to do. British courts have interpreted and applied the Human Rights Act wisely, without encroaching on the executive and legislative branches of government.

Source: Adapted from an article by Anthony Lester in *The Observer*, 14 August 2005.

1 Why is Art. 3 of the European Convention important?
2 Who is Michael Howard?
3 Why are our judges in a weaker position than their European counterparts?
4 Who do you think should have the most power, the judges or Parliament?

Reading on the web

Copies of Public Bills currently being considered by Parliament can be found at:

www.parliament.uk/business/bills_and_legislation.cfm

Copies of recent legislation can be found at:

www.opsi.gov.uk/acts.htm

Useful explanatory notes prepared by the government to explain the implications of recent legislation can be found at:

www.opsi.gov.uk/legislation/uk-expa.htm

John Halliday has produced a report on the work of the Law Commission which has been published on the internet at:

www.dca.gov.uk/majrep/lawcom/halliday.htm

The Law Commission's website is:

www.lawcom.gov.uk/

Chapter summary

Introduction

The most important laws in the UK are made by Parliament.

Influences on Parliament

Different organisations and people try to influence Parliament to make changes to the law. These include:

- pressure groups;
- political parties;
- the media; and
- the Law Commission.

Making an Act of Parliament

All statutes begin as a Bill. There are three types of Bill:

- Public Bills;
- Private members' Bills;
- Private Bills.

The legislative process usually starts in the House of Commons and proceeds as follows:

- First reading
- Second reading
- Committee stage
- Report stage
- Third reading
- House of Lords
- Royal Assent.

Role of the House of Lords

The Parliament Acts of 1911 and 1949 lay down special procedures by which proposed legislation can go for Royal Assent without the approval of the House of Lords after specified periods of time. These procedures are only rarely used, because the House of Lords usually drops objections that are resisted by the Commons, though their use has increased in recent years.

The supremacy of Parliament

This means that Parliament is the highest source of English law, and statutes must be applied by the courts. Britain does not have a Bill of Rights which could restrict Parliament's powers to make laws. The Human Rights Act 1998 incorporated the European Convention on Human Rights but this does not give the Convention superiority over English law. Statutes which breach the Convention must still be applied by the courts.

One limit on parliamentary supremacy is now European law. As part of a process of devolution, Parliament has chosen to give legislative powers to the Scottish Parliament and the Northern Ireland Assembly. In theory, Parliament could take back these legislative powers and therefore remains supreme.

Advantages of parliamentary law-making

Parliament provides:

- a democratic process; and
- an opportunity for open debate.

Disadvantages of parliamentary law-making

■ There are problems with the House of Lords; and
■ Parliament only has limited time.

Question and answer guides

1

(a) Explain what is meant by the doctrine of parliamentary supremacy and briefly explain **one** limitation on this doctrine. *(10 marks)*

(b) Briefly explain the roles of the House of Commons, House of Lords and the monarch in the formal process of statute law creation. *(10 marks)*

(c) Discuss the advantages of the process of law making in Parliament.

(10 marks)

(from AQA Specimen Question Paper, 2007)

Here is a good, potentially A-grade answer to this question. Please note that this is not the only answer that could be written to this question and you are unlikely to get exactly the same question in your exam. So you need to practice developing your own skills in answering questions, in consultation with your teacher. You may want to attempt the question first, and then compare your answer with this one. This advice is not repeated in later chapters but applies to all questions in the book.

(a) The doctrine of parliamentary supremacy states that Parliament is the highest source of English law. So long as a law has been through the legislative process, it must be applied by the courts, regardless of what the courts might think about it. The reasoning behind this approach is that Parliament, unlike the judiciary, is democratically elected, and therefore ought to have the upper hand when making the laws that citizens have to live by.

One limitation on parliamentary supremacy is the Human Rights Act 1998. This Act incorporates the European Convention on Human Rights into domestic law, and requires the courts to interpret legislation as far as possible so as to keep it in line with the Convention's principles (s. 3(1) of the Human Rights Act 1998, discussed at p. 47). But if a court feels unable to place a compatible interpretation on a statute, it is not allowed to declare the statute invalid. All it can do is make a declaration of incompatibility, leaving it to Parliament to decide whether to rectify the position.

The Human Rights Act does not even prevent Parliament from passing Acts that are explicitly in conflict with the Convention. But if it does so then a Government Minister must formally acknowledge the conflict. Under s. 19 of the 1998 Act.

(Instead of the Human Rights Act, another limitation on parliamentary supremacy that you might discuss is the Scotland Act 1998.)

(b) The formal process of statute creation begins with a Bill receiving its first reading in the House of Commons. This involves the title being read to the House. The Bill then moves on to its second reading, at which it is debated, and members vote on whether it should proceed. The next stage is the committee stage, involving an examination of the Bill by a committee of the House. Next comes the report stage, when the committee reports back to the House, and any proposed amendments are voted upon. Finally there is the third reading, when the Bill is re-presented to the House and a vote taken on whether to accept it as it stands.

Assuming the Bill passes all its Commons stages, it then goes to the House of Lords, where it goes through a similar process. If the Lords alters anything, the Bill returns to the Commons for further consideration.

Once agreement between the Houses is reached, the Bill is presented for Royal Assent by the Monarch.

The Parliament Acts 1911 and 1949 lay down special procedures by which Bills can go for Royal Assent without the Lords' approval, after specified periods of time. To date there have been only four occasions when Acts have been passed relying on these procedures. The most recent was the Hunting Act 2004.

(c) One advantage of the process of law making in Parliament is that the House of Commons has been democratically elected and therefore the legislation that it issues should reflect the will of the majority of the general public.

Another advantage is that the legislative process takes place in public and provides an opportunity for the public to directly influence the content of new legislation.

It can also be argued that the legislative process provides many opportunities for Bills to be amended, thus hopefully ensuring that statutes do not contain too many mistakes. Often it is the Government itself that tables these amendments, in recognition of defects brought to its attention during the various legislative stages.

The scrutinising role of the House of Lords could also be said to be an advantage, with its discussions less dominated by party politics than in the Commons, enabling Bills to be considered in a more measured way. Despite a few well-publicised instances when the Commons and the Lords have fallen out, most of the time Lords' amendments to Bills are accepted by the Commons.

Finally, it can be argued that the legislative process commands a large measure of public support, so that even unpopular laws are obeyed, out of respect for the process by which they have been made.

2

(a) Outline **three** influences on Parliament as a law maker.   (*15 marks*)
(b) Identify and discuss **one disadvantage** of **each** of the **three** influences on the law-making process that you have outlined in your answer to question (a).

(*15 marks*)

(from AQA Exam Paper, June 2007)

Here is a possible outline plan of what you should include in a good answer to this question. You may want to try making your own plan first, and then compare your plan with this one. Don't worry if you don't get all the points; seeing what you have missed out will help you to remember the topic and tell you what you need to look at again. This advice is not repeated in later chapters but applies to all questions in the book.

(a)
Law Commission

- Describe its role and key features.
- Describe how it handles a typical project.
- For a good answer, give an example of how the Law Commission has influenced Parliament.

Pressure groups

- Give examples of pressure groups, drawn from a range of sectors.
- Give examples of the types of tactics pressure groups use.
- For a good answer, give an example of how pressure groups have influenced Parliament.

Media

- Mention the media's role in highlighting issues of concern.
- Mention how public opinion and media pressure interact.
- For a good answer, give an example of how the media has influenced Parliament.

(b)
Law Commission

- Refer to the Law Commission's declining success rate and the consequent 'implementation problem'.
- For a good answer, discuss who is to blame for this.

Pressure groups

- Refer to pressure groups' unrepresentative nature.
- Consider whether, if their influence is too great, it undermines the democratic process.
- For a good answer, suggest a case where pressure groups arguably exerted too much influence over Parliament.

Media

- Refer to the danger of the media whipping up public opinion.
- Refer to doubts over the media's motives for doing this.
- For a good answer, suggest a case where the media arguably exerted too much influence over Parliament.

Common errors in (a)

- including material that should be in (b);
- spending too much time on one influence.

Common errors in (b)

- writing about advantages instead of disadvantages;
- failing to adopt a balanced stance.

Group activity 1

Consider the following statement: 'This country has no need for the House of Lords as a legislative chamber and it should be abolished.'

Divide your friends (or class) into two groups. Choose one person to be the judge. One group must argue in favour of the House of Lords being retained as a legislative chamber and the other group must argue in favour of it being abolished. The judge will act as a referee, choosing who can speak and deciding at the end which group put forward the strongest arguments.

Group activity 2

Working in groups, look at the website of the Office of Public Sector Information to investigate the passage of the Hunting Act 2004 through Parliament:

www.opsi.gov.uk/acts/acts2004/20040037.htm

- Was the Hunting Bill preceded by a formal consultation process?
- What type of Bill was it?
- What problems did the Bill encounter on its way through Parliament?
- What does the Act state its purpose to be?

Group activity 3

Working in groups, find and read the Hunting Act 2004. This Act was the result of many years of protests by anti-hunting pressure groups, such as the League Against Cruel Sports and the Royal Society for the Prevention of Cruelty to Animals (RSPCA). The pro-hunting pressure group, the Countryside Alliance, ensured that their point of view was not ignored. Investigate the campaigns for and against hunting and consider how the pressure groups tried to influence the work of Parliament on the subject. You may find the following sites helpful:

http://www.opsi.gov.uk/acts/acts2004/20040037.htm
http://banhunting.rspca.org.uk/servlet/Satellite?pagename=RSPCA/
RSPCARedirect&pg=otherissues&marker=1&articleId=1181306037166
www.ifaw.org/ifaw/general/default.aspx?oid=199695
www.league.org.uk/content.asp?CategoryID=1511
www.countryside-alliance.org.uk/blogsection/hunting-campaigns/

mylawchamber

Visit **www.mylawchamber.co.uk/elliottaqa** to access interactive questions, quizzes and activities to test yourself on this chapter.

Part 2
DELEGATED LEGISLATION

Chapter 2

Delegated legislation

This chapter explains:

- the three forms of delegated legislation;
- why delegated legislation is necessary;
- how delegated legislation is controlled;
- criticism made of delegated legislation.

Introduction

In many cases, the statutes passed by Parliament lay down a basic framework of the law, with creation of the detailed rules delegated to government departments, local authorities, or public or nationalised bodies. There are three main forms of delegated legislation:

Statutory instruments

These are made by government departments.

Bye-laws

These are made by local authorities, public and nationalised bodies. Bye-laws have to be approved by central government.

Orders in Council

These are issued by the government in times of emergency. They are drafted by the relevant government department, approved by the Privy Council and signed by the Queen.

On an everyday basis, delegated legislation is an extremely important source of law. The output of delegated legislation far exceeds that of Acts of Parliament, and its provisions include rules that can substantially affect the day-to-day lives of huge numbers of people – safety laws for industry, road traffic regulations, and rules relating to state education, for example.

The power to make delegated legislation

Ordinary members of the public cannot decide on a whim to make delegated legislation. Instead, usually an Act of Parliament is required, known as an enabling Act, which gives this power to a branch of the state. The Act can be quite specific giving a limited power to make legislation on a very narrow issue, or it can be very general and allow for a wide range of delegated legislation to be made. An example of such a general provision is the European Communities Act 1972, s. 2, which allows the executive to make delegated legislation to bring into force in the UK relevant European legislation.

sourcebook p. 35 →

Parliament has recently passed an Act which gives the executive very wide powers to make delegated legislation, the Legislative and Regulatory Reform Act 2006. This Act was introduced following a report of the Better Regulation Task Force, *Regulation-Less is More* (2005). The official aim of the Act is to make it simpler and faster to amend existing legislation. It allows ministers to issue statutory instruments to amend existing legislation or implement recommendations of the Law Commission (with the possibility of some changes being added by the government). No vote in Parliament is required, though the statutory instrument can be blocked by a new parliamentary committee. The first draft of the Bill was severely criticised by a panel of MPs for giving excessive powers to make delegated legislation which were disproportionate to the Bill's stated aims. In the light of these criticisms, some amendments were made, but concerns remain that this is an unnecessary shift of power from a democratically elected Parliament, to the executive. The director of the pressure group, Justice, has commented:

'In its original form, the Bill went well beyond what the government says it wanted and was one of the most appallingly drafted Bills I've ever seen. It was just amazingly wide. Either that was the government's intention, in which case they really were trying to accumulate a major increase in power, or it wasn't, in which case it's pretty incompetent.'

Task 2.1

Statutory instruments are published on the website for the Office of Public Sector Information at:

www.opsi.gov.uk/stat.htm

Go to this website and find the Data Protection Act 1998 (Commencement) Order 2000 (SI 2000/183). This statutory instrument brought the main provisions of the Data Protection Act 1998 into force.

1 Under which legislative provisions was this piece of delegated legislation made?
2 On what date did these provisions come into force?

Why is delegated legislation necessary?

Delegated legislation is necessary for a number of reasons.

Insufficient parliamentary time

Parliament does not have the time to debate every detailed rule necessary for efficient government.

Speed

It allows rules to be made more quickly than they could by Parliament. Parliament does not sit all the time, and its procedure is slow and cumbersome. Delegated legislation often has to be made in response to emergencies and urgent problems.

Technicality of the subject matter

Modern legislation often needs to include detailed, technical provisions – those in building regulations or safety at work rules, for example. MPs do not usually have the technical knowledge required, whereas delegated legislation can use experts who are familiar with the relevant areas.

Need for local knowledge

Local bye-laws, in particular, can only be made effectively with awareness of the locality. Recognition of the importance of local knowledge can be found with the new devolved assemblies for Scotland, Wales and Northern Ireland. These new democratic bodies have important powers to make delegated legislation.

Flexibility

Statutes require cumbersome procedures for enactment, and can only be revoked or amended by another statute. Delegated legislation, however, can be put into action quickly, and be easily revoked if it proves problematic.

Future needs

Parliament cannot hope to foresee every problem that might arise as a result of a statute, especially concerning areas such as health provision or welfare benefits. Delegated legislation can be put in place as and when such problems arise.

Control of delegated legislation

Because it is not directly made by elected representatives, delegated legislation is subject to the following range of controls, designed to ensure that the power delegated is not abused.

Consultation

Those who make delegated legislation often consult experts within the relevant field, and those bodies who are likely to be affected by it. In the case of road traffic regulations, for example, Ministers are likely to seek the advice of police, motoring organisations, vehicle manufacturers and local authorities before making the rules. Often, the relevant statute makes such consultation obligatory and names the bodies who should be consulted. Under the National Insurance Act 1946, for example, draft regulations must be submitted to the National Insurance Advisory Committee, and any minister proposing to make rules of procedure for a tribunal within a department is required by the Tribunals and Inquiries Act 1971 to consult the Council on Tribunals. In other cases there may be a general statutory requirement for 'such consultation as the minister thinks appropriate with such organisations as appear to him to represent the interest concerned'.

Publication

All delegated legislation is published, and therefore available for public scrutiny. Alongside the statutory instrument, the government now publishes an explanatory memorandum detailing the statutory instrument's policy objective and legislative context.

Supervision by Parliament

There are a number of ways in which Parliament can oversee delegated legislation.

Revocation

Parliamentary sovereignty means that Parliament can at any time revoke a piece of delegated legislation itself, or pass legislation on the same subject as the delegated legislation.

The affirmative resolution procedure

Enabling Acts dealing with subjects of special, often constitutional, importance may require Parliament to vote its approval of the delegated legislation. This is called the affirmative resolution procedure, whereby delegated legislation is laid before one or both Houses (sometimes in draft), and becomes law only if a motion approving it is passed within a specified time (usually 28 or 40 days). Since a vote has to be taken, the procedure means that the government must find parliamentary time for debate, and opposition parties have an opportunity to raise any objections. In practice, though, it is very rare for the government not to achieve a majority when such votes are taken.

The negative resolution procedure

Much delegated legislation is put before Parliament for MPs under the negative resolution procedure. Within a specified time (usually 40 days), any member may put down a motion to annul it. An annulment motion put down by a backbencher is not guaranteed to be dealt with, but one put down by the Official

Opposition (the party with the second largest number of MPs) usually will be. If, after debate, either House passes an annulment motion, the delegated legislation is cancelled.

Committee supervision

Several parliamentary committees monitor new delegated legislation. The Joint Committee on Statutory Instruments watches over the making of delegated legislation and reports to each House on any delegated legislation which requires special consideration, including any regulations made under an Act that prohibit challenge by the courts, or which seem to make unusual or unexpected use of the powers granted by the enabling Act. However, the committee may not consider the merits of any piece of delegated legislation. This is the responsibility of the House of Lords' Merits of Statutory Instruments Committee. In addition, the House of Lords' Select Committee on Delegated Powers and Deregulation looks at the extent of legislative powers proposed to be delegated by Parliament to government ministers. It is required to report on whether the provision of any Bill inappropriately delegates legislative power, or subjects the exercise of legislative power to an inappropriate level of parliamentary scrutiny.

Questions from MPs

MPs can ask ministers questions about delegated legislation at a ministerial question time, or raise them in debates.

The House of Lords

Although the House of Lords cannot veto proposed Acts, the same does not apply to delegated legislation. In 1968 the House of Lords rejected an order imposing sanctions against the Rhodesian government made under the Southern Rhodesia Act 1965.

Control by the courts: judicial review

While the validity of a statute can never be challenged by the courts because of parliamentary sovereignty, delegated legislation can. In a judicial review hearing the courts undertake a review of the process that has been followed in making a decision and can make sure that the public authority had the power to make this decision. Delegated legislation may be challenged on any of the following grounds under the procedure for judicial review.

Procedural *ultra vires*

The term *ultra vires* is Latin and can be translated as 'beyond the powers'. It refers to the situation where a public authority has overstepped its powers. Procedural *ultra vires* occurs where the procedures laid down in the enabling Act for producing delegated legislation have not been followed. In **Agricultural, Horticultural and Forestry Training Board *v* Aylesbury Mushrooms Ltd** (1972), an order was declared invalid because the requirement to consult with interested parties before making it had not been properly complied with.

Substantive *ultra vires*

This is usually based on a claim that the measure under review goes beyond the powers Parliament granted under the enabling Act. In **Customs and Excise Commissioners** *v* **Cure & Deeley Ltd** (1962), the powers of the Commissioners to make delegated legislation under the Finance (No. 2) Act 1940 were challenged. The Act empowered them to produce regulations 'for any matter for which provision appears to them necessary for the purpose of giving effect to the Act'. The Commissioners held that this included allowing them to make a regulation giving them the power to determine the amount of tax due where a tax return was submitted late. The High Court invalidated the regulation on the grounds that the Commissioners had given themselves powers far beyond what Parliament had intended; they were empowered only to collect such tax as was due by law, not to decide what amount they thought fit.

> ✓ **Know your terms 2.2**
>
> Define the following terms:
> 1 Judicial review.
> 2 *Ultra vires*.
> 3 Bye-law.
> 4 Order in Council.
> 5 Enabling Act.

R *v* **Secretary of State for Social Security, ex parte Joint Council for the Welfare of Immigrants** (1996) concerned the Asylum and Immigration Appeals Act 1993, which provided a framework for determining applications for asylum, and for appeals after unsuccessful applications. It allowed asylum seekers to apply for social security benefits while they were waiting for their applications or appeals to be decided, at a cost of over £200 million per year to British taxpayers. This led to concern from some quarters that the provisions might attract those who were simply seeking a better lifestyle than that available in their own countries (often called economic migrants), as opposed to those fleeing persecution, whom the provisions were actually designed to help.

In order to discourage economic migrants, the then Secretary of State for Social Security exercised his powers to make delegated legislation under the Social Security (Contributions and Benefits) Act 1992, and produced regulations which stated that social security benefits would no longer be available to those who sought asylum after they had entered the UK, rather than immediately on entry, or those who had been refused leave to stay here and were awaiting the outcome of appeals against the decision.

The Joint Council for the Welfare of Immigrants challenged the regulations, claiming that they fell outside the powers granted by the 1992 Act. The Court of Appeal upheld the claim, stating that the 1993 Act was clearly intended to give asylum seekers rights which they did not have previously. The effect of the regulations was effectively to take those rights away again, since without access to social security benefits, most asylum seekers would have either to return to the countries from which they had fled, or to live on nothing while their claims were processed. The court ruled that Parliament could not have intended to give the Secretary of State powers to take away the rights it had given in the 1993 Act: this could only be done by a new statute, and therefore the regulations were *ultra vires*.

The decision was a controversial one, because the regulations had themselves been approved by Parliament, and overturning them could be seen as a challenge to the power of the legislature, despite the decision being explained by the court as upholding that power.

Unreasonableness

If rules are manifestly unjust, have been made in bad faith (for example, by someone with a financial interest in their operation) or are otherwise so perverse that no reasonable official could have made them, the courts can declare them invalid.

Quick quiz 2.3

1 Name the three main forms of delegated legislation.

2 Give three reasons why delegated legislation is necessary.

3 Explain what is meant by the affirmative resolution procedure.

4 Name the three grounds on which delegated legislation can be challenged before the courts.

Criticism of delegated legislation

Lack of democratic involvement

This argument is put forward because delegated legislation is usually made by civil servants, rather than elected politicians. This is not seen as a particular problem where the delegated legislation takes the form of detailed administrative rules, since these would clearly take up impossible amounts of parliamentary time otherwise. However, in the last years of the last Conservative government there was increasing concern that delegated legislation was being used to implement important policies.

Overuse

Critics argue that there is too much delegated legislation; this is linked to the point above, as there would be little problem with increasing amounts of delegated legislation if its purpose was merely to flesh out technical detail.

Sub-delegation

Delegated legislation is sometimes made by people other than those who were given the original power to do so.

Lack of control

Despite the above list of controls over delegated legislation, the reality is that effective supervision is difficult. First, publication has only limited benefits, given that the general public are frequently unaware of the existence of delegated legislation, let alone on what grounds it can be challenged and how to go about doing so. This in turn has an effect on the ability of the courts to control delegated legislation, since judicial review relies on individual challenges being brought before the courts. This may not happen until years after a provision is enacted, when it finally affects someone who is prepared and able to challenge it. The obvious result is that legislation which largely affects a class of individuals who are not given to questioning official rules, are unaware of their rights, or who lack the financial resources to go to court, will rarely be challenged.

A further problem is that some enabling Acts confer extremely wide discretionary powers on ministers; a phrase such as 'the minister may make such regulations as he sees fit for the purpose of bringing the Act into operation' would not be unusual. This means that there is very little room for anything to be considered *ultra vires*, so judicial review is effectively frustrated. Even where judicial review is available, this is frequently a slow and expensive process.

The main method of control over delegated legislation is therefore parliamentary, but this too has its drawbacks. Although the affirmative resolution procedure usually ensures that parliamentary attention is drawn to important delegated legislation, it is rarely possible to prevent such legislation being passed. The Select Committee on the Scrutiny of Delegated Powers makes an important contribution, and has been able to secure changes to a number of important pieces of legislation. However, it too lacks real power, as it is unable to consider the merits of delegated legislation (as opposed to whether the delegated powers have been correctly used) and its reports have no binding effect.

Reading on the web

Statutory instruments are published on the Office for Public Sector Information website at:

www.opsi.gov.uk/stat.htm

Chapter summary

There are three main forms of delegated legislation:

- statutory instruments;
- bye-laws; and
- Orders in Council.

Why is delegated legislation necessary?

Delegated legislation is necessary because it saves parliamentary time, constitutes a quick form of legislation, and is suited to technical subject areas or where local knowledge is needed.

Control of delegated legislation

Delegated legislation is controlled through:

- the consultation of experts;
- publication of the legislation;
- supervision by Parliament; and
- the courts with the judicial review procedure.

Criticism of delegated legislation

Delegated legislation has been criticised due to:

- lack of democratic involvement;
- overuse;
- sub-delegation; and
- lack of controls.

Question and answer guides

1

(a) Describe the main types of delegated legislation used in the English legal system.

(b) Explain the different ways that controls are exercised over delegated legislation.

(c) Discuss the problems with using delegated legislation.

(a) The most common form of delegated legislation is a statutory instrument. These are made by Government departments under powers conferred by Acts of Parliament. An example is The North Tees Primary Care Trust (Change of Name) Order 2007, which was made by the Secretary of State for Health under powers conferred on him by the National Health Service Act 2006. Another example is The Severn Bridges Tolls Order 2007, which was made by the Secretary of State for Transport under powers conferred on her by the Severn Bridges Act 1992.

The second form of delegated legislation is a bye-law. These are made by local authorities and public bodies. They have to be approved by central government. They are limited in their application to a particular area or to the operations of a particular body. An example is Basingstoke and Deane Borough Council's Pleasure Fairs Bye-law of 1978.

The third and final form of delegated legislation is an Order in Council. They are drafted by the relevant government department, approved by the Privy Council and signed by the Queen. Orders in Council can be used in times of emergency, for example, under the Civil Contingencies Act 2004. Or they can be used to give effect to European Union directives, under s. 2 of the European Communities Act 1972.

(b) The parliamentary controls on delegated legislation include the requirement that it be made in accordance with a specified procedure. One such is the affirmative resolution procedure, under which the legislation is laid before one or both Houses and becomes law only if a motion approving it is passed within a specified time. Another is the negative resolution procedure, whereby, within a specified time, any member may put down a motion to annul the legislation. If an annulment motion is then passed, the legislation is cancelled.

Another parliamentary control is committee supervision. Several parliamentary committees, including the Joint Committee on Statutory Instruments, monitor new delegated legislation and alert members to any which require special consideration.

Turning to the judicial controls, if a court is satisfied that one of two grounds has been made out, it can declare delegated legislation invalid. The first of these grounds – procedural *ultra vires* – involves the claimant alleging that the procedures laid down in the enabling Act have not been followed. The case of **Agricultural Training Board** *v* **Aylesbury Mushrooms** (1972) provides an example of this.

The second ground – substantive *ultra vires* – involves the claimant alleging that the measure exceeds the powers granted by the enabling Act. The case of **Customs and Excise Commissioners** *v* **Cure & Deeley Ltd** (1962) provides an example of this. In deciding what powers were granted, the courts presume that Parliament did not intend the delegate to make legislation that is unreasonable.

(c) One criticism made of delegated legislation is that it lacks democratic involvement, being made by unelected civil servants, not by elected politicians. This would not be so bad if delegated legislation was used merely to flesh-out policies already enshrined in statutes. But in recent years it has been increasingly used to implement those policies themselves.

Another problem with delegated legislation is the lack of adequate controls over it. The negative and affirmative resolution procedures rarely prevent delegated legislation being passed, while the various parliamentary committees that monitor new delegated legislation lack real power. As for the judicial controls on delegated legislation, they rely on someone who is affected by the legislation having the knowledge and the resources to challenge it in the courts. Even if a court case is mounted, it is likely to be a slow and expensive process.

Another criticism often made of delegated legislation is that the general public are frequently unaware of its existence. This is particularly true of bye-laws which, unlike statutory instruments and Orders in Council, are not required to be published centrally.

A final criticism that can be made of delegated legislation is its enormous volume. Not only is this a problem in itself, but it adds strength to those criticisms already mentioned.

2

(a) Using examples, briefly explain the meaning of delegated legislation. Include in your answer an outline description of how **Parliament** exercises control over the process of delegated legislation. (*20 marks*)
(b) Briefly discuss **three advantages** of delegated legislation as a source of law.
(*10 marks*)
(from AQA Exam Paper, January 2005)

(a)

- Give a definition of delegated legislation, e.g. 'legislation made by Government departments, local authorities, and public or nationalized bodies under powers given to them by Parliament'.
- Explain how powers are delegated, mentioning enabling Acts.
- For a good answer, give an example of an enabling provision, e.g. the European Communities Act 1972, s. 2.
- Name and describe the three types of delegated legislation, giving examples: see Q.1(a) above.
- Describe the affirmative and negative resolution procedures, and committee supervision: see Q.1(b) above.
- For a good answer, give one or two more examples of parliamentary controls on delegated legislation, e.g. the requirement on ministers to consult with interested parties on proposed delegated legislation, or Parliament's power at any time to revoke a piece of delegated legislation, or to repeal the enabling Act.

(b)

Time
Discuss how delegated legislation avoids the problem of Parliament not having the time to debate every detailed rule necessary for efficient government.

Speed
Discuss how delegated legislation allows laws to be made more quickly than they could be by Parliament, and when Parliament is not sitting.

Expertise
Discuss how modern legislation often needs to include detailed, technical provisions and how delegated legislation can use experts who are familiar with the relevant areas.

Common errors in (a)

- including judicial controls on delegated legislation;
- poorly describing the affirmative and negative resolution procedures.

Common errors in (b)

- writing about disadvantages instead of advantages;
- merely identifying advantages but not discussing them.

Group activity 1

You will often find new bye-laws listed in the classified section of the local newspapers. Take a look at your local newspaper and see if you can find a bye-law mentioned that has been passed recently. Alternatively, you could look at your local council website and look up bye-laws on the site index and select a recent bye-law from the website.

- What was the name of the bye-law?
- What was its purpose?
- Which enabling Act empowered the local authority to pass the bye-law?

Split up into small groups and report back your findings.

Group activity 2

- Divide your friends (or class) into groups of two or three people.
- Each group should visit the web page of the Joint Committee on Statutory Instruments:

  www.parliament.uk/parliamentary_committees/joint_committee_on_
  statutory_instruments.cfm.

- Read one of the Committee's recent reports, with each group choosing a different report.
- Make notes summarising your chosen report's contents.
- Compare your notes with those of the other groups.
- In the light of this comparison, how useful do you think the Committee is in controlling delegated legislation?

---

mylawchamber

Visit **www.mylawchamber.co.uk/elliottaqa** to access interactive questions, quizzes and activities to test yourself on this chapter.

Part 3
STATUTORY INTERPRETATION

Chapter 3

Statutory interpretation

When judges are faced with a new piece of legislation, its meaning is not always clear and they have to interpret it. Often in interpreting the Act, the judges say that they are looking for Parliament's intention.

In this chapter we will consider:

- the meaning of parliamentary intention;
- the rules of statutory interpretation;
- internal aids to statutory interpretation;
- external aids to statutory interpretation.

Introduction

Although Parliament makes legislation, it is left to the courts to apply it. The general public imagines that this is simply a case of looking up the relevant law and ruling accordingly, but the reality is not so simple. Despite the fact that Acts of Parliament are carefully written by expert draftsmen, there are many occasions on which the courts find that the implications of a statute for the case before them are not at all clear.

Where the meaning of a statute is uncertain, the job of the courts – in theory at least – is to discover how Parliament intended the law to apply and put that into practice. This is because, in our constitution, Parliament is the supreme source of law (excluding European law, which will be discussed later), and therefore the judiciary's constitutional role is to put into practice what it thinks Parliament actually intended when Parliament made a particular law, rather than simply what the judges themselves might think is the best interpretation in the case before them. However, as we shall see, the practice is not always as straightforward as the constitutional theory suggests.

What is parliamentary intention?

While the judges often say, when interpreting a piece of legislation, that they are looking for the intention of Parliament, it is not really clear what is meant by this. The idea of parliamentary intention is a very slippery concept in practice. Is it the intention of every individual member of Parliament at the time the law was passed? Obviously not, since not every MP will have voted for the legislation or even necessarily been present when it was passed. The intention of all those who did support a particular piece of legislation is no easier to assess; it is not feasible to conduct a questionnaire every time a legislative provision is found to be unclear. When judges say they are looking for the intention of Parliament, often what they really mean is that they are looking for the meaning of the words that Parliament used. They are seeking not what Parliament meant, but the true meaning of the words they used.

Statutory interpretation and case law

Once the courts have interpreted a statute, or a section of one, that interpretation becomes part of case law in just the same way as any other judicial decision, and subject to the same rules of precedent. A higher court may decide that the interpretation is wrong, and reverse the decision if it is appealed, or overrule it in a later case, but unless and until this happens, lower courts must interpret the statute in the same way.

Rules of interpretation

Parliament has given the courts some sources of guidance on statutory interpretation. The Interpretation Act 1978 provides certain standard definitions of common provisions, such as the rule that the singular includes the plural and 'he' includes 'she', while interpretation sections at the end of most modern Acts define some of the words used within them – the Police and Criminal Evidence Act 1984 contains such a section. A further source of help has been provided since the beginning of 1999: all Bills passed since that date are the subject of special explanatory notes, which are made public. These detail the background to the legislation and explain the effects particular provisions are intended to have.

Apart from this assistance, it has been left to the courts to decide what method to use to interpret statutes, and three basic approaches have developed, in conjunction with certain aids to interpretation.

The literal rule

This rule gives all the words in a statute their ordinary and natural meaning, on the principle that the best way to interpret the will of Parliament is to follow the literal meaning of the words it has used. Under this rule, the literal meaning must be followed, even if the result is absurd.

Advantages of the literal rule

The literal rule respects parliamentary sovereignty, giving the courts a restricted role and leaving law-making to those elected for the job.

Examples of the literal rule

Whitely *v* **Chapell** (1868). A statute aimed at preventing electoral malpractice made it an offence to impersonate 'any person entitled to vote' at an election. The accused was acquitted because he impersonated a dead person and a dead person was clearly not entitled to vote!

sourcebook
p. 26

Fisher *v* **Bell** (1961). After several violent incidents in which the weapon used was a flick-knife, Parliament decided that these knives should be banned. The Restriction of Offensive Weapons Act 1959 consequently made it an offence to 'sell or offer for sale' any flick-knife. The defendant had flick-knives in his shop window and was charged with offering these for sale. The court held that 'offers for sale' must be given its ordinary meaning in law, and that in contract law this was not an offer for sale but only an invitation to people to make an offer to buy. The defendant was therefore not guilty of a crime under the Act, despite the fact that this was obviously just the sort of behaviour the Act was set up to prevent.

Disadvantages of the literal rule

Where use of the literal rule does lead to an absurd or obviously unjust conclusion, it can hardly be said to be enacting the will of Parliament, since Parliament is unlikely to have intended absurdity and injustice.

In addition, the literal rule is useless where the answer to a problem simply cannot be found in the words of the statute.

The Law Commission in 1969 pointed out that interpretation based only on literal meanings 'assumes unattainable perfection in draftsmanship'; even the most talented and experienced draftsmen cannot predict every situation to which legislation may have to be applied. The same word may mean different things to different people, and words also shift their meanings over time.

In the case of **R (Haw)** *v* **Secretary of State for the Home Department** (2006), the Court of Appeal refused to apply a literal interpretation to a new piece of legislation as it considered that this would not reflect the intention of Parliament. The case was concerned with Brian Haw, who had been holding a protest in Parliament Square, opposite Parliament, against the war in Iraq since June 2001. He lived on the pavement and displayed a large number of placards protesting about government policy in Iraq. The demonstration had earlier been held to be lawful since it neither caused an obstruction nor gave rise to any fear that a breach of the peace might arise. The Serious Organized Crime and Police Act 2005 was subsequently passed, s. 133(1) of which required any person who intended to organise a demonstration in the vicinity of Parliament to apply to the police for authorisation to do so. Section 132(1) provided that a person who carried on a demonstration in the designated area was guilty of an offence if, when the demonstration started, appropriate authorisation had not been given:

'Any person who –
(a) organises a demonstration in a public place in the designated area, or
(b) takes part in a demonstration in a public place in the designated area, or
(c) carries on a demonstration by himself in a public place in the designated area is guilty
*of an offence if, when the demonstration **starts**, authorisation for the demonstration has*
not been given under section 134(2).'

Haw argued that the Act did not apply to his demonstration because it had started before the Act came into force. The Court of Appeal held that the Act did in fact apply to Haw's demonstration: 'Any other conclusion would be wholly irrational and could fairly be described as manifestly absurd.' Construing the statutory language in context, Parliament's intention was clearly to regulate all demonstrations in the designated area, whenever they began. Thus, rather than following a literal interpretation of the legislation, the courts looked at its context to determine the intention of Parliament. The court gave particular weight to the fact that the 2006 Act repealed a provision in the Public Order Act 1986. That provision had provided for controls to be placed on public demonstrations and would have applied to demonstrations which had been started since 1986. The Court of Appeal thought it was inconceivable that Parliament would have intended to repeal that power to control demonstrations started before 2006 and replace it with legislation which could only control demonstrations started after 2006, as this would leave a significant gap in the power of the state to control demonstrations. Conditions have now been imposed on Haw's demonstration in accordance with the provisions of the 2005 Act, aimed primarily at restricting the size of the demonstration. It is accepted that Haw's demonstration in itself does not pose a security risk, but if a large number of people joined his demonstration, this could be an opportunity for terrorists to join in and conceal an explosive device.

The golden rule

This provides that if the literal rule gives an absurd result, which Parliament could not have intended, then (and only then) the judge can substitute a reasonable meaning in the light of the statute as a whole.

Advantages of the golden rule

The golden rule can prevent the absurdity and injustice caused by the literal rule, and help the courts put into practice what Parliament really means.

Disadvantages of the golden rule

The Law Commission noted in 1969 that the 'rule' provided no clear meaning of an 'absurd result'. As in practice that was judged by reference to whether a particular interpretation was irreconcilable with the general policy of the legislature, the golden rule turns out to be a less explicit form of the mischief rule (discussed below).

Examples of the golden rule

R *v* **Allen** (1872). Section 57 of the Offences Against the Person Act 1861 stated that: 'Whosoever being married shall marry any other person during the life of the former husband or wife . . . shall be guilty of bigamy.' It was pointed out that it was impossible for a person already married to 'marry' someone else – he or she might go through a marriage ceremony, but would not actually be married; using the literal rule would make the statute useless. The court therefore held that 'shall marry' should be interpreted to mean 'shall go through a marriage ceremony'.

sourcebook p. 28

Adler *v* **George** (1964). The defendant was charged under s. 3 of the Official Secrets Act 1920, with obstructing a member of the armed forces 'in the vicinity of any prohibited place'. He argued that the natural meaning of 'in the vicinity of' meant near to, whereas the obstruction had actually occurred in the prohibited place itself, an air force station. The court held that while in many circumstances 'in the vicinity' could indeed only be interpreted as meaning near to, in this context it was reasonable to construe it as including being within the prohibited place.

Inco Europe Ltd *v* **First Choice Distribution** (2000). The House of Lords stated that words could be added to a statute by the judge to give effect to Parliament's intention where an obvious error had been made in drafting a statute.

The mischief rule

This rule was laid down in **Heydon's Case** in the sixteenth century, and provides that judges should consider three factors:

- what the law was before the statute was passed;
- what problem, or 'mischief', the statute was trying to remedy;
- what remedy Parliament was trying to provide.

The judge should then interpret the statute in such a way as to put a stop to the problem that Parliament was addressing.

Examples of the mischief rule

sourcebook p. 29

Smith *v* **Hughes** (1960). The Street Offences Act 1958 made it a criminal offence for a prostitute to solicit potential customers in a street or public place. In this case, the prostitute was not actually in the street, but was sitting in a house, on the first floor, and tapping on the window to attract the attention of the men walking by. The judge decided that the aim of the Act was to enable people to walk along the street without being solicited, and since the soliciting in question was aimed at people in the street, even though the prostitute was not in the street herself, the Act should be interpreted to include this activity.

Elliott *v* **Grey** (1960). The Road Traffic Act 1930 provided that it was an offence for an uninsured car to be 'used on the road'. The car in this case was not being used on the road, but jacked up, with its battery removed, but the court held that as it was nevertheless a hazard of the type which the statute was designed to prevent, it was covered by the phrase 'used on the road'.

Advantages of the mischief rule

The mischief rule helps avoid absurdity and injustice, and promotes flexibility. It was described by the Law Commission in 1969 as a 'rather more satisfactory approach' than the other two established rules.

Disadvantages of the mischief rule

Heydon's Case (1584) was the product of a time when statutes were a minor source of law, compared to the common law. Drafting was by no means as exact a process as it is today, and the supremacy of Parliament was not really established. At that time, too, statutes tended to include a lengthy preamble, which more or less spelt out the 'mischief' with which the Act was intended to deal. Judges of the time were very well qualified to decide what the previous law was and what problems a statute was intended to remedy, since they had usually drafted statutes on behalf of the king, and Parliament only rubber-stamped them. Such a rule may be less appropriate now that the legislative situation is so different.

 ## Quick quiz 3.1

Complete the following table by giving one case to illustrate each of the rules of interpretation.

Literal rule	
Golden rule	
Mischief rule	

Table 3.1 **The three rules of statutory interpretation**

Literal rule	The words are given their ordinary and natural meaning.
Golden rule	If the literal rule gives an absurd result that Parliament cannot have intended, then the judge can substitute a reasonable meaning in the light of the statute as a whole.
Mischief rule	This rule was laid down in **Heydon's Case**. Judges should consider three factors: ■ what the problem was before the statute was passed; ■ what problem, or 'mischief', the statute was trying to remedy; ■ what remedy Parliament was trying to provide. The judge should then interpret the statute in such a way as to put a stop to the problem that Parliament was addressing.

Aids to interpretation

Whichever approach the judges take to statutory interpretation, they have at their disposal a range of material to help. Some of these aids may be found within the piece of legislation itself, or in certain rules of language commonly applied in statutory texts – these are called internal aids. Others, outside the piece of legislation, are called external aids.

Internal aids

The literary rule and the golden rule both direct the judge to internal aids, though they are taken into account whatever the approach applied.

The statute itself

To decide what a provision of the Act means, the judge may draw a comparison with provisions elsewhere in the statute. Clues may also be provided by the long title of the Act or the subheadings within it.

Rules of language

Developed by lawyers over time, these rules are really little more than common sense, despite their intimidating names. As with the rules of interpretation, they are not always precisely applied. Some examples are given below.

Ejusdem generis

General words which follow specific ones are taken to include only things of the same kind. For example, if an Act used the phrase 'dogs, cats and other animals', the phrase 'and other animals' would probably include other domestic animals, but not wild ones.

Expressio unius est exclusio alterius

Express mention of one thing implies the exclusion of another. If an Act specifically mentioned 'Persian cats', the term would not include other breeds of cat.

Noscitur a sociis

A word draws meaning from the other words around it. If a statute mentioned 'cats, kittens and food', it would be reasonable to assume that 'food' meant cat food, and dog food was not covered by the relevant provision.

Presumptions

The courts assume that certain points are implied in all legislation. These presumptions include the following:

- statutes do not change the common law;
- the legislature does not intend to remove any matters from the jurisdiction of the courts;

- existing rights are not to be interfered with;
- laws which create crimes should be interpreted in favour of the citizen where there is ambiguity;
- legislation does not operate retrospectively: its provisions operate from the day it comes into force, and are not backdated.

sourcebook
p. 35 → It is always open to Parliament to go against these presumptions if it sees fit – for example, the European Communities Act 1972 makes it clear that some of its provisions are to be applied retrospectively. But unless the wording of a statute makes it absolutely clear that Parliament has chosen to go against one or more of the presumptions, the courts can assume that the presumptions apply.

External aids

The mischief rule directs the judge to external aids, including the following:

Historical setting

A judge may consider the historical setting of the provision that is being interpreted, as well as other statutes dealing with the same subjects.

Dictionaries and textbooks

These may be consulted to find the meaning of a word, or to gather information about the views of legal academics on a point of law.

Explanatory notes

Acts passed since the beginning of 1999 are provided with explanatory notes, published at the same time as the Act.

Reports

Legislation may be preceded by a report of a Law Commission or a public inquiry. The House of Lords stated in **Black Clawson International Ltd** *v* **Papierwerke Waldhof-Aschaffenburg AG** (1975) that official reports may be considered as evidence of the pre-existing state of the law and the mischief that the legislation was intended to deal with.

sourcebook
p. 153 → ### The Human Rights Act 1998

This Act incorporates into UK law the European Convention on Human Rights, which is an international treaty signed by most democratic countries, and designed to protect basic human rights. In many countries, the Convention has been incorporated into national law as a Bill of Rights, which means that the courts can overrule domestic legislation which is in conflict with it. This is not the case in the UK. Instead, s. 3(1) of the Human Rights Act requires that: 'So far as it is possible to do so, primary and subordinate legislation must be read and given effect in a way which is compatible with the Convention rights.' This means essentially that where a statutory provision can be interpreted in more than one way, the interpretation which is compatible with the European Convention should be the one chosen. Section 2 further requires that in deciding any question which arises in connection with a right protected by the Convention, the courts should take into account any relevant judgments made by the European Court of Human Rights. If it is impossible to find an interpretation which is compatible with the Convention, the court concerned can make a declaration of incompatibility. This does not affect the validity of the statute in question, but it is designed to draw attention to the conflict so that the government can change the law to bring it in line with the Convention (although the Act does not oblige the government to do this). There is a special 'fast track' procedure by which a minister can make the necessary changes.

To clarify interpretation, when new legislation is made, the relevant Bill must carry a statement from the relevant minister, saying either that its provisions are compatible with the Convention, or that even if they are not, the government wishes to go ahead with the legislation anyway. In the latter case, the government would be specifically saying that the legislation must override Convention rights if there is a clash, but clearly any government intent on passing such legislation would be likely to face considerable opposition and so would have to have a very good reason, in the eyes of the public, for doing so.

Hansard

This is the official daily report of parliamentary debates, and therefore a record of what was said during the introduction of legislation. For over 100 years, the judiciary held that such documents could not be consulted for the purpose of statutory interpretation. During his career, Lord Denning made strenuous efforts to do away with this rule, and in **Davis v Johnson** (1979) justified his interpretation of a piece of legislation by reference to the parliamentary debates during its introduction. The House of Lords, however, rebuked him for doing so, and maintained that the rule should stand.

sourcebook p. 30 → In 1993, the case of **Pepper v Hart** overturned the rule against consulting *Hansard*, and such consultation is clearly now allowed. The case was between teachers at a fee-paying school (Malvern College) and the Inland Revenue, and concerned the tax which employees should have to pay on perks (benefits related to their job). Malvern College allowed its teachers to send their sons there for one-fifth of the usual fee, if places were available. Tax law requires employees to pay tax on perks, and the amount of tax is based on the cost to the employer of providing the benefit, which is usually taken to mean any extra cost that the employer would not otherwise incur. The amount paid by Malvern teachers for their sons' places covered the extra cost to the school of having the child there (in books, food, etc.), but did not cover the school's fixed costs, for paying teachers, maintaining buildings and so on, which would have been the same whether the teachers' children were there or not. Therefore the perk cost the school little or nothing, and so the teachers maintained that they should not have to pay tax on it. The Inland Revenue disagreed, arguing that the perk should be taxed on the basis of the amount it saved the teachers on the real cost of sending their children to the school.

The reason why the issue of consulting parliamentary debates arose was that during the passing of the Finance Act 1976, which laid down the tax rules in question, the then Secretary to the Treasury, Robert Sheldon, had specifically mentioned the kind of situation that arose in **Pepper v Hart**. He had stated that where the cost to an employer of a perk was minimal, employees should not have to pay tax on the full cost of it. The question was, could the judges take into account what the minister had said? The House of Lords convened a special court of seven judges, which decided that they could look at *Hansard* to see what the minister had said, and that his remarks could be used to decide what Parliament had intended.

The decision in **Pepper v Hart** was confirmed in **Three Rivers District Council v Bank of England (No. 2) (1996)**, which concerned the correct interpretation of legislation passed in order to fulfil obligations arising from an EC directive. Although the legislation was not itself ambiguous, the claimants stated that, if interpreted in the light of the information contained in *Hansard*, the legislation imposed certain duties on the defendants, which were not obvious from the legislation itself. The defendants argued that *Hansard* could only be consulted where legislation contained ambiguity, but the court disagreed, stating that where legislation was passed in order to give effect to international obligations, it was important to make sure that it did so, and consulting legislative materials was one way of helping to ensure this. The result would appear to be that *Hansard* can be consulted not just to explain ambiguous phrases, but to throw light on the general purpose of legislation.

In **R v Secretary of State for the Environment, Transport and the Regions, ex parte Spath Holme Ltd (2001)** the House of Lords gave a restrictive interpretation of the application of **Pepper v Hart**. The applicant was a company that was the landlord of certain properties. It sought judicial review of the Rent Acts (Maximum Fair Rent) Order 1999, made by the Secretary of State under s. 31 of the Landlord and Tenant Act 1985. The applicant company contended that the 1999 Order was unlawful as the Secretary of State had made it to alleviate the impact of rent increases on certain categories of tenants, when a reading of *Hansard* showed that Parliament's intention was that such orders would only be made to reduce the impact of inflation. On the use of *Hansard* to interpret the intention of Parliament, the House of Lords pointed out that the case of **Pepper v Hart** was concerned with the meaning of an expression used in a statute ('the cost of a benefit'). The minister had given a statement on the meaning of that expression. By contrast, the present case was concerned with a matter of policy, and in particular the meaning of a statutory power rather than a statutory expression. Only if a minister were, improbably, to give a categorical assurance to Parliament that a power would not be used in a given situation would a parliamentary statement on the scope of a power be admissible.

sourcebook
p. 32

In **Wilson v Secretary of State for Trade and Industry (2003)** the House of Lords again gave a restrictive interpretation to **Pepper v Hart**. It held that only statements in *Hansard* made by a minister or other promoter of legislation could be looked at by the court, other statements recorded in *Hansard* had to be ignored.

Under the British constitution, Parliament and the courts have separate roles. Parliament enacts legislation, the courts interpret and apply it. Owing to the principle of the separation of powers (see p. 243), neither institution should stray into the other's domain. Thus, Art. 9 of the Bill of Rights 1689 provides that 'the freedom of speech and debates or proceedings in Parliament ought not to be impeached or questioned in any court or place out of Parliament'. In **Wilson** *v* **Secretary of State for Trade and Industry** (2003) the House of Lords emphasised the importance of the courts not straying into Parliament's constitutional role. It concluded from this that *Hansard* could be used only to interpret the meaning of words in legislation; it could not be used to discover the reasons for the legislation. The Court of Appeal in **Wilson** had used *Hansard* to look at the parliamentary debates concerning a particular Act. It was not trying to discover the meaning of words, as their meaning was not in doubt, but to discover the reason which led Parliament to think that it was necessary to pass the Act. The House of Lords held that the Court of Appeal had been wrong to do this. Referring to *Hansard* simply to check the meaning of enacted words supported the principle of parliamentary sovereignty (see p. 14). Referring to *Hansard* to discover the reasoning of Parliament, where there was no ambiguity as to the meaning of the words, would go against the sovereignty of Parliament.

The Human Rights Act 1998 requires the courts to exercise a new role in respect of Acts of Parliament. This new role is fundamentally different from interpreting and applying legislation. The courts are now required to determine whether the legislation violates a right laid down in the European Convention on Human Rights. If the Act does violate the Convention, the courts have to issue a declaration of incompatibility. In order to determine this question, the House of Lords stated in **Wilson** that the courts can only refer to *Hansard* for background information, such as the social policy aim of the Act. Poor reasoning in the course of parliamentary debate was not a matter which could count against the legislation when determining the question of compatibility.

Although it is now clear that *Hansard* can be referred to in order to find evidence of parliamentary intention, there is still much debate as to how useful it is, and whether it can provide good evidence of what Parliament intended.

Arguments for use of Hansard

■ **Usefulness.** Lord Denning argued in **Davis** *v* **Johnson** (1979) that to ignore the parliamentary debates would be to 'grope in the dark for the meaning of an Act without switching on the light'. When such an obvious source of enlightenment was available, it was ridiculous to ignore it.

■ **Media reports.** Parliamentary proceedings are reported in newspapers and on radio and television. Since judges are as exposed to these as anyone else, it seems ridiculous to blinker themselves in court, or to pretend that they are blinkered.

Arguments against the use of Hansard

■ **Lack of clarity.** The House of Lords, admonishing Lord Denning for his behaviour in **Davis** *v* **Johnson**, and directing that parliamentary debates were not to be consulted, stated that the evidence provided by the parliamentary debates might not be reliable; what was said in the cut and thrust of public debate was not 'conducive to a clear and unbiased explanation of the meaning of statutory language'.

■ **Time and expense.** Their Lordships also suggested that if debates were to be used, there was a danger that the lawyers arguing a case would devote too much time and attention to ministerial statements and so on, at the expense of considering the language used in the Act itself.

> 'It would add greatly to the time and expense involved in preparing cases involving the construction of a statute if counsel were expected to read all the debates in Hansard, and it would often be impracticable for counsel to get access to at least the older reports of debates in select committees in the House of Commons; moreover, in a very large proportion of cases such a search, even if practicable, would throw no light on the question before the court . . .'

■ **Parliamentary intention.** The nature of parliamentary intention is difficult, if not impossible, to pin down. Parliamentary debates usually reveal the views of only a few members, and even then, those words may need interpretation too.

Lord Steyn, a judge in the House of Lords, has written an article entitled '*Pepper v Hart: A Re-examination*' (2001). In that article he criticises the way the use of *Hansard* in **Pepper v Hart** gives pre-eminence to the government minister's interpretation of the statute and ignores any dissenting voices by opposition MPs. The minister only spoke in the House of Commons and the detail of what he said was unlikely to have been known by the House of Lords. He therefore queries how the minister's statement can be said to reflect the intention of Parliament, which is made up of both Houses. He points to the nature of the parliamentary process:

> 'The relevant exchanges sometimes take place late at night in nearly empty chambers. Sometimes it is a party political debate with whips on. The questions are often difficult but politician warfare sometimes leaves little time for reflection. These are not ideal conditions for the making of authoritative statements about the meaning of a clause in a Bill. In truth a Minister speaks for the government and not for Parliament. The statements of a Minister are no more than indications of what the Government would like the law to be. In any event, it is not discoverable from the printed record whether individual members of the legislature, let alone a plurality in each chamber, understood and accepted a ministerial explanation of the suggested meaning of the words.'

This criticism has been partly tackled by the House of Lords in **Wilson v Secretary of State for Trade and Industry** (2003). The House stated that the courts must be careful not to treat the ministerial statement as indicative of the intention of Parliament.

> 'Nor should the courts give a ministerial statement, whether made inside or outside Parliament, determinative weight. It should not be supposed that members necessarily agreed with the Minister's reasoning or his conclusions.'

The House emphasised that the will of Parliament is expressed in the language used in its enactments.

??? Quick quiz 3.2

1 Name the three main rules of statutory interpretation.

2 Give three examples of internal aids to statutory interpretation.

3 Give three examples of external aids to statutory interpretation.

4 What is the legal significance of the House of Lords' decision in **Pepper v Hart**?

How do judges really interpret statutes?

The so-called 'rules of interpretation' are not rules at all, but different approaches. Judges do not methodically apply these rules to every case, and the fact that the rules can conflict with each other and produce different results necessarily implies some choice as to which is used. The idea that statutory interpretation is an almost scientific process that can be used to produce a single right answer is simply non-sense. There is room for more than one interpretation (otherwise the question would never reach the courts) and judges must choose between them. For clear evidence of this, there is no better example than the recent litigation concerning Augusto Pinochet, the former President of Chile. He had long been accused of crimes against humanity, including torture and murder and conspiracy to torture and to murder. When he made a visit to the UK, the Spanish government requested his extradition to Spain so that it could put him on trial. This led to a protracted sequence of litigation concerning whether it was legal for Britain to extradite him to Spain, and eventually the question came before the House of Lords. Pinochet's defence argued on the basis of the State Immunity Act 1978, which gives other states with immunity from prosecution in English courts; the Act provides that 'states' includes heads of state. The Lords were therefore asked to decide whether this immunity extended to Pinochet's involvement in the acts he was accused of and, by a majority of three to two, they decided that it did not. Yet when the appeal was reopened (because one of the judges, Lord Hoffmann, was found to have links with Amnesty International, which was a party to the case), this time with seven Law Lords sitting, a different decision was reached. Although the Lords still stated that the General did not have complete immunity, by a majority of six to one, they restricted his liability to those acts which were committed after 1978, when torture committed outside the UK became a crime in the UK. This gave General Pinochet immunity for the vast majority of the torture allegations, and complete immunity for the allegations of murder and conspiracy to murder.

The reasoning behind both the decisions is complex and does not really need to concern us here; the important point to note is that in both hearings, the Lords were interpreting the same statutory provisions, yet they came up with significantly different verdicts. Because of the way it was reopened, the case gives us a rare insight into just how imprecise and unpredictable statutory interpretation can be, and it is hard to resist the implication that if you put any other case involving statutory interpretation before two separate panels of judges, they might well come up with different judgments too. Given then that judges do have some freedom over questions of statutory interpretation, what influences the decisions they make? The academic Griffith (1997) claims that where there is ambiguity, the judges choose the interpretation that best suits their view of policy and are therefore making a political decisions.

The purposive approach

Over the past three decades, the judiciary has come to acknowledge that it does have some degree of discretion in interpreting statutes, but there is still considerable debate as to how far it can, and should, take this.

Lord Denning was in the forefront of moves to establish a more purposive approach, aiming to produce decisions that put into practice the spirit of the law, even if that meant paying less than usual regard to the letter of the law, the actual words of the statute. He felt that the mischief rule could be interpreted broadly, so that it would not just allow the court to look at the history of the case, but would also allow the court to carry out the intention of Parliament, however imperfectly this might have been expressed in the words used.

Denning stated his view in **Magor and St Mellons *v* Newport Corporation** (1952):

> '*We do not sit here to pull the language of Parliament to pieces and make nonsense of it . . . we sit here to find out the intention of Parliament and carry it out, and we do this better by filling in the gaps and making sense of the enactment than by opening it up to destructive analysis.*'

This approach was roundly criticised by the House of Lords, with Lord Simonds describing 'filling in the gaps' as 'a naked usurpation of the judicial function, under the guise of interpretation . . . If a gap is disclosed, the remedy lies in an amending Act'.

Denning's views nevertheless contributed to the growth of a more purposive approach which has gained ground in the last 20 years, with courts seeking to interpret statutes in ways which will promote the general purpose of the legislation. However, the courts still maintain that this cannot be taken too far.

The introduction of the Human Rights Act 1998 is likely to prompt a shift to a purposive interpretation of legislation, as the courts weigh up important issues concerning the rights of the individual against the state, and take into account the judgments of the European Court of Human Rights, which itself takes a purposive approach to interpretation. Some experts have predicted that the House of Lords' role will become increasingly like that of the American Supreme Court, dealing with vital questions for society and the individual, rather than the detailed and technical commercial and taxation matters which form the bulk of its current work.

Reading on the web

Hansard is available at:

www.publications.parliament.uk/pa/pahansard.htm

Chapter summary

Parliamentary intention

When interpreting statutes the courts are looking for the intention of Parliament, but this intention is frequently difficult to find.

Rules of statutory interpretation

There are three rules of statutory interpretation:

- the literal rule;
- the golden rule; and
- the mischief rule.

Internal aids to statutory interpretation

Internal aids consist of the statute itself and rules of language.

External aids

These include:

- dictionaries and textbooks;
- the explanatory notes;
- reports that preceded the legislation;
- treaties; and
- *Hansard*, following the decision of **Pepper *v* Hart**.

How do judges really interpret statutes?

The idea that statutory interpretation is an almost scientific process that can be used to produce a single right answer is simply nonsense. There is room for more than one interpretation (otherwise the question would never reach the courts) and judges must choose between them. The academic Griffith (1997) claims that where there is ambiguity, the judges choose the interpretation that best suits their view of policy and are therefore making a political decisions.

The purposive approach

During his judicial career, Lord Denning was in the forefront of moves to establish a more purposive approach to statutory interpretation, aiming to produce decisions that put into practice the spirit of the law, even if that meant paying less than usual regard to the letter of the law, the actual words of the statute.

Question and answer guides

1

(a) Explain how the courts use two aids to statutory interpretation.
(b) Explain how the judges use any two rules of statutory interpretation.
(c) Discuss the advantages and disadvantages of the literal rule of statutory interpretation.

(a) The aids to interpretation are either internal (i.e. they are found within the Act) or external (i.e. found outside it). The internal aids include the presumption that legislation does not operate retrospectively. The courts presume that Parliament did not intend legislation to be backdated. Parliament can go against this presumption if it wishes, but it must use express words. For example, the European Communities Act 1972 makes it clear that some of its provisions are to be applied retrospectively. *(Another example is s. 75 of the Criminal Justice Act 2003, which abolished the double jeopardy rule: see p.128).*

As for the external aids, these include *Hansard*. This records what was said in Parliament during a bill's legislative process. For over 100 years the judiciary held that *Hansard* could not be consulted. But then in **Pepper *v* Hart** (1993) the House of Lords held that a report in *Hansard* of a minister's statements as to what legislation meant, made while it was going through Parliament, could be used to decide what Parliament had intended the legislation should mean. However, in **Wilson *v* Secretary of State for Trade and Industry** (2003) the House of Lords held that *Hansard* could only be used to interpret the meaning of words in legislation, and not to discover the reasons for it.

(b) The literal rule states that the words of a statute should be given their ordinary and natural meaning, even if this leads to an absurd result. Thus in **Fisher *v* Bell** (1961) a statute made it an offence to 'offer for sale' any flick-knife. The court held that this meant a contractual offer and that displaying a knife in a shop window was not such an offer but merely an invitation to treat.

(Another case illustrating the literal rule is **Whitely *v* Chapell** *(1868): see p.42)*

The mischief rule provides that a judge interpreting a statute should consider three factors: what the law was before the statute was passed, what 'mischief' or problem the statute was trying to remedy, and what remedy Parliament was trying to provide. The judge should then give the statute the meaning that will put a stop to that problem.

Thus in **Elliott *v* Grey** (1960) a statute made it an offence for an uninsured car to be 'used on the road'. A car was parked on the road, jacked up, with its battery removed. The court held that, as it was a hazard of the type which the statute was designed to prevent, it was covered by the phrase 'used on the road'.

(Another case illustrating the mischief rule is **Smith *v* Hughes** *(1960): see p.44)*

(c) The main argument used in support of the literal rule is that it respects parliamentary sovereignty and the doctrine of the separation of powers; it restricts the courts' role to interpreting legislation, while leaving legislation-making to those elected for the job.

But critics of the literal rule point to those situations where its use leads to an absurd or unjust result. They argue that this can hardly be said to be enacting the will of Parliament, as Parliament is unlikely to have intended absurdity or injustice. All that the literal rule does in such cases is cause Parliament to have to pass amending legislation, as happened following the decision in **Fisher *v* Bell**, above.

The Law Commission has pointed out that interpretation based only on literal meanings 'assumes unattainable perfection in draftsmanship'; even the most talented and experienced draftsmen cannot predict every situation to which legislation may have to be applied. The same word may mean different things to different people, and words also shift their meaning over time.

Perhaps the strongest criticism of the literal rule is that made by Professor Zander, who argues that it is defeatist and lazy; the judge gives up trying to understand the document at the first attempt. It is, he claims, an abdication of responsibility by the judge.

2

Judges use a variety of **aids**, intrinsic (internal) and extrinsic (external), and **rules** (approaches) when interpreting Acts of Parliament.

(a) Briefly describe the **aids** to interpretation used by judges.　　　　(*10 marks*)

(b) Describe **two** of the **rules** of (approaches to) statutory interpretation and discuss their advantages and disadvantages.　　　　(*20 marks*)

(from AQA Exam Paper, June 2006)

(a)

- Explain the distinction between internal and external aids.
- Briefly describe two (or, for a good answer, three) of the internal aids, e.g. the statute itself (including short title, long title, headings, marginal notes and definition sections), one of the rules of language and one of the presumptions.
- Briefly describe two (or, for a good answer, three) of the external aids, e.g. dictionaries, Law Commission reports and *Hansard*.

(b)
Golden rule

- State the rule.
- Briefly describe one (or, for a good answer, two) case examples.
- Discuss two advantages, e.g. it can prevent absurdity and help realise the will of Parliament.
- Discuss two disadvantages, e.g. there is no clear meaning of 'absurd', and the mischief rule makes it unnecessary.

Purposive approach

- State the approach, e.g. 'seeking to interpret statutes in ways which will promote their general purpose'.
- Refer to Lord Denning's promotion of it, e.g. in **Magor and St Mellons** *v* **Newport Corporation** (1952).
- For a good answer, refer to a recent case example, e.g. **Fitzpatrick** *v* **Sterling Housing Association** (1999).
- Discuss two advantages, e.g. it allows judges to reach just decisions and to keep statutes up-to-date.
- Discuss two disadvantages, e.g. it undermines parliamentary supremacy and increases uncertainty.

Common errors in (a)

- writing about the rules of/approaches to interpretation;
- writing more than the question's 10 marks justifies.

Common errors in (b)

■ mentioning more than two rules/approaches;
■ not writing enough to justify the question's 20 marks.

Group activity 1

Look at the bye-law on the website below restricting multiple dog walking:

www.wandsworth.gov.uk/Home/EnvironmentandTransport/Dogs/dogwalking.htm

Split up into three groups. One group should apply a literal interpretation to the bye-law, one should apply the golden rule and one should apply the mischief rule. Compare how each group interpreted the bye-law. Did you come to different conclusions as to its meaning depending on which approach was used?

Group activity 2

In **Royal College of Nursing** *v* **DHSS** (1980) the House of Lords had to interpret s. 1 of the Abortion Act 1967.

■ Divide your friends (or class) into five groups.
■ Each group should read one of the five Law Lords' judgments in the case. (You will find all the judgments at www.bailii.org/uk/cases/UKHL/1980/10.html, but each group should read only one!)
■ Each group should prepare notes stating what interpretation 'its' Law Lord put on s. 1 and summarising the reasons he gave for choosing that interpretation.
■ The groups should then meet to compare notes.
■ What conclusions can you draw from this comparison about the process of statutory interpretation?

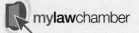

Visit **www.mylawchamber.co.uk/elliottaqa** to access interactive questions, quizzes and activities to test yourself on this chapter.

Part 4
JUDICIAL PRECEDENT

Chapter 4

Judicial precedent

> **This chapter contains:**
> - an introduction to judicial precedent;
> - an explanation of case names and law reporting;
> - a description of the hierarchy of the courts and judicial precedent;
> - an analysis of how judicial precedent works in practice;
> - an overview of the advantages and disadvantages of binding precedent.

Introduction

Judicial precedent, often known as case law, comes from the decisions made by judges in the cases before them. In deciding a case, there are two basic tasks; first, establishing what the facts are, meaning what actually happened; and, secondly, how the law applies to those facts. It is the second task that can make case law. Once a decision has been made on how the law applies to a particular set of facts, similar facts in later cases should be treated in the same way. This is the principle of *stare decisis*, which is a Latin term meaning 'let the decision stand'. This is obviously fairer than allowing each judge to interpret the law differently, and also provides predictability, which makes it easier for people to live within the law. In developing case law, the judges follow the decisions that preceded them and set precedents for the future, hence the name judicial precedent.

English judgments are frequently quite long, containing quite a lot of comment which is not strictly relevant to the case, as well as an explanation of the legal principles on which the judge has made a decision. The explanation of the legal principles on which the decision is made is called the *ratio decidendi* – Latin for the 'reason for deciding'. It is this part of the judgment, known as binding precedent, which forms case law.

All the parts of the judgment which do not form part of the *ratio decidendi* of the case are called *obiter dicta* – which is Latin for 'things said by the way'. These are often discussions of hypothetical situations: for example, the judge might say: 'Jones did this, but if she had done that, my decision would have been . . .' None of the *obiter dicta* forms part of the case law, though judges in later cases may be influenced by it, and it is said to be a persuasive precedent.

✓ **Know your terms 4.1**

Define these Latin terms:

1 *Stare decisis.*
2 *Ratio decidendi.*
3 *Obiter dicta.*

In deciding a case, a judge must follow any decision that has been made by a higher court in a case with similar facts. The rules concerning which courts are bound by which are known as the rules of judicial precedent, or *stare decisis*. As well as being bound by the decisions of courts above them, some courts must also follow their own previous decisions; they are said to be bound by themselves.

Case names

Each legal case that is taken to court is given a name. The name of the case is usually based on the family name of the parties involved. In essays, the name of the case should normally be put into italics or underlined, though in this book we have chosen to put them in bold.

If Ms Smith steals Mr Brown's car, then a criminal action is likely to be brought by the state against her. The written name of the case would then be **R *v* Smith**. The letter 'R' stands for the Latin *Rex* (King) or *Regina* (Queen), depending on whether there was a king or queen in office at the time of the decision. Sometimes the full Latin terms are used rather than the simple abbreviation R, so that the case **R *v* Smith**, if brought now while Queen Elizabeth is in office, could also be called **Regina *v* Smith**.

The 'v' separating the two parties' names is short for 'versus' (against), in the same way as one might write Manchester United *v* Arsenal Football Club when the two teams are going to play a match against each other. When speaking, instead of saying 'R versus Smith', one should really say 'The Crown against Smith'.

In civil law, if Mr Brown is in a neighbour dispute with Ms Smith and decides to bring an action against Ms Smith, the name of the case will be **Brown *v* Smith**.

The law reports

Because some cases lay down important legal principles, over 2,000 each year are published in law reports. Some of these law reports date back over 700 years. Perhaps the most respected series of law reports are those called *The Law Reports*, because before publication the report of each case included in them is checked for accuracy by the judge who tried it. It is this series that should be cited before a court in preference to any other.

The hierarchy of the courts

The European Court of Justice

Decisions of the European Court of Justice (ECJ) are binding on all English courts. It appears not to be bound by its own decisions.

The House of Lords

sourcebook
p. 6 →

Apart from cases concerning European law, this is the highest appeal court on civil and criminal matters, and all other English courts are bound by it. It was traditionally bound by its own decisions but, in 1966, the Lord Chancellor issued a practice statement saying that the House of Lords was no longer bound by its previous decisions. In practice, the House of Lords only rarely overrules one of its earlier decisions. This reluctance to do so is illustrated by the case of **R v Kansal (No. 2)** (2001). In that case the House of Lords held that it had probably got the law wrong in its earlier decision of **R v Lambert** (2001). The latter case had ruled

sourcebook
p. 153 →

that the Human Rights Act 1998 would not have retrospective effect in relation to appeals heard by the House of Lords after the Act came into force, but which had been decided by the lower courts before the Act came into force. Despite the fact that the majority thought the earlier judgment of **Lambert** was wrong, the House decided in **Kansal** to follow it. This was because **Lambert** was a recent decision, it represented a possible interpretation of the statute which was not unworkable and it only concerned a temporary transitional period.

There are, however, a range of cases where the House of Lords has been prepared to apply the 1966 practice statement. For example, in **R v R** (1991), it held that rape within marriage is a crime, overturning a legal principle that had stood for centuries.

In **Arthur JS Hall & Co v Simons** (2000), the House of Lords refused to follow the earlier case of **Rondel v Worsley** (1969), which had given barristers immunity against claims for negligence in their presentation of cases.

In **R v G and another** (2003), the House of Lords overruled an established criminal case of **R v Caldwell** (1981). Under **R v Caldwell**, the House had been prepared to convict people for criminal offences where the prosecution had not proved that the defendant personally had intended or seen the risk of causing the relevant harm, but had simply shown that a reasonable person would have had this state of mind on the facts. This was particularly harsh where the actual defendant was incapable of seeing the risk of harm, because, for example, they were very young or of low intelligence. **Caldwell** had been heavily criticised by academics over the years, but when the House of Lords originally reconsidered the matter in 1992 in **R v Reid**, it confirmed its original decision. However, when the matter again came to the House of Lords in 2003 in **R v G**, the House dramatically admitted that it had got the law wrong. It stated:

> 'The surest test of a new legal rule is not whether it satisfies a team of logicians but how it performs in the real world. With the benefit of hindsight the verdict must be that the rule laid down by the majority in **Caldwell** failed this test. It was severely criticised by academic lawyers of distinction. It did not command respect among practitioners and judges. Jurors found it difficult to understand; it also sometimes offended their sense of justice. Experience suggests that in **Caldwell** the law took a wrong turn.'

sourcebook
p. 65 →

An important case is **Re Pinochet** (1998), where the House of Lords stated that it had the power to reopen an appeal where one of the parties has been subjected to an unfair procedure. The case was part of the litigation concerning General Augusto Pinochet, the former Chilean president. The Lords reopened the appeal because one of the Law Lords who heard the original appeal, Lord Hoffmann, was connected with the human rights organisation, Amnesty International, which had been a party to the appeal. This meant that there was a possibility of bias and so the proceedings could be viewed as unfair. The Lords stressed, however, that there was no question of them being able to reopen an appeal because the decision made originally was thought to be wrong; the Pinochet appeal was reopened because it could be said that there had not been a fair hearing, and not because the decision reached was wrong (although at the second hearing of the appeal, the Lords did in fact come to a slightly different decision).

The government intends to abolish the House of Lords and replace it with a Supreme Court. This reform is contained in the Constitutional Reform Act 2005 and is discussed at p. 85.

sourcebook p. 326 →

Task 4.2

Visit the House of Lords' judicial business website at:

www.publications.parliament.uk/pa/ld/ldjudgmt.htm

Find the judgment **Re Pinochet** (1998). Who were the judges in that case?

Figure 4.1 **Demonstrators in favour of the deportation of the former Chilean President Augusto Pinochet**

Privy Council

The Privy Council was established by the Judicial Committee Act 1833. It is the final appeal court for many Commonwealth countries. The Privy Council currently has jurisdiction to hear devolution cases relating to the powers of the devolved legislative and executive authorities in Scotland, Northern Ireland and Wales. Once the Supreme Court has been established, this domestic jurisdiction will be transferred to the new court.

Under the traditional rules of precedent, the decisions of the Privy Council do not bind English courts, but have strong persuasive authority because of the seniority of the judges who sit in the Privy Council (**de Lasala v de Lasala** (1980)). This well-established rule of precedent has been thrown into doubt by the recent Court of Appeal judgment of **R v James and Karimi** (2006). The Court of Appeal held that in exceptional circumstances a Privy Council judgment can bind the English Courts and effectively overrule an earlier House of Lords' judgment. This conflicts with the traditional approach to such judgments, confirmed by the House of Lords in **Miliangos v George Frank (Textiles) Ltd** (1976) that 'the only judicial means by which decisions of this House can be reviewed is by this House itself'.

The Court of Appeal case of **James and Karimi** was concerned with provocation which can be a partial defence to murder. The defence is laid down in s. 3 of the Homicide Act 1957. This section has been interpreted as laying down a two-part test. The first part of the test requires the defendant to have suffered from a sudden and temporary loss of self-control when he or she killed the victim. The second part of the test provides that the defence will be available only if a reasonable person would have reacted as the defendant did. This is described as an objective test, because it is judging the defendant's conduct according to objective standards, rather than their own standards. However, in practice, reasonable people almost never kill, so if this second requirement was interpreted strictly the defence would rarely succeed. As a result, in **R v Smith (Morgan)** (2001) the House of Lords held that, in determining whether a reasonable person would have reacted in this way, a court could take into account the actual characteristics of the defendant. So if the defendant had been depressed and was of low intelligence, then the test would become whether a reasonable person suffering from depression and of low intelligence would have reacted by killing the victim.

sourcebook
p. 9 → In an appeal from Jersey on the defence of provocation, **Attorney-General for Jersey v Holley** (2005), the Privy Council had refused to follow the case of **Smith (Morgan)**, stating that the case misinterpreted Parliament's intention when it passed the Homicide Act 1957. It considered that the only characteristics that should be taken into account when considering whether the defendant had reacted reasonably, were characteristics that were directly relevant to the provocation itself, but not general characteristics which simply affected a person's ability to control him or herself.

The Court of Appeal in **James and Karimi** (2006) has now decided to apply the Privy Council's judgment in **Holley** rather than the House of Lords' judgment in **Smith (Morgan)**. The Court of Appeal acknowledged that this went against the established rules of judicial precedent. It gives various justifications for treating this as an exceptional case, in which those established rules should not apply. It pointed out that the Privy Council had realised the importance of its judgment and had chosen to have an enlarged sitting of nine judges all drawn from the House of Lords:

> 'The procedure adopted and the comments of members of the Board in **Holley** suggest that a decision must have been taken by those responsible for the constitution of the Board in **Holley** . . . to use the appeal as a vehicle for reconsidering the decision of the House of Lords in **Morgan Smith**, not just as representing the law of Jersey but as representing the law of England. A decision was taken that the Board hearing the appeal to the Privy Council should consist of nine of the twelve Lords of Appeal in Ordinary.'

The emphasis on the enlarged formation of the Privy Council potentially leaves the status of its decisions dependent upon an administrative decision as to how many judges should sit, a decision which has never been the subject of any legal controls.

The judges in **Holley** were divided in their verdict six to three. The start of the first judgment of the majority stated:

> 'This appeal, being heard by an enlarged board of nine members, is concerned to resolve this conflict [between the House of Lords and the Privy Council] and clarify definitively the present state of English law, and hence Jersey law, on this important subject.'

The dissenting judges stated: 'We must however accept that the effect of the majority decision is as stated in paragraph 1 of the majority judgment.' Thus, even the dissenting judges appear to accept that the majority decision lays down the law in England.

The Court of Appeal also considered that if an appeal was taken to the House of Lords, the outcome was 'a foregone conclusion' and the House would take the same approach as **Holley**:

> 'Half of the Law Lords were party to the majority decision in **Holley**. Three more in that case accepted that the majority decision represented a definitive statement of English law on the issue in question. The choice of those to sit on the appeal might raise some nice questions, but we cannot conceive that, whatever the precise composition of the Committee, it would do other than rule that the majority decision in **Holley** represented the law of England. In effect, in the long term at least, **Holley** has overruled **Morgan Smith**.'

This argument would be more convincing if the **Holley** case had been decided by a unanimous verdict. In fact, there are still potentially six House of Lords judges who could prefer the **Smith (Morgan)** approach: the three dissenting judges and the three House of Lords' judges who did not hear the **Holley** case.

Lord Woolf recognised in **R** v **Simpson** (2003) that the rules of judicial precedent must provide certainty but at the same time they themselves must be able to evolve in order to do justice:

> 'The rules as to precedent reflect the practice of the courts and have to be applied bearing in mind that their objective is to assist in the administration of justice. They are of considerable importance because of their role in achieving the appropriate degree of certainty as to the law. This is an important requirement of any system of justice. The principles

should not, however, be regarded as so rigid that they cannot develop in order to meet contemporary needs.'

The Court of Appeal presumably concluded in **James and Karimi** that this was a situation where justice could only be achieved by shifting the established rules of judicial precedent. The actual outcome of the case makes it more difficult for a partial defence to murder, reducing liability to manslaughter, to succeed. This may be considered to achieve justice for victims' families, but it may be an injustice to the mentally ill defendant.

The Court of Appeal

This is split into Civil and Criminal Divisions; they do not bind each other. Both divisions are bound by the House of Lords.

The Civil Division is usually bound by its own previous decisions, but there are four exceptions to this where:

1 the previous decision was made in ignorance of a relevant law (it is said to have been made *per incuriam*);
2 there are two previous conflicting decisions;
3 there is a later, conflicting House of Lords decision;
4 a proposition of law was assumed to exist by an earlier court and was not subject to argument or consideration by that court.

sourcebook
p. 6 → The first three of these exceptions were laid down in **Young v Bristol Aeroplane Co. Ltd** (1944). The fourth was added by **R v Brent London Borough Housing Benefit Review Board, ex parte Khadim** (2001).

In the Criminal Division, the results of cases heard may decide whether or not an individual goes to prison, so the Criminal Division takes a more flexible approach to its previous decisions and does not follow them where doing so could cause injustice.

Lord Denning would have liked the Court of Appeal to have had the power to overrule its own previous decisions wherever it felt it had got the law wrong, in the same way as the House of Lords has this power following the Practice Statement of 1966. He put forward this view in **Davis v Johnson** (1979). The Court of Appeal has not been prepared to take this stance, and Lord Simon was of the view that any such change to the rules of precedent concerning the Court of Appeal would require an Act of Parliament (**Miliangos v George Frank (Textiles) Ltd** (1976)).

The High Court

This court is divided between the Divisional Courts and the ordinary High Court. All are bound by the Court of Appeal and the House of Lords.

The Divisional Courts are the Queen's Bench Division, which deals with criminal appeals and judicial review, the Chancery Division and the Family Division, which both deal with civil appeals. The two civil Divisional Courts are bound by their previous decisions, but the Divisional Court of the Queen's Bench is more flexible about this, for the same reason as the Criminal Division of the Court of Appeal. The Divisional Courts bind the ordinary High Court.

The ordinary High Court is not bound by its own previous decisions. It can produce precedents for courts below it, but these are of a lower status than those produced by the Court of Appeal or the House of Lords.

The Crown Court

The Crown Court is bound by all the courts above it. Its decisions do not form binding precedents, though when High Court judges sit in the Crown Court, their judgments form persuasive precedents, which must be given serious consideration in subsequent cases, though it is not obligatory to follow them. Since the Crown Court cannot form binding precedents, it is obviously not bound by its own decisions.

Magistrates' and county courts

These are called the inferior courts. They are bound by the High Court, Court of Appeal and House of Lords. Their own decisions are not reported, and cannot produce binding precedents, or even persuasive ones; like the Crown Court, they are therefore not bound by their own decisions.

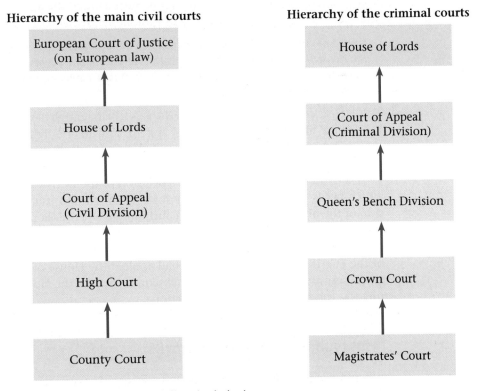

Figure 4.2 **The routes for civil and criminal cases**

European Court of Human Rights

The European Court of Human Rights (ECtHR) is an international court based in Strasbourg. It hears cases alleging that there has been a breach of the European Convention on Human Rights. This court does not fit neatly within the hierarchy of the courts. Under s. 2 of the Human Rights Act 1998 an English court is required to 'take account of' the cases decided by the ECtHR, though its decisions do not bind the English courts. In practice, when considering a Convention right, the domestic courts try to follow the same interpretation as that given by the ECtHR. In **R (Alconbury) v Secretary of State for the Environment, Transport and the Regions** (2001) the House of Lords said:

> '*In the absence of some special circumstances it seems to me the court should follow any clear and constant jurisprudence of the European Court of Human Rights. If it does not do so there is at least a possibility the case will go to that court which is likely in the ordinary case to follow its own constant jurisprudence.*'

Despite this, the House of Lords has refused to follow an earlier decision of the ECtHR. In **Morris v United Kingdom** (2002) the ECtHR ruled that the courts martial system (which is the courts system used by the army) breached the European Court of Human Rights, as it did not guarantee a fair trial within the meaning of Art. 6 of the European Convention. Subsequently, in **Boyd v Army Prosecuting Authority** (2002), three soldiers who had been convicted of assault by a court martial argued before the House of Lords that the court martial had violated their right to a fair trial under the Convention. Surprisingly, the argument was rejected and the House of Lords refused to follow the earlier decision of the ECtHR. It stated:

> '*While the decision in **Morris** is not binding on the House, it is of course a matter which the House must take into account (s. 2(1)(a) of the Human Rights Act 1998) and which demands careful attention, not least because it is a recent expression of the European Court's view on these matters.*'

The House considered that the ECtHR was given 'rather less information than the House' about the courts martial system, and in the light of this additional information it concluded that there had been no violation of the European Convention.

Where there is a conflict between a decision of the ECtHR and a national court which binds a lower court, then the lower court should usually follow the decision of the binding higher national court, but give permission to appeal. Thus, in **Kay v London Borough of Lambeth** (2006) the Court of Appeal had been faced with a binding precedent of the House of Lords which conflicted with a decision of the ECtHR. The Court of Appeal had applied the House of Lords' decision but given permission to appeal. In the subsequent appeal the House had agreed that this was the appropriate course of action.

How judicial precedent works

When faced with a case on which there appears to be a relevant earlier decision the judges can do any of the following:

- **Follow.** If the facts are sufficiently similar, the precedent set by the earlier case is followed, and the law applied in the same way to produce a decision.
- **Distinguish.** Where the facts of the case before the judge are significantly different from those of the earlier one, then the judge distinguishes the two cases and need not follow the earlier one.
- **Overrule.** Where the earlier decision was made in a lower court, the judges can overrule that earlier decision if they disagree with the lower court's statement of the law. The outcome of the earlier decision remains the same, but will not be followed.
- **Reverse.** If the decision of a lower court is appealed to a higher one, the higher court may change it if they feel the lower court has wrongly interpreted the law. Clearly, when a decision is reversed, the higher court is usually also overruling the lower court's statement of the law.

In practice, the process is rather more complicated than this, since decisions are not always made on the basis of only one previous case; there are usually several different cases offered in support of each side's view of the question.

How do judges really decide cases?

The independence of the judiciary was ensured by the Act of Settlement 1700, which transferred the power to sack judges from the Crown to Parliament. Consequently, judges should theoretically make their decisions based purely on the logical deductions of precedent, uninfluenced by political or career considerations.

The eighteenth-century legal commentator, William Blackstone, introduced the declaratory theory of law, stating that judges do not make law, but merely, by the rules of precedent, discover and declare the law that has always been. He thought there was always one right answer to a legal question, to be deduced from an objective study of precedent.

Today, however, this position is considered somewhat unrealistic. If the operation of precedent is the precise science Blackstone suggests, a large majority of cases in the higher courts would never come to court at all. The lawyers concerned could simply look up the relevant case law and predict what the decision would be, then advise whichever of the clients would be bound to lose not to bother bringing or fighting the case. In civil litigation no good lawyer would advise a client to bring or defend a case that they had no chance of winning. Evidence that more than one solution is possible is provided by reading a judgment of the Court of Appeal, argued as though it were the only possible decision in the light of the cases that had gone before, and then discover that this apparently inevitable decision has promptly been reversed by the House of Lords.

In practice, then, judges' decisions may not be as neutral as Blackstone's declaratory theory suggests: they have to make choices which are by no means spelt out by precedents. Yet, rather than openly stating that they are choosing between two or more equally relevant precedents, the courts find ways to avoid awkward ones, which give the impression that the precedents they do choose to follow are the only ones that could possibly apply. In theory, only the House of Lords, which can overrule its own decisions as well as those of other courts, can depart from precedent: all the other courts must follow the precedent that applies in a particular case, however much they dislike it. In fact, there are a number of ways in which judges may avoid awkward precedents that at first sight might appear binding. In particular, the courts may distinguish an earlier case by saying that its facts are different in some significant way. Since the facts are unlikely to be identical, this is the simplest way to avoid an awkward precedent, and the courts have made some extremely narrow distinctions in this way. Or the court may give the precedent a very narrow *ratio decidendi*.

Quick quiz 4.3

1 What are the three main sources of English law?

2 In what year did the House of Lords declare that it was no longer bound by its previous decisions?

3 What are the four situations where the Court of Appeal Civil Division is not bound by its own decisions?

4 Which of the following courts can create a binding precedent: the High Court, Crown Court, magistrates' court and county court?

5 What is the difference between a court overruling a previous decision and a court reversing a previous decision?

6 Which legal writer is traditionally associated with the declaratory theory of law?

Task 4.4

Read the Practice Statement that was issued by the House of Lords in 1966, stating that it was no longer bound by its previous decisions, and then answer the questions below:

> Their Lordships regard the use of precedent as an indispensable foundation upon which to decide what is the law and its application to individual cases. It provides at least some degree of certainty upon which individuals can rely in the conduct of their affairs, as well as a basis for orderly development of legal rules.
>
> Their Lordships nevertheless recognise that the rigid adherence to precedent may lead to injustice in a particular case and also unduly restrict the proper development of the law. They propose, therefore, to modify their present practice and while treating former decisions of this House as normally binding, to depart from a previous decision when it appears right to do so.
>
> In this connection they will bear in mind the danger of disturbing retrospectively the basis on which contracts, settlement of property and fiscal arrangements have been entered into and also the especial need for certainty as to the criminal law.
>
> This announcement is not intended to affect the use of precedent elsewhere than in the House.

Questions

1 Define the term 'retrospectively'.
2 What did the House of Lords consider to be the advantages of the doctrine of judicial precedent?
3 What disadvantages did they recognise exist in the strict application of the rules of judicial precedent?
4 In which areas of law did their Lordships state that they would be less willing to change their previous decisions?

Advantages of binding precedent

Certainty

Judicial precedent means litigants can assume that like cases will be treated alike, rather than judges making their own random decisions, which nobody could predict. This helps people plan their affairs.

Detailed practical rules

Case law is a response to real situations, as opposed to statutes, which may be more heavily based on theory and logic. Case law shows the detailed application of the law to various circumstances, and thus gives more information than statute.

Just and impartial rules

If the judges are accepted as independent and follow the rules of judicial precedent then if we accept Blackstone's declaratory theory, their decisions should be just and impartial.

Free market in legal ideas

The right-wing philosopher Hayek (1982) has argued that there should be as little legislation as possible, with case law becoming the main source of law. He sees case law as developing in line with market forces; if the *ratio* of a case is seen not to work, it will be abandoned, if it works it will be followed. In this way the law can develop in response to demand. Hayek sees statute law as imposed by social planners, forcing their views on society whether they like it or not, and threatening the liberty of the individual.

Flexibility

Law needs to be flexible to meet the needs of a changing society, and case law can make changes far more quickly than Parliament. The most obvious signs of this are the radical changes the House of Lords has made in the field of criminal law, since announcing in 1966 that it would no longer be bound by its own decisions.

Disadvantages of binding precedent

Complexity and volume

There are hundreds of thousands of decided cases, comprising several thousand volumes of law reports, and more are added all the time. Judgments themselves are long, with many judges making no attempt at readability, and the *ratio decidendi* of a case may be buried in a sea of irrelevant material. This can make it very difficult to pinpoint appropriate principles.

Rigid

The rules of judicial precedent mean that judges should follow a binding precedent even where they think it is bad law, or inappropriate. This can mean that bad judicial decisions are perpetuated for a long time before they come before a court high enough to have the power to overrule them.

Illogical distinctions

The fact that binding precedents must be followed unless the facts of the case are significantly different can lead to judges making minute distinctions between the facts of a previous case and the case before them, so that they can distinguish a precedent which they consider inappropriate. This in turn leads to a mass of cases all establishing different precedents in very similar circumstances, and further complicates the law.

Unpredictable

The advantages of certainty can be lost if too many of the kind of illogical distinctions referred to above are made, and it may be impossible to work out which precedents will be applied to a new case.

Dependence on chance

Case law changes only in response to those cases brought before it, so important changes may not be made unless someone has the money and determination to push a case far enough through the appeal system to allow a new precedent to be created.

Unsystematic progression

Case law develops according to the facts of each case and so does not provide a comprehensive code. A whole series of rules can be built on one case, and if this is overruled the whole structure can collapse.

Lack of research

When making case law the judges are presented only with the facts of the case and the legal arguments, and their task is to decide on the outcome of that particular dispute. Technically, they are not concerned with the social and economic implications of their decisions, and so they cannot commission research or consult experts as to these implications, as Parliament can when changing the law. In the US, litigants are allowed to present written arguments containing socio-economic material.

Retrospective effect

Changes made by case law apply to events which happened before the case came to court, unlike legislation, which usually only applies to events after it comes into force. This may be considered unfair, since if a case changes the law, the parties concerned in that case could not have known what the law was before they acted. US courts sometimes get round the problems by deciding the case before them according to the old law, while declaring that in future the new law will prevail: or they may determine with what degree of retroactivity a new rule is to be enforced.

In **SW v United Kingdom** (1996), two men, who had been convicted of the rape and attempted rape of their wives, brought a case before the European Court of Human Rights, alleging that their convictions violated Art. 7 of the European Convention on Human Rights, which provides that criminal laws should not have retrospective effect. The men argued that, when the incidents which gave rise to their convictions happened, it was not a crime for a man to force his wife to have sex; it only became a crime after the decision in **R v R** (1991) (see p. 62). The court dismissed the men's argument: Art. 7 did not prevent the courts from clarifying the principles of criminal liability, provided the developments could be clearly foreseen. In this case, there had been mounting criticism of the previous law, and a series of cases which had chipped away at the marital rape exemption, before the **R v R** decision.

The same issue again came before the courts in **R v C** (2004). In that case the defendant was convicted in 2002 of raping his wife in 1970. On appeal, he argued that this conviction breached Art. 7 of the European Convention and tried to distinguish the earlier case of **SW v United Kingdom** (1995). He said that, while in **SW v United Kingdom** the defendant could have foreseen in 1989 when he committed his offence that his conduct would be regarded as criminal, this was not the case in 1970. This argument was rejected by the Court of Appeal. It claimed, rather unconvincingly, that a husband in 1970 could have anticipated this development in the law. In fact, the leading textbooks at the time clearly stated that husbands were not liable for raping their wives.

Recent criminal cases have shown that the retrospective effect of case law can also work to the benefit of the defendant. In **R v Powell and English** (1998) the House of Lords clarified the law that should determine the criminal liability of accomplices. An earlier controversial case that had involved the criminal liability of an accomplice was that of **R v Craig and Bentley** (1952), whose story was made into the Hollywood film *Let Him Have It*. Bentley was caught and arrested after being chased across rooftops by police. Craig had a gun, and Bentley is alleged to have said to Craig, 'Let him have it'. Craig then shot and killed a policeman. Craig was charged with murdering a police officer (at that time a hanging offence) and Bentley was charged as his accomplice. In court Bentley argued that when he shouted 'Let him have it', he was telling Craig to hand over his gun, rather than, as the prosecution claimed, encouraging him to shoot the police officer. Nevertheless, both were convicted. Craig was under the minimum age for the death sentence, and was given life imprisonment. Bentley, who was older, was hanged. The conviction was subsequently overturned by the Court of Appeal in July 1998, following a long campaign by his family. In considering the trial judge's summing up to the jury, the Court of Appeal said that criminal liability 'must be determined according to the common law as now understood'. The common law that applied in 1998 to accomplice liability was more favourable than the common law that applied in 1952. The danger in practice is that every time the common law shifts to be more favourable to defendants the floodgates are potentially open for defendants to appeal against their earlier convictions.

Undemocratic

Lord Scarman pointed out in **Stock** *v* **Jones** (1978) that a judge cannot match the experience and vision of the legislator; and that unlike the legislator a judge is not answerable to the people. Theories, like Griffith's (1997), which suggest that precedent can actually give judges a good deal of discretion, and allow them to decide cases on grounds of political and social policy, raise the question of whether judges, who are unelected, should have such freedom.

Reading on the web

The House of Lords' recent judgments are available on the House of Lords' judicial business website at:

> www.publications.parliament.uk/pa/ld/ldjudgmt.htm

Some important judgments are published on the Court Service website at:

> www.hmcourts-service.gov.uk

Chapter summary

Introduction

In deciding a case, a judge must follow any decision that has been made by a higher court in a case with similar facts. Judges are bound only by the part of the judgment forming the legal principle that was the basis of the earlier decision, known as the *ratio decidendi*. The rest of the judgment is known as *obiter dicta* and is not binding.

The hierarchy of the courts

The European Court of Justice is the highest authority on European law, in other matters the House of Lords is the highest court in the UK. Following the 1966 Practice Statement, the House of Lords is not bound by its previous decisions.

How do judges really decide cases?

According to the traditional declaratory theory laid down by William Blackstone, judges do not make law but merely discover and declare the law that has always been, but this is open to debate.

Advantages of binding precedent

The doctrine of judicial precedent provides:

- certainty;
- detailed practical rules;
- just and impartial rules;
- a free market in legal ideas; and
- flexibility.

Disadvantages of binding precedent

Case law has been criticised because of its:

- complexity and volume;
- rigidity;
- illogical distinctions;
- unpredictability;
- dependence on chance;
- retrospective effect; and
- undemocratic character.

Question and answer guides

1

(a) Describe the doctrine of judicial precedent.

(b) Explain two situations when a lower court is not required to follow a legal precedent.

(c) Discuss the main benefits of having rules respecting judicial precedent.

(a) The doctrine of judicial precedent determines when courts are bound by the decisions of other courts. Its central rule is the principle of *stare decisis* – once a decision has been made on how the law applies to a set of facts, similar facts in later cases should be treated in the same way. To help achieve this courts have access to earlier judgments, via law reports. The most respected are *The Law Reports*, which should be cited in preference to any other.

Another rule of judicial precedent is that a court is bound by a decision of a higher court. 'Height' is determined by the hierarchy of the courts. At the top is the European Court of Justice (on matters relating to European law), then the House of Lords, then the Court of Appeal, then the High Court sitting as a Divisional Court, then the High Court sitting as a single judge. The Crown Court, magistrates' courts and county courts form the lowest tier of the hierarchy.

Another aspect of judicial precedent is the distinction between *ratio decidendi* and *obiter dicta*. The former refers to that part of a judgment which contains the legal principles on which the decision is made, while the latter refers to the rest of the judgment. Only the ratio is capable of being binding. The obiter is at best persuasive.

(b) One way in which judges can avoid following precedents is by distinguishing them. When judges distinguish a precedent they are saying that its facts are materially different from those of the case before them. Since the facts of two cases are unlikely to be identical, distinguishing is the simplest, and most commonly used, way to avoid an awkward precedent.

Another way a judge can avoid following a precedent is by redefining its ratio. When judges write a judgment they will hardly ever say which part is the ratio. It is left to later judges to decide this. This allows those later judges the discretion to give the ratio a very narrow definition, so narrow that it is no longer relevant to the case before them. This they might choose to do if the precedent is one that they do not want to have to follow.

(An alternative way of avoiding precedents that you might mention is overruling. But make sure you distinguish between overruling by a higher court of a lower court, which is always possible, and overruling by a court of one of its own previous decisions, which with some courts is only possible in certain limited situations, e.g. in the case of the House of Lords, where allowed by the 1966 Practice Statement.)

(c) One argument in support of the doctrine of judicial precedent is that it produces a degree of certainty. Litigants can assume that like cases will be treated alike, rather than judges making their own random decisions, which nobody could predict. This in turn helps people plan their affairs and avoid litigation.

Another alleged advantage of case law, as compared with statute law, is that it is made in response to real-life situations, whereas statute law tends to be based more on abstract theorising. Case law is created by the detailed application of the law to various practical circumstances, and thus is more likely to work than statute law.

It can also be argued that case law offers greater flexibility than statute law, allowing it to better reflect the needs of a changing society. The courts have shown themselves willing to make major changes to case law over-night, changes which might have taken years if left to Parliament. Examples are provided by such cases as **R** *v* **R** (1991) (abolition of the rule that a husband could not be convicted of raping his wife), **Hall** *v* **Simons** (2000) (abolition of the rule that protected barristers from liability for negligent advocacy) and **R** *v* **G and another** (2003) (abolition of the criminal law concept of objective recklessness).

2

(a) Describe the major features of the doctrine of judicial precedent in the English system of case law.   *(20 marks)*

(b) Consider **three disadvantages** of the doctrine of judicial precedent.

(10 marks)

(from AQA Exam Paper, January 2005)

(a)

- Describe the system of law reporting, emphasising the range of publications and the status of *The Law Reports*.
- Describe the hierarchy of the courts including, for a good answer, the position of the Privy Council following **R *v* James and Karimi** (2006).
- Describe the extent to which courts are bound by themselves, especially the position of the House of Lords under the 1966 Practice Statement and of the Court of Appeal under **Young *v* Bristol Aeroplane Co. Ltd** (1944).
- Explain *ratio decidendi* and *obiter dicta*. For a good answer, explain how House of Lords' *obiter dicta* carry almost as much weight in lower courts as ratios.
- Explain the difference between binding and persuasive precedents.
- For a good answer, explain how judges can avoid following precedent by distinguishing and redefining the ratio.

(b)
Complexity

- Mention the length of judgments and the difficulties in identifying the ratio.
- For a good answer, mention the special problems presented by House of Lords' judgments.

Rigidity

- Precedent means judges having to follow decisions that they might think are wrong.
- Bad decisions can therefore be perpetuated.

Undemocratic

- Is it wrong that unelected judges should have so much law-making power?
- Refer to Lord Scarman's comments discussed at p. 74.

Common errors in (a)

- failure to describe sufficient features in sufficient depth;
- confusion over extent to which courts are bound by themselves.

Common errors in (b)

- mentioning more than three disadvantages;
- mentioning advantages rather than disadvantages.

Group activity 1

- With your friends (or class), prepare a chart depicting the English civil court hierarchy in as simple a form as possible. It should make clear that all civil cases are tried in either the High Court or a county court, and that appeals go to the Court of Appeal and then to the House of Lords.

- Divide your friends (or class) into groups of two or three people.
- Each group should invite six people, having no knowledge of law, to study the chart and then answer the following questions. Try to get your interviewees to give reasoned answers, rather than just 'Yes' or 'No'.

  Q.1(a): Do you think that a court on the chart should be bound by the earlier decisions of a court that is higher than it? (You will need to explain what 'bound' means!)

  Q.1(b): Do you think that there should be any situations in which a court on the chart should be able to overrule an earlier decision of a court that is higher than it?

  Q.2(a): Do you think that a court on the chart should be bound by its own previous decisions?

  Q.2(b): Do you think that there should be any situations in which a court on the chart should be able to overrule one of its own previous decisions?

- With your friends (or class), prepare a table summarising all the answers obtained by all the groups.
- To what extent do these answers accurately reflect the legal position and what conclusions can you draw from this as to the current rules of judicial precedent?

Group activity 2

Look at Lord Bingham's judgment in the House of Lords' case **R (Countryside Alliance and others)** *v* **Attorney-General** (2007). Which strategies does he use to avoid following the following cases?

- **Pretty** *v* **United Kingdom** (2002).
- **Buckley** *v* **United Kingdom** (1996).
- **Chapman** *v* **United Kingdom** (2001).

---

mylawchamber

Visit **www.mylawchamber.co.uk/elliottaqa** to access interactive questions, quizzes and activities to test yourself on this chapter.

Section B
THE LEGAL SYSTEM

This section of the book looks at the different people involved in the English legal system. Some of these are in paid employment, such as the professional judges, barristers and solicitors. Others are essentially unpaid and include jurors and magistrates. It also looks at the formal and informal methods available in England and Wales to solve disputes. The formal methods pass through either the criminal justice system or the civil justice system and include a structured appeal process. Less formal methods fall within the concept of alternative methods of dispute resolution and include the tribunal system. All of these methods of resolving disputes require funding, and the different sources of funding are considered. Thus, this section looks at:

- the civil courts;
- tribunals;
- alternative methods of dispute resolution;
- criminal courts;
- magistrates;
- the jury;
- the legal profession;
- paying for legal services;
- the judges.

Part 5
THE CIVIL COURTS AND OTHER FORMS OF DISPUTE RESOLUTION

The civil courts

This chapter discusses:

- the division between civil and criminal courts;
- the civil courts;
- appeals in civil cases from the county court and the High Court;
- reform of the House of Lords.

Civil or criminal?

The laws that have developed in the English legal system can be divided between civil and criminal laws and often separate courts are responsible for civil and criminal matters. A crime is a wrong which is punished by the state; in most cases, the parties in the case are the wrongdoer and the state (called the Crown for these purposes), and the primary aim is to punish the wrongdoer. By contrast, a civil action is between the wrongdoer and a potential victim and the aim is to compensate the victim for the harm done. There are cases in which the same incident may give rise to both criminal and civil proceedings. An example would be a car accident, in which the driver might be prosecuted by the state for dangerous driving, and sued by the victim for the injuries caused.

This chapter looks at the civil courts which are responsible for dealing with civil legal issues. Chapter 8 looks at the criminal courts.

The civil courts

There are two main civil courts which hear civil cases at first instance. These are the county courts and the High Court. The county courts hear the cases where less money is involved, whereas the High Court hears the bigger financial cases. Thus, most civil cases start in the county court. They only start in the High Court if the claimant expects to recover more than £15,000, or £50,000 if it is a personal injury case.

There are currently around 300 county courts. The High Court is divided into three divisions: the Queen's Bench Division, the Family Division and the Chancery Division. The Family Division hears cases concerning marriage, children and the family, such as divorce, adoption and wills. The Chancery Division deals with

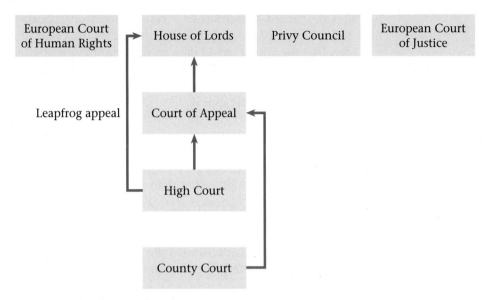

Figure 5.1 **The civil court system**

matters of finance and property, such as tax and bankruptcy. The Queen's Bench Division is the biggest of the three, with the most varied jurisdiction. The major part of its work is handling those contract and tort cases which are unsuitable for the county courts. Sitting as the Divisional Court of the Queen's Bench, its judges also hear certain criminal appeals and applications for judicial review. High Court judges usually sit alone, but the Divisional Court is so important that two or three judges sit together.

Trials in the High Court are heard either in London or in one of the 26 provincial trial centres. In theory, they are all presided over by High Court judges, but in fact there are not enough High Court judges to cope with the case load. Some cases, therefore, have to be dealt with by circuit judges and others by barristers sitting as part-time, temporary, deputy judges.

Although most civil cases are dealt with by either the county courts or the High Court, magistrates' courts have a limited civil jurisdiction, and some types of cases are tried by tribunals.

Appeals in civil law cases

Civil appeals may be made by either party to a dispute. Permission to appeal must be obtained for almost all appeals. This permission can be obtained either from the court of first instance or from the appellate court itself. Permission will be given where the appeal has a realistic prospect of success or where there is some other compelling reason why the appeal should be heard. The general rule is that appeal lies to the next level of judge in the court hierarchy.

The Access to Justice Act 1999 provides that in normal circumstances there will be only one level of appeal to the courts. Where the county court or High Court has already reached a decision in a case brought on appeal, there will be no further possibility for the case to be considered by the Court of Appeal, unless it considers that the appeal would raise an important point of principle or practice, or there is some other compelling reason for the Court of Appeal to hear it. Thus, in future, second appeals will become a rarity. Only the Court of Appeal can grant permission for this second appeal.

In the Court of Appeal cases are normally heard by three judges but, following the Access to Justice Act 1999, some smaller cases can be heard by a single judge.

Civil appeals will normally simply be a review of the decision of the lower court relying on the notes made by the earlier judge(s) and other documentary evidence of the proceedings, rather than a full rehearing, calling witnesses, etc., unless the appeal court considers that it is in the interests of justice to hold a rehearing. Written skeleton arguments should normally be provided to the court so that oral submissions can be kept brief to save time and costs. The appeal will only be allowed where the decision of the lower court was wrong, or where it was unjust because of a serious procedural or other irregularity in the proceedings of the lower court.

Appeals from the county court

Appeals from the county court based on alleged errors of law or fact are made to the Civil Division of the Court of Appeal. Appeals from a district judge's decision normally have to go first to a circuit judge and then to the High Court.

The Court of Appeal may affirm, vary (for example, by altering the amount of damages) or reverse the judgment of the county court. It is generally reluctant to overturn the trial judge's finding of fact because it does not hold a complete rehearing. As the trial judge will have had the advantage of observing the demeanour of witnesses giving their evidence, the Court of Appeal will hardly ever question his or her findings about their veracity and reliability as witnesses. From the Court of Appeal, there may be a further appeal to the House of Lords, for which leave must be granted.

Judicial review by the High Court is also possible.

Appeals from the High Court

Cases started in the High Court may be appealed to the Civil Division of the Court of Appeal. From there, a further appeal on questions of law or fact may be made, with permission, to the House of Lords.

The exception to this process is the 'leap-frog' procedure, provided for in the Administration of Justice Act 1969. Under this procedure, an appeal can go directly from the High Court to the House of Lords, missing out the Court of Appeal. The underlying rationale is that the Court of Appeal may be bound by a decision of the House of Lords, so that money and time would be wasted by going to the Court of Appeal when the only court that could look at the issue afresh is the House of Lords. In order to use this procedure, all the parties must consent to it and the High Court judge who heard the original trial must certify that the appeal is on a point of law that either:

(a) relates wholly or mainly to the construction of an enactment or of a statutory instrument, and has been fully argued in the proceedings and fully considered in the judgment of the judge in the proceedings; or

(b) is one in respect of which the judge is bound by a decision of the Court of Appeal or of the House of Lords in previous proceedings, and was fully considered in the judgments given by the Court of Appeal or the House of Lords (as the case may be) in those previous proceedings (s. 12(3)).

The trial judge has a discretion whether or not to grant this certificate, and there is no right of appeal against this decision. Even if a certificate is granted, leave will still need to be obtained from the House of Lords. If that leave is obtained, the appellant might decide that it has been given on such restrictive terms that it would prefer to follow the ordinary appeal procedure rather than go ahead with a leapfrog appeal: **Ceredigion County Council** *v* **Jones** (2007).

Quick quiz 5.1

1 Name the three divisions of the High Court.

2 Which court(s) can give permission to appeal for civil cases?

3 How many judges normally sit in the Court of Appeal?

4 Which court hears civil appeals from the High Court?

The House of Lords

Apart from cases concerning European law, this is the highest appeal court on civil matters, and all other English courts are bound by it. The government intends to abolish the House of Lords and replace it with a Supreme Court. This reform is contained in the Constitutional Reform Act 2005 and is discussed below.

sourcebook p. 326 →

Criticism and reform of the appeal system

A Supreme Court

Rather unexpectedly, the government announced in June 2003 that it was going to abolish the House of Lords and replace it with a Supreme Court. It subsequently issued a consultation paper, *Constitutional Reform: a Supreme Court for the United Kingdom* (2004), which considered the shape that this reform should take. The Constitutional Reform Act 2005 has now been passed, which contains provisions for the creation of the new court. It is expected to start hearing cases in October 2009.

sourcebook p. 293 →

The government was undoubtedly wrong to announce a decision, then consult afterwards merely on the detail, but the decision itself was probably right. There is a natural inclination towards the saying, 'If it isn't broke, don't mend it'. But, with the highest court in the land, one cannot afford to wait until it is broken before one starts to mend. It is now important that the new Supreme Court gets some quality accommodation that matches its status. The judges need space, computer support, research facilities and research assistants. The new court will have to work hard in its early years to establish its reputation nationally and internationally. It must be given all the resources necessary in order to be able to achieve this.

Reasons for abolishing the House of Lords

sourcebook p. 153 → The consultation paper stated that this reform was necessary to enhance the independence of the judiciary from both the legislature and the executive. It pointed to the growth of judicial review cases and the passing of the Human Rights Act 1998 as two key reasons why this reform was becoming urgent. Article 6 of the European Convention on Human Rights requires not only that the judges should be independent, but also that they should be seen to be independent. The fact that the Law Lords are currently a Committee of the House of Lords can raise issues about the appearance of independence from the legislature.

The government is, however, anxious to point out that the reform does not imply any dissatisfaction with the performance of the House of Lords as the country's highest court of law:

> 'On the contrary its judges have conducted themselves with the utmost integrity and independence. They are widely and rightly admired, nationally and internationally. The Government believes, however, that the time has come to establish a new court regulated by statute as a body separate from Parliament.'

Six of the current Law Lords are opposed to the reform, considering the change unnecessary and harmful.

Separation from Parliament

The new Supreme Court will be completely separate from Parliament. Its judges will have no rights to sit and vote in the upper House. Only the current Law Lords will have the right to sit and vote in the House of Lords after their retirement from the judiciary.

One advantage of this change will be that the court will no longer sit in the Palace of Westminster, where there is a shortage of space, and could be given more spacious accommodation elsewhere. It will be based in a refurbished gothic building opposite Parliament in Parliament Square.

Jurisdiction

The proposed court will be the Supreme Court for the whole of the UK. Its jurisdiction will remain the same as that of the House of Lords, but with the addition of jurisdiction in relation to devolution cases. At the moment, the Privy Council has the jurisdiction to hear cases concerning the devolution of Scotland, Wales and Northern Ireland. This jurisdiction will be transferred to the new Supreme Court. The reason for the transfer is to remove any perceived conflict of interest in which the UK Parliament, with an obvious interest in a dispute about devolution, appears to be sitting in judgment over the case.

There is no proposal to create a Supreme Court on the US model, with the power to overturn legislation. Nor is there any proposal to create a specific constitutional court. The new court will not have the power to give preliminary rulings on difficult points of law. It has been pointed out that English courts do not traditionally consider issues in the abstract, so giving such a power to the Supreme Court would sit very uneasily with our judicial traditions. This is despite the fact that we have become accustomed to this procedure for the European Court of Justice.

The government realised that there were already various entities in the United Kingdom that were known as supreme courts. In particular, the Court of Appeal, the High Court and the Crown Court were together known as the supreme court for the purposes of allocating jurisdiction to judges and routing between the courts. But this title was not in common usage and now the title of Supreme Court is reserved for the new court to be created as a result of this legislation.

Membership

The existing twelve full-time Law Lords will form the initial members of the new court. The government wants to keep the same number of full-time judges, but to continue to allow the court to call on the help of other judges on a part-time basis. The Lord Chancellor was a member of the Appellate Committee of the House of Lords, but does not have a right to sit in the Supreme Court. A President of the Court will be appointed.

The judges will no longer automatically become Lords. Members of the Supreme Court will be called 'Justices of the Supreme Court'.

Qualifications for membership will remain the same. The government has rejected the idea that changes should be made to make it easier for distinguished academics to be appointed in order to enhance the diversity of the court. This is disappointing, as the government itself acknowledges that the current pool of candidates for the post is very narrow, and the government's statistics themselves show that the current senior judiciary are not representative of society.

Candidates will not be subjected to confirmation hearings before Parliament as these would risk politicising the appointment process.

Do we need a second appeal court?

Do we need two courts with purely appellate jurisdiction? Could the House of Lords (or Supreme Court) be abolished altogether, leaving the Court of Appeal as the final appellate court? Efforts to abolish the appellate jurisdiction of the House of Lords date back over a hundred years – in fact the Judicature Act 1873 contained a section which did just that, but it was never brought into force. The following are some of the arguments on both sides.

Arguments for abolition

■ The Court of Appeal should be sufficient; a third tier is unnecessary and illogical. A. P. Herbert points out that giving appellants the chance to have their case decided by two appellate courts is like having your appendix taken out by a distinguished surgeon and then being referred to another who might confirm the first surgeon's decision, but might just as easily recommend the appendix be replaced! Reversing legal decisions might not pose the same practical problems as reversing medical ones but, nevertheless, it may seem odd that the decisions of the eminent judges in the Court of Appeal can be completely overturned by the House of Lords.

■ It adds cost and delay to achieving a decision. Usually, QCs are instructed in appeals to the House of Lords, substantially increasing costs, and extra time is taken up. This can add to emotional stress and financial hardship for one or both litigants.

Arguments against abolition

■ Its small membership allows the House of Lords to give a consistent leadership that the Court of Appeal, with its much greater number of judges, could not, and therefore to guide the harmonious development of the law. Louis Blom-Cooper QC (1972) has argued that, especially since the Practice Statement of 1966 allowing the House of Lords to overrule its own decisions, the Law Lords are in a unique position to be able to reform the law from the top. The much larger size of the Court of Appeal, and its division into different courts, means there would always be a danger of different courts within it applying different views of the law.

■ The combination of the two appellate courts allows the majority of appeals to be dealt with more quickly than the House of Lords could hope to deal with them, while still retaining the smaller court for those matters which require further consideration, and for promoting consistent development of the law.

Integration

The government is looking at whether to integrate the High Court and the county court to produce a simpler civil court system. In a unified court, all cases would start in the same way and be allocated to different sorts of judges on the basis of their complexity. In a consultation paper, *A single Civil Court?* (2005) the government considered abolishing the county courts, while giving the High Court a wider jurisdiction to hear all civil cases at first instance. The government is concerned that it is inefficient and costly for the Courts Service to administer two separate civil court systems.

Reading on the web

Any developments in the establishment of a Supreme Court are likely to be signalled on the website of the Ministry of Justice:

www.justice.gov.uk/

Chapter summary

Civil or criminal?

The laws that have developed in the English legal system can be divided between civil and criminal laws and often separate courts are responsible for civil and criminal matters.

The civil courts

There are two main civil courts which hear civil cases at first instance. These are the county courts and the High Court. The county courts hear the cases where less money is involved, whereas the High Court hears the bigger financial cases.

Appeals in civil law cases

Civil appeals may be made by either party to a dispute. Permission to appeal must be obtained for almost all appeals. The Access to Justice Act 1999 provides that, in normal circumstances, there will be only one level of appeal to the courts. Civil appeals will normally simply be a review of the decision of the lower court.

Appeals from the county court

Appeals from the county court based on alleged errors of law or fact are made to the Civil Division of the Court of Appeal. The Court of Appeal may affirm, vary or reverse the judgment of the county court. From the Court of Appeal, there may be a further appeal to the House of Lords, for which leave must be granted.

Appeal from the High Court

Cases started in the High Court may be appealed to the Civil Division of the Court of Appeal. From there, a further appeal on questions of law or fact may be made, with permission, to the House of Lords. The exception to this process is the 'leap-frog' procedure.

The House of Lords

Apart from cases concerning European law, this is the highest appeal court on civil matters, and all other English courts are bound by it.

Criticism and reform of the appeal system

The government intends to abolish the House of Lords and replace it with a new, independent Supreme Court. The provisions for this reform are contained in the Constitutional Reform Act 2005.

Integration

The government is looking at whether to integrate the High Court and the county court to produce a simpler civil court system.

Question and answer guide

For exam questions covering the material in this chapter, please see the Question and answer guide section of Chapter 22: Compensatory damages.

Group activity 1

- Divide your friends (or class) into six groups.
- Using the internet and any other available resources, each group should make notes on the membership and civil jurisdiction of one of the following courts:

  Supreme Court of the United States
  Supreme Court of Canada
  Supreme Court of India
  Supreme Court of Ireland
  Supreme Court of New Zealand
  High Court of Australia (= Australia's supreme court)

- Compare your notes with what this chapter tells you about the membership and civil jurisdiction of the new Supreme Court of the United Kingdom, looking for any significant similarities and differences.
- From these similarities and differences, what conclusions can you draw about the new Supreme Court of the United Kingdom?
- Compare your conclusions with those of the other groups.

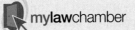

Visit www.mylawchamber.co.uk/elliottaqa to access interactive questions, quizzes and activities to test yourself on this chapter.

Tribunals

This chapter looks at:

- the history of tribunals;
- tribunals today following the Tribunals, Courts and Enforcement Act 2007;
- tribunal procedure, composition and status;
- the employment tribunals;
- the availability of appeals and judicial review;
- the advantages and disadvantages of the tribunal system.

Introduction

Many claims and disputes are settled, not by the courts, but by tribunals, each specialising in a particular area. The tribunal system handles over a million cases every year. Although tribunals have often been seen as an unimportant part of the legal system, this caseload clearly shows that they are now playing a major role. Employment tribunals are probably the best-known example, but there are many others, dealing with subjects ranging from social security and tax to forestry and patents. Not all are actually called tribunals – the category includes, for example, the Education Appeal Committee, which hears appeals concerning the allocation of school places, and the Criminal Injuries Compensation Authority, which assesses applications for compensation for victims of violent crime. The majority deal with disputes between the citizen and the state, though the employment tribunal is an obvious exception.

Tribunals are generally distinguished from the other courts by less formal procedures, and by the fact that they specialise. However, they are all expected to conduct themselves according to the same principles of natural justice used by the courts: a fair hearing for both sides and open and impartial decision-making.

Individual tribunals may differ quite markedly from each other in terms of procedure, workload and membership. For example, employment tribunals operate on an adversarial model, whereas the procedure in the Social Security tribunals is much more inquisitorial.

History

Tribunals were in existence as long ago as 1799, but the present system has really grown up since the Second World War. The main reason for this was the growth of legislation in areas which were previously considered private, and therefore rarely addressed by the state, such as Social Security benefits, housing, town and country planning, education and employment.

This legislation gave people rights – to a school place, to unemployment benefit, or not to be unfairly sacked, for example – but its rules also placed limits on these rights. Naturally, this leads to disputes: employer and employee disagree on whether the latter's dismissal was unfair under the terms of the legislation; a Social Security claimant believes he or she has been wrongly denied benefit; a landowner disputes the right of the local authority to purchase her field compulsorily.

Given the potentially vast number of disputes likely to arise, and the detailed nature of the legislation concerning them, it was felt that the ordinary court system would neither have been able to cope with the workload, nor be the best forum for sorting out such problems, hence the growth of tribunals.

As well as the administrative tribunals dealing with this kind of dispute, there are domestic tribunals, which deal with disputes and matters of discipline within particular professions – trade unions and the medical and legal professions all have tribunals like this. The decisions of these tribunals are based on the particular rules of the organisation concerned, but they are still required to subscribe to the same standards of justice as the ordinary courts and, in the case of those set up by statute, their decisions can be appealed to the ordinary courts – as can those of most administrative tribunals.

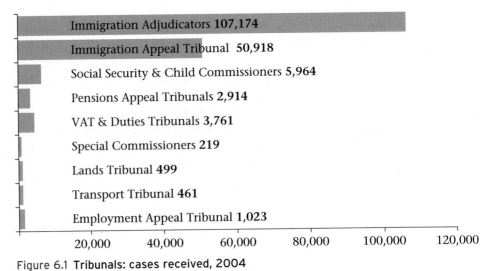

Figure 6.1 **Tribunals: cases received, 2004**

Source: 'Judicial Statistics Annual Report 2005', p. 106. © Crown Copyright 2006.

Tribunals today

Tribunals have recently been the subject of a major reform with the passing of the Tribunals, Courts and Enforcement Act 2007. This piece of legislation followed an important review of the tribunal service chaired by Sir Andrew Leggatt. Before that Act was passed, tribunals had been created by individual pieces of primary legislation, without any overarching framework.

Part 1 of the Act now creates a new, simplified statutory framework for tribunals. The Legatt Review had recommended that there should be a single Tribunal Service and the Act moves in this direction by creating two new, generic tribunals, the First-tier Tribunal and the Upper Tribunal. The Upper Tribunal is primarily, but not exclusively, an appellate tribunal from the First-tier Tribunal. The Act gives the Lord Chancellor power to transfer the jurisdiction of existing tribunals to the two new tribunals. Schedule 6 to the 2007 Act lists the tribunals which it is intended will be abolished and their jurisdiction transferred to one of the two new tribunals. These tribunals consist of most of the tribunals that have been administered by central government, such as the Mental Health Review Tribunal, the Meat Hygiene Appeals Tribunal and the Special Educational Needs and Disability Tribunal. The Act provides for the establishment of 'chambers' within the two tribunals so that the many jurisdictions that will be transferred into the tribunals can be grouped together appropriately. Each chamber will be headed by a Chamber President and the tribunals' judiciary will be headed by a Senior President of Tribunals. The Senior President is a new office and he or she will be the judicial leader of the tribunal system.

Some tribunals have been excluded from the new structures because of their specialist nature and tribunals run by local government have not been included for the time being while further consideration is given to their financial situation. The employment tribunals (discussed below) and the Employment Appeal Tribunal will keep their separate identity, though they will share the administrative arrangements of the new tribunals. These two tribunals have been retained because of the nature of the cases that come before them, which involve one private party against another, unlike most other tribunals which hear applications from citizens against decisions of the state.

All the tribunals that fall within the responsibility of central government will increasingly be administered by a centralised Tribunal Service, which was established in 2006 and is an executive agency of the Ministry of Justice.

An Administrative Justice and Tribunals Council has been created which supervises the tribunals as well as have responsibility for keeping the administrative justice system as a whole under review. It is required to consider and advise the government on how to make the system more accessible, fair and efficient.

Tribunal procedure

Until 2007, the tribunals all had their own rules of procedure. Under the 2007 Act, a new Tribunal Procedure Committee has been established with responsibility for tribunal rules of procedure. It is hoped that this Committee will establish a unified set of procedural rules.

Composition

Most tribunals consist of a legally trained chairperson, and two lay people who have some particular expertise in the relevant subject area – doctors in the Medical Appeal Tribunal, for example, and representatives of both employees' and employers' organisations in the employment tribunal. The lay members take an active part in decision-making. The legally trained members now have the title of 'judge' under the Tribunals, Courts and Enforcement Act 2007.

Tribunals composed entirely of lay people are considered to have been less effective than those with a legally qualified chairperson.

Status

Tribunals are regarded as inferior to the ordinary courts, even though they are largely independent from them in their own jurisdictions. This was confirmed in the case of **Peach Grey & Co.** v **Sommers** (1995), which concerned a claim of wrongful dismissal against a firm of solicitors, heard by an industrial tribunal. The person dismissed had tried to influence a witness due to appear before the tribunal, and his former employers claimed that this was contempt of court. The Divisional Court agreed and, in accepting that it had jurisdiction to punish this contempt, it confirmed that the tribunal is an inferior court.

Employment tribunals

Employment tribunals provide one example of a powerful tribunal playing a central role in today's society. The role of employment tribunals has altered radically since they were first established in 1964. The number of applications has risen dramatically, so that in 2001 there were 130,408 applications. The procedure is quicker than the civil courts, with 75 per cent of cases being heard within 26 weeks of receipt and only 4 per cent of cases are appealed. A MORI users' survey in 2002 found that both applicants and respondents were satisfied that cases were dealt with impartially and professionally. However, research into the employment tribunals has been carried out for the employers organisation, the Confederation of British Industry (CBI). This research, *Restoring Faith in Employment Tribunals* (2005), concluded that employers lacked confidence in the employment tribunal system and often chose to settle weak and vexatious claims to avoid using it. Among the 450 employers polled, the research found that all firms with fewer than 50 staff settled every claim, despite advice that they would win almost half the cases. Most employers felt that the tribunal system had become too adversarial. Tribunal proceedings have become more legalistic and adversarial and no longer satisfy the original idea that they should be quick, informal hearings.

Appeals and judicial review

Historically, there was no uniform appeals procedure from tribunals, and there was no absolute right of appeal from a tribunal, though most did allow some right of appeal. An example of where there was no right of appeal was the vaccine damage tribunal, set up under the Vaccine Damage Payments Act 1971 to assess claimants' rights to damages for disabilities caused by a vaccination. The Tribunals and Inquiries Act 1992 provided for appeals to the High Court on points of law from some of the most important tribunals. These appeals are heard by the Queen's Bench Division. However, appeals to the High Court are expensive, complex and time-consuming, and are therefore inconsistent with the basic aims of tribunals. Some tribunal appeals could only be made to the relevant minister, who could hardly be seen as a disinterested party.

In addition to appeal rights, decisions of tribunals are always subject to judicial review by the High Court on the grounds that they have not been made in accordance with the rules of natural justice or are not within the powers of the tribunal to make. The controlling effect of the potential for judicial review is limited by the fact that it cannot consider the merits of decisions and that, where wide discretionary powers are given to a minister, government department or local authority, the court will find it difficult to prove that many decisions are outside those powers.

The Tribunals, Courts and Enforcement Act 2007 now provides a unified appeal structure for the tribunal system. Under the Act, in most cases, a decision of the First-tier Tribunal may be appealed to the Upper Tribunal and a decision of the Upper Tribunal may be appealed to a court. The grounds of appeal must relate to a point of law. The rights to appeal may only be exercised with permission from the tribunal being appealed from or the tribunal or court being appealed to.

It is also now possible for the Upper Tribunal to deal with some judicial review cases which would in the past have been dealt with by the High Court. The Upper Tribunal has this jurisdiction only where a case falls within a class specified in a direction given by the Lord Chief Justice or transferred by the High Court. It is hoped that this simplified appeal structure will enable the law to develop more consistently.

Task 6.1

When the Lord Chancellor established the Review of Tribunals by Sir Andrew Leggatt, he set its terms of reference. These terms of reference laid down the work that the Review had to carry out. Read the terms of reference of the Review and then answer the questions below:

Terms of Reference

To review the delivery of justice through tribunals other than ordinary courts of law, constituted under an Act of Parliament by a Minister of the Crown or for the purposes of ministers' functions; in resolving disputes, whether between citizen and the state, or between other parties, to ensure that:

There are fair, timely, proportionate and effective arrangements for handling those disputes, within an effective framework for decision-making which encourages the systematic development of the area of law concerned, and which forms a coherent structure, together with the superior courts, for the delivery of administrative justice; ▶

The administrative and practical arrangements for supporting those decision-making procedures meet the requirements of the European Convention on Human Rights for independence and impartiality;

There are adequate arrangements for improving people's knowledge and understanding of their rights and responsibilities in relation to such disputes, and that tribunals and other bodies function in a way which makes those rights and responsibilities a reality;

The arrangements for the funding and management of tribunals and other bodies by government departments are efficient, effective and economical; and pay due regard both to judicial independence, and to ministerial responsibility for the administration of public funds;

Performance standards for tribunals are coherent, consistent, and public; and effective measures for monitoring and enforcing those standards are established; and tribunals overall constitute a coherent structure for the delivery of administrative justice.

The review may examine, insofar as it considers it necessary, administrative and regulatory bodies which also make judicial decisions as part of their functions.

Questions

1 Why was the government particularly concerned that the tribunals' procedures met the requirements of the European Convention on Human Rights?
2 In this context, what is meant by the 'superior courts'?
3 The Review was required to consider whether there were 'adequate arrangements for improving people's knowledge and understanding of their rights and responsibilities' in relation to disputes between citizens and the state. If you had been refused a place in the school of your choice, would you have known where to take your dispute?
4 The Review was asked to consider whether 'tribunals overall constitute a coherent structure for the delivery of administrative justice'. Will the Tribunals, Courts and Enforcement Act 2007 achieve this?

Advantages of tribunals

Speed

Tribunal cases come to court fairly quickly, and many are dealt with within a day. Many tribunals are able to specify the exact date and time at which a case will be heard, so minimising time-wasting for the parties.

Cost

Tribunals usually do not charge fees, and each party usually pays their own costs, rather than the loser having to pay all. The simpler procedures of tribunals should mean that legal representation is unnecessary, so reducing cost, but that is not always the case (see below).

Informality

This varies between different tribunals but, as a general rule, wigs are not worn, the strict rules of evidence do not apply, and attempts are made to create an unintimidating atmosphere. This is obviously a help where individuals are representing themselves.

Flexibility

Although they obviously aim to apply fairly consistent principles, tribunals do not operate strict rules of precedent, so are able to respond more flexibly than courts.

Specialisation

Tribunal members already have expertise in the relevant subject area, and through sitting on tribunals are able to build up a depth of knowledge of that area that judges in ordinary courts could not hope to match.

Relief of congestion in the ordinary courts

If the volume of cases heard by tribunals was transferred to the ordinary courts, the system would be completely overloaded.

Awareness of policy

The expertise of tribunal members means they are likely to understand the policy behind legislation in their area, and they often have wide discretionary powers which allow them to put this into practice.

Privacy

Tribunals may, in some circumstances, meet in private, so that the individual is not obliged to have their circumstances broadcast to the general public (but see the first disadvantage below).

Disadvantages of tribunals

Despite the improvements made to the tribunal system by the Tribunals, Courts and Enforcement Act 2007, problems still remain with the tribunal system.

Lack of openness

The fact that some tribunals are held in private can lead to suspicion about the fairness of their decisions.

Unavailability of state funding

Full funding from the Legal Services Commission is available for only a small number of minor tribunals. Tribunals are, of course, designed to do away with the need for representation, but the fact is that in many of them the ordinary individual will be facing an opponent with access to the very best representation – an employer, for example, or a government department – and this clearly places them at a serious disadvantage. Even though the procedures are generally informal compared with those in ordinary courts, the average person is likely to be very much out of their depth, and research by Genn and Genn in 1989 found that much of the law with which tribunals were concerned was complex, and their adjudicative process sometimes highly technical; individuals who were represented had a much better chance of winning their case.

There is, however, some dispute as to the desirability of such representation necessarily involving lawyers; although in some cases this will be the more appropriate form of representation, there are fears that introducing lawyers could detract from the aims of speed and informality. If money for tribunal representation were to become available, it may be better spent on developing lay representation, such as that offered by specialist agencies such as the UK Immigration Advisory Service, or the Child Poverty Action Group, who can develop real expertise in specific areas, as well as general agencies such as the Citizens' Advice Bureaux.

Quick quiz 6.2

1 What is the most recent piece of legislation regulating tribunals?

2 Which body has responsibility for supervising the tribunals?

3 What is the normal composition of a tribunal?

4 Is funding from the Legal Services Commission available for legal proceedings before tribunals?

Reading on the web

The Report of the Review of tribunals by Sir Andrew Leggatt is available at:

 www.tribunals-review.org.uk

The website of the Tribunal Service is at:

 www.tribunals.gov.uk/

The Tribunals, Courts and Enforcement Act 2007 is published on the website of the Office for Public Sector Information at:

 www.opsi.gov.uk/acts/acts2007/20070015.htm

The explanatory notes to the Tribunals, Courts and Enforcement Act 2007 are published on the website of the Office of Public Sector information at:

 www.opsi.gov.uk/acts/acts2007/20070015.htm

Chapter summary

Introduction

Tribunals are generally different from ordinary courts because of their less formal procedures and the fact that they are very specialist.

History

Tribunals were in existence as long ago as 1799, but the present system has really grown up since the Second World War.

Tribunals today

Part 1 of the Tribunals, Courts and Enforcement Act 2007 creates a new, simplified statutory framework for tribunals. The Act establishes two new, generic tribunals, the First-tier Tribunal and the Upper Tribunal. The Upper Tribunal is primarily, but not exclusively, an appellate tribunal from the First-tier Tribunal. The Act provides for the establishment of 'chambers' within the two tribunals so that the many jurisdictions that will be transferred into the tribunals can be grouped together appropriately. The tribunals' judiciary will be headed by a Senior President of Tribunals.

Tribunal procedure

Under the 2007 Act, a new Tribunal Procedure Committee has been established with responsibility for tribunal rules of procedure.

Composition

Most tribunals consist of a legally trained chairperson, and two lay people who have some particular expertise in the relevant subject area.

Status

Tribunals are generally regarded as inferior to the ordinary courts.

Employment tribunals

Employment tribunals provide one example of a powerful tribunal playing a central role in today's society.

Appeals from tribunals

Historically, there was no uniform appeals procedure from tribunals, though most did allow some right of appeal. Improvements to the appeal system have been made by the Tribunals, Courts and Enforcement Act 2007.

Advantages of tribunals

The advantages of tribunals include:

- speed;
- cost;
- informality;
- flexibility;
- specialisation;
- relief of congestion in the ordinary courts;
- awareness of policy; and
- privacy.

Disadvantages of tribunals

The disadvantages of tribunals include:

- lack of openness;
- unavailability of funding from the Legal Services Commission.

Question and answer guide

For exam questions covering the material in this chapter, please see the Question and answer guide section of Chapter 7: Alternative methods of dispute resolution.

Group activity 1

- Divide your friends (or class) into groups of two or three people.
- Using the internet and any other available resources, each group should make notes on the membership and jurisdiction of any one type of tribunal. Make your choice from the list of tribunals on the Tribunal Service website: www.tribunals.gov.uk/tribunalatoz.htm.
- Compare notes with the other groups, looking for any common themes.
- What conclusions can you draw about the membership and jurisdiction of tribunals generally?

---

mylawchamber

Visit **www.mylawchamber.co.uk/elliottaqa** to access interactive questions, quizzes and activities to test yourself on this chapter.

Chapter 7

Alternative methods of dispute resolution

This chapter considers the alternatives to courts. In particular, it looks at:
■ the problems with court hearings;
■ the four main alternative dispute resolution (ADR) mechanisms;
■ examples of ADR;
■ the advantages and disadvantages of using ADR.

Introduction

Court hearings are not always the best method of resolving a dispute, and their disadvantages mean that, for some types of problem, alternative mechanisms may be more suitable. Under the rules of civil procedure the courts are required to encourage and facilitate the use of alternative methods of dispute resolution (ADR) and help the parties to settle a case out of court.

In **Halsey v Milton Keynes General NHS Trust** (2004) the Court of Appeal held that the courts do not, however, have the power to force parties to try ADR, as this might amount to a breach of a person's right to a fair trial under Art. 6 of the European Convention on Human Rights.

Problems with court hearings

Alternative methods of dispute resolution have become increasingly popular because of the difficulties of trying to resolve disputes through court hearings. Below are some of the specific problems posed by court hearings.

The adversarial process

A trial necessarily involves a winner and a loser, and the adversarial procedure, combined with the often aggressive atmosphere of court proceedings divides the parties, making them end up enemies even where they did not start out that way. This can be a disadvantage where there is some reason for the parties to sustain a relationship after the problem under discussion is sorted out – child custody cases are the obvious example, but in business, too, there may be advantages in resolving a dispute in a way which does not make enemies of the parties. The court system is often said to be best suited to areas where the parties are strangers and happy to remain so – it is interesting to note that in small-scale societies with close kinship links, court-type procedures are rarely used, and disputes are usually settled by negotiation processes that aim to satisfy both parties, and thus maintain the harmony of the group.

Technical cases

Some types of dispute rest on detailed technical points, such as the way in which a machine should be made, or the details of a medical problem, rather than on points of law. The significance of such technical details may not be readily understandable by an ordinary judge. Expert witnesses or advisers may be brought in to advise on these points, but this takes time, and so raises costs. Where detailed technical evidence is at issue, alternative methods of dispute resolution can employ experts in a particular field to take the place of a judge.

Inflexible

In a court hearing, the rules of procedure lay down a fixed framework for the way in which problems are addressed. This may be inappropriate in areas which are of largely private concern to the parties involved. Alternative methods can allow the parties themselves to take more control of the process.

Imposed solutions

Court hearings impose a solution on the parties, which, since it does not involve their consent, may need to be enforced. If the parties are able to negotiate a settlement between them, to which they both agree, this should be less of a problem.

Publicity

The majority of court hearings are public. This may be undesirable in some business disputes, where one or both of the parties may prefer not to make public the details of their financial situation or business practices because of competition.

Alternative dispute resolution mechanisms

Where, for one or more of the reasons explained above, court action is not the best way of solving a dispute, a wide range of alternative methods of dispute resolution (ADR) may be used. Four main forms of ADR can be identified: arbitration, mediation, conciliation and negotiation.

- **Arbitration** is a procedure whereby both sides to a dispute agree to let a third party, the arbitrator, decide. The arbitrator may be a lawyer, or may be an expert in the field of the dispute. He or she will make a decision according to the law and the decision is legally binding.

- **Mediation** involves the appointment of a mediator to help the parties to a dispute reach an agreement which each considers acceptable. Mediation can be 'evaluative', where the mediator gives an assessment of the legal strength of a case, or 'facilitative', where the mediator concentrates on assisting the parties to define the issues. When a mediation is successful and an agreement is reached, it is written down and forms a legally binding contract unless the parties state otherwise.
- **Conciliation** is similar to mediation but the conciliator takes a more interventionist role than the mediator in bringing the two parties together and in suggesting possible solutions to help achieve an agreed settlement. The term conciliation is gradually falling into disuse and the process is regarded as a form of mediation.
- **Negotiation** is one of the simplest forms of ADR involving discussions between the parties with or without the help of lawyers to try to resolve the dispute – the high numbers of civil cases settled out of court are examples of this.

Figure 7.1 **The ABTA logo**

Source: Association of British Travel Agents.

Formal ADR schemes include the Advisory, Conciliation and Arbitration Service (ACAS), which mediates in many industrial disputes and unfair dismissal cases; the role of ombudsmen in dealing with disputes in the fields of insurance and banking, and in complaints against central and local government and public services; the work done by trade organisations such as the Association of British Travel Agents (ABTA) in settling consumer complaints; inquiries into such areas as objections concerning compulsory purchase or town and country planning; the conciliation schemes offered by courts and voluntary organisations to divorcing couples; and the arbitration schemes run by the Institute of Arbitrators for business disputes. We will look at some of these in more detail below. Though procedural details vary widely, what they all have in common is that they are attempting to provide a method of settling disagreements that avoids some or all of the disadvantages of the court system listed above.

Examples of ADR

Below are some examples of ADR being used in practice.

Conciliation in unfair dismissal cases

A statutory conciliation scheme administered by ACAS operates before cases of unfair dismissal can be taken to an employment tribunal. ACAS conciliation officers talk to both sides, with the aim of settling the dispute without a tribunal hearing; they are supposed to procure reinstatement of the employee where possible, but in practice most settlements are only for damages.

A conciliation officer contacts each party or their representatives to discuss the case and advise each side on the strength or weakness of their position. They may tell each side what the other has said, but if the case does eventually go to a tribunal, none of this information is admissible without the consent of the party who gave it.

Evaluation

The success of the scheme is sometimes measured by the fact that two-thirds of cases are either withdrawn or settled by the conciliation process. However, this ignores the imbalance in power between the employer and the employee, especially where the employee has no legal representation – the fact that there has been a settlement does not necessarily mean it is a fair one, when one party is under far more pressure to agree than the other. Dickens's 1985 study of unfair dismissal cases found that awards after a hearing were generally higher than those achieved by conciliation, implying that employees may feel under pressure to agree to any settlement. The study suggested that the scheme would be more effective in promoting fair settlements – rather than settlement at any price – if conciliation officers had a less neutral stance and instead tried to help enforce the worker's rights.

> ✓ **Know your terms 7.1**
>
> Define the following terms:
>
> 1 Adversarial process.
> 2 Arbitrator.
> 3 ADR.
> 4 ACAS.

Mediation in divorce cases

In many ways, the court system is an undesirable forum for divorce and its attendant disputes over property and children, since the adversarial nature of the system can aggravate the differences between the parties. This makes the whole process more traumatic for those involved, and clearly is especially harmful where there are children. Consequently, conciliation has for some time been made available to divorcing couples, not necessarily to get them back together (though this can happen), but to try to ensure that any arrangements between them can be made as amicably as possible, reducing the strain on the parties themselves as well as their children.

The Family Law Act 1996 makes changes to the divorce laws and places a greater emphasis on mediation. The Act requires those seeking public funding for representation in family proceedings to attend a meeting with a mediator to consider whether mediation might be suitable in their case.

Evaluation

In divorce cases generally, success depends on the parties themselves and their willingness to cooperate. The parties may find that meeting in a neutral environment, with the help of an experienced, impartial professional helps them communicate calmly, and can make the process of divorce less painful for the couple and their children, by avoiding the need for a court battle in which each feels obliged to accuse the other of being unfit to look after their children – a battle which can be as expensive as it is unpleasant, at a time when one or both parties may be under considerable financial strain.

A three-year study undertaken as a pilot scheme for the new reforms found that eight out of ten couples reached agreement on some issues through mediation, and four in ten reached a complete settlement. However, the Solicitors' Family Law Association (SFLA) points out that because men are usually the main earners in a family, and women's earning abilities may be limited by the demands of childcare, women may need lawyers to get a fair deal financially; in fact the

SFLA says the reforms may well turn out to be 'a rogue's charter for unscrupulous husbands'.

Commercial arbitration

Many commercial contracts contain an arbitration agreement, requiring any dispute to be referred to arbitration before court proceedings are undertaken – the aim being to do away with the need for going to court. Arbitrators usually have some expertise in the relevant field, and lists of suitable individuals are kept by the Institute of Arbitration. The parties themselves choose their arbitrator, ensuring that the person has the necessary expertise in their area and is not connected to either of them. Once appointed, the arbitrator is required to act in an impartial, judicial manner just as a judge would, but the difference is that they will not usually need to have technical points explained to them, so there is less need for expert witnesses.

Disputes may involve disagreement over the quality of goods supplied, interpretation of a trade clause or point of law, or a mixture of the two. Where points of law are involved the arbitrator may be a lawyer.

The Arbitration Act 1996 aims to promote commercial arbitration, by providing a clear framework for its use. It sets out the powers of the parties to shape the process according to their needs, and provides that they must each do everything necessary to allow the arbitration to proceed properly and without delay. It also spells out the powers of arbitrators, which include limiting the costs to be recoverable by either party and making orders which are equivalent to High Court injunctions if the parties agree. Arbitrators are also authorised to play an inquisitorial role, investigating the facts of the case – many of them are, after all, experts in the relevant fields.

Arbitration hearings must be conducted in a judicial manner, in accordance with the rules of natural justice, but proceedings are informal and held in private, with the time and place decided by the parties. The arbitrator's decision, known as the award, is often delivered immediately, and is as binding on the parties as a High Court judgment would be, and if necessary can be enforced as one.

The award is usually to be considered as final, but appeal may be made to the High Court on a question of law, with the consent of all the parties, or with the permission of court. Permission will only be given if the case could substantially affect the rights of one of the parties, and provided (with some exceptions) that they had not initially agreed to restrict rights of appeal. The High Court may confirm, vary or reverse the award, or send it back to the arbitrator for reconsideration.

Evaluation

Arbitration fees can be high, but for companies this may be outweighed by the money they save through being able to get the problem solved as soon as it arises, rather than having to wait months for a court hearing. The arbitration hearing itself tends to be quicker than a court case, because of the expertise of the arbitrator – in a court hearing time, and therefore money, can be wasted in explanation of technical points to the judge.

The ability of the parties to choose their arbitrator promotes mutual trust in and respect for the decision, and arbitration is conducted with a view to compromise rather than combat, which avoids destroying the business relationship between the parties. Privacy ensures that business secrets are not made known to competitors. Around 10,000 commercial cases a year go to arbitration, which tends to suggest that business people are fairly happy with the system and the more detailed framework set out by the 1996 Act is thought likely to increase use even further.

Quick quiz 7.2

1 Which body administers the statutory conciliation scheme in cases of unfair dismissal?

2 Which Act introduced a greater emphasis on mediation in divorce proceedings?

3 If you had a disastrous holiday in Spain which you think is the fault of your travel agent, which body will arrange conciliation and arbitration of any subsequent dispute?

4 What is the name of the Act which lays down the main laws governing the use of arbitration procedures?

Advantages of ADR

Cost

Many procedures try to work without any need for legal representation, and even those that do involve lawyers may be quicker and therefore cheaper than going to court.

In 1998, Professor Genn carried out research into a mediation scheme at Central London County Court. The scheme's objective was to offer virtually cost-free court-annexed mediation to disputing parties at an early stage in litigation. This involved a three-hour session with a trained mediator assisting parties to reach a settlement, with or without legal representation. The scheme's purpose was to promote swift dispute settlement and a reduction in legal costs through an informal process that parties might prefer to court proceedings. Hazel Genn's research did not find clear evidence that mediation saved costs. The overall cost of cases which were settled through mediation was significantly less than those which were litigated; but where mediation was used and the parties failed to reach an agreement, and then went on to litigate, it was possible for costs to be increased.

Accessibility

Alternative methods tend to be more informal than court procedures, without complicated rules of evidence. The process can therefore be less intimidating and less stressful than court proceedings.

Speed

The delays in the civil court system are well known, and waiting for a case to come to court may, especially in commercial cases, add considerably to the overall cost, and adversely affect business.

The research carried out by Professor Genn (1998) found that mediation was able to promote and speed up settlement. The majority (62 per cent) of mediated cases were settled at the mediation appointment.

Expertise

Those who run alternative dispute resolution schemes often have specialist knowledge of the relevant areas, which can promote a fairer as well as a quicker settlement.

Conciliation of the parties

Most alternative methods of dispute resolution aim to avoid irrevocably dividing the parties, so enabling business or family relationships to be maintained.

Customer satisfaction

Research by Hazel Genn (2002) found that ADR generally results in a high level of customer satisfaction.

Problems with ADR

Imbalances of power

As the unfair dismissal conciliation scheme shows, the benefits of voluntarily negotiating agreement may be undermined where there is a serious imbalance of power between the parties – in effect, one party is acting less voluntarily than the other.

Lack of legal expertise

Where a dispute hinges on difficult points of law, an arbitrator may not have the required legal expertise to judge.

No system of precedent

There is no doctrine of precedent, and each case is judged on its merits, providing no real guidelines for future cases.

Enforcement

Decisions not made by courts may be difficult to enforce.

Low take-up rate

There is a low take-up rate for ADR, and the numbers have not increased as much as expected following the introduction of the Woolf reforms. Research carried out for the government, *Further Findings: a continuing evaluation of the civil justice reforms*, has found that after a substantial rise in the first year following the introduction of the Civil Procedure Rules 1998, there has been a levelling off in the number of cases in which alternative dispute resolution is used.

Hazel Genn's research (2002) found that, outside commercial practice: 'the profession remains very cautious about the use of ADR. Positive experience of ADR does not appear to be producing armies of converts.' She looked at the reasons why parties choose not to use ADR. For the Commercial Court ADR scheme, the most common reasons given for refusal to mediate were:

- a judgment was required for policy reasons;
- the appeal turned on a point of law;
- the past history or behaviour of the opponent.

The most common reasons given for not trying ADR following an ADR order in the Court of Appeal were:

- the case was not appropriate for ADR;
- the parties did not want to try ADR;
- the timing of the order was wrong (too early or too late); or
- there was no faith in ADR as a process in general.

In addition, Professor Hazel Genn has suggested that, following the Woolf reforms, the increased number of pre-trial settlements might mean that fewer people feel the need for ADR in 'run of the mill' cases. The research concluded that an individualised approach to the directing of cases towards ADR is likely to be more effective than general invitations at an early stage in the litigation process. This would require the development of clearly articulated selection principles. The timing of invitations or directions to mediate is crucial. The early stages of proceedings may not be the best time, and should not be the only opportunity to consider using ADR.

The future for ADR

Although ADR appears to meet many of the principles for effective civil justice, the proportion of people with legal problems who choose to use ADR has remained very low, even when there are convenient and free schemes available. It is not altogether clear why this is so. Hazel Genn's research (1998) found that in only 5 per cent of cases did the parties agree to try mediation, despite vigorous attempts to stimulate demand. It was least likely to be used where both parties had legal representation.

At present, many of those contemplating litigation will go first to a solicitor and Professor Genn's research shows widespread misunderstanding about mediation processes amongst solicitors. Many did not know what was involved and were therefore not able to advise clients on whether their case was suitable for any form of ADR, or the benefits that might flow from seeking to use it. Solicitors were apprehensive about showing weakness through accepting mediation in the context of traditional adversarial litigation. Litigants were also hostile to the idea of compromise, particularly in the early stages of litigation.

It is likely that, in the future, ADR will play an increasingly important role in the resolution of disputes. It is already widely used in the US, where the law frequently requires parties to try mediation before their case can be set down for trial. It is generally accepted that the UK will see a similar expansion in the use of ADR, as both the courts and the legal profession begin to take ADR more seriously than they once did. Following Lord Woolf's reforms of the civil justice system, the new rules of procedure in the civil courts impose on the judges a duty to encourage parties in appropriate cases to use ADR and to facilitate its use. Parties can request that court proceedings be postponed while they try ADR and the court can also order a postponement for this reason. Backing up this position is the fact that the government has said, in the explanatory notes to the Access to Justice Act 1999, that in time it hopes to extend public funding to increasingly cover the use of ADR.

Reading on the internet

The research carried out by Professor Genn in 1998 on the mediation scheme at Central London County Court is available on the former Department for Constitutional Affairs website:

www.dca.gov.uk/research/1998/598esfr.htm

Chapter summary

Introduction

Following Lord Woolf's reforms of the civil justice system, ADR should play a more important role in solving all types of civil disputes. ADR has become increasingly popular because of problems resolving disputes through court hearings.

Alternative dispute resolution mechanisms

Four main forms of ADR can be identified:

- arbitration;
- mediation;
- conciliation;
- negotiation.

Conciliation in unfair dismissal cases

A statutory conciliation scheme administered by the Advisory, Conciliation and Arbitration Service (ACAS) operates before cases of unfair dismissal can be taken to an employment tribunal.

Mediation in divorce cases

The Family Law Act 1996 has made changes to the divorce laws and places a greater emphasis on mediation.

Commercial arbitration

Many commercial contracts contain an arbitration agreement, requiring any dispute to be referred to arbitration before court proceedings are undertaken.

Advantages of ADR

The advantages of ADR include:

- cost;
- accessibility;
- speed;
- expertise;
- conciliation of the parties; and
- customer satisfaction.

Problems with ADR

The problems with ADR are that:

- there may be a serious imbalance of power between the parties;
- an arbitrator may lack legal expertise;
- there is no system of precedent;
- enforcement may be difficult; and
- there is low take-up rate.

The future of ADR

It is likely that in the future ADR will play an increasingly important role in the resolution of disputes.

Question and answer guides

1

(a) Explain the role of tribunals in the English legal system.

(b) Discuss two alternative methods of dispute resolution.

(c) Discuss the advantages, where there is a civil dispute, of using an alternative method of dispute resolution.

(a) Each type of tribunal specialises in a particular type of case. The majority deal with disputes between the citizen and the state: for example, the Social Security and Child Support Appeals Tribunal looks at, among other things, disputes over state benefits. But employment tribunals are an exception; they deal with disputes between employees and employers over, for example, dismissal or discrimination.

Most tribunals consist of a legally trained chairperson (who has the status of a professional judge following the Tribunals, Courts and Enforcement Act 2007 (TCEA)) and two lay people who have some particular expertise in the relevant subject area, for example, representatives of both employees' and employers' organisations in the employment tribunal.

The procedures followed in tribunals are generally less formal than in the courts. However, they are expected to conduct themselves according to the same principles of natural justice. Until 2007, the tribunals all had their own rules of procedure. But under the TCEA a new Tribunal Procedure Committee has been established with responsibility for tribunal rules of procedure. It is hoped that this committee will establish a unified set of procedural rules.

Historically, there was no uniform appeals procedure from tribunals, and there was no absolute right of appeal from a tribunal, though most did allow some right of appeal. The TCEA now provides a unified appeal structure for the tribunal system.

(b) Arbitration is a procedure whereby the parties to a dispute agree to it being resolved by a third party. The latter – an arbitrator – is agreed upon by the parties and will usually be an expert in the field of the dispute. Arbitration is most often used to resolve disputes arising out of commercial contracts. Indeed, the latter often contain a clause stating that if any dispute arises it must be referred to arbitration and not to the courts.

Arbitration hearings must be conducted in accordance with the rules of natural justice, but proceedings are informal and private, with the time and place decided by the parties. The arbitrator's award is final, but appeal may be made to the High Court on a question of law.

Mediation involves the appointment of a mediator to help the parties to a dispute reach an agreement which each considers acceptable. It can be either 'evaluative', where the mediator gives an assessment of the strength of a party's case, or 'facilitative', where the mediator simply helps the parties define the issues.

The types of disputes dealt with by mediation include disputes over wills, commercial disputes and disputes between neighbours. Mediation is also used in divorce cases, either to achieve a reconciliation or to settle the end of the relationship as amicably as possible.

(c) The informality of alternative dispute resolution (ADR) makes it less intimidating and less stressful than going to court. The parties are unlikely to be legally represented and this should help keep costs down. The location and timing of the hearings is likely to be more convenient than if the parties went to court, again saving them money.

Those who deliver ADR schemes (such as arbitrators and mediators) often have specialist knowledge of the relevant areas, which can promote a fairer as well as a quicker settlement. This is a particular advantage where the evidence involves a lot of technical and/or scientific information.

ADR avoids the delays of the civil court system, an advantage of particular importance in commercial or family disputes, as the quicker the dispute is settled the quicker the parties can get back to business or to leading their normal lives.

The fact that ADR is private means that it avoids the parties having to 'wash their dirty linen in public' and protects companies' commercial secrets. This further helps to reduce the collateral damage so often inherent in litigation.

Another advantage of ADR is that it frees up the courts, giving them more time to deal with those disputes which are not suitable for resolution by ADR, or in which ADR has been tried but failed.

2

(a) Explain any **three** forms of Alternative Dispute Resolution (ADR). Include a description of the types of case they deal with. (*20 marks*)

(b) Discuss the **disadvantages** of ADR as a form of dispute resolution. (*10 marks*)

(from AQA Exam Paper, January 2007)

(a)
Mediation

- Explain what it involves, mentioning use of independent/neutral mediator.
- Explain the difference between 'evaluative' and 'facilitative' mediation.
- Describe the types of disputes dealt with by mediation, e.g. commercial, neighbours, divorce.

Conciliation

- Explain how the terms 'mediation' and 'conciliation' are often treated as interchangeable.
- Explain how the only real difference between conciliation and mediation is that a conciliator is more interventionist than a mediator.
- Describe the types of disputes dealt with by conciliation.
- For a good answer, refer to ACAS (the Advisory, Conciliation and Arbitration Service).

Negotiation

- Explain what it involves.
- Emphasise its simplicity and popularity as a form of ADR.
- Explain how it is used to resolve all types of dispute.

- For a good answer, distinguish between formal negotiation (involving lawyers) and informal negotiation (not involving lawyers).

(b)
Bargaining power

- Discuss how voluntary participation in ADR may be undermined where there is an imbalance of power between the parties.

Expertise

- Discuss how, where a dispute hinges on difficult points of law, an arbitrator may not have the required legal expertise.

Take-up

- Discuss the low take-up rate for ADR, with usage not increasing as much as expected following the Woolf reforms. For a good answer, suggests reasons for this.

Common errors in (a)

- writing about more than three forms of ADR;
- writing about public inquiries.

Common errors in (b)

- writing about advantages instead of disadvantages;
- merely identifying disadvantages but not discussing them.

Group activity 1

- Divide your friends (or class) into groups of two or three people.
- Using the internet and any other available resources, prepare a short profile of one of the organisations listed as 'Accredited Mediation Providers' on the website of the Civil Mediation Council: www.civilmediation.org/provider-organisations.php.
- Your profile should concentrate on the type of ADR services the organisation offers and the type of people (qualifications, training, etc.) they employ to deliver those services. Try also to find out what the organisation charges for its services, though this may be difficult!
- Compare your profile with those of the other groups, looking for any common themes.

Group activity 2

Working in groups, look at the booking conditions of any ABTA member holiday tour operator either on a travel agent's website or in a holiday brochure. Find the clause dealing with 'disputes' or 'complaints'. Imagine that you had booked a cruise with this travel agent and had suffered severe food poisoning after eating from the ship's buffet. How will your subsequent complaint be handled by the travel agent? Look at the ABTA code of conduct on its website:

www.abta.com/download/codeofconduct.pdf

Looking at the ABTA code of conduct do you think an alternative method of dispute resolution might be used to try and resolve your complaint?

Visit **www.mylawchamber.co.uk/elliottaqa** to access interactive questions, quizzes and activities to test yourself on this chapter.

Part 6
THE CRIMINAL COURTS AND
LAY PEOPLE

Chapter

8 | Criminal courts

> **This chapter discusses:**
> - the two criminal trial courts: the magistrates' court and the Crown Court;
> - the classification of offences as summary, indictable or either-way offences;
> - the criminal trial process for adults and young people;
> - appeals from the magistrates' court and the Crown Court;
> - the powers of the prosecution to appeal following the acquittal of a defendant;
> - the criticism and reform plans for the appeal system.

Introduction

There are two main courts where people can be put on trial to decide whether they are guilty of committing a criminal offence: the magistrates' court and the Crown Court. In general terms, magistrates' courts hear the less serious cases (such as minor driving offences), while the Crown Court hears the more serious offences (such as murder and rape). In most magistrates' courts, three 'lay magistrates' (in other words, they are not qualified lawyers) hear the case. In the Crown Court, a jury hears the case with a professional judge presiding over the proceedings. When a person has committed a criminal offence, the classification of that offence determines which court will hear the case.

Classification of offences

There are three different categories of criminal offence: summary, indictable and triable either way.

Summary offences

Summary offences are the most minor crimes, and are only triable summarily in the magistrates' court. 'Summary' refers to the process of ordering the defendant to attend the court by summons, a written order usually delivered by post, which is the most frequent procedure adopted in the magistrates' courts. There has been some criticism of the fact that more and more offences have been made summary only, reducing the right to trial by jury in the Crown Court.

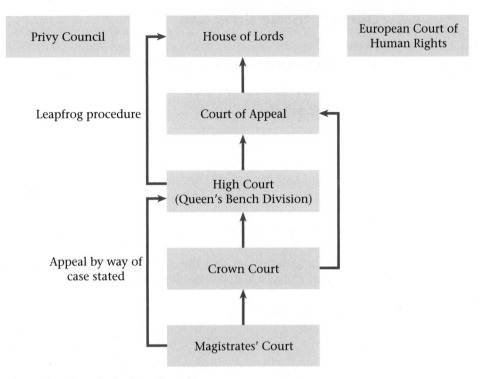

Figure 8.1 **The criminal court system**

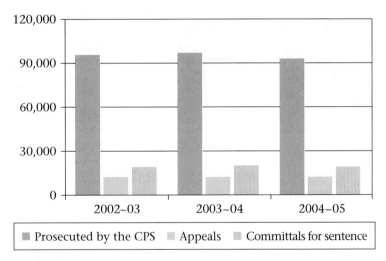

Figure 8.2 **Crown Court caseload**

Source: 'Crown Prosecution Service Annual Report 2004-2005', p. 38. © Crown Copyright 2005.

Indictable offences

These are the more serious offences, such as rape and murder. They can only be heard by the Crown Court. The indictment is a formal document containing the alleged offences against the accused, supported by brief facts.

Offences triable either way

These offences may be tried in either the magistrates' court or the Crown Court. Common examples are theft and burglary.

Mode of trial

Where a person is charged with an offence triable either way, he or she can insist on a trial by jury. If the person states that they wish to be tried in the magistrates' court, the magistrates can still decide that they think the Crown Court would be the more appropriate venue and send the case to be heard in a Crown Court despite the person's preference to be tried by a magistrates' court. In reaching this decision, the magistrates will take into account the seriousness of the case and whether they are likely to have sufficient sentencing powers to deal with it. Since 1996, the magistrates are also able to take into account the defendant's plea of guilty or not guilty, which will be given, for triable either-way offences, before the mode of trial decision. If the defendant indicates a guilty plea, the court proceeds to sentence or commits the case to the Crown Court for sentence. If the defendant pleads not guilty, or fails to indicate a plea, the court decides the mode of trial.

The Criminal Justice Act 2003, Sch. 3, has made certain changes to the mode of trial procedures. When deciding whether the case should stay in the magistrates' court, the magistrates will be informed of the defendant's prior convictions. If the magistrates decide summary trial is appropriate, defendants will have the right to ask for an indication of sentence on plea of guilty before deciding which court to choose. Committal for sentence has been abolished for less serious either-way cases. Magistrates' sentencing powers have been increased from six to twelve months' custody, in the hope that magistrates will send fewer cases to the Crown Court for sentencing.

Dr Andrew Herbert (2003) has carried out research into the magistrates' decision to send cases to the Crown Court. He has concluded that the reforms in the Criminal Justice Act 2003 are doomed to fail in reducing the number of cases referred to the Crown Court. The main Home Office reason for the recent reform attempts has been to reduce costs and increase efficiency. The chief finding of the research is that the magistrates overwhelmingly reject this reason for changing the court venue:

'There was a virtual consensus among those interviewed that there was no need for any significant change in the division of business between the higher and the lower courts.'

Magistrates felt that the existing law produced a fair and realistic choice of court. They resented reforms being made for economic or political reasons. Some of the magistrates interviewed pointed to the importance of their judicial independence, so that government policy would not persuade them to keep more cases. One of the magistrates said:

'I would never agree to retaining cases on economic grounds. I am fed up with political speak. There should not be pressure put on us. We are trained to do a job and should be left to do it.'

The lawyers interviewed thought that lay magistrates were already being asked to handle cases at the extreme of their ability and were not capable of dealing with more serious cases.

Task 8.1

Complete the following table.

Type of offence	Trial court
Summary	
Triable either way	
Indictable offence	

The Crown Prosecution Service

The Crown Prosecution Service was established in 1985 as a national prosecution service for England and Wales. Following the Criminal Justice Act 2003, the Crown Prosecution Service decides whether to charge an offender for most criminal offences in the light of the information that it receives from the police.

The trial

Apart from the role played by the jury in the Crown Court, the law and procedure in the Crown Court and magistrates' court are essentially the same. Defendants should normally be present at the trial, though the trial can proceed without them if they have chosen to abscond. A lawyer should usually represent them in their absence (**R** *v* **Jones** (2002)).

The trial begins with the prosecution outlining the case against the accused, and then producing evidence to prove its case. The prosecution calls its witnesses, who will give their evidence in response to questions from the prosecution (called examination-in-chief). These witnesses can then be questioned by the defence (called cross-examination), and then if required, re-examined by the prosecution to address any points brought up in cross-examination.

When the prosecution has presented all its evidence, the defence can submit that there is no case to answer, which means that on the prosecution evidence, no reasonable jury (or Bench of magistrates) could convict. If the submission is successful, a verdict of not guilty will be given straight away. If no such submission is made, or if the submission is unsuccessful, the defence then puts forward its case, using the same procedure for examining witnesses as the prosecution did. The accused is the only witness who cannot be forced to give evidence.

Once the defence has presented all its evidence, each side makes a closing speech, outlining their case and seeking to persuade the magistrates or jury of it. In the Crown Court, this is followed by the judge's summing up to the

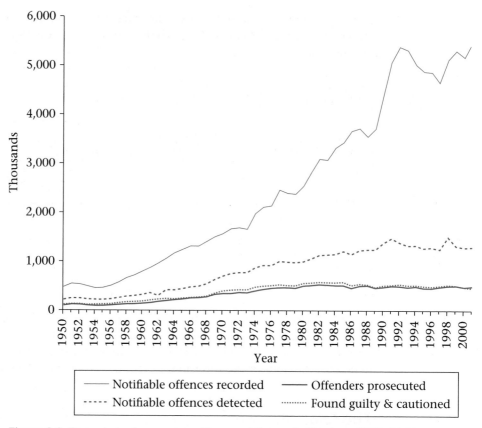

Figure 8.3 Recorded crime, prosecutions and 'known' offenders, 1950-2001
Source: 'Criminal Statistics England and Wales 2001', p. 16, [Figure 1.2]. © Crown Copyright 2002.

jury. The judge should review the evidence, draw the jury's attention to the important points of the case, and direct the jury on the law if necessary, but must not trespass on the jury's function of deciding the true facts of the case. At the end of the summing up, the judge reminds the jury that the prosecution must prove its case beyond reasonable doubt, and tries to explain in simple terms what this means.

Trial of young offenders

Young offenders are usually tried in youth courts, which are a branch of the magistrates' court. Other than those involved in the proceedings, the parents and the press, nobody may be present unless authorised by the court. Parents or guardians of children under 16 must attend court at all stages of the proceedings, and the court has the power to order parents of older children to attend.

In limited circumstances, young persons can be tried in a Crown Court; for example, if the offence charged is murder, manslaughter or causing death by dangerous driving. They may sometimes be tried in an adult magistrates' court or the Crown Court if there is a co-defendant in the case who is an adult. Following a Practice Direction discussed below, a separate trial should be ordered unless it is in the interests of justice to do otherwise. If a joint trial is ordered, the ordinary procedures apply 'subject to such modifications (if any) as the court might see fit to order'.

The trial procedures for young offenders have been reformed in the light of a recent ruling of the European Court of Human Rights. This found that John Venables and Robert Thompson, who were convicted by a Crown Court of murdering the two-year-old James Bulger in 1993, did not have a fair trial in accordance with Art. 6 of the European Convention on Human Rights. It concluded that the criminal procedures adopted in the trial prevented their participation:

> 'The public trial process in an adult court with attendant publicity was a severely intimidating procedure for 11-year-old children . . . The way in which the trial placed the accused in a raised dock as the focus of intense public attention over a period of three weeks, had impinged on their ability to participate in the proceedings in any meaningful manner.'

Following this decision, a Practice Direction was issued by the Lord Chief Justice, laying down guidance on how young offenders should be tried when their case is to be heard in the Crown Court. The language used by the Practice Direction follows closely that used in the European decision. It does not lay down fixed rules but states that the individual trial judge must decide what special measures are required by the particular case, taking into account 'the age, maturity and development (intellectual and emotional) of the young defendant on trial'. The trial process should not expose that defendant to avoidable intimidation, humiliation or distress. All possible steps should be taken to assist the defendant to understand and participate in the proceedings. It recommends that young defendants should be brought into the court out of hours in order to become accustomed to its layout. John Venables and Robert Thompson had both benefited from these familiarisation visits. The police should make every effort to avoid exposure of the defendant to intimidation, vilification or abuse.

As regards the trial, it is recommended that wigs and gowns should not be worn and public access should be limited. The courtroom should be adapted so that, ordinarily, everyone sits on the same level. In the Bulger trial, the two defendants sat in a specially raised dock. The decision to raise the dock had been done so that the defendants could view the proceedings, but the Court of Human Rights noted that, while it did accomplish this, it also made the defendants aware that everyone was looking at them. Placing everyone on the same level should alleviate this problem. In addition, the Practice Direction states that young defendants should sit next to their families or an appropriate adult and near their lawyers.

The Practice Direction suggests that only those with a direct interest in the outcome of the trial should be permitted within the court. Where the press is restricted, provision should be made for the trial to be viewed through a CCTV link to another court area.

Task 8.2

In 2003 the Youth Justice Board published its annual report, *Gaining Ground in the Community*. This report examined the types of crime being committed by young offenders and the experience of young people as victims of crime. The report states:

Types of offence

Both the annual MORI Youth Survey and the data from Young Offending Teams provide information on the types of crimes being committed by young people. The most common offences committed by young people brought into contact with the youth justice system fall into the following categories:

- Motoring offences (23 per cent).
- Theft and handling (17.8 per cent).
- Violence against the person (13 per cent).
- Criminal damage (10.2 per cent).
- Public order offences (6.7 per cent).

Victimisation and fears of young people

There are continuing high levels of fear among young people, according to the MORI Youth Survey, with a third of respondents saying that they felt unsafe in their local area after dark. Over half of young people in school are worried about being physically assaulted or being the victim of theft. A third worry about bullying and racism.

Some 46 per cent of young people in school and 61 per cent of excluded young people say that they have been a victim of crime in the last 12 months. Two-thirds of young people who have been victims of crime say that the perpetrator of the offence is another young person aged under 18.

Questions

1 What type of crime is a young person most likely to commit?
2 Are you frightened to go out in your local area after dark?
3 What percentage of young people have been the victim of a crime in the last 12 months?
4 Have you been the victim of a crime?

Appeals in criminal law cases

The appeal process is supposed to spot cases where there have been wrongful convictions at an early stage so that the injustice can be promptly remedied. A wrongful conviction could arise because of police or prosecution malpractice, a misdirection by a judge, judicial bias, or because expert evidence, such as forensic evidence, was misleading. Sadly, the Court of Appeal in particular failed in the past to detect such problems and this led to demands for reform. The Criminal Appeal Act 1995 was therefore passed to make major amendments to the criminal appeal procedure.

From the magistrates' court

There are four routes of appeal from a magistrates' court.

Rectification

The magistrates can rectify an error they have made under s. 142 of the Magistrates' Courts Act 1980. The case is retried before a different bench where it would be in the interests of justice to do so and the sentence can be varied.

Right to appeal to the Crown Court

A defendant who has pleaded not guilty may appeal as of right to the Crown Court on the grounds of being wrongly convicted or too harshly sentenced. Only appeals against sentence are allowed if the defendant pleaded guilty. The appeal has to be made within 28 days of the conviction. These appeals are normally heard by a circuit judge sitting with between two and four magistrates (not those who heard the original trial). Each person's vote has the same weight, except where the court is equally divided; in such a case the circuit judge has the casting vote.

The court will rehear the facts of the case and either confirm the verdict and/or sentence of the original magistrates, or substitute its own decision for that of the lower court. It can impose any sentence that the magistrates might have imposed – which can occasionally result in the accused's sentence being increased.

Appeals by way of case stated

Alternatively, either the prosecution or the accused may appeal on the grounds that the magistrates have made an error of law, or acted outside their jurisdiction. The magistrates are asked to 'state the case' for their decision to be considered by the High Court. This is, therefore, known as an appeal by way of case stated.

Appeals by way of case stated are heard by up to three judges of the Queen's Bench Division and the sitting is known as a Divisional Court. The court can confirm, reverse or vary the decision; give the magistrates its opinion on the relevant point of law; or make such other order as it sees fit, which may include ordering a rehearing before a different Bench.

Referral by the Criminal Cases Review Commission

sourcebook p. 340 → The Criminal Cases Review Commission can refer appeals from the magistrates' court to the Crown Court. This body is discussed in more detail from p. 125 onwards. In fact, only 5 per cent of new cases received by the Commission since 1997 have been against convictions by the magistrates.

Further appeals

If an appeal has been made to the Crown Court, either side may then appeal against the Crown Court's decision by way of case stated. If a party has already appealed to the High Court by way of case stated, the party may not afterwards appeal to the Crown Court.

From the Divisional Court there may be a further appeal, by either party, to the House of Lords, but only if the Divisional Court certifies that the question of law

Figure 8.4 The Criminal Cases Review Commission's offices in Alpha Tower, Birmingham

Source: © Roy Peters Photography.

is one of public importance and the House of Lords or the Divisional Court gives permission for the appeal to be heard.

Criminal cases tried by magistrates are also subject to judicial review.

In practice, appeals from the decisions of magistrates are taken in only 1 per cent of cases. This may be because most accused plead guilty, and since the offences are relatively minor and the punishment usually a fine, many of those who pleaded not guilty may prefer just to pay up and put the case behind them, avoiding the expense, publicity and embarrassment involved in an appeal.

From the Crown Court

There are three types of appeal for cases tried in the Crown Court.

To the Court of Appeal with judicial permission

An appeal on grounds that involve the facts, the law or the length of the sentence can be made to the Court of Appeal. The accused must get permission to appeal from the trial judge or the Court of Appeal. A sentence cannot be imposed that is more severe than that ordered by the Crown Court. An appeal against sentence will only be successful where the sentence is wrong in principle or manifestly severe; the court will not interfere merely because it might have passed a different sanction.

Task 8.3

Look at the diagram and answer the questions that follow.

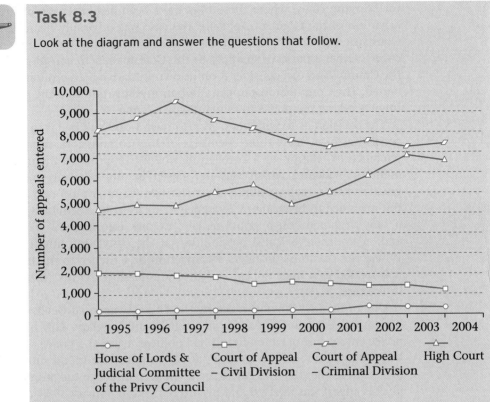

Figure 8.5 **Appellate Courts: Appeals entered, 1995–2004**

Source: 'Judicial Statistics Annual Report 2004', p. 6. © Crown Copyright 2005.

Questions

1 Which appellate court hears the fewest cases?
2 Which division of the Court of Appeal is the busiest?
3 Did the High Court's workload increase or decrease in 2003–04?
4 What is the trend in the workload of the House of Lords?

While only the accused can appeal to the Court of Appeal, from there either the accused or the prosecution may appeal on a point of law to the House of Lords, provided that either the Court of Appeal or the House of Lords grants permission for the appeal and that the Court of Appeal certifies that the case involves a matter of law of general public importance.

Referral by the Criminal Cases Review Commission

The Criminal Appeal Act 1995 established the Criminal Cases Review Commission (CCRC), following a proposal made by the Royal Commission on Criminal Justice 1993 (RCCJ). This body is not a court that decides appeals; rather it is responsible for bringing cases, where there may have been a miscarriage of justice, to the attention of the Court of Appeal if the case was originally heard by the Crown Court (or the Crown Court if the case was originally heard by a magistrates' court). Either a person can apply to the Commission to consider his/her case or the Commission can consider it on its own initiative if an ordinary appeal is time barred. The Commission can carry out an investigation into the case, which may involve asking the police to reinvestigate a crime.

The decision as to whether or not to refer a case will be taken by a committee consisting of at least three members of the Commission. It can make such a reference in relation to a conviction where it appears to them that any argument or evidence, which was not raised in any relevant court proceedings, gives rise to a real possibility that the conviction would not be upheld were the reference to be made. A reference in relation to a sentence will be possible if 'any argument on a point of law, or any information' was not so raised and, again, there is a real possibility that the conviction might not be upheld. Where the Commission refers a conviction or sentence to the Court of Appeal, it is treated as a fresh appeal and the Commission has no further involvement in the case.

One of the first referrals made by the CCRC concerned Derek Bentley. He had been involved with a friend in an unsuccessful burglary. This had resulted in a police chase, during which friend had pointed a gun at a police officer and Derek Bentley had said 'let him have it', at which point the friend shot and killed the officer. Derek Bentley was convicted as an accomplice to the murder. He appealed but his appeal was rejected and he was hanged in January 1953.

The circumstances of his conviction gave rise to a long campaign by his family, and numerous representations were made to the Home Office. He was given a royal pardon in 1993 but this was in respect of the sentence only. The family continued its campaign for the conviction itself to be quashed and, in 1998, the CCRC referred the case to the Court of Appeal which quashed the conviction, stating that the conviction was unsafe because of a defective summing-up by the trial judge to the jury, which had included such prejudicial comments about the defence case that Bentley had been denied a fair trial. This was a notable high-profile success for the CCRC, but it remains to be seen whether the Commission will have success with lower-profile referrals.

Case stated

Following the Access to Justice Act 1999, appeals by way of case stated have been introduced from the Crown Court to the High Court. Previously, these were available only from the magistrates' court.

Second appeal to the Court of Appeal

In exceptional circumstances the Court of Appeal will be prepared to hear an appeal twice: in other words, an appeal from its own earlier decision in the same case. This was decided in the landmark case of **Taylor** *v* **Lawrence** (2002). The

Court of Appeal had dismissed the first appeal which had been based on the fact that the judge at first instance had been a client of the claimants. After that first appeal, the appellant then discovered that the judge had not been asked to pay for work carried out the night before the case went to court. When this came to light, the Court of Appeal ruled that it would hear a second appeal. The Court of Appeal laid down guidelines for future cases on when it would be prepared to hear a second appeal in the same case. It must be clearly established that a significant injustice has probably been done, the circumstances are exceptional and there is no alternative effective remedy. There is no effective remedy if leave would not be available for an appeal to the House of Lords. Leave to appeal would not have been given by the House of Lords in **Taylor v Lawrence** because the case was not of sufficient general importance and merit.

> ✓ **Know your terms 8.4**
>
> Define the following terms:
>
> 1 The 'leap-frog' procedure.
> 2 Divisional Court.
> 3 Double jeopardy.
> 4 Criminal Cases Review Commission.

Procedure before the Court of Appeal

Whichever appeal route is taken to reach the Court of Appeal, once the case is before the court, it is dealt with under the same procedure, which will now be considered. The Court of Appeal in criminal cases does not rehear the whole case with all its evidence. Instead, it aims merely to review the lower court's decision. This is at least partly because the Court of Appeal is reluctant to overturn the verdict of a jury, apparently fearing that to do so might undermine the public's respect for juries in general. The Court of Appeal can admit fresh evidence 'if they think it necessary or expedient in the interests of justice' (Criminal Appeal Act 1968, s. 23(1)).

The appellate court can allow the appeal, dismiss it or order a new trial. Under s. 2 of the Criminal Appeal Act 1968 (as amended by the 1995 Act), an appeal should be allowed if the court thinks that the conviction is 'unsafe'. There is conflicting case law as to whether, if a person is found to have had an unfair trial under Art. 6 of the European Convention on Human Rights, this will automatically mean that the conviction is unsafe and should be quashed. Some English judges prefer the view that if the defendant is clearly guilty their conviction should be upheld as safe even if the trial was unfair. This seems to conflict with the view of the European Court of Human Rights, which suggested in **Condron v United Kingdom** (1999) that the conviction should always be quashed if there has been an unfair trial. The Court of Appeal may order a retrial where it feels this is required in the interests of justice. It will only do so if it accepts that the additional evidence is true but is not convinced that it is conclusive – in other words, that it would have led to a different verdict.

Appeals to the House of Lords

A small number of criminal appeals are heard each year by the House of Lords. Planned reforms to the House of Lords are discussed at page 85.

Powers of the prosecution following acquittal

In the past, there was a general rule that once a person had been tried and acquitted they could not be retried for the same offence, under the principle of double jeopardy. The rule aimed to prevent the oppressive use of the criminal justice system by public authorities. Following the unsuccessful private prosecution of three men suspected of killing Stephen Lawrence, the judicial inquiry into the affair recommended that the principle of double jeopardy should be abolished. It proposed that the Court of Appeal should have the power to permit prosecution after acquittal 'where fresh and viable evidence is presented'.

The Criminal Justice Act 2003, s. 75 has now abolished the double jeopardy rule. The Act introduces an interlocutory prosecution right of appeal against a ruling by a Crown Court judge that there is no case to answer or any other ruling made before or during the trial that has the effect of terminating the trial. A retrial is permitted in cases of serious offences where there has been an acquittal in court, but compelling new evidence subsequently comes to light against the acquitted person. Twenty-nine serious offences are listed in Sch. 5 to the Act, and are most of the offences which carry a maximum sentence of life imprisonment. This is wider than the recommendations of the Law Commission and Sir Robin Auld. The consent of the Director of Public Prosecutions is required to reopen investigations and to apply to the Court of Appeal. The first person in 800 years to be tried and convicted for a crime he was previously cleared of was a man called William Dunlop. He had been tried twice for the murder of Julie Hogg in 1989, but at these two earlier trials the jury were unable to reach a verdict and he had been formally acquitted at the end of the second trial. When new evidence arose, he was prosecuted again following the abolition of the double jeopardy rule and he pleaded guilty.

Certain other exceptions to the double jeopardy rule also existed prior to the 2003 Act:

- The prosecution can state a case for consideration of the High Court following the acquittal of a defendant by the magistrates' court. This is restricted to a point of law or a dispute on jurisdiction.
- The prosecution can also, with leave, appeal to the House of Lords against a decision of the Court of Appeal.
- The Criminal Justice Act 1972 gives the Attorney-General powers to refer any point of law which has arisen in a case for the opinion of the Court of Appeal, even where the defendant was acquitted. Defendants are not identified (though they may be represented) and their acquittal remains unaffected even if the point of law goes against them – so this procedure is not, strictly speaking, an appeal. The purpose of this power is to enable the Court of Appeal to review a potentially incorrect legal ruling before it gains too wide a circulation in the trial courts.
- The Criminal Justice Act 1988 enables the Attorney-General to refer to the Court of Appeal cases of apparently too lenient sentencing for certain offences, including cases where it appears the judge has erred in law as to their powers of sentencing. Leave from the Court of Appeal is required. The Court of Appeal may quash the sentence and pass a more appropriate one. This is the first time

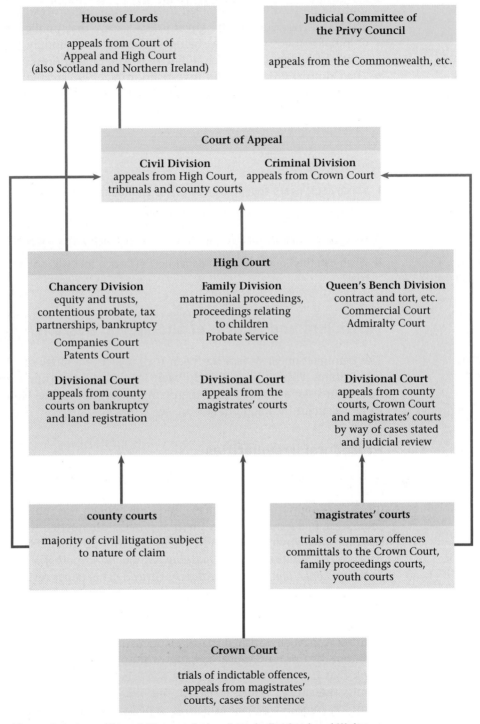

Figure 8.6 An outline of the court structure in England and Wales

This diagram is, of necessity, much simplified and should not be taken as a comprehensive statement on the jurisdiction of any specific court.

Source: 'Judicial Statistics Annual Report 2004', p. 3. © Crown Copyright 2005.

that the prosecution is involved in the sentencing process. The provision was enacted in response to the government's view that public confidence in the criminal justice system was being undermined by unduly lenient sentences, which had been given much publicity by the tabloid press.

■ The Criminal Procedure and Investigation Act 1996 created a power to order a retrial where a person has been convicted of an offence involving interference with, or intimidation of, a juror, witness or potential witness, in any proceedings which led to an acquittal.

Quick quiz 8.5

1 Which court hears appeals by way of case stated from the magistrates' court?

2 Which court hears appeals from the Divisional Court?

3 What percentage of magistrates' cases are the subject of an appeal?

4 When can the Court of Appeal admit new evidence that was not heard in the original trial?

Criticism and reform of the appeal system

The criminal appeal system has been the subject of a range of criticism over the years. Some reforms have already been introduced and others are likely in the near future. For a discussion of the planned abolition of the House of Lords and its replacement by a Supreme Court, see p. 85.

Procedural irregularities

In his *Review of the Criminal Courts* (2001), Sir Robin Auld highlighted the difference between a conviction which was unsafe, in the sense that it was incorrect (or lacked supporting evidence), and one which was unsatisfactory because something had gone wrong in the trial process. He queried whether in the latter situation the conviction should be quashed. In September 2006, the government issued a consultation paper, *Quashing convictions – report of a Review by the Home Secretary, Lord Chancellor and Attorney General*. This paper reviewed the legal test used by the Court of Appeal to quash criminal convictions. The Criminal Justice and Immigration Bill effectively accepts Sir Robin Auld's recommendations on this subject. Clause 26 of the Bill provides that 'a conviction is not unsafe if the Court of Appeal are satisfied that the appellant is guilty of the offence'. Clause 27 adds that the Court of Appeal can allow the appeal against conviction 'where they think that it would be incompatible with the appellant's Convention Rights to dismiss the appeal'. Thus, if passed, the Bill would alter the test applied by the Court of Appeal when considering appeals against conviction. A conviction would not be unsafe if the Court of Appeal is satisfied that the appellant is guilty of the offence. If it appears to the Court of Appeal, in determining an appeal, that there has been serious misconduct by any person involved in the investigation or prosecution of the offence, the court may refer the matter to the Attorney-General.

In support of this reform, the government has argued that to acquit defendants where the Court of Appeal considers that they are guilty is itself an injustice to the victim and the public, because the guilty are being allowed to walk free without punishment; their conviction is being quashed 'on a technicality'. In its consultation paper, the government observes: 'if the system or those who operate it are at fault it is they and not the public who should be punished or required to learn lessons, if appropriate.'

This proposed reform has proved highly controversial. Critics, such as the academic Ian Dennis (2006), have argued that it would remove an important safeguard in the criminal justice system, which effectively discourages abuse of procedural rules by representatives of the state, such as the police or prosecution. They have argued that a conviction is fundamentally unsatisfactory if it is gained in breach of the rule of law and to uphold such a conviction undermines the rule of law. Will the public be happy to see the criminal courts appear to sanction a flagrant illegality by an agent of the state? The Court of Appeal does not rehear the evidence of a case and is not therefore in a strong position to reach a view on whether a person is innocent or guilty. Alternative sanctions of, for example, the police for procedural irregularities have not always proved effective. Alarmingly, in **R** *v* **Mullen** (1993), the government seems to view unlawful rendition – when a person is removed from a country without following the lawful procedures – as a mere technicality, yet this constitutes a major violation of an individual's human rights.

The Criminal Cases Review Commission

sourcebook
p. 340 The Criminal Cases Review Commission (CCRC) was established in 1995 with the hope that it would detect miscarriages of justice more rapidly than the old procedures followed by the Home Office. But the CCRC has itself been the subject of some criticism. One weakness in the new arrangements is that the CCRC does not itself hear the appeals. Cases such as the Birmingham Six (where six Irishmen were wrongly convicted in the 1970s for planting bombs in Birmingham as part of an IRA bombing campaign) had to be repeatedly referred back to the Court of Appeal before the court would eventually overturn the original conviction. The establishment of the CCRC will not end this obstacle.

The pressure group, Justice, has criticised the fact that the CCRC has no power to assign in-house staff as investigating officers. It has argued that, without this power, the Commission could not guarantee the independence of an inquiry. The CCRC has no independent powers to carry out searches of premises, to check criminal records, to use police computers or to make an arrest. To do this it would have to appoint someone who had these powers, usually a police officer. The fact that investigations carried out on behalf of the CCRC will be by the police has caused concern. Many allegations of a miscarriage of justice involve accusations of malpractice by the police. Experience of police investigations into the high-profile miscarriages of justice suggests that these are not always effective, and there is a tendency for the police to close ranks and try to protect each other. Justice has also questioned the independence of the organisation, as its members are government appointees.

Task 8.6

The Chairman of the Criminal Cases Review Commission wrote in its third annual report an open letter to the Home Secretary. This stated:

'Although early stakeholder concerns regarding the Commission's likely independence, and ability to investigate miscarriages of justice thoroughly, are now only rarely repeated, there has been persistent, well-founded criticism of the Commission's accumulation of cases awaiting review. That accumulation derives directly from the fact that the Commission's initial funding and corresponding scale of operations were inadequate to cope with the case intake that materialised. The Commission can satisfy the legitimate expectations of Parliament and its other stakeholders only if the resources allocated to it are sufficient for it to minimise its case accumulation.

Projections made in February 1998 suggested that some 50 Case Review Managers (CRMs) would be needed for a few years to enable expeditious progress to be made towards that minimisation. Subsequent funding increases allowed that complement of CRMs to be reached just before 31 March 2002 . . .

There has been an unexpected 12% increase in applications to the Commission, combined with fast CRM turnover and slower recruitment than expected. These factors have retarded progress towards minimisation of the case accumulation.'

Questions

1 What is meant by 'stakeholders'?
2 What is meant by the term 'case accumulation'.
3 What problems have the CCRC encountered in reducing the backlog of cases?

The Criminal Cases Review Commission states that its values are:

- Independence
- Integrity
- Impartiality
- Professionalism
- Accountability
- Transparency

Figure 8.7 **The value of Criminal Cases Review Commission**
Source: Criminal Cases Review Commission Annual Report and Accounts 2004-5.

Quick quiz 8.7

1 When was the Criminal Cases Review Commission created?

2 What is the single test that the Court of Appeal applies in deciding whether to allow a criminal appeal?

3 Explain the case involving Derek Bentley.

4 Which court hears cases involving judicial review?

Reading on the web

Any developments in the establishment of a Supreme Court are likely to be signalled on the website of the Ministry of Justice:

www.justice.gov.uk/

The annual report of the Criminal Cases Review Commission is published on the Commission's website at:

www.ccrc.gov.uk/publications/publications_get.asp

Chapter summary

Introduction

There are two main courts where people can be put on trial to decide whether they are guilty of committing a criminal offence: the magistrates' court and the Crown Court.

Classification of offences

Summary offences

Summary offences are the most minor crimes, and are only triable summarily in the magistrates' court.

Indictable offences

These are the more serious offences, such as rape and murder. They can only be heard by the Crown Court.

Offences triable either way

These offences may be tried in either the magistrates' court or the Crown Court.

Mode of trial

Where a person is charged with an offence triable either way, he or she can insist on a trial by jury. If the person states that they wish to be tried in the magistrates' court, the magistrates can still decide that they think the Crown Court would be the more appropriate venue and send the case to be heard in a Crown Court.

The trial

Apart from the role played by the jury in the Crown Court, the law and procedure in the Crown Court and magistrates' court are essentially the same.

Trial of young offenders

Young offenders are usually tried in youth courts, which are a branch of the magistrates' court. In limited circumstances, young persons can be tried in a Crown Court. The trial procedures for young offenders have been reformed in the light of a recent ruling of the European Court of Human Rights.

Appeals in criminal cases

From the magistrates' court

There are four routes of appeal:

- the magistrates can rectify an error they have made;
- a defendant who has pleaded not guilty may appeal as of right to the Crown Court on the grounds of being wrongly convicted or too harshly sentenced;
- either the prosecution or the accused may appeal to the High Court on the grounds that the magistrates have made an error of law or acted outside their jurisdiction; and
- the Criminal Cases Review Commission can refer appeals from the magistrates' court to the Crown Court.

From the Crown Court

There are three types of appeal from the Crown Court:

- an appeal to the Court of Appeal;
- an application to the Criminal Cases Review Commission; and
- an appeal by way of case stated from the Crown Court to the High Court.

From both the Magistrate's Court and the Crown Court, final appeals are sometimes possible to the House of Lords.

Powers of the prosecution following acquittal

The general rule is that once a person has been tried and acquitted, he or she cannot be retried for the same offence, under the principle of double jeopardy. Major exceptions have now been developed.

Criticism and reform of the appeal system

The appeal system has been the subject of considerable criticism. The government intends to abolish the House of Lords and replace it with a new, independent Supreme Court. The government plans to restrict when a conviction can be quashed 'on a technicality'. There has been concern over the working of the Criminal Cases Review Commission.

Question and answer guide

For exam questions covering the material in this chapter, please see the Question and answer guide section of Chapter 19: Sentencing.

Group activity 1

On 15 February 1997, Billie-Jo Jenkins, aged 13, was battered to death on the patio at her home in Hastings, East Sussex. Sion Jenkins was prosecuted for the murder of his foster daughter. His case was the subject of two appeals, three trials and ended with no verdict from the final jury. Working in groups, investigate the appeals process in this murder case. You could start by looking at *The Times* website:

www.timesonline.co.uk/tol/news/uk/article728984.ece

What is the Criminal Cases Review Commission?

Group activity 2

- Divide your friends (or class) into groups of two or three people.
- Each group should visit the 'Cases We Have Referred' page of the website of the Criminal Cases Review Commission: www.ccrc.gov.uk/cases/case_referred.asp.
- Half of the groups should choose a case in which the original conviction was quashed by the Court of Appeal and the other half should choose a case in which the original conviction was upheld.
- Each group should read the judgment of the Court of Appeal (accessible via the CCRC website) in its chosen case and make notes summarising the reasons it gave for its decision to quash or uphold. (If you find that the judgment in your chosen case has not been posted on the CCRC website yet, pick another case.)
- The groups should then meet to compare notes, looking to see what conclusions they can draw about how the Court of Appeal deals with CCRC references.

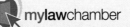

Visit **www.mylawchamber.co.uk/elliottaqa** to access interactive questions, quizzes and activities to test yourself on this chapter.

Chapter 9 — Magistrates

This chapter discusses:

- the existence of lay and professional magistrates;
- the selection and appointment of lay magistrates;
- their social background;
- the training provided;
- their powers;
- the work of justices' clerks and legal advisers;
- whether lay magistrates or professional judges should work in the magistrates' court.

Introduction

Lay magistrates have a long history in the English legal system, dating back to the Justices of the Peace Act 1361, which, probably in response to a crime wave, gave judicial powers to appointed lay people. Their main role then, as now, was dealing with criminals, but they also exercised certain administrative functions, and until the nineteenth century the business of local government was largely entrusted to them. A few of these administrative powers remain today.

There are over 28,000 lay magistrates (also called justices of the peace, or JPs), hearing over 1 million criminal cases a year – 95 per cent of all criminal trials, with the remaining being heard in the Crown Court. They are therefore often described as the backbone of the English criminal justice system. Lay magistrates do not receive a salary, but they receive travel, subsistence and financial loss allowances.

There are also 129 professional judges who sit in the magistrates' courts. These are now called 'district judges (magistrates' courts)' following a reform introduced by the Access to Justice Act 1999. They had previously been known as stipendiary magistrates. They receive a salary of over £90,000. Following the passing of the sourcebook p. 81 → Constitutional Reform Act 2005, the new Judicial Appointments Commission is involved in the appointment process of these professional judges. Applicants must have a relevant qualification and at least five years' post-qualification experience. They act as sole judge in their particular court, mostly in the large cities, especially London. They are part of the professional judiciary, and most of the comments about magistrates in this chapter do not apply to them.

Selection and appointment

Lay magistrates are appointed by the Lord Chancellor in the name of the Crown, on the advice of Local Advisory Committees. For historical reasons, magistrates in Lancashire, Greater Manchester and Merseyside are appointed by the Chancellor of the Duchy of Lancaster in the name of the Crown. Candidates are interviewed by the committee, which then makes a recommendation to the minister, who usually follows the recommendation.

Members of the Local Advisory Committees are appointed by the Minister of Justice. Two-thirds of them are magistrates, and the minister is supposed to ensure that they have good local knowledge, and represent a balance of political opinion. Their identity was at one time kept secret, but names are now available to the public.

Candidates are usually put forward to the committee by local political parties, voluntary groups, trade unions and other organisations, though individuals may apply in person. The only qualifications laid down for appointment to the magistracy are that the applicants must be under 65 and live within 15 miles of the commission area in which they will work. These qualifications may be dispensed with if it is considered to be in the public interest to do so. In practice, they must also be able to devote an average of half a day a week to the task, for which usually only expenses and a small loss of earnings allowance are paid. Legal knowledge or experience is not required; nor is any level of academic qualification.

Certain people are excluded from appointment, including police officers, traffic wardens and members of the armed forces; anyone whose work is considered incompatible with the duties of a magistrate; anyone who owing to a disability could not carry out all the duties of a magistrate; people with certain criminal convictions; undischarged bankrupts; and those who have a close relative who is already a magistrate on the same Bench.

In 1998 the procedures for appointing lay magistrates were reviewed. The reforms aimed to make the appointment criteria open and clear. Thus, a job description for magistrates was introduced which declares that the six key qualities defining the personal suitability of candidates are: having good character, understanding and communication, social awareness, maturity and sound temperament, sound judgement and commitment and reliability. Positions are now advertised widely, including in publications such as *Inside Soaps*, to attract a wider range of people.

The new Judicial Appointments Commission established by the Constitutional Reform Act 2005 is not yet involved in the appointment of lay magistrates, but there are plans that at a future stage it will take over responsibility for their appointment. It is already responsible for the appointment of district judges (magistrates' court).

??? Quick quiz 9.1

1 Who appoints lay magistrates?

2 What is the role of the Local Advisory Committees?

3 What qualifications does a person need to become a magistrate?

4 In the future, which body will have responsibility for the appointment of lay magistrates?

Background

Class

The 1948 Report of the Royal Commission on Justices of the Peace showed that approximately three-quarters of all magistrates came from professional or middle-class occupations. Little seems to have changed since. Research carried out by Rod Morgan and Neil Russell (2000) found that more than two-thirds of lay magistrates were, or had been until retirement, employed in a professional or managerial position. Their social backgrounds were not representative of the community in which they served. For example, in a deprived metropolitan area, 79 per cent of the Bench members were professionals or managers compared with only 20 per cent in the local population.

✓ **Know your terms 9.2**

Define the following terms:
1 Stipendiary magistrate.
2 Justice of the Peace.
3 The Bench.
4 Royal Commission.

One of the reasons for this may be financial; while employers are required to give an employee who is appointed as a magistrate reasonable time off work, not all employers are able or willing to pay wages during the employee's absence. To meet this difficulty, lay magistrates receive a loss of earnings allowance, but this is not overly generous and will usually be less than the employee would have earned.

A further problem is that employees who take up the appointment against the wishes of their employer may find their promotion prospects jeopardised. This means that only those who are self-employed, or sufficiently far up the career ladder to have some power of their own, can serve as magistrates without risking damage to their own employment prospects. The outcome is that those outside the professional and managerial classes are proportionately under-represented on the Bench, which is still predominantly drawn from the more middle-class occupations. The maximum age for appointment has been raised to 65 in the hope that working-class people, who were prevented from serving during their working lives, will do so in retirement, though so far the change has had little impact.

In the past, the government sought to achieve a social balance on the bench by taking into account a person's political affiliation when making appointments. This stemmed from the time when people tended to vote along class lines, with people from the working class voting predominantly for the Labour Party. Political opinion is no longer a reliable gauge of a person's social background and the government has therefore replaced the question about 'political associations' on the application form for magistrates. It has been replaced by a question about the applicant's employment. The Ministry of Justice believes that this will provide a better means of achieving a socially balanced Bench. The government has issued a White Paper, *Supporting Magistrates' Courts to Provide Justice*. This includes proposals to encourage the recruitment of more young magistrates to make them representative of the communities they serve. Legislation will be introduced to clarify the process of magistrates taking time off work to attend court, including a requirement for employers to explain a refusal to allow a person to take time off.

Age

There are few young magistrates – most are middle-aged or older. The average age of magistrates is 57, only 4 per cent are under the age of 40, and almost a third are in their 60s. The problems concerning employment are likely to have an effect on the age as well as the social class of magistrates; people at the beginning of their careers are most dependent on the goodwill of employers for promotion, and least likely to be able to take regular time off without damaging their career prospects. They are also more likely to be busy bringing up families.

While a certain maturity is obviously a necessity for magistrates, younger justices would bring some understanding of the lifestyles of a younger generation. The Government is concerned that 11,000 magistrates are due to retire within the next ten years.

Table 9.1 **Ethnicity: lay magistrates and population generally**

	White	Black Caribbean, Black African, Black other	Indian, Pakistani, Bangladeshi, Chinese	Other	Not known	Total
Magistrates England and Wales Number	21,950	430	541	186	2,825	25,932
Percentage	85%	2%	2%	1%	11%	100%
General population for England and Wales (1991 census)	94%	2%	3%	1%	–	100%

The data excludes magistrates in the Duchy of Lancaster.

Source: R. Morgan and N. Russell (2000), *The Judiciary in the Magistrates' Courts*, Home Office RDS Occasional Paper No. 66. © Crown Copyright 2000.

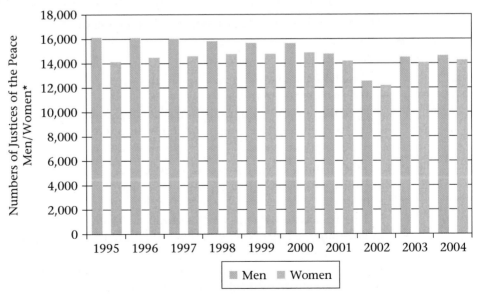

Figure 9.1 Justices of the Peace, 1995-2004

* As at 1 January of each year. From 2000 onwards figures compiled on a financial year basis.

Source: 'Judicial Statistics Annual Report 2004', p. 128. © Crown Copyright 2005.

Race

The government reported in 1987 that the proportion of black magistrates was only 2 per cent. The figures for 2003 show that lay magistrates increasingly reflect the ethnic diversity of contemporary Britain. Just over 6 per cent of magistrates come from ethnic minority communities, who make up 7.9 per cent of the general population, but there is considerable variation locally and the fit between the local benches and the local communities they serve is, in several instances, very poor.

Training

The Magistrates' Commission Committees are responsible for providing training under the supervision of the Judicial Studies Board. Magistrates are not expected to be experts on the law, and the aim of their training is mainly to familiarise them with court procedure, the techniques of chairing and the theory and practice of sentencing. They undergo a short induction course on appointment, and have to undergo basic continuous training comprising 12 hours every three years. Magistrates who sit in juvenile courts or on domestic court panels receive additional training. In order to chair a court hearing a magistrate must, since 1996, take a chairmanship course, the syllabus of which is set by the Judicial Studies Board. Since 1998 the training has included more 'hands on' practical experience, sessions in equality awareness and experienced magistrates act as monitors of more junior members of the Bench.

Magistrates' criminal powers

Magistrates have three main functions in criminal cases:

- Hearing applications for bail.
- Trial: magistrates mainly try the least serious criminal cases (see p. 116). They are advised on matters of law by a justices' clerk, but they alone decide the facts, the law and the sentence.
- Appeals: in ordinary appeals from the magistrates' court to the Crown Court, magistrates sit with a judge. But, following a reform by the Access to Justice Act 1999, they no longer have this role in relation to appeals against sentence.

Magistrates also exercise some control over the investigation of crime, since they deal with applications for bail and requests by the police for arrest and search warrants.

Lay magistrates generally sit in groups of three. However, s. 49 of the Crime and Disorder Act 1998 provides that certain pre-trial judicial powers may be exercised by a single justice of the peace sitting alone. These include decisions to extend or vary the conditions of bail, to remit an offender to another court for sentence and to give directions as to the timetable for proceedings, the attendance of the parties, the service of documents and the manner in which evidence is to be given. These powers of single justices were tested in six pilot studies and, having proved to be successful, were applied nationally in November 1999.

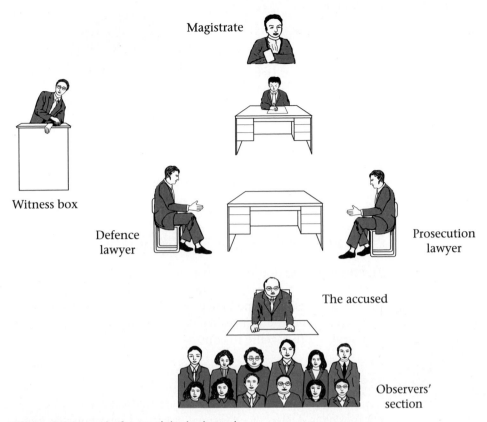

Magistrate

Witness box

Defence
lawyer

Prosecution
lawyer

The accused

Observers'
section

Figure 9.2 Layout of a magistrates' court

Source: F. Mahar and M. J. Duffy, *AQA General Certificate of Education Law Teachers' Guide 2001/2.*

The role of magistrates in the criminal justice system has been effectively increased in recent years. Some offences which were previously triable either way have been made summary only, notably in the Criminal Law Act 1977, where most motoring offences and criminal damage worth less than £2,000 were made summary only (since raised to £5,000 in the Criminal Justice and Public Order Act 1994). The government proposed at the time that thefts involving small amounts of money should also be made summary offences, but there was great opposition to the idea of removing the right to jury trial for offences which reflected on the accused's honesty. The proposal was dropped, but is still suggested from time to time.

The vast majority of new offences are summary only – there was controversy over the fact that the first offence created to deal with so-called 'joy-riding' was summary, given that the problem appeared to be a serious one, and critics assume that it was made a summary offence in the interests of keeping costs down. Since then, the more serious joy-riding offence, known as aggravated vehicle-taking, which occurs when joy-riding causes serious personal injury or death, has been reduced to a summary offence by the Criminal Justice and Public Order Act 1994. Other serious offences which are summary only include assaulting a police officer, and many of the offences under the Public Order Act 1986.

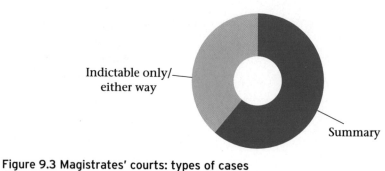

Figure 9.3 Magistrates' courts: types of cases
Source: 'Crown Prosecution Service Annual Report 2005-06', p. 80. © Crown Copyright 2006.

The justices' clerk and legal advisers

The primary function of the justices' clerk and legal adviser is to advise the lay magistrates on law and procedure. They are not supposed to take any part in the actual decision of the Bench; legal and procedural advice should be given in open court, and the justices' clerk and legal adviser should not accompany the magistrates if they retire to consider their decision.

Task 9.3

Visit a magistrates' court. You can find the address of a local magistrates' court by looking in a telephone directory. Write up a report of your visit by answering the following questions:

About the court

1 What was the name and address of the court?
2 What was the court building like? Was it old or modern? Was it clean and in good decorative order? Were the waiting areas comfortable? Was there access to refreshments? Was it easy to find your way around the building, with rooms clearly signposted and labelled?
3 Did you find the court staff helpful? Were there any explanatory leaflets available?

About the proceedings
Take one of the cases that you watched and answer the following questions:

1 Were the proceedings heard by lay magistrates or a professional judge? Were they male or female and what was their approximate age? What did they wear? Were they polite to the parties?
2 Was the case a civil or criminal matter?
3 Were the parties represented by a lawyer?
4 What was the case about?
5 Did any witnesses give evidence?
6 If you heard the whole case, what was its outcome?
7 Did you think that the court came to the right decision?

Lay magistrates versus professional judges

In recent years there has been some discussion as to whether lay magistrates should be replaced by professional judges. There have been suspicions that this may be on the government's political agenda. These suspicions have been fuelled by the increasing role of justices' clerks and the commission of research in the field by Rod Morgan and Neil Russell. Their report, *The Judiciary in the Magistrates' Courts* (2000), has provided some useful up-to-date information to support the debate on the future role of lay magistrates in the criminal justice system. That research concluded:

> 'At no stage during the study was it suggested that . . . the magistrates' courts do not work well or fail to command general confidence. It is our view, therefore, that eliminating or greatly diminishing the role of lay magistrates would not be widely understood or supported.'

Advantages of lay magistrates

Cost

It has traditionally been assumed that, because lay magistrates are unpaid volunteers, they are necessarily cheaper than their professional colleagues. However, it is not clear that this is the case. The research by Rod Morgan and Neil Russell (2000) found that a simple analysis of the direct costs for the Magistrates' Courts Service of using the two types of magistrates shows that lay magistrates are extraordinarily cheap compared to professional judges. The direct average cost of a lay justice is £495 per annum, that of a district judge £90,000. However, lay magistrates incur more indirect costs than professional judges. They are much slower than professional judges in hearing cases – as one professional judge handles as much work as 30 lay magistrates. Lay magistrates therefore make greater proportionate use of the court buildings. They need the support of legally qualified legal advisers. Administrative support is required for their recruitment, training and rota arrangements. When all the overheads are brought into the equation, the cost per appearance for lay and professional magistrates becomes £52.10 and £61.78 respectively. These figures have to be seen in the context that professional judges are currently more likely to send someone to prison which is more expensive than the alternative sentences frequently imposed by lay magistrates. They are almost twice as likely to remand defendants in custody and they are also twice as likely to sentence defendants to immediate custody, a finding that may be partly attributable to their hearing the most serious cases.

Switching to Crown Court trials would be extremely expensive. The Home Office Research and Planning Unit has estimated that the average cost of a contested trial in the Crown Court is around £13,500, with guilty pleas costing about £2,500. By contrast, the costs of trial by lay magistrates are £1,500 and £500 respectively. This is partly a reflection of the more serious nature of cases tried in the Crown Court, but clearly Crown Court trials are a great deal more expensive overall.

Table 9.2 **The cost of appearing before lay and professional magistrates (per appearance)**

	Lay magistrates £	Professional magistrates £
Direct costs (salary, expenses, training)	3.59	20.96
Indirect costs (premises, administration staff, etc.)	48.51	40.82
Direct and indirect costs	52.10	61.78

Source: R. Morgan and N. Russell (2000), *The Judiciary in the Magistrates' Courts*, Home Office RDS Occasional Paper No. 66. © Crown Copyright 2000.

Lay involvement

Lay magistrates are an ancient and important tradition of voluntary public service. They can also be seen as an example of participatory democracy. Lay involvement in judicial decision-making ensures that the courts are aware of community concerns. However, given the restricted social background of magistrates, and their alleged bias towards the police, the true value of this may be doubtful. Magistrates do not have the option, as juries do, of delivering a verdict according to their conscience.

Weight of numbers

The simple fact that magistrates must usually sit in threes may make a balanced view more likely.

Local knowledge

Magistrates must live within a reasonable distance of the court in which they sit, and therefore may have a more informed picture of local life than professional judges.

Disadvantages of lay magistrates

Inconsistent

There is considerable inconsistency in the decision-making of different Benches. This is noticeable in the differences in awards of state funding and the types of sentences ordered. To achieve the fundamental goal of a fair trial similar crimes committed in similar circumstances by offenders with similar backgrounds should receive a similar punishment. But in Teeside, 20 per cent of convicted burglars are sentenced to immediate custody, compared to 41 per cent in Birmingham.

In 1985, the Home Office noted in *Managing Criminal Justice* (edited by David Moxon) that, though Benches tried to ensure their own decisions were consistent, they did not strive to achieve consistency with other Benches. The researchers Flood-Page and Mackie found in 1998 that district judges (magistrates' courts) sentenced a higher proportion of offenders to custody than lay magistrates after allowing for other factors. There are also marked variations in the granting of bail applications: in 1985, magistrates' courts in Hampshire granted 89 per cent of bail applications, while in Dorset only 63 per cent were allowed.

The government announced that it intended to put an end to the disparity in sentencing patterns in different areas, a situation which was described as 'post-code sentencing'. In order to do this, a Sentencing Guidelines Council has been established to ensure greater consistency in sentencing across England and Wales.

Inefficient

Most of the public sampled in the research by Rod Morgan and Neil Russell (2000) were largely unaware that there were two types of magistrate. When enlightened and questioned, a majority considered that magistrates' court work should be divided equally between the two types of magistrate or that the type of magistrate did not matter. However, professional court users have significantly greater levels of confidence in the district judges (magistrates' court). They regard these judges as quicker than lay justices, more efficient and consistent in their decision-making, better able to control unruly defendants and better at questioning CPS and defence lawyers appropriately. In practice, straightforward guilty pleas to minor matters are normally dealt with by panels of lay magistrates, whereas serious contested matters are increasingly dealt with by a single, professional judge who decides questions of both guilt and sentence. Morgan and Neil Russell question whether the work should be distributed in the opposite way.

Bias towards the police

Police officers are frequent witnesses, and become well known to members of the Bench, and it is alleged that this results in an almost automatic tendency to believe police evidence. One magistrate was incautious enough to admit this: in **R v Bingham Justices, ex parte Jowitt** (1974), a speeding case where the only evidence was that of the motorist and a police constable, the chairman of the Bench said: 'Quite the most unpleasant cases that we have to decide are those where the evidence is a direct conflict between a police officer and a member of the public. My principle in such cases has always been to believe the evidence of the police officer, and therefore we find the case proved.' The conviction was quashed on appeal because of this remark.

Magistrates were particularly criticised in this respect during the 1984 miners' strike, for imposing wide bail conditions which prevented attendance on picket lines, and dispensing what appeared to be conveyor-belt justice.

Background

Despite the recommendations of two Royal Commissions (1910 and 1948) and the *Review of the Criminal Courts* (2001) that magistrates should come from varied social backgrounds, magistrates still appear to be predominantly middle class and middle-aged, with a strong Conservative bias.

The selection process has been blamed for the general narrowness of magistrates' backgrounds: Elizabeth Burney's 1979 study into selection methods concluded that the process was almost entirely dominated by existing magistrates who, over and over again, simply appointed people with similar backgrounds to their own.

The effect of their narrow background on the quality and fairness of magistrates' decisions is unclear. A survey of 160 magistrates by Bond and Lemon (1979) found no real evidence of significant differences in approach between those of different classes, but they did conclude that political affiliation had a noticeable effect on magistrates' attitudes to sentencing, with Conservatives tending to take a harder line. The research did not reveal whether these differences actually influenced the way magistrates carried out their duties in practice, but there is obviously a risk that they would do so.

In 1997, there was a slight controversy when, on winning the General Election, the Labour Lord Chancellor called for more Labour-voting candidates to be recommended for appointment as magistrates by Advisory Committees. His reasoning was that the political make-up of the magistrates needed to reflect that of the general population, which had shifted towards Labour. The Labour government has now reversed its position, having concluded that it is no longer necessary to seek a political balance among magistrates because people no longer vote along class lines.

Some feel that the background of the Bench is not a particular problem: in *The Machinery of Justice in England* (1989), Jackson points out that: 'Benches do tend to be largely middle to upper class, but that is a characteristic of those set in authority over us, whether in the town hall, Whitehall, hospitals and all manner of institutions.'

However, a predominantly old and middle-class Bench is unrepresentative of the general public and may weaken confidence in its decisions, on the part of society in general as well as the defendants before them. Jackson's argument that those 'set in authority over us' always tend to be middle to upper class is not a justification for doing nothing.

Quick quiz 9.4

1 Describe the three main functions of the magistrates in criminal matters.

2 How many lay magistrates normally sit to hear a case?

3 What is the role of the justices' clerk?

4 In what way has the magistrates' decision-making been found to be inconsistent?

Reading on the web

The research of Rod Morgan and Neil Russell, *The Judiciary in the Magistrates' Courts* (2000), is available on the Home Office website in the section dedicated to the Research Development and Statistics Directorate:

www.homeoffice.gov.uk/rds/pdfs/occ-judiciary.pdf

The website of the Magistrates Association, which represents the interests of magistrates, is available at:

www.magistrates-association.org.uk

General information about magistrates is available on the former Department for Constitutional Affairs' website.

www.dca.gov.uk/magistrates.htm

The report *Delivering Simple, Speedy, Summary Justice – An Evaluation of the Magistrates' Courts Tests* is available at:

www.dca.gov.uk/publications/reports_reviews/mag_courts_evaluation.pdf

Chapter summary

Introduction

There are over 28,000 lay magistrates and 129 professional judges who sit in the magistrates' courts.

Selection and appointment

Lay magistrates are appointed by the Lord Chancellor in the name of the Crown, on the advice of Local Advisory Committees.

Background

More than two-thirds of lay magistrates are employed in a professional or managerial position, or were until they retired. Almost a third of magistrates are in their sixties. Lay magistrates do, however, increasingly reflect the ethnic diversity of contemporary Britain.

Training

The Magistrates' Commission Committees are responsible for providing training under the supervision of the Judicial Studies Board.

Magistrates' criminal powers

Magistrates have three main functions in criminal cases:

- hearing applications for bail;
- hearing trials in the magistrates' court;
- hearing some appeals in the Crown Court alongside a professional judge.

The justices' clerk and legal adviser

The primary function of the justices' clerk and legal adviser is to advise the lay magistrates on law and procedure. They are not supposed to take any part in the actual decision of the Bench.

Lay magistrates versus professional judges

In recent years, there has been some discussion as to whether lay magistrates should be replaced by professional judges.

Question and answer guides

1

(a) Explain how lay magistrates are chosen and appointed.   (*15 marks*)

(b) Identify and discuss the advantages **and** disadvantages of using **lay magistrates** in the criminal justice process.   (*15 marks*)

(from AQA Exam Papers, January 2006 and January 2007)

(a) Lay magistrates are appointed by the Lord Chancellor and Secretary of State for Justice (the 'Lord Chancellor') in the name of the Crown, on the advice of Local Advisory Committees. Candidates are interviewed by the committee, which then makes a recommendation to the Lord Chancellor who usually follows the recommendation.

Members of the Local Advisory Committees are appointed by the Lord Chancellor. Two-thirds of them are magistrates, and the Lord Chancellor is required to ensure that they have good local knowledge, and represent a balance of political opinion. Candidates are usually put forward to the committee by local political parties, voluntary groups, trade unions and other organisations, though individuals may apply in person.

The only qualifications laid down for appointment to the magistracy are that applicants must be at least 18, under 65 and live within 15 miles of the commission area in which they will work. In practice, they must also be able to devote an average of half a day a week to the task. Legal knowledge is not required. Nor is any level of academic qualification.

Certain people are excluded from appointment, including police officers, traffic wardens and members of the armed forces; anyone whose work is considered incompatible with the duties of a magistrate; anyone who, due to a disability, could not carry out all the duties of a magistrate; people with certain criminal convictions; undischarged bankrupts; and those who have a close relative who is already a magistrate on the same Bench.

In 1998 a job description for magistrates was introduced. This declares that the six key qualities defining the personal suitability of candidates are: having good character, understanding and communication, social awareness, maturity and sound temperament, sound judgement and commitment and reliability.

The new Judicial Appointments Commission established by the Constitutional Reform Act 2005 is not yet involved in the appointment of lay magistrates, but there are plans that at a future stage it will take over this responsibility.

(b) Supporters of using lay magistrates in the criminal justice process often point to their low cost to the taxpayer, when compared with professional judges. While it is undoubtedly true that they are cheaper than professional judges, if one takes into account both direct and indirect costs, Rod Morgan and Neil Russell in their research, *The Judiciary in the Magistrates' Courts* (2000), have demonstrated that the difference is not as great as is sometimes assumed.

Another argument often advanced in favour of lay magistrates is that they help maintain an ancient and important tradition of voluntary public service.

Moreover, they can be seen as an example of participatory democracy. Lay involvement in judicial decision-making ensures that the courts are aware of community concerns. However, it needs to be remembered that magistrates do not have the option, as juries do, of delivering a verdict according to their conscience.

It is also argued that magistrates tend to have a more informed picture of local life than professional judges, by virtue of the requirement that they must live within a reasonable distance of the court in which they sit. The fact that they must usually sit in threes makes a balanced view more likely.

On the other hand, critics of using lay magistrates in the criminal justice process point to the considerable inconsistency in the decision-making of different Benches. Others argue, however, that some level of disparity is actually a strength of the system, as it allows for different Benches to reflect the different concerns of their respective areas.

Another criticism of lay magistrates is their alleged inefficiency. Professional court users regard professional judges as quicker, more efficient and more consistent than lay justices, better able to control unruly defendants and better at questioning CPS and defence lawyers appropriately.

It is also claimed that lay magistrates are biased towards the police. Police officers are frequent witnesses in magistrates' courts, and become well known to members of the Bench, and it is alleged that this results in an almost automatic tendency to believe police evidence.

2

(a) Describe how lay magistrates are selected and trained. *(15 marks)*
(b) Outline the range of duties undertaken by lay magistrates. Comment on how well lay magistrates carry out this 'valuable role'. *(15 marks)*
(from AQA Exam Papers, January 2004 and June 2002)

(a)
Selection

- Describe the roles of the Lord Chancellor and Local Advisory Committees.
- Describe the age and residency qualifications.
- Mention, and give examples of, the excluded categories.
- Mention, and give examples of, the six key qualities listed in the 1998 job description for magistrates.
- For a good answer, mention the future role of the Judicial Appointments Commission.

Training

- Describe the roles of the Magistrates' Commission Committees and Judicial Studies Board.
- Mention how magistrates attend a short induction course on appointment.
- Mention how they have to undergo 12 hours' basic continuous training every three years.
- For a good answer, give examples of the additional training that some receive.

(b)

Outline of duties *(criminal only, as civil are outside the new AQA specification)*

■ Describe magistrates' trial role – in magistrates' courts, sitting in threes, dealing with the least serious cases, deciders of law and fact, advised by the clerk or legal advisers.

■ Describe magistrates' appellate role – in the Crown Court, sitting with a judge, hearing appeals against conviction.

■ Describe how they deal with a range of miscellaneous matters – in magistrates' courts, often sitting alone – e.g. bail applications.

Evaluation of role

■ Discuss the advantages of lay magistrates, e.g. cost, lay involvement, local, balanced.

■ Discuss the disadvantages of lay magistrates, e.g. inconsistency, inefficiency, biased towards police.

Common errors in (a)

■ writing about the selection of jurors;

■ writing nothing or very little about training.

Common errors in (b)

■ describing magistrates' trial role only;

■ writing too little about the advantages and disadvantages of lay magistrates.

Group activity 1

■ Divide your friends (or class) into groups of two or three people.

■ Each group should visit 'The Magistrates' Blog', also known as 'The Law West of Ealing Broadway', at http://tlwoeb.blogspot.com. This blog describes itself as 'Musings and Snippets from an English Magistrate'.

■ Dip into the blog (do not attempt to read it all!) and make notes summarising the things that the author appears to like/dislike most about his/her work as a magistrate.

■ Compare your notes with the other groups to see if you have missed anything.

■ If you know any magistrates, ask them what they like/dislike most about their work and see how they compare with the blogger.

■ Warning: When reading this blog, bear in mind that it is anonymous and therefore we do not know whether the author is indeed a magistrate.

Group activity 2

Have a look at the following website, which provides information about being a lay magistrate:

www.dca.gov.uk/magistrates/index.htm

■ Would you be interested in becoming a magistrate, now or in the future? If in the future, at what stage in the future?

- If you decided that you would like to become a magistrate, what would you need to do to make this idea a reality?
- What qualifications would you need?
- Once you had been selected to become a magistrate, what training would you be offered?
- If you were working, could you insist that your employer gave you time off so that you could sit as a magistrate?

mylawchamber

Visit **www.mylawchamber.co.uk/elliottaqa** to access interactive questions, quizzes and activities to test yourself on this chapter.

The jury

This chapter discusses:

- the role of the jury;
- how the jury works in secret and reaches its verdict;
- the jury selection process;
- the advantages and disadvantages of jury service;
- some possible ways that the jury system could be reformed.

Introduction

The jury system was imported to Britain after the Norman conquest. Today the jury is considered a fundamental part of the English legal system though, as we shall see, only a minority of cases are tried by a jury. The main Act that now governs jury trial is the Juries Act 1974.

Today, the jury has attained symbolic importance, so that Lord Devlin wrote in 1956: 'Trial by jury is more than an instrument of justice and more than one wheel of the constitution; it is the lamp that shows that freedom lives.' This statement led to a classic rebuttal by the academic Penny Darbyshire (1991), who wrote an article entitled 'The Lamp that shows that Freedom Lives – Is it worth the Candle?' She argued in that article that juries are not random, not representative, but anti-democratic, irrational and haphazard legislators, whose erratic and secret decisions run counter to the rule of law.

Role of the jury

The jury has to weigh up the evidence and decide what are the true facts of the case – in other words, what actually happened. The judge directs the jurors as to what is the relevant law, and the jurors then have to apply the law to the facts that they have found and thereby reach a verdict. If it is a criminal case and the jury has given a verdict of guilty, the judge will then decide on the appropriate sentence.

In reaching their verdict, the jury are only entitled to consider evidence that arose in court, they cannot consider in the jury room evidence that has not been introduced in court. This issue arose in **R v Marshall and Crump** (2007). Two defendants had been convicted of offences including robbery and manslaughter. After their conviction material, printed off the internet, was found in the jury room. The defendants appealed on the basis that their convictions were unsafe as they had not had any opportunity to discuss this material in open court. While it was accepted that, in principle, a jury should not consider material that had not been considered in court, on the facts of the case the evidence had been printed off legitimate websites to which the public had general access and concerned only issues as to sentencing. Therefore, on the facts of the particular case, the convictions were found to have been safe.

Although juries are symbolically important in the criminal justice system, they actually only operate in a minority of cases and their role is constantly being reduced to save money. Criminal offences are classified into three groups: summary only offences, which are tried in the magistrates' courts; indictable offences, which are tried in the Crown Court; and either way offences, which, as the name suggests, may be tried in either the magistrates' courts or the Crown Court. The majority of criminal offences are summary only, and because these are, in general, the least serious offences, they are also the ones most commonly committed (most road traffic offences, for example, are summary only). As a result, 95 per cent of criminal cases are heard in the magistrates' courts, where juries have no role (this proportion also includes cases involving either way offences where the defendant chooses to be tried by magistrates). Juries only decide cases heard in the Crown Court. Even among the 5 per cent of cases heard there, in a high proportion of these the defendant will plead guilty, which means there is no need for a jury and, on top of that, there are cases where the judge directs the jury that the law demands that they acquit the defendant, so that the jury effectively makes no decision here either. The result is that juries actually decide only around 1 per cent of criminal cases.

On the other hand, it is important to realise that even this 1 per cent amounts to 30,000 trials, and that these are usually the most serious ones to come before the courts – though here too the picture can be misleading, since some serious offences, such as assaulting a police officer or drink-driving, are dealt with only by magistrates, while even the most trivial theft can be tried in the Crown Court if the defendant wishes.

Despite its historical role in the English legal system, and the almost sacred place it occupies in the public imagination, juries have come under increasing attack in recent years. Successive governments have attempted to reduce their use in criminal cases in order to save money. The Criminal Law Act 1977 removed the right to jury trial in a significant number of offences, by making most driving offences and relatively minor criminal damage cases summary only. Since 1977, more and more offences have been removed from the realm of jury trial by being made summary only. The sentencing powers of magistrates have been increased by the Criminal Justice Act 2003. Prior to that Act, magistrates could only sentence a person to six months' imprisonment for a single offence. Following the passing of the 2003 Act, magistrates can sentence offenders to up to 12 months' imprisonment for a single offence, and this could be increased further to 18 months by delegated legislation. The government hopes that, by increasing the magistrates' sentencing powers, more cases will be tried in the magistrates' court rather than being referred up to the Crown Court to be tried by an expensive jury.

sourcebook
p. 136 ➡ The Criminal Justice Act 2003 also allows trial by judge alone in the Crown Court in two situations:

Figure 10.1 **The Old Bailey, the Central Criminal Court in London**
Source: PA Photos.

- where a serious risk of jury tampering exists (s. 44); or
- where the case involves complex or lengthy financial and commercial arrangements (s. 43).

In this second scenario, trial by judge alone would be possible where the trial would be so burdensome upon a jury that it is necessary in the interests of justice for the case to be heard without a jury. Alternatively, it would be possible where the trial would be likely to place an excessive burden on the life of a typical juror. While s. 44 has been brought into force, the government agreed with the opposition not to implement s. 43 while alternative proposals for specialist juries and judges sitting in panels were investigated. The relevant legislative provisions can be brought into force only by a parliamentary order approving its implementation, which will require debates and a vote in both Houses of Parliament was initiated at the end of 2005 but, following strong opposition, the provision was not brought into force. Instead, in 2006 the government introduced a single issue Bill, the Fraud (Trials without Jury) Bill, aimed solely at abolishing the jury in complex fraud trials.

This Bill did not complete its progress through Parliament before Parliament close for the summer of 2007. It may be that government will not try to push this piece of legislation as no mention was made of it in the Queen's Speech when Parliament re-opened in November 2007 and it has not been reintroduced to Parliament.

The secrecy of the jury

Once they retire to consider their verdict, jurors are not allowed to communicate with anyone other than the judge and an assigned court official, until after the verdict is delivered. Afterwards they are forbidden by s. 8 of the Contempt of Court Act 1981 from revealing anything that was said or done during their deliberations. Breach of this section amounts to a criminal offence.

The arguments in favour of secrecy have been stated by McHugh J as:

- it ensures freedom of discussion in the jury room;
- it protects jurors from outside influences, and from harassment;
- if the public knew how juries reached a verdict, they might respect the decision less;
- without secrecy, citizens would be reluctant to serve as jurors;
- it ensures the finality of the verdict;
- it enables jurors to bring in unpopular verdicts;
- it prevents unreliable disclosures by jurors and misunderstanding of verdicts.

The arguments against secrecy and in favour of disclosure are that this reform would:

- make juries more accountable;
- make it easier to inquire into the reliability of convictions and rectify injustices;
- show where reform is required;
- educate the public;
- ensure each juror's freedom of expression.

The verdict

Ideally juries should produce a unanimous verdict, but in 1967 majority verdicts were introduced of ten to two (or nine to one if the jury has been reduced during the trial). This is now provided for in the Juries Act 1974. When the jury withdraws to consider its verdict, it must be told by the judge to reach a unanimous verdict. If, however, the jury has failed to reach a unanimous verdict after what the judge considers a reasonable period of deliberation, given the complexity of the case (not less than two hours), the judge can direct that it may reach a majority verdict. The foreman of the jury must state in open court the numbers of the jurors agreeing and disagreeing with the verdict.

Qualification for jury service

Before 1972, only those who owned a home which was over a prescribed rateable value were eligible for jury service. The Morris Committee in 1965 estimated that 78 per cent of the names on the electoral register did not qualify for jury service under this criteria, and 95 per cent of women were ineligible. This was either because they lived in rented accommodation or because they were the wife or other relative of the person in whose name the property was held. The Committee recommended that the right to do jury service should correspond with the right to vote. This reform was introduced in 1972, but nevertheless there continued to be a problem that in practice juries were not truly representative of the society which they served. While it was understandable that some people with criminal convictions were disqualified from jury service, a wide range of other people were either excluded or excused from jury service.

The basis of the use of juries in serious criminal cases is that the 12 people are randomly selected, and should therefore comprise a representative sample of the population as a whole. This ideal came closer with the abolition of the property qualification and with the use of computers for the random selection process. Despite this, research carried out for the Home Office (*Jury Excusal and Deferral* (2000)) found that each year only two-thirds of the people summoned for jury service made themselves available to do it. About 15 per cent of summoned jurors failed to attend court on the day or had their summonses returned as 'undelivered'. Because enforcement has been poor, it became widely known that a jury summons could be ignored with impunity.

sourcebook p. 130 → In his *Review of the Criminal Courts* (2001), Sir Robin Auld argued that the many exclusions and excusals from jury service deprived juries of the experience and skills of a wide range of professional and successful people. Their absence created the impression that jury service was only for those not important or clever enough to get out of it. He was keen to make juries more representative of the general population. He wanted jury service to become a compulsory public duty for all, to stop middle-class professionals opting out. He proposed that everyone should be eligible for jury service, save for the mentally ill.

The government accepted these recommendations. The Criminal Justice Act 2003, s. 321 and Sch. 33 amended the Juries Act 1974. This Act now provides that potential jury members must be:

- aged 18 to 70;
- on the electoral register;
- resident in the UK, Channel Islands or Isle of Man for at least five years since the age of 13;
- not a mentally disordered person; and not disqualified from jury service.

Most of the grounds for ineligibility and excusal have been removed. Only military personnel can be excused from jury service and only the mentally ill are ineligible for jury service. The rules disqualifying people with certain criminal convictions from jury service remain. As a result, in future juries should become much more representative of society. Following these reforms, increasing participation in the jury system, an appeal was brought before the Court of Appeal (**R v Abdroikov** (2005)), arguing that a trial was unfair where a police officer or employee of the Crown Prosecution Service acted as jurors. This appeal was rejected, as the court stated that such individuals were required to behave in the same way as any other randomly selected juror.

Sir Robin Auld also recommended that potential jurors should no longer only be selected from the electoral register. Many people are not registered to vote in elections, even though they are entitled to do so. To reach as many people as possible he therefore proposed that a range of publicly maintained lists and directories should be used. The government has not adopted this recommendation.

??? ## Quick quiz 10.1

1 Does the jury decide the sentence of an offender?

2 What age group can sit on a jury?

3 Can a police officer sit as a juror?

4 Do the jury have to reach a unanimous verdict in order to convict a defendant?

Summoning the jury

Every year almost half a million people are summoned to do jury service. In 2001 a Central Juror Summoning Bureau was established to administer the juror-summoning process for the whole of the country. Computers are used to produce a random list of potential jurors from the electoral register. Summons are sent out (with a form to return confirming that the person does not fall into any of the disqualified or ineligible groups), and from the resulting list the jury panel is produced. This is made public for both sides in forthcoming cases to inspect, though only names and addresses are shown. It is at this stage that jury vetting may take place (see below). Jurors also receive a set of notes which explain a little of the procedure of the jury service and the functions of the juror.

Jury service is compulsory and failure to attend on the specified date, or unfitness for service through drink or drugs, is contempt of court and can result in a fine.

The jury for a particular case is chosen by random ballot in open court – the clerk has each panel member's name on a card, the cards are shuffled and the first 12 names called out. Unless there are any challenges (see p. 158), these 12 people will be sworn in. In a criminal case there are usually 12 jurors and there must never be fewer than nine. In civil cases in the county court there are eight jurors.

Jury vetting

Jury vetting consists of checking that potential jurors do not hold 'extremist' views which some feel would make them unsuitable for hearing a case. It is done by checking police, Special Branch and security service records.

Attorney-General's guidelines exist stating when jurors should be vetted. These state that vetting might be necessary in certain special cases, such as terrorism. Authorisation is required by the Attorney-General, who will be acting on the advice of the Director of Public Prosecutions. Checking whether a person has a criminal record is permissible in a much wider range of cases without special permission.

Vetting for any purpose remains controversial. Supporters claim that it can promote impartiality by excluding those whose views might bias the other members of the jury, and make them put pressure on others, as well as protecting national security and preventing disqualified persons from serving. Opponents say it infringes the individual's right to privacy, and gives the prosecution an unfair advantage, since it is too expensive for most defendants to undertake, and they do not have access to the same sources of information as the prosecution.

Challenges

As members of the jury panel are called, and before they are sworn in, they may be challenged in one of two ways:

1 **Challenge for cause.** Either side may challenge for cause, on the grounds of privilege of peerage, disqualification, ineligibility or assumed bias. Jurors cannot be questioned before being challenged to ascertain whether there are grounds for a challenge. A successful challenge for cause is therefore only likely to succeed if the juror is personally known, or if jury vetting has been undertaken. If a challenge for cause is made, it is tried by the trial judge.
2 **Stand by.** Only the prosecution may ask jurors to stand by for the Crown. Although there are specified grounds for this, in practice no reason need be given, and this is generally how the information supplied by jury vetting is used.

This limited process of challenging the jury should be contrasted with the system in the US, where it can take days to empanel a jury, particularly where the case has received a lot of pre-trial media coverage. Potential jury members can be asked a wide range of questions about their attitudes to the issues raised by a case, and a great deal of money may be spent employing special consultants who claim to be able to judge which way people are likely to vote, based on their age, sex, politics, religion and other personal information.

In a high-profile case, **R v Andrews** (1998), the defence wanted to use the American approach to establish whether members of the jury panel were likely to be biased against the defendant. She was accused of murdering her boyfriend, and the case had received an enormous amount of publicity since Ms Andrew had initially told police that her boyfriend was killed by an unknown assailant in a 'road rage' incident, sparking off a media hunt for the killer. Her lawyers wanted to issue questionnaires to the jury panel to check whether any of them showed a

Figure 10.2 **Tracie Andrews, the defendant in R v Andrews** (1998), arrives at the High Court in London to find out if her Court of Appeal bid for freedom has succeeded, after being jailed for life for murdering her fiancé, Lee Harvey, who she had claimed was killed by a mystery motorist in a road rage attack

Source: © Fiona Hanson/PA Photos.

prejudice against her. The trial judge refused the request and when Ms Andrews was convicted, she appealed, arguing that the failure to allow questioning of the jury meant her conviction was unsafe. The argument was rejected by the Court of Appeal, which stated that questioning of the jury panel, whether orally or by written questionnaire, should be avoided in all but the most exceptional cases, such as where potential jurors might have a direct or indirect connection to the facts of the trial (for example, if they were related to someone involved in the trial, or had lost money as a result of the defendant's actions).

Advantages of the jury system

Public participation

Juries allow the ordinary citizen to take part in the administration of justice, so that verdicts are seen to be those of society rather than of the judicial system, and satisfy the constitutional tradition of judgment by one's peers. Lord Denning described jury service as giving 'ordinary folk their finest lesson in citizenship'.

sourcebook p. 117 → The Home Office has carried out research into the experience of being a juror: Matthews, Hancock and Briggs, *Jurors' Perceptions, Understanding, Confidence and Satisfaction in the Jury System: a study in six courts* (2004). The research questioned 361 jurors about their jury service. More than half (55 per cent) said they would be happy to do it again, 19 per cent said they would not mind doing jury service again, but 25 per cent said they would never want to be a juror again. About two-thirds felt that their experience had boosted their opinion of the jury system and they were impressed by the professionalism and helpfulness of the court staff and the performance of the judge. A minority were unhappy with the delays in the system, the trivial nature of some cases and the standard of facilities. Thirty-six per cent of jurors felt intimidated or very uncomfortable in the courtroom, primarily because they were worried about meeting defendants or their family members coming out of court or in the street.

When questioned by Professor Lloyd-Bostock about their experience, the jurors in the collapsed Jubilee line case were found to be enthusiastic about their role, committed to it, and furious when the trial was aborted. They were a remarkably cooperative and mutually supportive group. Two compared being on the jury with being on *Big Brother*. However, as the trial progressed, the jurors felt increasingly like 'jury fodder', on tap but not informed. They would be telephoned at short notice and told not to turn up for several days but no explanation would be given. Even more frustrating was when they turned up for jury service and then, after a lengthy delay, sent home again. The main difficulties suffered by the jurors were in relation to their employment. All seven jurors who were employed said their employers were very unhappy about the long trial. Most felt that the court should have more responsibility for communicating directly with their employers rather than placing the onus on the jurors. Uncooperative employers could cause problems over claims for allowances. One juror had been made redundant, one was in an employment dispute, one had missed a definite and much-desired promotion and was required to undertake extensive retraining, and one had been signed off by his doctor as suffering from stress as a result of his work situation. Most of the jurors had suffered financially as a result of the trial. One suggestion is that a juror liaison person could be appointed for long jury trials whose remit is to look after jurors' needs and alleviate the burden of jury service as much as possible.

Certainty

The jury adds certainty to the law, since it gives a general verdict which cannot give rise to misinterpretation. In a criminal case the jury simply states that the accused is guilty or not guilty, and gives no reasons. Consequently, the decision is not open to dispute.

Ability to judge according to conscience

A major milestone in the history of the jury was in **Bushell's Case** (1670). Before this, judges would try to bully juries into convicting the defendant, particularly where the crime had political overtones, but in **Bushell's Case** it was established that the jury's members were the sole judges of fact, with the right to give a verdict according to their conscience, and could not be penalised for taking a view of the facts opposed to that of the judge. The importance of this power now is that juries may acquit a defendant, even when the law demands a guilty verdict.

Because juries have the ultimate right to find defendants innocent or guilty, they have been seen as a vital protection against oppressive or politically motivated prosecutions, and as a kind of safety valve for those cases where the law demands a guilty verdict, but genuine justice does not. For example, in the early nineteenth century, all felonies (a classification of crimes used at the time, marking out those considered most serious) were in theory punishable by death. Theft of goods or money above the value of a shilling was a felony, but juries were frequently reluctant to allow the death penalty to be imposed in what seemed to them trivial cases, so they would often find that the defendant was guilty, but the property stolen was worth less than a shilling.

There are several well-known recent cases of juries using their right to find according to their consciences, often concerning issues of political and moral controversy, such as **R v Kronlid** (1996). The defendants were three women who broke into a British Aerospace factory and caused damage costing over £1.5 million to a Hawk fighter plane. The women admitted doing this – they had left a video explaining their actions in the plane's cockpit – but claimed that they had a defence under s. 3 of the Criminal Law Act 1967, which provides that it is lawful to commit a crime in order to prevent another (usually more serious) crime being committed, and that this may involve using 'such force as is reasonable in all the circumstances'.

The defendants pointed out that the plane was part of a consignment due to be sold to the government of Indonesia, which was involved in oppressive measures against the population of East Timor, a region forcibly annexed by Indonesia in 1975. They further explained that Amnesty International had estimated that the Indonesians had killed at least a third of the population of East Timor, and that the jet was likely to be used in a genocidal attack against the survivors. Genocide is a crime and therefore, they argued, their criminal damage was done in order to prevent a crime. However, the prosecution gave evidence that the Indonesian government had given assurances that the planes would not be used against the East Timorese, and the British government had accepted this and granted an export licence. Acquitting the women was therefore a criticism of the British government's position on the issue, as well as the actions of the Indonesian government, and in the face of the clear evidence that they had caused the damage, they were widely expected to be convicted. The jury found them all not guilty.

Other cases have involved what were seen to be oppressive prosecutions in cases involving the government, such as **R** *v* **Ponting** (1985), where the defendant, a civil servant, was prosecuted for breaking the Official Secrets Act after passing confidential information to a journalist – even though doing so exposed a matter of public interest, namely the fact that the then government had lied to Parliament. Ponting was acquitted.

Quick quiz 10.2

1 Give three arguments in favour of the secrecy of the jury and three arguments against.

2 What is the minimum number of jurors who must vote in favour of a conviction or an acquittal in order to reach a verdict?

3 Can juries carry out independent research into a case?

4 Give an example of a case where the jurors may have decided a case according to their conscience rather than the law.

Task 10.3

The Judicial Studies Board has issued a specimen direction which judges can give to a jury to explain their different roles during a jury trial. This specimen direction is as follows:

'Our functions in this trial have been and remain quite different. Throughout this trial the law has been my area of responsibility, and I must now give you directions as to the law which applies in this case. When I do so, you must accept those directions and follow them.

I must also remind you of the prominent features of the evidence. However, it has always been your responsibility to judge the evidence and decide all the relevant facts of this case, and when you come to consider your verdict you, and you alone, must do that.

You do not have to decide every point which has been raised; only such matters as will enable you to say whether the charge laid against the defendant has been proved. You will do that by having regard to the whole of the evidence and forming your own judgement about the witnesses, and which evidence is reliable and which is not.

The facts of this case are your responsibility. You will wish to take account of the arguments in the speeches you have heard, but you are not bound to accept them. Equally, if in the course of my review of the evidence, I appear to express any views concerning the facts, or emphasise a particular aspect of the evidence, do not adopt ▶

those views unless you agree with them; and if I do not mention something which you think is important, you should have regard to it, and give it such weight as you think fit. When it comes to the facts of this case, it is your judgement alone that counts.'

Questions

1 Does the jury have to follow the judge's directions on the law?
2 Does the jury have to follow the judge's view of the facts?

Disadvantages of the jury system

Lack of competence

Lord Denning argued, in *What Next in the Law?* (1982), that the selection of jurors is too wide, resulting in jurors that are not competent to perform their task. Praising the 'Golden Age' of jury service when only 'responsible heads of household from a select band of the middle classes' were eligible to serve, he claimed that the 1972 changes have led to jurors being summoned who are not sufficiently intelligent or educated to perform their task properly. In one unfortunate case, a jury hearing a murder trial had apparently set up an ouija board in an attempt to make contact with the spirit of the deceased: **R v Young** (1995). Denning suggested that jurors should be selected in much the same way as magistrates are, with interviews and references required. This throws up several obvious problems: a more complicated selection process would be more time-consuming and costly; finding sufficient people willing to take part might prove difficult; and a jury that is intelligent and educated can still be biased, and may be more likely to be so if drawn from a narrow social group.

Particular concern has been expressed about the average jury's understanding of complex fraud cases. The Roskill Committee concluded that trial by random jury was not a satisfactory way of achieving justice in such cases, with many jurors 'out of their depth'. However, the Roskill Committee was unable to find accurate evidence of a higher proportion of acquittals in complex fraud cases than in any other kind – many of their conclusions were based on research by Baldwin and McConville (1979), yet none of the questionable acquittals reported there was in a complex fraud case.

The academic, Terry Honess (2003), conducted an extended simulation study of jurors' comprehension of some of the evidence in the Maxwell fraud trial. He estimated that four out of five of the participants could be regarded as competent to serve on a major fraud trial, and concluded that abolition of the jury system for complex fraud trials was not justified on the grounds of 'cognitive unfitness'.

Following the collapse of the trial of six men prosecuted for alleged fraud in the awarding of contracts for the construction of the extension to the Jubilee underground line, **R v Rayment and others** (2005), the jurors were questioned about their experience of the trial as part of a government review of the case. This review found that 'when the case collapsed this jury, taken as a group, had a good understanding of the case, the issues and the evidence so far, as presented to them'. The jurors said they had no problem with technical language or documents. They displayed quite impressive familiarity with the charges, issues and evidence, and were able to engage in detailed discussion of the prosecution case nearly a year after it had closed. The chief difficulty expressed by the jurors was not in finding evidence too technical or complex, but in finding the pace of the trial extremely slow and parts of the defence evidence tedious. It is questionable whether the trial needed to be unmanageably long. In the preface to his report on the case, Stephen Wooler (2006) describes it as 'probably one of the best examples' of cases 'which are neither sufficiently complex to be beyond the comprehension of juries, nor necessarily lengthy'. Discussion was evidently facilitated by the provision of a jury deliberating room for much of the trial, where the jury went whilst at court but not in court. The jurors said they found discussion much more difficult, if not impossible, when they did not have use of this room. The jurors were not allowed to take their notes from the courtroom and several said it would have been helpful to do so. The academic, Professor Findlay, has noted that juror comprehension and memory for complex evidence can be assisted through, for example, the use of visual aids. Discussion amongst jurors, taking notes and asking questions can enhance juror comprehension (Horowitz (2001)). Professor Lloyd-Bostock has concluded:

> '. . . where the jury is concerned, the "problem" with the Jubilee Line case was not the jury's ability to cope, but the unnecessarily excessive length of the case with its consequences for the jurors' lives, together with some aspects of their treatment at court . . . Taken in context, the jurors' perspective on the ill-fated Jubilee Line trial does not indicate that the solution is to abandon jury trial for such cases. Rather, it confirms that jury trial is valued, and that improvements through trial preparation, and trial and jury management, should be fully explored before the jury itself is threatened.'

The 'perverse verdicts' problem

It is a matter of fact that juries acquit proportionately more defendants than magistrates do. Research from the Home Office Planning Unit suggests that an acquittal is approximately twice as likely in a jury trial. Many critics of the jury system argue that this is a major failing on the part of juries, arising either from their inability to perform their role properly, as discussed above, or from their sympathy with defendants, or both.

This is a difficult area to research, as the Contempt of Court Act 1981 prohibits asking jurors about the basis on which they reached their decision. What research there is generally involves comparing actual jury decisions with those reached by legal professionals, or by shadow juries, who sit in on the case and reach their own decision just as the official jurors are asked to do.

A piece of research commissioned by the Roskill Committee on fraud trials concluded that jurors who found difficulty in comprehending the complex issues involved in fraud prosecution were more likely to acquit. They suggested that the jurors characterised their own confusions as a form of 'reasonable doubt' leading them to a decision to acquit.

A study by McCabe and Purves, *The Jury at Work* (1972), looked at 173 acquittals, and concluded that 15 (9 per cent) defied the evidence, the rest being attributable to weakness of the prosecution case or failure of their witnesses, or the credibility of the accused's explanation. McCabe and Purves viewed the proportion of apparently perverse verdicts as quite small and, from their observations of shadow juries, concluded that jurors did work methodically and rationally through the evidence, and tried to put aside their own prejudices.

However, Baldwin and McConville's 1979 study (*Jury Trials*) examined 500 cases, both convictions and acquittals, and found that up to 25 per cent of acquittals were questionable (as well as 5 per cent of convictions), and concluded that, given the serious nature of the cases concerned, this was a problem. They describe trial by jury as 'an arbitrary and unpredictable business'.

Zander (1988) points out that the high rate of acquittals must be seen in the light of the high number of guilty pleas in the Crown Court. It must also be noted that many acquittals are directed or ordered by the judge: according to evidence from the Lord Chancellor's Department to the Runciman Commission, in 1990–1, 40 per cent of all acquittals were ordered by the judge because the prosecution offered no evidence at the start of the trial. A further 16 per cent of the acquittals were directed by the judge after the prosecution had made its case as there was insufficient evidence to leave to the jury. Thus the jury was only responsible for 41 per cent of the acquittals, which was merely 7 per cent of all cases in the Crown Court. Bearing in mind the pressures on defendants to plead guilty, it is not surprising that those who resist tend to be those with the strongest cases – and, of course, the standard of proof required is very high. Nor is it beyond the bounds of possibility that part of the difference in conviction rates between magistrates and juries is due to magistrates convicting the innocent rather than juries acquitting the guilty.

In a high-profile case the Court of Appeal overturned a jury decision in civil proceedings on the basis that the jury decision had been perverse. In **Grobbelaar *v* News Group Newspapers Ltd** (2001) a jury had awarded the professional goalkeeper, Bruce Grobbelaar, £85,000 on the basis that he had been defamed in *The Sun* newspaper. *The Sun* had published a story claiming that Grobbelaar had received cash to fix football matches. It had obtained secretly taped videos of Grobbelaar, in which he apparently admitted receiving money in the past to lose matches, and appeared to accept cash following a proposal to fix matches in the future. A criminal prosecution of Grobbelaar had failed and he sued in the civil courts for defamation. Grobbelaar accepted that he had made the confessions and accepted cash, but claimed that he had done so as a trick in order to bring the other person to justice. The jury accepted his claim and awarded damages. *The Sun*'s appeal was allowed on the basis that the jury's decision had been perverse. The Court of Appeal found Grobbelaar's story 'incredible'. The House of Lords allowed a further appeal. It considered it wrong to overturn the jury's verdict as perverse, as the verdict could have been given an alternative explanation.

Bias

Jurors may be biased for or against certain groups – for example, they may favour attractive members of the opposite sex, or be prejudiced against the police.

Bias appears to be a particular problem in libel cases, where juries prejudiced against newspapers award huge damages, apparently using them punitively rather than as compensation for the victim. Examples include the £500,000 awarded to Jeffrey Archer in 1987, and the £300,000 to Koo Stark a year later, as well as **Sutcliffe *v* Pressdram Ltd** (1991), in which *Private Eye* was ordered to pay £600,000 to the wife of the Yorkshire Ripper. In the latter case Lord Donaldson described the award as irrational, and suggested that judges should give more guidance on the amounts to be awarded – not by referring to previous cases or specific amounts, but by asking juries to think about the real value of money (such as what income the capital would produce, or what could be bought with it). The Courts and Legal Services Act 1990 now allows the Court of Appeal to reduce damages considered excessive.

For a discussion of the problem of potentially racist jurors, see p. 170.

Representation of ethnic minorities

Black defendants have no right to have black people sitting on the jury. In **R *v* Bansal** (1985) the case involved an Anti-National Front demonstration and the trial judge ordered that the jury should be drawn from an area with a large Asian population. However, this approach was rejected as wrong in **R *v* Ford** (1989). The Court of Appeal held that race could not be taken into account when selecting jurors, and that a judge could not discharge jurors in order to achieve a racially representative jury.

Manipulation by defendants

The government's consultation paper, *Determining Mode of Trial in Either Way Cases* (1998), suggests that manipulation of the right to jury trial by defendants is a major problem. It claims that many guilty defendants choose jury trial in a bid to make use of the delay such a choice provides. The report puts forward three reasons why guilty defendants want to do this. First, delay may put pressure on the Crown Prosecution Service to reduce the charge in exchange for the defendant pleading guilty and so speed up the process. Secondly, it may make it more likely that prosecution witnesses will fail to attend the eventual trial, or at least weaken their recollections if they do attend, so making an acquittal more likely. Thirdly, if a defendant is being held on remand, he or she is kept at a local prison, and allowed additional visits and other privileges not given to convicted prisoners. Time spent on remand is deducted from any eventual prison sentence, so for a defendant on remand who calculates that he or she is likely to be found guilty and sentenced to imprisonment, putting off the trial for as long as possible will maximise the amount of the sentence that can be spent under the more favourable conditions. Such manipulation is obviously undesirable from the point of view of justice, and it also wastes a great deal of time and money, since many defendants who manipulate the system in this way end up pleading guilty at the last minute (resulting in what is known as a 'cracked trial'), so that the time and money spent preparing the prosecution's case is wasted; in most cases, state funding will also have been spent on the defence case.

However, those who support jury trials argue that this is a declining problem. In 1987, defendants choosing jury trial accounted for 53 per cent of either-way cases sent to the Crown Court, but by 1997, the proportion had fallen to 28 per cent.

Jury nobbling

This problem led to the suspension of jury trials for terrorist offences in Northern Ireland, and has caused problems in some English trials. In 1982 several Old Bailey trials had to be stopped because of attempted 'nobbling', one after seven months, and the problem became so serious that juries had to sit out of sight of the public gallery, brown paper was stuck over the windows in court doors, and jurors were warned to avoid local pubs and cafés and eat only in their own canteen. In 1984, jurors in the Brinks-Mat trial had to have police protection to and from the court, and their telephone calls intercepted.

A new criminal offence was created under the Criminal Justice and Public Order Act 1994 to try to give additional protection to the jury. This provides under s. 51 that it is an offence to intimidate or threaten to harm, either physically or financially, certain people involved in a trial including jurors.

A more radical reform was introduced in the Criminal Procedure and Investigation Act 1996. Section 54 of the Act provides that where a person has been acquitted of an offence and someone is subsequently convicted of interfering with or intimidating jurors or witnesses in the case, then the High Court can quash the acquittal and the person can be retried. This is a wholly exceptional development in the law since traditionally acquittals were considered final, and subsequent retrial a breach of fundamental human rights. Following the Criminal Justice Act 2003, where there is a real risk of jury nobbling a case can be heard by a single judge.

Absence of reasons

When judges sit alone their judgment consists of a detailed and explicit finding of fact. When there is a jury it returns an unexplained verdict which simply finds in favour of one party or another. The former is more easily reviewed by appellate courts because the findings and the inferences of the trial judge can be examined. But when the appellate court is faced with a jury's verdict, it must support that verdict if there is any reasonable view of the evidence which leads to it.

Article 6 of the European Convention on Human Rights requires courts to give reasons for their judgments. In his review of the criminal courts, Sir Robin Auld considered this matter in relation to the unreasoned jury verdict. However, he concluded that the European Court of Human Rights would take into account the way the British jury trial works as a whole and not find a violation of Art. 6.

Problems with compulsory jury service

Jury service is often unpopular but a refusal to act as a juror amounts to a contempt of court. Resentful jurors might make unsatisfactory decisions: in particular, jurors keen to get away as soon as possible are likely simply to go along with what the majority say, whether they agree or not.

Cost and time

A Crown Court trial currently costs the taxpayer around £7,400 per day, as opposed to £1,000 per day for trial by magistrates. The jury process is time-consuming for all involved, with juries spending much of their time waiting around to be summoned into court.

Distress to jury members

Juries trying cases involving serious crimes of violence, particularly rape, murder or child abuse, may have to listen to deeply distressing evidence, and in some cases to inspect graphic photographs of injuries. One juror in a particularly gruesome murder case told a newspaper how he felt on hearing a tape of the last words of the victim as, fatally injured, she struggled to make herself understood on the phone to the emergency services:

> 'It was your worst nightmare. I've watched American police programmes where you have a murder every 15 seconds, pools of blood, chalk lines where the bodies were . . . that's nothing compared to the sound of this tape. You cannot believe the shock that runs through you, the fear when you know this is what happened.' (The Sunday Times, 13 April 1997)

At the end of the case, most members of the jury were in tears, and after delivering their verdict, it was over an hour before they could compose themselves sufficiently to leave the jury room. The problem is made worse by the fact that jurors are told not to discuss the case with anyone else.

The potential for distress to jurors was recognised in the recent trials of Rosemary West and the killers of James Bulger, where the jurors were offered counselling afterwards, and since these cases the Ministry of Justice has provided that court-appointed welfare officers should be made available. However, these are provided only in cases judges deem to be exceptional, and only if jurors request their help.

Quick quiz 10.4

1 On what basis did the Court of Appeal allow the appeal of *The Sun* newspaper in the case of **Grobbelaar v News Group Newspapers Ltd** (2001)?

2 Does the failure of the jury to give reasons violate the right to a fair trial contained in Art. 6 of the European Convention on Human Rights?

3 Which is cheaper, a Crown Court trial or a trial in a magistrates' court?

4 Do black defendants have a right to at least one black juror sitting on the jury to hear their case?

Reform of the jury

A wide range of reform proposals have been put forward for the reform of the jury system.

Serious fraud trials

The government would like to remove jury trials from most serious fraud cases (see p. 169), a reform that has been heavily criticised. There has been an ongoing debate as to whether juries are suitable for such cases. Public attention was drawn to this issue by the collapse of the trial of six men accused of fraud relating to the awarding of contracts for the construction of the Jubilee Line extension on the London Underground system (**R v Rayment** (2005)). The trial lasted two years – the longest ever jury trial – before it collapsed, having cost the taxpayer £60 million.

> ✓ **Know your terms 10.5**
>
> Define the following terms:
> 1 Jury vetting.
> 2 Stand by.
> 3 Summary offence.
> 4 Jury nobbling.

It had suffered from a range of delays due to illness, scheduled holidays and paternity leave among the jury and lawyers, since it began in February 2000. Legal arguments also involved substantial periods where the jury was not required to hear evidence. In the last seven months before the case was dropped, the jury heard evidence on only 13 days of the 140 available. The prosecution eventually dropped the case after deciding there had been so many interruptions that a fair trial had become impossible.

To try to prevent such a waste of time and money occurring again, the Lord Chief Justice issued a protocol requiring judges to exercise strong case management over cases likely to last more than eight weeks, including strict deadlines. The aim is to reduce the length of such trials to a maximum of three months. Trials would only be allowed to go on longer than six months in 'exceptional circumstances'. In addition, since April 2005 large criminal cases are monitored by a case management panel chaired by the Director of Public Prosecutions.

But the government decided not to wait to see whether this new Protocol led to shorter fraud trials with juries sitting, and instead decided to remove juries from such cases by trying to push through Parliament the Fraud (Trials Without Jury) Bill. However, it faced strong opposition and the Bill has not been enacted.

The use of a single judge has the advantages of making trials quicker, reducing the likelihood of 'perverse' verdicts, and defeating the problem of jury nobbling (in Northern Ireland single judges have long been used in some cases because of the problem of jury nobbling). However, the benefits of public participation in the legal system would be lost, and all the problems associated with judicial bias and the restricted social background of judges (described in Chapter 13) would be let loose on cases which involve vital questions for both the individuals concerned and society as a whole. The Bar Council believes that juries should be retained in all cases where the defendant faces serious loss of liberty or reputation. It considers that fraud cases can appear complex, but if they are properly managed, juries are capable of deciding the case, which usually comes down to determining whether the defendant has been dishonest.

Using a bench of perhaps three or five judges would give a little more protection against individual bias, but would still not give the benefit of community participation that the jury offers (and would also require massive investment to train the increased number of judges that would be required).

Abolishing juries

It can be argued that, since juries decide only 1 per cent of criminal cases, the system really no longer needs them at all and they should be abolished. The pros and cons of this argument naturally depend on what would be put in their place.

The government's 1998 consultation paper on the criminal justice system considered four possible options for serious fraud trials:

- abolishing the use of juries in fraud trials completely and replacing them with a specially trained single judge and two lay people with expertise in commercial affairs;
- replacing juries with a specially trained single judge or panel of judges, possibly with access to advisers on commercial matters;
- retaining jury trial but restricting the jury's role to deciding questions of dishonesty, with the judge deciding other matters; or
- replacing the traditional, randomly selected jury with a special jury, selected on the basis of qualifications or tests, or drawn from those who can demonstrate specialist knowledge of business and finance.

Task 10.6

If you were charged with committing a fraud, what type of trial would you prefer?

- Would you prefer your case to be heard in a magistrates' court or a Crown Court?
- Would you want your case to be heard by a professional judge, by a jury or by a combination of lay people sitting with a judge and jointly deciding your guilt?
- Why would you prefer this type of trial?

Improving the performance of the jury

sourcebook p. 130 → Sir Robin Auld has made a range of specific recommendations to improve the performance of the jury.

Help the jury to work effectively

The Auld Review recommended that, in order to assist a jury in their work, the prosecution and defence advocates should prepare a written summary of the case and the issues that needed to be decided. This 'case and issues' summary would be agreed by the judge and distributed to the jurors at the start of the trial.

The judge would sum up the case at the end of the trial by forming questions which needed to be considered by the jurors. Juries would reach verdicts by answering these questions during their deliberations. Where the judge thought it appropriate he or she would be able to require the jury publicly to answer each of the questions and to declare a verdict in accordance with those answers. Sir Robin Auld argues that this would strengthen the jury as a tribunal of fact, provide a reasoned basis for jury verdicts and reduce the risk of perverse verdicts. While there can only be benefits from presenting the case more clearly to the jury, the use of questions which the jury may be forced to answer publicly seems to be an unnecessary restriction on the jurors' freedom to reach a decision in accordance with their conscience as well as in accordance with the law.

Professor Zander (2001) has criticised these recommendations. He argues persuasively that Sir Robin Auld demonstrates:

> 'an authoritarian attitude that disregards history and reveals a grievously misjudged sense of the proper balance of the criminal justice system. For centuries the role of the jury has included the power to stand between the citizen and unjust law . . . [G]etting it right does not necessarily mean giving the verdict a judge would have given. . . . To want to inquire whether they reached their decision in the "right" way, is foolish because it ignores the nature of the institution.'

Prevent perverse verdicts

The Auld Review was concerned by the risk of juries reaching perverse verdicts. Rather than seeing these as a potential safeguard of civil liberties, the review seems to consider these as an insult to the law. It has therefore recommended that legislation should declare that juries have no right to acquit defendants in defiance of the law or in disregard of the evidence. The prosecution would be given a right to appeal against what it considered to be a perverse acquittal by a jury.

Sir Robin Auld recommended that, where appropriate, the trial judge and the Court of Appeal should be allowed to investigate any alleged impropriety or failure in the way the jury reached its verdict, even where this is supposed to have happened during the traditionally secret deliberations of the jury. Such an investigation might look at accusations that some jurors ignored or slept through the deliberation or that the jury reached its verdict because of an irrational prejudice or whim, deliberately ignoring the evidence.

These recommendations show insufficient respect for the jurors and have been rejected by the government.

Reserve jurors

One recommendation of the *Review of the Criminal Courts* (2001) was that, where appropriate, for long cases judges should be able to swear in extra jurors. These reserve jurors would be able to replace jurors who are unable to continue to hear a case because, for example, of illness.

Black jurors

It has been argued by the Commission for Racial Equality that consideration needs to be given to the racial balance in particular cases. They suggest that where a case has a racial dimension and the defendant reasonably believes that he or she cannot receive a fair trial from an all-white jury, then the judge should have the power to order that three of the jurors come from the same ethnic minority as the defendant or the victim. Both the Runciman Commission (1993) and Sir Robin Auld's *Review of the Criminal Courts* (2001) have given their endorsement to this proposal but it has never been implemented.

The Society of Black Lawyers had, in addition, submitted to the Runciman Commission that there should always be a right to a multiracial trial and that certain cases with a black defendant should be tried by courts in areas with high black populations, and panels of black jurors who would be available at short notice should be set up. These proposals have not been implemented either.

The problems caused by lack of racial representation on juries can be seen in the high-profile Rodney King case in Los Angeles, where a policeman was found not guilty of assaulting a black motorist despite a videotape of the incident showing brutal conduct. The case was tried in an area with a very high white population, while the incident itself had occurred in an area with a high black population. However, the decision in **R v Ford** (1989), that there is no principle that a jury should be racially balanced, still holds.

Reading on the web

The *Report on Interviews with Jurors in the Jubilee Line Case* (2006) by Professor Sally Lloyd-Bostock is available on the website of Her Majesty's Crown Prosecution Service Inspectorate at:

www.hmcpsi.gov.uk/reports/JLJury-IntsRep.pdf

The *Review of the Investigation and Criminal Proceedings Relating to the Jubilee Line Case* (2006) by Stephen Wooler is available on the website of Her Majesty's Crown Prosecution Service Inspectorate at:

www.hmcpsi.gov.uk/reports/JubileeLineReponly.pdf

The consultation document, *Jury Research and Impropriety* (2005), considering when the law should allow the secrecy of jury deliberations to be broken, can be found on the former Department for Constitutional Affairs' website at:

www.dca.gov.uk/consult/juryresearch/_cp0405.pdf

Leaflets on jury service are published on the Court Service website at:

www.hmcourts-service.gov.uk/

Chapter summary

The role of the jury

Juries decide only about 1 per cent of criminal cases.

The secrecy of the jury

Once they retire to consider their verdict, jurors are not allowed to communicate with anyone other than the judge and an assigned court official, until after the verdict is delivered.

The verdict

Ideally juries should produce a unanimous verdict, but in 1967 majority verdicts were introduced of ten to two (or nine to one if the jury has been reduced during the trial).

Qualifications for jury service

Potential jury members must be:

- aged 18 to 70;
- on the electoral register; and
- resident in the UK, Channel Islands or Isle of Man for at least five years since the age of 13.

Jury vetting

Jury vetting consists of checking that the potential juror does not hold 'extremist' views which some feel would make them unsuitable for hearing a case. It is done by checking police, Special Branch and security service records.

Advantages of the jury system

Juries allow ordinary citizens to participate in the administration of justice and decide cases according to their conscience.

Disadvantages of the jury system

In practice, juries are not representative of the general population. Some of their judgments are perverse; they can be biased and susceptible to manipulation.

Reform of the jury

Proposals have been put forward for restricting the role of juries or abolishing juries altogether. Significant reform proposals were drawn up by Sir Robin Auld but many of these have been rejected by the government. Parliament considered the Fraud (Trials Without Jury) Bill but this Bill to abolish the use of juries in many fraud trials, has not been passed.

Question and answer guides

1

(a) Alicia is charged with theft (an either-way offence). Her case could be tried either by magistrates or by a jury in the Crown Court.
Explain the work of lay magistrates in criminal courts. *(10 marks)*

(b) Explain the work of juries in criminal courts. *(10 marks)*

(c) Discuss advantages **and** disadvantages of using juries in criminal cases.

(10 marks)

(from AQA Specimen Question Paper, 2007)

(a) Lay magistrates perform three main types of work in criminal courts. First, they try the least serious criminal cases. These comprise all summary offences, plus those either-way offences where the defendant is tried summarily. Such cases represent about 95 per cent of all criminal trials. Trying them involves lay magistrates sitting in a magistrates' court, hearing the evidence, deciding guilt or innocence and, if the defendant is found guilty, deciding the sentence. Although they are advised on matters of law by a justices' clerk or legal adviser, the magistrates alone decide the facts and law. In performing their trial functions, lay magistrates usually sit in groups of three.

Secondly, lay magistrates, sitting in a magistrates' court, deal with a range of matters arising before, during or after trial, such as requests by the police for arrest and search warrants, applications for bail, remitting offenders to another court for sentence, and giving directions as to the timetable for proceedings, the attendance of the parties and the service of documents. Under the Crime and Disorder Act 1998 these powers may be exercised by a single lay magistrate sitting alone.

Finally, lay magistrates hear some appeals in the Crown Court, namely where the defendant is appealing against conviction in a magistrates' court. When performing this role they sit alongside a professional judge.

(b) The role of the jury is to weigh up the evidence and decide what actually happened. The judge directs them as to the relevant law, and the jurors then have to apply the law to the facts that they have found and thereby reach a verdict. If the jury has given a verdict of guilty, the judge alone will decide on the appropriate sentence.

In reaching their verdict, the jury are only entitled to consider evidence that arose in court; they cannot consider in the jury room evidence that has not been introduced in court: **R v Marshall and Crump** (2007).

Once they retire to consider their verdict, jurors are not allowed to communicate with anyone other than the judge and an assigned court official, until after the verdict is delivered.

When the jury withdraws to consider its verdict, it must be told by the judge to reach a unanimous verdict. If, however, the jury has failed to reach a unanimous verdict after what the judge considers a reasonable period of deliberation given the complexity of the case (not less than two hours), the judge can direct that it may reach a majority verdict under the Juries Act 1974. The foreman of the jury must state in open court the number of jurors agreeing and disagreeing with the verdict.

(c) Using juries in criminal cases gives the ordinary citizen a role in the justice system. This satisfies the constitutional tradition of being judged by your peers and means that verdicts are seen to be those of society as a whole.

The jury also adds certainty to the law. It states simply that the accused is guilty or not guilty, giving no reasons. Consequently, the decision is not open to misinterpretation or dispute.

Because juries have the unfettered right to find defendants innocent or guilty, they are seen by some as protecting against politically motivated prosecutions. Cases where juries have used their right to find according to their conscience include **R v Ponting** (1985) and **R v Kronlid** (1996).

Amongst the arguments against juries is concern that some jurors are not competent to perform their task. Worries about jurors' understanding of complex fraud cases has contributed to proposals by, for example, the Roskill Committee, to give judges the power to dispense with juries in such cases.

Many critics of the jury system, including Sir Robin Auld, point to its high rate of acquittal. They argue that this arises from jurors' inability to perform their role properly and/or their sympathy with defendants.

There is also the fear that jurors may be biased for or against certain groups – for example, they may be prejudiced against black defendants.

2

(a) Explain how jurors may or may not qualify for jury service, and describe how jurors are chosen to serve on a jury. *(15 marks)*
(b) Identify and explain the advantages and disadvantages of using lay people in the Magistrates' Court and the Crown Court. *(15 marks)*

(from AQA Exam Papers, June 2006 and January 2004)

(a)

- Describe the rules on qualification for jury service – age, electoral register, residence: Criminal Justice Act 2003, amending the Juries Act 1974.
- For a good answer, differentiate between, and give grounds for, excusal, ineligibility and disqualification from jury service, citing **R v Abdroikov** (2007) discussed on p. 156.
- Describe the juror-summoning process, including the role of the Central Juror Summoning Bureau.
- Describe the process of choosing jurors by random ballot in open court.
- Differentiate between jury vetting and jury challenging.
- For a good answer, differentiate between challenging for cause and stand by, citing **R v Andrews** (1998), discussed on p. 158.
- Describe the process of swearing in jurors.

(b)
Lay magistrates

- Discuss the claim that lay magistrates cost taxpayers less than professional judges.
- Discuss how lay magistrates provide the courts with lay involvement and local input.
- Discuss the problem of inconsistency between different benches.
- Discuss lay magistrates' alleged inefficiency.
- Discuss fears that lay magistrates may be biased in favour of the police.

Juries

- Consider how juries maintain the tradition of being judged by your peers.
- Look at how juries help protect the citizen from politically motivated prosecutions.

- Explain concerns over jurors' competence.
- Discuss juries' high rate of acquittal.
- Examine fears that jurors may be biased, e.g. against the police.

Common errors in (a)

- being out of date, only discussing the pre-2003 law on jury qualification;
- discussing the role of the jury.

Common errors in (b)

- discussing only juries, or only lay magistrates;
- failing to adopt a balanced stance.

Group activity 1

- With your friends (or class), prepare a brief but balanced summary of the arguments for and against the use of juries in the English criminal justice system. The summary should be written in a style that can be understood by someone who knows nothing about the law.
- Divide your friends (or class) into groups of two or three people.
- Each group should invite six people of at least 18 years of age, having no knowledge of law, to read the summary and then answer the following questions. Try to get your interviewees to give reasoned answers, rather than just 'Yes' or 'No'.
   Q.1: Do you think that the use of juries in the English criminal justice system is a good thing?
   Q.2: Do you think that there should be any changes made to the use of juries in the English criminal justice system?
   Q.3: Would you be happy to serve on a jury if asked to do so?
   Q.4: Have you ever served on a jury before and, if so, what did you think of the experience?
- With your friends (or class), prepare a table summarising all the answers obtained by all the groups.
- Does this summary cause you to reconsider your own views on the jury system?

Group activity 2

Imagine you receive a letter in the post one morning informing you that you have been summoned to act as a juror.

- What should you do next?
- Why were you selected?
- When you are sitting in the jury box, how many other people will be sitting next to you?
- How long will you be required to sit as a juror?
- What happens if you have already booked a holiday which clashes with your jury service?

The government website on the criminal justice system will provide you with some useful information to help you think about the answers to these questions:

   www.cjsonline.gov.uk/juror/

Part 7
THE LEGAL PROFESSION AND OTHER SOURCES OF ADVICE AND FUNDING

Chapter 11

The legal profession

This chapter discusses the three main professions in the legal field:
- solicitors - their work, qualifications and training;
- barristers - their work qualifications and training;
- the social background of barristers and solicitors;
- legal executives - their work, qualifications and training.

Introduction

The British legal profession, unlike that of most other countries, includes two separate branches: barristers and solicitors (the term 'lawyer' is a general one which covers both branches). They each do the same type of work – advocacy, which means representing clients in court, and paperwork, including drafting legal documents and giving written advice – but the proportions differ, with barristers generally spending a higher proportion of their time in court.

In addition, some types of work have traditionally been available to only one branch (conveyancing to solicitors, and advocacy in the higher courts to barristers, for example), and barristers are not usually hired directly by clients. A client's first point of contact will usually be a solicitor, who then engages a barrister on their behalf if it proves necessary. As we shall see, however, these divisions are beginning to break down.

In the past, the two branches of the profession have been fairly free to arrange their own affairs, but over the last 15 years this situation has changed significantly, with the government increasingly passing legislation to control the professions.

As well as barristers and solicitors, an increasingly important profession is that of the legal executives.

Solicitors

There are around 98,000 solicitors in England and Wales. Their governing body is the Law Society. Until recently, the Law Society acted both as the representative of solicitors and as the solicitor's regulator. A government-commissioned report by Sir David Clementi (2004) raised concerns that this dual function could cause a conflict of interests, with the Law Society putting the solicitor first, rather than

sourcebook
p. 93 →

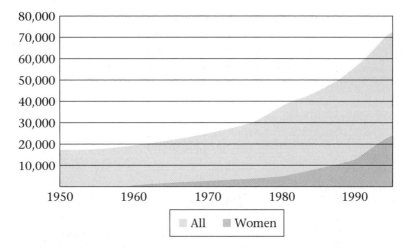

Figure 11.1 **Growth in the numbers of solicitors with practising certificates**
Source: The Law Society, Fact Sheet 2: Women in the profession [www.lawsociety.org.uk]. Reproduced with permission.

the consumer, when making decisions regarding the regulation of the profession. In response to these concerns, in 2005 membership of the Law Society became voluntary and the Law Society decided to separate its representative function from its regulatory function. The profession is now regulated by the Law Society Regulation Board.

Work

For most solicitors, paperwork takes up much of their time. It includes conveyancing (when solicitors deal with the legal aspects of the buying and selling of houses and other property) and drawing up wills and contracts, as well as giving written and oral legal advice. Until 1985, solicitors were the only people allowed to do conveyancing work, but this is no longer the case – people from different occupations can qualify as licensed conveyancers, and the service is often offered by banks and building societies.

Solicitors have traditionally been able to do advocacy work in the magistrates' court and the county court, but not generally in the higher courts. This situation was changed by the Courts and Legal Services Act 1990 and the Access to Justice Act 1999. These Acts put in place the mechanics for equalising rights of audience between barristers and solicitors. Now all barristers and solicitors automatically acquire full rights of audience, though they will be able to exercise these rights only on completion of the necessary training. There are currently 1,000 solicitor advocates. Many firms are sending their solicitors on courses, making advocacy training compulsory and designating individuals as in-house advocates. Thus, solicitors are increasingly doing the advocacy work themselves rather than sending it to a barrister. Where government funding has established fixed fees for work, solicitors are faced with a simple choice: keep the money or give it away. Even those solicitors who do not have full rights of audience can appear in the higher courts for a limited range of proceedings.

Traditionally, an individual solicitor did much less advocacy work than a barrister, but as more solicitors gain the necessary training, this is changing. In any case, solicitors as a group do more advocacy than barristers, simply because 98 per cent of criminal cases are tried in the magistrates' court, where the advocate is usually a solicitor.

Solicitors can, and usually do, form partnerships, with other solicitors. Alternatively, since 2001, they can form a limited liability partnership (LLP). Under an ordinary partnership a solicitor can be personally liable (even after retirement) for a claim in negligence against the solicitor firm, even if he or she was not involved in the transaction giving rise to the claim. Under a limited liability partnership a partner's liability is limited to negligence for which he or she was personally responsible.

> **✓ Know your terms 11.1**
>
> Define the following terms:
> 1 Law Society.
> 2 Conveyancing.
> 3 Rights of audience.
> 4 Solicitor advocate.

Solicitors work in ordinary offices, with, in general, the same support staff as any office-based business, and have offices all over England and Wales and in all towns. Practices range from huge London-based firms dealing only with large corporations, to small partnerships or individual solicitors, dealing with the conveyancing, wills, divorces and minor crime of a country town. The top city law firms are known as the 'magic circle' and a Sweet & Maxwell survey found nearly a quarter of all law students wanted to join one when they qualified, though in practice a much smaller percentage will succeed in doing so. Most law firms are small, with 85 per cent of them having four or fewer partners, and nearly half having only one partner. Some solicitors work in law centres and other advice agencies, government departments, private industry and education rather than in private practice.

Figures published in the journal *Commercial Lawyer* in September 2000 show that an elite group of 100 City solicitors working in central London are earning more than £1 million per year. But this figure has to be seen in the context of a profession that has over 80,000 members. The average annual salary for a solicitor is £51,463.

sourcebook p. 105 → ## Qualifications and training

Almost all solicitors have a university degree, though not necessarily in law. A number of universities introduced an admissions test in 2004, the National Admissions Test for Law, to help select students onto their popular law degrees. Students whose degree is not in law have to take a one-year conversion course leading to the Common Professional Examination (CPE).

The next step, for law graduates and those who have passed the CPE, is a one-year Legal Practice Course, designed to provide practical skills, including advocacy, as well as legal and procedural knowledge. The course costs between £5,000 and £9,000 and the vast majority of students are obliged to fund themselves or rely on loans.

After passing the Legal Practice exams, the prospective solicitor must find a place, usually in a solicitor firm, to serve a two-year apprenticeship under a training contract. There can be intense competition for these places, especially in times of economic difficulty when firms are reluctant to invest in training. Trainee solicitors should receive a minimum salary of £15,332 outside London and £17,110 in

London. In practice, the average salary for a trainee solicitor is £20,925. The work of a trainee solicitor can be very demanding, and a survey carried out for the Law Society found that a third work more than 50 hours a week.

It is possible to become a solicitor without a degree, by completing the one-year Solicitors First Examination Course, and the Legal Practice Course, and having a five-year training contract. Legal executives (see p. 197) sometimes go on to qualify this way.

Solicitors are required to participate in continuing education throughout their careers. They have to undertake 16 hours of education a year, with the subjects covered depending on each individual's areas of interest or need.

Lord Woolf, an influential judge, has observed that the solicitor profession is becoming 'increasingly polarised', depending on the nature of the work carried out, with lawyers working in City firms earning significantly more than those in high street practices. Specialist LPC courses are now being offered for some City law firms. Lord Woolf has criticised this development, as he fears it could undermine the concept of a single solicitor profession with a single professional qualification.

??? Quick quiz 11.2

1 How many solicitors are there?

2 Following the Access to Justice Act 1999, what rights of audience do solicitors have?

3 What percentage of criminal cases are heard in the magistrates' courts?

4 What does 'LPC' stand for?

Barristers

There are around 14,000 barristers in independent practice, known collectively as the Bar. Their governing body is the Bar Council, which acts as a kind of trade union, safeguarding the interests of barristers. The Bar Council, like the Law Society, has tried to separate its representative functions from its regulatory functions, and has therefore established a Bar Standards Board responsible for regulating the Bar. The Board makes the rules and takes the decisions affecting entry to, training for, and practice at the Bar, including disciplinary issues.

Work

Advocacy is the main function of barristers, and much of their time will be spent in court or preparing for it. Until the changes made under the Courts and Legal Services Act in 1990, barristers were, with a few exceptions, the only people allowed to advocate in the superior courts – the House of Lords, the Court of Appeal, the High Court, the Crown Court and the Employment Appeal Tribunal. We have seen that this has now changed, and they are increasingly having to compete with solicitors for this work. Barristers also do some paperwork, drafting legal documents and giving written opinions on legal problems.

Barristers must be self-employed and, under Bar rules, cannot form partnerships, but they usually share offices, called chambers, with other barristers. All the barristers in a particular chambers share a clerk, who is a type of business manager, arranging meetings with the client and the solicitor and also negotiating the barristers' fees. Around 70 per cent of practising barristers are based in London chambers, though they may travel to courts in the provinces; the rest are based in the other big cities.

Not all qualified barristers work as advocates at the Bar. Like solicitors, some are employed by law centres and other advice agencies, government departments or private industry, and some teach. Some go into these jobs after practising at the Bar for a time, others never practise at the Bar.

Traditionally, a client could not approach a barrister directly, but had to see a solicitor first, who would then refer the case to a barrister. In 2004 the ban on direct access to barristers was abolished. Members of the public can now contact a barrister without using a solicitor as an intermediary. Barristers are today able to provide specialist advice, drafting and advocacy without a solicitor acting as a 'middleman', although the management of litigation will still generally be handled by solicitors. Direct access to the client is permitted where the barrister has been in practice for three years, and has undertaken a short course preparing them for this new mode of operation.

Barristers work under what is called the 'cab rank' rule. Technically, this means that if they are not already committed for the time in question, they must accept any case which falls within their claimed area of specialisation and for which a reasonable fee is offered. In practice, barristers' clerks, who take their bookings, may manipulate the rule to ensure that barristers are able to avoid cases they do not want to take. The cab rank rule does not apply where a barrister is approached directly by a potential client, rather than being referred to them by a solicitor. In these circumstances, barristers must follow a principle of non-discrimination, under which they must not refuse work because of the way it is funded or because the client is unpopular.

Qualifications and training

The starting point is normally an upper-second class degree. If this degree is not in law, applicants must do the one-year course leading to the Common Professional Examination (the same course taken by would-be solicitors with degrees in subjects other than law). Mature students may be accepted without a degree, but applications are subject to very stringent consideration, and this is not a likely route to the Bar.

All students then have to join one of the four Inns of Court: Inner Temple; Middle Temple; Gray's Inn; or Lincoln's Inn, all of which are in London. The Inns of Court first emerged in the thirteenth century and their role has evolved over time. Their main functions now cover the provision of professional accommodation for barristers' chambers and residential accommodation for judges, discipline, the provision of law libraries and the promotion of collegiate activities.

Students take the year-long Bar Vocational Course, which can now be taken at eight different institutions around the country. The course includes oral exercises,

Figure 11.2 **One of the dining rooms of the Inns of Court**
Source: Photograph courtesy of The Honourable Society of Gray's Inn.

and tuition in interviewing skills and negotiating skills, and as with solicitors' training, more emphasis has been laid on these practical aspects in recent years.

Around 1,600 people take the Bar Vocational Course each year, and each one has to pay approximately £7,000 for the course alone, and then find living expenses on top. Local authority grants are discretionary and only rarely available. Limited financial assistance is available from the Inns of Court.

Students have to dine at their Inn 12 times. This rather old-fashioned and much-criticised custom stems from the idea that students will benefit from the wisdom and experience of their elders if they sit among them at mealtimes. The dinners are now linked to seminars, lectures and training weekends, in order to provide genuine educational benefit.

After this, the applicant is called to the Bar, and must then find a place in a chambers to serve his or her pupillage. This is a one-year apprenticeship in which pupils assist a qualified barrister, who is known as their pupil master. Competition for pupillage places can be fierce, with only about 600 pupillage vacancies available each year. In the past funding for pupillage has been a problem. But pupils should now normally be paid a minimum of £10,000 a year. Pupils are required to take a further advocacy course before the end of pupillage, as part of the increased emphasis on practical skills.

Pupillage completed, the newly qualified barrister must find a permanent place in a chambers, known as a tenancy. This can be the most difficult part, and some are forced to 'squat' – remaining in their pupillage chambers for as long as they are allowed, without becoming a full member – until they find a permanent place. There are only around 300 tenancies available each year – one to every two pupils.

In 1993, the Royal Commission on Criminal Justice recommended that barristers should have to undertake further training during the course of their careers, after noting that both preparation of cases and advocacy were failing to reach acceptable standards. In response, the Bar Council introduced a continuing education programme. Barristers must now complete a minimum of 45 hours of continuing education in the prescribed subjects by the end of their first three years of practice. The Bar Council has also introduced an established practitioners programme under which all barristers who have been qualified for over three years must undertake each year a minimum of 12 hours study.

Queen's Counsel

After ten years in practice, a barrister may apply to become a Queen's Counsel, or QC (sometimes called a silk, as they wear gowns made of silk). This usually means they will be offered higher-paid cases, and need do less preliminary paperwork. The average annual earnings of a QC are £270,000, with a small group earning over £1 million a year. Not all barristers attempt or manage to become QCs – those that do not are called juniors, even up to retirement age. Juniors may assist QCs in big cases, as well as working alone. Since 1995, solicitors can also be appointed as QCs, but there are currently only eight QCs who come from the solicitor profession.

Task 11.3

In July 2003 the government issued a Consultation Paper, *The Future of Queen's Counsel*. The Foreword to this Consultation Paper has been written by the Minister for Constitutional Affairs, Lord Falconer. It states:

> 'There has long been a debate about the relevance and use of the rank of Queen's Counsel. The time has come to bring that debate to a head, and to reach conclusions, after full consultation on the way ahead. Over the last four centuries, the QC system has become a well-established part of our legal structure. But the legal system must meet the needs of the public. The system must be capable of identifying those with the skills and expertise to deal with any particular dispute. In particular, it should be able to recognise the wide variety of skills needed to provide the public with the legal service it needs. This paper therefore explores whether the current QC system is objectively in the public interest and whether it commands public confidence.'

Questions

The Consultation Paper asked for views from the public on a range of questions. Consider how you would respond to these questions asked by the government:

1 Do you consider that the rank of QC in its current form benefits the public? What are the reasons for your view?
2 Do you think that the current QC system should be abolished or changed? What are the reasons for your view?
3 If you consider that the QC rank should be abolished, do you consider that it should be replaced by another form of quality mark (whether it be granted by the state, the professions, an independent body or the Judicial Appointments Commission)?

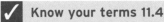 **Know your terms 11.4**

Define the following terms:

1 Limited liability partnership.
2 Bar Council.
3 Pupillage.
4 Queen's Counsel.

Background of barristers and solicitors

Lawyers have in the past come from a very narrow social background, in terms of sex, race and class; there have also been significant barriers to entrants with disabilities. In recent years the professions have succeeded in opening their doors to a wider range of people, so that they are more representative of the society in which they work.

White, middle-class men dominate in most professions, excluding many people who would be highly suited to such careers. A narrow social profile created particular problems for the legal professions in the past. First, it meant that the legal professions have been seen as unapproachable and elitist, which put off some people from using lawyers and thereby benefiting from their legal rights (this issue is examined in Chapter 12). Secondly, the English judiciary is drawn from the legal professions and, if their background is narrow, that of the judiciary will be too (this issue is examined in Chapter 13). Increasingly, the professions are becoming representative of the society in which they function.

Women

The number of women in the professions has increased dramatically since the 1950s. In 1987 women accounted for less than 20 per cent of all solicitors; now 41 per cent of solicitors are women. Today there are more women qualifying for the solicitor profession than men.

For the barrister profession in 2002 equal numbers of men and women qualified to practise and 32 per cent of barristers are women.

The problem now for women is less about entry into the professions and more about pay, promotion and working conditions. Female solicitors earn less than male solicitors. Despite the fact that there are more women achieving first and upper second class law degrees than men, in 1998 the Law Society's Annual Statistical Survey found that new female entrants were earning on average 4.4 per cent less than new male entrants. Women who become partners in law firms earn on average £6,000 less than men in the same position.

Fewer women are being promoted to become partners in their law firm. Over 50 per cent of male solicitors are partners in their firm, compared to only 23 per cent of female solicitors. This cannot simply be explained by the fact that the average age of women solicitors is younger: 88 per cent of male solicitors in private practice with 10–19 years of experience were partners, compared with 63 per cent of female solicitors with the same experience. There is a similar problem in the barrister profession. In 2003, 112 men were made Queen's Counsel, but only nine women.

A growing problem exists of women choosing to leave the profession early. This is either because they find it impossible to combine the demands of motherhood with a legal career or because they are frustrated at the 'glass ceiling' which seems to prevent women lawyers from achieving the same success as their male counterparts. Solicitor firms tend not to have provisions in place for flexible or part-time working for solicitors. Those that do, tend to discourage solicitors from taking advantage of them (*Research Study No. 26 of the Law Society Research and Policy Planning Unit* (1997)). The Law Society has recognised that, in order to retain women and to ensure that the investment in their training is not lost, the profession must consider more flexible work arrangements (including career breaks) to allow women (and men) to continue to work as well as carrying out caring responsibilities.

The legal profession also needs to tackle the long-hours culture to stem the flow of women lawyers leaving the profession. The macho culture of working long hours forces women, who often have to juggle work and family, out of the legal world.

Ethnic minorities

Again, the picture is improving. The number of solicitors from ethnic minority groups has increased recently. In 2003, 8 per cent of practising solicitors came from an ethnic minority. This compares with 4 per cent in 1995. In 2003, 17 per cent of trainee solicitors were from a minority ethnic group. There are still, however, very few male Afro-Caribbean solicitors.

As regards the Bar, in 1989, 5 per cent of practising barristers came from an ethnic minority, in 2003 they made up 11 per cent of practising barristers and 20 per cent of pupils. This compares favourably with other professions.

Regrettably, there have been some reports in the media of black candidates doing less well in legal examinations than white candidates, particularly at the Bar. It has been suggested that oral examinations may be particularly vulnerable to subjective marking.

The Law Society has recognised that obstacles still exist for ethnic minorities in the solicitor profession. This is because most solicitor firms do not follow proper recruitment procedures, do not have an equal opportunities policy and practice, and the levels of discrimination within society at large are reflected in the perception of solicitors and their clients.

Class

The biggest obstacle to a career in law now seems to be class background. Law degree students are predominantly middle class, with fewer than one in five coming from a working-class background. A 1989 Law Society Survey found that over a third of solicitors had come from private schools, despite the fact that only 7 per cent of the population attend such schools. In recent years, more lawyers have been educated in the state sector, but this progress could soon be reversed. This is

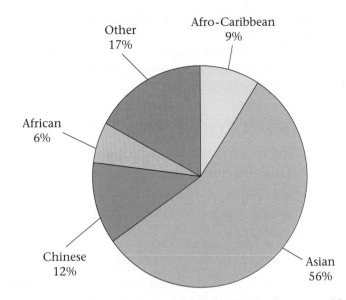

Figure 11.3 **The ethnic origin of solicitors from minority ethnic groups, 2002**

Source: The Law Society, Fact Sheet 3: Solicitors from minority ethnic groups [www.lawsociety.org.uk].
Reproduced with permission.

because the lack of funding for legal training has made it very difficult for
students without well-off parents to qualify, especially as barristers.

The chair of the Bar Council has warned that government plans to allow
universities to charge top-up fees will stop students from poorer backgrounds
pursuing a career in law.

One possible source of change for the future is the number of part-time law
degrees and Legal Practice Courses now available to mature students, who tend to
come from a much broader range of backgrounds than those who attend university straight from school. Students on part-time courses can support themselves
by continuing to work while they study in the evenings and at weekends.

Disability

Much attention has been paid to the under-representation of working-class
people, ethnic minorities and women in the legal profession, but disabled people
are less often discussed. Skill as a lawyer requires brains, not physical strength
or dexterity, yet it seems there are still significant barriers to entry for disabled
students, particularly to the Bar. Part of the problem is simply practical: a quarter
of court buildings are over 100 years old and were never designed to offer disabled
access. Most now have rooms adapted for disabled people, but need notice if they
are to be used, which is hardly feasible for junior barristers, who often get cases at
very short notice. The other main barrier is effectively the same as that for ethnic
minorities, working-class people and women: with fierce competition for places,
'traditional' applicants have the advantage.

Steps are being taken to address the problems of disabled applicants to the Bar.
In 1992, the Bar's Disability Panel was established. This offers help to disabled

people who are already within the profession or are hoping to enter it, by matching them to people who have overcome or managed to accommodate similar problems. The Inner Temple also gives grants for reading devices, special furniture and other aids, with the aim of creating a 'level playing field' for disabled and able-bodied people.

Increasing diversity through educational reforms

The Solicitors Regulation Authority is considering introducing a radical reform to the way people qualify as solicitors. The Law Society has observed:

> 'The existing training pathway – a degree in law, one year on a Legal Practice Course and a two-year training contract – has worked well, and will continue to be the route to qualification for many. But it is a system that favours the young school leaver with a traditional academic education who is prepared to take on a five figure debt. It makes law a difficult career choice for the rest. That is discriminatory – and not good for the profession.'

sourcebook p. 105 → In 2005 the Law Society published a consultation paper, *Qualifying as a Solicitor: a framework for the future.* The consultation paper suggested that it should no longer be necessary for a future solicitor to complete a Legal Practice Course or, in fact, to have any academic legal qualifications (such as a law degree). Instead, candidates would simply need to demonstrate they had acquired the necessary skills and knowledge by passing assessments set by the Law Society.

These proposals were the subject of considerable criticism, in particular that without the course structure for the Legal Practice Course, consistent standards would not be maintained. As a result, a further consultation paper has been issued, *A new framework for work based learning* (2006). This paper recommends that the current academic and vocational training qualifications should remain essentially the same. Changes would be made, instead, to the work experience aspect of the qualification process. At the moment when a person completes the Legal Practice Course they can only become fully qualified solicitors if they are able to find a training contract. Thousands of people each year fail to find such a position. The Solicitors Regulation Authority is considering establishing an alternative route to qualifying. Instead of having a training contract, individuals would be able to work in any legal environment and have that work supervised and accredited directly by the Authority. People taking this route could gain their work experience at any stage, including while they were actually studying on the Legal Practice Course. There would no longer be a requirement that the trainee solicitor gain their experience over two years; instead, the emphasis would be on the student demonstrating, through a portfolio of their work, that they had attained the relevant skills. In practice, this arrangement would allow paralegals to qualify as solicitors without having a training contract. Qualifying in this way is likely to take longer than the two-year training contract, and there is a risk that it might create a two-tier profession, with solicitors qualifying by the new route being viewed as inferior to those qualifying by the traditional route. This reform could help those people who pass their Legal Practice Course but are then unable to secure a training contract.

Changes would also be made to the training contract route to qualification, though it would still be necessary for these trainees to do the Legal Practice

Course first. Law firms would have to apply to become accredited training organisations. The accredited firm would assess the work of trainee solicitors four times at regular six monthly intervals.

The Solicitors Regulation Authority is proposing to carry out a small pilot scheme of its proposal in 2008 and review these proposals in 2010 in the light of the success (or otherwise) of the pilot. Sadly, the new proposals fail to tackle the problem of the cost of getting the academic and vocational qualifications which will continue to act as a barrier to students from lower income families.

It is undoubtedly important that the legal profession should be a career option for all able students from a wide range of backgrounds, and that people should not be prevented from entering the profession because their family is not rich. But there are other ways that this can be achieved. The Charter 88 constitutional reform pressure group has argued that students should be funded throughout their legal training. The Law Society and the Bar Council have made representations to the Department of Education, pointing out that training for other professions, such as medicine and teaching, is paid or involves reduced fees. In her book, *Eve was Framed*, Helena Kennedy QC argues that selection for the Bar, in particular, has always been based too much on 'connections' and financial resources than on ability. She recommends public funding for legal education and that there should be incentives for barristers' chambers to take on less conventional candidates.

Michael Zander (1988) argued that both the academic and the vocation stages of training could be improved, with a consequent rise in professional standards. Law degrees should include at least preliminary training in areas such as drafting documents and developing interviewing skills. Both pupillage and training contracts can be 'infinitely variable' in quality, according to Zander, 'ranging from excellent to deplorable' depending on where they are undertaken. He suggested that a more integrated training was needed, like that undertaken by medical students, with better links between academic and vocational stages.

The former Advisory Committee on Legal Education and Conduct (ACLEC) examined the whole issue of legal training. Its 1996 report suggested that the two branches should no longer have completely separate training programmes at the post-graduate stage. Instead, after either a law degree or a degree in another subject plus the CPE, all students would take a Professional Legal Studies course, lasting around 18 weeks. Only then would they decide which branch of the profession to choose, going on to a Legal Practice Course (for solicitors) or Bar Vocational Course (for barristers) which would be only 15–18 weeks long. This, ACLEC suggested, would prevent the problem of students having to specialise too early. It also recommended that funding should be made available for the CPE course and the vocational stage of training.

Performance of the legal professions

Over the past 30 years, the performance of lawyers has come in for a great deal of criticism. Barristers and solicitors involved in criminal work were criticised by the 1993 Royal Commission on Criminal Justice, which found that defence cases were frequently inadequately prepared, often because the work was delegated to unqualified staff and not properly supervised. Advocacy standards were also low, on the part of both barristers and solicitors, and the Commission suggested that inadequate training might be the reason for this. They particularly criticised the practice of allowing pupil barristers to take on cases during their second six months, and the lack of detailed assessment of pupils' experience during this time. They recognised that both branches of the profession were already increasing advocacy training, but suggested that more work might be needed.

In 1995, the Consumers' Association magazine *Which?* caused a stir with a survey of the standards of advice provided by solicitors. Its researchers phoned a number of solicitors, posing as members of the public seeking advice about simple consumer problems, and the advice given was assessed by the Association's own legal team. The verdict was not good, with much of the advice given being assessed as inadequate or simply wrong. Two years later, the magazine repeated the test and, once again, the results were bad: of the 79 solicitors approached by researchers, the majority gave advice which was incomplete, or in some cases incorrect. *Which?* accepted that lawyers cannot be expected to be experts in every area of law, but argued that if asked something outside their area of expertise, they should admit that and either find out the answer or refer the client to someone else.

The number of complaints made about lawyers continues to rise, according to the 2003 annual report from the Legal Services Ombudsman. Figures from the OSS seem to suggest that the problem is not spread throughout its branch of the profession. It claims 80 per cent of complaints made to the OSS concern the same 950 firms, out of the 8,500 in practice.

A survey undertaken for the Law Society in 2001 found that the public perceive lawyers as formal, expensive and predatory. It may be that they are now being accused of being predatory because of the intensive television advertising by companies who pass work on to solicitors.

One of the most common areas for complaint is costs. The Law Society's Written Practice Standard requires solicitors to give clients written information about all aspects of financing their case, including how the fee is calculated, arrangements for payment, and liability for the other side's costs. However, a 1995 report by the National Association of Citizens' Advice Bureaux (NACAB), *Barriers to Justice*, concluded that few clients actually received clear information about costs, and that this was part of the reason why fees were so often the cause of complaints. NACAB recommended that solicitors should have to agree with clients a timetable for regular updates on costs, confirm the arrangement in writing and provide leaflets giving information about costs.

Research carried out in 2005 for the consumer group *Which?*, showed that three out of ten people did not feel they got value for money from solicitors and one-third did not feel they received a good service.

Barristers' prices have also been the subject of considerable criticism and, in particular, the fees charged by what the press have called 'super silks' – QCs whose annual earnings can top £1 million. As a result of this criticism, the House of Lords looked into the issue, and reported in October 1998 that the fees being charged in some cases were excessive. The report accused barristers' clerks of 'deliberately pitching fees at a very high level' (a conclusion which was not all that surprising,

Figure 11.4 **Advertisement by the Law Society**

Source: The Law Society of England and Wales. Reproduced with permission.

since securing the best possible fee for his or her barrister is part of a clerk's job). The report was welcomed by the Legal Action Group, which said that the excessively high fees charged by some QCs were undermining public confidence in the legal system.

The legal profession suffers from a negative public image. A survey of over 1,000 consumers and 100 lawyers carried out in 2005 found that while most lawyers consider themselves forward-thinking and up to date, the public think quite the opposite. The consumers said the main attributes they associated with lawyers were that they were good with people but also ruthless and ambitious. The Law Society launched a pilot campaign in 2005 to try to change the public's view of the profession. The adverts portrayed solicitors as heroes to encourage the public to consult solicitors about their legal problems. Interestingly, research on the public's attitude to the campaign found that on average 78 per cent of respondents found the positioning of solicitors as heroes credible.

The future of the profession

A number of government reports have been published in recent years pushing for changes in the professions. In 2001 the Office of Fair Trading (OFT) issued a report entitled *Competition in the Professions* (2001). This looked primarily at the restrictive practices of barristers and solicitors. These professions were criticised for imposing unjustified restrictions on competition and urged to take prompt action to put an end to these practices.

Professor Zander (2001b) criticised the report, stating:

> *'What is deplorable about these developments is the simplistic belief that equating the work done by professional people to business will necessarily improve the position of the consumer, when the reality is that sometimes it may rather worsen it. Certainly one wants competition to ensure that professional fees are no higher than they need to be and that the professional rules did not unnecessarily inhibit efficiency. But what one looks for from the professional even more is standards, integrity and concern for the client of a higher order than that offered in the business world. To damage those even more important values in the name of value for the consumer in purely economic terms may be to throw out the baby with the bath water.'*

The government accepted that the legal professions should be subject to competition law. It subsequently issued a consultation paper, *In the Public Interests?*, which questioned the competitiveness of legal services given primarily by solicitors working in solicitor firms.

The Bar Council has made some changes in the light of the OFT report, but has rejected many of its key recommendations. Direct access to the Bar has been increased (see p. 182). Employed barristers can now under take litigation work for their employer. To exercise this right they will have to undertake 12 weeks' training with a practising litigator. The Office of Fair Trading considers this latter reform inadequate, and has confirmed it will continue to investigate the ban on independent barristers litigating without the intermediary of a solicitor. The stumbling block is over whether barristers should be allowed to handle clients' money – something the Bar Council is resolutely against.

In July 2003, the government established an independent review into the regulation of legal services. The review was chaired by Sir David Clementi and considered which regulatory framework 'would best promote competition, innovation and the public and consumer interest in an efficient, effective and independent legal sector'. Sir David published his final report in 2004, *Review of the regulatory framework for legal services in England and Wales.* The government subsequently published a White Paper in 2005 entitled *The Future of Legal Services – Putting Consumers First,* in which it accepted most of Clementi's recommendations. The Legal Services Act 2007 contains the key reforms, which will be considered in turn below.

Regulation of the legal professions

Sir David Clementi looked at how improvements in the provision of legal services could be made through changes to the regulation of the professions. At the moment, the professions regulate themselves through their professional bodies, the Law Society and the Bar Council. Clementi considered that the present regulatory arrangements did not prioritise the public's interest. He therefore considered whether the professions should be stripped of their right to regulate themselves and whether instead an independent regulator should be established. The professional bodies would have merely represented their professions and not regulated them. Clementi commented:

> '*Among the suggested advantages of this approach are the clear independence of the regulator, clarity of purposes for both regulator and representative bodies and consistency of rules and standards across the profession and services. An independent regulator would be well placed to make tough, fair enforcement decisions and to facilitate lay/consumer input into the decision making processes.*
>
> *Disadvantages might include creating an overly bureaucratic and inefficient organisation, with consequent issues of costs and unwieldy procedure. A further argument is that it fails to recognise the significance of strong roots within the profession and their importance on the international stage. Divorcing the regulatory functions from the profession might lessen the feeling of responsibility professionals have for the high standard of their profession and their willingness to give time freely to support the system.*'

Ultimately, Clementi concluded that an Independent Legal Services Board should be established, but this would just oversee the way the existing professional bodies regulated the professions. The Legal Service Board would have a duty to promote the public and consumer interests, and would be led by a part-time chair and a full-time chief executive, who would both be non-lawyers and the majority of the Board's members would be non-lawyers. All the members of the Board would be selected on merit by the relevant government minister. The professional bodies would be required to separate their regulatory and representative functions. They would still take care of the day-to-day regulation of the professions and disciplinary matters, though they could cease to be legally recognised if they failed to carry out their duties satisfactorily.

Sir David Clementi hopes that this reform would achieve consistency and transparency, while keeping costs down and leaving regulation close to those who provide the services. The proposal has been generally well received, though the Bar is unhappy that it is to lose the power to regulate itself. Front-line regulators, such as the Law Society and the Bar Council, are anxious that they should have primary responsibility for the day-to-day regulation of the professions, with the new Board taking only a light touch, supervisory approach to regulation (as recommended by Clementi), intervening merely when it is in the public interest. This light-touch approach would avoid costly duplication of effort, stifling innovation and burdening the front-line regulators. However, the Legal Services Act 2007 gives the Legal Services Board the power to set targets for front-line regulators and would have the power to remove a body's authorisation to regulate if the targets were not met. Front-line regulators would have to apply to the Legal Services Board for permission to carry out regulatory functions, such as the regulation of alternative business structures.

The Law Society and Bar Council were also concerned that the Legal Services Board should be clearly independent of government politics, but the Act gives considerable power to the Minister of Justice, including making appointments to the Board. The Law Society has argued that members of the Legal Services Board should be appointed by an independent appointment panel. The Legal Aid Practitioners Group commented that Clementi's proposals 'may give the government too much control over the lawyers whose challenges to them are essential in a free and democratic society'. For example, lawyers represent members of the public in criminal cases, when children are being taken into care and when local authorities seek to evict anti-social tenants.

With the passing of the Legal Services Act 2007, the government has started the recruitment process for people to sit on the Legal Services Board, as the first stage in the process of setting up the Board itself.

Business structures

Currently, most legal services can be delivered to the public only by solicitors working in a law firm or by barristers in independent practice at the Bar. The government's 2005 White Paper suggests that legal services could be provided to the public through a wide range of alternative business structures and provisions for this are contained in the Legal Services Act 2007. These provisions are likely to take effect in 2011. The aim is to increase competition to the benefit of consumers and to increase investment in legal service providers, so that they can invest in such areas as the use of IT for the delivery of legal services and expand to provide a better quality of service to the consumer. When alternative business structures are introduced, solicitors could be employed by such organisations as supermarkets, banks, insurance firms and accountants to provide legal services directly to the public. The plan has become known as the 'Tesco Law' because big organisations will be able to buy law firms. The government considers that bigger organisations will provide advice more efficiently. The Law Society sees the reform as an important means of attracting external investment into law firms and thereby facilitating business expansion. However, the Bar Council is unhappy with this reform. It has pointed out that outside commercial involvement does not always mean better and cheaper services.

The Co-op, the AA and Halifax have publicly announced that, when the legislation has been brought into force they intend to offer legal advice and assistance directly to the public. The Co-op plans to establish 'Co-operative Legal Services', offering a range of legal services, including conveyancing and will writing. It will be based in Bristol and employ approximately 150 people, including a team of 30 lawyers. It already offers a free legal services helpline to its customers, which has been praised by consumer groups but criticised by the Law Society for not offering face-to-face advice to its clients.

Fusion of the professions

The divided legal profession dates from the nineteenth century, when the Bar agreed to give all conveyancing work and all direct access to clients to the solicitors, in return for sole rights of audience in the higher courts and the sole right to become senior judges for barristers. However, since the late 1960s, there have been a series of moves towards breaking down this division. Following the Access to Justice Act 1999, solicitors automatically have rights of audience, though they still have to undertake training in order to exercise these rights. It is likely that an increasing number of solicitors will undertake this training to become solicitor-advocates.

There has been much discussion over recent years as to whether the professions will eventually fuse. When the Courts and Legal Services Act 1990 was passed, it was thought that it might be the first step in government plans to fuse the two professions by legislation. Until 1985, the two branches had been largely left alone to divide work between themselves, and had made their own arrangements for this; the abolition of the solicitors' monopoly on conveyancing was the first major government interference in this situation, and the Courts and Legal Services Act was obviously a much bigger step towards regulation by government rather than the professions themselves. Even if the government did not force fusion, it has been suggested, it could happen anyway if large numbers of solicitors take up rights of audience.

Alternatively, it has been suggested that the Bar might survive, but in a much reduced form, and there is much debate about which areas would suffer most. Barristers generally fall into two groups: those who specialise in commercial fields, such as company law, tax and patents; and those who have what is called a common law practice, which means that they deal with a fairly wide range of common legal issues, such as crime, housing and family law. Some legal experts believed that commercial lawyers would be most likely to survive, since they have a specialist knowledge that solicitors cannot provide. However, for several years now, solicitors in city firms have been becoming more specialist themselves, and if able to combine specialist knowledge with rights of audience, they would clearly be a threat to the commercial Bar. In addition, such firms offer high incomes, without the insecurity of self-employment at the Bar, and therefore they are able to attract first-rate students who once would have automatically been attracted to the more prestigious Bar. As these entrants work their way up through law firms, the Bar's traditional claim to offer the best expertise in high-level legal analysis will be difficult to sustain.

Task 11.5

One day a week the quality papers have a section dedicated to looking at legal issues. *The Times* law section comes out every Tuesday. Job advertisements for work in the legal field are placed in this section. Select two job advertisements and consider:

- Is the advertiser looking to recruit a barrister, solicitor or legal executive?
- In what area of law would the person recruited work?
- How much would they be paid?

Task 11.6

Professor Zander (2001b) has criticised the report of the Office of Fair Trading on anti-competitive practices in the legal professions. He has written:

> 'What is deplorable about these developments is the simplistic belief that equating the work done by professional people to business will necessarily improve the position of the consumer, when the reality is that sometimes it may rather worsen it. Certainly, one wants competition to ensure that professional fees are no higher than they need to be and that the professional rules do not unnecessarily inhibit efficiency. But what one looks for from the professions even more is standards, integrity and concern for the client of a higher order than that offered in the business world. To damage those even more important values in the name of value for the consumer in purely economic terms may be to throw out the baby with the bath water.'

Questions

1 In this context, who is the consumer?
2 What are the benefits identified of allowing competition among legal professionals?
3 What values does Zander argue need protecting by the legal professionals more than by the business world?
4 What is meant by the saying 'to throw out the baby with the bath water'?

Arguments for fusion of the professions

Expense

With the divided profession a client often has to pay both a solicitor and a barrister, sometimes a solicitor and two barristers, and as Michael Zander (1999) puts it: 'To have one taxi meter running is less expensive than to have two or three.' However, the Bar Council prepared a report entitled *The Economic Case for the Bar. A Comparison of the Costs of Barristers and Solicitors* (2000). This paper claimed that it was generally more economical to employ the services of a barrister, particularly a junior, for work within his or her area of expertise than to use a solicitor. In broad terms, it stated that the differences in charge-out rates make it from 25 per cent to 50 per cent cheaper to employ the services of a junior barrister than an assistant solicitor in London. A major factor is that barristers' overheads are approximately half those of solicitors. However, the paper is misleading, as without direct access to clients for barristers it is not an either/or situation. The reality is that a client does not pay for either a solicitor or a barrister, but if the client employs a barrister, the client must pay for both, along with the cost of the solicitor preparing the papers for the barrister.

Inefficiency

A two-tier system means work may be duplicated unnecessarily, and the solicitor prepares the case with little or no input from the barrister who will have to argue it in court. Barristers are often selected and instructed at the last moment. Research by Bottoms and McLean in Sheffield revealed that in 96 per cent of cases where the plea was guilty, and 79 per cent where it was not guilty, clients saw their barrister for the first time on the morning of the trial. In this situation important points may be passed over or misunderstood.

Arguments against fusion

Independence

The Bar has traditionally argued that its cab-rank principle guarantees this, ensuring that no defendant, however heinous the charges against them, goes undefended; and that no individual should lack representation because of the wealth or power of the opponent. The fact that barristers operate independently, rather than in partnerships, also contributes. However, the Courts and Legal Services Act 1990 does provide for solicitors with advocacy certificates to operate on a cab-rank basis, which has somewhat weakened the Bar's argument. In addition, successful barristers do get round the cab-rank rule in practice.

Importance of good advocacy

Our adversarial system means that the presentation of oral evidence is important; judges have no investigative powers and must rely on the lawyers to present the case properly.

The 1979 Royal Commission suggested that fusion would lead to a fall in the quality of the advocacy, arguing that, although many solicitors were competent to advocate in the magistrates' and county courts, arguing before a jury required different skills and greater expertise, and if rights were extended it was unlikely that many solicitors would get sufficient practice to develop these.

Table 11.1 **Comparison of barristers and solicitors**

	Barrister	*Solicitor*
Number	14,000	98,000
Professional organisation	Bar Council	Law Society
Professional course	Bar Vocational Course (BVC)	Legal Practice Course (LPC)
Apprenticeship	Pupillage	Training contract

Legal executives

Most firms of solicitors employ legal executives, who do much of the same basic work as solicitors. Their professional body is the Institute of Legal Executives. Although technically they are under the supervision of their employers, in practice many experienced executives specialise in particular areas – such as conveyancing – and take almost sole charge of that area. From the firm's point of view, they are a cheaper option than solicitors for getting this work done, and in many cases will be more experienced in their particular area than a solicitor. However, clients are usually unaware that, when they pay for a solicitor, they may be receiving the services of a legal executive.

Following the Courts and Legal Services Act 1990 and the Access to Justice Act 1999, the Institute of Legal Executives is now able to grant its members the rights to conduct litigation on the completion of suitable training. The first six legal executives qualified as advocates in the year 2000 and now have extended rights of audience in civil and matrimonial proceedings in the county court and magistrates' courts.

Legal executives are generally less well paid than solicitors. A survey carried out by the Institute of Legal Executives in 2001 found that a third of legal executives earned between £15,000 and £21,000, while 11 per cent earned over £27,000. If Legal Disciplinary Practices are introduced, legal executives may be able to own one of these.

Qualifications and training

To qualify as a legal executive, a person works full-time and studies part-time. Studying will be undertaken either at a local college or through distance learning with ILEX Tutorial College. It takes on average six years to qualify fully as a legal executive, though students with a law degree benefit from exemptions from some of the examinations. Only about 600 people qualify each year as legal executives, with many people failing to complete their education. Once qualified as a legal executive, a person can undertake further part-time study to become a solicitor, unless they have unsuccessfully attempted the Legal Practice Course before becoming a legal executive.

Reading on the web

Sir David Clementi's report, *Review of the Regulatory Framework for Legal Services in England and Wales*, is available at:

www.legal-services-review.org.uk

The consultation paper issued by the government in 2003 on the future of QCs is available on the former Department for Constitutional Affairs' website:

www.dca.gov.uk/consult/qcfuture/index.htm

The report of the Office of Fair Trading, *Competition in the Professions* (2001), is available on its website:

www.oft.gov.uk/shared-oft/reports/professional_bodies/oft32.pdf

The Bar Council's website can be found at:

www.barcouncil.org.uk

The Law Society's website can be found at:

www.lawsociety.org.uk/home.law

The website of the Solicitors Regulation Authority is at:

www.sra.org.uk/about/strategy.page

Chapter summary

The three main professions in the legal field are:

- solicitors
- barristers; and
- legal executives.

Solicitors

- *Work*: traditionally solicitors focused primarily on paperwork but they are now doing more advocacy.
- *Qualifications and training*: usually a university degree, followed by a conversion course if this was not in law. Then they take the one-year Legal Practice Course and a two-year training contract.

Barristers

- *Work*: traditionally advocacy, but they also do some paperwork.
- *Qualifications and training*: usually a university degree, followed by a conversion course if this is not in law. Then the one-year Bar Vocational Course and one-year pupillage.

Background of barristers and solicitors

Barristers and solicitors have traditionally come from a very narrow social background, in terms of class, race and sex, and disabled people are under-represented. They now come from a wider range of backgrounds, but there is a problem with promotion and retention of women and people from minority groups.

Increasing diversity through educational reforms

The Law Society is considering introducing a radical reform to the way people qualify as solicitors.

The future of the profession

A number of government reports have been published in recent years pushing for changes in the professions. In July 2003, the government established an independent review into the regulation of legal services, chaired by Sir David Clementi. Following the enactment of the Legal Services Act 2007, a range of reforms is likely to be introduced in the near future with a view to modernising the professions.

Moves towards fusion?

Since the late 1960s, there has been a series of moves towards breaking down the division between barristers and solicitors.

Question and answer guides

1

(a) Explain how **either** a solicitor **or** a legal executive is trained and qualifies.

(10 marks)

(b) 'The work of a solicitor is quite different from that of a barrister.' Outline the work of the two professions and consider whether this statement is accurate.

(20 marks)

(from AQA Exam Papers, June 2005 and January 2002)

(a) The usual route for qualifying as a legal executive involves working full-time while studying part-time. The work element must be for a minimum of five years and must be in 'qualifying employment'. Normally, this means employment in either a firm of solicitors or a legal department. The work done must be largely legal in nature.

The study element will be undertaken either at a local college (attending on a day release or evening class basis) or through distance learning. It will involve passing two sets of exams. The first is the ILEX Professional Diploma in Law, which is of A-level standard and normally takes two years. The second is the ILEX Professional Higher Diploma in Law, which is of degree standard, and again normally takes two years.

On passing the Higher Diploma, the candidate becomes a full member of the Institute of Legal Executives (having become a student member while doing his or her exams).

The candidate must then complete the rest of his/her period of qualifying employment. The rules state that a minimum of two of those five years must be undertaken after passing the Higher Diploma. On completion of the period of qualifying employment the applicant becomes a Fellow of the Institute of Legal Executives, this being the official title of legal executives.

(b) For most solicitors, much of their time is spent in an office doing paperwork, on non-contentious matters, in other words, matters unrelated to any court case. Examples of such matters are conveyancing (the legal aspects of buying and selling land), drawing up wills and contracts, and giving legal advice. Some of their time is also spent on contentious matters, such as undertaking litigation.

All solicitors have rights of audience (meaning the right to advocate) in the magistrates' and county courts. Also, since the 1990s, they can exercise rights of audience in the higher courts after completing some additional training. As more solicitors do this they are increasingly doing advocacy work themselves rather than sending it to barristers. In the lower courts much of the advocacy work is undertaken by solicitors.

Many solicitors work in the legal departments of companies and other organisations, in which case the kind of work they do will be determined by their employers' business.

Advocacy is the main function of barristers, and much of their time will be spent in court or preparing for court. They have full rights of audience, and so may undertake trial work or appeals. They also do some paperwork, drafting legal documents and giving expert opinions on legal problems.

Traditionally, one of the key differences between barristers and solicitors was that solicitors tended to have far more contact with the general public than barristers. Indeed, until recently barristers were unable to accept instructions directly from the public; the latter normally had to go through a solicitor, who would in turn instruct a barrister. This rule was relaxed in 2004 and members of the public can now, in many circumstances, instruct a barrister directly, provided the barrister has attended a short course and registered as willing to undertake direct access work.

Like solicitors, many barristers work in the legal departments of companies and other organisations. Some even work for firms of solicitors.

As for whether the work of a solicitor is 'quite different' from that of a barrister, the work of solicitors generally is still different from that of barristers generally, in that barristers tend to do more advocacy in the higher courts and tend to have less direct contact with the public. There are also some areas of law where barristers rarely practise; for example, conveyancing. However, for the reasons explained, these differences are changing and it is likely that in future the work of solicitors will become less and less different from that of barristers. The solicitor profession itself is becoming more divided between those who work in large city law firms and those who work in smaller high street offices.

2

(a) Describe the stages in qualifying as a solicitor.   *(10 marks)*
(b) Briefly describe and compare the roles played by solicitors, barristers **and** legal executives when acting for a defendant in a court case.   *(20 marks)*
                    (from AQA Exam Papers, January 2004 and January 2006)

(a)

- Explain how, for most people, the first stage in qualifying as a solicitor is to get a degree.
- Mention how non-law graduates also take the Common Professional Examination.
- Describe the nature and purpose of the Legal Practice Course.
- Describe the nature and purpose of the training contract.
- For a good answer, describe how it is possible to become a solicitor without a degree.

(b)
Solicitors

- Describe how a solicitor will usually be the client's first point-of-contact.
- Describe the solicitor's role in gathering evidence.
- Discuss how solicitors often do some advocacy at the early stages.
- Refer to the solicitor's role in instructing and liaising with the barrister.
- For a good answer, refer to the possibility of the solicitor exercising higher court rights of audience.

Barristers

- Describe how a barrister's involvement will probably be at the suggestion of the solicitor.
- Explain how barristers may be called upon for their expert opinion and/or for his advocacy skills.
- Explain how a barrister will probably advise on, and advocate, any appeals.

Legal executives

- Explain how legal executives work for/assist solicitors.
- For a good answer, refer to the possibility of legal executives having extended rights of audience.

Common errors in (a)

- omitting either the LPC or the training contract;
- confusing solicitors' and barristers' qualification process.

Common errors in (b)

- failing to make the comparisons that the question requires;
- omitting legal executives.

Group activity 1

- Divide your friends (or class) into groups of two or three people.
- Each group should choose a firm of solicitors to research. If you do not already know of one, you can find lists in telephone directories or on the internet (e.g. on the Law Society's website: www.lawsociety.org.uk).
- Using the Law Society's website, the firm's website, the firm's publicity material, media reports, etc., prepare a short profile of the firm, including information on its people, the type of work it does, and the number and location of its offices.
- Meet with the other groups to share and discuss profiles.

Group activity 2

There is a lot of controversy over court dress for barristers and judges. It has been suggested that their garments are too formal and intimidating for other participants in the case and should be changed:

- What is the standard court dress for junior barristers, Queen's Counsel and for judges?
- Does a judge's dress alter according to their seniority?
- What do you think judges and barristers should wear in court?

Work in groups and allocate tasks to answer these questions. You could visit the following websites to help you research this subject:

> **http://lcjb.cjsonline.gov.uk/area21/library/Court_Dress.pdf**
> **www.dca.gov.uk/consult/courtdress/annexd.htm**
> **www.judiciary.gov.uk/about_judiciary/court_dress/examples/index.htm**

Chapter 12

Paying for legal services

This chapter discusses:

- private funding of legal services;
- the Community Legal Service providing state funding for civil cases;
- the Criminal Defence Service providing state funding for criminal cases;
- conditional fee agreements as an alternative method of funding legal proceedings;
- alternative sources of legal advice;
- criticisms and reform of the current funding arrangements.

Introduction

When people have a legal problem or requirement then they may decide to see a lawyer. They may be able to pay for that lawyer out of their own savings or because they have insurance which covers their legal expenses in the case. If they are paying from their private funds then they will be able to choose the lawyer that they can afford and that they consider will be best able to do the job for them. For example, they might want a lawyer to do the conveyancing work on the sale of a house and a neighbour might recommend a good lawyer to them. But lawyers can be expensive and sometimes the state is prepared to foot the bill rather than expecting private individuals to pay because it is important that everyone should be able to enforce their legal rights.

Unfortunately, cost is not the only thing which stops many ordinary people from using the legal system. Other issues, such as awareness of legal rights, the elitist image of the legal profession and even its geographical situation, all contribute to the problem which legal writers call 'unmet legal need' – where people have a legal problem, but fail to see a lawyer to resolve that problem.

State-funded legal services

The system of state-funded legal help in this country goes back over half a century. After the Second World War, the Labour government introduced a range of measures designed to address the huge inequalities between rich and poor. These included the National Health Service, the beginnings of today's social security system and, in 1949, the first state-funded legal aid scheme. The legal aid scheme was designed to allow poorer people access to legal advice and representation in court: this would be provided by solicitors in private practice, but the state, rather than the client, would pay all or part of the fees. By the 1980s, the system had developed into six different schemes, covering most kinds of legal case, and administered by the Legal Aid Board. But the growing cost of these schemes was causing concern. In the 1990s the Conservative government sought to keep the escalating costs down by reducing financial eligibility for the schemes, which in turn led to criticisms that they were also reducing access to justice. As a result of all this, the Labour government passed the Access to Justice Act 1999, which made major changes to the system.

With the passing of this legislation the government hoped to improve the quality and accessibility of the legal services on offer, while keeping a tighter control on their budget. On 1 April 2000 the Legal Aid Board was replaced by the Legal Services Commission. It currently has a budget of approximately £2 billion a year – effectively each taxpayer is contributing £100 annually to legal aid work. The Commission is an executive non-departmental public body reporting to the Minister of Justice. The minister provides guidance to the Commission on his priorities but is not allowed to give guidance about the handling of any individual case.

The schemes

The Legal Services Commission administers two schemes: the Community Legal Service, which is concerned with civil matters, and the Criminal Defence Service, which is concerned with criminal matters. These two schemes will be considered in turn.

The Community Legal Service

Community Legal Service

Figure 12.1
The logo of the Community Legal Service
Source: Legal Services Commission.

Funding

Before 1999, legal aid in civil cases was available on a demand-led basis (meaning that all cases which met the merits and means tests would be funded), there is now a Community Legal Service Fund, containing a fixed amount of money, set each year as part of the normal round of government spending plans.

The detailed way in which the fund is to be spent is decided by a Funding Code, drawn up by the Legal Services Commission and approved by the Lord Chancellor, which sets out the criteria and procedures to be used when deciding whether a particular case should be funded. The Commission has a duty to obtain the best value for money, which the explanatory notes to the Access to Justice Act 1999 define as taking into account 'a combination of price and quality'. In other words, the Commission is not obliged to choose the cheapest possible service, but it is not obliged to choose the best quality one either; it has to find the best balance between the two.

Levels of funded legal services

Only solicitors or advice agencies holding a contract with the Legal Services Commission are able to provide advice or representation directly funded by the Commission. For specialist areas of law such as family law, immigration, mental health and clinical negligence, only specialist firms are funded to do the work. The merits test for civil legal aid has been replaced by the new Funding Code discussed above. This code lays down the rules as to which cases should receive funding. Direct funding is provided for different categories of legal service, as follows:

Legal Help

Legal Help provides initial advice and assistance with any legal problem. A means test is applied. This level of service covers work previously carried out under the 'green form' scheme.

Legal representation

Funding is available for a person to be represented in court proceedings. Both a means and a merits test are applied. This scheme replaces civil legal aid.

Help at Court

Help at Court allows somebody (a solicitor or adviser) to speak on another's behalf at certain court hearings, without formally acting for them in the whole proceedings. A means test is applied.

Approved Family Help

Approved Family Help provides help in relation to a family dispute, including assistance in resolving that dispute through negotiation or otherwise. This overlaps with the services covered by Legal Help, but also includes issuing proceedings and representation where necessary to obtain disclosure of information from another party, or to obtain a consent order where the parties have reached an agreement.

Family Mediation

This level of service covers mediation for a family dispute, including finding out whether mediation appears suitable or not.

Coverage

Certain types of case have been removed from the state-funded system altogether. These are:

■ Personal injury cases (with the exception of clinical negligence cases). Instead, these are funded by conditional fee agreements which are discussed later in this chapter.

■ Cases of defamation and malicious falsehood. Legal aid was never available for defamation. When the legal aid system was first established in 1949, defamation was excluded because the Attorney-General of the day was concerned that it would produce frivolous and unnecessary claims. While he accepted that the reputation of a poor person is just as deserving of legal protection as that of a wealthy person, he was worried that the legal aid scheme would be seriously overloaded if every slander uttered across the back garden wall could be pursued at the expense of the state. In some cases, behaviour which would normally be classed as defamation could be categorised as the related tort of malicious falsehood, for which legal aid was available. Now, neither is eligible for state funding. Under the Access to Justice Act 1999, legal aid can exceptionally be made available for such cases, but this has only happened once. Proceedings for defamation and malicious falsehood can, instead, be brought under a conditional fee agreement, discussed at p. 217.

■ Disputes arising in the course of a business. Business traders can insure against the cost of having to bring or defend a legal action, and the government believes that taxpayers should not be required to meet the legal costs of those who fail to do so.

■ Matters concerning the law relating to companies, partnerships, trusts (trusts are a way of holding property, and as such, tend mainly to affect wealthier people), or boundary disputes (for example, disputes between neighbours as to where each party's garden begins and ends).

The government considers that none of these types of case is sufficiently important to justify public funding. Approximately 80,000 people are injured each year at work, on the road or during a leisure activity. It has been estimated that personal injury cases accounted for around 60 per cent of cases previously funded by legal aid. However, the Access to Justice Act 1999 provides that a government minister can direct the Commission to provide services for excluded categories in exceptional circumstances.

Eligibility

Both a merits test and a means test are applied to determine whether funding for civil legal services will be awarded. A single means test applies. State funding is not available if a person earns more than £2,288 per month and if a person has £8,000 in savings.

The merits test is set out in the Funding Code and reflects the fact that certain cases should be given a higher priority for funding than others. For example, the chances of success might be relevant in many types of case, but would not be in cases about whether a child should be taken into local authority care.

Suppliers

In the past, a person who wanted help with a problem covered by legal aid could go to any lawyer and, provided the client met the relevant means and merits tests, that lawyer would be paid by the government for the help given in that particular case. This situation was beginning to change even before the 1999 Act was passed. Now only solicitors and advice agencies holding contracts with the Legal Services Commission are able to get state funding. Once they hold a contract, they are paid by the hour for their work.

The 1999 Act also gives the Commission power to make grants to service providers, such as advice centres, and to employ staff directly to deliver legal services to the public. This latter point means that the Commission could, if it wished, create a system of lawyers employed by the state to provide legal help to the public, though there appear to be no plans to do so with regard to civil cases at the moment.

Community Legal Advice

In 2004, Community Legal Advice was established. This is a national telephone and website service providing free legal advice on civil law matters. Members of the public can telephone the helpline on 0845 345 4345 for advice on such matters as housing, social security benefits and debt. Alternatively, they can visit the website at **www.communitylegaladvice.org.uk**. This website is visited over 50,000 times each month. Community Legal Advice is intended to provide an alternative to face-to-face advice, which will be particularly attractive to those with mobility problems, caring responsibilities or accommodation in a remote area. In addition, some people may feel more comfortable talking about their problems with the relative anonymity of a telephone line, rather than in a face-to-face meeting.

Quick quiz 12.1

1 When was the Community Legal Service established?

2 What is the name of the body that administers the Community Legal Service?

3 What is the Funding Code?

4 What are the five different categories of legal service that get direct funding as part of the Community Legal Service?

The Criminal Defence Service

In April 2001 a Criminal Defence Service was introduced, replacing the old system of criminal legal aid. This Criminal Defence Service is administered by the Legal Services Commission.

Funding

Unlike legal aid in civil cases, state-funded criminal defence work is still given on a demand-led basis; there is no set budget and all cases which fit the merits criteria and the means test are funded.

Levels of funded legal services

As part of this service, the Commission directly funds the provision of criminal legal services, employs public defenders and pays for duty solicitor schemes. Thus, under the Criminal Defence Service, legal services are provided by both lawyers in private practice and employed lawyers. The government believes that a mixed system of public and private lawyers will provide the best value for money for the taxpayer. The salaried service is intended to provide a benchmark to assess whether prices charged by private practice lawyers are reasonable, as well as filling in gaps in the system.

Direct funding

Only solicitor firms having a contract with the Legal Services Commission are able to offer state-funded criminal defence work. Unlike the contracts for civil matters, the contracts for criminal defence matters do not limit the number of cases that can be taken on, nor the total value of the payments that may be made. Contracted solicitors will be paid for all work actually undertaken in accordance with the contract. Solicitors with a contract should be able to provide the full range of criminal defence services, from the time of arrest until the end of the case (unlike under the previous system, where defendants could receive assistance relating to the same alleged offence under several different schemes, each resulting in a separate payment for the lawyers involved). In certain cases – such as serious fraud trials – there are panels of firms or individual lawyers who specialise in the relevant type of case, and defendants will be required to choose from that panel. State funding can support three types of service.

Advice and assistance. Funding is available for the provision of advice and assistance from a solicitor, including giving general advice, writing letters, negotiating, getting a barrister's opinion and preparing a written case. A means test is applied, but people who are eligible do not have to make any contribution to the legal costs. It does not cover representation in court.

When a person is questioned by the police, he or she has a right to free legal advice from a contracted solicitor and no means test is applied.

Advocacy assistance. Advocacy assistance covers the costs of a solicitor preparing a client's case and initial representation in certain proceedings in both the magistrates' court and the Crown Court and in certain other circumstances. There is no means test but there is a merits test.

Representation. When a person has been charged with a criminal offence, representation covers the cost of a solicitor to prepare the person's defence and to represent him/her in court. It may also be available for a bail application. It will sometimes pay for a barrister, particularly for the Crown Court and for the cost of an appeal.

Decisions to grant representation in individual cases are made by the magistrates' courts. Representation will be granted when it is in the 'interests of justice'. The court may decide that it is in the interests of justice to grant representation where, for example, the case is so serious that, on conviction, a person is likely to be sent to prison or to lose their job, where there are substantial questions of law to be argued, or where the defendant is unable to follow the proceedings and explain their case because they do not speak English well enough or are suffering from a psychiatric illness.

Means test

Before the Access to Justice Act 1999, criminal legal aid was means tested. The means test was criticised because most defendants were too poor to pay for their defence lawyers – only 1 per cent of applicants were refused criminal legal aid. As a result, the cost of administering the means test was more than the sum that was collected by defendants and the process also caused delays in the criminal system. The 1999 Act therefore abolished the means test for criminal cases. Instead, for cases heard in the Crown Court, orders could be issued at the end of a trial to recover the defence costs against wealthy people who have been convicted of an offence. Abolition of the means test lead to concern in the media that some wealthy defendants were receiving legal aid when they could have comfortably afforded to pay themselves. Following such criticisms, the Criminal Defence Service Act 2006 has reintroduced a means test for criminal cases (apart form the first hearing, to avoid court delays). There remains a risk that these reforms will cause delays in the criminal system, both because evidence of means will need to be obtained and because the number of unrepresented defendants is likely to increase. The Criminal Justice and Immigration Bill contains some provisions to try and improve how means testing works in practice.

Public defenders

Since May 2001, the Legal Services Commission directly employs a number of criminal defence lawyers, known as public defenders. The public defenders can provide the same services as lawyers in private practice and have to compete for work.

There was strong opposition to the introduction of public defenders. The explanatory notes to the Access to Justice Act state that the idea is to provide flexibility, so that employed lawyers could be used if, for example, there is a shortage of suitable private lawyers in remoter areas. The notes point out that using salaried lawyers will also give the Commission better information about the real costs of providing the services. Public defenders will provide an element of competition with solicitors in private practice. They are required to follow a code of conduct guaranteeing certain standards of professional behaviour, including duties to avoid discrimination, to protect the interests of those whom they are defending, to avoid conflicts of interest and to maintain confidentiality.

The government had planned to eventually set up a national network of public defender offices. People suspected of crime would then have had a choice only between these public defenders and lawyers who had a contract with the Legal Services Commission, though within that limited range it was intended that there would be some choice in all but the most exceptional circumstances. However, following research carried out by Lee Bridges and others, entitled *Evaluation of the Public Defender Service in England and Wales* (2007), the government concluded that four of the public defender offices were not delivering value for money and decided to close these down. It noted that all of the offices that were earmarked to be closed operated in areas with alternative criminal defence services, which was probably why they did not capture enough work to be cost effective. There are therefore four offices remaining and no plans at the moment to expand the scheme.

✓ **Know your terms 12.2**

Define the following terms:
1 Approved Family Help.
2 Means test.
3 Criminal Defence Service.
4 Public defender.

Duty solicitor schemes

Duty solicitors are available at police stations and magistrates' courts and offer free legal advice.

Criminal Defence Service Direct

A telephone service, known as Criminal Defence Service Direct (CDSD), was established in 2005 to provide telephone advice primarily to people detained by police for non-imprisonable offences who do not request to see their own lawyer. In addition, three pilot schemes have been established where telephone advice can be provided to any individual detained in a police station who is charged with a summary or either-way offence. For minor offences on the pilot scheme, the suspect will not be entitled to see their own solicitor, but will be obliged to use the telephone service. If these pilot schemes are successful, the role of the CDSD will be expanded nationally. The Legal Services Commission considers that telephone advice is a modern and appropriate way to assist people detained at police stations who are accused of less serious offences. It is also much cheaper than face to face advice. CDSD attempts to contact the client within 15 minutes of being informed of the case. In over half of cases the police fail to pick up the telephone, which causes delay.

Other participants in the Community Legal Service

There are a number of non-profit-making agencies which give legal advice and sometimes representation, and initiatives by the legal profession and other commercial organisations also address the issue of access to justice.

Law centres

Law centres offer a free, non-means-tested service to people who live or work in their area. They aim to be accessible to anyone who needs legal help, and in order to achieve this usually operate from ground floor, high street premises, stay open beyond office hours, employ a high proportion of lay people as well as lawyers and generally encourage a more relaxed atmosphere than that found in most private solicitors' offices. Most law centres are run by a management committee drawn from the local area, so that they have direct links with the community.

The first law centres were established in 1969; today there are around 50 of them. The Law Society allowed them to advertise (before the restriction on advertising was lifted for solicitors in general) in exchange for the centres not undertaking certain areas of work which were the mainstay of the average high street solicitor – small personal injury cases, wills and conveyancing. Their main areas of work are housing, welfare, immigration and employment.

Law centres are largely funded by grants from central and local government, though a few have also managed to secure some financial support from large local private firms. This method of funding means that they do not have to work on a case-by-case basis but can allocate funding according to community priorities.

Because they do not depend on case-by-case funding, law centres have developed innovative ways of solving legal problems. As well as dealing with individual cases, they run campaigns designed to make local people aware of their legal rights, act as a pressure group on local issues such as bad housing, and take action where appropriate on behalf of groups as well as individuals. The reasoning behind this approach is that resources and time are better used tackling problems as a whole, rather than aspects of those problems as they appear case by case. For example, if a council has failed to replace lead piping or asbestos in its council houses, it would seem more efficient to approach the council about all the properties rather than take out individual cases for each tenant as they become aware that they have a problem.

Law centres also provide valuable services in areas not covered by the statutory schemes, such as inquests, and several have set up duty solicitor schemes to deal with housing cases in the county court and help prevent evictions. They may offer a 24-hour general emergency service.

Most law centres face long-term problems with funding; several have closed, and others go through periodic struggles for survival. It is hoped that the Access to Justice Act, with its emphasis on making the most of voluntary advice services, will mean better funding in future. The danger is that local authorities will withdraw funding as funding becomes available from the Legal Services Commission.

Community Legal Advice Centres

In 2006 the Legal Service Commission established two pilot Community Legal Advice Centres (CLACs); it aims to establish a total of 75 in the future. The result would be a national network of legal aid suppliers working like the National Health Service. The idea is to tackle the full range of social welfare problems (such as debt, housing and employment) in a 'one-stop shop' for clients. CLACs will be situated in deprived areas. The director of the Law Centres Federation has observed that CLACs look remarkably like Law Centres and suggests that the government would be better off building on the strengths of the law centre 'brand' and funding more law centres, rather than creating competitors under a new brand.

Citizens' Advice Bureaux

There are around 700 Citizens' Advice Bureaux (CAB) across the country, offering free advice and help with a whole range of problems, though the most common areas at the moment are social security and debt. They are largely staffed by trained volunteers, who can become expert in the areas they most frequently deal with. Where professional legal help is required, some bureaux employ solicitors, some have regular help from solicitor volunteers and others refer individuals to local solicitors who undertake state-funded work. The bureaux are overseen by the National Association of Citizens' Advice Bureaux and must conform to its standards and codes of practice.

Task 12.3

Imagine that you are homeless with two children. You want to find out whether you have any rights to accommodation. Go to the Legal Services Commission website at **www.clsdirect.org.uk** and see whether you can find any useful information.

The Citizens' Advice Bureau provides advice on line at **www.adviceguide.org.uk**. Compare the information that is available on this website.

One of the major advantages of CABs is a very high level of public awareness – because they are frequently mentioned in the press and have easily recognisable high street offices, most people know where they are and what they do.

Like law centres, they have come under considerable financial pressure in recent years, with the result that many can only open for a very limited number of hours a week. The Access to Justice Act may mean better funding in future.

Alternative sources of legal help

Some local authorities run money, welfare, consumer and housing advice centres to provide both advice and a mechanism for dealing with complaints, while charities such as Shelter, the Child Poverty Action Group and MIND often offer legal help in their specialist areas. Other organisations, such as trade unions, motoring organisations, such as the AA and RAC, and the Consumers' Association give free or inexpensive legal help to their members. Some university law faculties run 'law clinics', where students, supervised by their tutors, give free help and advice to members of the public.

There are a number of internet sites giving basic legal advice for free, and some magazines publish legal advice lines, which charge a premium rate for readers to phone and get one-to-one legal advice from qualified solicitors. It is also possible to insure against legal expenses, either as a stand-alone policy or, more usually, as part of household, credit card or motor insurance.

As we saw earlier, cost is not the only cause of unmet legal need; a reluctance among many ordinary people to bring problems to lawyers is also recognised. In recent years, the profession has taken steps to address the issue, including the use of advertising and public relations campaigns. Many high street firms now advertise their services locally, while some of the firms currently involved in suing cigarette manufacturers for illnesses caused by smoking attracted potential clients by advertising specifically for people with smoking-related diseases.

Task 12.4

In 2003 the government issued a consultation paper, *Delivering Value for Money in the Criminal Defence Service*. The government wished to consult the public on proposed changes to the Criminal Defence Service. The end of the document contained a list of questions on which it wished to know the public's views before proceeding to introduce any reforms. These questions included the following:

1 Do you consider that access to free police station advice should be reduced? Would this adversely affect the rights of clients?
2 What types of police station advice should still be funded?
3 What impact would restricting the court duty solicitor scheme have upon the rights of the defendants?
4 What impact do you consider restricting the court duty solicitor scheme would have on the administration of the magistrates' courts?
5 What impact do you consider restricting the court duty solicitor scheme would have upon the number of defendants appearing without representation?

Question
If you were preparing a response to the government, how would you answer these questions?

The Access to Justice Act: an assessment

The Access to Justice Act 1999 was the subject of much opposition during the legislative process, and though some of the criticisms were addressed during the passing of the Act, some of this opposition remains. Below we detail the main criticisms, but first we look at some of the advantages claimed for the reformed system.

Advantages of the Access to Justice Act reforms

Control of costs

Before 1999 the cost of the legal aid system was considered a major problem. The government claims that the issuing of contracts, the fixed budget for state funding in civil cases and the fact that the Funding Code sets out clear criteria which reflect agreed priorities, will help keep costs under control.

A report from the National Audit Office (2003) has identified significant improvements that have taken place in the administration of state funding of legal services, with the creation of the Community Legal Service. The new funding arrangements have led to greater control and targeting of resources and better scrutiny of suppliers.

Better allocation of resources

The Funding Code for civil matters is designed to reflect agreed priorities, so money can be channelled into those areas which the government considers reflect best the needs of society.

Higher standards of work

By limiting state funding to contracted lawyers and firms who have passed quality control standards, the government claims that standards of work should be consistently high. The quality assurance mark will be used to spread high standards beyond law firms, to any organisation which might offer legal advice to the public. In addition, the Lord Chancellor suggested (*The Times*, 7 September 1999) that the creation of defence lawyers employed by the Commission would create a 'healthy rivalry' with private criminal lawyers and so stimulate them to give a better service.

Disadvantages of the reforms

Access to justice

The reforms were intended to improve access to justice, but they seem to have achieved the opposite. Because many state-funded legal services can only be obtained from lawyers who have a contract with the Legal Services Commission, members of the public are finding it increasingly difficult to find a state-funded lawyer with the relevant expertise close to their home.

Part of the problem is that many law firms have in the past done a small amount of legal aid work alongside their privately funded work. Such firms have not wanted to bid for block contracts because they have not wanted to increase the amount of comparatively poorly paid state-funded work they take on. There are now only 5,000 solicitor firms offering state-funded legal services, compared with 11,000 under the old legal aid system. Between January 2000 and June 2003 the number of civil contracts offered for housing law fell by a third from 743 to 489. In the same period, contracts for debt law fell by more than half, from 462 to 206. One result, many fear, will be the creation of a two-tier legal profession, with one set of firms doing poorly paid state-funded work and another doing exclusively private work.

The National Audit Office (2003) has identified a problem of lawyers opting out of contracting in family work. It also points to a need for more lawyers to under-take work in community care, housing and mental health. A study undertaken by the Citizens' Advice Bureaux (2004) has reinforced this picture of growing gaps in the supply of state-funded legal services, what it calls 'advice deserts'. Their sur-vey found that people were often having to travel up to 50 miles to find a lawyer. Over two-thirds of Citizens' Advice Bureaux said they had difficulty finding a legal aid immigration lawyer for clients, and 60 per cent reported problems finding solicitors to deal with housing and family law problems. The Legal Services Com-mission has, however, rejected the suggestion that there are legal aid 'advice deserts'. It has pointed out that almost 95 per cent of the population lives within five miles of a civil legal aid provider. It has also stated that the number of people who received civil legal help in 2005/06 was at a six-year high.

State funding is not available for legal representation at most tribunals.

Problems with conditional fee agreements

The Access to Justice Act 1999 removed personal injury cases from the state funding system, so that these can only be funded privately or by a conditional fee agreement. Much of the criticism of the current funding arrangements is concerned with the use of these conditional fee agreements which are discussed at pp. 217–223.

Cost-cutting

Critics, including the legal professions and some MPs, have accused the govern-ment of putting cost-cutting before access to justice. The chairperson of the Legal Aid Practitioners Group, Richard Miller, told *The Lawyer* newspaper in December 1998 that he believed the fixed budget for civil matters was designed to make it easy for the government to cut the amount spent in later years: 'The Legal Services Commission will simply be able to say, this is the budget and if there are any more cases, tough luck.'

Public defenders

The legal profession has fiercely opposed the idea of the Commission employing its own lawyers to do criminal defence work. Both the Bar Council and the Criminal Law Solicitors Association have expressed concern that lawyers who are wholly dependent on the state for their income cannot be sufficiently independ-ent to defend properly people suspected of crime – people who, by definition, are on the opposite side to the state.

The experience of foreign jurisdictions such as the US and Canada shows that any system of public defenders must be properly funded and staffed if it is to retain the confidence of providers, users and the courts. Unfortunately, they are frequently under-funded in practice, relying as a result on inexperienced lawyers with excessive case loads and who are not respected by their clients, opponents or the court.

sourcebook
p. 192 → Research carried out by Cyrus Tata and others (2004) has evaluated the success of the Public Defence Solicitors Office in Scotland in its first three years. The research compared the performance of the public defenders with that of solicitors in private practice receiving state funding. The conclusions of this research were mixed. It found that public defender clients pleaded guilty earlier than clients of solicitors in private practice. But it found no evidence to suggest that public defenders put explicit pressure on clients to plead guilty. Instead, the clients criticised the public defenders for being too neutral and too willing to go along with whatever the client decided. The change in economic incentives involved in receiving a salary rather than a legal aid payment appeared to produce a change in behaviour, because solicitors in private practice earn very little if a client immediately pleads guilty, so ending the case, compared to where there is a late guilty plea. Public defender clients were more likely to be convicted. Representation by a public defender increased the chances of a client being convicted from around 83 per cent to 88 per cent. This was primarily because clients of private solicitors were more likely to plead late, allowing for a greater chance in the meantime for the case against them to be dropped by the prosecution, for example because a witness fails to attend the trial. There was no difference between the sentences handed down.

The levels of trust and satisfaction expressed by public defender clients who had not volunteered to use the service, but been obliged to do so, was consistently lower than those expressed by clients using private practitioners. They were less likely to say that their solicitor had done 'a very good job' in listening to what they had to say; telling them what was happening; being there when they wanted them; or having enough time for them. They were also less likely to agree strongly that the solicitor had told the court their side of the story or treated them as though they mattered. Part of the problem appears to have been that clients resented not being able to choose their solicitor and this choice has now been reinstated. Those who had chosen to use the public defender service were more positive about the service. However, they were still significantly less likely than private clients to agree strongly that their lawyer had told the court their side of the story or had treated them as if they mattered, rather than as 'a job to be done'. Public defenders tended to be seen as more 'business-like' and less personally committed than private solicitors. Public defender clients were less likely to say that they would use the service again compared to clients of private solicitors.

The research concluded:

'From a managerial perspective, the fact that public defenders resolved cases at an earlier stage has advantages. It has the potential to save legal aid costs and also reduce court and prosecution costs, inconveniencing fewer witnesses. Clients were spared the wait and worry of repeated court [hearings] and were less likely to be held in detention pending the resolution of their case.'

At the moment, surprisingly, the public defender service is proving more expensive than private solicitors. The average cost of a case handled by the public defender service is over £800 compared to £506 for private practice. The Legal Aid Practitioners Group has suggested that this is because the tax payer has to pay the salary of public defenders even if they have failed to attract clients, while private solicitors are only paid for the work they do.

Poorer standards of work

A survey carried out in 1999 for the Legal Aid Practitioners Group found that 84 per cent of legal aid firms believed the Act's reliance on exclusive contracts would reduce the quality of legal services.

The Consumers' Association undertook research in 2001 into the experiences of people seeking help from the Community Legal Service. The research consisted of in-depth interviews of people who had sought help from the service, particularly those from vulnerable groups in society. It found that community centres and law centres provided the best help and advice, but many people felt that the legal system gave them a second-rate service. The research criticised the apparent lack of commitment and poor communication of some solicitors. There were still not enough solicitors and advisers specialising in areas like social security, housing, disability discrimination, employment and immigration law. People with disabilities complained of poor physical access to buildings.

The Legal Services Commission has paid for some research into the impact of different funding arrangements on the quality of the provision of legal services (*Quality and Cost: Final Report on the Contracting of Civil, Non-family Advice and Assistance Pilot* (Moorhead 2001)). A study was undertaken over two years of 80,000 cases handled by 43 not-for-profit agencies and 100 solicitor firms. The solicitor firms were randomly allocated to one of three payment groups: those who continued to be paid as under the old green form system; those paid a fixed sum and left to determine how many cases it was reasonable for them to do for the money; and those paid a fixed sum and given a specific number of cases which had to be undertaken. The research concluded that where the payment system gave firms an incentive to do work cheaply, the quality of work suffered. Thus firms in the third group performed worst on most indicators, with 20 per cent of the contracted advisers doing poor quality work. Group 2, in general, performed better than Group 1.

In his *Review of the Criminal Courts* (2001), Sir Robin Auld has recommended that changes should be made to the arrangements for the payment of defence lawyers so that they are rewarded for carrying out adequate case preparation.

??? Quick quiz 12.5

1 Give three advantages of the Access to Justice Act 1999 reforms.

2 Give three disadvantages of the Access to Justice Act 1999 reforms.

3 Research carried out by the Consumers' Association raised concerns about the standards of work carried out by the Community Legal Service. What were these concerns?

4 What does the Citizens Advice Bureau mean by an 'advice desert'.

Over-billing

Lawyers may be charging the government too much for their work. Audits conducted by the Legal Services Commission of case files kept by suppliers suggest that 35 per cent of suppliers were claiming 20 per cent more than they should have been, although some suppliers have complained about the basis of some of these decisions.

The cost of criminal cases

It seems that currently 1 per cent of criminal cases consume 49 per cent of the budget for the Criminal Defence Service. Following the publication of a consultation paper, *Delivering Value for Money in the Criminal Defence Service* (Lord Chancellor's Department, 2003), the government has tried to reduce the cost of these cases. Lawyers working on cases lasting more than five weeks, or costing more than £150,000 have to negotiate contracts for payment at each stage of the case.

The government paper, *A Fairer Deal for Legal Aid* (2003), gives details of plans to reduce the length of high cost criminal cases, by for example, removing juries from serious fraud cases and improving case management by judges. Lawyers will not be paid for time spent when a trial overruns.

Criminal barristers consider that they are underpaid for their work and in 2005 they effectively took strike action (they could not officially strike because they were self-employed and not members of a trade union). Fixed fees for Crown Court trials lasting up to ten days were introduced in 1997. The remuneration for these cases has been frozen since it came into force and this represents a 22.5 per cent pay cut in real terms. It has been estimated that junior criminal barristers relying on legal aid work, with up to five years experience, are earning only between £15,000 and £30,000 a year. They are paid just £46.50 to attend a Crown Court hearing which is not a trial, even though this can take up a whole day due to court delays.

At the moment, the government allocates a single budget to both civil and criminal state funding of legal services. Within this budget criminal defence work takes priority. So while the cost of criminal legal aid is expanding, this leaves less and less for civil legal aid. In 2004 the national legal aid budget was £2 billion, and 60 per cent of this was spent on criminal legal aid. Spending on civil legal aid fell by 22 per cent between 1997 and 2006.

Conditional fee agreements

In the US, a great many cases brought by ordinary individuals are funded by what are called contingency fees, or 'no win, no fee' agreements. Lawyers can agree with clients that no fee will be charged if they lose the case, but if they win, the fee will be an agreed percentage of the damages won. This obviously gives the lawyer a direct personal interest in the level of damages, and there have been suggestions that this is partly responsible for the soaring levels of damages seen in the US courts.

In the English legal system, contingency fees are banned, but in 1990 the Courts and Legal Services Act (CLSA) made provision for the introduction of conditional fee agreements. Under a conditional fee agreement, solicitors can agree to take no fee or a reduced fee if they lose, and raise their fee by an agreed percentage if they win, up to a maximum of double the usual fee. The solicitor calculates the extra fee (usually called the 'uplift' or 'success fee') on the basis of the size of the risk involved – if the client seems very likely to win, the uplift will generally be lower than in a case where the outcome is more difficult to predict. The rule that the losing party must pay the winner's costs remains, so a party using a conditional fee agreement will usually take out insurance to cover this if he or she should lose.

The Access to Justice Act 1999 makes some changes to the arrangements for conditional fee agreements in order to promote their use. Where a person who has made a conditional fee agreement wins his or her case, it will be possible for the court to order the losing party to pay the success fee, as well as the normal legal costs. Thus, the success fee is now only ever payable by the losing party, which is a complete reversal of the previous situation. This provision is designed to meet the criticism that damages are calculated to compensate the litigant for the damage done to him or her, so if the 'uplift' has to come out of the client's damages, the amount left will be less than the court calculated as necessary for the purpose of full compensation.

Similarly, where a winning litigant has taken out insurance to provide for payment of the other side's costs if he or she loses, the court can order that the other side also pays the cost of the insurance premium. As a result, people who are bringing actions for remedies other than the payment of money can use a conditional fee arrangement. These changes have caused problems in practice. The cost of after-the-event insurance has increased considerably, and some clients are finding it difficult to obtain such insurance. There has been a lot of litigation over paying these extra costs by the losing party. To try to reduce this problem, new rules of court have been written, which fix the success fee for particular types of litigation, such as road traffic accidents, depending on the circumstances of the case. For example, where litigation involves an accident at work and the employee brings a claim on the basis of a conditional fee agreement; if that action is successful, the employer's insurer will pay the employee's solicitor their normal costs, plus a success fee of 25 per cent of these costs if the case settled before trial, and a 100 per cent success fee for a riskier case that went to trial. It might be better if the sums were simply covered by judges increasing the award of damages to take into account these extra expenses.

There is no means test to determine whether a person is entitled to bring litigation on the basis of a conditional fee agreement. Naomi Campbell had brought legal proceedings against the publishers of the *Daily Mirror*. The case claimed that the newspaper had breached her right to privacy because it had published pictures of her leaving a support group for recovering drug users. Her claim was rejected by the Court of Appeal and she proceeded to appeal to the House of Lords. To pay for this appeal she reached a conditional fee agreement with her solicitors and her barrister. Her appeal to the House of Lords was successful and the publishing company was ordered to pay her £3,500 in damages and her costs. Her costs were £1,086,295.47 in total. The size of the bill for the appeal to the House of Lords was particularly high because the conditional fee agreement allowed for a success fee of 95 per cent for her solicitor and 100 per cent for her barrister. The publishers contested these costs, arguing that the success fee was so disproportionate that it infringed their rights to free speech under Art. 10 of the European Convention on Human Rights. They argued that, as Naomi Campbell was a rich celebrity, she could have afforded to fund her litigation without a conditional fee agreement, while the conditional fee agreement scheme was intended to help people who could not otherwise afford to sue. The House of Lords rejected this argument – conditional fee agreements were not means tested, and the publishers had to pay all the costs.

The Access to Justice Act 1999 made conditional fee agreements available for all cases apart from medical negligence. The government is now considering stopping state funding for medical negligence actions, so that these too would fall within the remit of conditional fee agreements. The consultation paper, *A New Focus for Civil Legal Aid: encouraging early resolution; discouraging unnecessary litigation* (2005), suggests that medical negligence cases could be transferred to the conditional fee agreement system after research into the possible impact of this change has been completed. It is questionable whether conditional fees are appropriate for such cases. They are generally very difficult for claimants to win – the success rate is around 17 per cent, compared with 85 per cent for other personal injury claims (often caused by road accidents). While the outcome of litigation arising from a road accident is often reasonably easy to predict, medical negligence cases require detailed reports before anyone can hazard a guess about whether any party is to blame. The evidence is that solicitors will only take on a case under a conditional fee agreement if they estimate there is at least a 70 per cent chance of being successful. It can cost between £2,000 and £5,000 simply to do the initial investigations necessary to assess accurately whether the case is worth pursuing. As a result, solicitors would be very unlikely to want to take on such cases on a conditional fee basis and, even if they did, the uncertainty of outcome means that insurance against losing would be extremely expensive, possibly amounting to thousands of pounds. On the other hand, removing state funding could be an effective way of reducing the National Health Service's legal costs. In 2003 the NHS was facing a record £4.4 billion bill in outstanding negligence claims.

The government is currently considering introducing collective conditional fee agreements. These are designed for bulk users of legal services such as trade unions and insurers.

Advantages of conditional fee agreements

Cost to the state

Conditional fee agreements cost the state nothing – the costs are entirely borne by the solicitor or the losing party, depending on the outcome. By removing the huge number of personal injury cases from state funding and promoting conditional fee agreements for them instead, the government claims it can devote more resources to those cases which still need state funding, such as tenants' claims against landlords, and direct more money towards suppliers of free legal advice, such as Citizens' Advice Bureaux.

Wider access to justice

The government believes that conditional fee agreements will allow many people to bring or defend cases, who would not have been eligible for state funding and who could not previously have afforded to bring cases at their own expense. As long as they can afford to insure against losing, and can persuade a solicitor that the case is worth the risk, anyone will be able to bring or defend a case for damages. Critics point out that there are a number of problems with this argument (see below).

Performance incentives

Supporters claim conditional fees encourage solicitors to perform better, since they have a financial interest in winning cases funded this way.

Wider coverage

Conditional fee agreements are allowed for defamation actions, and cases brought before tribunals: two major gaps in the provision of state funding.

Public acceptance

The Law Society suggests that clients have readily accepted conditional fee agreements in those areas where they have been permitted in the past. Within two years of the agreements being introduced, almost 30,000 conditional fee agreements had been signed, and by 1999 around 25,000 were in operation.

Fairness to opponents

There are restrictions on the costs state-funded clients can be made to pay to the other side, which can give them an unfair advantage, particularly in cases where both sides are ordinary individuals but only one has qualified for state funding. The requirement for insurance in conditional fee cases solves this problem.

Disadvantages of conditional fee agreements

Uncertain cases

Most of those who have criticised the legislation on conditional fee agreements accept that they are a good addition to the state-funded system, but are concerned that they may not be adequate as a substitute. In particular, critics – including the Bar, the Law Society, the Legal Action Group, and the Vice-Chancellor of the Supreme Court, Sir Richard Scott – have expressed strong concerns that certain types of case will lose out under the new rules. They suggest that solicitors will only want to take on cases under conditional fee agreements where there is a very high chance of winning. It was for this reason that medical negligence cases have been kept within the state-funded system.

Unfair trials

Where legal aid is refused, a subsequent trial may prove to be unfair if one party is unrepresented by a lawyer as a result, and the other party benefited from legal representation. This can amount to a breach of Art. 6 of the European Convention, which guarantees the right to a fair trial. The problem was highlighted

sourcebook
p. 187

by the case which has come to be known as the McLibel Two (**Steel** *v* **United Kingdom** (2005)). The defendants were two environmental campaigners who had distributed leaflets outside McDonald's restaurants. These leaflets criticised the nutritional content of the food sold in the restaurants. McDonald's sued the two defendants for defamation. The defendants were refused legal aid because it is not generally available for defamation cases (see p. 205). They therefore represented themselves throughout the proceedings, with only limited help from some sympathetic lawyers who provided a small amount of assistance for free. McDonald's were represented by a team of specialist lawyers. The libel trial lasted for 313 days and was the longest civil action in English legal history. The defendants lost the case and were ordered to pay £60,000 in damages (later reduced to £40,000 on appeal). They challenged the fairness of the UK proceedings in the European Court of Human Rights. That challenge was successful. The European Court held that the McLibel Two had not had a fair trial in breach of Art. 6 of the European Convention on Human Rights and there had been a breach of their right to freedom of expression under Art. 10 of the Convention.

Claimants misled

sourcebook
p. 183

The Citizens' Advice Bureau has issued a report entitled *No Win, No Fee, No Chance* (2005). This expresses concern that consumers are being misled by the term 'no win, no fee'. Often consumers find that the system costs them more than they gain. Consumers are subjected to aggressive and high-pressured sales tactics from unqualified employees of claims management companies. These companies receive a fee from solicitors for passing them a case. Consumers can be subjected to inappropriate marketing tactics, for example, accident victims have been approached in hospital. Consumers are not informed clearly of the financial risks that the legal proceedings will involve, and are misled into believing that the system will genuinely be 'no win, no fee'. In fact, consumers may need to take out an insurance policy to offset any legal expenses incurred if they lose the case and are required to pay the other side's costs. If the claim is, for example, against the council for failure to repair a council flat, a building surveyor may need to be paid as well as the lawyers. These legal expenses can be artificially inflated by unscrupulous claims management companies. The consumer can be encouraged to take out a loan to pay the monthly instalments of the insurance policy. The consumer frequently discovers that these expenses have wiped out any compensation they win. The injured person does not as a result benefit from the compensation they are entitled to. In some cases, the consumer even ends up owing money. In one case handled by the Citizens' Advice Bureau a woman was left with just £15 from a £2,150 compensation payout, and in another case a man received compensation of £1,250 for an accident at work, but owed nearly £2,400 for insurance relating to the litigation.

In **Bowen and ten others** *v* **Bridgend Borough Council** (2004) the litigation had arisen when employees of a claims management company had knocked on council tenants' doors suggesting that claims could be made. An action was brought against the council for failing to carry out housing repairs. The claimants had taken out loans to pay for insurance policies to cover any legal expenses they incurred. The average compensation paid to claimants was £1,631, but the claimants' solicitors sought an average of £8,000 in costs against the local authority. In fact, the court only ordered £250 to be paid, holding that many of the legal fees were unjustified and not payable.

The government has issued a consultation paper, *Making Simple CFAs a Reality* (2004). This is looking at how conditional fee agreements can be improved. It is also intending to improve the regulation of claims management companies through provisions contained in the Compensation Act 2006.

sourcebook p. 109

Insurance costs

There are concerns that insurance against losing can be expensive. In the area of personal injury, the Law Society provides an affordable insurance scheme, but in other areas the only suppliers are private insurance companies, which charge according to risk, so that clients with cases where the outcome is uncertain may be faced with very high premiums.

Both the Law Society and the Bar have suggested that a better idea would be the establishment of a self-financing contingency fund, which would pay for cases on the understanding that successful litigants would pay a proportion of their damages back to the fund. As mentioned above, this is allowed by the Act, but the government has said it has no plans to use the power at the moment.

Insurance pressures

There may also be pressure to settle from insurance companies, some of which have been known to threaten to withdraw their cover if a client refuses to accept an offer of settlement that the insurance company considers reasonable. Clearly, the insurance company's primary interest will be to avoid having to pay out, so it is not difficult to see that their idea of a reasonable settlement might be very different from the client's – or from what the client could expect to get if the case continued.

Financial involvement of lawyers

The Bar has criticised the idea of allowing lawyers a financial interest in the outcome of a case. In a letter to the Lord Chancellor, the Chair of the Bar Council argued that, since clients generally lack the knowledge to assess their chances of winning their case, lawyers will be able to charge whatever they think they can get away with (within the set limits). This seems a rather strange argument for a representative of the legal profession to put forward, and critics have widely suggested that the real reason behind this and the other criticisms made by the legal profession is that lawyers were reluctant to lose the no-risk income that state-funded legal aid allowed them.

The evidence on solicitors' approach to the uplift on fees is currently rather inconclusive. A report by Yarrow (1997) for the Policy Studies Institute on the effects of the changes made under the Courts and Legal Services Act 1990 found that the average uplift was 43 per cent, less than half the 100 per cent maximum allowed – but within that average, one in ten solicitors was charging between 90 per cent and 100 per cent. The author of the study, Stella Yarrow, commented that the number of cases assessed as having a low chance of success was surprisingly large, suggesting that solicitors might be underestimating the chances of winning in order to increase the uplift.

In 1999, the Forum of Insurance Lawyers (Foil) suggested that the chance to make extra money was encouraging solicitors to push clients into conditional fee agreements, even where the clients did not need such an agreement. Around 17 million people in Britain have some form of legal expenses insurance attached to their home, car or credit card insurance, and in many cases this will pay their legal costs for them. However, Foil points out, many people have this insurance without realising it, and it claims that instead of suggesting that clients check whether they have it, solicitors are persuading them into unnecessary conditional fee agreements.

Abuse in defamation proceedings

There is concern that conditional fee agreements are being used inappropriately in defamation proceedings, and thereby threatening the right to freedom of expression. Following a critical newspaper article, it is easy for a person to bring proceedings for defamation at no expense to themselves, but the newspaper is forced to incur considerable expense to defend such a claim. While it may be clear that a newspaper article damages the reputation of the claimant, the burden of proof will pass to the defendant to show, for example, that the article was true or fair comment. As a result, there needs to be strong case management by judges in defamation cases and the capping of costs where appropriate.

Lord Carter's reforms

In 2005, the Lord Chancellor asked Lord Carter to carry out a review of the legal aid system. Major reforms to the system have now been recommended by Lord Carter in his report, *Legal aid: a market-based approach to reform* (2006). Immediately after the publication of this report, the government issued a consultation paper, *Legal Aid: a sustainable future* (2006). This latter paper considers many of Lord Carter's recommendations.

Lord Carter has recommended that a new procurement regime should be introduced in 2009. To prepare for this procurement process a national system of peer review should be undertaken from 2007. Peer review means that law firms are assessed for the quality of their service by their peers, in other words other experienced and independent solicitors. This process of assessment would become the responsibility of the Law Society. The peer review system would identify firms who had attained the requisite quality thresholds, known as preferred suppliers, and they would be invited to apply for a contract with the Legal Services Commission. The tendering competition would be decided according to which firm bid to do the most work for the lowest price. A pilot scheme of a preferred supplier system, involving 25 firms throughout 2004–5, was shown to reduce bureaucracy and raise standards of service, as well as improve the relationship between the Legal Services Commission and legal aid firms. Legal aid lawyers have been strongly opposed to the introduction of competitive tendering and have pointed to hospital cleaning, school dinners and prison transport as examples of why tendering should not be used as a procurement mechanism.

Lord Carter criticised the current criminal legal aid system for spending money on 'unproductive time and anomalies in the system'. Payment is calculated on the basis of the number of hours spent on a case, and does not therefore reward efficiency. He recommends that criminal legal aid lawyers should no longer be paid by the hour, but by the case. Fixed fees will be introduced across the board for criminal cases, calculated according to the type of case. Fees will be front-loaded to encourage early preparation and discourage trials. It is argued that a fixed fee regime allows efficient firms to be more profitable since they expend less input to produce the same quality service and get the same fee as a less efficient firm.

> 'Fixed pricing rewards efficiency and suppliers who can deliver increased volumes of work. However, pricing should be graduated for more complex work so that cases genuinely requiring more expertise and effort are priced fairly.'

Also, under the new proposals, efficient firms would be able to win new contracts in the best value tendering process.

Lord Carter is also of the view that large law firms are more efficient than small ones. He predicts that his recommendations for procurement contracts, combined with the implementation of Sir David Clementi's recommendations (see p. 192) will lead to 'an increase in the average size of firms through growth and mergers, rationalization and harmonization of the way separate services are delivered'. To encourage this move towards larger law firms, the Legal Services Commission is proposing to grant legal aid contracts which are worth at least £25,000. Contracts could be awarded to either individual firms or a collection of firms formed to deliver the benefits of scale. Thus, there will be a move towards granting fewer and larger contracts. The number of people involved might not change dramatically but they would work for fewer employers.

Lord Carter considers that it is uneconomic for both the Legal Services Commission and solicitors to deliver small amounts of legal aid work. Grants should be made available to support this transition, including money for investment in computer technology and modernisation. The government's consultation paper suggests that it would be prepared to provide some practical support to law firms during this period of transition but not financial grants. Lord Carter argues that this reorganisation will be in the interests of legal aid lawyers, saying that sole practitioners (lawyers working in an office on their own) are likely to earn between £36,000 and £55,000, while equity partners in a legal aid firm with 40 fee earners could expect to earn between £120,000 and £150,000.

The aim of these reforms is to control the cost and quality of legal aid and to promote efficiency of service in the public interest. Lord Carter predicts that implementation of his proposals could lead to a saving of £100 million a year, with criminal legal aid costing 20 per cent less than in 2005. He suggests that, without these new procurement reforms, the same sort of price inflation as seen in the past decade would more than likely be repeated in the future.

The reform proposals have been the subject of considerable criticism from legal aid lawyers. Respondents to a consultation paper on price-competitive tendering issued by the Legal Services Commission in 2005, found that 85 per cent of respondents were opposed to this system. Sixty per cent said the proposals would have a negative effect on the quality of legal advice. Lord Carter's strategy has been dismissed by critics as 'pile them high, sell them cheap'. Black and minority ethnic solicitors frequently work as sole practitioners or in small legal aid firms, and this has lead to concern that such firms may suffer if these reforms are introduced. The reforms are likely to lead to a legal aid client having a narrower choice of lawyer. The contracts will only last for one or two years. Initially, there will be intense competition to obtain one of these contracts. Once the contracts have been allocated, a monopoly will have been created in each geographical area for the contract period – economically, an extremely unhealthy market structure and quite the opposite of the 'diverse and competitive market' intended. A criminal law firm which fails to get a contract, is unlikely to survive six months and it will be difficult for any new solicitor to enter the market given the emphasis on larger firms being preferred suppliers.

Reading on the web

The report of the Constitutional Affairs Committee criticising the government's plans to implement Lord Carter's legal aid reforms, *Implementation of the Carter Review of Legal Aid* (2007), is available on Parliament's website at:

www.publications.parliament.uk/pa/cm200607/cmselect/cmconst/223/223i.pdf

The report by Lee Bridges and others, *Evaluation of the Public Defender Service in England and Wales* (2007), is available on the website of the Legal Services Commission at:

www.legalservices.gov.uk/docs/pds/Public_Defenders_Report_PDFVersion6.pdf

Lord Carter's report, *Legal aid: a market-based approach to reform* (2006), is available at:

www.legalaidprocurementreview.gov.uk/publications.htm

The consultation paper, *Legal Aid: a sustainable future* (2006), is available at:

www.dca.gov.uk/consult/legal-aidsf/sustainable-future.htm

The website of Community Legal Advice is:

www.communitylegaladvice.org.uk

The judgment of the European Court of Human Rights in the McLibel Two case, was application number 6841/01 and can be found on the court's website at:

www.echr.coe.int/echr

The website of the Legal Services Commission is:

www.legalservices.gov.uk/

The website of the Community Legal Service is:

www.legalservices.gov.uk/civil.asp

Chapter summary

State funding of legal services

With the passing of the Access to Justice Act 1999, the Labour government introduced some major reforms to the provision of state-funded legal services. On 1 April 2000, the Legal Aid Board was replaced by the Legal Services Commission.

The Legal Services Commission administers two schemes: the Community Legal Service which is concerned with civil matters and the Criminal Defence Service which is concerned with criminal matters.

The Community Legal Service

Direct funding is provided for different categories of legal service as follows:

- Legal Help;
- Legal Representation;
- Help at Court;
- Approved Family Help; and
- Family Mediation.

The Criminal Defence Service

State funding can provide direct funding for three types of service in the criminal field:

- Advice and assistance;
- Advocacy assistance; and
- Representation.

In addition, the Legal Services Commission employs public defenders and pays for duty solicitor schemes.

Conditional fee agreements

In 1990 the Courts and Legal Services Act made provision for the introduction of conditional fee agreements. The scope for their use was increased by the Access to Justice Act 1999.

Reform

In his report, *Legal aid: a market-based approach to reform* (2006), Lord Carter has recommended the introduction of some important, money-saving reforms to the system of state funded legal services.

Question and answer guides

1

(a) Outline how a barrister is trained and qualifies. (*10 marks*)

(b) Paveen has been injured in an accident. Explain from whom she could get advice about a possible claim for damages. (*10 marks*)

(c) Briefly discuss advantages **and** disadvantages of both private funding and of 'no win – no fee' arrangements in a civil claim. (*10 marks*)

(from AQA Specimen Question Paper, 2007)

(a) The first stage in qualifying as a barrister – known as the academic stage – involves the applicant gaining an upper-second or first class degree. If this is not in law, applicants must also do the one-year course leading to the Common Professional Examination.

The second stage – known as the vocational stage – involves the applicant taking the year-long Bar Vocational Course. This course includes oral exercises, and tuition in advocacy, interviewing skills and negotiating skills.

However, before students can start the vocational stage, they must join one of the Inns of Court – Inner Temple, Middle Temple, Gray's Inn or Lincoln's Inn. Only the Inns of Court can confer the qualification of barrister-at-law, a process known as 'being called to the Bar'. To be called to the Bar, students must have successfully completed the BVC and undertaken 12 'qualifying sessions'. The latter are collegiate and educational activities organised by the Inn, the main purpose of which is to give students the opportunity to meet practising barristers.

The third and final stage in qualifying as a barrister is pupillage. This is a one-year apprenticeship spent in an authorised pupillage training organisation – either barristers' chambers or another approved legal environment such as the Government Legal Service. During pupillage the pupil receives practical training by assisting an experienced barrister, known as their pupil master.

(b) The traditional providers of legal advice to the public are solicitors in private practice. If Paveen does not know the name of a firm of solicitors she can consult the Law Society or find one by searching the internet or just finding an appropriate office on her local high street. Paveen will need to find a firm that handles personal injury claims like hers, as not all firms do such work.

If Paveen were to hire a firm of solicitors that firm might, with Paveen's permission, refer her case to a barrister if it required the barrister's specialist opinion. Alternatively, Paveen could consult a barrister directly without employing a solicitor. The barrister must be able and willing to undertake public access work. A list of such barristers is available from the Bar Council.

Some motor, household and credit card insurance gives the right to a limited amount of free legal advice on certain types of cases. Free or inexpensive legal help is also sometimes given to members of organisations such as the AA, the RAC, the Consumers' Association and trade unions.

Other possible sources of advice that Paveen might use are Law Centres, Citizens' Advice Bureaux and university law clinics. There are a number of internet sites giving basic legal advice for free, and some magazines publish legal advice lines, which charge a premium rate for readers to phone and get legal advice from a solicitor.

(c) The advantages of financing a civil claim from private funds are that it gives the client the greatest possible freedom of action, avoids the delays that arise when one is dependent on third party financing and, provided the clients' funds are large enough, gives them access to the best possible legal advice. The disadvantage is that civil litigation can be very expensive, especially given that the loser usually has to pay the winner's costs.

The main advantage claimed for 'no win, no fee' arrangements is that they allow many people to bring or defend cases who otherwise could not have done so, because they would not have been eligible for state funding and could not have afforded to finance the cases themselves.

Another advantage is that they cost the state nothing; the costs are borne by the solicitor or the losing party, depending on the outcome. This makes more resources available for those cases where state funding is still needed.

But the Citizens' Advice Bureau has issued a report, *No win, no fee, no chance* (2005), pointing out the high cost of insuring against losing in 'no win, no fee' cases. Clients with cases where the outcome is uncertain may be faced with very high premiums.

Critics also highlight the danger that solicitors will only want to take on cases under conditional fee agreements where there is a very high chance of winning.

2

Colin is arrested and detained at a police station on suspicion of committing a serious violent offence which is triable either way. He has to consider obtaining legal assistance for his present situation and for court appearances.

(a) Describe the different forms of legal advice and representation available to him. *(20 marks)*

(b) Briefly discuss how well the different forms of advice and representation will meet Colin's needs. *(10 marks)*

(from AQA Exam Paper, January 2003)

(a)

■ Private finance – refer to the possibility of Colin choosing to pay for a lawyer to advise and represent him at all stages.
■ State funding – explain Colin's entitlement to the following:
  ■ free, non-means-tested, advice and assistance at the police station, either from the duty solicitor or Colin's own choice of solicitor, provided the latter has a contract with the Legal Services Commission;
  ■ free but means-tested advice and assistance from an LSC-contracted solicitor while not at the police station but, e.g., on police bail;
  ■ free, non-means-tested, advocacy assistance, covering the cost of initial representation by an LSC-contracted solicitor in certain proceedings in the magistrates' court and Crown Court; subject to a merits test;

- free but means-tested representation by an LSC-contracted solicitor and perhaps also a barrister, if charged; subject to an 'interests of justice' test;
  - for a good answer, refer to the public defender service.
- Pro bono – explain how this might help Colin.

(b)

- Explain how the private finance option will meet Colin's needs in full, but at a cost.
- Refer to the financial attractions of state funding and pro bono.
- Refer to the unattractiveness of means testing, where it applies.
- Refer to criticisms of the duty solicitor scheme, especially doubts over the competence of some lawyers working under it.
- For a good answer, refer to criticisms of the public defender service, especially its limited availability.

Common errors in (a)

- mentioning civil legal aid;
- failing to mention private finance and *pro bono*.

Common errors in (b)

- discussing 'no win, no fee' agreements which are only relevant to civil litigation;
- repeating things already written in (a).

Group activity 1

- Divide your friends (or class) into groups of two or three people.
- Each group should choose a Law Centre in England and Wales from the list on the website of the Law Centres Federation – www.lawcentres.org.uk. It should prepare a profile of its chosen Law Centre, focusing on the types of legal problems with which it can help, the range of legal services that it offers, and the extent to which its services are funded by the State.
- The groups should then meet to compare profiles, looking for any common themes.

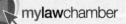

Visit **www.mylawchamber.co.uk/elliottqa** to access interactive questions, quizzes and activities to test yourself on this chapter.

Part 8
THE JUDICIARY

Chapter 13

The judges

This chapter discusses:

- the role of the judges;
- the different types of judges, known as the 'judicial hierarchy';
- how judges are appointed and trained;
- the five ways that a judge may cease to be a judge;
- the independence of the judiciary;
- criticisms of the judiciary.

The role of the judges

The judges play a central role under the British constitution. A basic principle of our constitution is known as the 'rule of law'. Under the rule of law, judges are expected to deliver judgments in a completely impartial manner, applying the law strictly, without allowing any personal preferences to affect their decision-making.

sourcebook p. 153 → The judges play a vital but sensitive role in controlling the exercise of power by the state. They do this, in particular, through the procedure of judicial review. The passing of the Human Rights Act 1998 significantly increased the powers of the judges to control the work of Parliament and the executive. A controversial judicial decision which highlights the tension between the roles of the judges, sourcebook p. 163 → Parliament and the executive is **A and others *v* Secretary of State for the Home Department (2004)**. Following fear over the increased risks of terrorism, Parliament had passed the Anti-Terrorism, Crime and Security Act 2001. This allowed the government to detain in prison suspected terrorists without trial. The subsequent detention of nine foreign nationals was challenged through the courts and the House of Lords ruled that their detention was unlawful because it violated the Human Rights Act. As a result, the legislation was repealed and replaced by the Prevention of Terrorism Act 2005. This established control orders, which can potentially amount to house arrest – the first time we have seen this measure in the UK.

Judicial hierarchy

sourcebook
p. 181 →
The judges are at the centre of any legal system, as they sit in court and decide the cases. At the head of the judiciary is the President of the Courts of England and Wales. This position was created by the Constitutional Reform Act 2005. Before that Act was passed, the Lord Chancellor had been the head of the judiciary. The new President of the Courts of England and Wales (in practice the Lord Chief Justice, discussed below) is now the head of the judiciary, being officially the president of the Court of Appeal, the High Court, the Crown Court, the county courts and the magistrates' courts. He or she is technically allowed to hear cases in any of these courts, though in practice he or she is only likely to choose to sit in the Court of Appeal. Under s. 7 of the Act, the President's role is to represent the views of the judiciary to Parliament and to government ministers. He or she is also responsible for the maintenance of appropriate arrangements for the welfare, training and guidance of the judiciary and for arranging where judges work and their workload.

The most senior judges are the 12 Lords of Appeal in Ordinary, more commonly known as the Law Lords. They currently sit in the House of Lords and the Privy Council. Their role will soon change, as the government has decided to abolish the House of Lords and replace it with a Supreme Court. The Constitutional Reform Act 2005 contains this reform and the new court is likely to be established in 2009. It is discussed in detail at p. 85.

At the next level down, sitting in the Court of Appeal, are 37 judges known as Lord Justices of Appeal and Lady Justices of Appeal. The Criminal Division of the Court of Appeal is presided over by the Lord Chief Justice who, following the Constitutional Reform Act 2005, is also known as the President of the Courts of England and Wales (discussed above). He or she can at the same time act as the Head of Criminal Justice or appoint another Court of Appeal judge to take this role.

The Civil Division of the Court of Appeal is presided over by the Master of the Rolls. There is also a head of civil justice and a head of family justice.

In the High Court, there are 107 full-time judges. As well as sitting in the High Court itself, they hear the most serious criminal cases in the Crown Court. Although – like judges in the Court of Appeal and the House of Lords – High Court judges receive a knighthood, they are referred to as Mr or Mrs Justice Smith (or whatever their surname is), which is written as Smith J.

The next rank down concerns the circuit judge, who travels around the country, sitting in the county courts and also hearing the middle-ranking Crown Court cases. The Criminal Justice and Public Order Act 1994 added a further role, allowing them occasionally to sit in the Criminal Division of the Court of Appeal.

The slightly less serious Crown Court criminal cases are heard by district judges, and then there are recorders, who are part-time judges dealing with the least serious Crown Court criminal cases. Recorders are usually still working as barristers or solicitors, and the role is often used as a kind of apprenticeship before becoming a circuit judge. Because of the number of minor cases coming before the Crown Court, there are now assistant recorders as well, and at times retired circuit

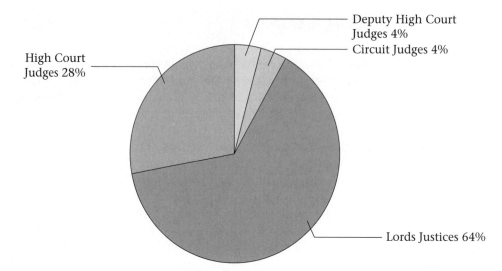

Figure 13.1 **Court of Appeal: days sat, 2004**

Source: 'Judicial Statistics Annual Report 2004', p. 131. © Crown Copyright 2005.

judges have been called upon to help out. Finally, in larger cities there are district judges (magistrates' courts), who were previously known as stipendiary magistrates, and are full-time, legally qualified judges working in the magistrates' courts.

In practice, there is some flexibility between the courts, so that judges sometimes sit in more senior courts than their status would suggest. This practice is illustrated in Table 13.1.

Table 13.1 **The hierarchy of the judiciary**

Judge	*Usual court*
Lord of Appeal in Ordinary	House of Lords and Privy Council
Lord Chief Justice	Criminal Division of the Court of Appeal
Master of the Rolls	Civil Division of the Court of Appeal
Lord Justice of Appeal	Court of Appeal
High Court judge	High Court and Crown Court
Circuit judge	County court and Crown Court
District judge	County court and Crown Court
District judge (magistrates' court)	Magistrates' court
Recorder	Crown Court

Moderniser swims into top judge's post

A brainy moderniser who keeps fit by swimming outdoors all year round is to become the new top judge in England and Wales when Lord Woolf retires at the end of September 2005.

Lord Phillips will take over as Lord Chief Justice for England and Wales from 1 October 2005. He will move from the number two post in the judiciary, Master of the Rolls, to the top job. Like Lord Woolf, he is seen as a liberal, while the other candidate who had been tipped for the job, the deputy Chief Justice, Lord Justice Judge, is regarded as more conservative.

The new Lord Chief Justice is less at ease with the media than Lord Woolf, but his friends say he will be equally effective in the top judge's most difficult role, standing up to the executive in defence of the rule of law.

'He's quite a shy, internal person with a very great sense of duty and obligation', said one judge who knows him well. 'He's very jolly with his friends, but finds it quite difficult to have a public persona.'

Source: Adapted from Claire Dyer, *The Guardian*, 18 June 2005.

Appointments to the judiciary

The way in which judges are appointed has been radically reformed by provisions in the Constitutional Reform Act 2005. In order to evaluate the new appointment procedures, it is useful to understand how judges were appointed before these reforms were introduced. We will therefore look first at the old procedures before looking at the new ones.

The old appointment procedures

Prior to the 2005 Act, the Lord Chancellor (who is the government minister at the head of the Ministry of Justice) played a central role in the appointment of judges. The Lords of Appeal in Ordinary and the Lord Justices of Appeal were appointed by the Queen on the advice of the Prime Minister, who in turn was advised by the Lord Chancellor. High Court judges, circuit judges and recorders were appointed by the Queen on the advice of the Lord Chancellor.

Over the years there had been considerable criticism of the way in which judges were appointed and, as a result, changes had been made even before the more radical reforms of the 2005 Act. In the past only barristers could become senior judges. The Courts and Legal Services Act 1990 widened entry to the judiciary, reflecting the changes in rights of audience (see p. 179), and (at least in theory) opening up the higher reaches of the profession to solicitors as well as barristers. The selection process for judges in the High Court involved the old Department for Constitutional Affairs gathering information about potential candidates over a period of time by making informal inquiries (known as 'secret soundings') from leading barristers and judges.

The normal procedure for recruiting for a job is to place an advertisement in a newspaper and to allow people to apply. By contrast, until recently, there were no advertisements for judicial office, one simply waited to be invited to the post. Advertisements have more recently been placed for junior and High Court judges, but still not for positions in the Court of Appeal and the House of Lords.

In the past, the final selection process consisted of a traditional job interview. For the appointment of most judges, this was replaced, in 2003, with the attendance at an assessment centre for a whole day. The centres require judicial applicants to sit through an interview, participate in role-play and pass a written examination and are meant to offer applicants a fairer opportunity to demonstrate their knowledge and skills and thereby reduce the danger of subjective judgments and resulting discrimination. Research carried out for the government has found that these assessment centres are, indeed, a fairer method of judicial selection than one relying solely on an interview process.

The Law Society, the professional body representing solicitors, considered the limited reforms made following Sir Leonard Peach's report in 1999 'inadequate', particularly as the new Commissioner was merely responsible for monitoring the existing system, rather than having any direct involvement in the appointments process itself.

The three main criticisms of the old system of selecting judges were that it was dominated by politicians and was secretive and discriminatory. On the first issue, the Lord Chancellor and the Prime Minister played central roles in this process but they were politicians and could be swayed by political factors in the selection of judges. The Lord Chancellor presented the Prime Minister with a shortlist of two or three names, listing them in the order of his or her own preference. Mrs Thatcher is known to have selected Lord Hailsham's second choice on one occasion.

On the second issue, the constitutional reform organisation Charter 88, among others, criticised the old selection process for being secretive and lacking clearly defined selection criteria. The process was handled by a small group of civil servants who, although they consulted widely with judges and senior barristers, nevertheless wielded a great deal of power. This process was considered to be unfair because it favoured people who had a good network of contacts, perhaps because of their education or family, rather than focusing on the individual's strength as a future judge. There was also a danger that too much reliance was placed on a collection of anecdotal reports from fellow lawyers, with candidates given no opportunity to challenge damning things said about them.

Since 1999 the Law Society had refused to participate in the secret soundings process. The president of the Law Society described the system as having 'all the elements of an old boys' network', and being inconsistent with an open and objective recruitment process: 'We suspect we were being used to legitimise a system where other people's views were more important than ours. It didn't really matter what we thought, it was the views of the senior judiciary and the Bar which counted.' The highest ranking solicitor among the judiciary is a single High Court judge.

As regards the third criticism, that the old appointments process was discriminatory, a 1997 study commissioned by the Association of Women Barristers is of interest. It found that there was a strong tendency for judges to recommend candidates from their own former chambers. The study looked at appointments to the High Court over a ten-year period (1986–96) and found that of the 104 judges appointed, 70 (67.3 per cent) came from a set of chambers which had at least one ex-member among the judges likely to be consulted. In addition, a strikingly high percentage of appointments came from the same handful of chambers: 28.8 per cent of new judges from chambers which represented 1.8 per cent of the total number of chambers in England and Wales. The fact that those who advised on appointments were already well established within the system could make it unlikely that they would encourage appointment from a wider base: Lord Bridge, the retired Law Lord, commented in a 1992 television programme that they tend to look for 'chaps like ourselves'. As Helena Kennedy QC has put it, 'the potential for cloning is overwhelming', and the outlook for potential female judges and those from the ethnic minorities not promising.

The process of 'secret soundings' gave real scope for discrimination, with lawyers instinctively falling back on gender and racial stereotypes in concluding whether someone was appropriate for judicial office. For example, individuals were asked whether they thought candidates showed 'decisiveness' and 'authority'. But these are very subjective concepts and Kamlesh Bahl has argued (*The Guardian*, 10 April 1995) that, as the judiciary is seen as a male profession, perceptions of judicial characteristics, such as 'authority', are also seen as male characteristics. 'Authority' is dependent more on what others think than on the person's own qualities. Indeed, research published by the Bar Council in 1992 concluded:

> *'It is unlikely that the judicial appointment system offers equal access to women or fair access to promotion to women judges . . . The system depends on patronage, being noticed and being known.'* (Holland (1992) Without Prejudice? Sex Equality at the Bar and in the Judiciary, para. 48(1))

However, in his book, *The Judge*, Lord Devlin (1979) says that, while it would be good to open up the legal profession, so that it could get the very best candidates from all walks of life, the nature of the job means that judges will still be the same type of people whether they come from public schools and Oxbridge or not, namely those 'who do not seriously question the status quo'.

In its second annual report published in 2003, the Commission for Judicial Appointments concluded that there was systemic bias in the way that the judiciary and the legal profession operated. This bias prevented women, ethnic minorities and solicitors from applying successfully for judicial office. The Commission was fundamentally unhappy with the appointment process for High Court judges and recommended that it should be stopped immediately because it was 'opaque, out-dated and not demonstrably based on merit'.

✓ **Know your terms 13.1**

Define the following terms:

1 Secret soundings.
2 Law Lord.
3 Master of the Rolls.
4 Lord Chief Justice.

The new appointment procedures

The government published a consultation paper, *Constitutional Reform: a new way of appointing judges* (2003). While some improvements had been made in recent years to the appointment procedures, the government concluded that:

> *'The most fundamental features of the system . . . remain rooted in the past. Incremental changes to the system can only achieve limited results, because the fundamental problem with the current system is that a Government minister, the Lord Chancellor, has sole responsibility for the appointments process and for making or recommending those appointments.*

However well this has worked in practice, this system no longer commands public confidence, and is increasingly hard to reconcile with the demands of the Human Rights Act.'

Following a limited consultation process, the Constitutional Reform Act 2005 was passed, containing provisions for the establishment of a new Judicial Appointments Commission responsible for a new judicial appointments process. This Commission started working in 2007. It is hoped that the creation of this body will help to put an end to the breaches of the principle of the separation of powers and reinforce judicial independence.

Under Sch. 12 to the Act, the Commission has 14 members: five lay members (including the chair), five judges, two legal professionals, a tribunal member and a lay magistrate. The members are appointed by the Queen on the recommendation of the Lord Chancellor. Candidates must be selected on the basis of merit and be of good character. Part 2 of the Tribunals, Courts and Enforcement Act 2007 contains provisions to try and widen the pool of lawyers eligible to become judges. In the past, to be eligible for appointment as a judge a person needed to have experience as a judge in a more junior court or rights of audience in a court (which effectively limited judicial appointments to barristers and solicitors). If these professions were dominated by white men from an upper-middle class background, then the judiciary would inevitably share this profile. Under the 2007 Act, eligibility is no longer based on the number of years candidates have had rights of audience before a court, but instead on their number of years' post-qualification experience. The latter is a much broader concept but equally reflects a person's experience of the law. The required number of years' experience has been reduced from seven to five years and ten to seven years depending on the seniority of the judicial office. In order to be considered for judicial office, a person must have a relevant qualification. Following the 2007 Act, the Lord Chancellor can provide that the qualification of a legal executive, for example, will be sufficient for judicial appointment in certain courts. Sixty per cent of legal executives are women, so this should help to increase the number of female judges.

In performing its functions the Commission must have regard to the need to encourage diversity in the range of persons available for selection (s. 64). It is allowed to encourage people it believes should apply for judicial posts to apply. The minister is able to issue guidance which the Commission must have regard to. This guidance can include directions on increasing diversity in the judiciary.

The Judicial Appointments Commission evaluates candidates and recommends, on the basis of merit only, one individual for each vacancy. The minister is not able to choose someone who has not been recommended to him or her by the Commission. He or she is, however, able to ask for a candidate who is not initially recommended by the Commission to be reconsidered, and can refuse the appointment of someone recommended and ask for a new name to be put forward. The minister has the ability to reject a candidate once, and to ask the Commission to reconsider once. Having rejected once, the minister must accept whichever subsequent candidate is selected.

There is special provision for the appointment of the Lord Chief Justice, the heads of Division and the Lord Justices of Appeal. The Commission establishes a selection panel of four members, consisting of two senior judges (normally including the Lord Chief Justice) and two lay members of the Commission.

Appointments of Lords Justices and above will continue to be made formally by the Queen on the advice of the Prime Minister, after the Commission has made a recommendation to the minister.

The new Appointments Commission will not be involved in the appointment of judges to the future Supreme Court. Instead, when there is a vacancy, the minister will appoint a temporary Commission. This Commission will include the President and Deputy President of the Supreme Court, as well as one member of each of the three judicial appointing bodies of England and Wales, Scotland and Northern Ireland. The temporary Commission will put forward between two and five recommended candidates to the minister, according to prescribed criteria. The minister must then consult with the senior judges, the First Minister in Scotland, the National Assembly for Wales, and the First Minister and deputy First Minister in Northern Ireland. The minister will afterwards notify the name of the selected candidate to the Prime Minister, who must recommend this candidate to the Queen for appointment.

The Law Society thinks that a choice of up to five gives too much scope for political interference, and thinks that only one name should be put forward for each job vacancy.

A Judicial Appointments and Conduct Ombudsman now oversees the recruitment process and has the power to investigate individual complaints about judicial appointments. The Commission for Judicial Appointments has been abolished.

The judicial appointment process has undoubtedly been improved by the reforms introduced by the Constitutional Reform Act 2005. However, there are some weaknesses in those reforms and the government could have gone much further in removing itself from the appointment process. The pressure group, Civil Liberties, is concerned that the Act only creates an advisory panel for judicial appointments, as the ultimate decision to appoint will still be made by the government minister (or effectively the Prime Minister for Court of Appeal and Supreme Court judges).

The government's consultation paper, *Constitutional Reform: a new way of appointing judges* (2003), considered the creation of three possible types of commission:

- An Appointing Commission.
- A Recommending Commission.
- A Hybrid Commission.

An Appointing Commission would itself make the decision whom to appoint with no involvement of a minister at any stage. This is similar to the arrangements that exist in some continental European countries.

A Recommending Commission would make recommendations to a minister as to whom he or she should appoint (or recommend that the Queen appoints). The final decision on who to appoint would rest with the minister.

A Hybrid Commission would act as an Appointing Commission in relation to the more junior appointments and as a Recommending Commission for the more senior appointments.

Ultimately, the government favoured the creation of a Recommending Commission, but an Appointing Commission would have more effectively removed government interference in the judicial appointment process.

Wigs and gowns

Traditionally, judges have been required to wear a wig made of horse hair and a gown when sitting in court. The government became concerned that this tradition could make the judges appear old-fashioned to court users. Following a consultation process, it has been decided that judges hearing civil court cases are no longer required to wear a wig. Judges hearing criminal cases will continue to wear a wig. This is because the wig provides a degree of anonymity for judges so that they are less likely to be recognised by defendants or their associates outside court, and also an important element of dignity to the court proceedings.

Training

Although new judges have the benefit of many years' experience as barristers or solicitors, they have traditionally received a surprisingly small amount of training for their new role, limited until recently to a brief training period, organised by the Judicial Studies Board. In the last few years, this has been supplemented in several ways: the advent of the Children Act 1989 has meant that social workers, psychiatrists and paediatricians have shared their expertise with new judges, while concern about the perception of judges as racist, or at best racially unaware, has led to the introduction of training on race issues. The reforms to the civil justice system and the passing of the Human Rights Act 1998 have led to the provision of special training to prepare for these legal reforms.

Pay

Judges are paid large salaries – £162,000 at High Court level – which are not subject to an annual vote in Parliament. The official justification for this is the need to attract an adequate supply of candidates of sufficient calibre for appointment to judicial office, and in fact some top barristers can earn more by staying in practice. One of the attractions for a barrister of becoming a judge is the security of a pensionable position after years of self-employment.

Table 13.2 **Judicial salaries**

Judge	Pay
Lord of Appeal in Ordinary (Law Lord)	£194,000
Lord Chief Justice	£225,000
Master of the Rolls	£200,800
Lord Justice of Appeal	£184,000
High Court judge	£162,000
Circuit judge	£120,300
District judge	£96,300
District judge (magistrates' court)	£96,300

Task 13.2

Read the following newspaper article and answer the questions below.

Wigs in court – it's time for this horseplay to stop

There are more important issues about the future of the legal system than whether lawyers and judges should continue to wear wigs and gowns. But the Lord Chancellor issued a consultation paper inviting us all to express our views. The legal bigwigs should be told by as many people as possible that fancy dress for lawyers is a nonsense that should have been mothballed long ago.

There is no positive case for retaining legal costume. As the consultation paper observes, tradition is no justification since 'our courts are not a tourist attraction'. The suggestion that the wearing of wigs and gowns symbolises the authority of office holders, instills respect for the law, and emphasises the impersonal and disinterested approach of the judge is impossible to sustain.

We are mature enough to understand that legal authority depends on the quality of the justice on offer, not on whether the judge and the lawyers have some horse hair on their head and a piece of cloth on their back. Indeed, it would be a sad reflection on the quality of the legal profession if its ability to command respect really did depend on its clothing.

Many courts of law perform their functions very satisfactorily without imposing a dress code. Neither the magistrates' courts nor employment tribunals require judges and lawyers to dress up for the occasion. The law lords sitting in the highest court of the land wear ordinary business suits. Without any noticeable effect on the quality of the product, judges of the High Court frequently make orders unrobed, indeed occasionally undressed (vice-chancellor Sadwell is said to have granted an injunction during the 1840s while bathing in the Thames).

Those judges and lawyers who argue that the wig and gown provide a welcome measure of anonymity which protects them from the antipathy of defendants and witnesses who may meet them out of court have no right to impose their lack of self-confidence on the rest of us. Anyone who insists on maintaining a disguise is free to wear fake spectacles, a false nose and an imitation moustache during court proceedings.

It is not simply that legal dress has no justification. It is positively damaging to the health of the legal system. The legal profession cannot convince its customers that it understands contemporary concerns and can provide a service for today's community when it looks as if it is still living in the eighteenth century.

Legal workers of the world unite. We have nothing to lose but our manes.

(Adapted from an article by David Pannick, published in *The Times* on 27 May 2003.)

Questions

1 Does the author of this article favour the wearing of wigs and gowns in court?
2 What are judges' wigs made out of?
3 Do the Law Lords wear wigs and gowns in the House of Lords?
4 Do you think judges should wear wigs and gowns in court?

Termination of appointment

There are five ways in which a judge may leave office:

Dismissal

Judges of the High Court and above are covered by the Act of Settlement 1700, which provides that they may only be removed from office by the Queen on the petition of both Houses of Parliament. The machinery for dismissal has been used successfully only once and no judge has been removed by petition of Parliament during the twentieth and twenty-first centuries.

Under the Courts Act 1971, circuit judges and district judges can be dismissed by the Lord Chancellor, if the Lord Chief Justice agrees, for 'inability or misbehaviour'. In fact, this has occurred only once since the passing of the Act: Judge Bruce Campbell (a circuit judge) was sacked in 1983 after being convicted of smuggling spirits, cigarettes and tobacco into England in his yacht. 'Misbehaviour' can include a conviction for drink-driving or any offence involving violence, dishonesty or moral turpitude. It would also include any behaviour likely to cause offence, particularly on religious or racial grounds or behaviour that amounted to sexual harassment.

In dismissing a judge, s. 108(1) of the Constitutional Reform Act 2005 provides that the Lord Chancellor will have to comply with any procedures that have been laid down to regulate this process.

In addition to dismissal there is, of course, also the power not to re-appoint those who have been appointed for a limited period only.

Discipline

In practice the mechanisms for disciplining judges who misbehave are more significant than those for dismissal, which is generally a last resort. There was concern in the past that there were no formal disciplinary procedures for judges. Over the years there had been a few judges whose conduct had been frequently criticised, but who had nevertheless remained on the Bench, and the lack of a formal machinery for complaints was seen as protecting incompetent judges. The pressure group Justice had recommended the establishment of a formal disciplinary procedure in its report on the judiciary in 1972. The Constitutional Reform Act 2005 contains provision for the establishment of such procedures. The Act gives the Lord Chancellor and the Lord Chief Justice joint responsibility for judicial discipline. Section 108(3) states:

> 'The Lord Chief Justice may give a judicial office holder formal advice, or a formal warning or reprimand, for disciplinary purposes (but this section does not restrict what he may do informally or for other purposes or where any advice or warning is not addressed to a particular office holder).'

A person can be suspended from judicial office for any period when they are subject to criminal proceedings, have been convicted, are serving a criminal sentence, are subject to disciplinary procedures or where it has been determined under prescribed procedures that a person should not be removed from office, but it appears to the Lord Chief Justice, with the agreement of the Lord Chancellor, that the suspension is necessary for maintaining public confidence in the judiciary. The Judicial Appointments and Conduct Ombudsman will consider complaints about disciplinary cases.

The Judicial Appointments and Conduct Ombudsman will be able to review the handling of complaints about judicial conduct.

As well as the formal procedures discussed above, judges may be criticised in Parliament, or rebuked in the appellate courts, and are often censured in the press. There may be complaints from barristers, solicitors or litigants, made either in court or in private to the judge personally. 'Scurrilous abuse' of a judge may, however, be punished as contempt of court.

Resignation

Serious misbehaviour has on occasion been dealt with not by dismissal, but by the Lord Chancellor suggesting to the judge that he or she should resign.

Retirement

Judges usually retire at 70.

Removal due to infirmity

The Lord Chancellor has the power to remove judges who are disabled by permanent infirmity from the performance of their duties and who are incapacitated from resigning their post.

Independence of the judiciary

In our legal system great importance is attached to the idea that judges should be independent and be seen to be independent. In addition to the common sense view that they should be independent of pressure from the government and political groups, and in order to decide cases impartially, judicial independence is required by the constitutional doctrine known as the separation of powers. Under this doctrine, the power of the state has to be divided between three separate and independent arms: the judiciary (comprising the judges), the legislature (Parliament in the UK); and the executive (the government of the day). The idea is that the separate arms of the state should operate independently, so that each one is checked and balanced by the other two, and none becomes all powerful. The doctrine of the separation of powers was first put forward in the eighteenth century by the French political theorist Montesquieu. Montesquieu argued that if all the powers were concentrated in the hands of one group, the result would be tyranny. Therefore, the doctrine requires that individuals should not occupy a position in more than one of the three arms of the state – judiciary, legislature and executive; each should exercise its functions independently of any control or interference from the others; and one arm of the state should not exercise the functions of either of the others.

In the past, the broad role of the Lord Chancellor was seen as both a threat to judicial independence and as the protector of judicial independence. He was a threat because he breached the doctrine of the separation of powers, but at the same time as the head of the judiciary, he was responsible for defending judges from government influence. When the government announced in 2003 that it planned to introduce major constitutional changes, including the abolition of the position of Lord Chancellor, this caused some concern among the judges. They were worried that, without the Lord Chancellor, there would be nobody with responsibility for protecting their independence, and that as a result their independence could be threatened. In response to these concerns, the Lord Chancellor signed an agreement with the senior judge, the Lord Chief Justice, known as the Concordat. This agreement provided that some of the key judicial functions of the Lord Chancellor would be handed to the Lord Chief Justice when the constitutional reforms were introduced and that key aspects of this agreement would be incorporated into the legislation which was subsequently done. Following political negotiations, the post of Lord Chancellor was not actually abolished, though the role of the Lord Chancellor has significantly changed. With the changes in the role of the Lord Chancellor introduced by the Constitutional Reform Act 2005, the government sought to reassure judges that their independence would still be guaranteed, by introducing a statutory guarantee of the independence of the judiciary. Section 3 states:

> 'The Lord Chancellor, other Ministers of the Crown and all with responsibility for matters relating to the judiciary or otherwise to the administration of justice must uphold the continued independence of the judiciary.'

It also provides that:

> 'The Lord Chancellor and other Ministers for the Crown must not seek to influence a particular judicial decision through any special access to the judiciary.'

Other safeguards of judicial independence include the security of tenure given to judges, which ensures they cannot be removed at the whim of one of the other branches of power (see p. 243); the fact that they are well paid and their salaries are not subject to a parliamentary vote; and the rule that they cannot be sued for anything done while acting in their judicial capacity. Independence in decision-making is provided through the fact that judges are accountable only to higher judges in appellate courts.

The importance of the independence of the judiciary can be seen, for example, in judicial review, where the courts can scrutinise the behaviour of the executive, and in some cases declare it illegal. If the judges were not independent from the executive, the judges might always make decisions on judicial review that favoured the executive, rather than decisions that were fair and impartial.

 Quick quiz 13.3

1 In which court does the Lord Chief Justice sit?

2 What is the Judicial Appointments Commission?

3 Which body is responsible for providing judicial training?

4 What is the doctrine of the separation of powers?

Problems with judicial independence

While the Constitutional Reform Act 2005 has now given statutory recognition to the independence of the judiciary, there remain a number of threats to judicial independence:

Supremacy of Parliament

Apart from where European law is involved, it is never possible for the courts to question the validity of existing Acts of Parliament. In the UK all Acts of Parliament are treated by the courts as absolutely binding, until such time as any particular Act is repealed or altered by Parliament itself in another statute or by a minister under the special fast-track procedure provided for under the Human Rights Act 1998. The judiciary is therefore ultimately subordinate to the will of Parliament.

The House of Lords

Lords of Appeal in Ordinary are also members of more than one arm of the state, since they take part in the legislative business in the House of Lords. However, they tend not to get involved in political controversy or ally themselves with a particular party, confining their contributions to technical questions of a legal nature. The Royal Commission on the House of Lords recommended in 2000 that the basic conventions restricting the role of the Law Lords should be put down in writing. The government announced in 2003 that it intended to replace the House of Lords with a Supreme Court and the Constitutional Reform Act 2005 contains provisions for the creation of this new court (see p. 85).

Non-judicial work

sourcebook
p. 202 → Judges also get involved in non-judicial areas with political implications, for example, chairing inquiries into Bloody Sunday in Northern Ireland, the Brixton riots or the Zeebrugge ferry disaster. Thus, Sir William Macpherson headed the inquiry into the handling of the police investigation of the death of the black teenager Stephen Lawrence, who was murdered in South London. This function can often be seen to undermine the political neutrality of the judiciary. The Hutton Inquiry, following the war against Iraq and Dr David Kelly's death raised questions about the future role of judges in public inquiries. There was wide public dissatisfaction with the Hutton Report (2003), and a general unease as to how independent the judge and chair, Lord Hutton, had been. As a result the Lord Chief Justice, Lord Woolf, wrote a memo to the House of Commons Public Administration Select Committee expressing concern that Lord Hutton had been used as a political tool by the government.

Cases with political implications

Although judges generally refrain from airing their political views, they are sometimes forced to make decisions that have political ramifications. Concerns have been expressed that too often such decisions defend the interests of the government of the day, sometimes at the expense of individual liberties.

Certain cases have borne out this concern. In **McIlkenny** *v* **Chief Constable of the West Midlands** (1981), Lord Denning dismissed allegations of police brutality against the six men accused of the Birmingham pub bombings with the words:

> *'Just consider the course of events if this action were to go to trial . . . If the six men fail, it will mean that much time and money and worry will have been expended by many people for no good purpose. If the six men win, it will mean that the police were guilty of perjury, that they were guilty of violence and threats, that the confessions were involuntary and were improperly admitted in evidence: and that the convictions were erroneous. That would mean that the Home Secretary would have either to recommend they be pardoned or he would have to remit the case to the Court of Appeal under section 17 of the Criminal Appeal Act 1968. This is such an appalling vista that every sensible person in the land would say: it cannot be right that these actions should go any further. They should be struck out.'*

In other words, Lord Denning was saying, the allegations should not be addressed, because if proved true, the result would be to bring the legal system into disrepute.

The danger of political bias has been increased with the passing of the Human Rights Act 1998. While judges already decide some politically sensitive cases, their number is likely to increase, with litigation directly accusing government actions and legislation of breaching fundamental human rights. Over time the changing role of the judiciary is most likely to be visible in the House of Lords (or the Supreme Court when this is established in 2009 – see p. 85). These judges currently decide about 100 cases a year, which are usually on technical commercial and tax matters. With the implementation of the Human Rights Act 1998, the House of Lords has moved closer to the US Supreme Court, deciding fundamental issues on the rights of the individual against the state.

At the moment there appear to be the greatest tensions between the judges and the government with regard to the application of the terrorist legislation and the judges' approach to sentencing. In 2006, the Attorney-General published a list of more than 200 judges who have given 'unduly lenient' sentences to criminals. The list was drawn up by looking at successful appeals against lenient sentences made by the Attorney-General to the Court of Appeal. In response, a spokesperson from the Judicial Communications Office stated:

> *'Figures on successful appeals against a judge's sentencing can only begin to have relevance if they are set against the total number of sentencing decisions made by the judge in question, and those where there has been no appeal or an appeal has been rejected. It should also be borne in mind that some judges have caseloads involving more complex and serious cases, so they might be more likely to feature in appeal cases. In any event, there are many cases where the Court of Appeal reduces sentences without implying any criticism of the sentencing judges, sometimes indeed because of changes of circumstances – such as new evidence – after the original sentencing decision.'*

At the same time, the then Constitutional Affairs Minister, Vera Baird, criticised the judiciary during an appearance on BBC Radio 4's *Any Questions* programmes. Baird attacked a trial judge for giving a convicted paedophile, Craig Sweeney, a sentence which potentially allowed him to be released after six years' imprisonment. The Lord Chancellor came to the defence of the trial judge and pointed out that he had simply applied the relevant sentencing guidelines to the case. Vera Baird subsequently apologised, in a letter to the Lord Chancellor, for her remarks.

The pressure group, Justice, has issued a *Manifesto for the rule of law*. This document seeks to remind politicians that there is a constitutional convention that the government should refrain from criticising the judiciary in any manner that would diminish public confidence. This convention was repeatedly breached by the former Home Secretaries John Reid and David Blunkett. Under their own rules of professional conduct, judges are not usually allowed to publicly respond to criticisms, so such remarks do not lead to a constructive debate. In addition, it is in everyone's interests that the judges who enforce the law are respected in society.

??? Quick quiz 13.4

1 What are the five ways in which a judge may leave office?

2 Who developed the doctrine of the separation of powers?

3 What is the average age of the Law Lords?

4 Can judges question the validity of an Act of Parliament?

Right-wing bias

In addition to its alleged readiness to support the government of the day, the judiciary has been accused of being particularly biased towards the interests traditionally represented by the right wing of the political spectrum. In his influential book, *The Politics of the Judiciary* (1997), Griffith states that: 'in every major social issue which has come before the courts in the last thirty years – concerning industrial relations, political protest, race relations, government secrecy, police powers, moral behaviour – the judges have supported the conventional, settled and established interests'.

Among the cases he cites in support of this theory is **Bromley London Borough Council *v* Greater London Council** (1983). In this case the Labour-run GLC had won an election on a promise to cut bus and tube fares by 25 per cent. The move necessitated an increase in the rates levied on the London boroughs, and one of those boroughs, Conservative-controlled Bromley, challenged the GLC's right to do this. The challenge failed in the High Court, but succeeded on appeal. The Court of Appeal judges condemned the fare reduction as 'a crude abuse of power', and quashed the supplementary rate that the GLC had levied on the London boroughs to pay for it. The House of Lords agreed, the Law Lords holding unanimously that the GLC was bound by a statute requiring it to 'promote the provision of integrated, efficient and economic transport facilities and services in Greater London', which they interpreted to mean that the bus and tube system must be run according to 'ordinary business principles' of cost-effectiveness. The decision represented a political defeat for the Labour leaders of the GLC and a victory for the Conservative councillors of Bromley.

Bias against women

In her book, *Eve was Framed* (1992), Helena Kennedy argues that the attitude of many judges to women is outdated, and sometimes prejudiced. Kennedy alleges that women are judged according to how well they fit traditional female stereotypes. Because crime is seen as stepping outside the feminine role, women are more severely punished than men, and women who do not fit traditional stereotypes are treated most harshly.

The Judicial Studies Board, responsible for the training of judges, has issued judges with the *Equal Treatment Bench Book*. This advises judges on equal treatment of people in court and the appropriate use of language to avoid causing offence by, for example, being sexist.

Influence of Freemasonry

Freemasonry is a form of secret society, which does not allow women to join. Among its stated aims is the mutual self-advancement of its members. There has long been concern about the extent of membership among the police, as well as the judiciary, on the basis that loyalty to other Masons – who might be parties in a case, or colleagues seeking promotion or other favours – could have a corrupting influence.

In an attempt to introduce greater transparency, a questionnaire was sent in 1998 to all members of the judiciary asking them to declare their 'Masonic status'. Five per cent of those who responded admitted to being Freemasons.

 Know your terms 13.5

Define the following terms:
1 Executive.
2 Freemasonry.
3 Law Society.
4 Stereotype.

Criticisms of the judiciary

Background, ethnic origin, sex and age

Judges are overwhelmingly white, male and middle- to upper-class, and frequently elderly, leading to accusations that they are unrepresentative of, and distanced from, the majority of society. In 1995, 80 per cent of Lords of Appeal, Heads of Division, Lord Justices of Appeal and High Court judges were educated at Oxford or Cambridge. Eighty per cent of judges appointed since 1997 were educated at a public school. The narrow background of the judges does mean that they can be frighteningly out of touch with the world in which they are working. One judge, who resigned in 1998, said in three different cases that he had not heard of the footballer Paul Gascoigne, the rock band Oasis and the singer Bruce Springsteen.

In 2004 only 16 per cent of judges were women and only 9 per cent of senior judges were women. There are still no women sitting as judges in the European Court of Justice. The first female judge, Lady Justice Hale, was appointed to the House of Lords in 2004. There are only two female judges in the Court of Appeal and ten female High Court judges. In 2006, the Equal Opportunities Commission warned that at the current rate, it will take 40 years for women to achieve equality in the senior judiciary. Just 3 per cent of court judges in 2004 came from an ethnic minority, with one member of the Court of Appeal coming from an ethnic

sourcebook p. 72 →

minority and one High Court judge. By comparison, 8 per cent of the population of England and Wales come from an ethnic minority. Lord Lane, the former Lord Chief Justice, said after his retirement that his regret at being forced off the bench was due, at least partly, to the fact that his colleagues were 'a jolly nice bunch of chaps'. This remark reinforces the view of many that the judiciary is actually a sort of rarefied gentlemen's club.

The age of the full-time judiciary has remained constant over many years with the average age of a judge being 58. With a retirement age of 70, judges are allowed to retire five years later than most other professions. David Pannick has written in his book, *Judges*, that 'a judiciary composed predominantly of senior citizens cannot hope to apply contemporary standards or to understand contemporary concerns'.

Before the Courts and Legal Services Act 1990, judges were almost exclusively selected from practising barristers. Since it is difficult for anyone without a private income to survive the first years of practice, successful barristers have tended to come from reasonably well-to-do families, who are, of course, more likely to send their sons or daughters to public schools and then to Oxford or Cambridge. Although the background of the Bar is gradually changing, the age at which judges are appointed means that it will be some years before this is reflected in the ranks of the judiciary.

The new opportunities provided for solicitors to join the judiciary, provided by the Courts and Legal Services Act 1990 and the new right of government lawyers to become junior judges may in time help to alter the traditional judicial background, since there are larger numbers of women, members of the ethnic minorities and those from less privileged backgrounds working as solicitors and government lawyers than in the barrister profession. Since April 2005, judges below High Court level are able to sit part-time, which may prove attractive to women combining work with childcare responsibilities.

sourcebook
p. 81 → Section 64 of the Constitutional Reform Act 2005 provides that the Judicial Appointments Commission 'must have regard to the need to encourage diversity in the range of persons available for selection for appointments'. The Lord Chancellor can issue guidance for the Commission in order to encourage a range of persons to be available for selection (s. 65). The Government issued a consultation paper, *Increasing Diversity in the Judiciary* (2004). At the launch of this paper, the Government Minister stated:

> 'It is a matter of great concern that the judiciary in England and Wales – while held in high regard for its ability, independence and probity, is not representative of the diverse society it serves. A more diverse judiciary is essential if the public's confidence in its judges is to be maintained and strengthened.
>
> We need to find out why people from diverse backgrounds and with disabilities are not applying for judicial appointment in the numbers we might expect and, once we have identified the barriers, we need to do something about removing them. Judicial appointments will continue to be made on merit. But I do not believe that there is any conflict between merit and diversity.'

sourcebook
p. 84 → A diversity strategy was launched by the Lord Chancellor in 2006 which aims to increase the number of women and black and ethnic minority judges. The strategy

seeks to achieve this by promoting fair and open selection processes based solely on merit and by ensuring that the culture and working environment for judicial office-holders encourages and supports a diverse judiciary. The Lord Chancellor is considering introducing flexible working hours for judges, career breaks, a work-shadowing programme and changes to age limits in order to try to attract a more diverse range of people to a judicial career. Part 2 of the Tribunals, Courts and Enforcement Act 2005 aims to widen the pool of lawyers eligible to become judges (see p. 238).

Training

Considering the importance of their work, judges receive very little training, even with recent changes. They may be experienced as lawyers, but the skills needed by a good lawyer are not identical to those required by a good judge.

Reading on the web

The website of the Judicial Appointments Commission is at:

www.judicialappointments.gov.uk/index.htm

The consultation paper, *Constitutional Reform: A New Way of Appointing Judges*, is available on the website for the former Department for Constitutional Affairs at:

www.dca.gov.uk/consult/jacommission/index.htm

The consultation paper, *Court Working Dress in England and Wales*, is available on the website for the former Department for Constitutional Affairs at:

www.dca.gov.uk/consult/courtdress

Sir Leonard Peach's report into judicial appointments is available on the website of the old Department for Constitutional Affairs:

www.dca.gov.uk/judicial/peach/indexfr.htm

General information on the judiciary is available on:

www.judiciary.gov.uk

The website of the Judicial Studies Board can be found at:

www.jsboard.co.uk

The booklet, *Judicial Appointments in England and Wales: policies and procedure*, is available on the former Department for Constitutional Affairs' website at:

www.dca.gov.uk/judicial/appointments/jappinfr.htm

Chapter summary

The role of the judges

The judges play a central role under the British Constitution, providing a vital but sensitive control over the exercise of power by the state.

Judicial hierarchy

At the head of the judiciary is the President of the Courts of England and Wales. The most senior judges are the 12 Lords of Appeal in Ordinary. They currently sit in the House of Lords and the Privy Council. At the next level down, sitting in the Court of Appeal, are 37 judges known as Lord Justices of Appeal and Lady Justices of Appeal.

Appointing the judges

The way in which judges are appointed has been radically reformed by provisions in the Constitutional Reform Act 2005. The Act contains provisions for the establishment of a new Judicial Appointments Commission. It is hoped that the creation of this body will help to put an end to the breaches of the principle of the separation of powers and reinforce judicial independence. Depending on their rank, judges are appointed by the Queen on the advice of the Prime Minister or by the Lord Chancellor.

Training

Training is provided by the Judicial Studies Board.

Termination of appointment

There are five ways in which a judge may leave office:

- dismissal;
- discipline;
- resignation;
- retirement; or
- removal due to infirmity.

Independence of the judiciary

In our legal system, great importance is attached to the idea that judges should be independent and be seen to be independent. Section 3 of the Constitutional Reform Act 2005 states:

> 'The Lord Chancellor, other Ministers of the Crown and all with responsibility for matters relating to the judiciary or otherwise to the administration of justice must uphold the continued independence of the judiciary.'

There are real concerns that the independence of the judiciary is not sufficiently protected. The academic, Griffith, has accused judges of being biased towards the interests traditionally represented by the right wing of the political spectrum. The lawyer, Baroness Kennedy, has argued that the attitude of many judges to women is outdated and sometimes prejudiced. There is also concern that some judges are members of the Freemasons.

Criticisms of the judiciary

Judges are overwhelmingly white, male and middle- to upper-class, and frequently elderly, leading to accusations that they are unrepresentative of the society they serve. The appointments process has been criticised for being dominated by politicians, secretive and discriminatory. Judges receive very little training.

Question and answer guides

1

(a) Naseem has been injured in a road accident. Briefly explain the role of the judge in Naseem's civil court claim for damages. (*10 marks*)

(b) Explain what is meant by the principle of judicial independence. (*10 marks*)

(c) Discuss the importance of the principle of judicial independence. (*10 marks*)

(from AQA Specimen Question Paper, 2007)

(a) From the moment the defence is filed it is the duty of the judge in a case such as Naseem's to proactively manage the litigation so as to bring it to trial quickly and efficiently. This role includes encouraging the parties to use an alternative dispute resolution procedure, if the judge considers that appropriate.

Assuming ADR is not used, or is unsuccessful, the judge will issue directions for the management of the case going forward. Depending on the track to which Naseem's claim is assigned, these directions may cover such matters as the date for the hearing, an estimate of the hearing time, the disclosure of documents and the exchange of witness statements.

Assuming that Naseem's case proceeds to trial, the judge will sit alone, hearing the evidence and any legal arguments. He or she will then prepare and deliver the judgment, containing the findings of fact and law. If the judge finds in favour of Naseem he or she will also decide what her damages should be.

Any appeal against the trial judge's decision will be heard by more senior judges. Appeals can normally only be on points of law, so the appeal judges will not need to rehear the evidence.

(*Note that most of the material needed to answer part (a) will be found in Chapter 21 of this book.*)

(b) The principle of judicial independence states that judges should be, and should be seen to be, independent from the government and political groups. In the English legal system there are many examples of the principle in operation.

First, there is the process for selecting and promoting judges. Under the Constitutional Reform Act 2005, this is now the responsibility of an independent

Judicial Appointments Commission (JAC), with the Lord Chancellor (a government minister) having only limited powers to reject the JAC's nominees.

Another example of judicial independence at work are the rules giving judges security of tenure, ensuring that they cannot be removed at the whim of the executive or the legislature. High Court judges and above are covered by the Act of Settlement 1700, which provides that they may only be removed from office by the Queen on the petition of both Houses of Parliament. Circuit and district judges can be dismissed by the Lord Chancellor, but only for 'inability or misbehaviour', and then only if the Lord Chief Justice agrees.

Other examples of judicial independence are the rule that judges cannot be sued for anything done while acting in their judicial capacity, their salaries are not subject to a parliamentary vote and they are only accountable to higher judges in appellate courts.

(c) The principle of judicial independence is important because it protects judges' impartiality, enabling them to decide cases solely on the basis of the facts before them and the applicable law. This in turn helps maintain public confidence in the judiciary, without which people would be unwilling to refer their disputes to the courts and would rely on self-help instead.

Judicial independence also helps maintain the constitutional doctrine of the separation of powers, which states that the three arms of the state – the judiciary, the legislature and the executive – should operate independently, with each controlling and balancing the others, and none becoming too powerful. Without the maintenance of this doctrine, argued Montesquieu (see p. 243), its originator, a tyranny would emerge.

Judicial independence also helps maintain the principle of the rule of law whereby the rights of individuals are determined by legal rules and not by the arbitrary behaviour of government. This in turn protects individual freedoms.

The practical importance of judicial independence can be seen most clearly in judicial review proceedings, where the courts are called upon to scrutinise the behaviour of the executive, and in some cases declare it illegal. If the judges were not independent from the executive they might always make decisions on judicial review that favoured the executive, rather than decisions that were fair and impartial.

2

(a) Describe how judges can be appointed and dismissed. (*15 marks*)
(b) Outline the role carried out by judges and discuss how well they carry out this role. (*15 marks*)

(from AQA Exam Paper, January 2003)

(a)
Appointment

- Explain the role of the Judicial Appointments Commission (JAC), and its selection criteria.
- Explain how JAC advertises for, evaluates and recommends candidates, one per vacancy.

- Explain the minister's limited power to reject JAC's recommendations.
- For a good answer, refer to the special procedures for appointment of judges to the new Supreme Court.

Dismissal

- Explain the position of judges of the High Court and above under the Act of Settlement 1700.
- Explain the position of circuit and district judges under the Courts Act 1971.
- Explain how a dismissal must comply with any procedures that have been laid down to regulate this process under the Constitutional Reform Act 2005.

(b)
Role

- Describe judges' pre-trial role, emphasising their case management responsibilities, especially in civil cases.
- Describe judges' trial role, distinguishing between cases where they sit alone and where they sit with a jury, and between civil and criminal cases.
- Describe judges' appellate role.
- Describe judges' other roles, e.g. conducting inquiries.

Evaluation

- Refer to the high regard in which UK judges are generally held, especially in upholding the rule of law.
- Refer to miscarriages of justice and whether judges are to blame.
- Refer to allegations of judges' right-wing and anti-women bias.
- Show an understanding of the difficulties judges face as the Human Rights Act 1998 increasingly draws them into politically sensitive matters.

Common errors in (a)

- failing to differentiate accurately between the JAC's and minister's roles;
- writing insufficient on dismissal.

Common errors in (b)

- writing only about the judges' trial role;
- providing insufficient evaluation of the judges' performance.

Group activity 1

- Divide your friends (or class) into groups of two or three people.
- In your groups, visit the 'Learning Resources' pages of the website of the Judicial Communications Office – www.judiciary.gov.uk/learning_resources – and familiarise yourself with their contents.
- Note that the first of these pages contains the following statement: 'We are seeking your feedback to help us develop our Learning Resources pages. Please email us with any comments or suggestions.'
- In your groups, prepare a draft email to the JCO containing your comments and suggestions on the Learning Resources pages.

■ Compare notes with the other groups and agree a final email for sending to the JCO.

Group activity 2

The system for appointing judges has become more formalised and 'secret soundings' for judicial appointments are a thing of the past. Visit the website of the Judicial Appointments Commission:

www.judicialappointments.gov.uk

Which judicial appointments are they advertising at the moment? How will they select the successful candidate? Which (if any) job would you be interested in applying for and why?

---

mylawchamber

Visit **www.mylawchamber.co.uk/elliottaqa** to access interactive questions, quizzes and activities to test yourself on this chapter.

Unit 2

THE CONCEPT OF LIABILITY

Section A
INTRODUCTION TO CRIMINAL LIABILITY

Criminal liability is imposed on conduct felt to be against the general interests of society. The crime is punished by the state (represented by the Crown for these purposes) and the primary aim is to punish the wrongdoer. This section explores the basic requirements of *actus reus* and *mens rea* in order for criminal liability to be imposed and introduces the exception of strict liability offences. It then applies these concepts of *actus reus* and *mens rea* to the non-fatal offences against the person. The formal procedures to trial are examined and the sentences available for people convicted of criminal offences explored. Thus, this section looks at:

- elements of a crime: *actus reus*;
- elements of a crime: *mens rea*;
- non-fatal offences against the person;
- strict liability in criminal law;
- criminal procedure and
- sentencing.

Part 9
UNDERLYING PRINCIPLES OF CRIMINAL LIABILITY

Chapter 14

Elements of a crime: *actus reus*

This chapter discusses:

- the guilty act that constitutes the *actus reus* of an offence;
- proving that the defendant caused the criminal harm;
- the imposition of criminal liability for failing to act, known as an omission.

Introduction

A person cannot usually be found guilty of a criminal offence unless two elements are present: an *actus reus*, Latin for 'guilty act'; and *mens rea*, Latin for 'guilty mind'. Both these terms actually refer to more than just moral guilt, and each has a very specific meaning, which varies according to the crime, but the important thing to remember is that to be guilty of an offence, an accused not only must have behaved in a particular way, but also must usually have had a particular mental attitude to that behaviour. The exception to this rule is a small group of offences known as crimes of strict liability, which are discussed in the next chapter.

The definition of a particular crime, either in statute or under common law, will contain the required *actus reus* and *mens rea* for the offence.

Actus reus

An *actus reus* can consist of more than just an act, it comprises all the elements of the offence other than the state of mind of the defendant. Depending on the offence, this may include the circumstances in which it was committed, and/or the consequences of what was done. For example, the crime of rape requires unlawful sexual intercourse by a man with a person without their consent. The lack of consent is a surrounding circumstance which exists independently of the accused's act.

Similarly, the same act may be part of the *actus reus* of different crimes, depending on its consequences. Stabbing someone, for example, may form the *actus reus* of murder if the victim dies, or of causing grievous bodily harm (GBH) if the victim survives; the accused's behaviour is the same in both cases, but the consequences of it dictate whether the *actus reus* of murder or GBH has been committed.

Conduct must be voluntary

If the accused is to be found guilty of a crime, his or her behaviour in committing the *actus reus* must have been voluntary. Behaviour will usually only be considered involuntary where the accused was not in control of his or her own body (when the defence of insanity or automatism may be available) or where there is extremely strong pressure from someone else, such as a threat that the accused will be killed if he or she does not commit a particular offence (when the defence of duress may be available).

In the much criticised decision of **R v Larsonneur** (1933), a Frenchwoman was arrested as an illegal immigrant by the authorities in Ireland, and brought back to the UK in custody where she was charged with being an alien illegally in the UK and convicted. This is not what most of us would describe as acting voluntarily, but it apparently fitted the courts' definition at the time. It is probably stricter than a decision would be today, but it is important to realise that the courts do define 'involuntary' quite narrowly on occasion.

Types of *actus reus*

Crimes can be divided into three types, depending on the nature of their *actus reus*.

Action crimes

The *actus reus* here is simply an act, the consequences of that act being immaterial. For example, perjury is committed whenever someone makes a statement which he/she does not believe to be true, while on oath. Whether or not that statement makes a difference to the trial is not important to whether the offence of perjury has been committed.

State of affairs crimes

Here the *actus reus* consists of circumstances, and sometimes consequences, but no acts – they are 'being' rather than 'doing' offences. The offence committed in **R v Larsonneur** is an example of this, where the *actus reus* consisted of being a foreigner who had not been given permission to come to Britain and was found in the country.

Result crimes

The *actus reus* of these is distinguished by the fact that the accused's behaviour must produce a particular result – the most obvious being murder, where the accused's act must cause the death of a human being.

Result crimes raise the issue of causation: the result must be proved to have been caused by the defendant's act. If the result is caused by an intervening act or event, which was completely unconnected with the defendant's act and which could not have been foreseen, the defendant will not be liable. Where the result is caused by a combination of the defendant's act and the intervening act, and the defendant's act remains a substantial cause, then he or she will still be liable.

Causation

With result crimes, the prosecution must prove that the defendant caused the result of the offence. In many cases this will be obvious: for example, where the defendant shoots or stabs someone, and the victim dies immediately of the wounds. Difficulties may arise where there is more than one cause of the result. This might be the act or omission of a third party which occurs after the defendant's act, and before the result constituting the offence, or some characteristic of the victim which means that the victim suffers a result which a fitter person would not have suffered.

In **R v D** (2006) the Crown Prosecution Service brought a test prosecution for manslaughter following the suicide of a woman after a lengthy period of domestic abuse. Mrs D committed suicide by hanging herself. On the evening of the suicide, her husband had struck her on the forehead, causing a cut from the bracelet he was wearing. He was subsequently prosecuted for manslaughter and inflicting grievous bodily harm under s. 20 of the Offences Against the Person Act 1861. In the Crown Court, the trial judge had ruled that the case should not proceed to trial as there was no basis on which a reasonable jury could convict the defendant of either offence. The Crown Prosecution Service appealed unsuccessfully against this ruling.

Under the traditional principles of causation, the free voluntary conduct of the victim breaks the chain of causation. This general principle was confirmed by the House of Lords in **R v Kennedy (No. 2)** (2007). The respected criminal law academic, Glanville Williams, has written in his *Textbook of Criminal Law* (1983):

> '*Underlying this rule [that the victim's voluntary conduct breaks the chain of causation] is, undoubtedly, a philosophical attitude. Moralists and lawyers regard the individual's will as the autonomous prime cause of his behaviour. What a person does (if he reaches adult years, is of sound mind and is not acting under mistake, intimidation or similar pressure) is his own responsibility, and is not regarded as having been caused by other people. An intervening act of this kind, therefore, breaks the causal connection that would otherwise have been perceived between previous acts and the forbidden consequences.*'

Despite this general rule, the trial judge suggested that, where a 'decision to commit suicide has been triggered by a physical assault which represents the culmination of a course of abusive conduct', it would be possible for the Crown 'to argue that that final assault played a significant part in causing the victim's death'. The prosecution, however, chose not to pursue this argument. The House of Lords judgment in **R v Kennedy (No. 2)** (2007) places considerable emphasis on personal autonomy and the assumption that intervening voluntary conduct of an informed adult will break the chain of causation.

In reality, there is a clear causal connection between domestic abuse and female suicides. Research carried out by Stark and Flitcraft, *Killing the beast within: Woman battering and female suicidality* (1995), concluded that domestic abuse could be the single most important cause of women committing suicide. It has been calculated that each year 188 suicides by women in the UK can be linked to domestic abuse: Sylvia Walby, *The Cost of Domestic Violence* (2004). This social reality should not be ignored by the criminal law.

Much of the case law in this field has been concerned with the offence of murder, where it must be shown that the offender caused the death of the victim, but the cases are equally relevant to any other result offence, including non-fatal offences against the person.

Defendants can only be held responsible for results where their acts are both a 'factual' and a 'legal' cause of the result constituting the offence.

Factual causation

In order to establish factual causation, the prosecution must prove two things:

- That *but for* the conduct of the accused, the result of the offence would not have occurred as and when it did. Thus, a defendant will not be liable for a death if the victim would have died at the same time regardless of the defendant's act (or omission). In **R v White** (1910), the defendant gave his mother poison but, before it had a chance to take effect, she died of a heart attack which was not caused by the poison. He was not liable for her death.
- That the original injury arising from the defendant's conduct was *more than a minimal cause* of the result constituting the offence. This is known as the *de minimis* rule. So, for example, pricking the thumb of a woman who was bleeding to death would hasten her death, but not enough to be the real cause of it.

Legal causation

Even if factual causation is established, the judge must direct the jury as to whether the defendant's acts are sufficient to amount in law to a cause of the result of the offence. Legal causation can be proved in any one of the following three ways or by a combination of them.

1. The original injury was an operative and significant cause of the result

Under this criterion the prosecution must show that at the time of the result of the offence occurring, the original harm caused by the defendant was still an 'operative and substantial' cause of the result. In **R v Smith** (1959), a soldier was stabbed in a barrack-room brawl. He was dropped twice as he was being taken to the medical officer, and then there was a long delay before he was seen by a doctor, as the doctor mistakenly thought that his case was not urgent. When he did eventually receive treatment, it was inappropriate for the injuries he was suffering from and harmful. Nonetheless, the court took the view that these intervening factors had not broken the chain of causation so that the original wound was still an operative cause and the accused was liable for murder.

The same principle was followed in **R v Malcherek and Steel** (1981). The victims of two separate attacks had been kept on life-support machines; these were switched off when tests showed that they were brain-dead. The two defendants argued that when the hospital switched off the machines the chain of causation was broken, thereby relieving the defendants of liability for murder. The court rejected this argument on the ground that the original injuries were still an operative cause of their victims' deaths.

In **R v Cheshire** (1991), a dispute developed in a fish and chip shop, ending with the defendant shooting his victim in the leg and stomach, and seriously wounding him. The victim was taken to hospital, where his injuries were operated on, and he was placed in intensive care. As a result of negligent treatment by the medical staff, he developed complications affecting his breathing, and eventually died. His leg and stomach wounds were no longer life-threatening at the time of his death. The court stated that the critical question for the jury to answer was: 'Has the Crown proved death?' Negligent medical treatment could only break the chain of causation if it was so independent of the accused's acts, and such a powerful cause of death in itself, that the contribution made by the defendant's conduct was insignificant. This means that medical treatment can only break the chain of causation in the most extraordinary cases; incompetent or even grossly abnormal treatment will not suffice if the original injury is still an operative cause of death.

An example of such an extraordinary case might be **R v Jordan** (1956). The defendant was convicted of murder after stabbing the victim, but the conviction was quashed by the Court of Appeal when it heard new evidence that, at the time of the death, the original wound had almost healed, and the victim's death was brought on by the hospital giving him a drug to which he was known to be allergic – treatment that was described as 'palpably wrong'. It was held that the wound was no longer an operative cause of death. **Jordan** was described in the later case of **R v Smith** as a very particular case dependent upon its exact facts, and in **Malcherek** as an exceptional case, and is therefore unlikely to be used as a precedent. It seems that the law still requires very extraordinary circumstances for medical treatment to break the chain of causation.

It was pointed out in **R v Mellor** (1996) that the burden of proof is on the prosecution, so the defence do not have to prove that there was, for example, medical negligence in order to avoid liability. In that case the accused attacked a 71-year-old man, breaking his ribs and facial bones. The victim died two weeks later of broncho-pneumonia, which would probably not have been fatal if, on the day of his death, he had been given oxygen. This failure may have constituted medical negligence. Certain passages in the judge's summing-up implied that there was a burden on the defence to prove medical negligence. He cited with approval the vital question on causation laid down in **Cheshire**, and it was accepted that the jury had been misdirected. Nevertheless, the conviction was upheld, as the evidence against the appellant was overwhelming so that a correctly directed jury would have convicted.

2. The intervening act was reasonably foreseeable

An intervening act which is reasonably foreseeable will not break the chain of legal causation. For example, if the defendant knocks the victim unconscious, and leaves him or her lying on a beach, it is reasonably foreseeable that, when the tide comes in, the victim will drown, and the defendant will have caused that death. However, the defendant would not be liable for homicide if the victim was left unconscious on the seashore and run over by a car careering out of control off a nearby road as this could not have been foreseen. In **R v Pagett** (1983), the defendant was attempting to escape being captured by armed police, and used his girlfriend as a human shield. He shot at the police, and his girlfriend was killed by shots fired at him in self-defence by the policemen. The defendant was found liable for the girl's death, as it was reasonably foreseeable that the police would shoot back and hit her in response to his shots. This is despite the fact that the police appear to have been negligent, as the mother of the girl subsequently succeeded in a claim for negligence in respect of the police operation in which her daughter was killed.

In cases involving medical treatment, only grossly abnormal treatment will be treated as not reasonably foreseeable, according to **Cheshire**. Treatment falling within the 'normal' band of incompetence will be regarded as foreseeable.

A defendant will avoid liability if a victim responds to their conduct in a way that is so daft that it could not have been foreseen. This issue arose in **R v Corbett** (1996) when a mentally disabled man had been drinking heavily with the defendant all day. An argument ensued and the defendant started to hit and head-butt the victim, who ran way. The victim fell into a gutter and was struck and killed by a car. At Corbett's trial for manslaughter the judge directed that he was the cause of the victim's death if the victim's conduct of running away was within the range of foreseeable responses to the defendant's behaviour. An appeal against this direction was rejected.

In **R v Dear** (1996) the Court of Appeal suggested that if the defendant's conduct was still an operative and significant cause of the death, the defendant would in law be the cause of that death, regardless of whether or not any intervening factors were foreseeable. The accused's daughter told him that she had been sexually assaulted. On hearing this allegation the accused stabbed the alleged abuser repeatedly with a knife. The victim died two days later. On appeal against his conviction for murder the appellant argued that he was not the cause of the death. He contended that the deceased had committed suicide either by reopening his wounds or, the wounds having reopened themselves, by failing to seek medical attention and the suicide broke the chain of causation. The appeal was dismissed as the injuries inflicted on the deceased were an operative and significant cause of the death. In such a case as this it was not necessary to consider the degree of fault in the victim or to consider how foreseeable the victim's conduct was. This approach has been criticised on the basis that it ignores previous authorities which state that the chain of causation is broken if the victim's conduct was so daft that it could not have been foreseen. It may be that this case will be distinguished from those authorities on the basis that the operative and substantive test had been satisfied on the facts of the case, and not in the earlier authorities; or it may be that **R v Dear** will not be followed.

3. The 'thin skull' test

Where the intervening cause is some existing weakness of the victim, the defendant must take the victim as he or she finds him. Known as the 'thin skull' rule, this means that if, for example, a defendant hits a person over the head with the kind of blow which would not usually kill, but the victim has an unusually thin skull which makes the blow fatal, the defendant will be liable for the subsequent death. The principle has been extended to mental conditions and beliefs, as well as physical characteristics. In **R v Blaue** (1975), the victim of a stabbing was a Jehovah's Witness, a church which, among other things, forbids its members to have blood transfusions. As a result of her refusal to accept a transfusion, the victim died of her wounds. The Court of Appeal rejected the defendant's argument

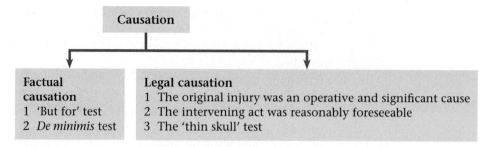

Figure 14.1 **Factual and legal causation compared**

that her refusal broke the chain of causation, on the ground that the accused had to take his victim as he found her.

Omissions

Criminal liability is rarely imposed for true omissions at common law, though there are situations where a non-lawyer would consider that there had been an omission but in law it will be treated as an act and liability will be imposed. There are also situations where the accused has a duty to act, and in these cases there may be liability for a true omission.

Act or omission?

It must first be decided whether in law you are dealing with an act or an omission. There are three situations where this question arises: continuing acts, supervening faults and euthanasia.

Continuing acts

The concept of a continuing act was used in **Fagan *v* Metropolitan Police Commissioner** (1969) to allow what seemed to be an omission to be treated as an act. The defendant was told by a police officer to park his car close to the kerb; he obeyed the order, but in doing so he accidentally drove his car on to the constable's foot. The constable shouted, 'Get off, you are on my foot'. The defendant replied, 'Fuck you, you can wait', and turned off the ignition. Convicted of assaulting the constable in the execution of his duty, the defendant appealed on the grounds that, at the time he committed the act of driving on to the officer's foot, he lacked *mens rea*, and though he had *mens rea* when he refused to remove the car, this was an omission, and the *actus reus* required an act. The appeal was dismissed, on the basis that driving on to the officer's foot and staying there was one single continuous act, rather than an act followed by an omission. So long as the defendant had the *mens rea* at some point during that continuing act, he was liable.

The same principle was held to apply in **Kaitamaki *v* R** (1985). The accused was charged with rape, and his defence was that, at the time when he penetrated the woman, he had thought she was consenting. However, he did not withdraw when he realised that she was not consenting. The court held that the *actus reus* of rape was a continuing act, and so when Kaitamaki realised that his victim did not consent (and therefore formed the necessary *mens rea*) the *actus reus* was still in progress.

Supervening fault

A person who is aware that he or she has done something which has endangered another's life or property, and does nothing to prevent the relevant harm occurring, may be criminally liable, with the original act being treated as the *actus reus* of the crime. In particular, this principle can impose liability on defendants who do not have *mens rea* when they commit the original act, but do have it at the point when they fail to act to prevent the harm they have caused.

This was the case in **R** *v* **Miller** (1983). The defendant was squatting in a building. He lay on a mattress, lit a cigarette and fell asleep. Some time later, he woke up to find the mattress on fire. Making no attempt to put the fire out, he simply moved into the next room and went back to sleep. The house caught fire, leading to £800-worth of damage. Miller was convicted of arson. As the fire was his fault, the court was prepared to treat the *actus reus* of the offence as being his original act of dropping the cigarette.

A rare example of the principle in **Miller** being applied by the courts is the case of **Director of Public Prosecutions** *v* **Santra-Bermudez** (2003). A police officer had decided to undertake a search of the defendant, as she suspected that he was a ticket tout. Initially, she had asked him to empty his pockets and in doing so he revealed that he was in possession of some syringes without needles attached to them. The police officer asked the defendant if he was in possession of any needles or sharp objects. He replied that he was not. The police officer proceeded to put her hand into the defendant's pocket to continue the search when her finger was pricked by a hypodermic needle. When challenged that he had said he was not in possession of any other sharp items, the defendant shrugged his shoulders and smirked at the police officer. The defendant was subsequently found guilty of an assault occasioning actual bodily harm (discussed on p. 289). This offence is defined as requiring the commission of an act, as opposed to an omission, but the appeal court applied the principles laid down in **Miller**. By informing the police officer that he was not in possession of any sharp items or needles, the defendant had created a dangerous situation, and he was then under a duty to prevent the harm occurring. He had failed to carry out his duty by telling the police officer the truth.

Offences capable of being committed by omission

Where the conduct in question is genuinely an omission, and not one of the categories just discussed, the next question is whether the particular offence can, in law, be committed by omission. The rules here are contained in both statute and common law with regard to the particular offences – for example, murder and manslaughter can be committed by omission, but assault cannot (**Fagan** *v* **Metropolitan Police Commissioner**, above).

An example of the offence of murder being committed by an omission is **R** *v* **Gibbins and Proctor** (1918). In that case, a man and a woman were living together with the man's daughter. They failed to give the child food and she died. The judge directed that they were guilty of murder if they withheld food with intent to cause her grievous bodily harm, as a result of which she died. Their conviction was upheld by the Court of Appeal.

A duty to act

Where the offence is capable in law of being committed by an omission, it can only be committed by a person who was under a duty to act (in other words, a duty not to commit that omission). This is because English law places no general duty on people to help each other or save each other from harm. Thus, if a man sees a boy drowning in a lake, it is arguable that under English criminal law the man is under no duty to save him, and can walk past without incurring criminal liability for the child's subsequent death.

A duty to act will only be imposed where there is some kind of relationship between the two people, and the closer the relationship the more likely it is that a duty to act will exist. So far, the courts have recognised a range of relationships as giving rise to a duty to act, and other relationships may in the future be recognised as so doing.

Special relationship

Special relationships tend to be implied between members of the same family. An obvious example of a special relationship giving rise to a duty to act is that of parents to their children. In **R v Lowe** (1973), a father failed to call a doctor when his nine-week-old baby became ill. He had a duty to act, though on the facts he lacked the *mens rea* of an offence, partly because he was of low intelligence.

Voluntary acceptance of responsibility for another

People may choose to take on responsibility for another. They will then have a duty to act to protect that person if the person falls into difficulty. In **R v Gibbins and Proctor** a woman lived with a man who had a daughter from an earlier relationship. He paid the woman money to buy food for the family. Sadly, they did not feed the child, and the child died of starvation. The woman was found to have voluntarily accepted responsibility for the child and was liable, along with the child's father, for murder.

In **R v Stone and Dobinson** (1977), Stone's sister, Fanny, lived with him and his girlfriend, Dobinson. Fanny was mentally ill, and became very anxious about putting on weight. She stopped eating properly and became bed-bound. Realising that she was ill, the defendants had made half-hearted and unsuccessful attempts to get medical help and, after several weeks, she died. The couple's efforts were found to have been inadequate. The Court of Appeal said that they had accepted responsibility for Fanny as her carers, and that once she became bed-bound the appellants were, in the circumstances, obliged either to summon help or else to care for her themselves. As they had done neither, they were both found to be liable for manslaughter.

Contract

A contract may give rise to a duty to act. This duty can extend not just for the benefit of the parties to the contract, but also to those who are not party to the contract, but are likely to be injured by failure to perform it. In **R v Pittwood** (1902), a gatekeeper of a railway crossing opened the gate to let a car through, and

Table 14.1 **Duty to act**

Existence of a duty to act	Case authority
Special relationship	**R v Lowe**
Voluntary acceptance of responsibility for another	**R v Stone and Dobinson**
Contract	**R v Pittwood**
Statute	
Defendant created a dangerous situation	**R v Miller**

then forgot to shut it when he went off to lunch. As a result, a haycart crossed the line while a train was approaching, and was hit, causing the driver's death. The gatekeeper was convicted of manslaughter.

Statute

Some pieces of legislation impose duties to act on individuals. For example, s. 1 of the Children and Young Persons Act 1933 imposes a duty to provide for a child in one's care. Failure to do so constitutes an offence.

Defendant created a dangerous situation

Where a defendant has created a dangerous situation, they are under a duty to act to remedy this. This duty is illustrated by the case of **R v Miller** (1983), which is discussed on p. 269.

Termination of the duty

The duty to act will terminate when the special relationship ends, so a parent, for example, probably stops having a duty to act once the child is grown up.

Criticism

It will depend on the facts of each case whether the court is prepared to conclude that the relationship is sufficiently close to justify criminal liability for a failure to act to protect a victim. This approach has been heavily criticised by some academics, who argue that the moral basis of the law is undermined by a situation which allows people to ignore a drowning child whom they could have easily saved, and incur no criminal liability so long as they are strangers. In some countries, legislation has created special offences which impose liability on those who fail to take steps which could be taken without any personal risk to themselves in order to save another from death or serious personal injury. The offence created is not necessarily a homicide offence, but it is an acknowledgement by the criminal law that the individual should have taken action in these circumstances. Photographers involved in the death of Princess Diana were prosecuted for such an offence in France.

??? Quick quiz 14.1

1 Explain the 'but for' test.

2 What is meant by the 'thin skull' test?

3 What was the *ratio decidendi* of **R v Miller** (1982)?

4 Does a stranger owe a duty to act to save a baby drowning in a puddle?

Reading on the web

The House of Lords' judgment of **R v Woollin** (1998) on intention is available on Parliament's website at:

www.publications.parliament.uk/pa/ld199798/ldjudgmt/jd980722/wool.htm

The House of Lords' judgment of **R v G and another** (2003) on recklessness is available on Parliament's website at:

www.publications.parliament.uk/pa/ld200203/ldjudgmt/jd031016/g-1.htm

Chapter summary

A person cannot usually be found guilty of a criminal offence unless two elements are present: an *actus reus* and a *mens rea*.

Actus reus

The *actus reus* comprises all the elements of the offence other than the state of mind of the defendant. The defendant's acts must have been voluntary.

Causation

With result crimes, the prosecution must prove that the defendant caused the result of the offence. Defendants can only be held responsible for results where their acts are both a 'factual' and a 'legal' cause of the result constituting the offence.

Factual causation

In order to establish factual causation, the prosecution must prove two things:

- that but for the conduct of the accused, the result of the offence would not have occurred as and when it did; and
- that the original injury arising from the defendant's conduct was more than a minimal cause of the result constituting the offence.

Legal causation

Legal causation can be proved in any one of the following three ways or by a combination of them:

- the original injury was an operative and significant cause of the result;
- the intervening act was reasonably foreseeable; and
- the 'thin skull' test.

Omissions

Criminal liability is rarely imposed for true omissions at common law, though there are situations where the accused has a duty to act, and in these cases there may be liability for a true omission.

Question and answer guide

For exam questions covering the material in this chapter, please see the Question and answer guides sections of Chapter 16: Non-fatal offences against the person, Chapter 17: Strict liability in criminal law and Chapter 19: Sentencing.

Group activity 1

- Divide your friends (or class) into groups of two or three people.
- Using the internet and any other available resources, make notes on the facts and decisions in the following two cases, noting that the courts in them came to opposite conclusions on very similar facts:

  Martin v State (1944) – this is a decision of a US court, the Alabama Court of Appeals.
  Winzar v Chief Constable of Kent (1983) – this is a decision of a UK court, the Queen's Bench Divisional Court.

- In your groups, decide which court's approach you prefer and why, and then record your group's views and reasons in writing.
- Meet with the other groups to compare notes. Does this cause you to reconsider your views on the two cases?

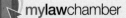 mylawchamber

Visit **www.mylawchamber.co.uk/elliottaqa** to access interactive questions, quizzes and activities to test yourself on this chapter.

Elements of a crime: *Mens rea*

This chapter discusses:

■ the state of mind of the person committing the crime, traditionally known as *mens rea*;

■ the meaning of intention for the purposes of criminal law;

■ the meaning of recklessness for the purposes of criminal law;

■ the concept of transferred malice;

■ the requirement that the *mens rea* of an offence must be present at the time the actus reus is committed.

Introduction

Mens rea is Latin for 'guilty mind' and traditionally refers to the state of mind of the person committing the crime. The required *mens rea* varies depending on the offence. We will consider the two most important forms of *mens rea*: intention and subjective recklessness.

When discussing *mens rea*, we often refer to the difference between subjective and objective tests. Put simply, a subjective test involves looking at what the particular defendant was thinking (or, in practice, what the magistrates or jury believe the defendant was thinking), whereas an objective test considers what a reasonable person would have thought in the defendant's position.

Intention

Intention is a subjective concept: a court is concerned purely with what the particular defendant was intending at the time of the offence, and not what a reasonable person would have intended in the same circumstances.

The case law in this field has developed in the context of the law of murder, where the *mens rea* required is that of an intention either to kill or to cause grievous bodily harm. But the law laid down in these cases applies more widely to any offence where intention can satisfy the *mens rea* element.

To help comprehension of the legal meaning of intention, the concept can be divided into two: direct intention and indirect intention.

Direct intention

Direct intention corresponds with the everyday definition of intention, and applies where the accused actually wants the result that occurs. An example of direct intention to kill is where Ann shoots at Ben because Ann wants to kill Ben.

Indirect intention

Indirect intention is less straightforward. It exists where the accused did not desire a particular result but, in acting as he or she did, realised to the point of virtual certainty that it might occur. For example, a mother wishes to frighten her children and so starts a fire in the house. She does not want to kill her children, but she realises that there is a virtually certain risk that they may die as a result of the fire. The courts are now quite clear that oblique intention can be sufficient for the imposition of criminal liability: people can intend a result that they do not necessarily want. But in a line of important cases, they have tried to specify the necessary degree of foresight required in order to provide evidence of intention.

In **R v Moloney** (1985), the defendant was a soldier who was on leave at the time of the incident that gave rise to his prosecution. He was staying with his mother and stepfather, with whom he was apparently on very good terms. The family held a dinner party, during which the appellant and his stepfather drank rather a lot of alcohol. They stayed up after everyone else had left or gone to bed; shortly after 4.00 am a shot was fired and the appellant was heard to say, 'I have shot my father'.

The court was told that Moloney and his stepfather had had a contest to see who could load his gun and be ready to fire first. Moloney had been quicker, and stood pointing the gun at his stepfather, who teased him that he would not dare to fire a live bullet; at that point Moloney, by his own admission, pulled the trigger. In evidence he said: 'I never conceived that what I was doing might cause injury to anybody. It was just a lark.' Clearly, he did not want to kill his stepfather, but could he be said to have intended to do so? Lord Bridge pointed out that it was quite possible to intend a result which you do not actually want. He gave the example of a man who, in an attempt to escape pursuit, boards a plane to Manchester. Even though he may have no desire to go to Manchester – he may even hate the place for some reason – that is clearly where he intends to go.

Foresight is merely evidence of intent

Moloney established that a person can have intention where he or she did not want the result but merely foresaw it, yet the courts are not saying that foresight is intention. Foresight is merely evidence from which intention can be found.

Before **Moloney**, in the case of **Hyam v DPP** (1975), it had looked as though foresight was actually intention, though the judgment in that case was not very clear. The defendant, Pearl Hyam, put blazing newspaper through the letterbox of the house of a Mrs Booth, who was going on holiday with Pearl Hyam's boyfriend; Mrs Booth's two children were killed in the fire. On the facts it appeared that Pearl Hyam did not want to kill the two children; she wanted to set fire to the house and to frighten Mrs Booth. The court held that she must have foreseen that death or grievous bodily harm were highly likely to result from her conduct, and that this was sufficient *mens rea* for murder. In **Moloney** the House of Lords held that **Hyam** had been wrongly decided, and that nothing less than intention to kill or cause grievous bodily harm would constitute the *mens rea* of murder: merely foreseeing the victim's death as probable was not intent, though it could be evidence of it.

Lord Bridge suggested that juries might be asked to consider the questions: was death or really serious injury a 'natural consequence' of the defendant's act, and did the defendant foresee that one or the other was a natural consequence of his/her act? If the answer was 'yes', the jury might infer from this evidence that the death was intended.

This guidance for juries in turn proved to be problematic. In **R v Hancock and Shankland** (1986) the defendants were striking miners who knew that a taxi, carrying men breaking the strike to work, would pass along a particular road. They waited on a bridge above it, and dropped a concrete block which hit the taxi as it passed underneath, killing the driver. At their trial the judge had given the direction suggested by Lord Bridge in **Moloney** and they were convicted of murder. On appeal, the House of Lords held that this had been incorrect, and a verdict of manslaughter was substituted. Their Lordships agreed with Lord Bridge that conviction for murder could result only from proof of intention, and that foresight of consequences was not in itself intention, but they were concerned that the question of whether the death was a 'natural consequence' of the defendants' act might suggest to juries that they need not consider the degree of probability. The fact that there might be a ten-million-to-one chance that death would result form the defendants' act might still mean that death was a natural consequence of it, in the sense that it had happened without any interference, but, with this degree of likelihood, there would seem to be little evidence of intention.

Lord Scarman suggested that the jury should be directed that: 'the greater the probability of a consequence, the more likely it is that the consequence was foreseen and that if that consequence was foreseen the greater the probability is that that consequence was also intended . . . But juries also need to be reminded that the decision is theirs to be reached upon a consideration of all the evidence.'

Thus, if a person stabs another in the chest, it is highly likely this will lead to death or grievous bodily harm, and since most people would be well aware of that, it is likely that they would foresee death or serious injury when they acted. If they did foresee this, then that is evidence of intent, from which a jury might conclude that that death was intended. But if you cut someone's finger, that person could die as a result – from blood poisoning, for example – but since this is highly unlikely, the chances are that you would not have foreseen that the person might die when you cut the finger, and your lack of foresight would be evidence that you did not intend the death.

The concept was further clarified in **R v Nedrick** (1986). The defendant had a grudge against a woman, and poured paraffin through the letterbox of her house and set it alight. The woman's child died in the fire. Lord Lane CJ said:

'Where the charge is murder and in the rare cases where the simple direction is not enough, the jury should be directed that they are not entitled to infer the necessary intention unless

they feel sure that death or serious bodily harm was a virtual certainty (barring some unforeseen intervention) as a result of the defendant's action and that the defendant appreciated that such was the case.

Where a man realizes that it is for all practical purposes inevitable that his actions will result in death or serious harm, the inference may be irresistible that he intended that result, however little he may have desired or wished it to happen . . . The decision is one for the jury to be reached on a consideration of all the evidence.'

In other words, Lord Lane considered that even if death or grievous bodily harm is not the defendant's aim or wish, the jury may infer intent if they decide that death or grievous bodily harm was virtually certain to result from what the defendant did, and the defendant foresaw that that was the case. Such foresight was still only evidence from which they might infer intent, and not intent itself, although it would be difficult not to infer intent where the defendant foresaw that death or grievous bodily harm was practically inevitable as a result of his or her acts.

The virtual certainty test in **Nedrick** became the key test on indirect intention. Then confusion was thrown into this area of the law by the Court of Appeal judgment in **R v Woollin** in 1996. Having given various explanations for his three-month-old son's injuries in the ambulance and in the first two police interviews, Woollin eventually admitted that he had 'lost his cool' when his son had choked on his food. He had picked him up, shaken him and thrown him across the room with considerable force towards a pram standing next to a wall about five feet away. He stated that he had not intended or thought that he would kill the child and had not wanted the child to die. The judge directed the jury that it was open to them to convict Woollin of murder if satisfied that he was aware there was a 'substantial risk' that he would cause serious injury. On appeal, the defence argued that the judge had misdirected the jury by using the term 'a substantial risk', which was the test for recklessness, and failing to use the phrase 'virtual certainty' derived from **Nedrick** for oblique intention. The appeal was rejected by the Court of Appeal, which held that in directing a jury a judge was obliged to use the phrase 'virtual certainty' if the only evidence of intent was the actions of the accused constituting the *actus reus* of the offence and their consequences on the victim. Where other evidence was available, the judge was not obliged to use that phrase, or a phrase that meant the same thing. The Court of Appeal felt that otherwise the jury function as laid down in s. 8 of the Criminal Justice Act 1967 would be undermined. This section states:

'A court or jury in determining whether a person had committed an offence,
(a) shall not be found in law to infer that he intended or foresaw a result of his actions by reason only of its being a natural and probable consequence of those actions; but
(b) shall decide whether he did intend or foresee that result by reference to all the evidence, drawing such inferences from the evidence as appear proper in the circumstances.'

Thus, Parliament had recognised in that provision that a court or jury could infer that a defendant intended a result of their actions by reason of its being a natural and probable result of those actions. In deciding whether the defendant intended the natural and probable result of his/her actions, s. 8 stated that the court or jury

Table 15.1 **Chronology of cases on indirect intention**

Case	Legal principle
Hyam v **DPP** (1975)	May have wrongly decided that foresight was intention.
R v **Moloney** (1985)	Overturned **Hyam** v **DPP**, as foresight is not intention, it is merely evidence of intent.
R v **Hancock and Shankland** (1986)	Lord Scarman suggested that the jury should be directed that: 'the greater the probability of a consequence, the more likely it is that the consequence was foreseen and that if that consequence was foreseen the greater the probability is that the consequence was also intended . . . But juries also need to be reminded that the decision is theirs to be reached upon a consideration of all the evidence.'
R v **Nedrick** (1986)	Indirect intention can exist where the defendant foresaw a result as a virtual certainty.
R v **Woollin** (1998)	The **Nedrick** test of virtual certainty was confirmed.

was to take into account all the evidence drawing such inferences as appeared proper. Section 8 contained no restrictive provision about the result being a 'virtual certainty'. The facts of **Woollin** fell within the category of cases where there was more evidence of intention than purely the conduct of the defendant constituting the *actus reus* of the offence and the result of the conduct, for in addition there was the conduct of the defendant in the first two interviews and his description of events to the ambulance controller.

A further appeal was made to the House of Lords. This ruled that the Court of Appeal and the trial judge had been mistaken. It said that the **Nedrick** direction was always required in the context of indirect intention. Otherwise, there would be no clear distinction between intention and recklessness, as both would be concerned simply with the foresight of a risk. The **Nedrick** direction distinguishes the two concepts by stating that intention will only exist when the risk is foreseen as a virtual certainty. Accordingly, a conviction for manslaughter was substituted.

Thus the **Nedrick** 'virtual certainty' direction was approved, though two amendments were made to it. First, the original **Nedrick** direction told the jury that 'they are not entitled to *infer* the necessary intention, unless they feel sure that death or serious bodily harm was a virtual certainty'. The House of Lords substituted the word 'find' for the word 'infer'. This change was to deal with the criticism that juries were told in the past that they could 'infer' intention from the existence of the foresight and this suggested that intention was something different from the foresight itself, but did not specify what it was. But the difficulties are not completely resolved by the change from 'infer' to 'find', as a jury is still only 'entitled' to make this finding, and it is still a question of evidence for the jury – it is not clear when this finding should be made. It might be more logical to oblige a jury to conclude that there is intention where a person foresaw a result as virtual certainty. The change of wording from 'infer' to 'find' was expressly followed by the Court of Appeal in **R** v **Matthews and Alleyne** (2003).

The second amendment was that the majority of the House of Lords felt that the first sentence of the second paragraph of Lord Lane's statement in **Nedrick**, quoted above ('Where a man realizes . . .'), did not form part of the model direction. So the jury will not normally be pressurised into finding intention by being told that a finding of intention 'may be irresistible'. Thus the model direction now reads as follows:

> *'Where the charge is murder and in the rare cases where the simple direction is not enough, the jury should be directed that they are not entitled to find the necessary intention unless they feel sure that death or serious bodily harm was a virtual certainty (barring some unforeseen intervention) as a result of the defendant's actions and that the defendant appreciated that such was the case. The decision is one for the jury to be reached on a consideration of all the evidence.'*

The House of Lords wanted less pressure to be put on the jury to find intention. Despite this, in **R v Matthews and Alleyne** the Court of Appeal still stated that a finding of indirect intention was 'irresistible' on the facts of the case. An 18-year-old A-level student had been robbed and then thrown over a bridge. He had told his attackers that he did not know how to swim and he drowned. The two appellants appealed against their conviction for murder on the basis that the jury had been misdirected on the law of intent. The guidance on indirect intention had been presented as a rule of law (the jury was told they must find intention when foresight as a virtual certainty was established) rather than as a rule of evidence (the jury should have been told they were entitled to find intention where foresight as a virtual certainty was established). The Court of Appeal stated that 'there is very little to choose between a rule of evidence and one of substantive law' and that on the facts a finding of intention was 'irresistible'.

It is also slightly puzzling that in the high-profile case of **Re A (Children) (Conjoined Twins: Medical Treatment)** (2000), concerning the legality of an operation to separate conjoined twins, the Court of Appeal included, as part of the direction on intention that should be given to the jury, the statement from **Nedrick** which the majority of the House of Lords had said no longer formed part of the model direction. The decision of the Court of Appeal had to be given under significant time constraints due to the urgent need to carry out the operation and, with due respect, it is suggested that this part of the Court of Appeal judgment is wrong.

Subjective recklessness

In everyday language, recklessness means taking an unjustified risk. However, its legal definition is not quite the same as its ordinary English meaning and careful direction as to its meaning in law has to be given to the jury.

Its legal definition has radically changed in recent years. It is now clear that it is a subjective form of *mens rea*, so the focus is on what the defendant was thinking. In 1981 in the case of **Metropolitan Police Commissioner v Caldwell**, Lord Diplock created an objective form of recklessness, but this was abolished in 2003 by the case of **R v G**. Following the House of Lords' judgment in **R v G**, recklessness will always be interpreted as requiring a subjective test. In that case, the House favoured the definition of recklessness provided by the Law Commission's draft Criminal Code Bill in 1989:

'A person acts recklessly . . . with respect to –
(i) a circumstance when he is aware of a risk that it exists or will exist;
(ii) a result when he is aware of a risk that it will occur; and it is, in the circumstances known to him, unreasonable to take the risk.'

Defendants must always be aware of the risk in order to satisfy this test of recklessness. In addition, their conduct must have been unreasonable. It would appear that any level of awareness of a risk will be sufficient, provided the court finds the risk taking unreasonable.

Until the case of **R v G**, the leading case on subjective recklessness was **R v Cunningham** (1957). In **R v Cunningham** the defendant broke a gas meter to steal the money in it, and the gas seeped out into the house next door. Cunningham's prospective mother-in-law was sleeping there, and became so ill that her life was endangered. Cunningham was charged under s. 23 of the Offences Against the Person Act 1861 with 'maliciously administering a noxious thing so as to endanger life'.

The Court of Appeal said that 'maliciously' meant intentionally or recklessly. They defined recklessness as where: 'the accused has foreseen that the particular kind of harm might be done and yet has gone on to take the risk of it.' This is called a subjective test: the accused must actually have had the required foresight. Cunningham would therefore have been reckless if he realised there was a risk of the gas escaping and endangering someone, and went ahead anyway. His conviction was in fact quashed because of a misdirection at the trial.

In order to define recklessness, the House of Lords in **R v G** preferred to use the words of the Law Commission's draft Criminal Code Bill (the draft Code), rather than the court's earlier words in **Cunningham**. It is likely, therefore, in future that the draft Code's definition will become the single definition of recklessness, and the phrasing in **Cunningham** will no longer be used.

There are three main differences between the definition of subjective recklessness in the draft Code and the definition in **Cunningham**. First, the **Cunningham** test refers only to taking risks as to a result and makes no mention of taking risks as to a circumstance. The Law Commission, in preparing its draft Code, felt that this was a gap in the law. It therefore expressly applies the test of recklessness to the taking of risks in relation to a circumstance. Secondly, the draft Code adds an additional restriction to a finding of recklessness: the defendant's risk-taking must have been 'unreasonable'. To determine whether the risk-taking was unreasonable, the courts will balance such factors as the seriousness of the risk and the social value of the defendant's conduct. William Wilson (2003) observes that: 'Jumping a traffic light is likely to be deemed reckless if actuated by a desire to get home quickly for tea but not if the desire was to get a seriously ill person to hospital.' Thirdly, the **Cunningham** test for recklessness only requires foresight of the type of harm that actually occurred. It is arguable that the Law Commission's Draft Code requires awareness of the risk that the actual damage caused might occur.

Transferred malice

If Ann shoots at Ben, intending to kill him, but happens to miss, and shoots and kills Chris instead, Ann will be liable for the murder of Chris. This is because of the principle known as transferred malice. Under this principle, if Ann has the *mens rea* of a particular crime and does the *actus reus* of the crime, Ann is guilty of the crime even though the *actus reus* may differ in some way from that intended. The *mens rea* is simply transferred to the new *actus reus*. Either intention or recklessness can be so transferred.

As a result, the defendant will be liable for the same crime even if the victim is not the intended victim. In **R *v* Latimer** (1886), the defendant aimed a blow at someone with his belt. The belt recoiled off that person and hit the victim, who was severely injured. The court held that Latimer was liable for maliciously wounding the unexpected victim. His intention to wound the person he aimed at was transferred to the person actually injured.

Where the accused would have had a defence if the crime committed had been completed against the intended victim, that defence is also transferred. So if Ann shot at Ben in self-defence and hit and killed Chris instead, Ann would be able to rely on the defence if charged with Chris's murder.

In **Attorney-General's Reference (No. 3 of 1994)** the defendant stabbed his girlfriend, who was to his knowledge between 22 and 24 weeks' pregnant with their child. The girlfriend underwent an operation on a cut in the wall of her uterus but it was not realised at the time that the stabbing had damaged the foetus's abdomen. She subsequently gave birth prematurely to a baby girl who later died from the complications of a premature birth. Before the child's death the defendant was charged with the offence of wounding his girlfriend with intent to cause her grievous bodily harm to which he pleaded guilty. After the child died, he was in addition charged with murdering the child. At the close of the prosecution's case, the judge upheld a defence submission that the facts could not give rise to a conviction for murder or manslaughter and accordingly directed the jury to acquit. The Attorney-General referred the case to the Court of Appeal for a ruling to clarify the law in the field. The Court of Appeal considered the foetus to be an integral part of the mother until its birth. Thus any intention to injure the foetus prior to its birth was treated as an intention to injure the mother. If, on birth, the baby subsequently died, an intention to injure the baby could be found by applying the doctrine of transferred malice. This approach was rejected by the House of Lords. It held that the foetus was not an integral part of the mother, but a unique organism. The principle of transferred malice could not therefore be applied, and the direction was criticised as being of 'no sound intellectual basis'.

> ✓ **Know your terms 15.1**
>
> Define the following terms:
> 1 *Actus reus*.
> 2 *Mens rea*.
> 3 **Cunningham** recklessness.
> 4 Transferred malice.

Mens rea and motive

It is essential to realise that *mens rea* has nothing to do with motive. To illustrate this, take the example of a man who suffocates his wife with a pillow, intending to kill her because she is afflicted with a terminal disease which causes her terrible and constant pain. Many people would say that this man's motive is not a bad one – in fact many people would reject the label 'murder' for what he has done. But there is no doubt that he has the necessary *mens rea* for murder, because he intends to kill his wife, even if he does not want to do so. He may not have a guilty mind in the everyday sense, but he does have *mens rea*. Motive may be relevant when the decision is made on whether or not to prosecute, or later for sentencing, but it makes no difference with regard to legal liability.

Proof of *mens rea*

Under s. 8 of the Criminal Justice Act 1967, where the definition of an offence requires the prosecution to prove that the accused intended or foresaw something, the question of whether that is proved is one for the court or jury to decide on the basis of all the evidence. The fact that a consequence is proved to be the natural and probable result of the accused's actions does not mean that it is proved that he or she intended or foresaw such a result; the jury or the court must decide.

Coincidence of *actus reus* and *mens rea*

The *mens rea* of an offence must be present at the time the *actus reus* is committed. So if, for example, Ann intends to kill Ben on Friday night, but for some reason fails to do so, then quite accidentally runs Ben over on Saturday morning, Ann will not be liable for Ben's murder. However, there are two ways in which the courts have introduced flexibility into this area: continuing acts, which are described above at p. 268, and the interpretation of a continuous series of acts as a single transaction. An example of the latter occurred in **Thabo Meli *v* R** (1954). The defendants had attempted to kill their victim by beating him over the head, then threw what they assumed was a dead body over a cliff. The victim did die, but from the fall and exposure, and not from the beating. Thus there was an argument that at the time of the *actus reus* the defendants no longer had the *mens rea*. The Privy Council held that throwing him over the cliff was part of one series of acts following through a preconceived plan of action and therefore the incident could not be seen as consisting of separate acts at all, but as amounting to a single transaction. The defendants had the required *mens rea* when that transaction began, and therefore *mens rea* and *actus reus* had coincided.

Quick quiz 15.2

1 What is the difference between direct and indirect intention?

2 What level of foresight is required for a finding of **Cunningham** recklessness and what level of foresight is required for a finding of indirect intention?

3 Name the most recent House of Lords' judgment on intention.

4 Is a person's motive relevant in determining whether he or she had *mens rea*?

Reading on the web

The full judgment of **R** v **Woollin** is available on the House of Lords' judicial business website at:

www.parliament.the-stationery-office.co.uk/pa/ld/ldjudgmt.htm#1998

Chapter summary

Mens rea

Mens rea traditionally refers to the state of mind of the person committing the crime.

Intention

Intention is a subjective concept.

- *Direct intention*. Direct intention exists where the accused actually wants the result that occurs.
- *Indirect intention*. Indirect intention exists where the accused did not desire a particular result but, in acting as he or she did, realised to the point of virtual certainty that it might occur. The 'virtual certainty' test was laid down by the Court of Appeal in **Nedrick** and approved by the House of Lords in **Woollin**.

Subjective recklessness

Defendants are reckless where they are aware of a risk and take that risk where it was unreasonable to do so.

Transferred malice

Under the principle of transferred malice, if the defendant has the *mens rea* of a particular crime and does the *actus reus* of the crime, the defendant is guilty of the crime even though the *actus reus* may differ in some way from that intended. The *mens rea* is simply transferred to the new *actus reus*.

Coincidence of *actus reus* and *mens rea*

The *mens rea* of an offence must be present at the time the *actus reus* is committed.

Question and answer guide

For exam questions covering the material in this chapter, please see the Question and answer guides sections of Chapter 16: Non-fatal offences against the person, Chapter 17: Strict liability in criminal law and Chapter 19: Sentencing.

Group activity 1

■ With your friends (or class), prepare a brief explanation of the rule that motive cannot be a defence to a crime. It should include examples (like the one given in this chapter) and be written in a style that can be understood by someone who knows nothing about the law.

■ Divide your friends (or class) into groups of two or three people.

■ Each group should invite six people, having no knowledge of law, to read the explanation and then, without the explanation in front of them, answer the following questions:

Q.1: Explain in your own words the rule that motive cannot be a defence to a crime. (The purpose of this question is simply to check that they have understood what they have just read!)

Q.2: Do you think it right that motive cannot be a defence to a crime?

Q.3: Can you think of any situations in which motive should be a defence to a crime?

■ With your friends (or class), prepare a table summarising all the answers obtained by all the groups to Q.2 and Q.3.

■ Does this summary cause you to reconsider your own views on whether motive should be a defence to a crime?

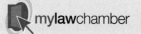 mylawchamber

Visit **www.mylawchamber.co.uk/elliottaqa** to access interactive questions, quizzes and activities to test yourself on this chapter.

Non-fatal offences against the person

This chapter discusses the five main non-fatal offences against the person, starting with the least serious and progressing to the most serious, where a life sentence can be imposed:

■ assault;

■ battery;

■ actual bodily harm;

■ inflicting grievous bodily harm or wounding;

■ causing grievous bodily harm or wounding.

Assault

The Criminal Justice Act 1988, s. 39 provides that assault is a summary offence with a maximum sentence on conviction of six months' imprisonment or a fine. It is a relatively common offence, with almost 12,000 adults convicted of this crime in 2003. The Act does not provide a definition of the offence; the relevant rules are found in the common law.

Actus reus

This consists of any act which makes the victim fear that unlawful force is about to be used against him or her. No force need actually be applied; creating the fear of it is sufficient, so assault can be committed by raising a fist at the victim, or pointing a gun. Nor does it matter that it may have been impossible for the defendant actually to inflict any force, for example if the gun was unloaded, so long as the victim is unaware of the impossibility of the threat being carried out.

Words alone can constitute an assault

Until the Court of Appeal decision in **R v Constanza** (1997), there was some uncertainty as to whether words alone could amount to an assault. **R v Constanza**, a case involving stalking, confirmed that they could. The House of Lords took this approach in **R v Ireland and Burstow** (1997), so that silent phone calls could amount to an assault. The offence would, for example, be committed if a man shouted to a stranger 'I'm going to kill you' – there is no need for an accompanying

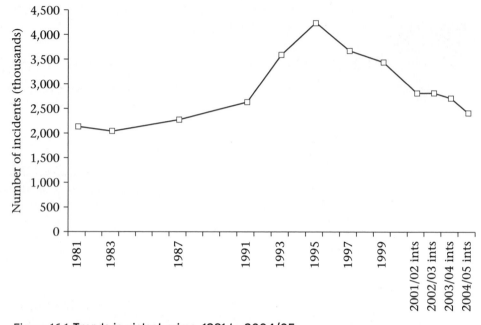

Figure 16.1 **Trends in violent crime, 1981 to 2004/05**

Source: Crime in England and Wales 2004/2005, p. 73, Figure 5.1. © Crown Copyright 2005.

act, such as raising a fist, or pointing a gun. The old case of **Meade and Belt** (1823), which had suggested the contrary, must now be viewed as bad law. Some people had gathered around another's house singing menacing songs, with violent language and the judge had said 'no words or singing are equivalent to an assault'.

Words can also prevent a potential assault occurring – so, if a person shakes a fist at someone, but at the same time states that they will not harm that person, there will be no liability for this offence. This was the situation in **Turberville** *v* **Savage** (1669). The defendant, annoyed by the comments someone had made to him, put his hand on his sword, which by itself could have been enough to constitute an assault, but also said, 'If it were not assize time I would not take such language', meaning that since judges were hearing criminal cases in the town at the time, he had no intention of using violence. His statement was held to negative the threat implied by putting his hand on his sword.

Fearing the immediate infliction of force

It has traditionally been said that the victim must fear the immediate infliction of force: fear that force might be applied at some time in the future would not be sufficient. The courts had often given a fairly generous interpretation of the concept of immediacy in this context. In **Smith** *v* **Chief Superintendent, Woking Police Station** (1983) the victim was at home in her ground-floor bedsit dressed only in her nightdress. She was terrified when she suddenly saw the defendant standing in her garden, staring at her through the window. He was found liable for assault, on the ground that the victim feared the immediate infliction of force, even though she was safely locked inside. The Court of Appeal said:

'It was clearly a situation where the basis of the fear which was instilled in her was that she did not know what the defendant was going to do next, but that, whatever he might be going to do next, and sufficiently immediately for the purposes of the offence, was something of a violent nature. In effect, as it seems to me, it was wholly open to the justices to infer that her state of mind was not only that of terror, which they did find, but terror of some immediate violence.'

However, the requirement that the victim must fear the immediate infliction of force was undermined by the House of Lords in **R v Ireland and Burstow** (1997). One of the defendants, Ireland had made a large number of unwanted telephone calls to three different women, remaining silent when they answered the phone. All three victims suffered significant adverse symptoms such as palpitations, cold sweats, anxiety, inability to sleep, dizziness and stress as a result of the repeated calls. He was convicted under s. 47 of the Offences Against the Person Act 1861. This offence is discussed below, but what is important here is that for Ireland to have been liable there must have been an assault. Ireland appealed against his conviction on the basis that there was no assault since the requirement of immediacy had not been satisfied. His appeal was dismissed by the Court of Appeal. The court stated that the requirement of immediacy was in fact satisfied as, by using the telephone, the appellant had put himself in immediate contact with the victims, and when the victims lifted the telephone they were placed in immediate fear and suffered psychological damage. It was not necessary for there to be physical proximity between the defendant and the victim. A further appeal was taken to the House of Lords in 1997 and, while the initial conviction was upheld, the House of Lords refused to enter into a discussion of the requirement for immediacy. They said that this was not necessary on the facts of the case as the appellant had pleaded guilty and that, in any case, the existence of immediacy would depend upon the circumstances in each case. It is not sufficient that the victim is immediately put in fear, the fear must be of immediate violence.

In **R v Constanza** (1997), a stalking case where the victim had been stalked over a prolonged period of time, the Court of Appeal stated that, in order to incur liability for assault, it is enough for the prosecution to prove a fear of violence at some time not excluding the immediate future. If the Court of Appeal in **Constanza**

Table 16.1 **Location of violent incidents (percentages)**

	All violence	*Domestic*	*Mugging*	*Stranger*	*Acquaintance*
Around the home	27	75	22	5	16
Around work	8	3	1	8	16
Street	24	6	49	25	25
Pub or club	21	3	8	38	23
Transport	4	-	8	7	2
Other location	15	13	12	16	17

Source: Adapted from C. Flood-Page and J. Taylor (eds.) (2003) *Crime in England and Wales 2001/2002: Supplementary Volume*, p. 57, Table 3g. Notes not included. © Crown Copyright 2003.

is followed, then there would be no need to fear the immediate infliction of force in the sense of a battery; the offence would include fearing some other type of injury, notably psychological damage. The concept of immediacy would also be considerably weakened.

Causation

Note that, as for all these offences against the person, the issue of causation may be relevant if there is any question that the defendant was not the cause of the relevant result. In the case of assault, the requirement of causation will not be satisfied if the victim was put in fear of immediate and unlawful force, but the defendant did not cause that fear.

Mens rea

The *mens rea* of assault is either intention or subjective recklessness. The defendant must have either intended to cause the victim to fear the infliction of immediate and unlawful force, or been aware of the risk that such fear would be created and unreasonably taken that risk. The meaning of intention is discussed at p. 274, and recklessness is discussed at p. 279.

Battery

By s. 39 of the Criminal Justice Act 1988, battery is a summary offence punishable with up to six months' imprisonment or a fine but, as with assault, it is left to the common law to define the offence.

Actus reus

The *actus reus* of battery consists of the application of unlawful force on another. Any unlawful physical contact can amount to a battery; there is no need to prove harm or pain, and a mere touch can be sufficient. Often the force will be directly applied by one person to another, for example if one person slaps another across the face, but the force can also be applied indirectly. This was the case in **Fagan v Metropolitan Police Commissioner** (discussed at p. 268), where the force was applied by running over the police officer's foot in the car.

A battery was also, therefore, committed in **Haystead v Director of Public Prosecutions** (2000). The defendant had punched a woman twice in the face while she was holding her three-month-old baby, causing her to drop her child. The baby hit his head on the floor. The defendant was convicted of the offence of battery against the child. He appealed the conviction, arguing that battery required a direct application of force, but this argument was rejected.

The force does not have to be applied to the victim's body; touching his or her clothes may be enough, even if the victim feels nothing at all as a result. In **R v Thomas** (1985) it was stated, *obiter*, that touching the bottom of a woman's skirt was equivalent to touching the woman herself.

Mens rea

Again, either intention or recklessness is sufficient, but here it is intention or recklessness as to the application of unlawful force.

Offences Against the Person Act 1861, s. 47

According to s. 47:

> 'Whosoever shall be convicted upon an indictment of any assault occasioning actual bodily harm shall be liable . . . [to imprisonment for five years].'

Section 47 of the Offences Against the Person Act 1861 (OAPA) provides that it is an offence to commit 'any assault occasioning actual bodily harm'. This offence is commonly known as ABH. The crime is triable either way and if found guilty the defendant is liable to a maximum sentence of five years.

Actus reus

Despite the fact that the Act uses the term 'assault' for this offence, s. 47 has been interpreted as being committed with either assault or battery. The first requirement is, therefore, to prove the *actus reus* of assault or battery, as defined above. In addition, the prosecution must show that the assault or battery caused ABH. Both **Ireland** and **Constanza**, discussed in the context of assault, were concerned with this offence as the issue of assault arose in the context of the *actus reus* of a s. 47 crime.

Actual bodily harm has been given a wide interpretation. In **R v Miller** (1954) the court stated: 'Actual bodily harm includes hurt or injury calculated to interfere with health or comfort.' Thus, ABH can occur simply where discomfort to the person is caused. However, this was qualified slightly in **R v Chan-Fook** (1994), where Hobhouse LJ said in the Court of Appeal: 'The word "actual" indicates that the injury (although there is no need for it to be permanent) should not be so trivial as to be wholly insignificant.' In **R v Donovan** (1934) the court stated that the injury had to be 'more than merely transient and trifling'. The defendant in **R v DPP** (2003) relied on this case to argue that he had not caused actual bodily harm because the victim had only momentarily lost consciousness following a kick to the head. He argued that this was only a transient harm and was not therefore sufficient. This argument was rejected by the court. **Donovan** merely required that the injury must not be both 'transient and trifling', on these facts the injury was transient but it was not trifling.

In **DPP v Smith** (2006) the High Court held that cutting someone's hair can fall within the s. 47 offence. Mr Smith had cut off his ex-girlfriend's ponytail without her consent after she went into his bedroom and woke him up. He argued that he had not caused any actual bodily harm because hair could not be part of the body as it was dead tissue, he had not caused any bruising, bleeding or cutting of the skin and no expert evidence had been submitted regarding psychological harm. But the High Court rejected these arguments. It treated human hair as part of the body and it stated that the s. 47 offence was committed not just when there was injury, but also when there was harm or damage.

In **Miller**, it was also accepted that ABH included not just physical harm, but also psychological injury, such as shock. In later cases, the courts have made it clear that psychological injury will only count as ABH if it is a clinically recognisable condition. The defendant in **R v Chan-Fook** aggressively questioned a man he suspected of stealing his fiancée's jewellery. He then dragged him upstairs and locked him in a room. The victim, frightened of what the defendant would do on his return, tried to escape through the window, but injured himself when he fell to the ground. Charged with an offence under s. 47, the defendant denied striking the victim. The trial judge said that, for liability to be incurred, it was sufficient if the victim suffered a hysterical or nervous condition at the time and the defendant was convicted at first instance. His appeal was allowed and Hobhouse LJ said: 'The phrase "actual bodily harm" is capable of including psychiatric injury. But it does not include mere emotions such as fear or distress or panic, nor does it include, as such, states of mind that are not themselves evidence of some identifiable clinical condition.'

In **R v D** (2006) the victim had committed suicide following a long period of domestic abuse. On the evening of the suicide, her husband had struck her on the forehead, causing a cut from the bracelet which he was wearing. He was subsequently prosecuted for manslaughter and inflicting grievous bodily harm under s. 20 of the Offences Against the Person Act 1861. The defendant was not convicted. The Court of Appeal held that in order for there to be liability for a s. 20 offence, the victim must have suffered bodily harm. This would include, following cases such as **Chan-Fook** (1994), medically recognisable psychiatric illnesses. From the evidence available to the court, while the victim had clearly suffered psychological harm, a jury could not be satisfied beyond reasonable doubt that she had suffered a clinically recognised psychiatric injury. Hobhouse LJ had stated in **Chan-Fook**:

> '. . . the phrase "actual bodily harm" is capable of including psychiatric injury, but it does not include mere emotions . . . nor does it include, as such, states of mind that are not themselves evidence of some identifiable clinical condition.'

The Court of Appeal found that there was insufficient evidence of a clinically recognised psychiatric injury in the case. But in reaching this conclusion it took an extremely narrow interpretation of **Chan-Fook**. None of the experts was of the opinion that Mrs D was suffering from 'mere emotion'; each recorded some form of psychological condition. The court's conclusion on this issue amounted to an inappropriate belittling of the horrendous experience of domestic violence by refusing to acknowledge that its consequences amounted to bodily harm. It is regrettable that a court should be prepared to accept that cutting a person's hair (**DPP v Smith** (2006)) can constitute actual bodily harm, but years of cruel domestic abuse may not be sufficient.

The offence of causing actual bodily harm has been applied in the context of stalking, but where the stalking consists of a course of conduct over a period of time, it can be difficult to identify the actual assault that caused the actual bodily harm. In **R v Cox** (1998) the Court of Appeal did not consider this problem insurmountable. The defendant's relationship with his girlfriend had ended. He started to make repeated telephone calls, some of which were silent, he prowled outside her flat, put through her letterbox a torn piece of a brochure showing details of a holiday she had booked, and, shortly before she was due to depart, he telephoned her to say that she was going to her death and he could smell burning. The complainant began to suffer from severe headaches and stress. The appellant was convicted of assault occasioning actual bodily harm and his conviction was upheld by the Court of Appeal even though it was difficult to identify an act that constituted the assault.

Mens rea

The *mens rea* of assault occasioning ABH is the same as for assault or battery. No additional *mens rea* is required in relation to the actual bodily harm, as the case of **R v Roberts** (1978) shows. Late at night, the defendant gave a lift in his car to a girl. During the journey he made unwanted sexual advances, touching the girl's clothes. Frightened that he was going to rape her, she jumped out of the moving car, injuring herself. It was held that the defendant had committed the *actus reus* of a s. 47 offence by touching the girl's clothes – sufficient for the *actus reus* of battery – and this act had caused her to suffer actual bodily harm. The defendant argued that he lacked the *mens rea* of the offence, because he had neither intended to cause her actual bodily harm, nor seen any risk of her suffering actual bodily harm as a result of his advances. This argument was rejected: the court held that the *mens rea* for battery was sufficient in itself, and there was no need for any extra *mens rea* regarding the actual bodily harm.

The point was confirmed in **R v Savage** (1992). The defendant went into a local pub, where she spotted her husband's new girlfriend having a drink with some friends. She went up to the table where the group was sitting, intending to throw a pint of beer over the woman. On reaching the table, she said 'Nice to meet you darling' and threw the beer but, as she did so, she accidentally let go of the glass, which broke and cut the woman's wrist. The defendant argued that she lacked sufficient *mens rea* to be liable for a s. 47 offence, because her intention had only been to throw the beer, and she had not seen the risk that the glass might injure the girlfriend. This was rejected because she intended to apply unlawful force (the *mens rea* of battery) and there was no need to prove that she intended or was reckless as to causing actual bodily harm. The conflicting case of **R v Spratt** (1990) was overruled on this point.

Offences Against the Person Act 1861, s. 20

This section states:

> '*Whosoever shall unlawfully and maliciously wound or inflict any grievous bodily harm upon any other person either with or without any weapon or instrument shall be guilty of an offence triable either way, and being convicted thereof shall be liable to imprisonment for five years.*'

Actus reus

The prosecution has to prove that the defendant either inflicted grievous bodily harm or wounded the victim.

Inflicting grievous bodily harm

In **DPP** *v* **Smith** (1961) the House of Lords emphasised that grievous bodily harm (GBH) is a phrase that should be given its ordinary and natural meaning, which was simply 'really serious harm'. This was confirmed in **R** *v* **Saunders** (1985) where the Court of Appeal said that there was no real difference between the terms 'serious' and 'really serious'. The point was again made in **R** *v* **Brown and Stratton** (1998), where the Court of Appeal stated that trial judges should not attempt to give a definition of the concept to the jury. The victim was a transsexual who had undergone gender reassignment treatment, and changed her name to Julie. Stratton was the victim's son and he had felt humiliated when his father had come to the supermarket where he worked, dressed as a woman. With his cousin, Stratton had gone round to Julie's flat and attacked her with fists and part of a chair, resulting in a broken nose, three missing teeth, bruising, a laceration over one eye and concussion. These injuries were found by the Court of Appeal to amount to grievous bodily harm and the defendants were liable under s. 20. **R** *v* **Ireland and Burstow** (1997) recognises that a really serious psychiatric injury can amount to grievous bodily harm.

In determining whether grievous bodily harm has been inflicted, the courts can take into account the particular characteristics of the victim, such as their age and health. In deciding the severity of the injuries, an assessment had to be made of the effect of the harm on the particular victim. Thus, in **R** *v* **Bollom** (2003) the victim was a 17-month-old child who had bruises over her body. In determining whether these bruises amounted to grievous bodily harm, the court could take into account the frailty of the child.

The difference between actual bodily harm under s. 47 and grievous bodily harm in this section is one of degree – grievous bodily harm is clearly the more serious injury.

The meaning of the word 'inflict' in this section has caused considerable difficulty. For many years it was held that 'inflict' implied the commission of an actual assault. Thus, in **R** *v* **Clarence** (1888) the Queen's Bench Division decided that a husband could not be said to have inflicted GBH on his wife by knowingly exposing her to the risk of contracting gonorrhoea through intercourse; the wife had not feared the infliction of lawful force at the time of the sexual intercourse. In **R** *v* **Wilson** (1984) the House of Lords stated that an assault is not necessary, the word 'inflict' simply required 'force being violently applied to the body of the victim, so that he suffers grievous bodily harm'. Thus it was thought that, under s. 20, grievous bodily harm had to be caused by the direct application of force. This meant, for example, that it would cover hitting, kicking or stabbing a victim, but not digging a hole for the victim to fall into. In practice, the courts often gave a wide interpretation as to when force was direct. In **R** *v* **Martin** (1881), while a play was being performed at a theatre, the defendant placed an iron bar across the exit, turned off the staircase lights and shouted 'Fire! Fire!' The audience panicked and, in the rush to escape, people were seriously injured. The defendant was found liable under s. 20, even though, strictly speaking, it is difficult to view the application of force as truly direct on these facts.

A similarly wide interpretation was given in **R v Halliday** (1889). In that case, the defendant's behaviour frightened his wife so much that she jumped out of their bedroom window to get away from him. The injuries that she suffered as a result of the fall were found to have been directly applied, so that he could be liable under s. 20.

However, following the decisions in **R v Ireland and Burstow** (1997), the word 'inflict' no longer implies the direct application of force. Burstow had become obsessed with a female acquaintance. He started to stalk her, following her, damaging her car and breaking into her house. He was convicted for this conduct but after his release from prison he continued to stalk her, following her and subjecting her to further harassment, including silent telephone calls, sending hate mail, stealing clothes from her washing line and scattering condoms over her garden. His behaviour caused his victim to suffer severe depression, insomnia and panic attacks. For this subsequent behaviour he was charged with inflicting grievous bodily harm under s. 20 of the Offences Against the Person Act 1861. The trial court convicted, stating that there was no reason for 'inflict' to be given a restrictive meaning. On appeal against his conviction, the appellant argued that the requirements of the term 'inflict' had not been satisfied. The appeal was dismissed by both the Court of Appeal and the House of Lords. The House stated that s. 20 could be committed where no physical force had been applied (directly or indirectly) on the body of the victim.

The offence can be committed when somebody infects another with HIV. A prosecution was brought under s. 20 in **R v Dica** (2004). The defendant knew that he was HIV positive and had unprotected sexual intercourse with two women. He was prosecuted under s. 20 of the Offences Against the Person Act 1861. His initial conviction was quashed on appeal and a retrial ordered because of a misdirection on the issue of consent, but the Court of Appeal accepted that a person could be liable under s. 20 for recklessly infecting another with HIV.

Wounding

Wounding requires a breaking of the skin, so there will normally be bleeding, though a graze will be sufficient. In **C (A Minor) v Eisenhower** (1984), the defendant fired an air pistol, hitting the victim in the eye with a pellet. This ruptured a blood vessel in the eye, causing internal bleeding, but the injury was not sufficient to constitute a wounding, as the skin had not been broken. This may seem odd, given that for this serious offence the *actus reus* can be satisfied simply by pricking somebody's thumb with a pin.

Mens rea

The *mens rea* for this offence is defined by the word 'maliciously'. In **R v Cunningham** (1957) it was stated that, for the purpose of the 1861 Act, maliciously meant 'intentionally or recklessly'.

The case of **R v Mowatt** (1967) established that there is no need to intend or be reckless as to causing GBH or wounding. The defendant need only intend or be reckless that his or her acts could have caused some physical harm. As Lord Diplock said: 'It is quite unnecessary that the accused should have foreseen that his unlawful act might cause physical harm of the gravity described in the section, i.e. a wound or serious physical injury. It is enough that he should have foreseen that some physical harm to some person, albeit of a minor character, might result.' The leading case on the point is now the House of Lords' judgment in **R v Savage**; **DPP v Parmenter** (1992).

> ✓ **Know your terms 16.1**
>
> Define the following terms:
>
> 1 Assault.
> 2 Battery.
> 3 Actual bodily harm.
> 4 Maliciously.

In **R v Grimshaw** (1984) the defendant was in a pub when she heard someone insult her boyfriend. She pushed the glass he was holding into his face. She was found guilty of an offence under s. 20: she had inflicted grievous bodily harm and she had the *mens rea* because she had at least foreseen that he might suffer some harm.

The Divisional Court decision in **Director of Public Prosecutions v A** (2000) highlighted the fact that the defendant is only required to have foreseen that some harm *might* occur, not that it *would* occur. In that case the defendant was a 13-year-old boy who had been playing with two air pistols with his friend. He shot his friend in the eye, causing him to lose his sight in that eye. The defendant was charged with committing an offence under s. 20 of the Offences Against the Person Act 1861. He argued that he lacked the requisite *mens rea*. On the issue of *mens rea*, the magistrates were referred by the court clerk to a passage in *Stone's Justices' Manual*, a book frequently used in the magistrates' courts. This passage stated: 'In order to establish an offence under s. 20 the prosecution must prove either that the defendant intended or that he foresaw that his act would cause some physical harm to some person, albeit of a minor nature.' The prosecution appealed against the defendant's acquittal and the appeal was allowed. The passage in *Stone's Justices' Manual* was wrong, as it required too high a level of *mens rea*. It was only necessary for the prosecution to show that the defendant had foreseen that some harm *might* occur, not that it *would* occur. In fact, if the defendant had foreseen that the harm would occur, the court could have found an intention to commit that harm under the **Nedrick** test for indirect intention, which exists where the harm is foreseen as a virtual certainty.

Where the offence is concerned with the infection of HIV, the defendant need not have known that he was actually infected, provided he was aware that there was a high risk that he was infected. In the Crown Court case of **R v Adaye** (2004), Mr Adaye had been informed by his wife that she was HIV positive. Shortly afterwards, he started a new sexual relationship with another woman and failed to use condoms. His new partner contracted HIV and he was prosecuted for the s. 20 offence. Mr Adaye had not taken a HIV antibody test and did not conclusively know of his HIV status at the time of transmission. However, the Crown Court held that knowledge of a higher level of risk of HIV infection was sufficient to hold that the defendant had acted recklessly.

Offences Against the Person Act 1861, s. 18

Section 18 provides:

> *'Whosoever shall unlawfully and maliciously by any means whatsoever wound or cause any grievous bodily harm to any person, with intent to do some grievous bodily harm to any person, or with intent to resist or prevent the lawful apprehension or detainer of any person, shall be guilty of an offence triable only on indictment, and being convicted thereof shall be liable to imprisonment for life.'*

This is similar to the offence of s. 20 and, like that offence, requires proof of either grievous bodily harm or wounding. The crucial difference is in the *mens rea*: while recklessness can be sufficient for s. 20, intention is always required for s. 18. It is for this reason that s. 18 is punishable with a life sentence, while the maximum sentence for s. 20 is only five years – a person acting with intent is considered to have greater moral fault than a person merely acting recklessly.

Actus reus

Wounding and grievous bodily harm are given the same interpretation as for s. 20. In **R v Ireland and Burstow** (1997) Lord Steyn said that the word 'cause' in s. 18 and 'inflict' in s. 20 were not synonymous, but it is difficult to see how they differ in practice. Both refer to the need for causation.

Mens rea

As noted above, the prosecution must prove intention. The intent must be either to cause grievous bodily harm (by contrast with s. 20, where an intention to cause some harm is sufficient), or to avoid arrest.

In addition, the section states that the defendant must have acted 'maliciously'. This bears the same meaning as discussed for s. 20, so if the prosecution has already proved that the defendant intended to cause grievous bodily harm, 'maliciously'

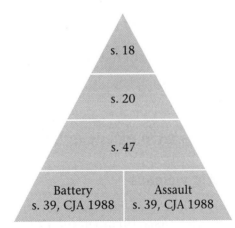

Figure 16.2 **Non-fatal offences against the person**

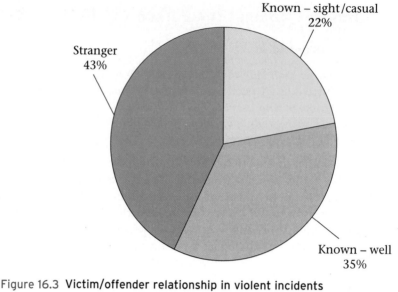

Figure 16.3 **Victim/offender relationship in violent incidents**

Source: C. Flood-Page and J. Taylor (eds.) (2003), *Crime in England and Wales 2001/2002: Supplementary Volume*, p. 57, Figure 3.8. Home Office, © Crown Copyright 2003.

imposes no further requirement: a defendant who intends to cause grievous bodily harm obviously intends to cause some harm. If the prosecution has proved the other form of intent, the intent to avoid arrest, then the requirement that the defendant acts maliciously does impose a further requirement: an intent to avoid arrest does not necessarily imply intention, or recklessness as to whether you cause some harm. Therefore, where the prosecution proves intent to avoid arrest, it must also show that the defendant intended to cause some harm, or was reckless as to whether harm was caused.

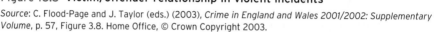

Quick quiz 16.2

1 If a person shouts at you 'I'm going to beat you up', has that person committed an assault?

2 What is the *mens rea* of an assault?

3 What is the *mens rea* of a s. 47 actual bodily harm offence?

4 What is the difference between the s. 20 and s. 18 offences in the Offences Against the Person Act 1861?

Problems with offences against the person

Domestic violence

Domestic violence accounts for 16 per cent of all violent crime (*Crime in England and Wales 2003/2004*, Home Office). This form of violence is defined by the Home Office as: 'Any violence between current and former partners in an intimate relationship, wherever and whenever the violence occurs. The violence may include physical, sexual, emotional and financial abuse.' One in four women and one in six men will be the victims of domestic violence at some point in their lives (Mirlees-Black (1999)). Every minute the police receive a 999 emergency telephone call reporting an incident of domestic violence (Stanko, 2000). Between a quarter and a third of victims of homicide are killed by a partner or former partner (Criminal Statistics (2000)). In 90 per cent of incidents where the couple have children, a child is present or in the next room. Domestic abuse occurs throughout the whole of our society, regardless of social class.

While the law itself does not distinguish between these victims and the person who gets attacked in the streets by a stranger, in practice the victims of domestic assaults rarely receive the law's protection. The first reason for this is simply that very few domestic assaults – research suggests around 2 per cent – are reported to the police. On average, a woman will be assaulted 35 times before she contacts the police (Yearnshire (1997)). If the offences are not reported, obviously they cannot be prosecuted, and the violent partner escapes punishment.

Research among battered wives suggests a variety of reasons for this under-reporting. Women are embarrassed by what the violence says about their relationship, and often blame themselves – a feeling frequently supported by a violent partner's claims that he has been provoked into violence by the woman's behaviour. In the early stages, a woman may make excuses for a man's behaviour, and tell herself that it will not happen again; by the time the violence has been repeated over a long period, she may feel powerless and unable to escape or take any steps towards reporting the offence. This situation can lead to a recognised psychological state, often called battered woman's syndrome, in which the victim loses the ability to see beyond the situation or any means of changing it.

Equally important is the fact that victims may fear that reporting the offence will simply lead to further beatings, given that even if charges are brought, the partner will usually be granted bail, and is highly likely to arrive home and attack her again in revenge for her making the complaint.

These problems are intensified by the traditional police approach to domestic violence which is to avoid involvement, leaving the partners to sort things out themselves. This is prompted partly by the emphasis on the privacy of the home and the family which has been a traditional part of British culture where 'an Englishman's home is his castle'. The expression 'rule of thumb' comes from a rule that a man was allowed to hit his wife with a stick if it was no thicker than this thumb. In addition, there were concerns that the intervention of the legal system might lead to increased marriage breakdown. The assumption was that a couple might divorce if a prosecution were brought, but left alone, they would patch up their differences. The police also claimed that, where prosecutions were brought, by the time the case came to court wives and girlfriends were refusing to give evidence leading to cases collapsing.

In recent years some changes have been made in an attempt to address these problems. A spouse can now be compelled to give evidence against their partner in court proceedings, following the passing of s. 80 of the Police and Criminal Evidence Act 1984, and orders can be made prohibiting violence against a partner and even ousting the violent person from the home, though the effect of such an order in practice may be minimal where the violent partner is really determined to get at the victim.

The Crown Prosecution Service has issued policy guidance on prosecuting cases of domestic violence. This encourages prosecutors to not just rely on the victim's evidence, but to also collect such evidence as medical reports and tape recordings of 999 calls. The prosecution can then proceed even where the victim no longer wishes to pursue the complaint. Special measures can be used during the trial to help the victim give evidence, such as allowing the victim to give evidence behind a screen. Bail conditions can be applied which order the defendant to keep away from the family home and the children's school.

In June 2003 the government published a consultation paper, *Safety and Justice: the Government's proposals on domestic violence*. This focuses on improving the legal protection available to the victims of domestic violence, using both the civil and criminal systems. This consultation process was followed by the Domestic Violence, Crime and Victims Act 2004, which introduces a range of practical reforms to try and improve the protection afforded to people who are the victim of domestic violence.

The government promised in its 2005 election manifesto to promote the use of 'advocates' in domestic violence, murder and rape cases. These advocates would be volunteers providing support to the victims during the criminal justice process. It also promised to develop specialist courts to deal with domestic violence.

The law and legal procedure alone cannot deal with this problem; a cultural change is required that would make domestic violence as unacceptable as any other kind of violent behaviour. Society tends to ignore domestic abuse or even consider it acceptable. One boy in five believes it is alright to hit a woman. One girl in ten agrees with this view.

Task 16.3

Read the following newspaper article and then answer the questions below:

Grim facts of domestic violence

The figures make depressing reading. One in four women and one in six men experience domestic violence in their lifetimes. An average of two women a week in England and Wales are killed by current or former partners. Domestic violence incidents make up nearly a quarter of all violent crimes and yet surveys say that only between 11 and 35 per cent of such events are reported to the police. This crime degrades both victim and perpetrator. And it is no respecter of age, race, sex or nationality. There are no significant differences in numbers between ethnic groups and it is the under-25s in all sections of society who are most likely to be affected. A study among Asian, Afro-Caribbean and Arab women found that half of those who had experienced domestic violence waited five years before they sought help.

Perhaps most depressing of all, a survey of 1,300 schoolchildren found that one in three boys thought violence against women was acceptable.

Academic research estimated the cost of dealing with domestic violence in the Hackney area alone in 1996 was £90 per household, equivalent to £278 million a year for Greater London alone. Multiply that nationally and the financial costs are huge.

So what are we to do to improve this state of affairs? The Government is committed to tackling domestic violence on every front. There are initiatives by the Department for Constitutional Affairs, the Home Office, the Crown Prosecution Service and the police. Type the words 'domestic violence' into an internet search engine and it will throw up the contact details of dozens of aid groups covering every race, religious, ethnic, sexual, geographic and national grouping.

Education is the only solution. If we are serious about reducing the rate of domestic violence, we need to tackle the issue in the classroom, not the police interview room.

(Article written by Marilyn Stowe and published in *The Times* on 1 July 2003.)

Questions

1 What is meant by 'domestic violence'?
2 Can men be victims of domestic violence?
3 Which age group is more likely to be the victim of domestic violence?
4 Research suggested that one in three schoolboys thought violence against women is acceptable. Do you think violence against women is acceptable?
5 What do you think is the best way of reducing domestic violence?

Definitions of the offences

Criticism is also often made of the way the offences themselves are defined. There is still no clear statutory definition of assault and battery, while the definitions of the more serious offences are contained in an Act passed back in 1861, with much of the vocabulary antiquated and even misleading, such as 'assault' in s. 47 and 'maliciously' in s. 18.

The requirement that the threat must be of immediate force in order to fall within an assault means that there is a gap in the law. Currently, if a person shouts that he or she is going to kill you, that may be an assault; but if the threat is to kill you tomorrow, it is not. The Law Commission has produced a draft Criminal Law Bill in the belief that prompt reform of this area is necessary, and which creates an offence that would cover this example.

Structure of the offences

The 1861 Act was merely a consolidating Act which gathered together a whole host of unrelated provisions from existing statutes. No attempt was made to rationalise the provisions. As a result, the offences lack a clear structured hierarchy. First, while assault and battery can only be punished with a maximum of six months' imprisonment, and a s. 47 offence can be punished by five years, the only real difference between them is that ABH is caused – yet ABH can mean as little as causing discomfort to the person. Secondly, the s. 20 offence is defined as a much more serious offence than one covered by s. 47, and yet they share the same maximum sentence of five years.

A third problem is that the only significant difference between s. 20 and s. 18 offences is arguably a slightly more serious *mens rea*, and yet the maximum sentence leaps from five years to life. This can perhaps be justified by the fact that a defendant

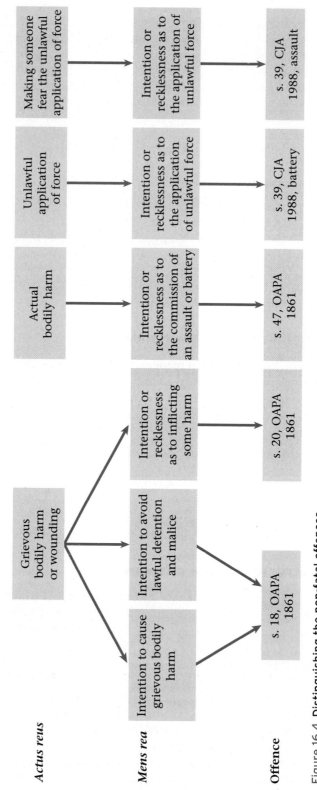

Figure 16.4 Distinguishing the non-fatal offences

Table 16.2 **Trial and sentence of the non-fatal offences**

Offence	Type of offence	Maximum sentence
Assault	Summary	Six months
Battery	Summary	Six months
s. 47, OAPA 1861	Summary	Five years
s. 20, OAPA 1861	Triable either way	Five years
s. 18, OAPA 1861	Indictable only	Life

who intends to cause GBH within s. 18 has the *mens rea* of murder, and it is merely chance which dictates whether the victim survives, leading to a charge under s. 18, or dies, leading to a charge of murder and a mandatory life sentence if convicted.

Reform

Modernising the legislation

In 1980 the Criminal Law Revision Committee recommended that this area of the law should be reformed. Its proposals were incorporated into the draft code of the criminal law prepared by the Law Commission. The Law Commission again considered the matter at the beginning of the 1990s, producing a report and draft Criminal Law Bill on the issue in 1993. In February 1998, the Home Office produced a consultation document in furtherance of its commitment to modernise and improve the law. This presents a draft Offences Against the Person Bill modelled largely, but not entirely, on the Law Commission's 1993 draft Criminal Law Bill. There now looks as if there is a real possibility that legislation may follow. The draft Bill updates the language used for these offences by talking about serious injury rather than grievous bodily harm, and avoiding the words 'maliciously' and 'wounding' altogether. Under the draft Bill, s. 18 is replaced by 'intentionally causing serious injury', with a maximum sentence of life (clause 1); s. 20 by 'recklessly causing serious injury', with a maximum sentence of seven years (clause 2); and s. 47 by 'intentionally or recklessly causing injury', with a maximum sentence of five years (clause 3). Thus the offence replacing s. 47 would remove the requirement of an 'assault', which would be tidier and avoid the problem of finding an assault where there is a course of conduct (see **R v Cox** on p. 290). The draft Bill still proceeds to use the term 'assault' for conduct which would better be described as two separate offences of assault and battery (clause 4).

Task 16.4

The Home Office consultation document, *Violence: Reforming the Offences Against the Person Act 1861*, includes an annexe with a draft Offences Against the Person Bill. You can find this draft Bill on the Home Office website at www.old.homeoffice.gov.uk/docs/vroapa.htm.

Look at the Bill and find out how 'intention' is defined for the purposes of this Bill.

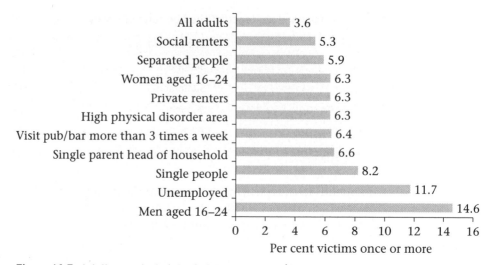

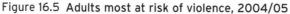

Per cent victims once or more

Figure 16.5 Adults most at risk of violence, 2004/05

Source: S. Nicholas, D. Povey, A. Walker and C. Kershaw, 'Adults most at risk of violence, 2004/05', British Crime Survey Interviews, *Crime in England and Wales 2004/2005*, p. 84, Figure 5.7. © Crown Copyright 2005.

Statutory definitions are given for the mental elements of the offences which would continue to give recklessness a subjective meaning. Difficulties could arise as the statutory definitions differ from the common law definitions and if, for example, a jury was also faced with an accusation of murder, they would have to understand and apply two different tests for intention. The most serious offence in clause 1 could be committed by an omission but not the lesser offences. Injury is defined (clause 15) to include physical and mental injury, but 'anything caused by disease' is not an injury of either kind, except for the purpose of clause 1. So it would be an offence under clause 1 intentionally to infect another with AIDS but no offence to recklessly do so under clause 2.

Liability for infecting another with a disease

In the case of **R** *v* **Dica** the Court of Appeal accepted that, in principle, a defendant could be liable under s. 20 of the Offences Against the Person Act 1861 for recklessly infecting another with AIDS. There is, however, much debate on whether criminal liability should be imposed for infecting another with a disease, particularly sexually transmitted diseases, such as AIDS. The World Health Report lists AIDS as the fourth biggest world killer, with an estimated 5,000 new infections every day, and the number of HIV patients in Britain is increasing. Clearly, it is in everybody's interests to stop the spread of AIDS, but there is much controversy over whether the criminal law can help to achieve this. The United Nations has put forward a range of reasons why the criminal law should get involved in preventing the transmission of AIDS in a document entitled *Criminal Law, Public Health and HIV Transmission: a policy options paper*. However, there are concerns that criminalising this type of activity risks discriminating against the ill. Where the relevant disease is AIDS, many of those infected belong to some of the more vulnerable groups in society. Prior to the **Dica** case, the Home Office had rejected criminalising the reckless transmission of disease because: 'the government is particularly concerned that the law should not seem to discriminate against those who are HIV positive, have AIDS or viral hepatitis or who carry any kind of disease.' A counter-argument to this is that the criminal law will only step in if an ill person behaves in a reprehensible manner, not simply because they are ill.

Another concern is that criminalising such conduct could prove to be counter-productive in terms of protecting public health. The involvement of the criminal law in the field, may encourage secrecy and constitute an obstacle to educating the public about AIDS. If the reckless transmission of a disease is criminalised, people might avoid having health checks, so that they can claim that they were not reckless in having unprotected sexual intercourse, because they did not know that they were carrying an infection. It could also encourage those who know they are infected, to engage in casual sexual intercourse after which they cannot be traced, rather than being in a long-term sexual relationship. Following a criminal conviction for HIV transmission in Scotland, two academics, Bird and Brown (2001), carried out research into the impact of the case on HIV transmission in Scotland. They suggested that following the conviction there was evidence of a 25 per cent reduction in HIV testing. They also found that even a modest fall in the uptake of HIV testing as a result of the judgment could produce a third increase in sexually transmitted HIV infections.

It may be appropriate to impose criminal liability where a person has intentionally infected another, but it will frequently be difficult to prove this intention in this type of case, and it is much more controversial to impose liability for reckless infection. In 1993 the Law Commission proposed the creation of an offence of recklessly causing serious injury, which would have covered the reckless transmission of disease (*Legislating the Criminal Code: Offences Against the Person and General Principles*, Law Com. No. 218). Five years later, however, the Home Office rejected this proposal (*Violence: Reforming the Offences Against the Person Act 1861*). It would have restricted liability for the transmission of a disease to where there was intention to cause serious injury. An intention to cause a lesser harm would not be sufficient and recklessness would not be sufficient. The government considered that 'it would be wrong to criminalise the reckless transmission of normally minor illnesses such as measles or mumps'.

In the context of AIDS, its transmission can be prevented by the use of a condom, and it is not unreasonable to expect people to use a condom when they know that failure to do so risks giving their partners a disease that will ultimately kill them.

Task 16.5

The following extract is the introduction to the Home Office consultation paper, *Violence: Reforming the Offences Against the Person Act 1861*. Read the passage and answer the questions that follow. (The underlined words are the subject of questions.)

1.1 This paper sets out proposals for the reform of the criminal offences used to prosecute violence against individual people. The vocabulary of offences of violence against the person is part of the common currency of everyday life. <u>Court reports and drama</u> have made the very words grievous bodily harm and actual bodily harm deeply familiar. However, familiarity does not mean that such time-hallowed offences are readily understood or that they provide an effective means for the courts to deal with violent behaviour. Criminal law that applies to violence against the person derives from both common and statute law, but the <u>unrepealed</u> parts of the Offences Against the Person Act 1861 provide the bulk of the statutory offences. That Act was itself not a coherent restatement of the law, but a <u>consolidation</u> of much older law. It is therefore not surprising that the law has been widely criticised as archaic and unclear and that it is now in urgent need of reform.

1.2 Reforming the law on violence against the person is not just an academic exercise – criminal cases involving non-fatal offences against the person make up a large part of the work of the courts and cost a great deal of taxpayers' money. In 1996, 83,000 cases came before the courts. It is therefore particularly important that the law governing such behaviour should be robust, clear and well understood. Unclear or uncertain criminal law risks creating injustice and unfairness to individuals, as well as making the work of the police and courts far more difficult and time-consuming. The Government's aim is that the proposed new offences should enable violence to be dealt with effectively by the courts and that the law should be set out in clear terms and in plain, modern language. That is what the draft Bill contained in this consultation paper does. It is intended to help not only practitioners of the law but anyone who finds themselves involved in court cases, whether as a defendant, victim or witness.

1.3 The proposals in this paper are based on the work of the Law Commission as set out in its report No. 218: *Offences Against the Person and General Principles*. That report examined the current state of the law in great detail and proposed a new set of offences ranging from intentional serious injury to assault, as well as rationalising and codifying other offences. The Government is deeply grateful to the Law Commission for the careful and painstaking work that they have done on this subject, and for the principled way they have approached it.

1.4 The purpose of this consultation paper is to set out both the rationale and the detail of the Government's proposals, how they relate to those of the Law Commission, and to invite comments on them. The Government recognises that reforming the law in this area can raise important questions of policy, principle and practice and wishes to ensure that the implications of its proposals are fully appreciated and that all those affected have an opportunity to contribute their views.

Questions

1 What is meant by 'court reports and drama'?
2 What does 'unrepealed' mean?
3 What is meant by 'consolidation' of the law?
4 What type of law does the government want to introduce?

Stalking

The problems of stalking have attracted considerable media attention. 'Stalking', like 'shoplifting' and 'football hooliganism', is not a technical legal concept but one used in everyday language. It describes a campaign of harassment, usually with sexual undertones. Such conduct raises two important questions which concerned western legal systems in the late twentieth century: what are the boundaries of acceptable sexual behaviour and how far should psychiatric damage be recognised by the law? So any legal developments in this area are very sensitive.

In response to public concern, the Protection from Harassment Act 1997 was passed. As well as enacting certain civil wrongs, it creates several new criminal offences. Section 1 prohibits a person from pursuing a course of conduct which they know or ought to know amounts to harassment of another. This is punishable by a maximum of six months' imprisonment. Section 4 contains the offence of aggravated harassment where, in addition, the defendant knows or ought to know that they placed the victim in fear of violence on at least two occasions. This is punishable with up to five years' imprisonment.

It is questionable whether this piece of legislation was necessary. The Act follows a pattern witnessed in other areas (for example, joyriding and dangerous dogs) of addressing a narrowly conceived social harm, backed by a single issue pressure group campaign, with a widely drawn provision which overlaps with existing offences. The new offences in the 1997 Act are broadly defined and there is a danger that they could impinge upon other activities hitherto regarded as legitimate, such as investigative journalism and door-to-door selling. Cases such as **R v Ireland and Burstow** and **R v Constanza** show that the courts were prepared to adapt existing criminal law offences to include this type of harmful conduct. On the other hand, some people feel that these cases artificially distorted the existing law, ignoring accepted authorities, and that a fresh legislative approach was required with this specific problem in mind. In practice, the value of the 1997 Act may be that it includes a power to make restraining orders forbidding the defendant from pursuing any conduct which amounts to harassment and a power of arrest to enforce these orders.

Reading on the web

The Home Office consultation paper *Violence: Reforming the Offences Against the Person Act 1861* (1998) is available on the Home Office website at:

   www.old.homeoffice.gov.uk/docs/vroapa.htm

The decision of **R v Ireland and Burstow** can be found on the House of Lords' website at:

   www.publications.parliament.uk/pa/ld/ldjudgmt.htm#1997

Chapter summary

There are five main non-fatal offences against the person:

- assault;
- battery;
- actual bodily harm;
- inflicting grievous bodily harm or wounding; and
- causing grievous bodily harm or wounding.

Assault

Actus reus

This consists of any act which makes the victim fear that unlawful force is about to be used against them.

Mens rea

The *mens rea* of assault is either intention or subjective recklessness. The defendant must have either intended to cause the victim to fear the infliction of immediate and unlawful force, or seen the risk that such fear would be created.

Battery

Actus reus

The *actus reus* of battery consists of the application of unlawful force on another.

Mens rea

Again, either intention or subjective recklessness is sufficient, but here it is intention or recklessness as to the application of unlawful force.

Offences Against the Person Act 1861, s. 47

Actus reus

The first requirement is to prove the *actus reus* of assault or battery. In addition, the prosecution must show that the assault or battery caused actual bodily harm.

Mens rea

The *mens rea* is the same as for assault or battery. No additional *mens rea* is required in relation to the actual bodily harm.

Offences Against the Person Act 1861, s. 20

Actus reus

The prosecution has to prove that the defendant either inflicted grievous bodily harm or wounded the victim.

Mens rea

The *mens rea* for this offence is defined by the word 'maliciously'. In **R v Cunningham** it was stated that, for the purposes of the 1861 Act, maliciously meant 'intentionally or recklessly' and the test for recklessness is subjective.

Offences Against the Person Act 1861, s. 18

Actus reus

The defendant must have caused grievous bodily harm or wounded the victim.

Mens rea

The defendant must have intended to cause grievous bodily harm or to avoid arrest. If the defendant intended to avoid arrest, there is an additional requirement that he or she acted maliciously.

Question and answer guides

1

Alan was reversing his lorry into a narrow entrance to park against a wall. He suddenly heard people standing on the pavement shout 'Stop!' Alan stopped immediately and looked to see what the fuss was about. He found that he had trapped Denis against the wall. When he saw that it was Denis, he shouted, 'I hate you, you can stay there!' He kept Denis trapped against the wall for several minutes and then drove off. As a result, Denis suffered a fractured spine and was permanently paralysed.

(a) Criminal offences usually require *actus reus* and *mens rea*. Explain, using examples, the meaning of these **two** terms **and** the principle that these two must coincide (the contemporaneity rule). *(15 marks)*

(b) Taking into account the explanations in your answer to part (a), and ignoring any possible driving offences, discuss the criminal liability of Alan for the injuries caused to Denis. *(10 marks)*

(from AQA Exam Paper, January 2007)

(a)

Actus reus

To say that a criminal offence requires an *actus reus* is to say that an accused must usually have acted in a particular way in order to incur criminal liability. An *actus reus* can include the circumstances in which the act was committed (e.g. lack of consent in rape) or the consequences of the act (e.g. causing grievous bodily harm in Offences Against the Person Act 1861, s. 20).

The *actus reus* must have been voluntary, although 'voluntary' has sometimes been widely defined: **Larsonneur**.

An omission usually cannot constitute an *actus reus*. However, where defendants know they have done something which has endangered life, and do nothing to prevent the harm occurring, their original act may be treated as the *actus reus*: **Miller**. Moreover, the courts have held that some offences can be committed by omission, e.g. manslaughter, although the omission must be by someone who is under a duty to act, e.g. because of a contract (**Pittwood**).

Mens rea

To say that an offence requires a *mens rea* is to say that an accused must have performed the *actus reus* with a particular state of mind. What that state of mind is varies, depending on the offence. The two most commonly encountered forms of *mens rea* are intention and subjective recklessness.

When the *mens rea* of an offence is intention that intention may be either direct or indirect. Direct intention corresponds with the everyday definition of intention, and applies where the accused actually wants the result that occurs. A jury is entitled to find indirect intention where the accused did not desire a particular result but, in acting as he or she did, realised to the point of virtual certainty that it might occur: **Woollin**.

When the *mens rea* of an offence is subjective recklessness then it means that the defendant must have been aware of a risk that something would happen, and yet unreasonably took that risk: **R v G**.

Coincidence

Defendants must have the *mens rea* of the offence at the same time that they commit the *actus reus*. If the two do not coincide (i.e. are not contemporaneous), they are not guilty of the offence.

However, the courts have qualified this rule in two ways. First, they will sometimes treat the *actus reus* as a continuing situation rather than a momentary event. This will enable them to find that, although the *actus reus* started before the *mens rea* was present, it was still continuing by the time the *mens rea* came into existence: **Fagan**.

Secondly, where the *actus reus* comes at the end of a pre-planned course of action, the court will sometimes treat it as having started when the course of action started. In this way, provided defendants had the necessary *mens rea* when they started, it will not matter that they had ceased to have it by the time they finished: **Thabo Meli**.

(b) The most serious offence for which Alan may be liable is causing grievous bodily harm (GBH) or wounding under s. 18 of the Offences Against the Person Act 1861 (OAPA). The *actus reus* is causing GBH or wounding. Wounding requires a breaking of the skin, and it is unclear whether that happened here. As for GBH, the courts have held that grievous means serious: **Saunders**. Given the nature of Denis' injuries, and that they were 'as a result' of Alan's conduct, the *actus reus* of s. 18 is clearly satisfied.

The *mens rea* of s. 18 is, so far as relevant, intention to cause GBH. When he first reversed his lorry into Denis, Alan had no such intention; he did not even realise that he had trapped Denis against the wall. At worst, Alan was, at this point in time, merely negligent. It was only when he saw what he had done and deliberately delayed releasing Denis that he could be said to have had the necessary intent to cause Denis GBH. But delaying doing something is a mere omission, for which generally there is no criminal liability.

However, applying the principles on coincidence explained in (a) and in particular in **Fagan** (the facts of which are similar to those of the scenario), the court might be prepared to treat the *actus reus* here as a continuing situation rather than a momentary event. This would enable the court to find that, although the *actus reus* (reversing the lorry into Denis) started before the *mens rea* was present, it was still continuing by the time the *mens rea* came into existence. Alternatively, a court could rely on **Miller** as Alan had created a dangerous situation.

But even if the court was prepared to adopt this approach, it might find that, by delaying releasing Denis, Alan did not intend to cause Denis **serious** harm but intended merely to cause him harm. Or it might find that he was merely **reckless** as to whether he caused Denis serious harm. Either finding would entitle Alan to be acquitted of the s. 18 offence.

Turning therefore to consider the next most serious offence for which Alan might be liable, this is causing GBH or wounding under OAPA s. 20. The *actus reus* is the same as s. 18's. However, the *mens rea* is intention **or** recklessness. Moreover, the prosecution does not need to prove that, by delaying releasing Denis, Alan was reckless as to causing Denis **serious** harm. He need only have been reckless as to whether his action could have caused Denis **some** harm: **Savage**. The evidence strongly suggests he was, given the words he shouted at Denis and the fact that he drove off without checking to see whether Denis was injured. Therefore it is likely that he would be found liable of the s. 20 offence.

2 Anna was walking alongside Tara, when she tripped Tara up with her foot. Tara fell over and grazed her knee. She ignored the graze until three days later, when her knee became swollen by an infection. She went to her doctor, who prescribed her a drug to deal with the infection. Tara's doctor did not check her medical records. Tara is in fact allergic to this drug and has become paralysed as a result of her reaction to taking the drug.

(a) Criminal offences generally require proof of both ***actus reus*** and ***mens rea***.
   (i) Briefly explain the meaning of these two terms.   (*5 marks*)
   (ii) Anna might be prosecuted for an offence. Explain what is meant by **causation** and discuss whether Anna's actions were the factual and legal cause of Tara's paralysis.   (*10 marks*)
(b) Taking into account your answer to (a), discuss Anna's criminal liability in this incident involving Tara.   (*10 marks*)

(from AQA Exam Paper, January 2005)

(a) (i)
Actus reus

- Define *actus reus*, and refer to the possibility of it including circumstances and consequences, giving examples of each.
- Refer to the need for the *actus reus* to be voluntary and, for a good answer, to the decision in **Larsonneur**.
- Refer to the fact that an omission cannot constitute an *actus reus* and to the exception laid down in **Miller**.
- For a good answer, explain how some offences can be committed by omission, provided the defendant was under a duty to act, giving an example of such a duty.

Mens rea

- Define *mens rea*.
- Refer to intention and subjective recklessness as being the two most commonly encountered forms of *mens rea*.
- Explain how intention may be either direct or indirect, explaining both and, for a good answer, cite **Woollin** in the context of indirect intention.
- Explain the meaning of subjective recklessness and, for a good answer, cite **R** *v* **G**.

(a) (ii)
Causation – meaning

- Define causation, referring to the need for both 'factual' and 'legal' causation.
- Explain factual causation, including the 'but for' test and citing **White**.
- Explain how legal causation involves proving that the original injury was an operative and significant cause of the result, contrasting **Smith** and **Jordan**.
- For a good answer, explain the 'thin skull' test, citing **Blaue**.

Causation – application

- Using the 'but for' test, briefly show why there was factual causation here.
- Emphasise that the more difficult issue is whether there was legal causation.
- Explain how Anna's tripping of Tara was clearly not the only cause of Tara's paralysis, mentioning the other causes, especially the medical treatment.
- Discuss whether the latter broke the chain of causation, as in **Jordan**, or did not do so, as in **Smith**.
- For a good answer, discuss the doubtful value of **Jordan** as a precedent, mentioning the comments made about it in **Smith** and **Malcherek**.

(b)

- Point out that, if Anna's tripping of Tara was an accident, Anna has no criminal liability at all.
- Explain how, on the assumption that the tripping was deliberate and that there was causation as between the tripping and the paralysis, s. 20 of the Offences Against the Person Act 1861 is the most serious relevant offence here, explaining briefly why s. 18 is not relevant.
- Explain the *actus reus* and *mens rea* of s. 20, citing relevant cases, and apply the relevant legal principles to the facts of the scenario.
- Identify s. 47 OAPA as the next most serious offence for which Anna might be liable if, for example, there was no causation as between the tripping and the paralysis.
- Explain the *actus reus* and *mens rea* of s. 47, citing relevant cases, and apply the relevant legal principles to the facts of the scenario.
- Identify battery as the next most serious offence for which Anna might be liable.
- Explain the *actus reus* and *mens rea* of battery, citing relevant cases, and apply the relevant legal principles to the facts of the scenario.

Common errors in (a) (i)

- spending longer on this part of the question than its 5 marks justifies.

Common errors in (a) (ii):

■ failing to explain factual causation correctly;
■ confusing factual and legal causation in the application part of the question.

Common errors in (b):

■ repeating material on causation that was already covered in (a) (ii);
■ failing to identify, explain and apply a relevant offence.

Group activity 1

■ Divide your friends (or class) into groups of two or three people.
■ Each group should pick one of the five offences covered in this chapter.
■ Using both the information in this chapter and any other information you can find in other publications and the internet, prepare a short note identifying your chosen offence's deficiencies and making recommendations as to how the offence could be improved.
■ Meet with the other groups that have chosen the same offence as you and produce a composite note summarising all of the groups' findings.
■ Meet with the groups that have chosen the other offences and compare notes, looking for any common themes.

mylawchamber

Visit **www.mylawchamber.co.uk/elliottaqa** to access interactive questions, quizzes and activities to test yourself on this chapter.

Chapter 17

Strict liability in criminal law

This chapter discusses:

- which crimes are crimes of strict liability;
- arguments in favour of strict liability;
- arguments against strict liability.

Introduction

Some crimes can be committed without any *mens rea*, or without *mens rea* regarding at least one aspect of the *actus reus*. These offences are known as strict liability crimes, and most of them have been created by statute, though public nuisance and blasphemous libel are examples of common law strict liability offences.

Which crimes are crimes of strict liability?

Unfortunately, statutes are not always so obliging as to state 'this is a strict liability offence'. Occasionally, the wording of an Act does make this clear, but otherwise the courts are left to decide for themselves. The principles on which this decision is made were considered in **Gammon (Hong Kong) Ltd** *v* **Attorney-General of Hong Kong** (1985). The defendants were involved in building works in Hong Kong. Part of a building they were constructing fell down, and it was found that the collapse had occurred because the builders had failed to follow the original plans exactly. The Hong Kong building regulations prohibited deviating in any substantial way from such plans, and the defendants were charged with breaching the regulations, an offence punishable with a fine of up to $250,000 or three years' imprisonment. On appeal they argued that they were not liable because they had not known that the changes they made were substantial ones. However, the Privy Council held that the relevant regulations created offences of strict liability, and the convictions were upheld.

Explaining the principles on which they had based the decision, Lord Scarman confirmed that there is always a presumption of law that *mens rea* is required before a person can be held guilty of a criminal offence. The existence of this presumption was reaffirmed in very strong terms by the House of Lords in **B (A Minor)** *v* **Director of Public Prosecutions** (2000). A 15-year-old boy had sat next to a

13-year-old girl and asked her to give him a 'shiner'. The trial judge observed that '[t]his, in the language of today's gilded youth, apparently means, not a black eye, but an act of oral sex'. The boy was charged with committing an act of gross indecency on a child under the age of 14. Both the trial judge and the Court of Appeal ruled that this was a strict liability offence and that there was therefore no defence available that the boy believed the girl to be over 14. The House of Lords confirmed that there was a presumption that *mens rea* was required, and ruled that the relevant offence was not actually one of strict liability. The House stated that, in order to rebut the presumption that an offence required *mens rea*, there needed to be a 'compellingly clear implication' that Parliament intended the offence to be one of strict liability. As the offence had a very broad *actus reus*, carried a serious social stigma and a heavy sentence, it decided that Parliament did not have this intention. Soon afterwards, the House of Lords confirmed its reluctance to find strict liability offences in **R** *v* **K** (2001).

The case has thrown doubt on the old case of **R** *v* **Prince** (1874), which was also concerned with an offence against the person that could only be committed on a girl under a certain age. That offence had been treated as one of strict liability and the reasonable but mistaken belief of the defendant as to her age was therefore found to be irrelevant. The House of Lords described that case as 'unsound' and a 'relic from an age dead and gone'. In **R** *v* **K** the House of Lords described **Prince** as a 'spent force'.

There are certain factors which can, on their own or combined, displace the presumption that *mens rea* is required. These can be grouped into four categories which will be considered in turn.

Regulatory offence

A regulatory offence is one in which no real moral issue is involved, and usually (though not always) one for which the maximum penalty is small – the mass of rules surrounding the sale of food are examples. In **Gammon** it was stated that the presumption against strict liability was less strong for regulatory offences than for truly criminal offences.

This distinction between true crimes and regulatory offences had previously been made in the case of **Sweet** *v* **Parsley** (1970). Ms Sweet, a teacher, took a sub-lease of a farmhouse outside Oxford. She rented the house to tenants, and rarely spent any time there. Unknown to her, the tenants were smoking cannabis on the premises. When they were caught, she was found guilty of being concerned in the management of premises which were being used for the purpose of smoking cannabis, contrary to the Dangerous Drugs Act 1965 (now replaced by the Misuse of Drugs Act 1971).

Ms Sweet appealed, on the grounds that she knew nothing about what the tenants were doing, and could not reasonably have been expected to have known. Lord Reid acknowledged that strict liability was appropriate for regulatory offences, or 'quasi-crimes' – offences which are not criminal 'in any real sense', and are merely acts prohibited in the public interest. But, he said, the kind of crime to which a real social stigma is attached should usually require proof of *mens rea*; in the case of such offences it was not in the public interest that an innocent person should be prevented from proving that innocence in the interests of making it easier for guilty people to be convicted.

Since their Lordships regarded the offence under consideration as being a 'true crime' – the stigma had, for example, caused Ms Sweet to lose her job – they held that it was not a strict liability offence, and since Ms Sweet did not have the necessary *mens rea*, her conviction was overturned.

Unfortunately, the courts have never laid down a list of those offences which they will consider to be regulatory offences rather than 'true crimes'. Those generally considered to be regulatory offences are the kind created by the rules on hygiene and measurement standards within the food and drink industry, and regulations designed to stop industry from polluting the environment, but there are clearly some types of offences which will be more difficult to categorise.

Issue of social concern

According to **Gammon**, where a statute is concerned with an issue of social concern (such as public safety), and the creation of strict liability will promote the purpose of the statute by encouraging potential offenders to take extra precautions against committing the prohibited act, the presumption against strict liability can be rebutted. This category is obviously subject to the distinctions drawn by Lord Reid in **Sweet** *v* **Parsley** – the laws against murder and rape are to protect the public, but this type of true crime would not attract strict liability.

The types of offences that do fall into this category cover behaviour which could involve danger to the public, but which would not usually carry the same kind of stigma as a crime such as murder or even theft. The breach of the building regulations committed in **Gammon** is an example, as are offences relating to serious pollution of the environment. In **R** *v* **Blake** (1997), the defendant was accused of making broadcasts on a pirate radio station and was convicted of using wireless telegraphy equipment without a licence, contrary to s. 1(1) of the Wireless Telegraphy Act 1949. His conviction was upheld by the Court of Appeal, which stated that this offence was one of strict liability. This conclusion was reached as the offence had been created in the interest of public safety, given the interference with the operation of the emergency services that could result from unauthorised broadcasting.

In **Harrow London Borough Council** *v* **Shah** (1999), the offence of selling National Lottery tickets to a person under the age of 16 was found to be an offence of strict liability. The Divisional Court justified this by stating that the legislation dealt with an issue of social concern.

These crimes overlap with regulatory offences in subject area, but unlike regulatory offences, may carry severe maximum penalties. Despite such higher penalties, strict liability is seen to be a necessary provision given the need to promote very high standards of care in areas of possible danger.

The wording of the Act

Gammon states that the presumption that *mens rea* is required for a criminal offence can be rebutted if the words of a statute suggest that strict liability is intended. The House of Lords said in **Sweet** *v* **Parsley**: 'the fact that other sections of the Act expressly required *mens rea*, for example, because they contain the word "knowingly", is not in itself sufficient to justify a decision that a section which is silent as to *mens rea* creates a [strict liability] offence.' At present it is not always clear whether a particular form of words will be interpreted as creating an offence of strict liability. However, some words have been interpreted fairly consistently, including the following.

'Cause'

In **Alphacell** *v* **Woodward** (1972), the defendant was a company accused of causing polluted matter to enter a river. It was using equipment designed to prevent any overflow into the river, but when the mechanism became clogged by leaves, the pollution was able to escape. There was no evidence that the defendant company had been negligent or even knew that the pollution was leaking out. The House of Lords stated that where statutes create an offence of causing something to happen, the courts should adopt a common-sense approach – if reasonable people would say that the defendant has caused something to happen, regardless of whether he or she knew he or she was doing so, then no *mens rea* is required. Their Lordships held that in the normal meaning of the word, the company had 'caused' the pollution to enter the water, and the company's conviction was upheld.

'Possession'

There are many offences which are defined as 'being in possession of a prohibited item', the obvious example being drugs. They are frequently treated as strict liability offences.

'Knowingly'

Clearly, use of this word tells the courts that *mens rea* is required, and it tends to be used where Parliament wants to underline the fact that the presumption should be applied.

The smallness of the penalty

Strict liability is most often imposed for offences which carry a relatively small maximum penalty, and it appears that the higher the maximum penalty, the less likely it is that the courts will impose strict liability. However, the existence of severe penalties for an offence does not guarantee that strict liability will not be imposed. In **Gammon** Lord Scarman held that where regulations were put in place to protect public safety, it was quite appropriate to impose strict liability, despite potentially severe penalties.

Relevance of the four factors

Obviously, these four factors overlap to a certain extent – regulatory offences usually do have small penalties, for example. And in **Alphacell** *v* **Woodward**, the House of Lords gave its decision the dual justification of applying the common-sense meaning of the term 'cause', and recognising that pollution was an issue of social concern.

It is important to note that all these categories are guidelines rather than clear rules. The courts are not always consistent in their application of strict liability, and social policy plays an important part in the decisions. During the 1960s, there was intense social concern about what appeared to be a widespread drug problem, and the courts imposed strict liability for many drug offences. Ten years later, pollution of the environment had become one of the main topics of concern, hence the justification for the decision in **Alphacell** v **Woodward**.

Today, there appears to be a general move away from strict liability, and some newer statutes imposing apparent strict liability contain a limited form of defence, by which an accused can escape conviction by proving that he or she took all reasonable precautions to prevent the offence being committed. However, the courts could begin to move back towards strict liability if it seems that an area of social concern might require it.

Crimes of negligence

Following the decision of **Attorney-General's Reference (No. 2 of 1999)**, it is arguable that crimes of negligence, such as gross negligence manslaughter, are actually crimes of strict liability. This is because in that case the Court of Appeal stated that gross negligence was not a form of *mens rea* and that a person could be found to have been grossly negligent without looking at their state of mind but simply by looking at the gross carelessness of their conduct.

The effect of mistake

Where strict liability applies, an accused cannot use the defence of mistake, even if the mistake was reasonable. The House of Lords' judgment of **B (A Minor)** v **Director of Public Prosecutions** is slightly misleading on this issue, as it seems to blur the distinction between mistakes made in relation to strict liability offences and mistakes made in relation to offences requiring *mens rea*. This distinction is, however, fundamental. As the case was concerned with an offence that required *mens rea*, anything it stated in relation to strict liability offences was merely *obiter dicta* and therefore not binding on future courts.

The European Convention on Human Rights

In **R** v **Mithun Muhamad** (2002) the Court of Appeal stated that strict liability offences did not automatically breach the European Convention on Human Rights. In **Salabiaku** v **France** (1988) the European Court of Human Rights stated: 'the Contracting States may, under certain conditions, penalise a simple or objective fact as such, irrespective of whether it results from criminal intent or from negligence.'

Quick quiz 17.1

1 What is meant by a strict liability offence?

2 In law is there a presumption that *mens rea* is required or is there a presumption that *mens rea* is not required?

3 Give three examples of words that can rebut the presumption that *mens rea* is required.

4 If a person makes a mistake, what impact can this have on his or her liability for a strict liability offence?

Arguments in favour of strict liability

Promotion of care

By promoting high standards of care, it is argued, strict liability protects the public from dangerous practices. Social scientist Barbara Wootton (1981) has defended strict liability on this basis, suggesting that if the objective of criminal law is to prevent socially damaging activities, it would be absurd to turn a blind eye to those who cause the harm due to carelessness, negligence or even an accident.

Deterrent value

Strict liability is said to provide a strong deterrent, which is considered especially important given the way in which regulatory offences tend to be dealt with. Many of them are handled not by the police and the Crown Prosecution Service (CPS), but by special government bodies, such as the Health and Safety Inspectorate, which checks that safety rules are observed in workplaces. These bodies tend to work by putting pressure on offenders to put right any breaches, with prosecution, or even threats of it, very much a last resort. It is suggested that strict liability allows enforcement agencies to strengthen their bargaining position, since potential offenders know that if a prosecution is brought, there is a very good chance of conviction.

Easier enforcement

Strict liability makes enforcing offences easier; in **Gammon** the Privy Council suggested that if the prosecution had to prove *mens rea* in even the smallest regulatory offence, the administration of justice might very quickly come to a complete standstill.

Difficulty of proving *mens rea*

In many strict liability offences, *mens rea* would be very difficult to prove, and without strict liability, guilty people might escape conviction. Obvious examples are those involving large corporations, where it may be difficult to prove that someone knew what was happening.

No threat to liberty

In many strict liability cases, the defendant is a business and the penalty is a fine, so individual liberty is not generally under threat. Even the fines are often small.

Profit from risk

Where an offence is concerned with business, those who commit it may well be saving themselves money, and thereby making extra profit by doing so – by, for example, saving the time that would be spent on observing safety regulations. If a person creates a risk and makes a profit by doing so, he or she ought to be liable if that risk causes or could cause harm, even if that was not the intention.

Arguments against strict liability

Injustice

Strict liability is criticised as unjust on a variety of different grounds. First, that it is not in the interests of justice that someone who has taken reasonable care, and could not possibly have avoided committing an offence, should be punished by the criminal law. This goes against the principle that the criminal law punishes fault.

Secondly, the argument that strict liability should be enforced because *mens rea* would be too difficult to prove is morally doubtful. The prosecution often find it difficult to prove *mens rea* on a rape charge, for example, but is that a reason for making rape a crime of strict liability? Although many strict liability offences are clearly far lesser crimes than these, some do impose severe penalties, as **Gammon** illustrates, and it may not be in the interests of justice if strict liability is imposed in these areas just because *mens rea* would make things too difficult for the prosecution. It is inconsistent with justice to convict someone who is not guilty, in the normal sense of the word, just because the penalty imposed will be small.

Even where penalties are small, in many cases conviction is a punishment in itself. Sentencing may be tailored to take account of mitigating factors, but that is little comfort to the reputable butcher who unknowingly sells bad meat, when the case is reported in local papers and customers go elsewhere. However slight the punishment, in practice there is some stigma attached to a criminal conviction (even though it may be less than that for a 'true crime') which should not be attached to a person who has taken all reasonable care.

In addition, as Smith and Hogan (2005) point out in their criminal law text-book, in the case of a jury trial, strict liability takes crucial questions of fact away from juries, and allows them to be considered solely by the judge for the purposes of sentencing. In a magistrates' court, it removes those questions from the requirement of proof beyond reasonable doubt, and allows them to be decided according to the less strict principles which guide decisions on sentencing.

Strict liability also delegates a good deal of power to the discretion of the enforcement agency. Where strict liability makes it almost certain that a prosecution will lead to a conviction, the decision on whether or not to prosecute becomes critical, and there are few controls over those who make this decision.

Ineffective

It is debatable whether strict liability actually works. For a start, the deterrent value of strict liability may be overestimated. For the kinds of offences to which strict liability is usually applied, the important deterrent factor may not be the chances of being convicted, but the chances of being caught and charged. In the food and drinks business particularly, just being charged with an offence brings unwelcome publicity, and even if the company is not convicted, it is likely to see a fall in sales as customers apply the 'no smoke without fire' principle. The problem is that in many cases the chances of being caught and prosecuted are not high. In the first place, enforcement agencies frequently lack the resources to monitor the huge number of potential offenders – the Factory Inspectorate in 1980 had 900 inspectors who were responsible for reporting on at least 600,000 different workplaces. Even where offenders are caught, it appears that the usual response of enforcement agencies is a warning letter. The most serious or persistent offenders may be threatened with prosecution if they do not put matters right, but only a minority are actually prosecuted. Providing more resources for the enforcement agencies and bringing more prosecutions might have a stronger deterrent effect than imposing strict liability on the minority who are prosecuted.

In other areas too, it is the chance of getting caught which may be the strongest deterrent – if people think they are unlikely to get caught speeding, for example, the fact that strict liability will be imposed if they do is not much of a deterrent.

In fact in some areas, rather than ensuring a higher standard of care, strict liability may have quite the opposite effect: knowing that it is possible to be convicted of an offence regardless of having taken every reasonable precaution may reduce the incentive to take such precautions, rather than increase it.

As Professor Hall points out, the fact that strict liability is usually imposed only where the possible penalty is small means that unscrupulous companies can simply regard the criminal law as 'a nominal tax on illegal enterprise'. In areas of industry where the need to maintain a good reputation is not so strong as it is in food or drugs, for example, it may be cheaper to keep paying the fines than to change bad working practices, and therefore very little deterrent value can be seen. In these areas it might be more efficient, as Professor Hall says, 'to put real teeth in the law' by developing offences with more severe penalties, even if that means losing the expediency of strict liability.

Justifying strict liability in the interests of protecting the public can be seen as taking a sledgehammer to crack a nut. It is certainly true, for example, that bad meat causes food poisoning just the same whether or not the butcher knew it was bad, and that the public needs protection from butchers who sell bad meat. But while we might want to make sure of punishment for butchers who knowingly sell bad meat, and probably those who take no – or not enough – care to check the condition of their meat, how is the public protected by punishing a butcher who took all possible care (by using a normally reputable supplier, for example) and could not possibly have avoided committing the offence?

Task 17.2

The Health and Safety Executive is responsible for the enforcement of a wide range of strict liability offences. Its website can be found at **www.hse.gov.uk/**.
Visit its website and find information on its work in this field.

Little administrative advantage

It is also open to debate whether strict liability really does contribute much to administrative expediency. Cases still have to be detected and brought to court, and in some cases selected elements of the *mens rea* still have to be proved. And although strict liability may make conviction easier, it leaves the problem of sentencing. This cannot be done fairly without taking the degree of negligence into account, so evidence of the accused's state of mind must be available. Given all this, it is difficult to see how much time and manpower is actually saved.

Inconsistent application

The fact that whether or not strict liability will be imposed rests on the imprecise science of statutory interpretation means that there are discrepancies in both the offences to which it is applied, and what it actually means. The changes in the types of cases to which strict liability is applied over the years reflect social policy – the courts come down harder on areas which are causing social concern at a particular time. While this may be justified in the interests of society, it does little for certainty and the principle that like cases should be treated alike.

The courts are also inconsistent in their justifications for imposing or not imposing strict liability. In **Lim Chin Aik v R** (1963) the defendant was charged with remaining in Singapore, despite a prohibition order against him. Lord Evershed stated that the subject matter of a statute was not sufficient grounds for inferring that strict liability was intended; it was also important to consider whether imposing strict liability would help to enforce the regulations, and it could only do this if there were some precautions the potential offender could take to prevent him from committing the offence: 'Unless this is so, there is no reason in penalising him and it cannot be inferred that the legislature imposed strict liability merely in order to find a luckless victim.'

In the case of **Lim Chin Aik**, the precaution to be taken would have been finding out whether there was a prohibition order against him, but Lord Evershed further explained that people could only be expected to take 'sensible' and 'practicable' precautions: Lim Chin Aik was not expected to 'make continuous enquiry to see whether an order had been made against him'.

Presumably, then, our hypothetical butcher should only be expected to take reasonable and practicable precautions against selling bad meat, and not, for example, have to employ scientific analysts to test every pork chop. Yet just such extreme precautions appear to have been expected in **Smedleys v Breed** (1974). The defendants were convicted under the Food and Drugs Act 1955, after a very small caterpillar was found in one of three million tins of peas. Despite the fact that even individual inspection of each pea would probably not have prevented the offence being committed, Lord Hailsham defended the imposition of strict liability on the grounds that: 'To construe the Food and Drugs Act 1955 in a sense less strict than that which I have adopted would make a serious inroad on the legislation for consumer protection.' Clearly, the subject areas of these cases are very different, but the contrast between them does give some indication of the shaky ground on which strict liability can rest – if the House of Lords had followed the reasoning of **Lim Chin Aik**, Smedleys would not have been liable, since they had taken all reasonable and practical precautions.

Better alternatives are available

There are alternatives to strict liability which would be less unjust and more effective in preventing harm, such as better inspection of business premises and the imposition of liability for negligence (see below).

Reform

The Law Commission's draft Bill

The Law Commission's draft Criminal Liability (Mental Element) Bill of 1978 requires that Parliament specifically state if it is creating an offence of strict liability. Where this is not done, the courts should assume that *mens rea* is required. The practice of allowing the courts to decide when strict liability should be applied, under cover of the fiction that they are interpreting parliamentary intention, is not helpful, and leads to a mass of litigation with many of the cases irreconcilable with each other – as with **Lim Chin Aik** and **Smedleys** *v* **Breed**, above. If legislators knew that the courts would always assume *mens rea* unless specifically told not to, they would be more likely to adopt the habit of stating whether the offence was strict or not.

> ✓ **Know your terms 17.3**
>
> Define the following terms:
> 1 Regulatory offence.
> 2 Stigma.
> 3 Draft Bill.
> 4 Law Commission.

Restriction to public danger offences

Strict liability could perhaps be more easily justified if the tighter liability were balanced by real danger to the public in the offence – the case of **Gammon** can be justified on this ground.

Liability for negligence

Smith and Hogan in their criminal law textbook (2005) suggest that strict liability should be replaced by liability for negligence. This would catch defendants who were simply thoughtless or inefficient, as well as those who deliberately broke the law, but would not punish people who were genuinely blameless.

Defence of all due care

In Australia a defence of all due care is available. Where a crime would otherwise impose strict liability, the defendant can avoid conviction by proving that he or she took all due care to avoid committing the offence.

Extending strict liability

Baroness Wootton (1981) advocates imposing strict liability for all crimes, so that *mens rea* would only be relevant for sentencing purposes.

Reading on the web

The website of the Health and Safety Executive can be found at:

www.hse.gov.uk/

The decision of **B (A Minor)** v **Director of Public Prosecutions** (2000) is available on the House of Lords' website at:

www.publications.parliament.uk/pa/ld/ldjudgmt.htm#2000

Chapter summary

Strict liability crimes are crimes which can be committed without any *mens rea*, or without *mens rea* regarding at least one aspect of the *actus reus*.

Which crimes are crimes of strict liability?

The wording of an Act will sometimes make it clear that an offence is one of strict liability; otherwise the courts must decide. There is always a presumption of law that *mens rea* is required before a person can be held guilty of a criminal offence. There are certain factors which can, on their own or combined, displace the presumption that *mens rea* is required. These can be grouped into the four following categories:

- the crime is a regulatory offence;
- the statute deals with an issue of social concern;
- the wording of the Act suggests that *mens rea* is not required; and
- the smallness of the penalty suggests *mens rea* is not required.

Crimes of negligence

Following the decision of **Attorney-General's Reference (No. 2 of 1999)**, it is arguable that crimes of negligence are actually crimes of strict liability.

The effect of mistake

Where strict liability applies, an accused cannot use the defence of mistake, even if the mistake is reasonable.

The European Convention on Human Rights

Strict liability offences do not automatically breach the European Convention.

Arguments in favour of strict liability

Arguments have been put forward in favour of strict liability including:

■ promotion of care;
■ deterrent value;
■ easier enforcement; and
■ difficulty in proving *mens rea*.

Arguments against strict liability

Arguments against strict liability include that such offences:

■ cause injustice;
■ are ineffective;
■ have little administrative advantage;
■ are applied inconsistently; and
■ should be replaced by better alternatives.

Question and answer guide

1

Jo, her boyfriend Peter, and Karen shared a flat. Jo was angry and upset because she believed that Peter and Karen had slept together. Jo heard the door to the flat being opened, and assumed that Karen or Peter had come in. In fact it was the landlord, Richard, who was delivering a new fridge. Without looking, Jo threw a pan full of boiling water in the direction of the door to the flat, and Richard was badly scalded.

(a) At a criminal trial, the prosecution is required to prove **mens rea** unless the crime is one of **strict liability**. Explain, with the help of decided cases, what **each** of these **two** terms means. (*15 marks*)
(b) Discuss Jo's criminal liability for Richard's injuries. (*10 marks*)

(from AQA Exam Paper, June 2006)

(a)
Mens rea
To say that an offence requires a *mens rea* is to say that an accused must have performed the *actus reus* with a particular state of mind. What that state of mind is

varies depending on the offence. The two most commonly encountered forms of *mens rea* are intention and subjective recklessness.

When the *mens rea* of an offence is intention that intention may be either direct or indirect; either will be sufficient. Direct intention corresponds with the everyday definition of intention, and applies where the accused actually wants the result that occurs. A jury is entitled to find indirect intention (sometimes called oblique intention) where the accused did not desire a particular result but, in acting as he or she did, realised to the point of virtual certainty that it might occur: **Woollin**.

When the *mens rea* of an offence is subjective recklessness then it means that the defendant must have been aware of a risk that something would happen, and yet unreasonably took that risk: **R *v* G**.

Under the principle known as transferred malice, the *mens rea* of one *actus reus* can be transferred to another *actus reus*. For example, if Ann shoots at Ben, intending to kill him, but happens to miss, and shoots and kills Chris instead, Ann will be liable for the murder of Chris, even though she did not intend to kill Chris. The law transfers her intention to kill from the *actus reus* of killing Ben to the *actus reus* of killing Chris. Either intention or recklessness can be transferred in this way: **Latimer**.

Strict liability

Strict liability crimes are those that can be committed without any *mens rea*, or without *mens rea* regarding at least one aspect of the *actus reus*.

Most strict liability offences are statutory. Sometimes the statute makes clear whether the offence is one of strict liability. But usually the courts are left to decide for themselves. In making this decision the courts start from the presumption that *mens rea* is required: **Sweet *v* Parsley**. To rebut this presumption they require a 'compellingly clear implication' that Parliament intended the offence to be one of strict liability: **B (A Minor) *v* DPP**.

The presumption that *mens rea* is required is less strong for 'regulatory offences' than for true crimes: **Gammon *v* Attorney-General of Hong Kong**. The courts have never laid down a complete list of those offences which they will consider to be regulatory. But they appear to be those in which no real moral issue is involved, and usually (though not always) one for which the maximum penalty is small, e.g. selling unfit food.

Where a statutory offence is concerned with an issue of social concern (such as public safety), and the creation of strict liability will promote the purpose of the statute by encouraging potential offenders to take extra precautions against committing the prohibited act, the presumption against strict liability can be rebutted. Examples of crimes that have been held to fall within this category are breaching building regulations (**Gammon**), using wireless telegraphy equipment without a licence (**R *v* Blake**) and selling National Lottery tickets to a person under the age of 16 (**Harrow London Borough Council *v* Shah**).

(b) The most serious offence for which Jo may be liable is causing grievous bodily harm (GBH) or wounding under s. 18 of the Offences Against the Person Act 1861 (OAPA). The *actus reus* is causing GBH or wounding. Wounding requires a breaking of the skin, and a bad scald would usually involve this. As for GBH, the courts have held that grievous means serious: **Saunders**. So a bad scald might well amount to GBH as well as wounding.

The *mens rea* of s. 18 is, so far as relevant, intention to cause serious harm. It is unclear whether Jo had such an intention when she threw the pan full of boiling water in the direction of the door to the flat. She may not have realised how hot the water was, or she may not have intended to hit anyone with it. Even proof that she was reckless would not be sufficient, as s. 18 requires nothing less than intent.

Assuming, however, that intent **could** be proved, it would not matter that Jo's intent had been to hit Karen or Peter; as explained in (a), the principle of transferred malice would operate to transfer her intention to cause serious harm from the *actus reus* of seriously harming Karen or Peter to the *actus reus* of seriously harming Richard.

Given the uncertainty over whether intent could be proved, it is necessary to consider the next most serious offence for which Jo might be liable. This is causing GBH or wounding under OAPA s. 20. The *actus reus* is the same as s. 18's. However, the *mens rea* is intention **or** recklessness. Moreover, the prosecution does not need to prove that Jo was reckless as to causing **serious** harm. She need only have been reckless as to whether her action could have caused **some** harm: **Savage**. Moreover, the principle of transferred malice would operate to transfer her recklessness from the *actus reus* of harming Karen or Peter to the *actus reus* of harming Richard.

If Richard's injuries were not serious enough to satisfy the *actus reus* of s. 18 or s. 20, it would be necessary to consider the next most serious offence for which Jo might be liable. This is assault occasioning actual bodily harm under OAPA, s. 47. 'Actual bodily harm' has been widely defined as including any 'hurt or injury calculated to interfere with health or comfort': **Miller**. There can be little doubt that a bad scald passes this threshold. As for the *mens rea* of s. 47, subjective recklessness regarding the battery would be sufficient.

Group activity 1

- Divide your friends (or class) into groups of two or three people.
- Each group should choose one case from List A below and one from List B. List A are cases where the courts held the offence in question to be one of strict liability, whereas List B are cases where they held that the prosecution had to prove *mens rea*.

List A – strict liability:
  Alphacell *v* Woodward (1972)
  Smedleys *v* Breed (1974)
  Gammon (Hong Kong) Ltd *v* Attorney-General of Hong Kong (1985)
  Pharmaceutical Society *v* Storkwain (1986)
  R *v* Blake (1996)
  Harrow London Borough Council *v* Shah (1999)

List B – *mens rea* must be proved:
  Sweet *v* Parsley (1970)
  B (A Minor) *v* Director of Public Prosecutions (2000)

- Using the information in this chapter and any other information you can find in other publications and the internet, make notes on the facts and decisions in your chosen cases. Concentrate on finding out why the court found strict liability in one case but not in the other.
- Meet with the other groups and compare notes, looking for any common themes.

---

mylawchamber

Visit **www.mylawchamber.co.uk/elliottaqa** to access interactive questions, quizzes and activities to test yourself on this chapter.

Part 10
THE CRIMINAL COURTS, PROCEDURE AND SENTENCING

Chapter 18 Criminal procedure

> **This chapter discusses:**
>
> - the classification of the non-fatal offences for the purposes of determining the trial court;
> - pre-trial procedures: bail, plea before venue and sending for trial;
> - the burden and standard of proof in criminal cases.

Classification of the non-fatal offences

It was seen in Chapter 8 that there are two main criminal courts: the magistrates' court and the Crown court. The magistrates' courts hear summary offences and the Crown Court hears indictable offences. Triable either way offences are heard either in the magistrates' court or the Crown Court depending on the outcome of the mode of trial procedures. As regards the non-fatal offences against the person, assault and battery are summary offences only and therefore must be tried in the magistrates' court. The offences of assault occasioning actual bodily harm (OAPA 1861, s. 47) and reckless GBH (OAPA 1861, s. 20) are both triable either way offences. Section 18 of the Offences Against the Person Act 1861 is an indictable only offence and will therefore always be tried in the Crown Court.

Pre-trial matters

Bail

A person accused, convicted or under arrest for an offence may be granted bail, which means they are released under a duty to attend court or the police station at a given time. The right to bail has been reduced in recent years amid concern that individuals on bail reoffend and fail to turn up at court for their trial. Fourteen per cent of those bailed to appear at court fail to do so (*Criminal Justice Statistics 2003*) and nearly 25 per cent of defendants commit at least one offence while on bail (Brown (1998) *Offending While on Bail*, Home Office, Report No. 72). The criteria for granting or refusing bail are contained in the Bail Act 1976. There is a general presumption in favour of bail for unconvicted defendants, but there are some important exceptions. Bail need not be granted where there are substantial grounds for believing that, unless kept in custody, the accused would fail to surrender to bail, or would commit an offence, interfere with witnesses or otherwise obstruct the course of justice. In assessing these risks, the court may take account of the nature and seriousness of the offence and the probable sentence, along with the character, antecedents, associations and community ties of the defendant. Following the Criminal Justice and Court Services Act 2000, a court considering the question of bail must take into account any drug misuse by the defendant. The Criminal Justice Act 2003 has created a presumption against bail for a person charged with an imprisonable offence, who tests positive for a specified Class A drug and refuses treatment, unless there are exceptional circumstances. This provision may breach Art. 5 of the European Convention on Human Rights, which guarantees the right to freedom of the person.

The courts need not grant bail when the accused should be kept in custody for their own protection, where the accused is already serving a prison sentence or where there has been insufficient time to obtain information as to the criteria for bail. If the court does choose to grant bail in such cases, its reasons for doing so must be included in the bail record. The presumption in favour of bail is reversed where someone is charged with a further indictable offence which appears to have been committed while on bail.

The Criminal Justice and Public Order Act 1994, following concern at offences being committed by accused while on bail, provided that a person charged or convicted of murder, manslaughter, rape, attempted murder or attempted rape could never be granted bail if they had a previous conviction for such an offence. This complete ban breached the European Convention on Human Rights. The law has now been reformed by the Crime and Disorder Act 1998, under which such a person may only be granted bail where there are exceptional circumstances which justify doing so. Thus, Sion Jenkins, who was convicted of the murder of his foster-daughter Billy-Jo, was on bail throughout most of the proceedings.

When bail is refused for any of the stated reasons, other than insufficient information, the accused will usually be allowed only one further bail application; the court does not have to hear further applications unless there has been a change in circumstances. Where the remand in custody is on the basis of insufficient information, this is not technically a refusal of bail, so the accused may still make two applications.

Bail can be granted subject to conditions, such as that the accused obtain legal advice before their next court appearance or that the accused or a third party give a security (which is a payment into court that will be forfeited if the accused fails to attend a court hearing). The Police and Justice Act 2006 increased the range of conditions that can be imposed when granting bail. When a defendant fails to attend court any money held by the court is immediately forfeited and it is up to the person who paid that money to show why it should not be forfeited. A defendant refused bail, or who objects to the conditions under which it is offered, must be told the reasons for the decision, and informed of their right to appeal. The prosecution also has increasing rights to appeal against a decision to grant bail.

The Criminal Justice Act 2003 has given the police the power to grant bail at the place of arrest. This is called 'street bail'. It means that the police do not have to take suspects to the police station and undertake lengthy paperwork. A form is completed on the street and later entered in police records. The power has not been used much by the police and is unlikely to be used much until compulsory ID cards have been introduced.

In 1992 the average proportion of unconvicted and unsentenced prisoners was 22 per cent of the average prison population. Many of these remand prisoners, who have not been convicted of any offence, are kept in prison for between six months and a year before being tried, despite the fact that 60 per cent of them go on to be acquitted or given a non-custodial sentence.

Plea before venue procedure

The plea before venue procedure was introduced in 1997 to try to reduce the number of cases that were sent to the Crown Court and then the defendant sub-sequently pleaded guilty, as this was felt to incur unnecessary delay and expense. A plea before venue hearing is held in the magistrates' court. At this hearing defendants are asked to indicate whether they wish to plead guilty or not guilty. They are not obliged to answer this question and if they choose not to do so then the court will proceed to a full mode of trial hearing. If they plead guilty the court will then hear some more detail about the case and either sentence the defendant themselves there and then (or after they have adjourned until they have received a pre-sentence report); or alternatively commit for sentence to the Crown Court if the magistrates consider their powers of punishment insufficient. If defendants enter a plea of guilty they have themselves no right to demand that the case be sent up to the Crown Court for sentencing, only the magistrates can decide to do this. The advantage for the defendant of pleading guilty at this stage is that they can expect to benefit from a reduced sentence because they pleaded guilty at the earliest opportunity.

If the accused pleads not guilty then the case will proceed to a full trial.

Task 18.1

Complete the following table by writing each of the non-fatal offences in the appropriate box.

Type of offence	Offence
Summary	
Triable either way	
Indictable offence	

Sending for trial

The 'sending for trial' is a procedure created by s. 51 of the Crime and Disorder Act 1998, and is intended to be quicker than the old committal procedures which were finally abolished by the Criminal Justice Act 2003. Until this reform was introduced, a case might have given rise to half a dozen hearings in a magistrates' court before being sent up to the Crown Court for trial. Under the reformed system, every adult charged with an indictable offence has to appear only once in a magistrates' court to determine issues concerning funding from the Legal Services Commission, bail, and the use of statements and exhibits. The magistrates' court provides defendants with a statement of the evidence against them as well as a notice setting out the offence(s) for which they are to be sent for trial and the place where they are to be tried. They are then sent immediately for trial in the Crown Court. The Crown Court has taken over from the magistrates' court all remaining case management duties.

Burden and standard of proof

In order for a person to be convicted of a criminal offence, the prosecution must prove its case beyond reasonable doubt. If this is not done, the person will be acquitted, as in English law all persons are presumed innocent until proven guilty – **Woolmington** *v* **DPP** (1935).

Reading on the web

The research report *Offending on bail and police use of conditional bail* (1998) is available on the home office website at:

www.homeoffice.gov.uk/rds/pdfs/r72.pdf

The Police and Justice Act 2006 is available on the website of the Office for Public Sector Information at:

www.opsi.gov.uk/acts/acts2006/20060048.htm

Chapter summary

Introduction

There are two main courts where people can be put on trial to decide whether they are guilty of committing a criminal offence: the magistrate' court and the Crown Court.

Classification of the non-fatal offences

Assault and battery are summary offences, ss. 47 and 20 of the OAPA 1861 are triable either way and s. 18 is indictable only.

Pre-trial matters

Bail

A person accused, convicted or under arrest for an offence may be granted bail, which means they are released under a duty to attend court or the police station at a given time.

Plea before venue procedure

A plea before venue hearing is held in the magistrates' court. At this hearing defendants are asked to indicate whether they wish to plead guilty or not guilty.

Sending for trial

Every adult charged with an indictable offence has to appear only once in a magistrates' court to determine issues concerning funding from the Legal Services Commission, bail, and the use of statements and exhibits.

Burden and standard of proof

In order for a person to be convicted of a criminal offence, the prosecution must prove its case beyond reasonable doubt.

Question and answer guide

For exam questions covering the material in this chapter, please see the Question and answer guides section of Chapter 19: Sentencing.

Group activity 1

- Divide your friends (or class) into groups of two or three people.
- In your groups, visit the website www.cjsonline.gov.uk, which is maintained by the Ministry of Justice, and take the virtual tour in the site's 'Defendant' section. You can take either the interactive version of the tour or, if your computer will not run this, the text version.
- As you are watching the tour, imagine that you are a person who has been charged with a crime, that you have never had any involvement with the law before and that you strongly deny any wrongdoing. In that role, make notes on what you think you would want to know and how well the tour answers your questions.
- Meet with the other groups and compare notes, looking for any common themes.

Group activity 2

Take a look at the police recruitment website:

www.policecouldyou.co.uk

On this website you will see that the police force are recruiting for a number of different ancillary positions as well as the regular police service. In groups, look at the positions on offer on the site. Compare the pay that is being offered and the qualifications that are being required. If you had to apply for a position which job would you choose and why?

---

mylawchamber

Visit **www.mylawchamber.co.uk/elliottaqa** to access interactive questions, quizzes and activities to test yourself on this chapter.

Chapter 19

Sentencing

This chapter discusses:

- government reforms to the sentencing process;
- the aims of sentencing;
- sentencing practice in the courts;
- fines;
- custodial sentences;
- community sentences;
- some problems with sentencing.

The Criminal Justice Act 2003

The Home Office undertook a review of sentencing that was carried out by John Halliday and published in 2001. A wide range of recommendations were contained in his report, *Making Punishment Work, Report of the Review of the Sentencing Framework for England and Wales*. Central to the approach of the Halliday Review is that the courts should have a greater role in the implementation of sentences and that offenders should spend more time under supervision after their release from custody. He also wanted to see a greater predictability in sentencing so that the sentencing practice would have a stronger deterrent effect on potential offenders. He was particularly concerned by the approach of the courts to persistent offenders, whom he thought committed a disproportionate amount of crime.

The government accepted many of the report's recommendations and introduced significant reforms to the sentencing system in the Criminal Justice Act 2003. Politicians are continually tinkering with the sentencing system and the process of consultation and reform is ongoing. The latest consultation paper on the topic is called *Making Sentencing Clearer* (2006) and considers, among other things, giving back some sentencing discretion to judges.

Aims of sentencing

This chapter is concerned with the sentencing of those convicted of crimes, including the types of punishment available, and how the choice between them is made by the sentencer. But, first, we need to consider why people are punished at all – what is the punishment supposed to achieve? Section 142 of the Criminal Justice Act 2003 states that:

'Any court dealing with an [adult] offender in respect of his offence must have regard to the following purposes of sentencing –
(a) the punishment of offenders,
(b) the reduction of crime (including its reduction by deterrence),
(c) the reform and rehabilitation of offenders,
(d) the protection of the public, and
(e) the making of reparation by offenders to persons affected by their offences.'

Each of these purposes of sentencing will now be examined in turn.

Punishment of offenders

Punishment is concerned with recognising that the criminal has done something wrong and taking revenge on behalf of both the victim and society as a whole. This can also be described as retribution. Making punishments achieve retribution was a high priority during the last years of the Conservative government with Michael Howard as the Home Secretary. In the White Paper of 1990, *Crime, Justice and Protecting the Public*, reference was made to the need for sentences to achieve 'just deserts', stating that punishments should match the harm done, and show society's disapproval of that harm. The problem with this is that other factors all too often intervene: for example, those from stable homes, with jobs, are more likely to get non-custodial sentences than those without, who may be sent to prison even though their crime more properly fits a non-custodial sentence.

The reduction of crime

Crime is a harm which society wishes to eradicate. One way of reducing crime is through using a sentence as a deterrent. Deterrence is concerned with preventing the commission of future crimes; the idea is that the prospect of an unpleasant punishment will put people who might otherwise commit crime off the idea. Punishments may aim at individual deterrence (dissuading the offender in question from committing crime again), or general deterrence (showing other people what is likely to happen to them if they commit crime).

One problem with the use of punishment as a deterrent is that its effectiveness depends on the chances of detection: a serious punishment for a particular crime will not deter people from committing that offence if there is very little chance of being caught and prosecuted for it. This was shown when Denmark was occupied during the Second World War. All the Danish police were interned, drastically cutting the risk for ordinary criminals of being arrested. Despite increases in punishment, the number of property offences soared.

Linked with this problem is the fact that a deterrent effect requires the offender to stop and think about the consequences of what they are about to do, and, as the previous government's 1990 White Paper pointed out, this is often unrealistic:

'Deterrence is a principle with much immediate appeal . . . But much crime is committed on impulse, given the opportunity presented by an open window or unlocked door, and it

is committed by offenders who live from moment to moment; their crimes are as impulsive as the rest of their feckless, sad or pathetic lives. It is unrealistic to construct sentencing arrangements on the assumption that most offenders will weigh up the possibilities in advance and base their conduct on rational calculation. Often they do not.'

The deterrent effect of punishment on individuals becomes weaker each time they are punished. The more deeply a person becomes involved with a criminal way of life, the harder it is to reform and, at the same time, the fear of punishment becomes less because they have been through it all before.

It has been argued that, to deal with this problem, offenders should be given a severe sentence at an early stage – which politicians like to call a 'short, sharp, shock' – rather than having gradually increased sentences which are counterbalanced by the progressive hardening of the offender to the effects of punishment. Successive attempts at the 'short, sharp, shock' treatment have, however, shown it to have no meaningful effect on reconviction rates. The approach was introduced under the Detention Centre Order, created by the Criminal Justice Act 1982; it was abolished in the Criminal Justice Act 1988.

Where a specific crime is thought to be on the increase, the courts will sometimes try to stem this increase by passing what is called an exemplary sentence. This is a sentence higher than that which would normally be imposed, to show people that the problem is being treated seriously, and make potential offenders aware that they may be severely punished. There is some debate as to whether exemplary sentences actually work; their effectiveness depends on publicity, yet British newspapers tend to highlight only those sentences which seem too low for an offence which concerns society, or which seem too high for a trivial offence. In addition, even where there is publicity, the results may be negligible – Smith and Hogan (2002) point to an exemplary sentence passed for street robbery at a time when mugging was the subject of great social concern. The sentence was publicised by newspapers and television, yet there was no apparent effect on rates of street robbery even in the area where the case in question took place. We should also question whether exemplary sentences are in the interests of justice, which demands that like cases be treated alike; the person who mugs someone in the street when there has not been a public outcry about that offence is no better than one who mugs when there has.

Reform and rehabilitation

The aim of rehabilitation is to reform offenders, so that they are less likely to commit offences in the future – either because they learn to see the harm they are causing, or because, through education, training and other help, they find other ways to make a living or spend their leisure time. During the 1960s, a great deal of emphasis was placed on the need for rehabilitation, but the results were felt by many to be disappointing. By 1974 the American researcher Robert Martinson was denouncing rehabilitation programmes for prisoners in his paper *What Works*, in which he came to the conclusion that 'nothing works'.

Although rehabilitation sounds like a sensible aim, Bottoms and Preston argue, in *The Coming Penal Crisis* (1980), that rehabilitative sentences are fundamentally flawed. First, such sentences assume that all crime is the result of some deficiency or fault in the individual offender; Marxist academics argue that crime is actually a result of the way society is organised. Secondly, they discriminate against the less advantaged in society, who are seen as in need of reform, whereas when an offender comes from a more privileged background, their offence tends to be seen as a one-off, temporary slip. This means that punishment is dictated not by the harm caused, but by the background of the offender. Thirdly, in some cases the pursuit of reform can encourage inexcusable interference with the dignity and privacy of individuals. This has included, in some countries, implanting electrodes in the brain, and in the UK in the 1970s experiments were carried out involving hormone drug treatment for sex offenders.

In light of the fact that there is a growing prison population, there seems to be a renewed interest in the idea of rehabilitation. Over the past five years, offending behaviour programmes have been developed in many of the prisons of England and Wales. From an initial fragmented range of courses on such matters as anger management, alcohol and drug abuse, domestic violence and victim awareness, the emphasis is now on programmes aimed at changing the way the prisoners think, such as 'Reasoning and Rehabilitation' and 'Enhanced Thinking Skills'. 'Reasoning and Rehabilitation' courses do not look directly at the prisoners' offending; instead, over a 35-session course, run by prison probation officers and psychologists, they focus on six key areas – impulse control, flexible thinking (learning from experience), means-end testing (predicting probable outcomes of behaviour), perspective taking (seeing other people's points of view), problem solving and social skills. 'Enhanced Thinking Skills' courses follow a similar pattern, but over 20 sessions. Attendance on the courses is voluntary – but a long-term prisoner is unlikely to be released early without having completed one.

In 1998–99, 3,000 prisoners successfully completed one of these programmes, but this still represents only a very small proportion of the prison population. The number completing a programme is expected to increase significantly over the next few years. Whether a prisoner has the opportunity to undertake a course depends on the establishment in which he or she is being held. Not all prisons run these courses and in most of the ones that do, priority is given to prisoners serving four years or more – in other words, those who have to apply for early release. Yet many persistent offenders are in prison for less than four years. It is common to find people who have had a series of successive two- and three-year sentences, separated by mere weeks and often only days of freedom before they have reoffended and returned to prison. The senior judge, Lord Bingham, would like to see offending behaviour programmes made a legal requirement for all prisoners.

But how far will efforts to change the way a prisoner thinks reduce reoffending? One of the main problems faced by prisoners on release is a lack of work and consequent lack of an honest income or legitimate ways to spend their time. Many prisoners come out with the best of intentions but faced with empty days and even emptier pockets, they soon succumb to their old temptations. There is a danger that prisoners released into their old environment without having acquired any practical or vocational skills to help them on their way will fall back into a life of crime.

A report of the Parliamentary Penal Affairs Group, *Changing Offending Behaviour – Some Things Work* (1999), found that 'cognitive behavioural' programmes did work. But, in addition, they argued that there is increasing evidence that programmes focused directly on the needs of the offender in relation to the offending behaviour are successful in reducing the risk of reoffending. The types of needs that can be tackled include the need for employment, education, improved social skills and a break from negative peer groups. The need to tackle alcohol and drug problems was also highlighted.

Protection of the public

By placing an offender in custody, he or she is prevented from committing further offences and the public are thereby protected. While this has its merits where highly dangerous offenders are concerned, it is an extremely expensive way of dealing with crime prevention and, since prison is often the place where criminals pick up new ideas and techniques, may be ultimately counter-productive.

Reparation

The government has been developing ways in which offenders can provide remedies to their victims or the community at large. This is known sometimes as restorative justice, and has been pioneered for young offenders. So far, it seems to have been surprisingly successful in reducing reoffending and increasing victim satisfaction with the criminal justice system. Offenders can be required, for example, to write letters of apology to their victims, help to repair damage they have caused or take part in other community work.

Research has been carried out into the effectiveness of restorative justice which was published in a report, *Restorative Justice: the Evidence* (Sherman, 2007). This concluded that many violent criminals are less likely to commit further offences after participating in a restorative justice programme. The victim's symptoms of post-traumatic stress disorder are reduced, partly because meeting their offender demystifies the offence. Restorative justice was also cheaper than traditional criminal sentences.

??? Quick quiz 19.1

1 What are the five purposes of sentencing identified by the Criminal Justice Act 2003?

2 The White Paper, *Crime, Justice and Protecting the Public* (1990), identified one practical reason why a sentence might not act as a deterrent in practice. What reason was this?

3 What problems are identified by Bottoms and Preston in the use of rehabilitative sentences?

4 Is restorative justice cheaper or more expensive than traditional criminal sentences?

Sentencing practice

When an offender is convicted in the Crown Court, it is the trial judge alone (without the help of the jury) who determines the appropriate sentence. On conviction in the magistrates' court, the magistrates can determine the sentence themselves or, under s. 3 of the Powers of Criminal Courts (Sentencing) Act 2000 (PCC(S)A), the defendant can be committed to the Crown Court for sentence. If sentenced by the magistrates' court, the maximum sentence that can be imposed for a summary offence has been increased from six months to 12 months by the Criminal Justice Act 2003, s. 154. The minimum is five days (s. 132 of the Magistrates' Courts Act 1980).

Once the defendant has been found guilty, it must be decided first what category of sentence is appropriate and then the amount, duration and form of that sentence.

In recent years there has been a considerable amount of legislation trying to control and regulate the sentencing practices of the judges. The legislature has increasingly sought to reduce the discretion available to the judiciary in selecting the sentence. We will look first at the common law practice known as the tariff system.

The tariff system

To determine the type and length of a sentence, as well as looking at the relevant legislation and guidance from the Sentencing Guidelines Council, judges will also rely on what has been called the tariff principle, first recognised by Dr David Thomas in his book *Principles of Sentencing* (1970). The tariff system is based on treating like cases alike: people with similar backgrounds who commit similar offences in similar circumstances should receive similar sentences. That does not mean that judges apply a rigid scale of penalties, but that for most types of criminal offence it is possible to identify a range within which the sentence for different factual situations will fall. The system works in two stages: calculation of the initial tariff sentence; and then the application of secondary tariff principles which can be either aggravating or mitigating factors.

Aggravating and mitigating factors

The circumstances of the offence may include aggravating factors which may lead the offender to have a heavier sentence. Under the Criminal Justice Act 2003, a court must treat the fact that an offence was racially or religiously motivated as an aggravating factor which increased the seriousness of the offence. Any previous convictions, which are recent and relevant, should be regarded as an aggravating factor which will increase the severity of the sentence.

Mitigating factors are reasons why the defendant should be punished less severely than the facts of the case might suggest (Criminal Justice Act 2003, s. 166). These include youth or old age; previous good character; provocation; domestic or financial problems; drink, drugs or ill-health; and any special hardship offenders may have to undergo in prison, such as the fact that sex offenders and police informers may have to be held in solitary confinement for their own protection. The offender's behaviour after committing the offence may also be a factor, including efforts to help the police and/or compensate the victim. A plea of guilty is usually taken as a sign of remorse and an offender's sentence can now be reduced by up to a third in the light of the stage at which they indicate an intention to plead guilty and the circumstances in which that indication was given (Criminal Justice Act 2003, s. 144). The application of s. 144 has proved politically sensitive, as the reduction in sentence is available even where the offender has been caught red-handed. As a result, the government is considering amending s. 144 in the near future. As far as the offence itself is concerned, the fact that it was committed on impulse and not premeditated may be a mitigating factor. Offenders benefit from a reduced sentence, or even immunity from sentence, if they give evidence against other criminals (Serious Organized Crime and Police Act 2005). This is sometimes called 'Queen's evidence'.

Sentences available for adult offenders

There are four main categories of sentence: custodial sentences; community sentences; fines; and other miscellaneous sentences. The death penalty has been abolished. We will now look in detail at the different types of sentences that can be imposed on an offender.

Fines

A fine may be imposed for almost any offence other than murder. Offences tried in the magistrates' court carry a set maximum, depending on the offence; the highest is £5,000. There is no maximum in the Crown Court. The courts must ensure that the amount of the fine reflects the seriousness of the offence, and also takes account of the offender's means, reducing or increasing it as a result (Criminal Justice Act 2003, s. 167). Magistrates' courts can arrange for the automatic deduction of a fine from the offender's earnings, known as an 'attachment of earnings order', when imposing the fine or following a failure to pay. Under ss. 300 and 301 of the Criminal Justice Act 2003 the court has the power to impose unpaid work or curfew requirements on a fine defaulter or to disqualify them from driving, rather than sending them to prison.

The Courts Act 2003 seeks to improve the information available to magistrates on offenders' means prior to sentence, and to ensure that enforcement action is taken promptly. The Act has introduced a new framework for fine enforcement. When a collection order is issued by the court, fine officers manage and collect fines instead of the court. Discounts of up to 50 per cent are given to those who pay promptly. If the offender fails to pay promptly, the fine can be increased by the fines officer by up to 50 per cent without the case being referred back to the courts. The fines officer may also issue a 'further steps notice'. This can, for example, require payments to be deducted automatically from an offender's pay, for their property to be seized and sold, or their car clamped. Once clamped the car can be removed for sale or other disposal and any proceeds are used to discharge or reduce the offender's outstanding fine.

The fine is the most common sentence issued by the court, with three-quarters of all offenders sentenced at magistrates' courts in 2000 being issued a fine. The number of fines issued has decreased in recent years and the researchers Flood-Page and Mackie (1998) concluded that 'there seems to have been a general disenchantment with financial penalties'.

Since 2007, alongside every fine issued by the magistrates, the defendant also has to pay an additional £15 towards services for victims and witnesses. Some magistrates have been unhappy with this requirement, as they feel like unofficial tax collectors and the amount collected cannot be adapted to reflect the financial means of the convicted person.

Advantages

Evidence suggests that people are less likely to reoffend after being sentenced to a fine than following other sentences, though this can be partly explained by the type of offenders that are given fines in the first place. Fines also bring income into the system, and they do not have the long-term disruptive effects of imprisonment.

Disadvantages

There have been high rates of non-payment, a problem which the Courts Act 2003 is intended to tackle. A third of fines are never paid, so that in 2000–01, according to the National Audit Office, £74 million of fines were written off (mainly because the offender could not be traced). Not only does this make the sentence ineffective, but repeated non-payment of a fine can lead to a custodial sentence, with the result that some inmates of English prisons are there for very minor offences, such as failure to pay for a television licence.

Research carried out for the Home Office, *Enforcing Financial Penalties* (Whittaker, 1997), found that the majority of fine defaulters were out of work (only 22 per cent of the men and 11 per cent of the women had any paid employment, even part time). Predominant among reasons for non-payment were changes in circumstances through illness or job loss, and financial difficulties brought on by other debts.

A wide range of enforcement methods are available to the courts, including attachment of earnings orders and the automatic deduction of fines from social security benefits. In practice, these enforcement methods are only rarely used. The 1997 Home Office study highlighted practical difficulties in trying to arrange the deduction of fines from social security benefits. Some magistrates felt that attachment of earnings orders removed the responsibility from the defaulter for ensuring that the fine was paid, which was seen as part of the punishment. The government is now planning to establish a National Enforcement Service, which should be fully operational in 2007. This will employ 4,000 enforcement officers who will wear a uniform and be responsible for ensuring fines are paid and other court orders obeyed.

Fines can be unfair, since the same fine may be a very severe punishment to a poor defendant, but make little impact on one who is well off. In an attempt to address this problem, the Criminal Justice Act 1991 originally laid down a system of unit fines for the magistrates' courts. A maximum number of units was allocated to each offence, up to a total of 50. Within that maximum, the court had to determine the number of units which was commensurate with the seriousness of the case. The value of the unit depended on the offender's disposable weekly income (their income after having deducted any regular household expenses), with the minimum value of a unit being £4, and the maximum £100. The unit fines system aimed to even out the effects of fines so that, although the sums to be paid were different, the impact on the offender would be similar. The pilot schemes for the unit fines suggested that fines were paid more quickly and there was a drop in debtors ending up in prison, because of the more realistic assessment of the fines.

Unfortunately, the idea aroused huge public opposition after press coverage of what seemed to be high fines for relatively minor offences and very low fines for the unemployed – despite the fact that even if some of these were unfair, they were less unfair than the previous system. There was public uproar when a man received a £1,200 fine for dropping a crisp packet. As a result, unit fines were abolished, and the courts reverted to their previous practice, except that they are now required to take into account ability to pay when setting fines.

The government has been considering the reintroduction of the unit fine scheme. The relevant legislative provisions were contained in the Management of Offenders and Sentencing Bill, but this part of the Bill was subsequently dropped.

Fixed-penalty fines

In order to clamp down on loutish behaviour, the police have been given the power to impose fixed-penalty fines by the Criminal Justice and Police Act 2001. These fines can be imposed for such offences as being drunk in a public place and being drunk and disorderly. A police officer may give a person aged 16 and over a penalty notice if there is reason to believe that the person has committed a penalty offence (s. 2). The fine for each offence is fixed by the Home Secretary and can be for up to a quarter of the maximum fine applicable to the offence. Recipients must either pay the fine within 21 days or opt for trial (they will not be marched off to the cash machine by the police officer, as was originally suggested). If they fail to do either, then a sum which is one and a half times the penalty will be registered against them for enforcement as a fine. If the person pays the fixed-penalty fine, there is no criminal conviction or admission of guilt associated with the payment of the penalty.

The system of fixed-penalty fines is currently being piloted, and if these pilot schemes are successful they will be extended nationwide. The pilots have been criticised by the police. Fifty per cent of the fines have not been paid, and there is a problem with people giving false names and addresses.

Advantages

In the past, much minor offending escaped sanction because of the need to focus police and court resources on more important matters. It is hoped that fixed-penalty fines will provide a quick and efficient way of dealing with low-level, but disruptive criminal behaviour.

Disadvantages

Fixed-penalty fines take place outside the protective framework of the court system, and there is therefore a danger of abuse and corruption.

Figure 19.1 Wormwood Scrubs, an example of a Victorian prison
Source: © Williams Justin Williams/PA Photos.

Custodial sentences

For adult defendants, a custodial sentence means prison; for young offenders, it usually means being detained in a young offenders' institution. A court should not pass a custodial sentence unless it considers that the crime was so serious that only a custodial sentence is justified (s. 152, Criminal Justice Act 2003). Section 153 of the Criminal Justice Act 2003 directs the court to impose the shortest custodial term that is commensurate with the seriousness of the offence(s), subject to certain exceptions. Section 143 of the 2003 Act states that:

> *'In considering the seriousness of any offence, the court must consider the offender's culpability in committing the offence and any harm which the offence caused, was intended to cause or might foreseeably have caused.'*

The court also has to take into account previous convictions, failure to respond to previous sentences and the commission of an offence while on bail (Criminal Justice Act 2003, s. 143).

Where a judge intends to impose a custodial sentence (unless the sentence is fixed by law), a pre-sentence report must normally be prepared by the probation service, containing background information about the defendant. This will assist the judge in selecting the appropriate sentence.

Most of those given custodial sentences do not serve the full sentence in custody, but are released early on licence. If they breach the terms of that licence, then they can be recalled to prison.

The Criminal Justice Act 2003 has introduced a new scheme for the sentencing of dangerous adults. The scheme applies to offenders who have committed a

343

specified sexual or violent offence and have been assessed as dangerous. Such offenders can receive an extended sentence and their release is at the discretion of the Parole Board. The most dangerous offenders who continue to pose a risk to the public may be kept in prison for an indeterminate period. These measures will allow the state to hold offenders in prison for longer than is required by the gravity of their offence in order to protect the public. In practice, the heavy use of indeterminate sentences has increased the problem of prison overcrowding.

Task 19.2

Read the following extract from a newspaper article and answer the questions that follow.

Tagging is harder than prison because I have to make an effort every day

'I don't like tagging. It's harder than prison because I have to make an effort every day', Mark, 27, who has a long list of drug-related burglaries on his record, says. But it imposed a strict, disciplined framework on his life for the first time in years. This would not, on its own, keep him out of trouble – but it would give Mark and his probation officer the chance to start other longer-term programmes that might.

Tagging's intrusion into family life has produced mixed results. Some women, in particular, found the enforced presence of their partner added to both tension in their relationship and the risk of violence. Others welcomed a period in which the partner learnt to see more of his children.

'He really resented our home being his prison', one wife said, 'and when I went out to work part time and left him to put the children to bed it was – well, he thought it was the end of the world. But after a bit, when he saw how they responded, he was really proud. It won't change everything, but it has done a lot of good.'

Not everyone agrees and research in Scotland revealed that some parents of tagged young adults were resentful about the role of unpaid jailers which they felt had been forced upon them.

Extensive Home Office research has concluded that tagging is 'offence neutral' – that is, it has no real impact on longer-term reoffending rates. But electronic monitoring can be positively used. Politicians have capitalised on its usefulness in terms of crisis management of prison numbers.

In technology terms, electronic tagging schemes are basic – much more sophisticated technology, using satellites to track offenders rather than simply enforcing a curfew, is already in use in the US and could soon be available here.

If all tagging can do is provide a short-term fix, the enormous investment already made will simply have been wasted. Using technology in ways that make a real impact on crime figures and on reoffending rates must be the aim.

(Adapted from an article by Dick Whitfield which was published in *The Times*, 11 March 2003.)

Questions

1 Why did some parents in Scotland resent the tagging of their children?
2 Does tagging currently reduce the longer-term reoffending rates?
3 What does the author consider should be the aim of using technology?
4 Do you think that tagging is a good idea?

Custody plus

John Halliday's report on sentencing (discussed at p. 334) argued that prison sentences of less than 12 months had little meaningful impact on criminal behaviour, because only half of the sentence time was actually served in prison, and the person was then released without conditions. The Prison Service had little opportunity to tackle criminal behaviour as the period served in custody was so short. In addition, such sentences could have long-term adverse effects on family cohesion, employment and training prospects – all of which are key to the rehabilitation of offenders. This was particularly regrettable, as these sentences are used for large numbers of persistent offenders who are likely to reoffend.

Halliday recommended that, to tackle this weakness in short prison sentences, there should be a new sentence which he described as 'custody plus'. The government has adopted this reform in the Criminal Justice Act 2003. Under s. 181, all sentences for less than 12 months' custody are replaced by custody plus (or intermittent custody, discussed below). After spending a maximum of three months in custody, the offender will be released and subjected to at least six months' post-release supervision in the community. The court can attach specific requirements to the sentence, based upon those available under a community sentence. If an offender fails to comply with the terms of the community part of the sentence, he or she will be returned to custody.

Sentences for more than 12 months require the offender to spend half their time in custody (unless they obtain early release on home detention curfew), and the remainder of their sentence under supervision in the community. It is hoped that these reforms will provide a more effective framework within which to address the needs of offenders. Following negative media coverage, this automatic reduction of a custodial sentence by half is currently being reconsidered by the Home Office with regard to the most serious offenders and may be removed in the near future.

Suspended sentence

Under ss. 189–194 of the Criminal Justice Act 2003, a custodial sentence can be suspended. A court is able to suspend a short custodial sentence for between six months and two years. The offender can be required to undertake certain activities in the community.

If the offender breaches the terms of the suspension, the suspended sentence will be activated. The commission of a further offence during the entire length of suspension will also count as breach, and the offender's existing suspended sentence will be dealt with at the time the court sentences him or her for the new offence. Courts have a discretion to review an offender's progress under a suspended sentence.

Suspended sentences were created in 1967 and were intended to be used as an alternative to a custodial sentence. In practice, they have sometimes been used where a community sentence would have been adequate. If the offender then commits another offence the suspended sentence is activated, so that the offender ends up in prison. The Criminal Justice and Immigration Bill contains a provision to abolish suspended sentences for summary only offences to reduce this problem.

Home detention curfew

Home detention curfews were introduced by the Crime and Disorder Act 1998. Prisoners sentenced to between three months' and four years' imprisonment can be released early (usually 60 days early) on a licence that includes a curfew condition. This requires the released prisoners to remain at a certain address at set times, during which period they will be subjected to electronic monitoring. Most curfews are set for 12 hours between 7 p.m. and 7 a.m. The person can be recalled to prison if there is a failure to comply with the conditions of the curfew condition or in order to protect the public from serious harm. Private contractors fit the electronic tag to a person's ankle, install monitoring equipment which plugs into the telephone system in their home and connects with a central computer system, and notify breaches of curfew to the Prison Service.

Research has been carried out by Dodgson (2001) and others into the first 16 months' experience of home detention curfew. It found that only 5 per cent were recalled to prison. The main reasons for recall were breach of the curfew conditions (68 per cent) or a change of circumstances (25 per cent). The use of home detention curfew appeared to have eased the transition from prison to the community. Offenders were very positive about the scheme, with only 2 per cent saying that they would have preferred to have spent their time in prison. Prior to release, over a third of prisoners said that the prospect of being granted home detention curfew influenced their behaviour in prison. Other household members were also very positive about the scheme.

Sentences for murder

An area that has caused considerable controversy and litigation in recent years is the question of the release of prisoners sentenced to life imprisonment, and in particular the Home Secretary's involvement in this decision. In the recent past, the final decision as to when murderers should be released on licence lay with a politician, the Home Secretary. This was found to be in breach of the European Convention on Human Rights in the case of **R (Anderson)** *v* **Secretary of State for the Home Department** (2002). The danger was that Home Secretaries might be influenced by issues of political popularity rather than the justice in the particular case. The matter was highlighted in the case of Myra Hindley, who was convicted for life in 1966 for the murder of two children and for her involvement in the killing of a third.

The Home Secretary, however, seems anxious to retain some control in this area. Provisions have been added to the Criminal Justice Act 2003 which aim to promote consistency in the sentencing of murderers. Under these provisions, judges are required to slot offenders into one of three categories according to the severity of their crime. For the first category, actual life will be served by those convicted of the most serious and heinous crimes: multiple murderers, child killers and terrorist murderers. For the second category, there is a starting point of 30 years. This category includes murders of police and prison officers and murders with sexual, racial or religious motives. For the third category, the starting point is 15 years. In addition, there are 14 mitigating and aggravating factors which will affect the sentence imposed. Judges are able to ignore these guidelines, provided they explain why. Once the minimum term has expired, the Parole Board will consider the person's suitability for release. If the Parole Board considers that the person no longer poses a significant risk of reoffending, it can order their release. They are released on licence for the rest of their lives, and are supervised by the probation service until they are assessed as being fully reintegrated into the community. If they reoffend while under supervision, or if they fail to cooperate, or to keep in contact with the probation service, the licence is revoked by the Lifer Review and Recall Section at the Home Office; a warrant of arrest is issued by Scotland Yard and they are classed as unlawfully at large until arrested and returned to prison.

There are at present 22 people serving whole-life tariffs in England and Wales, none in Europe and 25,000 in the US (along with 3,500 people under sentence of death).

Quick quiz 19.3

1 Does the jury, the judge or both together select the offender's sentence in the Crown Court?

2 What is the automatic sentence for murder?

3 What is a fixed penalty fine?

4 Which academic first recognised the tariff principle in sentencing?

Advantages of custodial sentences

The previous Conservative government claimed that prison 'works', in the sense that offenders cannot commit crime while they are in prison, and so the public is protected. The current government claims that prison can be made to work both by protecting the public and by making use of the opportunity for rehabilitation.

Disadvantages of custodial sentences

Fifty-nine per cent of prisoners are reconvicted within two years of being released. In her book, *Bricks of Shame* (1987), Vivienne Stern highlights several reasons why imprisonment lacks any great reformative power, and may even make people more, rather than less, likely to reoffend. Prisoners spend time with other criminals, from whom they frequently acquire new ideas for criminal enterprises; budget cuts have meant there is now little effective training and education in prisons, while the stigma of having been in prison means their opportunities for employment are fewer when they are released; and families often break down, so that the ex-prisoner may become homeless. The result, says Stern, is that 'going straight can present the quite unattractive option of a boring, lonely existence in a hostel or rented room, eking out the Income Support'. All this can also mean that prison punishes the innocent as well as the guilty, with the prisoner's family suffering stigma, financial difficulties, the misery of being parted from the prisoner and often family breakdown in the end. The research, *Poverty and Disadvantage Among Prisoners' Families* (Smith, 2007), noted that about 4 per cent of children experience

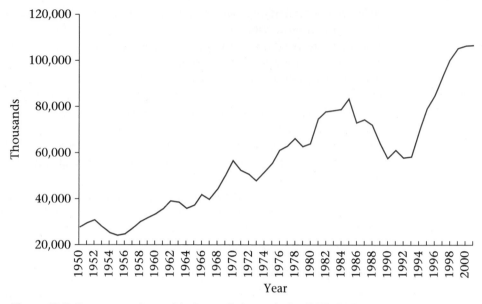

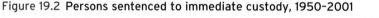

Figure 19.2 **Persons sentenced to immediate custody, 1950–2001**
Source: 'Criminal Statistics England and Wales 2001', p. 18 [Figure 1.3]. © Crown Copyright 2002.

the imprisonment of their father during their school years. It found that this frequently caused them to suffer emotional and economic hardship, with a negative effect on their personal development.

Stern rejects the idea that prison works because it protects the public. She points out that although it may prevent the individual offending for a while, the percentage of crime that is actually detected and prosecuted is so small that imprisonment has little effect on the crime rate.

Prisons are also extremely expensive – at £36,000 a year per prisoner, three weeks in prison costs as much as a lengthy community sentence. To this must be added the costs associated with the family breakdown and unemployment that imprisonment frequently causes. As well as those who find themselves in prison through non-payment of fines, many of those actually sentenced to prison have committed relatively minor offences and could be dealt with just as effectively, and far more cheaply, in the community.

The conditions within prisons continue to cause concern. While all prisoners are now supposed to have 24-hour access to toilet facilities, the practice of 'slopping out' having ended in 1996, other problems remain. A continuing area of concern that has been highlighted in the Prison Ombudsman's report for 1998 is the failure of the Prison Service's internal complaints system to investigate complaints adequately. Lord Woolf, in his inquiry into the prison disturbances that took place in 1990, found that one of the root causes of the riots was that prisoners believed they had no other effective method of airing their grievances.

Where prison conditions are poor, there is an increased risk of suicide. Between 1999 and 2003 a total of 434 people committed suicide in prison. There were over 16,000 incidents of self-harm recorded in 2003. A report of the Joint Committee on deaths in custody in 2004 found that the young, the mentally unstable and women are most at risk.

The number of people in prison has been growing at an alarming rate over recent years. In 2004 the UK was holding over 75,000 prisoners, an increase of more than 50 per cent in the previous ten years. This figure is expected to reach 80,000 by 2009. Seventy per cent of sentenced prisoners are serving 12 months or less. This increase in the prison population is not due to an increase in criminal activity, but simply that heavier sentences are being imposed. A Home Office bulletin issued in 2000 showed the courts in England and Wales to be among the toughest in western Europe in terms of numbers imprisoned, while a Council of Europe study revealed that defendants in English courts get longer sentences for assault, robbery or theft than they do elsewhere in Europe. Average prison populations in Europe are approximately one-third lower as a proportion of the population to that of the UK. A report carried out by the businessman Patrick Carter in 2003 estimated that the increased use of custody had only reduced crime by 5 per cent at the most.

The Chief Inspector of Prisons claimed, in an interview for *The Guardian* in 2001, that the prison population could be cut to 40,000 if 'the kids, the elderly, the mentally ill, the asylum seekers, those inside for trivial shoplifting or drug offences' were taken away. The inevitable result of a growing prison population is prison overcrowding. In 1996 matters reached crisis point and this led to a

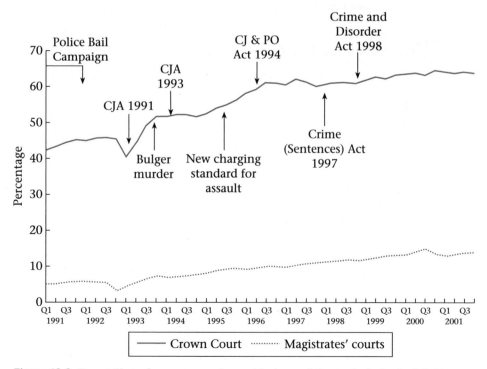

Figure 19.3 **Proportion of persons sentenced to immediate custody for indictable offences by type of court, 1991–2001**

Source: 'Criminal Statistics England and Wales 2001', p. 81 [Figure 7.4]. © Crown Copyright 2002.

controversial scheme whereby a converted ship was used as a floating prison. In *Prison Sardines* (1996), a Howard League report, it was noted that, at the end of February 1996, 46 prisons were overcrowded, with Usk Prison in Gwent being 75 per cent overcrowded. By 2007 the prison population had increased further and the government decided to put some prisoners in police cells. This was an unsatisfactory solution to prison overcrowding because it is more expensive than prisons, while providing no facilities for education and rehabilitation.

The Home Office has issued a five-year strategic plan (*Cutting Crime – Delivering Justice: Strategic Plan for Criminal Justice 2004–08*). This states that the government wishes to stop the drift towards longer custodial sentences. In fact, the prison population has continued to rise rapidly.

In recent years there has been concern that dangerous offenders have been released on licence, and have subsequently reoffended. There have been suggestions that the Parole Board has been wrong to agree the release of certain individuals and, when they have been released, they have not been adequately supervised by the probation service. Such concerns were expressed in the media following the murder of the wealthy banker, John Monckton, at his home in Chelsea by Damien Hanson when he was on probation. The Parole Board may be giving undue weight to the human rights of the offender rather than the rights of potential victims, but they may also not have sufficient information to make a fully informed decision. Some of the criticism of the probation service may reflect an unrealistic expectation of the level of supervision that can be provided with the level of funding available.

??? Quick quiz 19.4

1 Do you think that 'prison works'?

2 How much does it cost to keep a person in prison for a year?

3 In 2004 how many people were in prison in the UK?

4 What percentage of children experience the imprisonment of their father during their school years?

Community sentence

Section 148 of the Criminal Justice Act 2003 states that a community sentence can only be imposed if the offence was 'serious enough to warrant such a sentence'. Where a court passes a community sentence, the particular requirements of the sentence must be the most suitable for the offender. The restrictions on liberty imposed by the order must be 'commensurate with the seriousness of the offence, or the combination of the offence and one or more offences associated with it'.

Recent governments have been anxious to emphasise that community sentences impose substantial restrictions on the offender's freedom and should not be seen as 'soft options'. Home Office statistics show that 56 per cent of offenders given community sentences reoffend within two years.

The Criminal Justice Act 2003 has established a single community order which can be applied to an offender aged 16 or over. This order can contain a range of possible requirements. These are:

- an unpaid work requirement;
- an activity requirement;
- a programme requirement;
- a prohibited activity requirement;
- a curfew requirement;
- an exclusion requirement;
- a residence requirement;
- a mental health treatment requirement;
- a drug rehabilitation requirement;
- an alcohol treatment requirement;
- a supervision requirement.

Each of these requirements will now be considered in turn.

Unpaid work requirement

The offender can be required to perform, over a period of 12 months, a specified number of hours of unpaid work for the benefit of the community. The number of hours must be between 40 and 300. The kind of work done includes tasks on conservation projects, archaeological sites and canal clearance. This requirement allows useful community work to be done, and may give offenders a sense of achievement which helps them stay out of trouble afterwards. There is a recurring discussion as to whether people carrying out work as part of a community sentence should be required to wear uniforms so that they can be recognised as offenders contributing to the community by the public, or whether this is unnecessarily humiliating to the offender.

Activity requirement

Under an activity requirement, offenders must present themselves to a specified person, at a specified place, for a maximum of 60 days, and/or take part in specified activities for a certain number of days. An activity requirement may include such tasks as receiving help with employment, group work on social problems and providing reparation to the victim.

Programme requirement

A programme requirement obliges the offender to participate in an accredited programme on a certain number of days. Programmes are courses which address offending behaviour, such as anger management, sex offending and drug abuse.

Prohibited activity requirement

The court can instruct an offender to refrain from participating in certain activities. For example, it might forbid an offender from contacting a certain person, or from participating in specified activities during a period of time. The court can make a prohibited activity requirement which prohibits a defendant from possessing, using or carrying a firearm.

Curfew requirement

An offender can be ordered to remain in a specified place or places for periods of not less than two hours or more than 12 hours in any one day for up to six months. The court should avoid imposing conditions which would interfere with the offender's work or education, or cause conflict with their religious beliefs. A specified person must be made responsible for monitoring the offender's whereabouts. Courts can require offenders to wear electronic tags, in order to monitor that they are conforming to their curfew order.

Advantages

Tagging costs about £4,000 a year, compared with £24,000 for a prison place. Curfew orders have the potential to keep offenders out of trouble and protect the public, without the disruptive effects of imprisonment. In the US city of Atlanta, a night curfew has been imposed on anyone under 16. This was introduced to protect children, but has also had the effect of considerably reducing juvenile crime. While such use of curfew orders on those who have not been convicted of crimes intrudes on the right to freedom of movement, the results show that, as a sentence, it could prove very useful.

At the moment, electronic tags are used that set off an alarm if a curfew is breached, but cannot identify where the criminal has then gone. The government is now considering a more technologically advanced system which can track the precise movements of the offender. This could have the advantage, for example, of making sure that a convicted paedophile does not enter a school building.

Disadvantages

The Penal Affairs Consortium have argued that the money spent on electronic tagging would be better spent on constructive options such as supervision requirements, which work to change offenders' long-term attitudes towards offending. Opponents of electronic tagging claim it is degrading to the person concerned, but its supporters – including one or two well-known former prisoners – point out that it is far less degrading than imprisonment. This argument applies only where tagging is used as an alternative to imprisonment: its opponents claim that it is likely to be used in practice to replace other non-custodial measures. Existing research suggests, however, that curfew orders with tagging are being seen as a genuine alternative to custody (Nuttall *et al.* (1998)).

Exclusion requirement

An offender can be required to stay away from a certain place or places at set times. Electronic tags can be used to monitor compliance with this requirement. It is aimed at people, such as stalkers, who present a particular danger or nuisance to a victim. An exclusion requirement is similar in many respects to a curfew requirement. However, whereas under a curfew requirement an offender has to remain at a specified place, an exclusion requirement prohibits an offender from entering a specific place.

Residence requirement

A residence requirement obliges the offender to reside at a place specified in the order for a specified period.

Mental health treatment requirement

A court can direct an offender to undergo mental health treatment for a certain period(s) as part of a community sentence or suspended sentence order, under the treatment of a registered medical practitioner or chartered psychologist. Before including a mental health treatment requirement, the court must be satisfied that the mental condition of the offender requires treatment and may be helped by treatment, but is not such that it warrants making a hospital or guardianship order (within the meaning of the Mental Health Act 1983). The offender's consent must be obtained before the requirement is imposed.

Drug rehabilitation requirement

As part of a community sentence or suspended sentence, the court may impose a drug rehabilitation requirement, which includes drug treatment and testing. In order to impose such a requirement, the court must be satisfied that the offender is dependent on or has a propensity to misuse any controlled drug and therefore requires and would benefit from treatment. In addition, the court must be satisfied that the necessary arrangements are or can be made for the treatment and that the offender has expressed a willingness to comply with the drug rehabilitation requirement. The treatment provided must be for a minimum of six months.

A court may provide for the review of this requirement, and such reviews must take place if the order is for more than 12 months. Review hearings provide the court with information about the offender's progress, including the results of any drug tests.

Alcohol treatment requirement

A court can require an offender to undergo alcohol treatment to reduce or eliminate the offender's dependency on alcohol. The offender's consent is required. This requirement must last at least six months.

Supervision requirement

The offender can be placed under the supervision of a probation officer for a fixed period of between six months and three years. Home Office research into the probation service (Mair and May, *Offenders on Probation* (1997)) found that 90 per cent of the people supervised thought that their supervision had been useful. The most common reason given for this view was that it offered them someone independent to talk to about their problems. A third mentioned getting practical help or advice with specific problems and about 20 per cent mentioned being helped to keep out of trouble and avoid reoffending. The research concluded:

> *'The message contained in this report is a good one for the probation service; it is viewed favourably by most of those it supervises, and seems to work hard at trying to achieve its formal aims and objectives as stated in the National Standards. However, this should not*

lead to any sense of complacency. It is arguable that any agency which provided similar help to that provided by the probation service to the poor and unemployed would be seen in an equally positive light.'

Owing to staff shortages, particularly in London, some offenders who are subject to a supervision requirement, are merely being required to turn up and have their names ticked off.

Miscellaneous sentences

A range of other sentences are also available to the court. These include the following.

Compensation orders

Where an offence causes personal injury, loss or damage (unless it arises from a road accident), the courts may order the offender to pay compensation. This may be up to £1,000 in a magistrates' court and is unlimited in the Crown Court. Orders can also be made for the return of stolen property to its owner, or, where stolen property has been disposed of, for compensation to be paid to the victim from any money taken from the offender when arrested.

Binding over to be of good behaviour

This order dates back to the thirteenth century and the relevant legislative provisions can be found in the Justices of the Peace Act 1361 and the Magistrates' Courts Act 1980. A binding over order can be made against any person who is before a court and has 'breached the peace' – not just the defendant, but also any witness or victim. People who are bound over have to put up a sum of money and/or find someone else to do so, which will be forfeited if the undertaking is broken. A person who refuses to be bound over can be imprisoned, despite the fact that they may not have been convicted of any offence. The order usually lasts for a year.

Absolute and conditional discharges

If the court finds an offender guilty of any offence (except one for which the penalty is fixed by law), but believes that in the circumstances it is unnecessary to punish the person and a community rehabilitation order is inappropriate, it may discharge the defendant either absolutely or conditionally.

An absolute discharge effectively means that no action is taken at all, and is generally made where the defendant's conduct is wrong in law, but no reasonable person would blame them for doing what they did. A conditional discharge means that no further action will be taken unless the offender commits another offence within a specified period of up to three years. This order is commonly made where the court accepts that the offender's conduct was wrong as well as illegal but the mitigating circumstances are very strong. If an offender who has received a conditional discharge is convicted of another offence during the specified period, they may, in addition to any other punishment imposed, be sentenced for the original offence. A discharge does not count as a conviction unless it is conditional and the offender reoffends within the specified period.

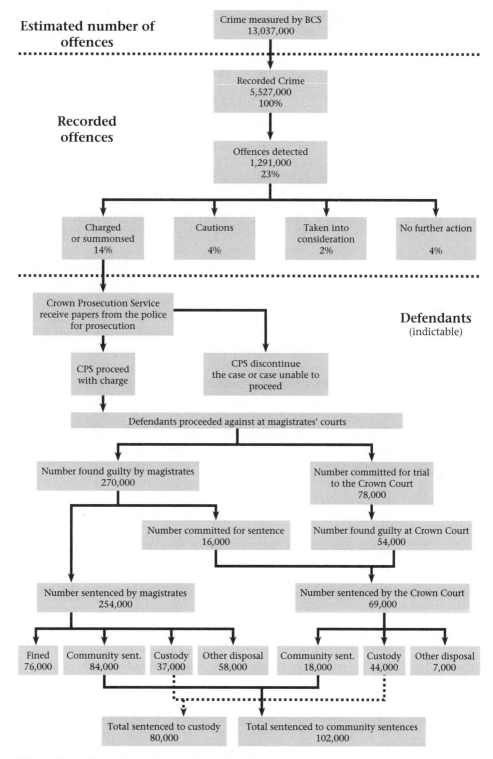

Figure 19.4 Flows through the criminal justice system, 2001

Source: 'Criminal Statistics England and Wales 2001', p. 15 [Figure 1.1]. © Crown Copyright 2002.

Disqualification

This is most common as a punishment for motoring offences, when offenders can be disqualified from driving. Under ss. 146–147 of the PCC(S)A 2000, a court may disqualify a person from driving as a punishment for a non-motoring offence. A conviction for offences concerning cruelty to animals may also lead to disqualification from keeping pets or livestock.

Anti-social behaviour orders

Anti-social behaviour orders are civil orders issued by a court to protect the public from behaviour that causes harassment, alarm and distress. Section 1 of the Crime and Disorder Act 1998 provides that bodies such as local authorities or the police may apply under civil procedures to a court for an anti-social behaviour order (ASBO). An ASBO can also be ordered as part of a criminal sentence. The order will be made against a person aged 10 or over who has acted in an anti-social manner, that is, a manner which is likely to cause harassment, alarm or distress to someone not in the same household as the person described in the order, and who is likely to do so again. Guidance on the legislation provided by the Home Office suggests that typical behaviour which might fall within this provision includes 'serious vandalism or persistent intimidation of elderly people'. The court has power to prohibit that person from doing anything described in the order for a period of not less than two years. For example, a person could be prohibited from entering a certain geographical area. Thus, in 2002, a woman was banned from going near her local police station for three years, as she had been harassing police officers. While the ASBO is obtained using civil procedures, breach of the ASBO can give rise to the criminal sanctions of a fine or five years' imprisonment.

There has been much controversy over the way ASBOs have been used in practice. The pressure groups Liberty, the National Association of Probation Officers (Napo) and the Howard League for Penal Reform have together formed a campaign group, ASBO Concern, calling for a public review of the way anti-social behaviour orders are used. Initially, ASBOs were intended to deal primarily with anti-social behaviour by neighbours and young people, but they are increasingly being used for a wider range of problems. For example, an anti-social behaviour order was issued in 2004 against Sony Music Entertainment (UK) Ltd, to stop flyposting around the country.

A survey published by the probation officers union, NAPO, has revealed that ASBOs are being inappropriately used against the mentally ill (*Anti-Social Behaviour Orders: analysis of the first six years* (2004)). As a result, people who are unable to control their behaviour owing to mental ill-health are being sanctioned, when treatment would actually be more effective and humane. NAPO give an example of a man who had been standing on a windowsill and moaning while pretending to dance with a Christmas tree. An ASBO was issued against him banning him from shouting, swearing and banging windows. He breached the order in August 2004, and was imprisoned for two months for continuing to moan in public. He breached the order again and was imprisoned for four months.

By the end of 2003, 42 per cent of all ASBOs were breached and 55 per cent of the breaches resulted in custody. Forty-five per cent of ASBOs have been issued against children. Nearly half of children subject to such an order have breached it, with ten young people each week being placed in custody for breaching an ASBO. Custodial sentences are being handed down for breach of an ASBO where the triggering anti-social conduct was not actually criminal.

The local authorities and police feel that it is necessary for photographs of people sanctioned with an ASBO to be made public in order for the ASBO to be effectively enforced. Photographs have been posted on council websites, leaflets distributed and local newspapers informed. There is concern that such publicity simply stigmatises families, could lead to a surge in vigilantism and does nothing to tackle the underlying causes of a person's anti-social behaviour. In **R (Stanley, Marshall and Kelly *v* Metropolitan Police Commissioner** (2004) the High Court held that the authorities were entitled to 'name and shame' people who have been subjected to an ASBO, and it did not amount to a breach of their right to a private and family life which are guaranteed by Art. 8 of the European Convention.

Task 19.6

Try to visit a Crown Court. This will give you an opportunity both to see a jury at work and to see defendants being sentenced. You can find the address of your local Crown Court by looking in a telephone directory. Alternatively, Crown Court addresses are available on the Court Service's website at: www.courtservice.gov.uk/HMCSCourtFinder.

You are unlikely to be able to see a whole case from beginning to end, as they tend to spread over several days. Near the entrance to the court will be a list of cases that are going to be heard and employees at the reception will also be able to help advise you on suitable cases to watch. Some cases will merely be concerned with sentencing an offender, who has been convicted at an earlier stage. Try to see at least one sentencing hearing, as well as trying to see a case where a jury is sitting. Note that the jury are never involved in the sentencing decision. Write up a report of your visit by answering the following questions:

About the court

1 What was the name and address of the court?
2 What was the court building like? Was it old or modern? Was it clean and in good decorative order? Were the waiting areas comfortable? Was there access to refreshments? Was it easy to find your way around the building, with rooms clearly signposted and labelled?
3 Did you find the court staff helpful? Were there any explanatory leaflets available?

About the proceedings involving a jury
Choose one hearing involving a jury and answer the following questions:

1 How many men and how many women were sitting on the jury?
2 Were there any black jurors?
3 How did the jurors behave during the case?

▶

4 Did the jurors take notes?

5 Did the jurors ask any questions?

6 Did the jurors appear to be paying attention?

7 Was the professional judge male or female?

8 What was the ethnic origin of the judge?

9 What did you think of the way the judge behaved during the case?

About the sentencing process

Choose one hearing where the offender was sentenced and answer the following questions:

1 What offence had the offender committed?

2 Was the offender male or female?

3 Approximately how old do you think the offender was?

4 Was the offender represented by a lawyer?

5 Did the court refer to a pre-sentence report?

6 Did the defence lawyer present any arguments in mitigation in favour of a lighter sentence?

7 What sentence did the offender receive?

8 How did the offender react to his or her sentence?

9 Did the judge explain the choice of sentence?

10 Do you think that the court gave the right sentence?

Write up a short oral presentation about your visit to present to the other students with whom you are studying.

Problems with sentencing

The role of the judge

We have seen that the sentence in England is traditionally a decision for the judge, which can lead to inconsistent punishments, especially among magistrates' courts. This situation clearly offends against the principle of justice that requires like cases to be treated alike.

The government has tried to restrict judicial discretion through legislative guidelines and has also set up a Sentencing Advisory Panel, a Sentencing Guidelines Council and a Judicial Studies Board. Overseen by the Ministry of Justice, the Judicial Studies Board has functions that include running seminars on sentencing, which seek to reduce inconsistencies; courses for newly appointed judges; and refresher courses for more experienced members of the judiciary. The Board also publishes a regular bulletin, summarising recent legislation, sentencing decisions, research findings and developments in other countries, while the Magistrates' Association issues a *Sentencing Guide for Criminal Offences* to its members.

Other jurisdictions generally allow judges less discretion in sentencing. In the US, for example, many states use 'indeterminate' sentencing by which a conviction automatically means a punishment of, say, one to five years' imprisonment, and the exact length of the sentence is decided by the prison authorities. However, in this country, control of sentencing is seen as an important aspect of judicial independence, and the introduction of more legislative controls has been criticised as interfering with the judiciary's constitutional position.

Racism

Critics of sentencing practice in England have frequently alleged that members of ethnic minorities are treated more harshly than white defendants. For example, in 2001, 21 per cent of the prison population was from an ethnic minority, which is significantly higher than their representation in the general population. This difference becomes much less if only UK nationals are considered, because one in four black people in prison is a foreign national, often imprisoned for illegally importing drugs. Whether these figures actually point to racial discrimination in sentencing is the subject of much debate.

What is clear from recent research is that some members of the ethnic minorities perceive the sentencing process as racist. Research undertaken in 2003 by Roger Hood and others (*Ethnic Minorities in the Criminal Courts: Perceptions of Fairness and Equality of Treatment*) investigated how far black and Asian defendants considered that they had been treated unfairly by the courts because of their race. Most complaints about racial bias concerned sentences perceived to be more severe than those imposed on a similar white defendant.

In addition to any racism in the system, the legal and procedural factors which affect sentencing may account for some of the differences in the punishment of black and white offenders. More black offenders elect for Crown Court trial and plead not guilty, which means that, if convicted, they would probably receive harsher sentences, because the sentences in the Crown Court are higher than those in the magistrates' court and they would not benefit from a discount for a guilty plea. Research by Flood-Page and Mackie in 1998 found that there was no evidence that black or Asian offenders were more likely than white offenders to receive a custodial sentence when all relevant factors were taken into account.

The experience of black people when in the prison system has also given rise to concern. An internal report commissioned by the Prison Service in 2000 found a blatantly racist regime at Brixton prison, where black staff as well as inmates suffered from bullying and harassment. The head of the Prison Service acknowledged that the service is 'institutionally racist' and that 'pockets of malicious racism exist'. He promised to sack all prison officers found to be members of extreme right-wing groups such as the British National Party. Prison officers' training now includes classes on race relations.

sourcebook p. 245 → ## Sexism

There is enormous controversy over the treatment of women by sentencers. On the one hand, many claim that women are treated more leniently than men. In 2001, 19 per cent of known offenders were women. In 2003, women made up only 6 per cent of the prison population, but their numbers are growing. A Home Office study carried out by Hedderman and Hough in 1994 reported that, regardless of their previous records, women were far less likely than men to receive a custodial sentence for virtually all indictable offences except those concerning drugs, and that, when they do receive prison sentences, these tend to be shorter than those imposed on men. Flood-Page and Mackie also found in 1998 that women were less likely to receive a prison sentence or be fined when all relevant factors were taken into account. This has been variously attributed to the fact that women are less likely to be tried in the Crown Court; chivalry on the part of sentencers; assumptions that women are not really bad, but offend only as a result of mental illness or medical problems; and reluctance to harm children by sending their mothers to prison.

On the other hand, some surveys have suggested that women are actually treated less leniently than men. A 1990 study by the National Association for the Care and Resettlement of Offenders (NACRO) found that one-third of sentenced female prisoners had no previous convictions, compared with 11 per cent of men, and most of them were in prison for minor, non-violent offences. Because they are usually on lower incomes than men, women are thought more likely to end up in prison for non-payment of fines.

Several critics have suggested that women who step outside traditional female roles are treated more harshly than both men and other women. Sociologist Pat Carlen (1983) studied the sentencing of a large group of women, and found that judges were more likely to imprison those who were seen as failing in their female role as wife and mother – those who were single or divorced, or had children in care. This was reflected in the comments made by sentencers, including, 'It may not be necessary to send her to prison if she has a husband. He may tell her to stop it', and 'If she's a good mother we don't want to take her away. If she's not, it doesn't really matter.'

Today, women represent the fastest-growing sector of the prison population; their numbers nearly trebled in the space of nine years from 1,300 in 1992 to 4,300 in 2002. About one-fifth of the total female prison population have been sentenced as drugs couriers and, of these, some seven out of every ten are foreign nationals (Penny Green, *Drug Couriers: A New Perspective* (1996)). HM Chief Inspector of Prisons, Sir David Ramsbotham, has commented: 'There is considerable doubt whether all the women in custody [at Holloway] really needed to be there in order for the public to be protected' (*Report on Holloway Prison* (1997)). Helen Edwards, the Chief Executive of NACRO, has observed that: 'the vast majority of women in prison do not commit violent offences and much of their offending relates to addiction and poverty. Prison is not an appropriate, necessary or cost-effective way of dealing with these problems.'

The needs of women prisoners have wrongly been assumed to be the same as those of men. The Chief Inspector of Prisons has emphasised that female prisoners have different social and criminal profiles, as well as different health care, dietary and other needs. The Home Office published a study of women in prison: *Women in Prison: A Thematic Review* (Ramsbotham, 1997). Their survey revealed that the great majority of women in prison come from deprived backgrounds. Over half had spent time in local authority care, had attended a special school or had been in an institution as a child. A third had had a period of being homeless, half had run away from home, half reported having suffered violence at home (from a parent or a partner) and a third had been sexually abused. Forty per cent of sentenced women prisoners had a drug dependency, and alcohol problems were also found to be very common. Almost 20 per cent had spent time in a psychiatric hospital prior to being imprisoned and 40 per cent reported receiving help or treatment for a psychiatric, nervous or emotional problem in the year before coming into prison. Nearly two in five reported having attempted suicide.

The government has established a three-year plan, called 'The Women's Offending Reduction Programme'. This aims to increase the opportunities for tackling women's offending in the community. Each year about 17,000 children are separated from their mother when she is put into prison.

Privatisation

Criminal justice has, historically, been regarded as a matter for the state. Recently, however, first under the Conservative government in the early 1990s, and now under Labour, various parts of the system have been privatised, including ten prisons. The Home Secretary said in 1998 that all new prisons would be privately built and run. Such moves have not generally been seen as runaway successes. Privatised prison escort services have come in for severe criticism, with prisoners managing to escape or not being brought to the court on time.

Reading on the web

The guide entitled *Restorative Justice: helping to meet local need* (2004), published by the Office for Criminal Justice Reform, is available on the Home Office website at:

www.crimereduction.gov.uk/criminaljusticesystem12.htm

The report of the National Association of Probation Officers, entitled *Anti-Social Behaviour Orders: analysis of the first six years*, is available on their website at:

www.napo.org.uk

The report of John Halliday on sentencing is available at:

www.homeoffice.gov.uk/documents/halliday-report-sppu

Information about the confiscation powers can be found at:

www.assetsrecovery.gov.uk

The consultation paper, *Making Sentencing Clearer* (2006), is available on the website of the National Offender Management Service:

www.noms.homeoffice.gov.uk

The report by L. Sherman and H. Strang, *Restorative Justice: the Evidence* (2007), is available on the website of the Esmée Fairbairn Foundation at:

www.esmeefairbairn.org.uk/docs/RJ_full_report.pdf

The report by R. Smith and others, *Poverty and Disadvantage Among Prisoners' Families* (2007), is available on the website of the Joseph Rowntree Foundation at:

www.jrf.org.uk/knowledge/findings/socialpolicy/2065.asp

Chapter summary

The Home Office undertook a review of sentencing that was carried out by John Halliday and published in 2001. The government accepted many of Halliday's recommendations and introduced significant reforms to the sentencing system in the Criminal Justice Act 2003.

Aims of sentencing

Section 142 of the Criminal Justice Act 2003 states that:

> 'any court dealing with an [adult] offender in respect of his offence must have regard to the following purposes of sentencing –
> (a) the punishment of offenders;
> (b) the reduction of crime (including its reduction by deterrence);
> (c) the reform and rehabilitation of offenders;
> (d) the protection of the public; and
> (e) the making of reparation by offenders to persons affected by their offences.'

Aggravating and mitigating factors

The circumstances of the offence may include aggravating factors, which may lead the offender to have a heavier sentence. Mitigating factors are reasons why the defendant should be punished less severely than the facts of the case might suggest.

Sentences available for adult offenders

The judge has the power to impose a wide range of sentences:

Fines

The fine is the most common sentence issued by the court, but there is a major problem with fines not being paid.

Custodial sentences

Adult offenders can be sent to prison. Some offenders will be released early on home detention curfew. The Criminal Justice Act 2003 has introduced 'custody plus'.

Community sentence

The Criminal Justice Act 2003 has established a single community order that can be applied to an offender aged 16 or over. This order can contain a range of possible requirements. These are:

- an unpaid work requirement;
- an activity requirement;
- a programme requirement;
- a prohibited activity requirement;

- a curfew requirement;
- an exclusion requirement;
- a residence requirement;
- a mental health treatment requirement;
- a drug rehabilitation requirement;
- an alcohol treatment requirement; and
- a supervision requirement.

Miscellaneous sentences

A range of other sentences is also available to the court. These include:

- compensation orders;
- binding over to be of good behaviour;
- absolute and conditional discharges;
- disqualification;
- anti-social behaviour orders.

Problems with sentencing

The role of the judge

There has been concern that there is inconsistency in sentencing.

Racism

Critics of sentencing practice in England have frequently alleged that members of ethnic minorities are treated more harshly than white defendants.

Sexism

There is enormous controversy over the treatment of women by sentencers.

Privatisation

Criminal justice has, historically, been regarded as a matter for the state. Recently, however, various parts of the system have been privatised, including ten prisons.

Question and answer guide

1

Sally had a fight with a colleague at work called Frank. Frank picked up a chair and hit Sally with the chair, breaking Sally's leg. When questioned by the police Frank said that he had not been in the office at the time of the incident. Frank already has a number of convictions for violent behaviour.

(a)	(i)	Explain the concept of *actus reus*, giving examples.	*(6 marks)*
	(ii)	Explain the concept of *mens rea*, giving examples.	*(7 marks)*
	(iii)	Explain the concept of strict liability, giving examples.	*(7 marks)*

(b) (i) Discuss Frank's criminal liability for his fight with Sally.   *(10 marks)*

(ii) Describe briefly the procedures that would be followed after Frank is charged with the offence until the start of the criminal trial.   *(5 marks)*

(c) (i) Should Frank be convicted, describe the full range of sentences which a court could choose from when sentencing Frank.   *(5 marks)*

(ii) Discuss how a court will choose which sentence to impose on Frank.

(5 marks)

(a) (i)

To say that a criminal offence requires an *actus reus* is to say that an accused must usually have acted in a particular way. An *actus reus* can include the circumstances in which the act was committed (e.g. lack of consent in rape) or the consequences of the act (e.g. causing grievous bodily harm in Offences Against the Person Act 1861, s. 20).

The *actus reus* must have been voluntary, although 'voluntary' has sometimes been widely defined: **Larsonneur**.

An omission usually cannot constitute an *actus reus*. However, where defendants know that they have done something which has endangered life, and do nothing to prevent the harm occurring, their original act may be treated as the *actus reus*: **Miller**. Moreover, the courts have held that some offences can be committed by omission, e.g. manslaughter, although the omission must be by someone who is under a duty to act, e.g. because of a contract (**Pittwood**).

(a) (ii)

To say that an offence requires a *mens rea* is to say that an accused must have performed the *actus reus* with a particular state of mind. What that state of mind is varies, depending on the offence. The two most commonly encountered forms of *mens rea* are intention and subjective recklessness.

When the *mens rea* of an offence is intention that intention may be either direct or indirect. Direct intention corresponds with the everyday definition of intention, and applies where the accused actually wants the result that occurs. A jury is entitled to find indirect intention where the accused did not desire a particular result but, in acting as he or she did, realised to the point of virtual certainty that it might occur: **Woollin**.

When the *mens rea* of an offence is subjective recklessness then it means that the defendant must have been aware of a risk that something would happen, and yet unreasonably took that risk: **R *v* G**.

(a) (iii)

Strict liability crimes are those that can be committed without any *mens rea*, or without *mens rea* regarding at least one aspect of the *actus reus*.

Most strict liability offences are statutory. Sometimes the statute makes clear whether the offence is one of strict liability. But usually the courts are left to decide for themselves. In making this decision, the courts presume that *mens rea* is required: **Sweet *v* Parsley**. To rebut this presumption they require a 'compellingly clear implication' that Parliament intended the offence to be one of strict liability: **B (A Minor) *v* DPP**. This presumption is less strong for regulatory offences than for true crimes: **Gammon** *v* **Attorney-General of Hong Kong**. Regulatory offences are those in which no real moral issue is involved, e.g. selling unfit food.

(b) (i)

The most serious offence for which Frank may be liable is causing grievous bodily harm or wounding under s. 18 of the Offences Against the Person Act 1861 (OAPA). The *actus reus* is causing GBH or wounding. Wounding requires a breaking of the skin, and it is unclear whether that happened here. As for GBH, the courts have held that grievous simply means serious: **Saunders**. Given that Sally's leg has been 'very badly broken' and 'needed surgery', the *actus reus* of s. 18 can probably be satisfied.

The *mens rea* of s. 18 is, so far as relevant, intention to cause GBH. In Frank's case this means that the prosecution must prove that, in hitting Sally, he intended to cause her serious harm. The fact that he used a cricket bat is evidence of this, but not conclusive evidence.

The next most serious offence for which Frank may be liable is causing GBH or wounding under OAPA, s. 20. The *actus reus* is the same as s. 18's. However, the *mens rea* is intention **or** recklessness. Moreover, the prosecution does not need to prove that Frank was reckless as to causing **serious** harm. He need only have been reckless as to whether his acts could have caused **some** harm: **Savage**. Frank's use of a cricket bat strongly suggests he was.

(b) (ii)

Assuming Frank is charged under s. 20, an either-way offence, he will be brought before a magistrates' court and asked to plead guilty or not guilty. If he pleads guilty, the court will hear the details of his offence and sentence him. Or it can commit him for sentence to the Crown Court if it considers that its powers of punishment are insufficient. If Frank chooses not to plead, or pleads not guilty, the court will decide the mode of trial. Frank can insist on jury trial. If he does not do so the magistrates will decide the mode of trial. If jury trial is decided upon (or chosen by Frank), the magistrates will deal with any bail application, but leave all pre-trial matters to the Crown Court. If summary trial is decided upon, the magistrates will decide all pre-trial matters themselves.

(c) (i)

The first type of sentence available to the criminal courts if Frank were to be convicted of an offence is a custodial sentence. If Frank is assessed as dangerous, which is possible given that he has several previous convictions for violence, the court may impose an indeterminate sentence of imprisonment under the Criminal Justice Act 2003.

Secondly, the court could impose a community sentence. The Criminal Justice Act 2003 has established a single community order, to which the court can attach a range of requirements, e.g. a curfew requirement and/or an exclusion requirement. In Frank's case these requirements might be designed to keep him away from Sally.

The other main types of sentence that the courts could impose are a fine, an absolute or a conditional discharge and a compensation order.

(c) (ii)

The factors that the court will take into account in sentencing Frank include, first, whether he changed his plea to guilty. If he did, this will probably result in a more lenient sentence, though not if it came very late in the day.

A second factor are Frank's antecedents. These will include his previous convictions for violence and any other convictions he may have.

The court must also consider any aggravating or mitigating factors. Aggravating factors in Frank's case would include his use of a weapon. A mitigating factor might be that he appears to have acted impulsively.

The court will also take into account any pre-sentence reports and any medical reports on Frank that it might call for.

Group activity 1

- Divide your friends (or class) into groups of two or three people.
- In your groups, visit the website www.crimeinfo.org.uk, which is maintained by the Centre for Crime and Justice Studies at King's College London.
- Click on 'Judge for Yourself' and you will find an interactive exercise on sentencing.
- Work through this exercise in your group, making notes as you go along that record the sentencing decisions you made and why you made them. At the end of the exercise, ask yourself, 'What has this exercise taught me about the sentencing process?'
- Meet with the other groups and compare notes, looking for any common themes.

Group activity 2

The *Adult Court Bench Book* is a substantial book prepared by the Judicial Studies Board to support magistrates in carrying out their work. The aim of the *Bench Book* is to assist in the judicial process and promote national consistency of approach to increase the confidence the public have in the administration of justice. It is available on line at:

www.jsboard.co.uk/downloads/acbb_complete_07.pdf

Working in groups, take a look at this book. See if you can find out the procedure the magistrates must follow before they impose a custodial sentence – look at pages 201–3 for some useful guidance on this subject. When you visited a magistrates' court, did the magistrates follow that procedure?

Group activity 3

Look at recent copies of your local newspaper. There will be reports about criminal cases heard in the local courts. List the variety of sentences passed on those convicted. Repeat the exercise using a national paper. Contrast and compare the sentences handed down and consider the reasons for any differences that you note.

Section B
INTRODUCTION TO TORT

Tort law is concerned with the imposition of civil liability. Civil liability is imposed either for the commission of a tort or for breach of a contract and this section concentrates on the former. A tort involves breach of a duty which is fixed by the law. It can give rise to litigation between the wrongdoer and the victim and the aim is to compensate the victim for the harm done.

The grounds for imposing liability for negligence are analysed and the remedy of damages in tort law examined. The civil courts and rules of civil procedure are also examined. Thus, this section looks at:

- negligence;
- civil procedure; and
- compensatory damages.

Part 11
LIABILITY IN NEGLIGENCE

Chapter 20

Negligence

This chapter discusses the three main requirements for the imposition of liability for negligence:

■ the existence of a duty of care;

■ breach of the duty;

■ damage caused by the breach;

■ the burden of proof in negligence claims;

■ criticisms of negligence law.

Introduction

Negligence is the most important tort in modern law. It was first recognised in the 1932 case of **Donoghue** *v* **Stevenson**, and concerns breach of a legal duty to take care, with the result that damage is caused to the claimant. Examples of the type of case which might be brought in negligence are people injured in a car accident who sue the driver and patients who sue doctors when medical treatment goes wrong.

The tort of negligence has three main elements:

■ the defendant must owe the claimant a duty of care;

■ the defendant must breach that duty of care;

■ that failure must cause damage to the claimant.

The duty of care

Negligence is essentially concerned with compensating people who have suffered damage as a result of the carelessness of others, but the law does not provide a remedy for everyone who suffers in this way. One of the main ways in which access to compensation is restricted is through the doctrine of a duty of care. Essentially, this is a legal concept which dictates the circumstances in which one party will be liable to another in negligence: if the law says you do not have a duty of care towards the person (or organisation) you have caused damage to, you will not be liable to that party in negligence.

It is interesting to note that in the vast majority of ordinary tort cases which pass through the court system, it will usually be clear that the defendant does owe the claimant a duty of care, and what the courts will be looking at is whether the claimant can prove that the defendant breached that duty – for example, in the huge numbers of road-accident cases that courts hear every year, it is established that road users owe a duty to other road users, and the issues for the court will generally revolve around what the defendant actually did, and what damage was caused. Yet flick through the pages of this or any other law book, and you soon see that duty of care occupies an amount of space which seems disproportionate to its importance in real-life tort cases. This is because when it comes to the kinds of cases which reach the higher courts and therefore the pages of law books, duty of care arises frequently, and that in turn is because of its power to affect the whole shape of negligence law. Every time a new duty of care is recognised (or declined), that has implications for the numbers of tort cases being brought in the future, the types of situations it can play a part in, and therefore the role which the tort system plays in society.

As a result, the law in this field has caused the courts considerable problems and we can analyse its development in three main stages: the original neighbour principle as established in **Donoghue v Stevenson**; a two-stage test set down in **Anns v Merton London Borough** (1978), which greatly widened the potential for liability in negligence; and a retreat from this widening following the case of **Murphy v Brentwood District Council** (1990).

Development of the duty of care

The neighbour principle

The facts of **Donoghue v Stevenson** began when Mrs Donoghue and a friend went into a café for a drink. Mrs Donoghue asked for a ginger beer, which her friend bought. It was supplied, as was usual at the time, in an opaque bottle. Mrs Donoghue poured out and drank some of the ginger beer, and then poured out the rest. At that point, the remains of a decomposing snail fell out of the bottle. Mrs Donoghue became ill, and sued the manufacturer.

Up until this time, the usual remedy for damage caused by a defective product would be an action in contract, but this was unavailable to Mrs Donoghue because the contract for the sale of the drink was between her friend and the café. Mrs Donoghue sued the manufacturer, and the House of Lords agreed that manufacturers owed a duty of care to the end-consumer of their products. The ginger beer manufacturer had breached that duty, causing harm to Mrs Donoghue, and she was entitled to claim damages.

For the benefit of future cases, their Lordships attempted to lay down general rules for when a duty of care would exist. Lord Atkin stated that the principle was that: 'You must take reasonable care to avoid acts or omissions which you can reasonably foresee would be likely to injure your neighbour.' By 'neighbour', Lord Atkin did not mean the person who lives next door, but 'persons who are so closely and directly affected by my act that I ought to have them in contemplation as being so affected when I am directing my mind to the acts or omissions which are called in question'. This is sometimes known as the neighbour principle.

The test of foreseeability is objective; the court does not ask what the defendant foresaw, but what a reasonable person could have been expected to foresee.

Claimants do not have to be individually identifiable for the defendant to be expected to foresee the risk of harming them. In many cases, it will be sufficient if the claimant falls within a category of people to whom a risk of harm was foreseeable – for example, the end-user of a product, as in **Donoghue** *v* **Stevenson**. The ginger beer manufacturer did not have to know that Mrs Donoghue would drink its product, only that someone would.

Task 20.1

A headnote is a summary of a case that appears at the beginning of a law report. Below is a headnote from the *All England Law Reports* of the judgment of **Donoghue** *v* **Stevenson**. The section in italics is a list of the key issues that are considered in the case. A lawyer can look at this list to decide whether the case contains any law relevant to the area they are researching. Read the headnote and answer the questions that follow (the words that are the subject of the questions have been underlined).

```
        DONOGHUE (or McALISTER) v STEVENSON

[House of Lords (Lord Buckmaster, Lord Atkin, Lord Tomlin, Lord
Thankerton and Lord Macmillan), December 12, 1931, May 26, 1932]
   [Reported [1932] AC 562; 101 LJPC 119; 147 LT 281; 48 TLR 494;
76 Sol Jo 396; 37 Com Cas 350]
```

Negligence – Duty of manufacturer to consumer – No contractual relation – No possibility of examination of product before use – Knowledge that absence of reasonable care in preparation of production will result in injury to consumer – Bottle of ginger-beer purchased from retailer – Dead snail in bottle – Purchaser poisoned by drinking contents – Liability of manufacturer.

A manufacturer of products which he sells in such a form as to show that he intends them to reach the ultimate consumer in the form in which they left him, with no reasonable possibility of intermediate examination, and with the knowledge that the absence of reasonable care in the preparation or putting up of the products will result in injury to the consumer, owes a duty to the consumer to take reasonable care, although the manufacturer does not know the product to be dangerous and no contractual relations exist between him and the consumer.

Per LORD ATKIN: <u>The rule that you are to love your neighbour</u> becomes in law: You must not injure your neighbour; and the lawyer's question: Who is my neighbour? receives a restricted reply. You must take reasonable care to avoid acts or omissions which you can reasonably foresee would be likely to injure your neighbour. Who, then, in law is my neighbour? The answer seems to be persons who are so closely and directly affected by my act that I ought reasonably to have them in contemplation as being so affected when I am directing my mind to the acts or omissions which are called in question.

Per LORD MACMILLAN: A person who for gain engages in the business of manufacturing articles of food and drink intended for consumption by members of the public in the form in which he issues them is under a duty to take care in the manufacture of those articles. That duty he owes to those whom he intends to consume his products. He manufactures his commodities for human consumption; he intends and contemplates that they shall be consumed. By reason of that very fact he places himself in a relationship with all potential consumers of his commodities, and that relationship which he assumes and desires for his own ends, imposes on him a duty to take care to avoid injuring them. He owes them a duty not to convert by his own carelessness an article which he issues to them as wholesome and innocent into an article which is dangerous to life and health.

The appellant and a friend visited a café where the friend ordered for her a bottle of ginger-beer. The proprietor of the café opened the ginger-beer bottle, which was of opaque glass so that it was impossible to see the contents, and poured some of the ginger-beer into a tumbler. The appellant drank some of the ginger-beer. Then her friend poured the remaining contents of the bottle into the tumbler and with it a decomposed snail came from the bottle. As a result of her having drunk part of the impure ginger-beer the appellant suffered from shock and gastric illness. In an action by her for negligence against the manufacturer of the ginger-beer.

Held by LORD ATKIN, LORD THANKERTON, and LORD MACMILLAN (LORD BUCK-MASTER and LORD TOMLIN dissenting), on proof of these facts <u>the appellant would be entitled to recover</u>.

Questions

1 In which court was this case heard?
2 What is meant by 'Reported [1932] AC 562'.
3 How many judges heard the case, and what were their names?
4 What is meant by the phrase 'Per LORD ATKIN'?
5 Which judges disagreed with the majority decision?
6 The headnote provides summaries of Lord Atkin's judgment and Lord Macmillan's judgment. In the light of the discussion of the case in this textbook at p. 371, which judgment has been the most influential in the development of the law?
7 Lord Atkin refers to the 'rule that you must love your neighbour'. Where is this rule laid down?
8 What is meant by the phrase 'the appellant would be entitled to recover'?

A two-stage test

The issue of reasonable foresight was never the only criterion for deciding whether a duty of care is owed. As time went on, and a variety of factual situations were established in which a duty of care arose, the courts began to seek precedents in which a similar factual situation had given rise to the existence of a duty of care. For example, it was soon well established that motorists owe a duty of care to other road users, and employers owe a duty to their employees, but where a factual situation seemed completely new, a duty of care would only be deemed to arise if there were policy reasons for doing so. 'Policy reasons' simply mean that the courts take into account not just the legal framework, but also whether society would benefit from the existence of a duty. The apparent need to find such reasons was said to be holding back development of the law.

This view was addressed in **Anns** *v* **Merton London Borough** (1978), where Lord Wilberforce proposed a significant extension of the situations where a duty of care would exist, arguing that it was no longer necessary to find a precedent with similar facts. Instead, he suggested that whether a duty of care arose in a particular factual situation was a matter of general principle.

In order to decide whether this principle was satisfied in a particular case, the courts should use a two-stage test. First, they should establish whether the parties satisfied the requirements of the neighbour test – in other words, whether the claimant was someone to whom the defendant could reasonably be expected to foresee a risk of harm. If the answer was yes, a *prima facie* duty of care arose. The second stage would involve asking whether there were any policy considerations which dictated that no duty should exist.

This two-stage test changed the way in which the neighbour test was applied. Previously, the courts had used it to justify new areas of liability, where there were policy reasons for creating them. After **Anns** *v* **Merton London Borough**, the test would apply unless there were policy reasons for excluding it. This led to an expansion of the situations in which a duty of care could arise, and therefore in the scope of negligence. This expansion reached its peak in **Junior Books** *v* **Veitchi** (1983), where the House of Lords seemed to go one step further. The House appeared to suggest that what were previously good policy reasons for limiting liability should now not prevent an extension where the neighbour principle justified recovery. It therefore allowed recovery for purely economic loss (meaning financial loss that did not result from injury or damage to property) when previously this kind of claim had not been permitted.

As the first stage was relatively easy to pass, it seemed likely that the bounds of liability would be extended beyond what was considered to be reasonable, particularly given the judiciary's notorious reluctance to discuss issues of policy – a discussion that was necessary if the second stage was to offer any serious hurdle. As a result, the growth in liability for negligence set all sorts of alarm bells ringing. Eventually, the problems of insuring against the new types of liability, and the way in which tort seemed to be encroaching on areas traditionally governed by contractual liability, led to a rapid judicial retreat and in a series of cases, the judiciary began restricting new duties of care.

The judicial retreat

In 1990, the case of **Murphy** *v* **Brentwood District Council** came before a seven-member House of Lords. The House invoked the 1966 Practice Statement (which allows them to depart from their own previous decisions) to overrule **Anns**. They quoted the High Court of Australia in **Sutherland Shire Council** *v* **Heyman** (1985), a case in which the High Court of Australia had itself decided not to follow **Anns**:

> 'It is preferable, in my view, that the law should develop novel categories of negligence incrementally and by analogy with established categories, rather than by a massive exten-sion of a prima facie *duty of care, restrained only by indefinable "considerations" which ought to negative, or to reduce or limit the scope of the duty or the class of person to whom it is owed.'*

The broad general principle with its two-part test envisaged in **Anns** was thereby swept aside, leaving the courts to impose duties of care only when they could find precedent in comparable factual situations.

Rejection of the **Anns** test did not mean that the categories of negligence were closed, but the creation of new duties of care was intended to involve a much more gradual process, building step by step by analogy with previous cases involving similar factual situations. Issues of policy would still arise, as such consideration of policy is an inescapable result of the importance of the judge's position.

The law today

Over the years, case law has established that there are a number of factual situations in which a duty of care is known to be owed. For example, drivers owe a duty of care not to injure pedestrians, and employers owe a duty of care to take reasonable steps to protect their employees from injury. However, there are still situations in which it is not clear whether there is a duty of care, and following the moves towards a tighter test after **Anns** was overruled, the House of Lords set down a new test in **Caparo Industries plc** v **Dickman** (1990).

The case is explained in more detail below but, essentially, the test requires the courts to apply a three-stage process, asking whether the damage caused was reasonably foreseeable, whether there was a relationship of 'proximity' between the claimant and the defendant, and whether it is just and reasonable to impose a duty of care.

The **Caparo** test is now accepted as the basic test to be applied when a court is presented with a new factual situation in which it needs to decide whether a duty of care exists. However, the courts have developed more detailed, and more restrictive, rules which apply in certain types of case. We will now look first at the basic **Caparo** test.

Quick quiz 20.2

1 Which case established the tort of negligence?

2 What three elements need to be proved for a finding of negligence?

3 What is the 'neighbour principle'?

4 In determining whether a duty of care is owed, are the courts likely to follow **Anns** v **Merton London Borough** or **Murphy** v **Brentwood District Council?**

Duties of care

The *Caparo* test

As explained above, the basic test for a duty of care is now the one set down in **Caparo** v **Dickman**. This will usually be applied to duty of care questions in cases involving physical injury and/or damage to property, and those which do not fall into any of the special categories listed above. In some cases, it is also applied alongside the special rules in those categories, and some experts suggest that those special rules are in fact simply a more detailed application of the principles in the **Caparo** test.

The test requires the courts to ask three questions:

1 Was the damage reasonably foreseeable?
2 Was there a relationship of proximity between defendant and claimant?
3 Is it just, fair and reasonable to impose a duty in this situation?

As we shall see from the cases in this section, in many situations one or more of these elements may overlap, and so the test is not always applied as a clear, three-step process.

Reasonable foreseeability

This element of the test has its foundations in the original 'neighbour principle' developed in **Donoghue v Stevenson** (see p. 371). Essentially, the courts have to ask whether a reasonable person in the defendant's position would have foreseen the risk of damage. A modern case which shows how this part of the test works is **Langley v Dray** (1998), where the claimant was a policeman who was injured in a car crash when he was chasing the defendant, who was driving a stolen car. The Court of Appeal held that the defendant knew, or ought to have known, that he was being pursued by the claimant, and therefore in increasing his speed he knew, or should have known, that the claimant would also drive faster and so risk injury. The defendant had a duty not to create such risks and he was in breach of that duty.

In order for a duty to exist, it must be reasonably foreseeable that damage or injury would be caused to the particular defendant in the case, or to a class of people to which he or she belongs, rather than just to people in general. In other words, the duty is owed to a person or class of persons, and not to the human race in general. A good, if old, example of this principle can be seen in **Palsgraf v Long Island Railroad** (1928). The case arose from an incident when a man was boarding a train, and a member of the railway staff negligently pushed him, which caused him to drop a package he was carrying. The box contained fireworks, which exploded, and the blast knocked over some scales, several feet away. They fell on the claimant and she was injured. She sued, but the court held that it could not reasonably be foreseen that pushing the passenger would injure someone standing several feet away. It was reasonably foreseeable that the passenger himself might be injured, but that did not in itself create a duty to other people.

That does not, however, mean that the defendant has to be able to identify a particular individual who might foreseeably be affected by their actions; it is enough that the claimant is part of a class of people who might foreseeably be affected. This was the case in **Haley v London Electricity Board** (1965). The defendants dug a trench in the street in order to do repairs. Their workmen laid a shovel across the hole to draw pedestrians' attention to it, but the claimant was blind, and fell into the hole, seriously injuring himself. It was agreed in court that the precautions taken would have been sufficient to protect a sighted person from injury, so the question was whether it was reasonably foreseeable that a blind person might walk by and be at risk of falling in. The Court of Appeal said that it was:

the number of blind people who lived in London and were used to walking about by themselves meant that the defendants owed a duty to this class of people.

Proximity

In normal language, proximity means closeness, in terms of physical position but, in law, it has a wider meaning which essentially concerns the relationship, if any, between the defendant and the claimant. In **Muirhead v Industrial Tank Specialities** (1985), Goff LJ pointed out that this does not mean that the defendant and claimant have to know each other, but that the situations they were both in meant that the defendant could reasonably be expected to foresee that his or her actions could cause damage to the claimant.

In this sense, proximity can be seen as simply another way of expressing the foreseeability test, as the case of **Caparo v Dickman** itself shows. The claimants, Caparo, were a company who had made a takeover bid for another firm, Fidelity, in which they already owned a large number of shares. When they were deciding whether to make the bid, they had used figures prepared by Dickman for Fidelity's annual audit, which showed that Fidelity was making a healthy profit. However, when the takeover was complete, Caparo discovered that Fidelity was in fact almost worthless. They sued Dickman, and the House of Lords had to decide whether Dickman owed them a duty of care. They pointed out that the preparation of an annual audit was required under the Companies Act 1985, for the purpose of helping existing shareholders to exercise control over a company. An audit was not intended to be a source of information or guidance for prospective new investors, and therefore could not be intended to help existing shareholders, like Caparo, to decide whether to buy more shares. The audit was effectively a statement that was 'put into more or less general circulation and may foreseeably be relied on by strangers to the maker of the statement, for any one of a variety of purposes which the maker of the statement has no reason to contemplate'. As a result, the House of Lords held that there was no relationship of proximity between Caparo and Dickman, and no duty of care.

Proximity may also be expressed in terms of a relationship between the defendant, and the activity which caused harm to the claimant, defined by Lord Brennan in **Sutradhar v Natural Environment Research Council** (2004) as 'proximity in the sense of a measure of control over and responsibility for the potentially dangerous situation'. An example of this kind of proximity can be seen in **Watson v British Boxing Board of Control** (2000), where the claimant was the famous professional boxer Michael Watson, who suffered severe brain damage after being injured during a match. He sued the Board, on the basis that they were in charge of safety arrangements at professional boxing matches, and evidence showed that if they had made immediate medical attention available at the ringside, his injuries would have been less severe. The Court of Appeal held that there was sufficient proximity between Mr Watson and the Board to give rise to a duty of care, because they were the only body in the UK which could license professional boxing matches, and therefore had complete control of and responsibility for a situation which could clearly result in harm to Mr Watson if the Board did not exercise reasonable care.

In **Sutradhar**, the claimant was a resident of Bangladesh, who had been made ill by drinking water contaminated with arsenic. The water came from wells near his home, and his reason for suing the defendants was that, some years earlier, they had carried out a survey of the local water system, and had neither tested for, nor revealed the presence of, arsenic. The claimant argued that the defendants should have tested for arsenic, or made public the fact that they had not done so, so as not to lull local people into a false sense of security. The House of Lords, however, held that the defendants had no duty of care to users of the water system, because there was insufficient proximity. Mr Sutradhar himself had never seen the defendants' report, and so his claim had to be based on the idea that they owed a duty to the whole population of Bangladesh. The House of Lords said this could not be the case: the defendants had no connection with the project that had provided the wells, and no one had asked them to test whether the water was safe to drink. They had no duty to the people or the government of Bangladesh to test the water for anything, and were simply doing general research into the performance of the type of wells that happened to be used in that area. The fact that someone had expert knowledge of a subject did not impose on them a duty to use that knowledge to help anyone in the world who might require such help. Proximity required a degree of control of the source of Mr Sutradhar's injury, namely the drinking water supply of Bangladesh, and the defendants had no such control.

Justice and reasonableness

In practice, the requirement that it must be just and reasonable to impose a duty often overlaps with the previous two – in **Watson** and **Sutradhar**, for example, the arguments made under the heading of proximity could equally well be seen as arguments relating to justice and reasonableness. It was obviously more just and reasonable to expect the Boxing Board to supervise a match properly, since that was their job, than it was to expect the researchers in **Sutradhar** to take responsibility for a task that was not their job, and which they never claimed to have done.

Where justice and reasonableness are specifically referred to, it is usually because a case meets the requirements of foreseeability and proximity, but the courts believe there is a sound public policy reason for denying the claim. An example is **McFarlane v Tayside Health Board** (1999). The claimant had become pregnant after her partner's vasectomy failed, and claimed for the costs of bringing up the child. The courts denied her claim, on the basis that it was not just and reasonable to award compensation for the birth of a healthy child – something most people, they said, would consider a blessing.

In **Customs Commissioners and Excise v Barclays Bank plc** (2006), the government's Customs and Excise department was owed large sums in unpaid VAT by two companies, who had accounts with the defendant bank. Customs and Excise had gone to court and obtained what are called 'freezing' injunctions, which restricted the two companies' access to the money they had in the bank. The bank was notified of the orders, and should have prevented the companies from withdrawing money, but, apparently because of negligence, they failed to do so, which meant that the two companies were able to take out over £2 million, and Customs and Excise were unable to recover all the money owed. They sued the bank, claiming that it owed them a duty of care. The House of Lords held that it was foreseeable that Customs and Excise could lose money if the bank was negligent in handling the freezing injunction, and that this suggested there was also a degree of proximity. However, the decisive issue was whether it was just and reasonable to impose a duty. The House stated that where a court order was breached, the court had power to deal with that breach; this would usually be enough to ensure that banks complied with such orders, and there was nothing to suggest that the order created any extra cause of action. In addition, it was unjust and unreasonable that the bank should become exposed to a liability which could amount to very much more than the £2 million that was at stake in this case, when it had no way of resisting the court order, and got no reward for complying with it.

Physical injury and damage to property

The most straightforward kind of tort case as far as the existence of a duty of care is concerned (and in practice the most common) is one where the defendant has done something which physically injures the claimant, or damages his or her property. In these cases a duty of care will exist where the damage was reasonably foreseeable – essentially, the original neighbour test – and there are no policy reasons against imposing liability (though it is important to remember, in all negligence cases, that establishing the existence of a duty is only a step towards liability; the claimant still needs to prove that the duty was breached and that the breach caused damage). Thus, for example, a motorist automatically owes a duty of care not to cause physical injury to other road users, even though they are likely to be strangers to him or her. The operation of the test can be seen in **Langley** v **Dray** (1998), where the claimant was a policeman who was injured in a car crash when he was chasing the defendant, who was driving a stolen car. The Court of Appeal held that the defendant knew, or ought to have known, that he was being pursued by the claimant, and therefore in increasing his speed he knew or should have known that the claimant would also drive faster and so risk injury. The defendant had a duty not to create such risks and he was in breach of that duty.

Omissions

As a general rule, the duties imposed by the law of negligence are duties not to cause injury or damage to others; they are not duties actively to help others. And if there is no duty, there is no liability. If, for example, you see someone drowning, you generally have no legal duty to save them, no matter how easy it might be to do so (unless there are special reasons why the law would impose such a duty on you in particular, such as under an employment contract as a lifeguard). This means tort law generally holds people liable for acts (the things people do), not omissions (the things they fail to do).

However, there are some situations in which the courts have recognised a positive duty to act, arising from the circumstances in which the parties find themselves. Although the categories are loose and at times overlap, the following are the main factors which have been taken into consideration.

Control exercised by the defendants

Where the defendants have a high degree of control over the claimant, they may have a positive duty to look after them which goes beyond simply taking reasonable steps to ensure that the defendants themselves do not cause injury. A key case in this area is **Reeves v Commissioner of Police for the Metropolis** (1999). The case was brought by the widow of a man who had committed suicide while in police custody. Although previous case law had accepted that the police had a duty of care to prevent suicide attempts by prisoners who were mentally ill, Mr Reeves was found to have been completely sane, and the police therefore argued that, while clearly they had a duty of care not to cause his death, they could not be held responsible for the fact that he chose to kill himself, and had no duty to prevent him from doing so. However, the Court of Appeal held that their duty of care to protect a prisoner's health did extend to taking reasonable care to prevent him or her from attempting suicide; they accepted that to impose a positive duty like this was unusual, but explained that it was justified by the very high degree of control which the police would have over a prisoner, and the well-known high risk of suicide among suspects held in this way.

In **Orange v Chief Constable of West Yorkshire Police** (2001), the Court of Appeal emphasised that the duty established in **Reeves** did not amount to a general obligation to treat every prisoner as a suicide risk. The case involved the suicide of a married man with young children, who was arrested for being drunk and disorderly, and placed in a police cell. The custody officer who came to release him found that he had used his belt to hang himself from the horizontal bar of a grille inside the cell door. There had been no reason to suspect that he was a suicide risk, but his widow sued the police, claiming that they had been negligent in failing to take away his belt, or to monitor him properly, and in leaving him in a cell with a suspension point.

The Court of Appeal rejected this argument, stating that the duty laid down in **Reeves** was a duty to take reasonable steps to discover whether an individual prisoner was a suicide risk, and act accordingly. As there was no reason to suspect this prisoner might try to commit suicide, there was no duty to take steps to prevent him from doing so.

The 2001 prize for the cheekiest legal action must surely go to the claimant in another case in this area, **Vellino v Chief Constable of Greater Manchester** (2001). Mr Vellino was a career criminal, with an extensive record, and was well known to the local police. On several occasions the police had gone to his flat to arrest him, and he had tried to escape by jumping from the second floor windows to the ground floor below. On the occasion that gave rise to the case, the police arrived and Mr Vellino jumped, as usual, but this time he seriously injured himself, ending up with brain damage and paralysis, which made him totally dependent on others for his needs. He sued the police, arguing that they were under a duty to prevent him from escaping, and their failure to do so had caused his injuries. It was, his counsel argued, foreseeable that he would try to escape, and foreseeable injury could result.

The Court of Appeal rejected the argument entirely, pointing out that it would mean that arresting officers had a duty to hold a suspect in the lightest possible grip, just in case he or she wrenched a shoulder in struggling to break free. Equally, it would mean prisons could be sued if prisoners hurt themselves jumping off high boundary walls, since it was foreseeable that prisoners might try to escape and that jumping off high walls tends to cause injury.

In any case, the court said, Mr Vellino was not actually under the control of the police when he jumped. He was trying to escape police custody, which was a crime, and therefore the defence of illegality applied.

Assumption of responsibility

Although in English law people generally have no duty actively to help each other, such a duty will be implied where the courts find that one of the parties has assumed responsibility for the other in some way. A common reason for finding such an assumption is where a contract implying such responsibility exists, or where such responsibility clearly arises from the defendant's job.

In **Costello v Chief Constable of Northumbria Police** (1999), the claimant was a police constable who was attacked by a prisoner in a police station cell. A police inspector was nearby but, despite her screams, he failed to come to her aid. The claimant sued the Chief Constable, alleging that the inspector had a duty of care towards her in that situation (the Chief Constable was sued as being vicariously liable. The Court of Appeal agreed; as a police officer, the inspector had assumed a responsibility to help fellow officers in circumstances like these, and where a member of the police force's failure to act would result in a fellow officer being exposed to unnecessary risk of injury, there was a positive duty to act.

A defendant may also be deemed to have assumed responsibility for another person by virtue of his or her actions towards that person. In **Barrett v Ministry of Defence** (1995), the Ministry of Defence (MOD) was sued by the widow of a naval pilot, who had died by choking on his own vomit after becoming so drunk that he passed out. He had been found unconscious and an officer had organised for him to be taken up to his own room, but nobody had been told to watch over him and make sure he did not choke. The court heard that extreme drunkenness was common on the remote Norwegian base where the death happened, and the officer in charge admitted that he had not fulfilled his responsibility, imposed by Royal Navy regulations, of discouraging drunkenness at the base. At trial, the judge found the defendant was negligent in tolerating the excessive drinking, but reduced the damages by one-quarter because the dead man had been contributorily negligent in getting so drunk. The MOD appealed.

The Court of Appeal disagreed with the first instance court's finding that the officer could be liable for failing to prevent drunkenness, and held that it was fair, just and reasonable to expect an adult to take responsibility for their own consumption of alcohol and the consequences of it. However, the court stated that once the officer had ordered the unconscious man to be taken up to the room, he had from that point assumed responsibility for his welfare, and had been negligent in not summoning medical help or watching over him. Bearing in mind that the defendant would never have had to assume this responsibility had it not been for the dead man's own actions, they decided that there was contributory negligence, and damages were reduced accordingly.

Creation of a risk

Where a defendant actually creates a dangerous situation – even if this risk is created through no fault of the defendant – the courts may impose a positive duty to deal with the danger. This issue was explored in **Capital and Counties plc v Hampshire County Council** (1997). The case concerned the question of whether fire brigades had a duty of care towards people whose property was on fire. The court concluded that in general they did not, but said that where a fire brigade had actually done something which either created a danger or made the existing danger worse, they then had a positive duty to take reasonable steps to deal with that danger. In the case itself, this meant that a fire brigade whose employee had ordered the claimant's sprinkler system to be turned off, and thereby enabled the fire to spread more rapidly than it would otherwise have done, was liable in negligence.

Breach of a duty of care

At the very beginning of this chapter, we explained that negligence has three elements: a duty of care; breach of that duty; and damage caused by the breach. Now that we have looked at the various tests for establishing whether a duty exists between the claimant and the defendant, we can move on to consider what, assuming a duty has been found in any particular circumstances, will constitute a breach of that duty.

Breach of a duty of care essentially means that the defendant has fallen below the standard of behaviour expected in someone undertaking the activity concerned, so, for example, driving carelessly is a breach of the duty owed to other road users, while bad medical treatment may be a breach of the duty owed by doctors to patients. In each case, the standard of care is an objective one: the defendant's conduct is tested against the standard of care which could be expected from a reasonable person. This means that it is irrelevant that the defendant's conduct seemed fine to them; it must meet a general standard of reasonableness.

As the test is objective, the particular defendant's own characteristics are usually ignored. A striking example of this is that the standard of care required of a driver is that of a reasonable driver, with no account taken of whether the driver has been driving for 20 years or 20 minutes, or even is a learner driver. In **Nettleship v Weston** (1971) the claimant was a driving instructor, and the defendant his pupil. On her third lesson, she drove into a lamp post and the claimant was injured. The court held that she was required to come up to the standard of the average competent driver, and anything less amounted to negligence: 'The learner driver may be doing his best, but his incompetent best is not good enough. He must drive in as good a manner as a driver of skill, experience and care.' However, there are a limited number of situations in which special characteristics of the defendant will be taken into account (see below).

The standard of reasonableness

It is important to realise that the standard of care in negligence never amounts to an absolute duty to prevent harm to others. Instead, it sets a standard of reasonableness: if a duty of care exists between two parties, the duty is to do whatever a reasonable person would do to prevent harm occurring, not to do absolutely anything and everything possible to prevent harm.

An example of this principle in operation is **Simonds v Isle of Wight Council** (2003). The claimant here was a five-year-old boy, who was injured while playing, unsupervised, on swings during a school sports day. The boy had had a picnic lunch with his mother near to where the sports day was taking place, and afterwards his mother sent him back to rejoin the supervised activities. Unknown to her, the little boy instead headed for some nearby swings. While playing there alone, he fell off and broke his arm. The court rejected the mother's claim that the school had a duty of care to prevent accidents happening on the swings. The sports day had been well supervised, and the school had in place measures to prevent children playing on the swings; it was not possible to make a playing field completely free of hazards, only to take reasonable precautions, and the school had done that.

In deciding what behaviour would be expected of the reasonable person in the circumstances of a case, the courts consider a number of factors, balancing them against each other. These include:

- special characteristics of the defendant;
- special characteristics of the claimant;
- the size of the risk;
- how far it was practical to protect against the risk;
- common practice in the relevant field;
- any benefits to society that might be gained from taking the risk.

None of the factors is conclusive by itself; they interact with each other. For example, if a type of damage is not very serious nor very likely to occur, the precautions required may be quite slight, but the requirements would be stricter if the damage, though not serious, was very likely to occur. Equally, a risk of very serious damage will require relatively careful precautions even if it is not very likely to occur.

Special characteristics of the defendant

Children

Where the defendant is a child, the standard of care is that of an ordinarily careful and reasonable child of the same age. In **Mullin v Richards** (1998), the defendant and claimant were 15-year-old schoolgirls. They were fencing with plastic rulers during a lesson, when one of the rulers snapped and a piece of plastic flew into the claimant's eye, causing her to lose all useful sight in it. The Court of Appeal held that the correct test was whether an ordinarily careful and reasonable 15-year-old would have foreseen that the game carried a risk of injury. On the facts, the practice was common and was not banned in the school, and the girls had never been warned that it could be dangerous, so the injury was not foreseeable.

Illness

A difficult issue is what standard should be applied when a defendant's conduct is affected by some kind of infirmity beyond their control. In **Roberts v Ramsbottom** (1980), the defendant had suffered a stroke while driving and, as a result, lost control of the car and hit the claimant. The court held that he should nevertheless be judged according to the standards of a reasonably competent driver. This may seem extremely unjust, but remember that motorists are required by law to be covered by insurance; the question in the case was not whether the driver himself would have to compensate the claimant, but whether his insurance company could avoid doing so by establishing that he had not been negligent. This is also one explanation for the apparently impossible standard imposed in **Nettleship** (p. 382).

Even so, in a more recent case, **Mansfield v Weetabix Ltd** (1997), the Court of Appeal took a different approach. Here the driver of a lorry was suffering from a disease which, on the day in question, caused a hypoglycaemic state (a condition in which the blood sugar falls so low that the brain's efficiency becomes temporarily impaired). This affected his driving, with the result that he crashed into the defendant's shop. The driver did not know that his ability to drive was impaired, and there was evidence that he would not have continued to drive if he had known. The Court of Appeal said that the standard by which he should be measured was that of a reasonably competent driver who was unaware that he suffered from a condition which impaired his ability to drive; on this basis he was found not to be negligent.

Professionals and special skills

Account will also be taken of the fact that a particular defendant has a professional skill, where the case involves the exercise of that skill. In such a case, the law will expect the defendant to show the degree of competence usually to be expected of an ordinary skilled member of that profession, when doing their duties properly. A defendant who falls short of that level of competence, with the result that damage is done, is likely to be held negligent. It would be ridiculous to demand of a surgeon, for example, no more than the skill of the untrained person in the street when carrying out an operation.

In **Vowles v Evans** (2003), a rugby player was injured as a result of a decision made by the referee. The Court of Appeal said that the degree of care a referee was legally expected to exercise would depend on his grade, and that of the match he was refereeing; less skill would be expected of an amateur stepping in to help out, than of a professional referee. This means that the same accident might amount to a breach of duty if the referee was a trained professional, but not if he was an amateur. The referee in the case was a professional and was found liable. Similarly, in **Gates v McKenna** (1998), a stage hypnotist was expected to take the precautions that a 'reasonably careful exponent of stage hypnotism' would take to prevent psychiatric injury to members of his audience, while in **Watson v Gray** (1998), a defendant professional footballer could only be liable for negligently injuring another player if a reasonable professional footballer would have known that what the defendant did carried a significant risk of serious injury.

Differences of opinion

In assessing the standard of care to be expected in areas where the defendant is exercising special skill or knowledge, the courts have accepted that within a profession or trade there may be differences of opinion as to the best techniques and procedures in any situation. This issue was addressed in **Bolam v Friern Barnet Hospital Management Committee** (1957), a case brought by a patient who had had electric shock treatment for psychiatric problems and had suffered broken bones as a result of the relaxant drugs given before the treatment. These drugs were not always given to patients undergoing electric shock treatment; some doctors felt they should not be given because of the risk of fractures; others, including the defendant, believed their use was desirable. How was the court then to decide whether, in using them, the defendant had fallen below the standard of a reasonable doctor?

Their answer was a formula which has been taken as allowing the medical profession (and to a certain extent other professions, as the test has been adopted in other types of case too) to fix their own standards. According to McNair J: 'A doctor is not guilty of negligence if he has acted in accordance with a practice accepted as proper by a responsible body of medical men skilled in that particular art.' Providing this was the case, the fact that other doctors might disagree could not make the conduct negligent. The practical effect of this decision (which was only given in a High Court case, but was adopted in several later House of Lords cases) was that so long as a doctor could find a medical expert prepared to state that the actions complained of were in keeping with a responsible body of medical opinion, it would be impossible to find him or her negligent.

The House of Lords has, however, now modified this much-criticised decision in **Bolitho v City and Hackney Health Authority** (1997). This case involved a two-year-old boy, who was admitted to hospital suffering breathing difficulties. He was not seen by a doctor. Shortly after his second attack of breathing problems, his breathing failed completely, he suffered a heart attack and died. His mother sued the health authority on his behalf, arguing that he should have been seen by a doctor, who should have intubated him (inserted a tube into his throat to help him breathe), and that it was the failure to do this which caused his death. The doctor maintained that even if she had seen the boy she would not have intubated him, which meant that the court had to decide whether she would have been negligent in not doing so. The doctor was able to produce an expert witness to say that intubation would not have been the correct treatment, and the claimant was able to produce one who said it would.

In this situation, the **Bolam** principle had always been taken as suggesting that the doctor was therefore not negligent – other medical opinion might disagree with what she did, but she could produce evidence that it was a practice accepted by a responsible body of medical opinion. Lord Browne-Wilkinson, delivering the leading judgment with which the others agreed, thought differently. While agreeing that the **Bolam** test was still the correct one to apply, he said that the court was not obliged to hold that a doctor was not liable for negligence simply because some medical experts had testified that the doctor's actions were in line with accepted practice. The court had to satisfy itself that the medical experts' opinion was reasonable, in that they had weighed up the risks and benefits, and had a logical basis for their conclusion. He then went on, however, to water down this statement by suggesting that, in most cases, the fact that medical experts held a particular view would in itself demonstrate its reasonableness, and that it would only be in very rare cases that a court would reject such a view as unreasonable. The case before the House of Lords, he concluded, was not one of those rare situations, and so the claimant's claim was rejected.

However, there are some signs that **Bolitho** is now being used more forcefully, to hold medical opinion to a proper standard of reasonableness. In **Marriott** *v* **West Midlands Regional Health Authority** (1999), the claimant had suffered a head injury after a fall at home; he spent the night in hospital but was discharged the next day after tests. After continuing to feel ill for a week, he called his GP, who could find nothing wrong but told Mrs Marriott to call him again if her husband's condition got any worse. Four days later, Mr Marriott became partially paralysed, and this was later discovered to be a result of the original injury. He claimed that the GP had been negligent in not referring him back to the hospital, given that the GP did not have the resources to test for the condition which he was eventually found to have. At trial, Mr Marriott's expert witness claimed that, given the symptoms Mr Marriott had shown, the GP should have sent him back to the hospital for more tests; however, the GP brought expert evidence to suggest that, although this would have been a reasonable course of action, keeping a patient at home for review was equally reasonable in the circumstances.

The old **Bolam** approach would have required the judge to find for the GP, given that he could prove that a reasonable body of medical opinion supported his actions, but, following **Bolitho**, the trial judge looked at the reasonableness of this opinion, given the risk to Mr Marriott, and concluded that, in the circumstances, deciding to review his case at home, without asking for further tests, was not a reasonable use of a GP's discretion. He therefore found the GP negligent. The Court of Appeal upheld his approach: a trial judge was entitled to carry out his own assessment of the risk in the circumstances, and was not bound to follow the opinion of a body of experts.

The influence of this shift may also be seen in a case which attracted much media attention in 2004: **AB and others** *v* **Leeds Teaching Hospitals NHS Trust** (2004). The case was brought after it was revealed that some hospitals had been routinely retaining the organs of children who had died in their care, for research purposes. The parents had not been told that this was happening; many were devastated when they found out. The case was brought by some of the parents who had suffered psychiatric injury as a result of the shock of finding out what had happened.

The hospital stated that the practices they had followed were considered by the medical profession to be in the best interests of bereaved parents, who might be upset to hear about the unpleasant details of a post-mortem examination. The judge accepted that they had acted in good faith, and genuinely believed they were doing what was best for the parents. But, he said, they were wrong; they had a duty to give the parents full information and allow them to make an informed decision on whether they wanted their children's organs to be retained.

The use of the **Bolam** test has been extended to cover not just other professionals, but also defendants who do not have the skills of a particular profession, but have made a decision or taken an action which professionals in the relevant area might disagree about. In **Adams and another *v* Rhymney Valley District Council** (2000), the claimants were a family whose children died when fire broke out in the house they rented from the defendant council. The house had double-glazed windows which could only be opened with a key, and the claimants had been unable to smash the glass quickly enough to save the children. They argued that the council had been negligent in providing this type of window, and the issue arose of whether it was correct to decide this by applying the **Bolam** test, given that the council were not window designers. The court held that it was. They pointed out that, in deciding on the window design, the council had to balance the risk of fire against the risk of children falling out of a more easily opened window, and professional opinions varied on how this balance should be struck. If a reasonable body of experts in the field would consider that the council's window design struck this balance in an acceptable way, and the court accepted this view as reasonable, there was no negligence, even though other experts might disagree, and even though the council had neither consulted experts, nor gone through the same processes when choosing the design as an expert would have done.

Standards of skill

It was also established in **Bolam** (and **Bolitho** does not affect this point) that where a defendant is exercising a particular skill, he or she is expected to do so to the standard of a reasonable person at the same level within that field. No account is taken of the defendant's actual experience, so that a junior doctor is not expected to have the same level of skill as a consultant, but is expected to be as competent as an average junior doctor, whether he or she has been one for a year or a week. This principle was upheld in **Djemal *v* Bexley Heath Health Authority** (1995), where the standard required was held to be that of a reasonably senior houseman acting as a casualty officer (which was the defendant's position at the time), regardless of how long the defendant had actually been doing that job at that level.

The standard of care imposed is only that of a reasonably skilled member of the profession; the defendant is not required to be a genius, or possess skills way beyond those normally to be expected. In **Wells *v* Cooper** (1958) the defendant, a carpenter, fixed a door handle on to a door. Later the handle came away in the claimant's hand, causing him injury. It was held that the carpenter had done the work as well as any ordinary carpenter would, and therefore had exercised such care as was required of him; he was not liable for the claimant's injury.

In **Balamoan *v* Holden & Co** (1999) the defendant was a solicitor who ran a small town practice, in which he was the only qualified lawyer. The claimant consulted him over a claim for nuisance. During the following two years, he had two 30-minute interviews with non-qualified members of the solicitor's staff, but no contact with the defendant himself. At the end of that time, he was advised that his claim was worth no more than £3,000, and when he refused to accept that advice, his legal aid certificate was discharged and he stopped using the firm. He went on to conduct the nuisance case himself, and won a settlement of £25,000.

He then sued the solicitor, arguing that, but for the solicitor's negligence in, for example, failing to gather all the available evidence at the time, he could have won £1 million in damages. The Court of Appeal held that the solicitor was to be judged only by the standard to be expected of a solicitor in a small country town (rather than, for example, a specialist firm which might have expert knowledge of big claims). However, if such a solicitor delegated the conduct of claims to unqualified staff who could not come up to that standard, the solicitor could be held negligent.

A duty to explain?

In **Chester** *v* **Afshar** (2004), the House of Lords seemed to be suggesting that professionals had a duty not only to take reasonable steps to make sure their advice was right, but also to explain the thinking behind that advice. The claimant had been operated on by the defendent surgeon to treat a back problem. When recommending the surgery, the surgeon had made no mention of any risk of things going wrong. After the operation, the claimant suffered severe nerve damage, which caused paralysis in one leg. She later discovered that this was a known, if unusual, risk of the surgery. She sued the doctor.

The House of Lords found that the doctor had not been negligent in the way he carried out the operation; the paralysis was something that could happen even when the surgery was carried out properly, as it had been here. But they stated that the surgeon had been negligent in not warning the claimant of the risk, however slight it might be. The patient had a right to choose what was or was not done to her, and she could only exercise this right if given full information. Providing such information was therefore part of the doctor's duty of care.

It was not clear from the judgment in **Chester** whether the duty to warn applied only in medical negligence cases, or in all cases involving professionals, but subsequent cases have suggested that it is, at the very least, much less likely that a duty to warn would be owed in non-medical situations. In **Moy** *v* **Pettman Smith** (2005), the defendant was a barrister, who was sued by a client. The claim arose out of another case in which the claimant, Mr Moy, was suing a health authority for medical negligence over an operation that went wrong, and the defendant was his barrister. Part of the evidence in the case was to be a report from an orthopaedic surgeon, but Mr Moy's solicitors failed to get it in time. The barrister's application to have the trial adjourned so that the report could be obtained had initially been refused, but she planned to apply again. At the door of the court, the health authority made a settlement offer of £150,000, but the defendant advised the claimant not to accept it, and said she was hopeful that there would be no problem getting time to present the medical report. In fact, she thought there was around a 50:50 chance of that application being accepted by the court, but reasoned that if the report could not be used, and the result was that Mr Moy won less than he should have, he could sue the solicitors. However, she did not explain any of this to Mr Moy.

On her advice, Mr Moy refused the offer but, once the hearing got under way, it soon became obvious that the application to produce the extra evidence was not going to succeed, which would weaken the claimant's case. The barrister therefore advised Mr Moy to settle, but by this point, the health authority had reduced their offer to £120,000. Mr Moy then sued the barrister, and the question arose as to whether she was negligent in failing to explain fully her thinking about the likelihood of the court accepting the application to submit the medical report. The House of Lords held that she was not. The advice she had given was within the range of advice that could be given by a reasonably competent barrister, and as long as a barrister gave clear and understandable advice about their recommended course of action, it was not necessary to spell out all the reasoning behind that advice. Similarly, in **Paul Davidson Taylor v White** (2004), the Court of Appeal considered whether the **Chester** duty to explain applied to a claim against a solicitor, and in **Beary v Pall Mall Investments** (2005), to a claim against a financial adviser. In both cases, the answer was no.

Changes in knowledge

In areas such as medicine and technology, the state of knowledge about a particular subject may change rapidly, so that procedures and techniques which are approved as safe and effective may very quickly become outdated, and even be discovered to be dangerous. The case of **Roe v Ministry of Health** (1954) established that, where this happens, a defendant is entitled to be judged according to the standards that were accepted at the time when they acted.

The claimant in the case was left paralysed after surgery, because a disinfectant, in which ampoules of anaesthetic were kept, leaked into the ampoules through microscopic cracks in the glass, invisible to the naked eye. Medical witnesses in the case said that until the man's accident occurred, keeping the ampoules in disinfectant was a standard procedure, and there was no way of knowing that it was dangerous; it was only the injuries to the claimant that had revealed the risk. Therefore, the defendant was held not to be liable.

In **Maguire v Harland and Wolff plc** (2005), the claimant was a woman who had contracted the fatal disease mesothelioma, as a result of being exposed to asbestos fibres brought home on her husband's clothes. The husband worked for the defendant shipbuilding firm, and it was accepted that the firm had been in breach of their duty of care to him, in exposing him to asbestos. Could they also be expected to foresee injury to members of his family from exposure to his work clothes? Today, it is well known that such exposure can result in injury, but the court found that at the time when Mr Maguire was working at the shipyard there had been no information from specialists in workplace safety, or from the medical profession, to suggest that it was necessary or even sensible to protect family members from exposure. Therefore, the defendants were not liable to Mrs Maguire.

However, once a risk is suspected, the position may change. In **N v UK Medical Research Council** (1996), the Queen's Bench Division looked at this issue. In 1959, the Medical Research Council (MRC) started a medical trial of human growth hormone, which involved giving the hormone to children with growth problems. The children were each given the hormone by one of four different methods. In 1976, the MRC were warned that the hormone could cause Creutzfeldt–Jakob Disease (CJD, which most readers will know is the human form of BSE, the fatal brain disease generally known as mad cow disease – though this litigation has no connection with the controversy over BSE-infected beef). A year later, the MRC were told that two of the four methods of giving the hormone carried a particular risk of transmitting CJD. Ultimately, several of the children who received the hormone died from CJD, and their parents alleged that the MRC had been negligent in not investigating the risk when it was first suggested in 1976, and suspending the programme until it was proved safe.

The court held that the failure to look into the risk was negligent, and if the MRC had looked into it then, failure to suspend the trial programme would also have been negligent.

Special characteristics of the claimant

The standard of care requires that a reasonable person would have due regard to the fact that a claimant has some characteristic or incapacity which increases the risk of harm. In **Paris v Stepney Borough Council** (1951), the claimant was employed by the defendants in a garage. As a result of a previous injury at work, he could only see with one eye. His job included welding, and while doing this one day, a piece of metal flew into his good eye and damaged it. No goggles had been provided by the defendant. The House of Lords accepted that failing to provide goggles would not have made the defendants liable to a worker with no previous sight problems, but said that in this case the defendants were liable. The risk of injury was small, but the potential consequences to this particular employee if such injury did occur were extremely serious, as he could easily end up completely blind; moreover, the provision of goggles was not difficult or expensive.

In a number of recent cases the courts have looked at the issue of claimants who are drunk, and whether this amounts to a characteristic which in some way increases a defendant's duty towards them. In **Barrett v Ministry of Defence**, the case of the drunken naval pilot discussed on p. 381, the Court of Appeal took the view that there is no duty to stop someone else from getting drunk, but once the claimant was drunk, it accepted that the defendant had assumed some responsibility for protecting him from the consequences of his intoxication, by virtue of the relationship between them and the fact that the defendant had ordered the claimant to be taken to lie down.

However, without such a relationship, it seems there is no general duty to give extra protection to a drunken claimant. In **Griffiths v Brown** (1998), the claimant had got drunk and asked a taxi driver to take him to a particular cashpoint machine. The driver dropped him off on the opposite side of the road from the machine, and he was injured while crossing. He argued that the driver, knowing he was drunk, had a duty not to expose him to the danger of crossing a road. The court rejected this argument: the duty of a taxi driver was to carry a passenger safely during the journey, and then stop at a place where they can get out of the car safely; that duty should not be increased by the fact that the claimant was drunk. However, the court accepted that the duty might be extended if, for example, a passenger who intended to spend the evening drinking arranged for a taxi driver to collect them and see them home safely; this clearly accords with the **Barrett** approach that there may be a duty to protect a claimant from the effects of drunkenness where the defendant has actually done something which amounts to assuming responsibility for such protection.

Size of the risk

This includes both the chances of damage occurring, and the potential seriousness of that damage. In **Bolton *v* Stone** (1951), the claimant was standing outside her house in a quiet street when she was hit by a cricket ball from a nearby ground. It was clear that the cricketers could have foreseen that a ball would be hit out of the ground, and this had happened before, but only six times in the previous 30 years.

Taking into consideration the presence of a 17-foot fence, the distance from the pitch to the edge of the ground, and the fact that the ground sloped upwards in the direction in which the ball was struck, the House of Lords considered that the chances of injury to someone standing where the claimant was were so slight that the cricket club was not negligent in allowing cricket to be played without having taken any other precautions against such an event. The only way to ensure that such an injury could not occur would be to erect an extremely high fence, or possibly even a dome over the whole ground, and the trouble and expense of such precautions were completely out of proportion to the degree of risk.

A case in which the potential seriousness of an injury was decisive is **Paris *v* Stepney Borough Council** (above).

Practicality of protection

The magnitude of the risk must be balanced against the cost and trouble to the defendant of taking the measures necessary to eliminate it. The more serious the risk (in terms of both the chances of it happening and the degree of potential harm), the more the defendant is expected to do to protect against it. Conversely, as **Bolton *v* Stone** shows, defendants are not expected to take extreme precaution against very slight risks. This was also the case in **Latimer *v* AEC Ltd** (1952). Flooding had occurred in a factory owned by the defendants following an unusually heavy spell of rain. This had left patches of the floor very slippery. The defendants had covered some of the wet areas with sawdust, but had not had enough to cover all of them. The claimant, a factory employee, was injured after slipping on an uncovered area, and sued, alleging that the defendants had not taken sufficient precautions; in view of the danger, they should have closed the factory. The House of Lords agreed that the only way to eradicate the danger was to close the factory, but held that, given the level of risk, particularly bearing in mind that the slippery patches were clearly visible, such an onerous precaution would be out of proportion. The defendants were held not liable.

Where the defendant is reacting to an emergency, they are then judged according to what a reasonable person could be expected to do in such a position and with the time available to decide on an action, and this will clearly allow for a lesser standard of conduct than that expected where the situation allows time for careful thought.

Common practice

In deciding whether the precautions taken by the defendant (if any) are reasonable, the courts may look at the general practice in the relevant field. In **Wilson** *v* **Governors of Sacred Heart Roman Catholic Primary School, Carlton** (1997), the claimant, a nine-year-old boy, was hit in the eye with a coat by a fellow pupil as he crossed the playground to go home at the end of the day. The trial judge had looked at the fact that attendants were provided to supervise the children during the lunch break, and inferred from this that such supervision should also have been provided at the end of the school day. The Court of Appeal, however, noted that most primary schools did not supervise children at this time; they also pointed out that the incident could just as easily have happened outside the school gates anyway. Consequently, the school had not fallen below the standard of care required.

In **Thompson *v* Smith Shiprepairers (North Shields) Ltd** (1984), it was made clear that companies whose industrial practices showed serious disregard for workers' health and safety would not evade liability simply by showing that their approach was common practice in the relevant industry. The case involved a claimant who suffered deafness as a result of working in the defendants' shipyard, and the defendants argued that the conditions in which he worked were common across the industry and therefore did not fall below the required standard of care. Mustill J disagreed, stating that they could not evade liability simply by proving that all the other employers were just as bad. He pointed out that their whole industry seemed to be characterised by indifference to the problem, and held that there were some circumstances in which an employer had a duty to take the initiative to look at the risks and seek out precautions which could be taken to protect workers. He pointed out, however, that this approach must still be balanced against the practicalities; employers were not expected to have standards way above the rest of their industry, though they were expected to keep their knowledge and practices in the field of safety up to date.

Another area where common practice is taken into account is in accidents which take place during sports. In **Caldwell *v* Maguire and Fitzgerald** (2001), the claimant, Caldwell, was a professional jockey, as were the two defendants. All three were in a race with a fourth jockey, Byrne. At the point where the incident which gave rise to the case happened, Maguire, Fitzgerald and Byrne were neck and neck, with Caldwell close behind. As they approached a bend, Maguire and Fitzgerald pulled ahead in such a way as to leave no room for Byrne. Seeing its path ahead closed off, Byrne's horse veered across Caldwell's path, causing him to fall. The defendants were found to have committed the offence of careless riding under the rules of the Jockey Club, which regulates racing practice; this was the least serious of five possible offences concerning interfering with other riders.

Caldwell sued Maguire and Fitzgerald for causing his injuries, but the Court of Appeal found their conduct did not amount to negligence. They confirmed that a player of sports owes a duty to all the other players, and approved the test of negligence in sports used in the earlier case of **Condon *v* Basi** (1985), which stated that the duty on a player of sports is to exercise such care as is appropriate in the circumstances. The court went on to explain that this would depend on the game or sport being played, the degree of risk associated with it, its conventions and customs, and the standard of skill and judgement reasonably to be expected of players. As a result, the standard of care would be such that a momentary lapse of judgement or skill would be unlikely to result in liability and, in practice, it might be difficult to prove a breach unless the player's conduct amounted to a reckless disregard for others' safety. Therefore, in this case, the defendants were not negligent, as within the circumstances of the horseracing world, careless riding was accepted as part of the sport, even if not approved of.

Players of sport also have a duty to spectators, but the court stated that as, in the normal course of events, spectators would be at little or no risk from players, a player would have to have behaved with a considerable degree of negligence before he or she could be said to have failed to exercise such care as was reasonable in the circumstances.

Potential benefits of the risk

Some risks have potential benefits for society, and it has long been the practice of the courts to weigh such benefits against the possible damage if the risk is taken. This principle was applied in **Watt** *v* **Hertfordshire County Council** (1954). The claimant was a firefighter. He was among others called to the scene of an accident where a woman was trapped under a car; a heavy jack was needed to rescue her. The vehicle in which the fire officers travelled to the scene was not designed to carry the jack, and the claimant was injured when it slipped. He sued his employers, but the court held that the risk taken in transporting the jack was outweighed by the need to get there quickly in order to save the woman's life. However, the court stated that if the same accident had occurred in a commercial situation, where the risk was taken in order to get a job done for profit, the claimant would have been able to recover.

The Compensation Act 2006 now confirms this position. Section 1 of the Act states that when considering whether a defendant should have taken particular steps to meet a standard of care, a court:

'may . . . have regard to whether a requirement to take such steps might –
(a) prevent a desirable activity from being undertaken at all, to a particular extent, or in a particular way, or
(b) discourage persons from undertaking functions in connection with a desirable activity.'

As the case of **Watt** shows, s. 1 of the Act does not actually change the law, since the courts already considered the issue of public benefit where they felt it was necessary to do so, and s. 1 does not oblige them to take it into account, but merely confirms that they may.

The Act was passed in July 2006, so it is too early to see its impact, but critics have warned that it could lead to increased litigation. It has been suggested that it may end up being used to create two different standards of care, according to whether or not an activity is deemed 'desirable' or not. In his article 'What compensation?' (2006), John Leighton Williams QC cites the example of a firefighter trying to claim compensation for being injured at work. Would the fact that fighting fires is likely to be considered a desirable activity mean that he or she would have to prove a higher degree of negligence than workers in other fields would have to? Firefighting might well be something society wants to encourage, but is preventing those injured as a result of such work from claiming compensation really the best way to do so?

Leighton Williams also makes the point that differentiating between desirable activities and others may lead individuals to believe they can take unacceptable risks, on the assumption that, if anything goes wrong, they will not be held to account because they are leading Scouts on a climbing holiday, or taking a group of pupils skiing, and those activities would be considered desirable.

Quick quiz 20.3

1 When is a duty of care breached?

2 List three factors that the courts will take into account when deciding what behaviour would be expected of the reasonable person in the circumstances of a case.

3 In determining whether a defendant has breached a duty of care, will the courts take into account the age of the defendant?

4 What standard of care is expected of a doctor when treating a patient?

Damage

The negligence must cause damage; if no damage is caused, there is no claim in negligence, no matter how careless the defendant's conduct. In the vast majority of cases this is not an issue: there will be obvious personal injury, damage to property or economic loss. However, there are cases where the claimant perceives that the defendant's negligence has caused damage, yet the law does not recognise the results of that negligence as damage. The cases discussed in this section give an insight into how the law decides what is damage and what is not.

The issue of damage to property was the subject of **Hunter v Canary Wharf Ltd and London Docklands Development Corporation** (1997). The case arose from the construction of the big tower block known as Canary Wharf in East London. An action concerning the effects of the construction work was brought by local residents, and one of the issues that arose from the case was whether excessive dust could be sufficient to constitute damage to property for the purposes of negligence. The Court of Appeal concluded that the mere deposit of dust was not in itself sufficient because dust was an inevitable incident of urban life. In order to bring an action for negligence, there had to be damage in the sense of a physical change in property, which rendered the property less useful or less valuable. Examples given by the court included excessive dust being trodden into the fabric of a carpet by householders in such a way as to lessen the value of the fabric, or excessive dust causing damage to electrical equipment.

A very different issue was examined in **R v Croydon Health Authority** (1997) and **McFarlane v Tayside Health Board** (1999); could the birth of a child be considered damage? In **R v Croydon Health Authority**, an employee of the defendant had routinely examined the claimant, a woman of childbearing age, and found that she was suffering from a life-threatening heart condition, which could be made worse by pregnancy. The claimant was not told this, and went on to become pregnant and have a child. Although she did want a child, the claimant claimed she would not have become pregnant if she had known of the danger to herself in doing so. In addition to claiming for the fact that her heart condition was made worse by the pregnancy, she claimed for the expenses of pregnancy and the cost of bringing up the child, and was successful at first instance. The defendant appealed against the award of damages for the costs of pregnancy and bringing up the child. The Court of Appeal supported its view: where a mother wanted a healthy child and a healthy child was what she got, there was no loss. The court emphasised that a key factor in this case was that the claimant had wanted a child; the decision might be different, it was suggested, when a child was not wanted.

However, when this issue was addressed in **McFarlane v Tayside Health Board**, the House of Lords found it impossible to view as damage the birth of a healthy child, even to parents who had expressly decided that they did not want more children (the case is a Scottish one, but has been treated as representing English law too). The claimants were a couple who had four children, and decided that they did not want any more, so Mr McFarlane had a vasectomy. After he was wrongly advised that the operation had been successful, Mrs McFarlane became pregnant again, and gave birth to a healthy daughter. The couple sought to sue the health authority, with Mrs McFarlane claiming damages for the pain and discomfort of pregnancy and birth, and both claimants claiming for the costs of bringing up the child.

The House of Lords allowed the claim for pain and discomfort, pointing out that tort law regularly compensated for pain arising from personal injury, and there was no reason to treat pregnancy as involving a less serious form of pain. But they refused to allow the claim for the costs of bringing up the child, though there was some difference of opinion as to why. Lords Slynn and Hope simply argued that this was pure economic loss and it was not fair, just and reasonable to impose a duty on the health board to prevent such loss. Lords Steyn and Millett based their decision more on policy grounds, stating that the birth of a normal, healthy baby was universally regarded as a blessing, not a detriment, and therefore could not be viewed as damage. Lord Millett pointed out that although there were disadvantages involved in parenthood (cost being one), they were inextricably linked with the advantages, and so parents could not justifiably seek to transfer the disadvantages to others while themselves having the benefit of the advantages.

Both cases focused on the fact that the baby was healthy, and in **McFarlane** the House of Lords specifically declined to consider what the position is when a baby is born handicapped, who would not have been born at all if it were not for a defendant's negligence. The implication seemed to be that they might be prepared to allow that the birth of a child with disabilities could be considered damage in a way that having a healthy child did not, which said little for their approach to disabled people. (Note that what we are talking about here are cases where a disabled baby would not have been born at all, but for the defendant's negligence; this is not the same as cases where a baby would have been born healthy, but the defendant's negligence has caused its disability. There is no question that the latter type of case is accepted as damage, in the form of personal injury to the child.)

Not long afterwards, the question of whether the situation would be different if an unwanted child born as a result of negligence did turn out to be disabled arose before the Court of Appeal in **Parkinson** v **St James and Seacroft University Hospital** (2001). The claimant, Mrs Parkinson, and her husband had four children, and had decided they neither wanted nor could afford any more, so Mrs Parkinson was sterilised. Because of the hospital's admitted negligence, the operation did not work, and Mrs Parkinson became pregnant again. The child was born with severe disabilities, and Mrs Parkinson claimed for the costs of bringing him up. At first instance the court refused to allow her to claim the basic costs of his maintenance (the amount it would have cost to bring him up if he had not been disabled), following **McFarlane**. However, the judge said she could claim the extra costs which arose from her son's disability. The hospital appealed.

The Court of Appeal allowed Mrs Parkinson's claim for these extra costs (though not the basic costs) and, in her judgment, Hale LJ addressed the issue of whether the birth of a disabled child could be considered damage, if that of a healthy one could not. In doing so, she looked again at the reasoning in **McFarlane**. She argued that one of the most important rights protected by the law of tort was that of bodily integrity – the right to choose what happens to one's own body, and not to be subjected to bodily injury by others. The processes of pregnancy and childbirth, if unwanted, were a serious violation of this right, denying a woman the chance to decide what happened to her own body, and causing discomfort and pain. In addition, she pointed out that childbearing impacts on a woman's personal autonomy, saying that: 'One's life is no longer just one's own, but also someone else's.' Mothers-to-be are expected to alter what they eat, drink and do to safeguard the baby, while after the birth there is a legal responsibility to look after the child, which includes a financial burden. As a result, she said, it was clear that where an unwanted pregnancy happened as a result of negligence, its consequences were capable of giving rise to damages. However, she went on, it was also necessary to take into account the fact that children bring benefits to their parents, and since it was impossible to calculate these, the fairest assumption was that they were sufficient to cancel out the costs. This was what the House of Lords had assumed in **McFarlane**.

Applying this reasoning to the birth of a disabled child, she said that allowing a claim for the extra costs associated with disability made sense. It was acknowledging that a disabled child brought as much benefit to his or her family as any other child, but that, as he or she would cost more to bring up, the costs were not cancelled out. Therefore, the extra expense should be recoverable.

The same issue took a slightly different shape in **Rees** v **Darlington Memorial Hospital NHS Trust** (2002). Here the claimant was a disabled woman, who was almost blind as a result of a hereditary condition. Because of her disability, she did not want to have children, and so chose to be sterilised. The operation was performed negligently, and the claimant had a son, who was not disabled. She was a single parent, and claimed, not for the basic costs of bringing up her son, but for the extra costs of doing so that were caused by her disability.

The Court of Appeal had said that Ms Rees was entitled to compensation for these extra costs, but the House of Lords rejected the claim. As in **McFarlane**, they allowed the claimant compensation for the pain and stress of pregnancy and birth, but they refused to give compensation for any of the costs of bringing up a child. By a majority, they confirmed the reasoning in **McFarlane**, that a child should not be seen in terms of an economic liability, and that the benefits of having a child could not be quantified. They said that the idea of giving someone compensation for the birth of a healthy child would offend most people, especially as that money would come from the hard-pressed resources of the NHS.

However, they said that it was clear that where a defendant's negligence had brought about a pregnancy and birth which the mother did not want and had asked them to prevent, a legal wrong had been done that went beyond the pain and suffering of birth and pregnancy. As examples of the harm this could cause, Lord Bingham cited the situation of a single mother who might already be struggling to make ends meet and would now not only have another child to feed, but would face a longer period before she could work longer hours and earn more money; or the situation of a woman who had been longing to start or resume a much-wanted career, and was now prevented from doing so. The House of Lords held that there should be a financial recognition of this loss, and awarded Ms Rees £15,000 in addition to the compensation for pain and suffering.

The House also took the opportunity to consider whether **Parkinson** had been correctly decided, and said that it was; where a child born as the result of a defendant's negligence was disabled, the parents could claim for the extra costs associated with his or her disability.

Causation

In order to establish negligence, it must be proved that the defendant's breach of duty actually caused the damage suffered by the claimant, and that the damage caused was not too 'remote' from the breach (a legal test which is covered on p. 407 below). The rules on causation covered in this section also apply to every other tort where proof of damage is required. In practice, the rules are also applied in torts which are actionable *per se* (which means actionable merely because they have been committed, whether or not damage is caused) because where no damage is caused, compensation is usually a token amount, known as nominal damages, so most cases are likely to involve damage of some kind and to require proof of it. We discuss the issue here in the chapter on negligence so that you can get a complete overview of the first tort you study (and also because most of the cases on causation are in negligence), but remember when you look at the other torts that these rules apply there too.

The 'but for' test

Causation is established by proving that the defendant's breach of duty was, as a matter of fact, a cause of the damage. To decide this issue the first question to be asked is whether the damage would have occurred but for the breach of duty; this is known as the 'but for' test.

The operation of the test can be seen in **Barnett v Chelsea and Kensington Hospital Management Committee** (1968). A night-watchman arrived early in the morning at the defendants' hospital, suffering from nausea after having a cup of tea at work. The nurse on duty telephoned the casualty doctor, who refused to examine the man, and simply advised that he should go home, and consult his GP if he still felt unwell in the morning. The man died five hours later, of arsenic poisoning: he had been murdered. The hospital was sued for negligence, but the action failed. The court accepted that the defendants owed the deceased a duty of care, and that they had breached that duty by failing to examine him. However, the breach did not cause his death. There was evidence that, even if he had been examined, it was too late for any treatment to save him, and therefore it could not be said that but for the hospital's negligence he would not have died.

A similar result was reached in **Brooks** *v* **Home Office** (1999). The claimant was a woman in prison, who was pregnant with twins. Her pregnancy had been classified as high risk, so she needed regular ultrasound scans. One of these scans showed that one of the twins was not developing properly, but the prison doctor, who had little experience in this area of medicine, waited five days before seeking specialist advice. It was then discovered that the affected twin had died two days after the scan. Ms Brooks sued the Home Office (which is responsible for the prison service), arguing that she was entitled to receive the same standard of health care as a woman outside prison, and that the prison doctor's five-day delay in seeking expert advice fell below this standard. The court agreed with these two points, but it was found that a wait of two days before getting expert advice would have been reasonable for a woman outside prison, and as the baby had actually died within this time, the doctor's negligence could not be said to have caused its death.

Of course, it is not always clear what would have happened but for the defendant's negligence. This was the situation in **Chester** *v* **Afshar** (2004), the case described on p. 388, concerning the surgeon who failed to warn a patient of the possible risks of an operation. The defendants argued that causation could only be proved if the claimant could show that, had she been warned of the risk, she would have decided against having the operation at all. In that case, it could be said that, but for the surgeon's failure to warn, her injuries could not have happened. But the claimant did not say that she would not have had the operation: she said that she would have sought further advice on what to do. As it was not possible to say what that advice would have been or how she would have responded to it, the defendants argued that causation was not proved. The surgeon's failure to warn that the operation could go wrong did not in any way increase the risk associated with the operation; that risk was there anyway, and it was a risk the claimant would have taken had she chosen to have the operation later, which she may well have done.

The House of Lords disagreed. They pointed out that the scope of the surgeon's duty of care to his patient included a duty to warn of any risks. Therefore, there had to be a remedy where a doctor failed to fulfil that part of the duty, and a patient was injured as a result of the risk, otherwise that aspect of the duty was meaningless. The House of Lords accepted that it was very difficult to prove causation on conventional principles, and said that this was a case where legal policy required a judge to decide whether justice required the normal approach to causation to be modified. In this case it did. To find otherwise would mean that only those claimants who could categorically say that they would not have had the surgery would benefit from the existence of the duty of care, whereas those who needed time to think or more advice would not. This would leave the duty of care useless where it was needed most. On policy grounds, therefore, the test of causation was satisfied and the claimant won her case.

The decision in **Chester** caused shockwaves through the legal profession, with several experts claiming that it meant the House of Lords had effectively abolished any meaningful requirement for factual causation. However, the subsequent case of **Paul Davidson Taylor v White** (2004) makes it clear that **Chester** should be viewed as an exceptional case, in which the House of Lords was prepared to play with the rules on causation for policy reasons because there was no other way to get justice for the claimant.

The claimant in **White** was suing his solicitors, whom he said had been negligent in giving him incomplete advice about a tenancy dispute. He admitted that he could not prove that he would have acted differently if given different advice and, on traditional principles, this meant he could not satisfy the 'but for' test. However, he argued that the effect of **Chester** was that he could still have a claim, on the basis that the solicitor had denied him the chance to make up his mind after being given the full facts. The Court of Appeal rejected this argument. Arden LJ stated that **Chester** did not establish a new general rule on causation, pointing out that the House of Lords in that case had not said they were overruling any traditional rules on causation. There were policy reasons for the **Chester** decision, not least the fact that, within medicine, it is an established principle that patients asked to consent to surgery should have the risks explained to them. There were no such policy reasons in this case, and the general rule remained that a defendant can only be liable if their wrongful conduct actually caused harm.

An odd attempt to use the 'but for' test to a defendant's advantage was made in **Bolitho v City & Hackney Health Authority** (1997), the case discussed on p. 385, concerning the little boy brought to hospital with breathing difficulties. The doctor in the case had argued that, even if she had turned up to examine the little boy, she would not have intubated him, so her failure to attend could not be a cause of his death. Had this argument been allowed to succeed, it would have meant that a patient who could prove that a doctor was negligent in not attending could lose the action on the basis that, even if the doctor had attended, she would have behaved negligently. The House of Lords rightly refused to accept this, and stated that causation could be established if the claimant proved either that the doctor would have intubated if she had attended, or that she *should* have intubated if she had attended, because it would have been negligent not to do so.

Multiple causes

In some cases, damage may have more than one possible cause. As an example, take the facts of **McGhee v National Coal Board** (1972). The claimant's job brought him into contact with brick dust, which caused him to develop the skin condition dermatitis. It was known that contact with brick dust could cause dermatitis, but it was not suggested that merely exposing workers to the dust was negligent, as that was an unavoidable risk of the job they did. However, it was known that the risk of developing dermatitis could be reduced if workers could shower before leaving work, as this would lessen the amount of time the dust was in contact with their skin. The defendants had not installed any showers, and the claimant argued that they had been negligent in not doing so. To succeed in his claim, he had to prove that this negligence had caused his dermatitis – but because showers would only have lessened the risk, not removed it, the 'but for' test did not work. It was impossible to say that the damage would not have happened 'but for' the defendant's negligence, but equally impossible to say that it would definitely still have happened without the negligence.

As a result, in cases where there is more than one possible cause of damage, the courts have modified the 'but for' test, in an attempt to find a fair way to decide whether liability should be imposed. Unfortunately, they have come up with not one test, but several. In many cases, the result will differ according to which test is applied, yet it remains difficult to predict which approach a court will take in a particular case. This is bad for litigants, but not quite as bad as it sounds for law students tackling problem questions; as long as you can say what the possible tests are, and what result each one is likely to lead to, you are not expected to be able to predict which a court would actually opt for.

The simplest approach is that which was actually taken by the House of Lords in **McGhee**. They said that in cases where there was more than one possible cause, causation could be proved if the claimant could show that the defendant's negligence had materially increased the risk of the injury occurring; it was not necessary to show that it was the sole cause. In that case, the lack of showers was held to substantially increase the risk to Mr McGhee, and he won his case.

A similar test was used in **Page v Smith (No. 2)** (1996) involving an accident victim who claimed that the shock reactivated a previous physical illness, ME. The defendant claimed that the claimant had not proved that the accident had caused the recurrence of his illness. The Court of Appeal held that the question to be answered was, as in **McGhee**: 'did the accident, on the balance of probabilities, cause or materially contribute to or materially increase the risk of' the claimant developing the symptoms he complained of?

As we can see, the **McGhee** test has been used in cases over the past 30 years (and continues to be good law). During the same period, however, the courts have also used a completely different test, which in many cases would give the opposite result to the **McGhee** rule. This test was used in **Wilsher v Essex Health Authority** (1988), a tragic case concerning a claimant who was born three months early, with a number of health problems associated with premature birth. He was put on an oxygen supply and, as a result of a doctor's admitted negligence, was twice given too much oxygen. He eventually suffered permanent blindness, and the hospital was sued. However, medical evidence suggested that, although the overdoses of oxygen could have caused the claimant's blindness, it could also have been caused by any one of five separate medical conditions which he suffered from. The House of Lords held that the claimant had to prove, on a balance of probabilities, that the defendant's breach of duty was a material cause of the injury; it was not enough to prove that the defendant had increased the risk that the damage might occur, or had added another possible cause of it. On the facts of the case, the defendant's negligence was only one of the possible causes of the damage, and this was not sufficient to prove causation.

'Loss of a chance' cases

A third approach is taken to causation in cases which involve what is called 'loss of a chance'. Often these are medical negligence cases, and a typical example might involve a claimant being diagnosed with cancer, who has a certain percentage chance of being cured, but has that chance reduced by their doctor's delay in diagnosing or treating the illness. In such cases the court then has to decide whether the delay can be said to have caused the patient not to have been cured, or whether that would have been the situation even if the doctor had not acted negligently. Loss of a chance can also involve financial losses, where a claimant misses out on the chance of a lucrative deal, or a well-paid job, because of the defendant's negligence.

The key case on loss of chance with respect to injury or illness is **Hotson *v* East Berkshire Health Authority** (1987). Here the claimant, a young boy, had gone to hospital after falling from a rope and injuring his knee. An X-ray showed no apparent injury, so he was sent home. Five days later, the boy was still in pain, and when he was taken back to the hospital, a hip injury was diagnosed and treated. He went on to develop a condition known as avascular necrosis, which is caused when the blood supply to the site of an injury is restricted, and eventually results in pain and deformity. This condition could have arisen as a result of the injury anyway, but medical evidence showed that there was a 25 per cent chance that if he had been diagnosed and treated properly on his first visit to the hospital, the injury would have healed and the avascular necrosis would not have developed. The Court of Appeal treated this evidence as relevant to the issue of damages, holding that it meant his action could succeed but he should receive only 25 per cent of the damages he would have got if the condition was wholly due to the defendant's negligence.

The House of Lords, however, ruled that this was the wrong approach; what was really in issue was whether the claimant had proved that the defendant's negligence caused his condition. The House held that he had not: the law required that he should prove causation on a balance of probabilities, which means proving that it was more likely that they had caused his condition than that they had not. What the medical evidence showed was that there was a 75 per cent chance of him developing the condition even if the negligence had not occurred; proving causation on a balance of probabilities required at least a 51 per cent chance that the negligence caused the damage.

This approach was challenged in **Gregg *v* Scott** (2005). The claimant had visited his GP, complaining of a lump under his left arm, but the doctor said it was nothing to worry about. Nine months later, the lump was still there, so the claimant consulted another GP, who referred him to a surgeon. The lump was diagnosed as cancer, and it was shown to have grown during the time between visiting the first and second GP. The claimant was treated, and the cancer went into remission, but it was not known whether he was actually cured.

The claimant sued the doctor on the basis that the delay had made it less likely that he would be cured, but it was not possible to prove this was the case. Statistics showed that out of every 100 people who developed the same kind of tumour, 17 would be cured if they had prompt treatment, but not if their treatment was delayed by a year; 25 would be cured even if their treatment was delayed by a year; and 58 would be incurable regardless of how much treatment they had and when. The claimant therefore argued that he had originally had a 42 per cent chance of being cured (adding together the figures for those who would be cured even if treatment was delayed, and those who would only be cured if they received prompt treatment). By delaying his treatment, the doctor had reduced his chances to 25 per cent.

The House of Lords rejected this argument, and said that the claimant could succeed only if he could prove that the defendant's negligence made it more likely than not that he would not be cured. Since the statistics showed that it was more likely than not that his cancer would not have been curable (a 58 per cent chance against a 42 per cent one), this had not been proved. The claimant also argued that even if it could not be proved that the doctor's negligence caused the spread of his cancer, he should be able to claim for 'loss of a chance', meaning a reduction in his chances of survival. The House of Lords said this could not form the basis of a claim in medical negligence.

Damages for loss of a chance have been allowed in cases where the loss is purely financial. In **Stovold v Barlows** (1995), the claimant claimed that the defendant's negligence had caused him to lose the sale of his house. The Court of Appeal decided that there was a 50 per cent chance that the sale would have gone ahead had the defendant not been negligent, and on this basis they upheld the claimant's claim, but awarded him 50 per cent of the damages that he would normally have won (thus following the approach it had taken in **Hotson**, and not that taken by the House of Lords in that case).

In **Allied Maples Group v Simmons & Simmons** (1995), the claimants hoped to make a particular business deal, but were prevented from doing so by the defendant's negligence; it was possible that the deal might not have gone ahead for other reasons even if the negligence had not happened. The Court of Appeal held that where the damage alleged depends on the possible action of a third party (in this case the other party to the deal), the claimant must prove that the chance was a substantial one, as opposed to pure speculation on what might have happened. If so, the action can succeed on causation, and the evaluation of the chance will be taken into account when calculating damages.

This approach was clarified in **Dixon v Clement Jones** (2004). The claimant had started a business which very soon ran into trouble, and eventually resulted in her house being repossessed. She had consulted a firm of accountants, Dyer, when buying the business, and claimed that they had assured her that there was no way that the financial arrangements she was making could result in her losing her house; this advice turned out to be wrong. Clement Jones, a firm of solicitors, advised her to sue Dyer, but due to negligence on their part the claim was not made in time. She then sued Clement Jones. The Court of Appeal found that this was a case of loss of a chance, in that Mrs Dixon had lost the opportunity to sue Dyer. They explained that in such cases, there were three possibilities: it might be 'overwhelmingly clear' that the claimant would have lost the case, or won the case, or the prospects might be somewhere in between. If it was overwhelmingly clear that the claimant would have won, they could be awarded the amount they would have received if that case had gone to court; if it was overwhelmingly clear that they would have lost, they should be awarded no damages. In intermediate cases, the court did not need to decide whether, on the balance of probabilities, the claimant would have won or lost. Instead, they should assess the chance of success, and put a percentage on that figure in order to calculate the damages.

Multiple tortfeasors

In the cases discussed above, the question has been whether damage was caused by the defendant, or by one or more non-negligent acts or situations, such as accident or illness. What happens when the damage was definitely caused by negligence, but there is more than one party which could have been responsible? This often arises in cases concerning work-related illnesses which take many years to develop, so that it is not always clear at which point during the claimant's working life the damage was done. In **Holtby v Brigham & Cowan** (2000), the claimant suffered asbestosis as a result of breathing asbestos dust at work over a long period. He had been employed by the defendants for approximately half that time, and by other firms doing similar work for the rest; for reasons which are not important here, he was only suing the defendants. The Court of Appeal stated that the defendants were liable if it was proved that their negligence had made a material contribution to the claimant's disability; their negligence did not have to be the sole cause of it. However, if the injury had also been partially caused by the negligence of others, the defendants would only be liable for the proportion they had caused. In deciding how big this proportion was, the judge followed the practice of insurance companies and related it to the amount of time the claimant had been exposed to the defendants' negligence and, erring on the side of the claimant, set the proportion of liability at 75 per cent.

This approach can, however, work harshly against claimants, and this was revealed – and eventually to some extent corrected – in **Fairchild v Glenhaven Funeral Services** (2002). This case also concerned employees who had worked with asbestos, but here the disease caused was mesothelioma, an invariably fatal cancer that is almost always caused by asbestos. It is not entirely clear how mesothelioma is caused, but it is believed to be triggered by a single fibre of asbestos penetrating a cell in the lining of the lung, which then becomes malignant and eventually grows into a tumour. This makes it different from asbestosis, which generally gets worse the more asbestos the person is exposed to; with mesothelioma, the single event of the fibre entering the lung causes the disease. It may take up to 30 years to do so, but essentially the person's fate is sealed when the fibre enters the lung, and the amount of previous or subsequent exposure is irrelevant. This was what caused problems for the claimants in **Fairchild**.

The claimants (some of the men had already died, so their cases were brought by their widows) had been exposed to asbestos over long periods during their working lives, as a result of negligence by a series of different employers. By the time they sued, many of the companies were no longer worth claiming against, so the claimants sued only those who were. Previously, in mesothelioma cases, the courts had taken the approach that all significant exposure to asbestos up to around ten years before the symptoms developed could be said to have contributed to the causation of the disease. But in **Fairchild**, the High Court held that it was necessary for the claimant to prove which fibre had caused the disease, and only the employer at that time would be liable. Since it was impossible to know, let alone prove, which fibre had caused the disease, this ruling had the potential to mean that mesothelioma sufferers would never be able to sue those who had caused their disease unless they had been exposed to asbestos by only one employer.

As there are over 1,300 cases of the disease each year, and the figure is expected to more than double over the next 20 years, the decision caused considerable anxiety. But to many people's surprise, the Court of Appeal upheld the High Court's approach, and confirmed that where a claimant with mesothelioma has been exposed to asbestos by different employers at different times, and it cannot be proved, on a balance of probabilities, which period of exposure caused the illness, he or she cannot recover damages from any of the employers.

On a strict definition of causation, this at first sight looks plausible, if callous, but a closer look shows a number of problems. First, although the disease is caused by one inhalation of fibres and not cumulative exposure, you do not have to be a mathematical genius to work out that the more times you are exposed to asbestos, the higher the chance that, on one of those occasions, you will breathe some in. On this basis, it would not seem difficult to argue that each of the employers had increased the claimants' risk of getting the disease, just as the employer in **McGhee** did.

Secondly, the focus on the one 'guilty fibre' somehow suggests that only the employer who the claimant was working for at the time the fibre was inhaled did anything wrong – whereas in fact all of them had negligently exposed their employees to a substance which had the potential to kill them, prematurely and painfully. Ignoring this fact does not sit well with tort's claim to act as a deterrent to careless and dangerous behaviour.

Thirdly, the parties who would actually be paying any damages would be insurance companies, who had been taking premiums for decades during which the risks of asbestos were well known, and now wanted to escape liability. In fact, while the case was awaiting its House of Lords hearing, the insurance companies concerned offered the claimants a full settlement, which, if accepted, would have meant the cases would not be heard. As a result, although the **Fairchild** claimants would have been compensated, thousands of other victims would have remained at the mercy of the Court of Appeal judgment. The president of the Association of Personal Injury Lawyers, Frances McCarthy, called the offer 'a cynical and underhanded attempt to prevent the cases being heard'.

In the event, the House of Lords did hear the case, and came to a different view. They said that where an employee had been negligently exposed by different defendants, during different periods of employment, to inhalation of asbestos, a modified approach to proof of causation was justified. In such a case, proof that each defendant's wrongdoing had materially increased the risk of contracting the disease was sufficient to satisfy the causal requirements for liability. Applying that approach, the claimants could prove causation on a balance of probabilities, and the defendants were liable.

However, the benefits for claimants of the **Fairchild** decision were then restricted by the House of Lords decision in **Barker** *v* **Corus** (2006). In this case, a group of defendant employers sought to argue that, where an employee was negligently exposed to asbestos by more than one different employer, each employer's liability should be calculated according to the length of time the employer spent with them and, where relevant, to the type of asbestos involved (some kinds being more hazardous than others). In addition, one of the employees in the case had been self-employed for part of his career, and the companies which had employed him for the rest of the time argued that exposure to asbestos during his period of self-employment was his own responsibility, so they should not be liable for it.

The House of Lords rejected the argument about self-employment, basing their finding on the principle explained in **McGhee** (see p. 399). They pointed out that, in **McGhee**, there had been both negligent and non-negligent exposure to brick dust. The firm was not negligent in exposing the claimant to the dust during his working hours, because it was an unavoidable part of the job, but they were negligent in allowing the exposure to last longer than necessary, by not providing showers. As **Fairchild** had built on **McGhee**, the same principle should apply here, so that the fact that the defendant had had some non-negligent exposure to asbestos did not mean that the **Fairchild** principle could not apply.

More controversially, the House accepted the argument that damages should be apportioned according to the extent to which each company had contributed to the claimants' exposure to asbestos. The practical effect of this on claimants was potentially devastating, as it meant that unless they were able to sue every employer who had exposed them to asbestos, they could not hope to claim the full amount of damages appropriate to their illness. For example, where a claimant had worked for a roughly equal amount of time for three different employers and two had gone out of business by the time the claimant developed mesothelioma, the claimant would only be able to get a third of the damages that would normally be awarded for such a serious illness. The need, where possible, to trace all employers would add to the cost of cases, and the time they took, which was a particularly important issue given that, by the time mesothelioma was diagnosed, claimants usually did not have many years left to live.

The decision was, not surprisingly, welcomed by the insurance industry, which stood to save millions of pounds as a result, but was widely criticised by personal injury lawyers as being unfair to claimants. The government agreed, and inserted an amendment into the Compensation Bill, which was going through Parliament at the time, effectively reversing the **Corus** decision. Section 3 of the resulting Compensation Act 2006 now provides that where a person is responsible for negligently exposing another to asbestos, and that person goes on to contract mesothelioma as a result of exposure to asbestos, the person responsible for the negligent exposure can be fully liable, even if it cannot be proved that it was that episode of exposure and not another that caused the disease. Where there are several people who have negligently exposed the victim, the one who is sued can claim a contribution from the other(s), but there is no need for the victim to sue more than one of them.

Intervening events

In some cases, an intervening event may occur after the breach of duty, and contribute to the claimant's damage. Where such an event is said to break the chain of causation, the defendant will be liable only for such damage as occurred up to the intervening event. In such cases the intervening event is sometimes called a *novus actus interveniens*.

In **Thompson** *v* **James** (1997), the defendant was a doctor, who was sued by the parents of a child on the basis that he had been negligent in advising them not to have the child immunised against measles. The child had caught measles and as a result developed a rare condition which caused brain damage. The defendant had given the advice because the child's medical history made her more likely than most to suffer damage as a result of the immunisation. She was six months old at the time, and the decision not to immunise her was not taken until a year later, after the parents had talked to other doctors. The Court of Appeal held that the advice given by the other doctors was an intervening event which broke the chain of causation because it showed that the parents were not relying on the defendant's advice.

Where there is an intervening event but the original tort is still a cause of the damage, the defendant remains liable. In **Baker** *v* **Willoughby** (1969) the claimant injured his left leg in a road accident as a result of the defendant's negligence. After the accident he was shot in the left leg by an armed robber, and ended up having his leg amputated. The robber was not caught and so could not be sued for the incident.

The defendant argued that his liability only extended to the point at which the armed robbery occurred, when the effects of his negligence were overtaken by the robber's shooting. However, in this context the 'but for' test is not strictly applied: it would be inaccurate to suggest that the damage would not have occurred but for the breach of duty, for the claimant's leg would have been damaged later anyway, as a result of the robbery. However, the House of Lords took the approach that tort law compensates as much for the inability to lead a full life as for the specific injury itself. This inability continues even where the original injury had been superseded by a later one.

However, **Baker** *v* **Willoughby** was not followed in the decision of **Jobling** *v* **Associated Dairies** (1982). As a result of the defendant's breach of duty, the claimant hurt his back at work in 1973, which rendered him disabled and reduced his earning capacity by 50 per cent. In 1976, the claimant was diagnosed as suffering from a back condition, known as myelopathy, which had no connection with the accident. By the end of that year he was unable to work. The defendants argued that they should be liable for the effects of the back injury only up to the point at which the myelopathy occurred, to which the claimant responded that the case of **Baker** *v* **Willoughby** should apply. The House of Lords found unanimously in favour of the defendants' argument, applying the 'but for' test strictly. The risk of unrelated medical conditions occurring was habitually taken into account when calculating damages for future loss of earnings. It could therefore not be ignored when it had already developed. Interestingly, both **Baker** and **Jobling** were followed in **Murrell** *v* **Healy** (2001), though with reference to different aspects of the case. Murrell was injured in a car accident in May 1995. It was obviously not his year, as he was involved in another car accident in November, causing new injuries. He settled out of court with the driver in the first accident, and was paid compensation of £58,500. One of the questions at issue was how far the damages payable by the second driver should be reduced because of the payment Murrell had received from the first. The Court of Appeal held that the second driver was liable to compensate Murrell for the additional damage that the accident caused to an already injured victim. So if, for example, Murrell had originally been capable of heavy work, and after the first accident was only capable of light work, the second driver had no liability for that loss. But if the second accident had meant that he was then not even capable of light work, the second driver was liable to compensate him for that. This was held to be the other side of the rule in **Baker**; if the first tortfeasor's liability is not reduced by the second tort, then the second tortfeasor cannot be liable for losses caused by the first tortfeasor.

A second problem in the case was that Murrell's inability to work was also caused by a knee and hip problem, which had not been proved to be caused by either of the accidents. Here the court followed **Jobling**, holding that where a claimant has been injured by a tort but is also suffering from an unrelated condition that makes them unable to work, that condition reduces the damages payable by the tortfeasor. The correct approach was to try to assess what the claimant's life would have been like if the tort had not happened, so problems which would have existed then could not be ignored.

In **Corr v IBC Vehicles** (2006), the Court of Appeal was asked to assess whether a person's decision to commit suicide was an intervening event. The claimant's husband had worked for the defendants, and suffered a workplace accident that was due to their negligence. He was very nearly decapitated and, as a result of the accident, developed post-traumatic stress disorder, which caused serious depression. Eventually, six years after the accident, he committed suicide. It was clear that his employers were liable for the depression, but were they also liable for his death, or was his suicide an intervening act which broke the chain of causation between their negligence and his death? The Court of Appeal found that the defendants were liable. Suicide was not an uncommon consequence of severe depression, and depression was a reasonably foreseeable result of the accident, so there was no break in the chain of causation. It was not necessary to prove that suicide itself was reasonably foreseeable.

Remoteness of damage

As well as proving that the defendant's breach of duty factually caused the damage suffered by the claimant, the claimant must prove that the damage was not too remote from the defendant's breach. Like the issue of duty of care, the remoteness test is a legal test (rather than a factual one) which forms one of the ways in which the law draws the line between damage which can be compensated in law, and that which cannot. This means that there are some circumstances where the defendant will undoubtedly have caused damage in fact, but in law it is considered that they should not have to compensate the claimant for it.

There are two tests for remoteness in tort:

- the direct consequence test;
- the reasonable foreseeability test.

The test in negligence is now reasonable foreseeablity, but the direct consequence test applies to some other torts, so for convenience it is explained here. The chapters on other torts detail which test applies to each one.

The direct consequence test

The traditional test of whether damage was too remote was laid down in **Re Polemis** (1921), and essentially imposed liability for all direct physical consequences of a defendant's negligence; it became known as the direct consequence test. The case concerned the renting of a ship, an arrangement known as a charter. The people renting the ship, called the charterers, had loaded it with tins of petrol, and during the voyage these leaked, releasing large amounts of petrol vapour into the hold. The ship docked at Casablanca, and was unloaded. The workers unloading it had positioned some heavy planks as a platform over the hold and, as a result of their negligence, one of the planks fell into the hold. It caused a spark, which ignited the petrol vapour, and ultimately the ship was completely burnt, causing the owners a loss of almost £200,000. They sued the charterers.

The trial judge had found as a fact that the charterers could not reasonably have foreseen that the fire was likely to occur as a result of the plank falling into the hold, though they might reasonably have foreseen that some damage to the ship might result from that incident. However, the Court of Appeal held that this was irrelevant; the charterers were liable for any consequence that was a direct result of their breach of duty, even if such consequences might be different and much more serious from those which they might reasonably have foreseen. A consequence would be too remote only if it was 'due to the operation of independent causes having no connection with the negligent act, except that they could not avoid its results'.

The reasonable foreseeability test

As time went on and the tort of negligence grew, the direct consequence test came to be seen as rather hard on defendants. As a result, a new test was laid down in **Overseas Tankship (UK) v Morts Dock & Engineering Co (The Wagon Mound)** (1961), which is usually referred to as **Wagon Mound No. 1** (a second case, **Wagon Mound No. 2**, arose from the same incident, but raised different issues and is discussed later). The incident which gave rise to the litigation was an accident which occurred in Sydney Harbour, Australia. In **Wagon Mound No. 1**, the defendants were the owners of a ship which was loading oil there, and owing to the negligence of their employees, some of it leaked into the water and spread, forming a thin film on the surface. Within hours, the oil had spread to a neighbouring wharf, owned by the claimants, where another ship was being repaired by welders. It caused some damage to the slipway, but then a few days later, further and much more serious damage was caused when the oil was ignited by sparks from the welding operations.

The trial judge found that the damage to the slipway was reasonably foreseeable, but given that the evidence showed that the oil needed to be raised to a very high temperature before it would catch fire, the fire damage was not reasonably foreseeable. Nevertheless, as the Australian courts were also following **Re Polemis**, he found the defendants liable for both types of damage.

The Privy Council, however, took a different view, stating that **Re Polemis** was no longer good law. The new test of remoteness was the foresight of the reasonable person: was the kind of damage suffered by the claimant reasonably foreseeable at the time of the breach of duty? Under this test, the defendants in **Wagon Mound No. 1** were liable only for the damage to the slipway, and not for the fire damage. The reasonable foreseeability test as set down in **Wagon Mound No. 1** is now the standard test for remoteness of damage in negligence.

Type of damage

Under the reasonable foreseeability test as laid down in **Wagon Mound No. 1**, a defendant will be liable only if it was reasonable to foresee the type of damage that in fact happened – in **Wagon Mound No. 1**, it was clear that this covered the damage to the slipway, but not the fire damage. However, this has led to some difficult distinctions in other cases, as the contrasting decisions in **Doughty v Turner Manufacturing Co** (1964) and **Hughes v Lord Advocate** (1963) show.

In **Doughty**, the claimant was an employee who was injured when an asbestos cover was knocked into a vat of hot liquid. A chemical reaction between the asbestos and the liquid caused the liquid to bubble up and erupt over the edge of the vat, burning the claimant. The chemical reaction was not foreseeable, but the claimant argued that it was foreseeable that the lid falling in would cause some liquid to splash out, and the result of this was likely to be burning, the same injury as resulted from the liquid erupting. The court disagreed, holding that an eruption was different in kind to a splash.

In **Hughes**, Post Office employees had opened a manhole in the street, and left it open when they finished work for the day, covering it with a canvas shelter and surrounding it with paraffin lamps. The claimant, an eight-year-old boy, picked up one of the lamps and took it into the shelter. While playing there, he knocked the lamp into the manhole, and paraffin vapour from the lamp ignited, causing an explosion in which the claimant fell into the hole and was badly burnt. The defendants claimed that although they could have foreseen a risk that someone might be burnt, they could not have foreseen injuries caused by an explosion, and so the damage was too remote. The House of Lords rejected this view: if it was reasonably foreseeable that the damage would be burning, it did not matter that the burns were produced in an unforeseeable way.

Recent cases seem to suggest that the less narrow **Hughes** approach is gaining favour. In **Page v Smith (No. 2)** (1996) (see p. 400), it was argued that where some form of personal injury was foreseeable, the fact that the damage suffered was psychiatric rather than physical did not make it too remote; they were both types of personal injury and that was foreseeable. Similarly, in **Margereson v J W Roberts Ltd** (1996), the Court of Appeal considered the case of claimants who had contracted the lung disease mesothelioma as a result of playing near the defendant's asbestos factory as children. The court held that it was not necessary for mesothelioma to be a reasonably foreseeable result of exposure to the asbestos dust, it was sufficient that some form of lung damage was reasonably foreseeable.

It is worth noting that although apparently conflicting cases like **Hughes** and **Doughty** can seem confusing, as a student you are not expected to know which path a court would take when faced with this issue; what you have to do is show that you are aware that the cases illustrate different approaches. So when you tackle a problem question, you can do this by stating that there are conflicting cases, and describing how the decision on the facts that are before you might go if the courts took, for example, the **Hughes** approach, and how this might differ if the view expressed in **Doughty** was preferred.

Extent of damage

So long as the type of damage sustained is reasonably foreseeable, it does not matter that it is in fact more serious than could reasonably have been foreseen. The extreme application of this principle is the gruesome-sounding 'eggshell-skull' rule, which essentially establishes that defendants will be liable even if the reason why the damage is more serious than could be expected is due to some weakness or infirmity in the claimant. In **Smith** *v* **Leech Brain & Co Ltd** (1962), the claimant was burnt on the lip as a result of the defendant's negligence. He had a pre-cancerous condition, which became cancerous as a result of the burn, and the defendant was held liable for the full result of the negligence.

Until recently, it was not clear whether a version of the 'eggshell-skull' rule applied in economic loss cases, where the claimant's lack of funds results in the financial loss being greater than it might otherwise have been. The traditional view was that a defendant was not liable to pay any extra losses caused by the claimant's lack of money, as explained in **Liesbosch Dredger** *v* **SS Edison** (1933). The defendants negligently sank the claimants' ship, and because the claimants had already made contracts which required the use of the ship, they had to hire another vessel to do the work. It would have been cheaper overall to buy another ship, but the claimants' funds at the time did not allow them to do this. They therefore claimed for the cost of a new ship, plus the expenses of hiring the one they had used to fulfil their contractual obligations. The House of Lords refused to compensate them for the cost of the hired ship, on the ground that this loss was caused by their own financial circumstances, and was not foreseeable by the defendants.

However, a number of cases had seemed to suggest that a more generous view was appropriate, and in **Lagden** *v* **O'Connor** (2003) the House of Lords confirmed that the 'thin skull' principle now applies to economic weakness as well as to physical. The claimant, Mr Lagden, was involved in a car accident which was the fault of the defendant, and needed a replacement car while his own was being repaired. In normal circumstances there would be no argument about the fact that the defendant would be liable to compensate the claimant for the cost of doing this, but the problem was that in this case Mr Lagden was unemployed and had very little money, and could not afford to pay to hire a car, or to take out a personal loan to buy a new one. His only option was to replace his car through what is called credit hire, where the payment is deferred for a long period. However, this option was more expensive than the other two, and the defendants, relying on **Liesbosch**, argued that they should not be liable for the extra costs, only what it would have cost to hire a car in the normal way.

The House of Lords disagreed. While not saying that **Liesbosch** was wrong, they pointed out that it had been decided at a time when the test for remoteness of damage was direct causation (the **Polemis** test). The law had moved on since then and, as the test was now reasonable foreseeability, that meant that defendants had to take claimants as they found them, including their financial situation. If a defendant was hard up, and as a result of that they incurred extra costs, the defendant was liable to pay those costs, so long as they were reasonable. Costs would be considered reasonable if the claimant could not have avoided incurring them without making unreasonable sacrifices.

Quick quiz 20.4

1 What is the 'but for' test?

2 Which case lays down the current test on remoteness?

3 What is the current test for remoteness?

4 If it was reasonably foreseeable that about £10,000 worth of damage would be caused by a fire started by the defendant, will the defendant be liable to pay £1 million in compensation when this amount of damage was actually caused by the fire?

Risk of damage

The case of **Overseas Tankship (UK)** v **Miller Steamship Co (The Wagon Mound No. 2)** (1967) establishes that, so long as a type of damage is foreseeable, it will not be too remote, even if the chances of it happening were slim. The case arose from the accident in Sydney Harbour discussed on p. 408 when we looked at **Wagon Mound No. 1**; the defendants were the same, but in this case the claimants were the owners of some ships which were also damaged in the fire. When this case was heard, different evidence was brought which led the trial judge to conclude that it was foreseeable that the oil on the water would ignite, and when the case was appealed to the Privy Council, it held that on the evidence before that judge he was entitled to reach this conclusion. The risk was small but it clearly existed, and therefore the damage was not too remote.

Intervening events

An intervening event will only make damage too remote if the event itself was unforeseeable. The old case of **Scott** v **Shepherd** (1773) is still one of the best illustrations of this. The defendant threw a lighted firework into a market hall while a fair was being held there. It landed on a stall, and the stall owner picked it up and tossed it away from his stall; it landed on another, whose owner did the same, and after the firework had done a lively tour of the market, it eventually exploded in the claimant's face, blinding him in one eye. The court held that the defendant was liable; the actions of the stallholders were a foreseeable result of throwing the firework and therefore could not be considered intervening events.

In **Humber Oil Terminal Trustee Ltd** *v* **Owners of the ship Sivand** (1998), the defendants' ship had damaged the claimants' wharf as a result of negligent navigation. The claimants engaged contractors to repair the wharf, and their agreement with the contractors included a clause that obliged the claimants to pay any extra repair costs which might be necessary if the repairers encountered physical conditions which could not have been foreseen. This in fact happened, as the seabed proved unable to take the weight of the jack-up barge the repairers used, and so the barge sank. The claimants were claiming against the defendants for damage caused to the wharf by their negligence, and they sought to add this increased cost to their claim. The defendants argued that the loss of the barge was not foreseeable, and was an intervening act which broke the chain of causation. The Court of Appeal disagreed: although the precise circumstances were not reasonably foreseeable, it was the kind of circumstance envisaged by the contract, and the loss of the barge was not caused by an intervening event, but an existing state of affairs, namely the condition of the seabed, so it did not break the chain of causation.

Proving negligence

The claimant normally has the burden of proof in relation to proving negligence, which can be a considerable obstacle for a claimant. However, there are two exceptions to this rule: where the defendant has a criminal conviction related to the incident in question, and where the principle of *res ipsa loquitur* (Latin for 'the facts speak for themselves') applies.

Criminal convictions

Under s. 11 of the Civil Evidence Act 1968, a defendant's criminal conviction is admissible evidence in a subsequent civil case based on the same facts. This means that if a defendant whose conduct is alleged to have been negligent has already been convicted of a crime for that conduct, that is evidence of negligence, and it is for the defendant to disprove it if he or she can. A common example is where a defendant in a motor accident case has already been convicted of dangerous driving as a result of the accident.

Res ipsa loquitur

There are circumstances in which the facts of the case are such that the injury complained of could not have happened unless there had been negligence, and in such cases, the maxim *res ipsa loquitur* may apply. One example is the case of **Scott** *v* **London and St Katherine's Docks** (1865), where the claimant was injured by some bags of sugar which fell from the open door of the defendant's warehouse above. There was no actual evidence of negligence, but the Court of Appeal held that negligence could be inferred from what had happened, since the bags of sugar could not have fallen out of the door all by themselves. Similarly, in **Mahon v Osborne** (1939) it was held that a swab left inside the claimant after a stomach operation could not have got there unless someone had been negligent. In such circumstances, the courts may treat the facts themselves as evidence of negligence (but only evidence, which may be rebutted), provided that two other conditions are satisfied: the events are under the control of the defendant or the defendant's employees, and there is no direct evidence of negligence.

Under the control of the defendant

This point is illustrated by two contrasting cases. In **Gee v Metropolitan Railway Co.** (1873) the claimant fell out of a train just after it left a station, when the door he was leaning against flew open. The railway staff clearly had a duty to ensure that the door was properly shut, and since the train had so recently left the station, it could be inferred from the fact of what happened that they had not shut it properly. However, in a similar case, **Easson v London and North Eastern Railway** (1944), the train was seven miles past the last station when the door flew open. It was held that the fact that the door had opened in this way did not necessarily mean that railway staff had been negligent, because the situation was not under their exclusive control; any passenger could have interfered with the door during the time since the train had left the station. The staff might have been negligent, but the facts alone were not enough to act as reasonable evidence to that effect.

No direct evidence of negligence

If there is direct evidence of what caused the damage, the courts will examine that, rather than inferring it from the facts alone. In **Barkway v South Wales Transport Co. Ltd** (1950) the claimant was injured when the bus he was travelling in burst a tyre and crashed. The tyre burst because of a defect that could not have been discovered beforehand, but there was evidence that the bus company should have told drivers to report any blows to their tyres, which could weaken them, and they had not done so. The court held that it should examine this evidence rather than rely on *res ipsa loquitur*.

Using *res ipsa loquitur*

The operation of *res ipsa loquitur* was explained by the Court of Appeal in **Ratcliffe v Plymouth and Torbay Health Authority** (1998). Here the claimant had gone into hospital for an ankle operation, and had ended up with a serious neurological condition which it was agreed had been triggered by the injection of a spinal anaesthetic. He argued that this was a case of *res ipsa loquitur*; the injection must have been given negligently, or it could not have caused the problem. The health authority produced expert evidence which stated that the condition might be due to the claimant already having a susceptibility to spinal cord damage, and the injection triggering such damage even though it was not given negligently. The Court of Appeal, referring back to **Scott**, stated that where there was no direct evidence of negligence, but a situation was under the management of the defendant and/or the defendant's employees, and the damaging event was such that in the ordinary course of things would not happen if proper care was taken, that in itself could be taken as evidence of negligence, and in the absence of any other explanation, a judge would be entitled to infer that negligence had taken place. However, the defendant could prevent the judge from inferring negligence by either showing that he or she took reasonable care, or supplying another explanation for the events. The court stressed that nothing in the application of *res ipsa loquitur* changed the rule that the burden of proof was on the claimant. The defendant's alternative explanation would have to be plausible, and not merely theoretically possible, but the defendant is not required to prove that it was more likely to be correct than any other. In this case the defendant had provided a plausible explanation and it was up to the claimant to prove that negligence, rather than the claimant's explanation, had caused his injury, which he could not do.

By contrast, a claimant's case succeeded on the basis of *res ipsa loquitur* in **Widdowson v Newgate Meat Corporation** (1997). Here the claimant, who suffered from a serious mental disorder, was knocked down by the defendant's van while he was walking along the side of a dual carriageway at night. Because of his disorder, the claimant was not considered a reliable witness and was not called at the trial; the defendant pleaded that there was no case to answer and offered no evidence. The trial judge declined to apply *res ipsa loquitur* on the ground of a lack of evidence regarding the events leading up to the trial. The Court of Appeal disagreed with this approach: case law had established that where it was impossible to pinpoint an exact act or omission that was negligent, but the circumstances were such that it was more likely than not that the damage was caused by the defendant's negligence, it was up to the defendant to rebut this inference. In this case, the road was deserted and the defendant would have had a clear view of the claimant, so it was more likely than not that his negligence caused the action. The defendant driver had failed to rebut the inference by providing a credible explanation of what happened.

Rebutting the inference of negligence

An inference of negligence under the doctrine of *res ipsa loquitur* can be rebutted by the defendant. In **Ng Chun Piu v Lee Chuen Tat** (1988), a coach driver swerved while travelling along a dual carriageway, and crossed the central reservation, hitting a bus that was moving in the opposite direction. A passenger on the bus was killed, and his personal representatives sued the driver and owner of the coach. The Privy Council ruled that on the facts negligence could be inferred, but the coach driver was able to rebut this inference by explaining that he had had to swerve to avoid a car which had cut in front of him. Therefore, the burden of proving negligence remained with the claimant.

In **Ward v Tesco Stores Ltd** (1976), the claimant slipped on some yogurt which had been spilt on the floor of the defendant's supermarket. She put forward evidence that, three weeks later, another spill, this time of orange juice, was left on the supermarket's floor for 15 minutes, though she had no evidence of the circumstances leading up to her own accident. The defendant gave evidence that the floor was swept five or six times a day, and that staff were instructed that if they saw a spillage, they should stay by it, and call someone to clean it up. Nevertheless, the Court of Appeal relied on the doctrine of *res ipsa loquitur* to find that negligence could be inferred, and this inference was not rebutted by the defendant's evidence.

The Highway Code

Following the Road Traffic Act 1988, s. 38(7), where a road user fails to comply with any provision of the Highway Code, that fact may be submitted as evidence of negligence.

Criticisms of negligence law

In order to highlight the general problems with the law of negligence, we need to look first at what the aims of this area of the law are, so as to provide a gauge by which its success can be measured. The law of negligence has several aims, not all of which are necessarily consistent with each other:

- to compensate victims of harm caused by others;
- to mark the fault of those who cause harm;
- to deter carelessness;
- to spread the financial costs of harm caused by carelessness;
- to do all these things quickly and fairly.

To judge how well it achieves these aims, we need to look at both the law itself, and the context in which it operates.

Compensating victims of harm

Considering that compensation is generally seen to be its most important function, the law of negligence is remarkably inefficient in this area and, in practice, only a small proportion of victims of harm get compensation through it.

The first reason for this is that, if we take a wide view of harm, many people are caused harm by circumstances in which nobody can be blamed, for example those with genetic illnesses or those who suffer damage of any kind in accidents which are genuinely nobody's fault. You might well ask why they should be compensated, but the wider picture is that, as we shall see, society as a whole spends a lot of money on negligence cases, yet the result is that a few people get large amounts of money in damages, while many other people whose needs are the same, but result from different causes, do not. The question is therefore whether the system we currently have gives good value for our money.

Added to those people who cannot prove fault in anyone are those who possibly could, but whom the law of negligence will not compensate. Examples include those victims of psychiatric injury and economic loss who fall outside the rules on compensating these types of damage, and those whose damage is the result of carelessness by categories of defendant to whom the law gives special protection in certain circumstances, such as the police and local authorities.

Even among those who have suffered damage in circumstances where some-one else might be liable, only a small proportion take legal action. This might come as a surprise, given that most of the media seems to be convinced that suing is the most popular hobby in Britain. However, the government's own task force concluded that the compensation culture was a myth (see p. 443), and a 2004 survey by Datamonitor found that the number of personal injury claims was decreasing, from 743,595 per year in 2001, to 706,715 in 2003. Despite the availability of 'no win, no fee' arrangements, the majority of people injured through negligence never make a claim. A 1999 study by the Centre for Policy Studies found that only one in seven people who were sufficiently badly injured to need hospital treatment even took legal advice, let alone went on to claim, and the TUC says that only one in ten of people injured at work claim for compensation.

The reasons for this will be well known to those students who have studied access to justice on English Legal System courses: people are often unaware of the possibility of legal action, or are put off by the inaccessible image of the legal world, and the cost of legal action is extremely expensive. In recent years, 'no win, no fee' actions, and more accessible legal advice (from, for example, accident management companies, who advertise widely and lack the sometimes forbid-ding image of solicitors) have probably eased these problems to some extent, but a survey by MORI in 2000 suggests that such barriers still play an important part. The survey found that almost 72 per cent of people would consider making a claim if they were injured through someone else's negligence – but the likelihood of this actually translating into a similar proportion of actual claims seems slim, given that over 60 per cent thought they would probably not be able to afford legal action, and almost 70 per cent said they knew little or nothing about how to go about making a claim.

Among those who do bring cases, the chances of success are sometimes slim. This is particularly the case in medical negligence, where the **Bolam** ruling has essentially meant that, if doctors stick together, it is extremely difficult to prove them negligent. How far this will eventually change in the light of **Bolitho** (see p. 385 above) still remains to be seen; certainly the judgment in **Bolitho** leaves plenty of room to keep the old standard in all but exceptional cases. Yet there seems no compelling reason why medical negligence should be treated so differ-ently from other areas of negligence, and English law is alone among the major common law jurisdictions in giving doctors this privileged status.

In practice the vast majority of negligence cases are settled without going to court – sometimes early on, but often almost literally at the door of the court. This saves a lot of money for the side which would have lost the case, since a trial can drastically raise the costs, and the loser must pay those of the winner as well as their own. From the point of view of adequately compensating those injured though, out of court settlements can be problematic. Hazel Genn's 1987 study, *Hard Bargaining*, showed that in cases where the defendant is an insurance com-pany (which is the case in the vast majority of accident and professional negli-gence claims, for example) and the claimant an ordinary member of the public, the insurance companies, with their vast experience of these cases, are able to manipulate the pre-trial process in order to achieve not a fair settlement but the lowest offer they can get away with. What seems to happen is that small claims are over-compensated because it is not cost-effective for insurance companies to fight them, while very big claims (such as, for example, those brought by parents of children damaged by negligence at birth, who will need care throughout their lives) are often under-compensated because the claimants need compensation quickly, and so can effectively be forced to accept a lower settlement than they might get if they went to court.

Because the law on negligence is complicated, cases can be long and involved. Specialist legal representation is usually required, and the expert witnesses often needed to prove fault add to the cost. The result in practice is that only a fraction of the money spent on negligence cases actually goes to the victims of harm.

Marking fault

The original basis of the law of negligence was claimed to be essentially moral: those who carelessly cause harm to others should bear the responsibility for that harm. In fact, this was always debatable; for example, the direct consequence test for remoteness of damage, laid down in **Re Polemis** (1921), created cases where the damage the defendant was required to compensate could be violently out of proportion to their fault, and even though this test has been superseded, the 'eggshell-skull' rule can have a similar effect.

What makes the shift away from a moral basis much clearer though are the cases on economic loss and psychiatric injury. They show that where new sources of potential liability arise, what the courts look at now is not the rights and wrongs of the situation, but what the economic effects of such liability would be. In **Alcock v Chief Constable of South Yorkshire Police** (1992), the lines drawn with regard to closeness of relationship took no account of the degree of careless-ness involved in the police decision that caused the tragedy: the decision was no more or less careless because the relationship between some of the deceased victims and their relatives was or was not factually close. What the court was looking for was a way to limit liability, and it based its decision not on degree of fault, but essentially on the effect it would have on insurance premiums for the police and the workloads of the courts.

The very existence of insurance is a double-edged sword for the law of negli-gence. Without it, far fewer claims would be brought, because the majority of defendants would not have the money to pay damages, and in terms of com-pensation this would make the law even more inadequate. But in terms of fault, insurance causes a problem because the damages are usually paid by insurance companies, and not by the party whose carelessness has caused harm. Insurance premiums may rise slightly as a result of a claim, but not usually by anything like the cost of that claim, and in many cases premiums are indirectly paid for by all of us, rather than the individual policyholder anyway: employers' insurance is paid for in higher prices to customers, for example; insurance for health author-ities is paid for by our taxes; and the damages paid out by motor insurance companies are funded by all of us who have motor insurance, whether we claim or not. As a result, it is rarely the case that damages are actually paid by the party who has been careless.

Deterring carelessness

The argument here seems obvious: the tort system means that people and organisations know they are liable to be sued if their carelessness causes damage, and therefore its existence should mean that they are more likely to take care to avoid causing harm. In practice, however, the deterrence issue is not so straightforward.

First, the possibility of being sued for negligence can only really act as a deterrent if it is clear that everybody who suffers damage through negligence will sue, and, as we have seen, that is not the case. Secondly, the presence of insurance means that even if you are sued, your carelessness is quite likely not to cost you anything, giving you little incentive to be careful.

Thirdly, the market system on which our society is run actually makes it much more difficult for businesses to take sufficient care, where such care costs (and it usually does). This is because in a market system companies have to keep their costs in line with those of other competing firms. Any company which went out on a limb and spent a lot more money on safety precautions than its competitors were spending would soon be put out of business (a fact which was implicitly acknowledged by the courts in **Thompson _v_ Smith Shiprepairers (North Shields)** (1984), see p. 392 above).

A fourth problem is that in many cases the objective approach can mean that it is actually impossible for the tortfeasor to reach the required standard; in **Nettleship _v_ Weston** (1971), and **Djemal _v_ Bexley Heath Health Authority** (1995) (see pp. 382 and 387 above), the defendants were judged by standards that, in reality, they could not have been expected to attain. The decisions may have been right, given that both defendants would have been protected by insurance, but as far as deterrence is concerned, they were meaningless.

Similarly, in many cases the standard of care imposed is too vague to be of much use in deterring careless behaviour. In practice, most tortfeasors do not sit and balance the magnitude of the risk against its seriousness, while taking into account their own special characteristics and those of the potential claimant, and contemplating the possible benefits to society of what they are about to do. In an ideal world perhaps they should, but in practice they do not. What the law of negligence really does is not so much deter carelessness as attempt to mop up the mess that carelessness leaves behind.

Spreading risk

This is one area where the law of negligence can be seen to work very well at times; rather than leaving loss to lie where it falls, it can pass it on to those most able to bear it financially. The fine judgements needed to do this are not always easy, but there are many cases where the courts have shown obvious good sense in this area. An example is the case of **Smith _v_ Eric S. Bush** (1990) where the courts explicitly considered who was best able to bear the loss, and concluded that it was the surveyors, since they were insured, and their liability was in any case limited to the value of the house.

Having said that, it is worth bearing in mind that, as we have explained, when loss is shifted to insurers, in practice it is actually shifted from them to all of us. This is not necessarily a bad thing, since it spreads the costs of harm thinly – but if this is what society wants to do, it might be more efficiently done by compensating all victims of harm, however caused, through welfare systems based on need and paid for by taxes. In this way much more of the money spent would go to victims of harm, because there would be no need to take out the element of profit for insurance companies, nor the costs of legal actions. It would also mean that money would go to all those who need it to cope with their injury or illness, and not just those who can prove that someone else was to blame.

Individualism and negligence

Supporters of the school of thought known as critical legal theory criticise negligence law for the way it focuses almost exclusively on individual fault, when in fact there may be wider issues involved. For example, many of the activities which crop up in negligence cases – transport, industry and medicine, for example – are activities which benefit society as a whole, but also necessarily carry risks. As the judge in **Daborn v Bath Tramways** (1946) put it: 'If all the trains in this country were restricted to a speed of five miles per hour, there would be fewer accidents, but our national life would be intolerably slowed down.' It can be argued then that those people who are injured as a result of such risks bear the brunt of the convenience and other benefits which the relevant activities provide for all members of society, and that it might therefore be appropriate for society to compensate such victims automatically, rather than making them jump through the hoops of negligence law.

This argument becomes even stronger when the harm suffered by the claimant itself results in a benefit to society, through better knowledge of possible risks. For example, in **Roe v Ministry of Health** (1954) (see p. 389), it was only the injury caused to the claimant that revealed the danger of keeping ampoules of anaesthetic in disinfectant. Because the hospital could not have known of the risk beforehand, they were not liable. As a direct result of what happened, they had changed their procedures so that it could not happen to any future patients, but the patient whose suffering had caused this progress went uncompensated.

Critical theorists argue that since society benefits in all these cases, society should pay; this would require an acceptance that we have social, as well as individual responsibilities.

An economic solution?

It has been suggested that negligence should be assessed on the basis of an economic formula: if the likelihood of the injury, multiplied by its seriousness, exceeds the cost to the defendant of taking adequate precautions, they would be liable. The rationale behind this approach is that finding negligence effectively transfers the loss from the claimant to the defendant, and for economic reasons, this should only happen where the cost of avoiding the accident is less than paying compensation for it.

While this approach may have practical attractions, it lacks any concept of disapproving the wrongdoer's conduct, and could also raise difficulties when it came to calculating (or guessing) the cost of preventing an accident.

Reading on the web

The House of Lords' judgment in **Bolitho** v **City and Hackney Health Authority** can be found on the House of Lords' judicial business website at:

www.publications.parliament.uk/pa/ld/ldjudgmt.htm#1997

The Compensation Act 2006 can be read at:

www.opsi.gov.uk/acts/acts2006/ukpga_20060029_en.pdf

The House of Lords judgment in **Barker** v **Corus** (2006) can be read at:

www.publications.parliament.uk/pa/ld200506/ldjudgmt/jd060503/barker-1.htm

The House of Lords judgment in **Chester** v **Afshar** (2004) can be read at:

www.publications.parliament.uk/pa/ld200304/ldjudgmt/jd041014/cheste-1.htm

The House of Lords judgment in **Sutradhar** v **Natural Environmental Research Council** (2006) can be read at:

www.publications.parliament.uk/pa/ld200506/ldjudgmt/jd060705/sutrad-1.htm

Chapter summary

Negligence has three main elements:

- a duty of care;
- breach of the duty;
- damage caused by the breach.

Duty of care

Duty of care is a legal concept which dictates whether one party can be liable to another in negligence. The test for a duty of care has varied over the years, but the current main test comes from **Caparo** v **Dickman** (1990):

- Is the damage reasonably foreseeable?
- Was there a relationship of proximity between claimant and defendant?
- Is it just and reasonable to impose a duty of care?

Omissions

Negligence generally imposes liability for things people do, not things they fail to do, but there are some situations where a defendant may be liable for an omission to act:

- where the defendant has a high degree of control over the claimant;
- where the defendant has assumed responsibility for the claimant in some way;
- where the defendant creates a dangerous situation, and fails to deal with it.

Breach of a duty of care

A defendant will be in breach of their duty of care if their behaviour falls below the standard of behaviour reasonably to be expected in someone doing what they are doing. The test is objective, and is known as the standard of reasonableness; it requires the defendant to take reasonable precautions, not to eliminate every possible risk.

In deciding on the standard to be expected, the courts weigh up a number of factors:

- special characteristics of the defendant;
- special characteristics of the claimant;
- the size of the risk;
- how far it was practical to prevent the risk;
- common practice in the relevant field;
- any potential benefits to society from the activity that caused the risk.

Damage

The negligence must cause damage. If no damage is caused, there is no claim in negligence no matter how careless the defendant's conduct.

Causation

The claimant must prove that the defendant's negligence caused the damage. The rules on causation apply to all torts which require proof of damage. The basic test is the 'but for' test: would the damage have happened if the defendant had not been negligent?

More complex rules apply in cases where:

- the damage has more than one cause;
- the negligence causes 'loss of a chance';
- there are multiple tortfeasors;
- there is an intervening event after the negligence which contributes to the damage.

Remoteness of damage

The claimant must also prove that the defendant's negligence is not too remote from the damage: a legal, rather than factual test. The remoteness test in negligence is reasonable foreseeability; was the kind of damage suffered reasonably foreseeable at the time the duty was breached? So long as the type of damage is reasonably foreseeable, it does not matter that it is more serious than the defendant could have foreseen.

Proving negligence

The claimant has the burden of proof except where:

■ the defendant has a criminal conviction based on the same facts;
■ the principle *res ipsa loquitur* applies.

Criticisms of negligence law

Problems with the law on negligence arise in each one of its aims:

■ compensating victims of harm;
■ marking fault;
■ deterring carelessness;
■ spreading the costs of harm caused by carelessness;
■ fulfilling these tasks quickly and fairly.

Question and answer guides

1
Abdul invited his neighbour's children to swim in his pool. Abdul had just finished cleaning around the pool, and the surrounding paving was very slippery. As the children ran in, he shouted to them to be careful as the surround was slippery. Tom, aged four, immediately slipped and suffered a broken leg.

(a) In negligence cases, there has to be proof of **duty**, **breach** and **damage**. Outline what **each** of these **three** terms means. *(15 marks)*

(b) Using the rules set out in your answer to part (a) above, discuss whether Abdul has been negligent towards Tom. *(10 marks)*

(from AQA Exam Paper, June 2007)

(a)
Duty
'Duty' is short for 'duty of care'. In negligence cases, a duty of care is a legal obligation to take reasonable care not to cause someone damage. There are many categories of situation in which it is well established that someone owes someone else a duty of care, e.g. drivers to other road users.

Where the situation is not covered by precedent or statute, the courts apply the test laid down in **Caparo** *v* **Dickman** in order to decide whether a duty of care is owed. This requires the court to ask itself three questions, all of which must be answered 'Yes' in order for a duty of care to arise. First, 'Would a reasonable person in the defendant's position have foreseen the risk of damage?' Secondly, 'Was there a relationship of proximity between the defendant and the claimant?' Proximity means more than physical closeness, but concerns the relationship between the parties. Finally, 'Is it just, fair and reasonable to impose a duty in this situation?' This allows the courts to use public policy reasons to deny a claim, even where the other two conditions are satisfied.

Breach

'Breach' is short for 'breach of a legal duty of care'. In negligence cases, breach of a legal duty of care means failing to take the standard of care expected from someone undertaking the activity concerned. For example, in an action brought by one car driver against another, the defendant driver must be shown to have driven carelessly and thus breached the legal duty of care that he owes to other road users such as the claimant.

The standard of care is an objective one, so the particular defendant's own characteristics are usually ignored: **Nettleship v Weston**. But the defendant is not expected to do everything possible to prevent harm: **Simonds v Isle of Wight Council**.

In deciding what behaviour would be expected of the reasonable person in the circumstances of a case, the courts consider a number of factors. These include any special characteristics of the claimant (**Paris v Stepney Borough Council**), the size of the risk (**Bolton v Stone**), how far it was practical to protect against the risk (**Latimer v AEC Ltd**) and any benefits to society that might be gained from taking the risk (**Watt v Hertfordshire County Council**).

Damage

In requiring proof of damage, the law is saying that if no damage is caused to the claimant, he has no claim in negligence, no matter how careless the defendant's conduct. Proof of damage involves proving two things: that the defendant's breach caused the claimant's damage, and that the damage caused was not too 'remote' a consequence of the breach.

To establish causation, the claimant must prove that the damage would not have happened but for the defendant's breach of duty: **Barnett v Chelsea and Kensington Hospital Management Committee**.

To establish that the damage was not too remote, the claimant must prove that the kind of damage suffered by him was reasonably foreseeable at the time of the defendant's breach of duty: **Wagon Mound No. 1**. It does not matter that the precise sequence of events leading from the breach to the damage could not have been reasonably foreseen: **Hughes v Lord Advocate**.

(b)

The first question is whether Abdul owed Tom a duty of care. Applying the three-stage test in **Caparo v Dickman**, this requires asking, firstly, 'Would a reasonable person in Abdul's position have foreseen the risk of damage?' The answer is clearly 'Yes'. Secondly, 'Was there a relationship of proximity between Abdul and Tom?' Again, there clearly was, given their physical proximity. Finally, 'Is it just, fair and reasonable to impose a duty in this situation?' There is no public policy reason to deny Tom's claim, so the answer to this question is also 'Yes'.

The second question is whether Abdul breached his duty of care to Tom. Did his behaviour fall below the standard expected from a reasonable person in his position? In answering this question we need to consider the factors which the courts take into account when deciding whether a breach has occurred: see answer to (a). The factors of particular relevance here are the claimant's special characteristics, and how far it was practical to protect against the risk. On the first, Tom's youth would lead a court to expect Abdul to do more to protect him than simply shout a last-minute warning. On the second, Abdul could easily have protected Tom by simply not inviting him to swim in his pool until the surround had dried. Or he could have insisted that Tom's parents supervise him. The facts are distinguishable from those in **Latimer v AEC Ltd**, as in that case the closure of the factory would have caused great hardship, the slippery patches were clearly visible and the claimant was an adult.

The next question is the causation question – assuming that Abdul is in breach, did his breach cause Tom's damage (i.e. his broken leg)? Applying the 'but for' test, it clearly did.

The final question is the remoteness question – was Tom's damage too 'remote' a consequence of Abdul's breach? Applying the **Wagon Mound** test, it clearly was not. In particular, Abdul could not claim that Tom's running was an intervening event, as it was in the circumstances foreseeable.

In conclusion, therefore, it is likely that Abdul has been negligent towards Tom.

2

Pearl is a singer with a rock band. At the end of the band's concert at a big festival, Pearl decided to leap into the crowd, who were prepared to catch her. Unfortunately, Pearl misjudged the distance and landed on top of Tom, a security guard. Tom was facing the crowd at the time, as required by his job, and had no idea of what was about to happen. Tom suffered a severe neck injury.

(a) Explain what is meant by **a duty of care** in negligence, and discuss whether Pearl owes a duty of care to Tom. *(10 marks)*

(b) Assuming Pearl owes a duty of care to Tom, explain the legal principles relating to **breach of duty**. Discuss whether or not she is in breach of that duty.

(15 marks)

(from AQA Exam Paper, January 2006)

(a)

Meaning of 'duty of care'

- Define 'duty of care', e.g. a legal obligation to take reasonable care not to cause someone damage.
- Explain how there are many well-established duty of care situations, giving an example.
- Explain how, in new situations, the courts apply the **Caparo v Dickman** test.
- Explain the test's three stages.
- For a good answer, explain the meaning of 'proximity' in the second stage of the test, using the facts of **Caparo** as an illustration.

Does Pearl owe a duty of care to Tom?

- Pose the question 'Would a reasonable person in Pearl's position have foreseen the risk of damage?' and answer 'Almost certainly, yes', giving reasons.
- Pose the question 'Was there a relationship of proximity between Pearl and Tom?' and answer 'Almost certainly, yes', giving reasons.

- Pose the question, 'Is it just, fair and reasonable to impose a duty in this situation?' and answer 'Yes', giving reasons; for a good answer, distinguish this case from cases such as **McFarlane *v* Tayside Health Board**.
- Conclude by saying that Pearl almost certainly owes a duty of care to Tom.

(b)
Principles relating to 'breach of duty'

- Define 'breach of duty', emphasising that it involves testing the defendant's conduct against what could be expected of a reasonable person undertaking the same activity.
- Explain that the standard is objective, citing **Nettleship *v* Weston**.
- Explain how the standard does not require perfection, citing **Simonds *v* Isle of Wight Council**.
- Explain how, in applying the standard, the courts consider a number of factors; for a good answer, stress how these factors interact with each other, giving an example.
- Explain some of these factors, especially the size of the risk and how far it was practical to protect against the risk, citing relevant cases.

Is Pearl in breach of her duty to Tom?

- Pose the question 'What was the size of the risk to Tom?', explaining that this includes both the chances of him being injured and the potential seriousness of that injury.
- Answer that both were high, especially as Tom was 'facing the crowd at the time, as required by his job, and had no idea of what was about to happen'.
- Pose the question 'How great would have been the cost and trouble to Pearl of taking the measures necessary to eliminate the risk?'
- Answer 'Not at all great', explaining some of the simple things that she could have done to protect Tom.
- Conclude by saying that Pearl is almost certainly in breach of her duty to Tom.

Common errors in (a)

- treating **Donoghue *v* Stevenson** as the leading case on duty of care.
- failing to properly apply the **Caparo** test to the facts of the scenario.

Common errors in (b)

- incorrectly explaining how 'the size of the risk' operates as a factor relevant to breach.
- failing to apply 'the size of the risk' and 'eliminating the risk' to the facts of the scenario.

Group activity 1

- Divide your friends (or class) into groups of two or three people.
- Using the Internet and any other available resources, make notes on the facts and decision in the House of Lords case of **Rothwell *v* Chemical and Insulating Co. Ltd** (2007), concentrating on understanding why this action for negligence failed.

- Then, using the search phrase 'pleural plaques' (which is what this case was about), find the answers to the following questions:
  1 Why was the Association of British Insurers pleased with the decision in **Rothwell**?
  2 Why did the TUC (Trades Union Congress) describe the decision as 'a disgrace'?
  3 Why did Irwin Mitchell (a firm of personal injury lawyers) say that they were 'extremely disappointed' with the decision?
  4 What reaction did the decision produce from the Scottish Parliament?
- Once you have answered these questions, compare your answers with those of the other groups.

---

mylawchamber

Visit **www.mylawchamber.co.uk/elliottaqa** to access interactive questions, quizzes and activities to test yourself on this chapter.

Civil court procedure

This chapter discusses:

- an introduction to the civil justice system;
- the civil courts;
- the requirement that the courts deal with cases 'justly';
- civil procedure;
- problems with the civil court system.

The civil justice system

The civil justice system is designed to sort out disputes between individuals or organisations. One party, known as the claimant, sues the other, called the defendant, usually for money they claim is owed or for compensation for a harm to their interests. Typical examples might be the victim of a car accident suing the driver of the car for compensation, or one business suing another for payment due on goods supplied. The burden of proof is usually on the claimant, who must prove his or her case on a balance of probabilities – that it is more likely than not. This is a lower standard of proof than the 'beyond reasonable doubt' test used by the criminal courts and, for this reason, it is possible to be acquitted of a criminal charge yet still be found to have breached the civil law. This happened to the celebrity O. J. Simpson in America who, having been acquitted by the criminal courts of murdering his ex-wife and her friend, was successfully sued in the civil courts for damages by the victim's family. The rules on *res ipsa loquitur* discussed at p. 412 can affect the burden of proof in the context of the tort of negligence.

Major changes have been made to the civil justice system in recent years. After the Civil Justice Review of 1988, reforms were made by the Courts and Legal Services Act 1990. Following continued criticism of the civil justice system, the previous Conservative government ten years later appointed Lord Woolf to carry out an in-depth review of the civil justice system. Lord Woolf's inquiry was the sixty-third such review in a hundred years. Lord Woolf made far-reaching recommendations in his report, *Access to Justice*, which was published in 1996. As with the Civil Justice Review, his aim was to reduce the cost, delay and complexity of the system and increase access to justice. Most of his recommendations were implemented in April 1999.

The civil courts

There are two main civil courts which hear civil cases at first instance. These are the county courts and the High Court. The county courts hear the cases where less money is involved, whereas the High Court hears the bigger financial cases. Thus, most civil cases start in the county court. They start in the High Court only if the claimant expects to recover more than £15,000, or £50,000 if it is a personal injury case.

Quick quiz 21.1

1 What is the burden of proof in civil cases?

2 What major piece of legislation followed the Civil Justice Review of 1988?

3 What is the name of Lord Woolf's final report on the civil justice system?

4 Name the three divisions of the High Court.

Dealing with cases 'justly'

On 26 April 1999 new Civil Procedure Rules and accompanying Practice Directions came into force. These rules constitute the most fundamental reform of the civil justice system in the twentieth century, introducing the main recommendations of Lord Woolf in his final report, *Access to Justice*. He described his proposals as providing 'a new landscape for civil justice for the twenty-first century'. The general approach of Lord Woolf is reflected in his statement: 'If "time and money are no object" was the right approach in the past, then it certainly is not today. Both lawyers and judges, in making decisions as to the conduct of litigation, must take into account more than they do at present, questions of cost and time and the means of the parties.' Lord Woolf has said that the reforms should lead to a reduction in legal bills by as much as 75 per cent, though it might also mean that some lawyers would lose their livelihoods.

The ultimate goal is to change the litigation culture fundamentally. Thus, the first rule of the new Civil Procedure Rules lays down an overriding objective which is to underpin the whole system. This is that the rules should enable the courts to deal with cases 'justly'. This objective prevails over all other rules in case of a conflict. The parties and their legal representatives are expected to assist the judges in achieving this objective. The Woolf Report heavily criticised practitioners, who were accused of manipulating the old system for their own convenience and causing delay and expense to both their clients and the users of the system as a whole. Lord Woolf felt that a change in attitude among the lawyers was vital for the new rules to succeed. According to r. 1.1(2):

> *'Dealing with a case justly includes, so far as is practicable –*
> *a. ensuring that the parties are on an equal footing;*
> *b. saving expense;*

    c. dealing with the case in ways which are proportionate –
      i. to the amount of money involved;
      ii. to the importance of the case;
      iii. to the complexity of the issues; and
      iv. to the financial position of each party;
    d. ensuring that it is dealt with expeditiously and fairly; and
    e. allotting to it an appropriate share of the Court's resources, while taking into account the need to allot resources to other cases.'

The emphasis of the new rules is on avoiding litigation through pre-trial settlements. Litigation is to be viewed as a last resort, with the court having a continuing obligation to encourage and facilitate settlement. Lord Woolf had observed that it was strange that, although the majority of disputes ended in settlement, the old rules had been directed mainly towards preparation for trial. Thus the new rules put a greater emphasis on preparing cases for settlement rather than a trial.

    The new approach to civil procedure will now be examined in more detail.

Quick quiz 21.2

1 Do the new rules of procedure prioritise preparation for a settlement or for a trial?

2 When did the new Civil Procedure Rules come into force?

3 What is the overriding objective contained in the first rule of the new Civil Procedure Rules?

4 Before 1999 a person bringing an action was called a plaintiff. What is such a person called now?

Civil procedure

Before proceedings are commenced, claimants should send a letter to the defendants warning them that they are considering bringing legal proceedings. Almost all proceedings then start with the same document, called a claim form. The claim form informs the defendant that an action is being brought against them. When claimants are making a claim for money, they must provide a statement as to the value of the claim in the claim form.

    For non-personal injury actions, a claim may be started in the High Court where the claimant expects to recover more than £15,000 (this limit is expected to be raised to £50,000 in the near future). For personal injury actions, a claim can be started in the High Court only where the claimant expects to recover at least £50,000 for pain, suffering and loss of amenity.

    The claim form is served on the defendant to a case. The methods of service have been liberalised to reflect modern modes of communication, including the use of fax and emails. Service will normally be carried out by the court through postage by first class post, unless a party notifies the court that they will serve the documents. Defendants must acknowledge service. The claimant (known before 1999 as the plaintiff) must then serve on the defendant the particulars of claim.

The defendant should respond within 14 days by filing either an acknow-ledgement of service or a defence with the court. If the defendant fails to do either of these within that period of time, the claimant can enter judgment in default against the defendant.

If the defendant files a defence, the court will serve an allocation questionnaire on each party. This is designed to enable the court to allocate each claim to one of the three tracks discussed at p. 433.

The disclosure procedures are then followed, under which the parties are required to disclose the documents on which they intend to rely and also the documents which go against their case. Either party may seek more details from the other, through a 'request for information'. If the case is not settled out of court, the case proceeds to trial.

The different formal documents are described as the statement of case. All state-ments of case must be verified by a statement of truth. This is a statement signed by the claimant (or his/her legal representative) in the following words: 'I believe that the facts stated in these particulars of claim are true.' The purpose of the statement of case is to prevent parties from putting in facts for purely tactical purposes which they have no intention of relying upon. If a party makes a false statement in a statement of case verified by a statement of truth, the party will be guilty of contempt of court.

Either party can apply for a summary judgment on the ground that the claim or defence has no real prospect of success. The court can also reach this conclu-sion on its own initiative. At any stage of the proceedings the parties can enter into 'without prejudice' negotiations to try and settle the dispute out of court. The without prejudice rule makes all negotiations genuinely aimed at settlement, whether oral or in writing, inadmissible in evidence at any subsequent trial. The rule lets litigants make whatever concessions or admissions are necessary to achieve a compromise, without fear of these being held against them if negotia-tions break down and the case goes to court. It is hoped that this will help and encourage the parties to settle their disputes early.

Pre-action protocols

The pre-trial procedure is perhaps the most important area of the civil process, since few civil cases actually come to trial. To push the parties into behaving reasonably during the pre-trial stage, Lord Woolf recommended the develop-ment of pre-action protocols to lay down a code of conduct for this stage of the proceedings. The pre-action protocols aim to encourage:

- more pre-action contact between the parties;
- an earlier and fuller exchange of information;
- improved pre-action investigation;
- a settlement before proceedings have commenced.

They strive to achieve this through establishing a timetable for the exchange of information, by setting standards for the content of correspondence and by pro-viding schedules of documents that should be disclosed, along with a mechanism for agreeing a single joint expert. The pre-action protocols seek to encourage a

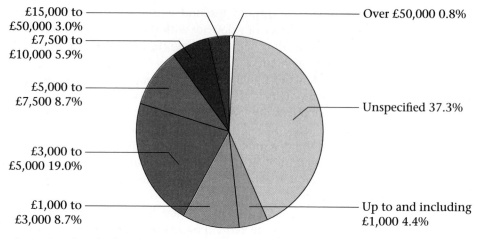

£15,000 to £50,000 3.0%
£7,500 to £10,000 5.9%
£5,000 to £7,500 8.7%
£3,000 to £5,000 19.0%
£1,000 to £3,000 8.7%
Over £50,000 0.8%
Unspecified 37.3%
Up to and including £1,000 4.4%

Figure 21.1 County Court claims issued by amount of claim, 2005

Figures are based on three months' sample data from selected county courts

Source: 'Judicial Statistics Annual Report 2005', p. 44. © Crown Copyright 2006.

Task 21.3

Look at the diagram (Figure 21.1) and answer the questions that follow.

Questions

1 In 2004, which types of cases were the most likely to be heard by the county court?
2 Which types of cases were least likely to be heard by the county court?

culture of openness between the parties. This should lead to the parties being better informed as to the merits of their case so that they will be in a position to settle cases fairly, and thereby reduce the need for litigation. Compliance with a pre-action protocol is not compulsory, but if a party unreasonably refuses to comply, then this can be taken into account when the court makes orders for costs.

Alternative dispute resolution

At various stages in a dispute's history, the court will actively promote settlement by alternative dispute resolution (ADR). For a detailed discussion of ADR in the English legal system, see Chapter 2. There is a general statement in the new rules that the court's duty to further the overriding objective by active case management includes both encouraging the parties to use an alternative dispute resolution procedure (if the court considers that appropriate) and facilitating the use of that procedure. Also, when filling in the allocation questionnaire, the parties can request a one-month stay of proceedings while they try to settle the case by ADR or other means. The parties will have to show that they genuinely attempted to resolve their dispute through ADR and have not just paid lip-service to the idea, as has been the tendency in the past.

Case management

This is the most significant innovation of the 1999 reforms. Case management means that the court will be the active manager of the litigation. The main aim of this approach is to bring cases to trial quickly and efficiently. Traditionally, it has been left to the parties and their lawyers to manage the cases. The current rules firmly place the management of a case in the hands of the judges, with r. 1.4 emphasising that the court's duty is to take a proactive role in the management of each case.

Once proceedings have commenced, the court's powers of case management will be triggered by the filing of a defence. When the defence has been filed and case management has started, the parties are on a moving train, trial dates will be fixed and will be difficult to postpone, and litigants will not normally be able to slow down or stop the case unless they settle. The court first needs to allocate the case to one of the three tracks – the small claims track, the fast track or the multi-track – which will determine the future conduct of the proceedings. To determine which is the appropriate track, the court will serve an allocation questionnaire on each party. The answers to this questionnaire will form the basis for deciding the appropriate track.

Quick quiz 21.4

1 What is the name of the document used to commence civil proceedings?

2 If a person wishes to bring an action for £26,000 compensation for a head injury, which court will normally hear the case?

3 What happens if a party does not comply with a pre-action protocol?

4 Under the system of case management, who controls the progress of a case through the civil justice system?

The three tracks

The court allocates the case to the most appropriate track, depending primarily on the financial value of the claim, but other factors that can be taken into account include the case's importance and complexity. Normally:

- small claims track cases deal with actions with a value of less than £5,000 (or £1,000 for personal injury cases);
- fast-track cases deal with actions of a value between £5,000 and £15,000;
- multi-track cases deal with actions with a value higher than £15,000.

The three tracks will now be considered in turn.

The small claims track

The handling of small claims was largely unchanged by the Woolf reforms. In the small claims track, directions will be issued for each case providing a date for the hearing and an estimate of the hearing time, unless the case requires a preliminary hearing appointment to assist the parties in the conduct of the case. This track was previously known as the small claims court, though it was never actually a separate court, but a procedure used by county courts to deal with relatively small claims. It was introduced in response to a report from the Consumers' Association in 1967 which claimed that county courts were being used primarily as a debt-collection agency for businesses: 89.2 per cent of the summonses were taken out by businesses and only 9 per cent by individuals, who were put off by costs and complexity.

Established in 1973, this special procedure aims to provide a cheap, simple mechanism for resolving small-scale consumer disputes. Disclosure is dispensed with and, if the litigation continues to trial, it is usually held in private rather than in open court. The hearing is simple and informal, with few rules about the admissibility or presentation of evidence. No experts may be used without leave.

It is usually a very quick process, with 60 per cent of hearings taking less than 30 minutes. Costs are limited except where, by consent, a case with a financial value such that it would normally be allocated to the fast track was allocated to the small claims track. The procedure is designed to make it easy for parties to represent themselves without the aid of a lawyer, and state funding for representation is not available. A party can choose to be represented by a lay person, though the party must also attend.

> **✓ Know your terms 21.5**
>
> Define the following terms:
> 1 Queen's Bench Division.
> 2 The Woolf Report.
> 3 Pre-action protocol.
> 4 Case management.

The fast track

Fast-track cases will normally be dealt with by the county court. Upon allocation to the fast track, the court gives directions for the management of the case, and sets a timetable for the disclosure of documents, the exchange of witness statements, the exchange (and number) of expert reports, and the trial date or a period within which the trial will take place, which will be no more than 30 weeks later (compared to an average of 80 weeks before 1999).

A typical timetable that a court may give under this track is:

- disclosure: 4 weeks;
- exchange of witness statements: 10 weeks;
- exchange of experts' reports: 14 weeks;
- hearing: 30 weeks.

Although the parties can vary certain matters by agreement, such as disclosure or the exchange of witness statements, the rules are quite clear that an application must be made to court if a party wishes to vary the date for the trial.

Under this track the maximum length of the trial is normally one day. The relevant Practice Direction states that the judge will normally have read the papers in the trial bundle and may dispense with an opening address. Witness statements will usually stand as evidence-in-chief. Oral expert evidence will be limited to one expert per party in relation to any expert field and expert evidence will be limited to two expert fields.

In an attempt to keep lawyers' bills down, fixed costs for fast-track trials have been introduced, but the introduction of pre-trial fixed costs has been delayed until additional information is available to inform the development of the revised costs regime. Lord Woolf had recommended that there should be a £2,500 limit on costs for fast-track cases (though clients could enter a written agreement to pay

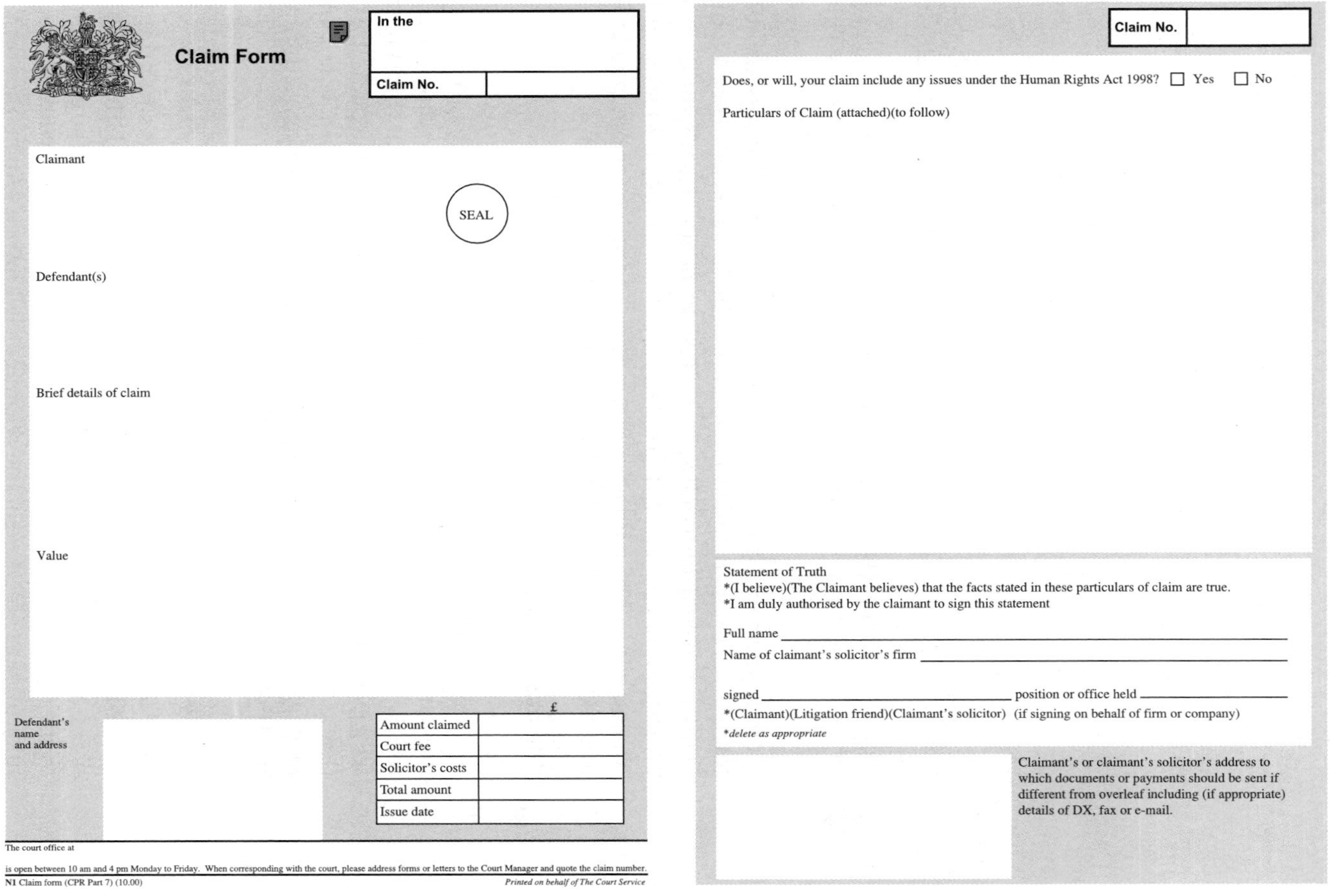

Claim Form

Claim No.

In the

Claim No.

SEAL

Claimant

Defendant(s)

Brief details of claim

Value

	£
Amount claimed	
Court fee	
Solicitor's costs	
Total amount	
Issue date	

Defendant's name and address

The court office at

is open between 10 am and 4 pm Monday to Friday. When corresponding with the court, please address forms or letters to the Court Manager and quote the claim number.

N1 Claim form (CPR Part 7) (10.00)

Printed on behalf of The Court Service

Does, or will, your claim include any issues under the Human Rights Act 1998? ☐ Yes ☐ No

Particulars of Claim (attached)(to follow)

Statement of Truth

*(I believe)(The Claimant believes) that the facts stated in these particulars of claim are true.
*I am duly authorised by the claimant to sign this statement

Full name

Name of claimant's solicitor's firm

signed _____ position or office held _____

*(Claimant)(Litigation friend)(Claimant's solicitor) (if signing on behalf of firm or company)

*delete as appropriate

Claimant's or claimant's solicitor's address to which documents or payments should be sent if different from overleaf including (if appropriate) details of DX, fax or e-mail.

Figure 21.2 A claim form

Source: Court Service website at www.mcsi.gov.uk. © Crown Copyright.

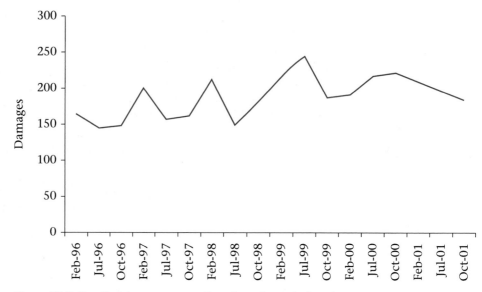

Figure 21.3 Small claims – average time from issue to hearing

Source: 'Further Findings: a continuing evaluation of the Civil Justice Reforms', August 2002 [Figure 12]. © Crown Copyright 2002.

more to their solicitors). Apart from the trial itself, litigants are still committing themselves to open-ended payment by the hour, which Lord Woolf described as being equivalent to handing out a blank cheque. He observed: 'If you and I are having our house repaired, we don't do it on a time and materials basis, because we know it will be a disaster. There is no incentive for the builder to do it in the least time and do it with the most economical materials.'

The multi-track

Upon allocation to the multi-track, the court can give directions for the management of the case and set a timetable for those steps to be taken. Alternatively, for heavier cases, the court may fix a case management conference or a pre-trial review or both. Unlike the fast track, the court does not at this stage automatically set a trial date or a period within which the trial will take place. Instead, it will fix this as soon as it is practicable to do so. Thus, this track offers individual case management with tailor-made directions according to the needs of the case. Only the High Court hears multi-track cases.

A proactive approach

Gone are the days when the court waited for the lawyers to bring the case back before it or allowed the lawyers to dictate without question the number of witnesses or the amount of costs incurred. In managing litigation, the court must have regard to the overriding objective, set out in Part 1, which is to deal with cases justly. To fulfil this key objective of the reformed civil justice system, the court is required to:

- identify the issues at an early stage;
- decide promptly which issues require full investigation and dispose summarily of the others;

- encourage the parties to seek alternative dispute resolution where appropriate;
- encourage the parties to cooperate with each other in the conduct of the procedures;
- help the parties to settle the whole or part of the case;
- decide the order in which issues are to be resolved;
- fix timetables or otherwise control the progress of the case;
- consider whether the likely benefits of taking a particular step will justify the cost of taking it;
- deal with a case without the parties' attendance at court if this is possible;
- make appropriate use of technology;
- give directions to ensure that the trial of a case proceeds quickly and efficiently.

A lot of the preliminary hearings, such as allocation hearings and case management conferences, are now dealt with by the judge over the telephone, rather than people having to attend court. This saves time and money by taking advantage of modern technology.

Disclosure

Before the 1999 reforms, disclosure was known as 'discovery'. The procedure used to involve each party providing the other with a list of all the documents which they had in relation to the action. The parties could then ask to see some or all of this material. The process could be time-consuming and costly. Pre-action disclosure was also available in claims for personal injury and death. Lord Woolf recommended that disclosure should generally be limited to documents which were readily available and which to a 'material extent' adversely affected or supported a party's case, though this could be extended for multi-track cases. This change would have significantly altered the disclosure process and risked going against the philosophy of openness between the parties generally advocated by Lord Woolf. He also favoured extending pre-action disclosure to be available for all proceedings and against people who would not have been parties to the future proceedings. However, the new Civil Procedure Rules are actually very similar to the old rules. These require the disclosure of documents on which they rely or which adversely affected or supported a party's case. It is not necessary for this impact to be to a 'material extent'. As under the old rules, additional disclosure will be ordered where it is 'necessary in order to dispose fairly of the claim or to save costs'. The availability of pre-action disclosure was not extended despite the fact that the Civil Procedure Act 1997 provided for its extension. The pre-action protocols are designed to ensure voluntary disclosure is made between likely parties. It seems that the government wishes to see how the pre-action protocols operate in practice before implementing such changes.

Sanctions

Tough rules on sanctions give the courts stringent powers to enforce the new rules on civil procedure to ensure that litigation is pursued diligently. The two main sanctions are an adverse award of costs, and an order for a case or part of a case to be struck out. These sanctions were available under the old rules, but the novelty of the new regime lies in the commitment to enforce strict compliance. There is an increasing willingness of the courts to manage cases with a stick rather than a carrot. The courts can treat the standards set in the pre-action protocols as the normal approach to pre-action conduct and have the power to penalise parties for non-compliance.

Money Claim Online

In 2002, Money Claim Online (MCOL) was established. It provides a debt recovery service over the Internet for sums up to £100,000. The debts might be for unpaid goods or services, or rent arrears, for example. Claimants can issue money claims via the internet at **www.moneyclaim.gov.uk**. Fees are paid electronically by debit or credit card. The defence can use the online service to acknowledge service and file a defence. Most debt claims are undefended and if no defence is filed then the claimant can apply online for a judgment and enforcement. The parties can use the website to check the progress of their case, such as whether a defence has been filed. The service is available 24 hours a day, seven days a week. The new service has proved very popular with creditors, who have issued thousands of claims to date using the new service.

> **✓ Know your terms 21.6**
>
> Define the following terms:
> 1 Multi-track.
> 2 Fast track.
> 3 Disclosure.
> 4 MCOL.

Task 21.7

Read the following extract from Lord Woolf's Report, *Access to Justice*, and answer the questions that follow.

The principles
I have identified a number of principles which the civil justice system should meet in order to ensure access to justice. The system should:

(a) be *just* in the results it delivers;
(b) be *fair* in the way it treats litigants;
(c) offer appropriate procedures at a reasonable cost;
(d) deal with cases with reasonable *speed*;
(e) be *understandable* to those who use it;
(f) be *responsive* to the needs of those who use it;
(g) provide as much *certainty* as the nature of particular cases allows; and
(h) be *effective*, adequately resourced and organised.

The basic reforms
The **interim report** set out a blueprint for reform based on a system where the courts with the assistance of litigants would be responsible for the management of cases. I recommended that the courts should have the final responsibility for determining what procedures were suitable for each case; setting realistic timetables; and ensuring that procedures and timetables were complied with.

The recommendations in my final report, together with the new code of rules, form a comprehensive and coherent package for the reform of civil justice. Each contributes to and underpins the others. Their overall effectiveness could be seriously undermined by piecemeal implementation. My overriding concern is to ensure that we have a civil justice system which will meet the needs of the public in the twenty first century.

   (Adapted from Lord Woolf's report, *Access to Justice*)

Questions

1 What is the goal that Lord Woolf hopes his reforms will achieve?
2 One of the principles on which Lord Woolf thinks a civil justice system should be based is that it offers 'appropriate procedures at a reasonable cost'. How far do you think the issue of cost should be taken into account when trying to achieve justice?
3 What is meant by an 'interim report'?
4 Lord Woolf was anxious that his reforms should not be undermined by piecemeal implementation. Has this proved to be a problem?

Problems with the civil court system

Out-of-court settlements

The use of pre-action protocols and claimant offers to encourage pre-trial settlements has diverted cases from being litigated in the courts. As a result only 8 per cent of cases listed for trial settle at the trial, while 70 per cent settle much earlier. The reforms put considerable emphasis on the use of out-of-court settlements which can have the advantage of providing a quick end to the dispute, and a reduction in costs. For the claimant, a settlement means they are sure of getting something, and do not have to risk losing the case altogether and probably having to pay the other side's costs as well as their own. But they must weigh this up against the chances of being awarded a better settlement if the case goes to trial and they win. The defendant risks the possibility that they might have won and therefore had to pay nothing, or that they may be paying more than the judge would have awarded had the claimant won the case, against the chance that the claimant wins and is awarded more than the settlement would have cost.

The high number of out-of-court settlements creates injustice, because the parties usually hold very unequal bargaining positions. In the first place, one party might be in a better financial position than the other, and therefore under less pressure to keep costs down by settling quickly.

Secondly, as Galanter's 1984 study revealed, litigants can often be divided into 'one-shotters' and 'repeat players'. One-shotters are individuals involved in litigation for probably the only time in their life, for whom the procedure is unfamiliar and traumatic; the case is very important to them and tends to occupy most of their thoughts while it continues. Repeat players, on the other hand, include companies and businesses (particularly insurance companies), for whom litigation is routine. They are used to working with the law and lawyers and, while they obviously want to win the case for financial reasons, they do not have the same emotional investment in it as the individual one-shotter. Where a repeat player and a one-shotter are on opposing sides – as is often the case in personal injury litigation, where an individual is fighting an insurance company – the repeat player is likely to have the upper hand in out-of-court bargaining.

A third factor was highlighted by Hazel Genn's 1987 study of negotiated settlements of accident claims. She found that having a non-specialist lawyer could seriously prejudice a client's interests when an out-of-court settlement is made. A non-specialist may be unfamiliar with court procedure and reluctant to fight the case in court. They may, therefore, not encourage their client to hold out against an unsatisfactory settlement. Specialist lawyers on the other side may take advantage of this inexperience, putting on pressure for the acceptance of a low settlement. Repeat players are more likely to have access to their own specialist lawyers, whereas, for the one-shotter, finding a suitable lawyer can be something of a lottery, since they have little information on which to base their choice.

Clearly, these factors affect the fairness of out-of-court settlements. In court, the judge can treat the parties as equals, but for out-of-court negotiations one party often has a very obvious advantage.

The government's first evaluation of the new Civil Procedure Rules has found that overall the reforms have been beneficial: *Emerging Findings: an early evaluation of the Civil Justice Reforms* (2001). It seems that cases are settling earlier, rather than at the door of the court. Lawyers and clients are now regarding litigation as a last resort, and making more use of alternative methods of dispute resolution. The pre-action protocols have been a success. Their effect has been to concentrate the minds of defendants and make them deal properly with a claim at the early stages rather than months after the issue of proceedings (conditional fee agreements could also be an explanation for this). While generally cases are being heard more quickly after the issue of the claim, small claims are taking longer. But the picture is not quite as straightforward as it looks. Lawyers know that as soon as they issue the claim form they will lose control of the pace of the negotiations and are going to be locked into timetables and procedures which they may find burdensome as well as costly. There is evidence that lawyers are therefore delaying issuing the claim. It is not yet clear whether litigation has become cheaper. The report quotes practitioners who believe the front-end loading of costs caused by the pre-action protocols means that overall costs have actually gone up.

In their research paper, *More Civil Justice: the impact of the Woolf reforms on pre-action behaviour* (2002), the Law Society and the Civil Justice Council assessed the success of the new pre-action procedures. Most of the respondents were positive about their introduction. In particular, personal injury practitioners and insurers have welcomed the additional information the protocol requires be disclosed during the early stages of proceedings, as it facilitates early settlement.

The latest research into the civil justice system, *The Management of Civil Cases: The Courts and the Post-Woolf Landscape* (2005), concludes that the reforms have lead to a better litigation culture. They have significantly reduced the amount of litigation going to court from 2.2 million cases in 1997 to 1.5 million cases in 2003. However, costs have increased, they have become front loaded (in other words, more costs are incurred at the earlier stages of the litigation process) and the cost of each case is higher overall.

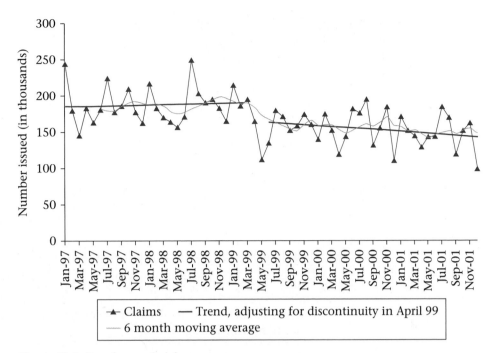

Figure 21.4 County court claims

Source: 'Further Findings: a continuing evaluation of the Civil Justice Reforms, August 2002 [Figure 1]. © Crown Copyright 2002.

Small claims track

The small claims procedure is an important part of the civil procedure system, involving around 80,000 actions each year. The procedure is quicker, simpler and cheaper than the full county court process, which is helpful to both litigants and the overworked court system. It gives individuals and small businesses a useful lever against creditors or for consumer complaints. Without it, threats to sue over small amounts would be ignored on the basis that going to court would cost more than the value of the debt or compensation claimed. Public confidence is also increased, by proving that the legal system is not only accessible to the rich and powerful. The academic, John Baldwin, has carried out research into the small claims track, *Lay and Judicial Perspectives on the Expansion of the Small Claims Regime* (2002). He noted that the official statistics show that the recent rises in the small claims limit have not led, as many feared, to the county courts being inundated with new cases. There has been only a slight increase in the number of small claims cases. Most small claims litigants involved in relatively high-value claims are satisfied with the experience. However, there are long-standing concerns about the small claims procedure, which have not been tackled by the 1999 reforms. Small claims are not necessarily simple claims; they may involve complex and unusual points of law. Is the small claimant entitled to be judged by the law of the land or by speedier, more rough-and-ready concepts of fairness?

The Consumers' Association magazine is of the view that the small claims procedure is not simple enough. It reported in 1986 that the process was still 'quite an ordeal', and the level of formality varied widely. The submissions of both the

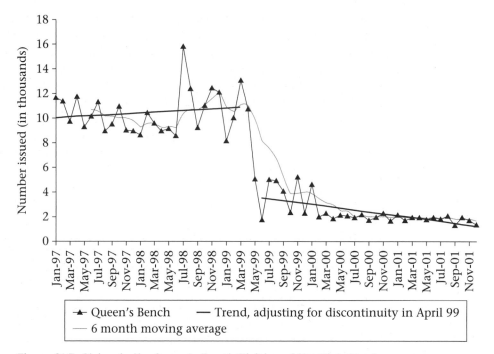

Figure 21.5 Claims in the Queen's Bench Division of the High Court

Source: 'Further Findings: a continuing evaluation of the Civil Justice Reforms', [Figure 2]. © Crown Copyright 2002.

National Consumer Council and the National Association of Citizens' Advice Bureaux to the Civil Justice Review echoed this feeling. The Civil Justice Review recommended that court forms and leaflets should be simplified. The system is still largely used by small businesses chasing debtors, rather than by the individual consumer for whom it was set up. A consultation paper was issued in 1995 suggesting that, in limited cases, the judge might be given the power to award an additional sum of up to £135 to cover the cost of legal advice and assistance in the preparation of the case. If this reform were to be introduced, it might assist individual consumers to bring their cases.

There are also problems with enforcement. A survey by the old Lord Chancellor's Department in 1986 found that 25 per cent of parties were failing to get the payment owed to them from the defendant following a successful application. A report by the Consumers' Association (November 1997) suggests that many people using the small claims procedure are being denied justice because of slow and inefficient enforcement procedures. The court is not responsible for enforcement, which is left to the winning party to secure. The report found that only a minority of defendants paid up on time and that after six months a substantial minority of people still had not paid their debts. The report's author, Professor John Baldwin, concluded that the enforcement problem was so serious that it threatened to undermine the small claims procedure itself by deterring people from using it.

The government considered raising the financial level of personal injury cases that can be considered by the small claims procedures from £1,000 to £5,000. The Better Regulation Taskforce (an independent advisory body established in 1997) published a report *Better Routes to Redress* (2004). This suggested that the government should consider raising the limits for personal injury cases to bring them into line with most other civil claims, which can already be considered by the small claims court when they involve claims of up to £5,000. The Taskforce suggested that the reform would 'increase access to justice for many as it will be less expensive, less adversarial and less stressful'. The government is concerned that procedures and costs should be proportionate to the size of the claim.

At the moment, most personal injury cases are heard under the fast track procedure which means costs can be recovered and lawyers can represent clients on a no-win, no-fee basis. If the financial limits were changed about 70 per cent of personal injury cases would be heard by the small claims procedure. On the small claims track, court costs cannot be recovered and lawyers are not able to represent clients on a no-win, no-fee basis. Litigants would therefore frequently be forced to represent themselves. The Association of Personal Injury Lawyers has argued that personal injury cases are complex and people want and need the help of a lawyer to prepare their case. The person being sued is likely to have been insured and will benefit from the specialist help of the insurer's lawyers.

Baldwin's research (2002) concluded that the informal small claims procedures inevitably involve a sacrifice in the standards of judicial decision making. He questioned whether this could be justified in claims involving more than the existing financial limits.

The Civil Justice Council spent three years looking at the funding of civil claims and how to keep costs in proportion. In 2005 it published its report, *Improved Access to Justice – Funding Options and Proportionate Costs* (2005). It recommends that the small claims track limit for personal injury cases should be retained at £1,000. It considers that the fast track limit for personal injury cases should be increased from £15,000 to £25,000 though parties could opt to have their cases on this track for claims up to £50,000.

In 2007, the government announced that it no longer intended to raise the small claims limit to £5,000 because this would not be in the interests of consumers. It is, however, considering increasing the fast track limit to £25,000. It is also looking at introducing a streamlined claims process for personal injury claims under £25,000. A consultation paper has been issued on the subject, entitled *Case track limits and the claims process for personal injury claims* (2007).

Compensation culture

There has been some concern that the UK might be developing a compensation culture, which has historically been associated with the US. A compensation culture implies that people with frivolous and unwarranted claims bring cases to court with a view to making easy money. The phenomenon of a more litigious society can be interpreted in two very different ways. It can be seen as a good thing because more people are asserting their rights and obtaining stronger legal protection. At the same time it can be seen as a bad thing because the law is pushing people into relationships which lack trust and creating confrontational communities.

The government has concluded that the UK does not have an unhealthy compensation culture (accident claims actually fell by 10 per cent in 2004), but the increased number of threats to sue and the resulting fear of being sued is having a negative effect on people's work and behaviour, and this trend needs to be reversed. In 2004 the Lord Chancellor commented:

'If you have a genuine claim – where someone else is to blame – you should be able to get compensation from those at fault. This is only fair. The victim or taxpayer shouldn't have to pay out where someone else is to blame. But there is not always someone else to blame. Genuine accidents do happen. People should not be encouraged to always "have a go" however meritless the claim. The perception that there is easy money just waiting to be had – the so-called "compensation culture" – creates very real problems. People become scared of being sued; organizations avoid taking risks and stop perfectly sensible activities. It creates burdens for those handling claims and critically it also undermines genuine claims.'

The Compensation Act 2006 contains provisions to encourage the courts to consider whether a successful negligence claim in a particular case might prevent a desirable activity, such as a school trip, from taking place in future.

The government is concerned that the problems relating to a compensation culture are being aggravated by the unscrupulous sales tactics of some claims management companies, which encourage people who have suffered minor personal injuries to bring litigation. Advertisements are frequently broadcast on television asking the viewers if they have suffered an accident in the last three years. A report on the issue, *Better Routes to Redress*, was published in 2004. This recommended that stronger guidelines regarding appropriate advertisements needed to be issued, and that the claims management companies needed to be more carefully regulated. However, it did feel that these companies and advertisements should be allowed to continue, as they helped improve access to legal services by spreading information about the services available and the ways that these could be paid for. Claims management companies are now regulated following the passing of the Compensation Act 2006.

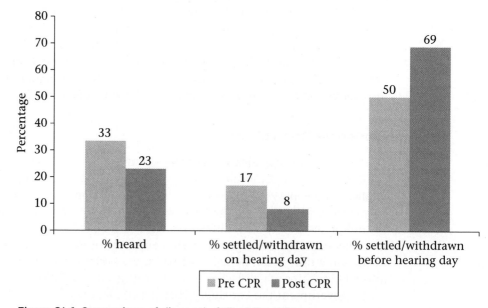

Figure 21.6 Comparison of disposal of 'Fast Track' cases

Source: 'Further Findings: a continuing evaluation of the Civil Justice Reforms', [Figure 6]. © Crown Copyright 2002.

The insurers, Norwich Union, have suggested a radical solution to the compensation culture, of abolishing all claims for under £1,000 (*A Modern Compensation System: moving from concept to reality* (2004)). The Law Society has rejected this suggestion, pointing out that denying people their right to seek compensation for claims under £1,000 would prevent the courts from getting to the root cause of injuries and falsely assumes that a loss of £1,000 is a trivial matter.

The Bar Council is concerned that plans to allow private companies to own law firms (see p. 193) would fuel the move towards a compensation culture, because such companies would seek to stimulate demand for legal services to increase profits. The legal sector could as a result become more commercialised with franchising, national brand-building and more television advertising.

Open to the public

There has been some controversy over whether the family courts are too secretive. This debate stems from the concern of fathers who feel that they have been treated unfairly by the courts. They have argued that the courts have been biased in favour of mothers when determining such issues as access to their children. Some fathers managed to get support for their cause in the media, but there were suggestions that, actually, the public were not able to get a full picture of the case because many of the court proceedings took place in private, so journalists might not be aware of good reasons why access to the father's children was being restricted, such as that he had been violent in the past. These issues raised the question of whether the public would have a better understanding of the court proceedings if they were open to the public. A balance needs to be achieved between the public's interest and the interests of the children in a case. This balance has been

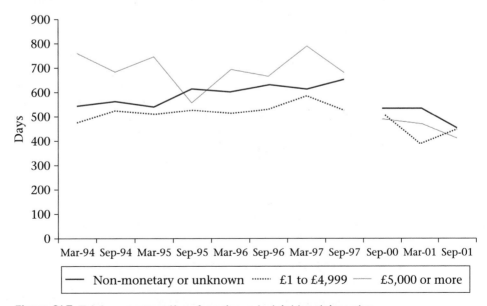

Figure 21.7 Trials – average time from issue to trial by claim value

Source: 'Further Findings: a continuing evaluation of the Civil Justice Reforms', [Figure 10]. © Crown Copyright 2002.

highlighted where children have been taken into care by social services when there has been a suspicion of abuse and the family have claimed their innocence. While the family are free to speak to the media and put their side of the case, the social services have an obligation to respect the privacy of the children and fear that the public are getting a very one-sided perspective of the case.

In the light of these debates, the government issued a consultation paper on whether the court privacy rules should be reformed. The paper is entitled *Confidence and Confidentiality: Improving Transparency and Privacy in Family Courts* (2006) and looks at how to find the delicate balance between the need for a transparent and open justice system while maintaining an individual's right to privacy.

Professor Zander's concern

Professor Zander (1998), a leading academic, felt that the reforms were fundamentally flawed, rather than prone to temporary hiccups, and was very vociferous in expressing his opposition to the reforms prior to their implementation. He is reported to have said that they amounted to taking a sledgehammer to crack a nut. Below is an analysis of the main concerns he has expressed.

Task 21.8

Visit a county court. You can find the address of a local county court by looking in a telephone directory. Alternatively, you can find the addresses of county courts on the court service website at:

www.courtservice.gov.uk/notices/county/ccadd/circuits.htm

Write up a report of your visit by answering the following questions:

About the court

1 What was the name and address of the court?
2 What was the court building like? Was it old or modern? Was it clean and in good decorative order? Were the waiting areas comfortable? Was there access to refreshments? Was it easy to find your way around the building, with rooms clearly signposted and labelled?
3 Did you find the court staff helpful? Were there any explanatory leaflets available?

About the proceedings

Take one of the cases that you watched and answer the following questions:

1 Was the judge male or female and what was their approximate age? What did the judge wear? Was he or she polite to the parties?
2 Were the parties represented by a lawyer?
3 What was the case about?
4 Did any witnesses give evidence?
5 If you heard the whole case, what was its outcome?
6 Did you think that the court came to the right decision?

Use the material you have gathered to prepare an oral presentation about your visit for your fellow students.

Case management

Zander feels that court management is appropriate in only a minority of cases and that the key is to identify these. He has remarked that judges do not have the time, skills or inclination to undertake the task of case management. The court does not know enough about the workings of a solicitor's office to be able to set appropriate timetables. In addition, litigants on the fast track may feel that the brisk way in which a three-hour hearing deals with the dispute is inadequate. Most will feel that justice has not been done by a short, sharp trial with restricted oral evidence and an interventionist judge chivvying the parties to a resolution of their dispute.

A move towards judicial management has already been seen in America, Australia and Canada. A major official study was published by the Institute of Civil Justice at the Rand Corporation in California (Kakalik, 1996). This research was not available to Lord Woolf while he was compiling his report. The study was based on a five-year survey of 10,000 cases looking at the effect of the US Civil Justice Reform Act 1990. This Act required certain federal courts to practise case management. Judicial case management has been part of the American system for many years so that, compared with this country, the procedural innovations being studied operated from a different starting point.

The study found that judicial case management did lead to a reduced time to disposition. Its early use yielded a reduction of one and a half or two months to resolution for cases that lasted at least nine months. Also, having a discovery timetable and reducing the time within which discovery took place significantly reduced both the time to disposition and the number of hours spent on the case by a lawyer. These benefits were achieved without any substantial change in the lawyers' or litigants' satisfaction or views of fairness.

On the other hand, case management led to an approximate 20-hour increase in lawyers' work hours overall. Their work increased with the need to respond to the court's management directions. In addition, once judicial case management had begun, a disclosure cut-off date had usually been established and lawyers felt an obligation to begin disclosure on a case which might be settled.

Thus, the Rand Report found that case management, by generating more work for lawyers, tended to increase rather than reduce costs. If the fixed costs did not reflect the extra cost, then this would be unjust to the lawyers and their clients. The danger is that case management will front-load costs on to cases which would have been settled anyway before reaching court, and which therefore did not need judicial management.

The Rand Report noted that the effectiveness of implementation depended on judicial attitudes. Some judges viewed these procedural innovations as an attack on judicial independence and felt that they emphasised speed and efficiency at the possible expense of justice. The report concluded, among other things, that judicial management should wait a month after the defence has been entered in case the action settles.

In the research carried out for the Law Society, *The Woolf Network Questionnaire* (2002), 84 per cent of solicitors questioned said they thought the new procedures were quicker and 70 per cent said they were more efficient than the old ones. Greater use of telephone case management conferences was cited as leading to greater efficiency.

Sanctions

Procedural timetables for the fast track are, according to Professor Zander, doomed to failure because a huge proportion of solicitors, for a range of reasons, will fail to keep to the prescribed timetables. This will necessitate enforcement procedures and sanctions on a vast scale which, in turn, will lead to innumerable appeals. Sanctions will be imposed that are disproportionate and therefore unjust, and will cause injustice to clients for the failings of the lawyers. Furthermore, if the judges did impose severe sanctions when lawyers failed to comply with timetable deadlines, it would usually be the litigants rather than the lawyers who would be penalised.

Professor Zander has pointed to the courts' experience of Order 17 under the old County Court Rules as evidence that lawyers are not good at time limits, and sanctions were unlikely to change that. Under that order, an action would be automatically struck out if the claimant failed to take certain steps within the time limits set by the rule. From its introduction in 1990 until 1998, roughly 20,000 cases had been struck out on this basis leaving 20,000 people either to sue their lawyers for negligence or to start all over again. In relation to Order 17, the Court of Appeal stated in **Bannister v SGB plc** (1997):

> 'This rule has given rise to great difficulties and has generated an immense amount of litigation devoted to the question whether a particular action has been struck out and if so, whether it should be reinstated. In short, the rule has in a large number of cases achieved the opposite of its object, which was to speed up the litigation process in the county courts.'

There is the danger that, if a court does not exercise its power temperately and judiciously, then in its eagerness to dispose of litigation it will actually generate more litigation. This danger is particularly acute where a court exercises powers on its own initiative. If, for example, a court moves to strike out a statement of case on its own initiative, the likely result is that the party affected will apply to have its case reinstated; and if, in fact, it was not a suitable case for striking out, unnecessary cost and delay will be the result.

There is a risk that unrealistic trial dates and timetables will be set, particularly in heavy litigation, at an early stage, and of the judges insisting on their being adhered to thereafter, regardless of the consequences.

In research carried out for the Law Society, *The Woolf Network Questionnaire* (2002), some solicitors said they were reluctant to apply for sanctions against those who did not stick to the pre-action protocols. This was because they felt that the courts were unwilling to impose sanctions for non-compliance in all but the most serious cases, judges were inconsistent in their approach to sanctions and an application for sanctions was likely to cause more delays and additional costs.

Costs

Litigation can be very costly and state funding is often not available (see Chapter 12). Research carried out for the Law Society, *The Woolf Network Questionnaire* (2002), suggests that the cost of engaging in civil litigation has not been reduced by the civil justice reforms. In many cases, especially those involving personal injury, the defendant's costs, and sometimes those of the claimant, will be paid by an insurance company – for example, the parties in a car accident are likely to have been insured and professionals such as doctors are insured against negligence claims. As Hazel Genn's 1987 study showed, where only one party is insured, this can place great pressure on the other, unless the other has been granted state funding. The insured side may try to drag out the proceedings for as long as possible, in the hope of exhausting the other party's financial reserves and forcing a low settlement.

Professor Zander has argued that in many civil cases the claimant wins and the defendant is an insurance company, which currently pays the claimant's costs. If, in future, the court can only order the loser to pay fixed and fairly low costs, then the claimant's lawyers will not be able to claim back everything that it was in fact necessary to spend on the case in order to win. He predicts that, as a result, either the work will not be done or the client will have to pay for it out of their damages. Either way, justice will not have been served.

Quick quiz 21.9

1 Name the three tracks for the purposes of case management.

2 If you wish to bring an action for compensation following a disastrous package holiday, claiming £4,000 compensation, to which track would your case be allocated?

3 What is meant by a 'compensation culture'?

4 Did the Rand Report into case management find that it tended to increase or reduce costs?

Reading on the web

The research, *Emerging Findings: An Early Evaluation of the Civil Justice Reforms* (2001), is available on the Lord Chancellor's website at:

www.dca.gov.uk/civil/emerge/emerge.htm

Lord Woolf's final report, *Access to Justice*, is available on the website of the Lord Chancellor's Department at:

www.dca.gov.uk/civil/final/index.htm

The website for Money Claim Online can be found at:

www.moneyclaim.gov.uk/csmc02/index.jsp

A useful source of information about court matters is the Court Service Annual Report:

www.courtservice.gov.uk

The research, *The Management of Civil Cases: The Courts and the Post-Woolf Landscape* (2005) is available, on the Department for Constitutional Affairs' website at:

www.dca.gov.uk/research/2005/9_2005_full.pdf

The report of the Civil Justice Council, *Improved Access to Justice - Funding Options and Proportionate Costs* (2005), is available at:

www.costsdebate.civiljusticecouncil.gov.uk

The consultation paper, *Case track limits and the claims process for personal injury claims* (2007), is available on the website of the former Department for Constitutional Affairs at:

www.dca.gov.uk/consult/case-track-limits/cp0807.pdf

The consultation paper, *Confidence and Confidentiality: Improving Transparency and Privacy in Family Courts* (2006), is available on the website of the former Department for Constitutional Affairs at:

www.dca.gov.uk/consult/courttransparencey1106/consultation1106.pdf

Chapter summary

Civil or criminal?

The laws that have developed in the English legal system can be divided between civil and criminal laws and often separate courts are responsible for civil and criminal matters.

The civil justice system

The civil justice system is designed to sort out disputes between individuals or organisations. The burden of proof is usually on the claimant, who must prove his or her case on a balance of probabilities. Major reforms were introduced following Lord Woolf's report, *Access to Justice*, which was published in 1996.

The civil courts

There are two main civil courts which hear civil cases at first instance. These are the county courts and the High Court. The county courts hear the cases where less money is involved, whereas the High Court hears the bigger financial cases.

Dealing with cases 'justly'

The first rule of the new Civil Procedure Rules lays down an overriding objective which is to underpin the whole system. This overriding objective is that the rules should enable the courts to deal with cases 'justly'.

Civil procedure

Almost all proceedings start with the same document, called a claim form. If the defendant files a defence, the court will serve an allocation questionnaire on each party. This is designed to enable the court to allocate each claim to one of the three tracks. For non-personal injury actions, a claim may be started in the High

Court where the claimant expects to recover more than £15,000. For personal injury actions a claim can be started in the High Court only where the claimant expects to recover at least £50,000.

Pre-action protocols

To push the parties into behaving reasonably during the pre-trial stage pre-action protocols have been developed. These lay down a code of conduct for this stage of proceedings.

Alternative dispute resolution

At various stages in a dispute's history, the court will actively promote settlement by alternative dispute resolution (ADR).

Case management

Case management has been introduced, whereby the court plays an active role in managing the litigation. To determine the level and form of case management cases have been divided into three types:

- small claims track;
- fast track; and
- multi-track.

Sanctions

The courts now have tough powers to enforce the new rules on civil procedure to ensure that litigation is pursued diligently.

Money Claim Online

In 2002 Money Claim Online (MCOL) was established. It provides a debt recovery service over the internet for sums up to £100,000.

Problems with the civil court system

The high number of out-of-court settlements creates injustice, because the parties usually hold very unequal bargaining positions. The small claims procedure is quicker, simpler and cheaper than the full county court process, but the Consumer's Association is of the view that the small claims procedure is not simple enough. In 2007 the government announced that it no longer intended to raise the small claims limit to £5,000 because this would not be in the interests of consumers. There has been some concern that the UK might be developing a compensation culture, which has historically been associated with the US.

Professor Zander has been a vociferous critic of Lord Woolf's reforms, suggesting that they would not succeed in reducing delays and expense.

Question and answer guide

For exam questions covering the material in this chapter, please see the Question and answer guides section of Chapter 22: Compensatory damages.

Group activity 1

■ Divide your friends (or class) into groups of two or three people.
■ Each group should choose a claims management firm ('CMF') operating in England and Wales. If you do not already know of one, look in the telephone directory or on the internet. (A complete list of all authorised CMFs can be found on the website www.claimsregulation.gov.uk, which is maintained by the Ministry of Justice.)
■ Starting from the firm's website, prepare a profile of your chosen CMF, focusing on its size and location, the services that it offers and its terms of business. Ask yourself, 'Is it clear to me how this CMF makes its money?'
■ Once you have prepared your profile, meet with the other groups to compare notes, looking for any common themes.

Group activity 2

Imagine you bought a pair of boots for £100 which fell apart the second time you wore them. You took them back to the shop and was told you should not have worn them in the rain so there is no refund or repair possible.

Having received no response to your letter of complaint to the shop, you have decided to make a legal claim for the ruined boots on the grounds that they were 'not fit for purpose' under the Sale of Goods Act 1979. Working in groups, look at how you could go about making a small claim in a civil court. Print off a claim form and complete it with details of your claim. You will find the form you need on the following website:

www.hmcourts-service.gov.uk/courtfinder/forms/n1_0102.pdf32+/76

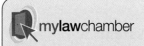

Visit **www.mylawchamber.co.uk/elliottqa** to access interactive questions, quizzes and activities to test yourself on this chapter.

Chapter 22

Compensatory damages

This chapter discusses:

- the financial remedy of damages where a tort has been committed;
- compensation for pecuniary losses, including pre-trial expenses and loss of earnings;
- compensation for non-pecuniary losses, including physical injury, pain and suffering;
- deductions from an award of damages to prevent a person being better off as a result of the injury (known as a set-off).

A person who is the victim of a tort may seek a remedy from the courts. The principal remedy awarded by a court for a tortious wrong is damages. Damages aim to compensate the claimant financially for the tort they have suffered.

Damages

In the vast majority of cases where damages are claimed they are what is known as compensatory. The principle behind compensatory damages is that they should put the claimant in the position they would have been in if the tort had never been committed. An award of compensatory damages may be composed of either general or special damages, or both. General damages are designed to compensate for the kinds of damages which the law presumes to be a result of the tort, such as pain and suffering from a personal injury, and loss of future earnings where the claimant's injuries mean that he or she cannot return to a previous employment or cannot work at all. Obviously, the amount of such damages cannot be calculated precisely, but the courts use the awards given for similar injuries in the past as a guideline.

Special damages are those which do not arise naturally from the wrong complained of, and must be specifically listed in pleadings, and proved in court. They generally cover the claimant's financial loss up until the date of trial, and any expenses incurred up to that point, and are therefore susceptible of more exact calculation.

453

Compensatory damages

The principle of restoring the claimant to the position they would have held if the tort had not been committed is called *restitutio in integrum*. There are essentially two different sorts of losses: pecuniary, which simply means financial, and non-pecuniary, which means losses other than those of money. Examples of pecuniary losses would be loss of earnings as a result of an injury, or a house being worth less than you paid for it because your surveyor negligently failed to spot defects in it. Non-pecuniary losses include pain and suffering after an injury, and what is called loss of amenity (see p. 465). They are usually seen in connection with personal injury cases, and rarely arise in cases concerning money or property, but in **Farley *v* Skinner (No. 2)** (2001), damages were given for non-pecuniary losses. The claimant had asked the defendant, a surveyor, to prepare a report on a home he was thinking of buying. Because of where the house was, the claimant was worried that it might be affected by aircraft noise, and he specifically asked the surveyor to check this out. The surveyor negligently reported that it was very unlikely that aircraft noise would be a problem. The claimant bought the house, spent a lot of money on doing it up, then moved in – and discovered that in fact there was a very severe problem with aircraft noise. He decided not to move, but claimed damages from the surveyor.

The House of Lords held that the whole purpose of the claimant in choosing the house had been to buy a place where he could enjoy peace and quiet, and if the surveyor had reported correctly, he would not have bought it. That being the case, the claimant was awarded £10,000 damages.

Calculating the loss

Pecuniary damages are clearly easier to calculate than non-pecuniary ones, since the claimant's loss can be measured in money. Even so, there are cases where the loss is purely financial, but the issue of what will amount to *restitutio in integrum* is not straightforward. In **Gardner *v* Marsh & Parsons** (1997), the claimants had bought a leasehold flat after having it surveyed by the defendants. The surveyor was negligent, failing to discover a serious structural defect, which did not come to light for three years. The lease contained a clause making the freeholder respons-ible for structural repairs, and the freeholder eventually repaired the defect, but not until two years later. The claimants sued the surveyors for negligence, claim-ing the difference between the price they paid, and the lower market value of the flat with the defect, but the surveyors claimed that no damages were required since the defect had been repaired, albeit not by them, and there was no loss.

The Court of Appeal disagreed, stating that loss could not be avoided by the claimant's own actions, unless those actions flowed from the original transaction between the parties, and were really part of a continuous course of dealing arising from it. In this case the claimants were only able to put right the problem because they had a contract with the freeholder, and even then they had had to go to the trouble of hassling the freeholder to do the repairs; they had also waited a long time for them to be done, during which time they could not sell the flat. The means by which they solved the problem were too remote to be taken into account when deciding the defendants' liability.

In **South Australia Asset Management Corporation** *v* **York Montague Ltd** (1997), the House of Lords heard three appeals, each arising from similar facts: the defendants had each negligently valued a property, and the claimants lent money for the purchase of the property on the strength of those valuations. Soon afterwards, property prices dropped, and the borrowers in each case defaulted on the loan, leaving the lenders with a property worth less than the money they were owed on it. Each of the lenders gave evidence that they would not have granted the loans if they had known the true value of the property, and claimed that therefore their damages should include the loss that they had made through the general drop in property prices, since if they had not made the loan, they would not have made that loss either. For our purposes, the details of one of the cases is sufficient: here the lenders lent £1.75 million on a property that was valued at £2.5 million, but was actually worth £1.8 million. By the time the property market had dropped, it was worth only £950,000.

The Court of Appeal analysed the cases on the basis of whether the loans would have been granted if the true valuations had been known, and said that where the lenders would not have gone ahead with the loans had it not been for the negligent valuation, the lenders were entitled to recover the difference between the sum lent, and the sum recovered when the property was sold, together with a reasonable rate of interest, so that they would be compensated for the drop in market prices. Where a lender would still have gone ahead with the loan even if the correct valuation had been given, but lent a smaller sum, they would only be able to recover the difference between what they actually lost and what they would have lost had they lent a lesser amount; any fall in the market could not be compensated.

The House of Lords rejected this argument. Their Lordships said that in order to calculate damages for breach of a duty of care, it was first necessary to determine exactly what the duty consisted of; a defendant would only be liable for consequences arising from negligent performance of that duty. In this case, the defendants did not have a duty to advise the claimants whether or not to make the loan; their duty was to inform the claimants of the value of the property offered as security, and so their liability was limited to the consequences of that advice being wrong, and not to the entire consequences of the loan being made. The consequence of the advice being wrong was that the claimants had less security for the debt than they thought, and that loss should be compensated; in the case detailed above, the correct figure would be £700,000. This would give the claimants the amount of security they thought they had at the time the loan was made, but would not compensate for the drop in property prices, since this was not a consequence of the negligent valuation, but would have happened anyway. If the defendants had had a duty to advise the claimants whether or not to make the loan, they would have been liable for all losses arising from the fact that the loan was made, including the drop in property prices, but here their duty did not extend that far so their liability could not either.

In a case with similar facts, **Platform Home Loans Ltd** *v* **Oyston Shipways Ltd** (2000), the House of Lords held that where part of the loss was due to the claimants' own negligence in making the loans in the first place without adequately assessing the borrowers' ability to repay it, the damages could be reduced for contributory negligence.

The main difficulty with applying the principle established in **South Australia** is how the courts identify the duty that was owed. Sometimes this will be obvious, but the case of **Aneco Reinsurance Underwriting Ltd** *v* **Johnson and Higgins** (2001) illustrates how complex this question can be. The case concerned a practice common in the insurance industry, called reinsurance. Where an insurer gives cover for a particular risk, they will often seek to protect themselves by reinsuring the same risk, or part of it, with another insurer, so that if the worst happens and the client claims on the insurance, the insurer will get some of their money back by claiming on their reinsurance. The claimants, Aneco, had been asked to provide insurance for a company we will call B. They were happy to do so, but wanted to reinsure part of the risk, and asked the defendants to arrange this for them. Believing this to have been done, they went ahead and issued the policy to B. B later claimed £35 million on the policy, and Aneco then sought to recover some of this under their reinsurance: the policy they believed had been arranged would have given them £11 million. In fact there was no reinsurance cover, because of the defendants' negligence.

The question then arose of how much they could claim in damages. The defendants claimed that, under the principle established in **South Australia**, their duty to Aneco was to ensure that, if B claimed on their insurance policy, Aneco could reduce their own losses by £11 million, by claiming on the reinsurance. They therefore maintained that the damages owed would be £11 million. Aneco, however, sought to claim the whole £35 million. Their reasoning was that when a company seeks reinsurance, they are not just looking for actual cover, but for an impression of how the insurance industry sees the risk in question; if it proves impossible to get reinsurance for a certain risk, it is very probably unwise to offer insurance for it yourself. They argued that, had Johnson and Higgins taken reasonable steps to arrange the reinsurance cover, they would have discovered that no one was willing to provide it, and had they told Aneco that it was proving impossible to reinsure the risk, Aneco themselves would not have gone ahead with the insurance policy, and would never have had to pay out £35 million.

The House of Lords agreed with Aneco, stating that, in agreeing to arrange reinsurance, the defendants owed Aneco a duty to advise on the availability of such cover, and in failing to do so they had breached that duty, and were liable to pay the full £35 million. Unfortunately, the House of Lords did not give any guidance as to quite how the extent or content of a duty is to be decided, which makes it very difficult to predict how the principle will be applied in future cases.

Preventing over-compensation

The fact that compensatory damages are designed to put the claimant in the position they would have enjoyed had the tort not happened does not just mean they should not end up worse off as a result of the tort; it also means that they should not end up better off than they would otherwise have been. In **Southampton Container Terminals Ltd** *v* **Schiffarts-Gesellschaft Hansa Australia MBH & Co.** (2001), the defendants' ship collided with the quayside in Southampton and destroyed the claimants' crane. The defendants admitted liability and the judge awarded the claimants the amount which the crane would have been worth if the claimants had sold it. The claimants appealed, arguing that the principle of *restitutio in integrum* meant they were entitled to the much higher cost of replacing the crane, including transport and installation costs. However, the Court of Appeal found that there was no evidence that the claimants had actually intended to replace the crane, and that its loss had caused inconvenience, but no serious financial loss. The court said that the overriding principle had to be that damages should be reasonable between the parties, and in this case allowing the appeal would result in compensation that was out of all proportion to the loss.

Similarly, although the courts will order compensation for special expenses which the claimant has reasonably incurred as a result of the tort, they will not compensate for expenses which he or she would have faced anyway.

In **Patel *v* Hooper & Jackson** (1999), the Court of Appeal allowed the buyer of a residential property, who was unable to live in it as a result of a negligent survey, to claim the cost of alternative accommodation up until such time as the house could reasonably be expected to have been sold, as well as the difference between the true value of the house and the price paid as a result of the negligent survey. The court held that, in the circumstances, the cost of alternative accommodation was part of the reasonable cost of the buyer extricating himself from the purchase.

Where loss is non-pecuniary (such as pain and suffering), *restitutio in integrum* is even more difficult, and the general aim is to provide fair and reasonable compensation for the damage done, taking into account all the circumstances. In each case, the exact calculation of damages is a question of fact, and the judge has discretion over whether to allow counsel to refer to decisions in previous similar cases. In practice, such references are frequent.

An (admittedly extreme) example of the difficult questions that can be faced in deciding just how to compensate for a non-pecuniary loss can be seen in **Briody *v* St Helen's and Knowsley Area Health Authority** (2001). Medical negligence by the defendant's employee had left the claimant unable to get pregnant naturally. Awards to cover infertility treatment such as *in vitro* fertilisation (IVF) had been made in previous cases, but the claimant's condition was such that she could not be helped by such treatments, so she sought damages to cover the cost of a surrogacy procedure, in which an embryo created from the claimant's egg and her partner's sperm would be implanted into a surrogate mother. The agreement arranging this procedure was illegal in England, and was to be carried out in America, though there was evidence that the chances of it working were very small. An alternative option was a procedure that was legal in England, but involved using donor eggs from another woman, rather than the claimant's own; this was said to have a slightly higher chance of success.

The Court of Appeal ruled that damages could not be awarded to cover either option. They agreed that, for a woman who wanted children, being deprived of the chance to have them was a very serious loss of amenity, which entitled the claimant to damages for that loss, over and above the pain and suffering arising from her injuries. However, they said that because there was such a slim chance of the first procedure working, it was very different from a claim for IVF treatment, which would usually offer a reasonable chance of success. It was not reasonable to expect the defendant to pay the costs of a treatment which was in fact very unlikely to compensate the claimant's loss. As for the second procedure, since this would not, even if it worked, produce a child that was biologically the claimant's own, the court said that it would not represent *restitutio in integrum*, and would in fact be little different from adoption. This seems rather odd reasoning, given that the claimant herself clearly viewed a baby from a donor egg as some compensation for the inability to have her own child.

Mitigation

A person who falls victim to a tort is expected to take reasonable steps to mitigate any loss; the defendant will not be liable for compensatory damages in respect of any losses that could have been prevented by such steps. However, since the situation is the fault of the defendant, not the claimant, the standard of reasonableness is not particularly high, and the claimant is certainly not required to make huge efforts to avoid a loss that is the defendant's fault.

In **Emeh *v* Kensington Area Health Authority** (1985), the claimant underwent a sterilisation operation carried out by the defendants' employees, but afterwards became pregnant. The defendants rather bizarrely argued that she could have mitigated her financial loss by having an abortion, thereby saving the cost of bringing up the child. Rejecting this argument, the court accepted that in the circumstances it was reasonable to refuse to have an abortion.

In **Ronan *v* Sainsbury's Supermarkets Ltd** (2006), the claimant was injured while working for Sainsbury's, at the age of 19, and had to have a number of operations as a result of his injuries. He started a career in banking, and was doing well, but still needed further surgery. Eventually, his injury began to cause more problems, which surgery was unable to solve, and this caused depression, leading him to leave his job. He decided to have a change of career, and went to university. There was evidence that, about a year later, his health improved to the extent that he could have gone back to his old career. His case against Sainsbury's came to court after he had finished university, and as part of his compensatory damages the court included a sum to cover loss of earnings for the three years at university. Sainsbury's argued that this money should not have been included, because the claimant should have mitigated his loss by giving up his studies and going back to his old job once his health allowed it. The court disagreed: the decision to change careers had been a direct result of the injuries caused by the accident, and once Mr Ronan had started his course it was unreasonable to expect him to leave it.

Compensation for personal injury

Damages for personal injury (which covers physical or psychiatric harm, disease and illness) raise problems not encountered with other types of loss. In the case of damage to property, for example, financial compensation is both easy to calculate, and an adequate way of making good the loss, by allowing the claimant to buy a replacement or pay for repairs. It is not so easy to calculate the value of a lost limb or permanent loss of general good health, and even if it were, money can never really compensate for such losses. In addition, the court may be required to estimate the amount of future earnings which will be lost, and the future development of the injury; even though personal injury cases may take years to come to trial, the degree of recovery to be expected may still be unclear, and new symptoms may not appear until years later.

Damages for personal injury are divided into pecuniary and non-pecuniary losses. Pecuniary damages are those which can be calculated in financial terms, such as loss of earnings, and medical and other expenses, while non-pecuniary damages cover damages that are less easy to calculate, such as loss of physical amenity, pain, shock and suffering. Within these two broad categories, the courts have defined the following 'heads of damage'.

Pecuniary losses

Pre-trial expenses

The claimant is entitled to recover all expenses actually and reasonably incurred as a result of the accident up to the date of the trial. This includes, for example, loss of, or damage to, clothing and any medical expenses.

Expenses incurred by another

In some cases the claimant will have had to be looked after by a friend or relative. Such carers cannot bring an action themselves directly against the defendant to seek compensation. But in **Donnelly v Joyce** (1972) the Court of Appeal recognised that the claimant could normally claim for this loss as part of his or her own claim. In that case the claimant was a child and his mother had to give up work to look after him when he was seriously injured by the defendant's negligence. The claimant succeeded in claiming for the financial loss that his mother had suffered as a result of caring for him.

This principle was extended to cover a slightly more complicated situation in **Lowe v Guise** (2002). Here, the claimant had been acting as a carer to his disabled brother, for around 77 hours a week. After being injured as a result of the defendant's negligence, he was only able to help his brother for around half that time, and their mother had to take over for the remainder of the time. There was no financial loss as a result of this arrangement, but Mr Lowe nevertheless claimed the value of the services provided to his brother by his mother as part of the amount required to compensate him for his injuries. The court agreed, holding that the help he had been giving his brother was not just a favour, it was a serious responsibility owed by him to his family. Loss of part of it was therefore the loss of something of real value to himself and to his family's welfare, and should be compensated.

The House of Lords decided in **Hunt v Severs** (1994) that any damages received under this head are awarded to the claimant to compensate the carer and not the claimant. When the claimant received this award, he or she should hand the money over to the carer and until he or she did so the money was held under an obligation to do so, known as being held on trust. On this point the House of

Lords reversed **Donnelly v Joyce**, which had viewed such an award as being to compensate the claimant's loss and therefore placing him or her under no legal obligation to hand it over to the carer.

In **Hunt v Severs** the claimant was the defendant's girlfriend. She was riding on the back of his motorbike when they had an accident and she was seriously injured. On leaving the hospital, she started to live with the defendant and they married three years later. At the trial the defendant admitted liability. The claimant claimed £77,000 as the value of the care that the defendant had given her and would give her in future. The trial judge had awarded this amount but the appeal was allowed by the House of Lords, because once it was accepted that the award was made to compensate the carer, it made no sense to make such an award if the carer was also the defendant, for he would be merely making a payment to himself. The fact that in reality it is not the defendant's money but the insurance company's money is traditionally ignored by the court.

This conclusion runs counter to the approach preferred by the Pearson Commission (see p. 470), which argued that damages should be the absolute property of the claimant. The Commission pointed out that any duty to hand some of it over to someone else, such as a carer, would be extremely difficult to supervise. It might also constitute an incentive for members of a family not to help each other but to employ people from outside the family to care for their relations.

Where a spouse provides services in a business context, the courts have decided that there must be an actual loss before the claimant can claim for the cost of the services. In **Hardwick v Hudson** (1999), the claimant was injured in a car accident. He was a partner in a garage business, and while he was recovering, his wife took over his role at work, without being paid. The claimant argued that this was comparable to carer services supplied free by a relative, but the Court of Appeal disagreed. The claimant's wife was supplying services which the business would otherwise have had to pay for, and in doing that, she could be seen as providing a benefit to the business and actually preventing the claimant from suffering the loss he would have done if he had paid someone to do the work. In fact, the couple would have been better off if the wife had been properly employed and paid by the business, under an express or implied contract, as then there would have been a loss and, the court said, the claimant could have sought to recover this from the defendant.

The same principle applies to other benefits provided by third parties. In **Dimond v Lovell** (2000), the claimant was involved in an accident for which the defendant was responsible and, as a result, she had to hire a car. Due to irregularities with the hire contract, it was held to be unenforceable and she ended up not having to pay the hire charges, but she attempted to claim them from the defendant anyway, on the basis that she had had to hire the car because of his negligence. The court compared the situation to that in cases where care was provided free by, for example, a partner, as in **Hunt v Severs**, and held that the same rule applied. Where claimants have received services from a third party at no cost to themselves, the court can award damages to be held in trust for that third party – but where it is not possible to impose a trust for the third party, the damages cannot be awarded to claimants instead. In this case, imposing a trust for the benefit of the car-hire company would have amounted to enforcing an unenforceable contract, and the court could not impose a trust for this purpose.

Pre-trial loss of earnings

The claimant can receive damages for the loss of the earnings or profits which would otherwise have been earned up to the date of the judgment. The amount awarded will be that which the claimant would actually have taken home, after tax and National Insurance contributions have been deducted. Both pre-trial expenses and pre-trial loss of earnings are considered to be special damages.

Future loss of earnings

Claims for future pecuniary loss almost always comprise loss of future earnings, and are regarded as general damages. Obviously they are difficult to calculate, since there is no real way of knowing what the future would have held for the claimant if the accident had not happened.

Damages are usually awarded as a lump sum, but clearly the purpose of damages for loss of future earnings due to personal injury is usually to give the claimant an income to replace the one he or she would have had if the injury had not happened. The courts therefore calculate a figure which, given as a lump sum, would be sufficient to buy an investment called an annuity that would give the claimant the right level of income for life, or however long the effects of the injury were expected to last (an annuity is an arrangement under which a lump sum is invested so as to produce an income).

The starting point for calculating future loss of earnings is the difference between income before the accident and afterwards, which is called the net annual loss. Obviously in some cases the claimant may be so badly injured that no income can be earned, but the principle also covers those who can work, but at less highly paid employment than before. Predicting future earnings can be a matter of guesswork, as the case of **Doyle v Wallace** (1998) shows. In this case the claimant was badly injured in a road accident and was unable to work. She had been planning to train as a drama teacher if she could get the necessary qualifications and, if not, she planned to get a clerical job. Her income would have been substantially higher as a teacher than as a clerk but, at the time of the accident, it was too early to know whether she would have obtained the necessary qualifications. The trial judge found that she had a 50 per cent chance of qualifying as a drama teacher, and calculated the damages for loss of future earnings on the basis of an income that was halfway between that of a drama teacher and that of a clerical worker. The Court of Appeal upheld this approach.

Similarly, in **Skipper v Calderdale Metropolitan Borough Council** (2006), the Court of Appeal held that it was at least arguable that a claimant could win compensation for damages to her employment prospects, based on the argument that if her dyslexia had been diagnosed at school she would have achieved better exam results and had a better-paid career, though in this case they believed the loss was likely to be small.

Another example of the kind of complications courts can face in 'loss of a chance' cases can be seen in **Langford v Hebran** (2001). Here, the claimant, then 27, had just started training to be a bricklayer, but was also a competitive kickboxer, and had recently won his first (and only) professional fight. After being injured in a car accident caused by the defendant's negligence, he was no longer able to do his job, or his sport, to the same standard. He claimed that, had he not been injured, he would have gone on to become a champion kickboxer, which meant that the court had to assess just how far the claimant was likely to go in his sport. The Court of Appeal, with the help of expert evidence, found that there were four possible levels of success which the claimant could have reached, ranging from holding one national title, to becoming world champion. They then had to assess the chances of him reaching each stage, and decide what that would have been worth to him financially.

The loss of a chance approach is generally used in cases where there is a fairly high degree of uncertainty as to whether the claimant's financial prospects would have improved if the accident had not happened; where it is fairly obvious that they would have improved, there is no need for loss of a chance calculations. In **Herring** *v* **Ministry of Defence** (2004), a part-time soldier was badly injured during a parachute jump. He had intended to apply to join the police force, and therefore claimed damages for loss of future earnings on the basis of the typical police officer's salary. The defendants argued that, as it was not clear whether he would have been accepted into the police force, the claim should be assessed on the basis of loss of a chance, but the Court of Appeal disagreed. On the evidence, it was clear that even if the claimant had not got into the police force, he would have got a job with similar earning power. His damages could therefore be calculated on the basis of a police officer's salary, with a small reduction for what are called the 'vicissitudes of life' (see below).

Once the court has the net annual loss figure, it adjusts that sum to take into account factors which might have altered the claimant's original earnings, such as promotion prospects, and the figure that they reach as a result of doing so is called the multiplicand. The court then takes the number of years that the disability is likely to continue (which may be the rest of the claimant's life) and reduces this number by taking into account what are called the 'contingencies (or vicissitudes) of life' – basically, the fact that even if the accident had not happened, the claimant might not have lived or worked until retirement age.

At this stage, the court has before it the annual amount that will compensate the claimant, and the number of years for which this amount should be payable. However, simply to multiply the first figure by the second would actually over-compensate the claimant. If we take, for example, an annual loss of £10,000, to be payable over 20 years, simple multiplication of these figures gives us £200,000. But a claimant does not actually need a lump sum of £200,000 to produce an annual income of £10,000 over 20 years, because the assumption is that the lump sum is invested and so makes more money during the 20 years, with the result that the claimant would end up over-compensated. To avoid this, the court assumes that the investment will earn a particular rate of return (called the discount rate), and reduces the lump sum to one which, on the basis of the assumed rate of return, will provide the right rate of compensation, nothing more and nothing less. The figure arrived at is called the multiplier, and the multiplicand multiplied by the multiplier gives the sum necessary to compensate the claimant for loss of future earnings.

Within these calculations, the rate of return on investments that the court assumes is very important – the higher the assumed rate of return, the smaller the lump sum, and if for some reason the claimant in practice is unable to achieve this rate of return on their investments, they will be under-compensated.

Until recently, the courts generally assumed a rate of interest of 4–5 per cent per year. This practice was criticised by, among others, the Law Commission in its 1995 report *Structured Settlements and Interim and Provisional Damages* (Law Com No. 224). It said that the assumed rate of interest was an arbitrary figure; it was possible to achieve this rate of interest, but only with a relatively sophisticated understanding of investments which few claimants would possess, and so many claimants were likely to end up under-compensated. The Commission recommended that the courts should use as their guideline the return given to investors on a type of investment called an Index Linked Government Security (ILGS), which would give a more accurate picture of the kind of returns claimants could hope to get on their lump sums. The practical effect of this would be that multipliers would go up and so, as a result, would damages.

The Damages Act 1996 responded to this recommendation by providing that the Lord Chancellor can prescribe a rate of interest for the purposes of calculating multipliers, and in June 2001 the rate was set at 2.5 per cent. To appreciate how important the precise figure is, it might help to know that if we take, for example, a 20-year-old man who is awarded a multiplicand of £70,000, the difference between the damages paid with a discount rate of 2 per cent and the amount paid with one of 2.5 per cent would be £225,400.

The Damages Act provides, in s. 1(2), that a court may use a different discount rate 'if any party to the proceedings shows that it is more appropriate to the question'. An attempt to make use of this provision was made in **Warriner v Warriner** (2002). The claimant had suffered serious brain damage in a road accident and was claiming damages of over £2 million. His lawyers wanted to put forward expert evidence to show that a different discount rate should be used, because the amount claimed was large and the claimant's life expectancy was long; it was claimed that the effect of a 2.5 per cent discount rate in this situation would be to under-compensate the claimant. The Court of Appeal refused to hear the evidence, stating that this was not the kind of circumstance intended to be covered by s. 1(2).

They held that the Lord Chancellor had given very careful consideration to setting the discount rate, and that the certainty offered by a set rate was extremely important. This being the case, the court said that a case could only activate the discretion allowed in s. 1(2) if there was material that supported changing the rate of return, and the Lord Chancellor had not considered that material when setting the rate. That was not the case here: the Lord Chancellor had considered the problems raised by large sums intended to cover long periods and allowed for them when setting the rate; the set rate assumed a relatively low level of investment performance, and in practice, claimants could do better, with prudent investing, and so even out the problem of under-compensation.

In **Cooke v United Bristol Healthcare NHS Trust; Sheppard v Stibbe and another; Page v Lee** (2003), the Court of Appeal heard three similar cases in which the claimants had all been very severely injured and were likely to need care for the rest of their lives. They argued that, in their circumstances, using the conventional method of assessing damages with the discount rate would leave them substantially under-compensated, because although the discount rate took into account the effects of inflation, the costs of care were increasing at a much faster rate than that of inflation. Again, the Court of Appeal held that it was not possible to take evidence of this into account. Parliament had authorised the Lord Chancellor to set the rate; he had done so, taking inflation into account, and the courts had to respect that.

Non-pecuniary losses

These are losses which are not financial, although the courts can only compensate for them in a financial way. They do this by reference to guidelines produced by the Judicial Studies Board, based on awards in previous cases. The Law Commission's 1995 Report No. 225, *How Much is Enough?*, argued that compensation paid for these losses had fallen behind inflation and should be substantially increased. The Commission suggested that there was no real problem with the very smallest awards, those currently under £2,000, but that above that, claimants were being undercompensated.

In **Heil** *v* **Rankin** (2001), the House of Lords took the opportunity to look into this claim and agreed with the Law Commission that there was a problem. However, it was held that only those awards currently worth £10,000 or more needed adjustment, with the biggest problem being at the very top end of the scale, with the compensation for what the House of Lords called 'catastrophic injuries'. Where previously £150,000 had been regarded as the top level, this should be raised to £200,000; below that, there should be a tapering scale of increases down to awards of £10,000 or less, which would stay at current levels.

Non-pecuniary losses fall into the following heads of damage.

The primary injury

Damages for the actual injury are usually calculated with reference to a tariff, so that recognised values are placed on similar injuries. For example, minor or temporary eye injuries are 'worth' £1,000–£2,500, a broken leg £4,000–£7,000, lung disease £1,000–£65,000, and quadriplegia £160,000–£200,000. For most sorts of injuries, there is a broad range within which damages can fall, allowing courts to take into account factors such as the seriousness of the injury, and how long the effects are likely to last.

Pain and suffering

Damages will be awarded for any pain and suffering which results from the injury itself, or from medical treatment of that injury. The claim may cover pain which the claimant can expect to suffer in the future, and mental suffering arising from the knowledge that life expectancy has been shortened or that the ability to enjoy life has been reduced by disability resulting from the injury.

Where the injury has caused a period of unconsciousness, that period will be excluded from any claim for pain and suffering, as it is assumed that an unconscious person is unaware of pain.

Loss of amenity

Loss of amenity describes the situation where an injury results in the claimant being unable to enjoy life to the same extent as before. It may include an inability to enjoy sport or any other pastime the claimant enjoyed before the injury, impairment of sight, hearing, touch, taste or smell, reduction in the chance of finding a marriage partner, and impairment of sexual activity or enjoyment. Calculation of these damages is based on a tariff laid down by the Court of Appeal, though the tariff figure can be adjusted to take into account the claimant's individual circumstances.

Damages for loss of amenity are not affected by whether the claimant is actually aware of the loss, so unconscious claimants may claim damages as if they had not been unconscious. This was the case in **H West & Son** *v* **Shephard** (1964). The claimant was a married woman, who was 41 when she was injured. Serious head injuries left her at least partially unconscious, and paralysed in all four limbs. There was no hope of recovery, and her life expectancy was only five years. She was unable to speak, but there was evidence to suggest that she had some awareness of her circumstances. An award of £17,500 for loss of amenity was upheld by a majority in the House of Lords.

Quick quiz 22.1

1 How are compensatory damages calculated?

2 Give two examples of the types of things that can be compensated by pecuniary damages following personal injury caused by negligence.

3 If damages are awarded for 'loss of amenity', what are they compensating?

4 Will tort damages take into account psychiatric harm?

Alternative methods of payment

The standard method of paying damages is as a single lump sum, paid after the trial, but this can cause problems in certain cases. There are three alternative methods of payment each aiming to deal with a different problem:

- Interim awards.
- Periodical payments.
- Provisional damages.

Interim awards are designed to deal with the problems caused by the fact that personal injury cases can take years to come to trial, which often leaves claimants without financial help when they most need it. In situations where the defendant has admitted liability, but there is still a dispute about the level of damages, the Supreme Court Act 1981 allows the courts to award interim damages before the case comes to trial. This provision can only be used where the defendant is insured, is a public body, or has the resources to make an interim payment.

Periodical payments are made not as a one-off sum, but in the form of a series of regular payments for the whole of the claimant's life. This form of damages is particularly useful in cases where the claimant has a serious injury which will mean they need lifelong care, but which does not shorten their lifespan. In these cases, providing a lump sum means there is a risk that at some point the money will run out, whereas periodical payments continue throughout their life. Even in less serious cases, lump sums almost always either over- or under-compensate the claimant because, as we saw on p. 463, they rely on an assumption of their lifespan, which is unlikely ever to be completely accurate.

Until April 2005, courts could only order periodical payments with the consent of both parties, and because defendants tended not to like the idea of such long-term liability such settlements were used only in around 100 cases a year. However, ss. 100 and 101 of the Courts Act 2003, which amend s. 2 of the Damages Act 1996 and came into force in April 2005, now give the courts a duty to consider whether a case is suitable for periodical payments, and a power to order that damages should be paid this way, either wholly or partly. They can also order that damages for past losses are paid as periodical payments, with the parties' consent. The power was used in **Walton** *v* **Calderdale Healthcare NHS Trust** (2005), where the claimant was 19 years old, would need lifelong care, and had a life expectancy of 70 years.

Provisional damages are designed to address the problem that, in some personal injury cases, the long-term effect of the injuries may not be known at the time of the trial. The Supreme Court Act 1981 gives the courts power to award provisional damages. Where there is a possibility that the injured person will, as a result of the tort, develop a serious disease, or serious physical or mental deterioration in the future, the court can award initial damages based on the claimant's condition at the time of trial, but retain the power to award further damages if the possible future deterioration does in fact happen. The award can only be adjusted once.

Set-offs

As we have said, tort damages are generally calculated to put the claimant in the position they would have enjoyed if the tort had never been committed. They are not designed to put the claimant in a better position than if the tort had never been committed, and so the courts will generally take steps to make sure that any other money paid as a result of the injury will be deducted from the damages: this is known as a set-off. The following principles are followed.

Tax

Where a claimant is awarded damages for loss of earnings, the amount payable will be what the claimant would have earned after paying tax and National Insurance (**British Transport Commission** *v* **Gourley** (1956)).

Payments by an employer

Sick pay from an employer is taken into account in assessing damages, and damages are reduced accordingly. In **Hussain** *v* **New Taplow Paper Mills Ltd** (1988) the House of Lords stated that long-term sick pay from the employer according to the terms of the employment contract could be deducted, as such payments were the equivalent of receiving a salary.

Social security benefits

When the social security system was first set up, the Law Reform (Personal Injuries) Act 1948 provided that the value of certain social security benefits received by claimants should be deducted from the compensation payable to them, and as time went on, the courts extended this approach, so that all benefits were covered by the rule. This prevented claimants being double-compensated, but it meant that the social security system (and therefore the taxpayer) was in effect subsidising defendants. From the late 1980s, new legislation was enacted, which deducted the value of social security benefits from the compensation received, but gave it to the state, rather than back to the defendant.

The situation is now covered by the Social Security (Recovery of Benefits) Act 1997. This provides that the value of social security benefits received by the claimant during the five years immediately following the accident or until the making of the compensation payment (whichever is the earlier) should be deducted from the compensation ordered by the court, and paid back to the state.

The Act treats compensation as having three elements – loss of earnings, cost of care, and loss of mobility – and the value of benefits received can only be set off against the corresponding element in the damages award. This means, for example, that if a claimant who has received £7,000 in income support and £3,000 in attendance allowance is awarded £10,000 for loss of earnings and £2,000 for cost of care, they will end up with £3,000, because the scheme will not take the outstanding £1,000 in attendance allowance away from the sum awarded for loss of earnings. In addition, no part of the value of social security benefits can be deducted from damages awarded for pain and suffering. The previous legislation did not apply to awards of up to £2,500, but the 1997 Act brings such payments within the scheme.

Exceptions

Apparent exceptions to the rule that damages should not make a claimant better off than they would have been if the tort had not been committed are made in the case of disability pensions paid by a claimant's employers, insurance pay-outs and payments made on a charitable basis. Sometimes known as the 'benevolence exception', this was established in **Parry v Cleaver** (1970), where Lord Read explained the decision on the grounds that set-offs of these kinds of payments would discourage charity and sensible investment in insurance, and might allow tortfeasors to benefit.

The rule has been criticised by the Law Commission in its 1997 consultation paper *Damages for Personal Injury: Collateral Benefits*. The Commission argued that it over-compensates victims, which is both contrary to the aims of tort law, and a waste of resources. It doubted that anyone would be put off buying insurance by the prospect of set-offs, since people buy insurance against income loss generally, not just loss as a result of a tort, so they would still want the cover.

In **Longden v British Coal Corporation** (1998), the House of Lords ignored such criticisms. The claimant in the case had suffered an injury at work which meant he had to retire at 36. Under a scheme run by his employers, he became entitled to receive a disability pension from that point, instead of the ordinary pension he would have started receiving when he became 60. The defendants accepted that they could not set off the disability pension against the damages for loss of earnings, following **Parry** v **Cleaver**, but argued that the disability pension could be set off against the claimant's claim for loss of the pension he would have started receiving at 60. The House of Lords held that the amounts he would receive from the disability pension after he reached 60 could be set off against the claim for loss of the normal pension, but the payments he received before he was 60 could not.

However, in **Gaca** v **Pirelli** (2004), the Court of Appeal said that the rule could not apply to pay-outs from insurance policies which had been paid for by the injured person's employer. Mr Gaca had been injured at work, and had received £122,000 from a group insurance scheme paid for by his employers, which covered employees who were disabled at work. Employees were not required to pay for the insurance cover. When Mr Gaca successfully sued his employers for causing his injuries, they sought to deduct the insurance pay-out from his damages. The Court of Appeal held that they could do so. The situation did not fall within the 'benevolence exception' because allowing the deduction did not discourage benevolence; in fact, failing to allow it might well discourage companies from making such payments to injured employees.

Benefits provided by the tortfeasor

In **Hunt** v **Severs** (1994), the claimant was very seriously injured in a car accident caused by her fiancé, whom she went on to marry. She sued him (which may seem odd, but bear in mind it would actually be his insurance company that stood to pay damages), and the issue arose of whether she could claim the cost of care that had been provided by him, and would continue to be given by him in the future. There is usually no problem with compensating the cost of care, even if that care is provided by a relative and so not actually paid for, but in this case the House of Lords held that such compensation could not be awarded, because it would amount to double compensation, just as if the defendant had, for example, given the claimant a wheelchair and then been asked to pay compensation for the cost of it.

 Quick quiz 25.2

1 When are provisional damages awarded?

2 When are interim damages awarded?

3 Can the courts order compensation to be paid as a structured settlement?

4 Give two examples of money that will be deducted from a person's award of damages.

Fatal accidents

When a claimant dies as a result of a tort, the claim he or she would have had against the tortfeasor passes to that person's estate, meaning that it becomes part of what is inherited as a result of the death. Whoever inherits the estate can recover the losses that the claimant would have claimed for the period between the injury and the death, provided that it is not too brief (see Law Reform (Miscellaneous Provisions) Act 1934, s. 1). So if, for example, someone is injured in an accident and dies six months later, the estate can claim damages for pecuniary and non-pecuniary losses, based on the usual principles, for that six-month period.

In addition, the Fatal Accidents Act 1976 establishes two further claims: a claim by dependants of the deceased for financial losses and a claim for the bereavement suffered. As well as the spouse and children of the deceased, dependants can include other relatives, so long as they can prove financial dependence on him or her. A partner who lived as husband or wife with the deceased for at least two years is also classed as a dependant. Dependants will have a claim only if the deceased would have had one, and any defence which could have been used by the defendant can be used against them.

Dependants can claim for financial losses to themselves caused by the death, including earnings spent on the dependants, savings made for their future use, non-essential items such as holidays, and the value of services rendered. So, for example, a man who loses his wife can claim the value of any domestic services she provided for the family. In **Martin v Grey** (1998), a 12-year-old girl was awarded a record amount of damages for loss of the services provided by her mother, who had been killed. The court held that in calculating the award it was necessary to look at the cost of providing the services a mother would normally provide, whether or not these services had actually been replaced; this might include, for example, the cost of employing a housekeeper or the loss of earnings of the father if he gave up work.

Assessing the loss can be a difficult task, and in **Davies v Powell Duffryn Associated Collieries Ltd** (1942) Lord Wright laid down some guidance. The court must start with the earnings of the deceased; from this it deducts an amount estimated to cover the deceased's personal and living expenses. The sum left will be the multiplicand. This is then multiplied by the multiplier, which is calculated using the rules described at p. 462, except that the multiplier runs from the date of the death. Benefits received by the dependants, such as social security or insurance payments, are not deducted.

The second claim allowed by the Fatal Accidents Act 1976 is for a fixed award of £10,000 damages for bereavement, which is designed to provide some compensation for the non-pecuniary losses associated with bereavement. It is only available to the husband or wife of the deceased, or, if the deceased was unmarried and a minor, to the parents. It does not give children a claim for the death of a parent.

Problems with damages

Lump sums

The fact that damages are paid in a lump sum has disadvantages for the claimant, particularly where the effects of injury worsen after the award is made. The introduction of provisional damages has gone some way towards dealing with this problem, but still does not cover cases where at the time of trial there is no reason to believe that further deterioration will occur.

As well as the future prospects of the claimant's health, the lump sum system requires the court to predict what the claimant's employment prospects are likely to be; in reality this can never be known, so the compensation may well turn out to represent much more or less than the claimant should have had. Perhaps more importantly, there is no way to predict the result of inflation on the award, so that when inflation is high, the award's value can soon be eroded.

A further problem is that there is no way to ensure that the claimant uses the lump sum in such a way as to make sure it provides a lifelong income, where necessary. If the money is used unwisely, the claimant may end up having to live on state benefits, which partly defeats the object of making the tortfeasor compensate for the damage caused.

These issues were considered by the Pearson Commission (1978), which recommended that in cases of death or serious, long-term injury, claimants should be able to receive damages in the form of periodic payments. Assuming that the defendant was insured, the insurer would be responsible for administering the payments, which would be revalued annually to reflect average earnings. In addition, the Commission recommended that the courts should be able to vary awards where changes in the claimant's medical condition affected the level of pecuniary loss. These recommendations were not taken up by the government.

Degrees of fault

Because the aim of tort damages is to compensate the claimant, rather than punish the defendant, compensation does not take into account the degree of fault involved in the defendant's action. As a result, a defendant who makes a momentary slip may end up paying the same damages as one who shows gross carelessness. The system as it stands seems unable to provide justice for the claimant without injustice to some defendants.

West & Son v Shephard and loss of amenity

The case of **West & Son v Shephard** (1964), and the principle that a person who is unaware of his or her loss of amenity can still be compensated for it, have been strongly criticised. The main criticism is that the compensation cannot actually be used by the unconscious person, and in most cases will simply end up forming part of his or her estate when that person dies. This being the case, it seems inequitable that relatives in this situation may end up with considerably more than the relatives of someone killed immediately as the result of a tort. But if no such award was made, the court would be treating the claimant like a dead person.

The Law Commission has recommended that this aspect of the law be kept, but the Pearson Commission suggested that awards for non-pecuniary loss should no longer be made to unconscious claimants. The Pearson Commission's recommendation has not been implemented.

Damages for bereavement

The standard payment for bereavement (see p. 469) was raised from £7,500 to £10,000 in 2002, but the Association of Personal Injury Lawyers (APIL) has criticised this as inadequate and unfair. The Association had been pushing for a complete review of bereavement damages, arguing that such damages should be at least equal to those for the most serious injuries; at £10,000, bereavement compensation is a fraction of the £35,000 typically awarded for loss of one eye, for example, or the £200,000 for paralysis. The current situation means that it is cheaper for defendants to kill than to injure.

APIL has also criticised the fact that parents are denied damages for children over 18, which means that unless the child has another next of kin – such as a spouse – defendants do not have to pay anybody bereavement compensation.

Reading on the web

A report of the Law Commission entitled *Damages for Personal Injury: Non-pecuniary Loss* (1999) is available on the Law Commission's website at:

www.lawcom.gov.uk/lc_reports.htm

The House of Lords' judgment in **Farley** v **Skinner** (1998) is available on the House of Lords' judicial business website at:

www.publications.parliament.uk/pa/ld/ldjudgmt.htm#2001

The Court of Appeal judgment in **Khodaparast** v **Shad** (1999) can be read at:

www.alpha.bailii.org/ew/cases/EWCA/Civ/1997/1544.html

Chapter summary

The principal remedy awarded by a court for a tortious wrong is damages.

Damages

In the vast majority of cases where damages are claimed they are what is known as *compensatory*, aiming to put claimants in the position they would have been in if the tort had never been committed. Where the loss suffered is non-pecuniary, it is very difficult to calculate how much compensation is appropriate, but the general aim is to provide fair and reasonable compensation for the damage done, taking into account all the circumstances.

Compensation for personal injury

Damages for personal injury are divided into pecuniary and non-pecuniary losses. Pecuniary losses are those which can be calculated in financial terms, while non-pecuniary losses are not financial and cover damages that are less easy to calculate, such as loss of physical amenity, pain, shock and suffering. Pecuniary losses are divided into the following categories:

- pre-trial expenses;
- expenses incurred by another;
- pre-trial loss of earnings; and
- future loss of earnings.

Non-pecuniary losses are grouped into the following categories:

- the primary injury;
- pain and suffering; and
- loss of amenity.

The following sources of money will be deducted from an award of damages to prevent a person from being better off as a result of the injury (known as a set-off):

- tax;
- payments by an employer; and
- social security benefits.

Question and answer guide

1

Having bought herself a cheap sail board, Olga decided to teach herself to windsurf on a lake near her home. After several hours' practice, she began to tire and decided to have one last attempt at crossing the lake. She failed to notice Petra, who was fishing from a boat on the lake. Unfortunately, Olga crashed into the boat, which capsized, and Petra lost her fishing equipment, worth £3,000, in the lake.

(a) Negligence requires proof of **duty**, **breach** and **damage**.
    (i)   Explain, using examples, the meaning of the term **duty of care**.
                                                    (7 marks)
    (ii) Explain, using examples, the meaning of the term **breach of duty**.
                                                    (7 marks)
    (iii) Explain, using examples, the meaning of the term **damage**.   *(7 marks)*
(b) Using the explanations given in your answers to (a), discuss whether Olga has been negligent towards Petra.   *(10 marks)*
(c) Assuming Olga was found to be liable in negligence:
    (i)   Identify which court would hear Petra's claim and outline the procedure that would be followed before a trial.   *(7 marks)*
    (ii) Outline how the court would calculate an award of damages, if appropriate, to Petra in the situation given.   *(7 marks)*
                                      (from AQA Specimen Question Paper, 2007)

(a) (i) A 'duty of care' is a legal obligation to take reasonable care not to cause someone damage. There are many categories of situations in which it is well established that someone owes someone else a duty of care, e.g. drivers to other road users.

Where the situation is not covered by precedent or statute, the courts apply the test laid down in **Caparo** *v* **Dickman**. This requires the court to ask itself three questions, all of which must be answered 'Yes' in order for a duty of care to arise. First, 'Would a reasonable person in the defendant's position have foreseen the risk of damage?' Secondly, 'Was there a relationship of proximity between defendant and claimant?' Proximity means more than physical closeness, but concerns the relationship between the parties. Finally, 'Is it just, fair and reasonable to impose a duty in this situation?' This allows the courts to use public policy reasons to deny a claim, even where the other conditions are satisfied.

(a) (ii) 'Breach of duty' is short for 'breach of a legal duty of care'. The defendant must be shown to have fallen below the standard of care expected from someone undertaking the activity concerned. For example, driving carelessly is a breach of the duty owed to other road users.

The standard of care is an objective one, so the particular defendant's own characteristics are usually ignored: **Nettleship** *v* **Weston**. But the defendant is not expected to do everything possible to prevent harm: **Simonds** *v* **Isle of Wight Council**.

In deciding what behaviour would be expected of the reasonable person in the circumstances of a case, the courts consider a number of factors. These include the size of the risk (**Bolton** *v* **Stone**), how far it was practical to protect against the risk (**Latimer** *v* **AEC Ltd**) and any benefits to society that might be gained from taking the risk (**Watt** *v* **Hertfordshire County Council**).

(a) (iii) In requiring proof of damage, the law is saying that if no damage is caused to the claimant, he has no claim in negligence, no matter how careless the defendant's conduct.

Proof of damage involves proving two things – that the defendant's breach caused the claimant's damage, and that the damage caused was not too 'remote' a consequence of the breach.

To establish causation, the claimant must prove that the damage would not have happened but for the defendant's breach of duty: **Barnett** *v* **Chelsea and Kensington Hospital Management Committee**.

To establish that the damage was not too remote, the claimant must prove that the kind of damage suffered by him was reasonably foreseeable at the time of the defendant's breach of duty: **Wagon Mound No. 1**. It does not matter that the precise sequence of events leading from the breach to the damage could not have been reasonably foreseen: **Hughes** *v* **Lord Advocate**.

(b) The first question is whether Olga owed Petra a duty of care. Applying the three-stage test in **Caparo** *v* **Dickman**, this requires asking, first, 'Would a reasonable person in Olga's position have foreseen the risk of damage?' The answer is clearly 'Yes'. Secondly, 'Was there a relationship of proximity between Olga and Petra?' Again, there clearly was, given their physical proximity. Finally, 'Is it just, fair and reasonable to impose a duty in this situation?' There is no public policy reason to deny Petra's claim, so the answer to this question is 'Yes' also.

The second question is whether Olga breached her duty of care to Petra. Did her behaviour fall below the standard expected from a windsurfer of reasonable competence? The answer is almost certainly 'yes', given that she carried on wind-surfing when she had begun to tire and that she failed to notice Petra. Because the test is objective, no allowance need be made for Olga's inexperience as a windsurfer.

The next question is the causation question – 'Did Olga's breach cause Petra's damage (i.e. the loss of her fishing equipment)?' Applying the 'but for' test, it clearly did.

The final question is the remoteness question – 'Was Petra's damage too "remote" a consequence of Olga's breach?' Applying the **Wagon Mound** test, it clearly was not.

(c) (i) Civil cases are only heard in the High Court if the claimant expects to recover more than £15,000, or £50,000 if it is a personal injury case. The only damage that Petra appears to have suffered is the loss of her fishing equipment, worth £3,000. Therefore, her case would be heard in a county court.

The proceedings start with Petra completing a claim form. This informs Olga that an action is being brought against her, and provides a statement as to the value of Petra's claim.

The claim form is then served on Olga, by the court using first class post, unless Petra elects to serve it herself. Olga will need to acknowledge service.

Petra must then serve on Olga her particulars of claim. Olga must respond by filing either an acknowledgement of service or a defence. If she fails to do either within 14 days, Petra can enter judgment in default.

If Olga files a defence, the court will serve an allocation questionnaire on both parties. This is designed to enable the court to decide to which track it should assign the claim.

The disclosure procedures are then followed, under which the parties are required to disclose the documents on which they intend to rely and also the documents which go against their case.

If the case is not settled out of court or by alternative dispute resolution (which the court will actively promote) it proceeds to trial. The small claims track is the one to which actions with a value of less than £5,000 are assigned, so this is how Petra's claim will be dealt with (see p. 433).

(c) (ii) In calculating an award of damages to Petra, the court would seek to put her in the position she would have been in if Olga's tort had never been committed.

The award may be composed of either general or special damages, or both.

General damages are designed to compensate Petra for the kind of damage which the law presumes to be a result of the tort, such as pain and suffering from a personal injury, and loss of future earnings where the claimant's injuries mean that she cannot return to a previous employment or cannot work at all. Also recover-able under this head would be an amount for loss of amenity, to compensate for the fact that the claimant's injuries prevent her from enjoying life to the same extent as before. There is nothing in the question to say that Petra has suffered any losses of these kinds, so general damages would seem inappropriate in her case.

Special damages are those which do not arise naturally from the wrong com-plained of, and must be specifically listed in pleadings and proved in court. They generally cover the claimant's financial loss (including lost earnings) up until the date of trial, and any expenses incurred up to that point, and are therefore susceptible of more exact calculation. The cost of Petra's lost fishing equipment would be recoverable under this head.

Petra is under a duty to mitigate, i.e. to take reasonable steps to keep her damages as low as possible (see p. 458).

There are three main ways in which the court can structure an award of damages – as a single lump sum, as periodical payments or as a combination of the two. In Petra's case, given that the only damage she has suffered appears to be the loss of her fishing equipment, a single lump sum would be the appropriate structure for the court to adopt.

---

mylawchamber

Visit **www.mylawchamber.co.uk/elliottaqa** to access interactive questions, quizzes and activities to test yourself on this chapter.

Section C
INTRODUCTION TO CONTRACT

Please note that if you are studying *Section C: Introduction to Contract* of the AQA specifications you will also need to study Chapter 20, Civil Court Procedure, above, which is part of the 'Introduction to Contract' specifications.

This section of the book provides an introduction to contract law. Ask most people to describe a contract, and they will talk about a piece of paper – the documents you sign when you start a job, buy a house or hire a car, for example. While it is certainly true that these documents are often contracts, in law the term has a wider meaning, covering any legally binding agreement, written or unwritten. In order to be legally binding, an agreement must satisfy certain requirements, of which the main ones will be discussed in this section:

- **An agreement** between the parties (which is usually shown by the fact that one has made an offer and the other has accepted it).
- **An intention** to be legally bound by that agreement (often called intent to create legal relations).
- **Consideration** provided by each of the parties – put simply, this means that there must be some kind of exchange between the parties. If I say I will give you my car, and you simply agree to have it, I have voluntarily made you a promise (often called a gratuitous promise), which you cannot enforce in law if I change my mind. If, however, I promise to hand over my car and you promise to pay me a sum of money in return, we have each provided consideration.

With a very few exceptions, being in writing is not a requirement for a binding contract. We make contracts when we buy goods at the supermarket, when we get on a bus or train, and when we put money into a machine to buy chocolate or drinks – all without a word being written down, or sometimes even spoken. A contract is an agreement, not a piece of paper.

Part 13
FORMATION OF CONTRACT

Chapter 23

Offer and acceptance

This chapter discusses:

■ how, for a contract to exist, one party must have made an offer, and the other must have accepted it;

■ unilateral and bilateral contracts;

■ when an offer exists;

■ the distinction between an offer and an invitation to treat;

■ how long an offer lasts;

■ when an offer is accepted;

■ the requirement that an acceptance must be communicated;

■ the time of the formation of the contract.

Introduction

For a contract to exist, usually one party must have made an offer, and the other must have accepted it. Once acceptance takes effect, a contract will usually be binding on both parties, and the rules of offer and acceptance are typically used to pinpoint when a series of negotiations has passed that point, in order to decide whether the parties are obliged to fulfil their promises. There is generally no halfway house – negotiations have either crystallised into a binding contract, or they are not binding at all.

Unilateral and bilateral contracts

In order to understand the law on offer and acceptance, you need to understand the concepts of unilateral and bilateral contracts. Most contracts are bilateral. This means that each party takes on an obligation, usually by promising the other something – for example, Ann promises to sell something and Ben to buy it. (Although contracts where there are mutual obligations are always called bilateral, there may in fact be more than two parties to such a contract.)

By contrast, a unilateral contract arises where only one party assumes an obligation under the contract. Examples might be promising to give your mother £50 if she gives up smoking for a year, or to pay a £100 reward to anyone who finds

Bilateral contract:	Unilateral contract:
All the parties assume an obligation under the contract	Only one party assumes an obligation under the contract

Figure 23.1 **Bilateral and unilateral contracts**

your lost purse, or, as the court suggested in **Great Northern Railway Co.** *v* **Witham** (1873), to pay someone £100 to walk from London to York. What makes these situations unilateral contracts is that only one party has assumed an obligation – you are obliged to pay your mother if she gives up smoking, but she has not promised in turn to give up smoking. Similarly, you are obliged to pay the reward to anyone who finds your purse, but nobody need actually have undertaken to do so.

A common example of a unilateral contract is that between estate agents and people trying to sell their houses – the seller promises to pay a specified percentage of the house price to the estate agent if the house is sold, but the estate agent is not required to promise in return to sell the house, or even to try to do so.

Offer

The person making an offer is called the offeror, and the person to whom the offer is made is called the offeree. A communication will be treated as an offer if it indicates the terms on which the offeror is prepared to make a contract (such as the price of the goods for sale), and gives a clear indication that the offeror intends to be bound by those terms if they are accepted by the offeree.

An offer may be express, as when Ann tells Ben that she will sell her CD player for £200, but it can also be implied from conduct – a common example is taking goods to the cash desk in a supermarket, which is an implied offer to buy those goods.

> **✓ Know your terms 23.1**
>
> Define the following terms:
> 1 Unilateral contract.
> 2 Bilateral contract.
> 3 An offeror.
> 4 An offeree.

Offers to the public at large

In most cases, an offer will be made to a specified person – as when Ann offers to sell her computer to Ben. However, offers can be addressed to a group of people, or even to the general public. For example, a student may offer to sell her old textbooks to anyone in the year below, or the owner of a lost dog may offer a reward to anyone who finds it.

In **Carlill** *v* **Carbolic Smoke Ball Co.** (1893) the defendants were the manufacturers of 'smokeballs' which they claimed could prevent flu. They published

Offeror = person making the offer	**Offeree** = person receiving the offer

Figure 23.2 **Offeror and offeree**

advertisements stating that if anyone used their smokeball for a specified time and still caught flu, they would pay that person £100, and that to prove they were serious about the claim, they had deposited £1,000 with their bankers.

Mrs Carlill bought and used a smokeball, but nevertheless ended up with flu. She therefore claimed the £100, which the company refused to pay. They argued that their advertisement could not give rise to a contract, since it was impossible to make a contract with the whole world, and that therefore they were not legally bound to pay the money. This argument was rejected by the court, which held that the advertisement did constitute an offer to the world at large, which became a contract when it was accepted by Mrs Carlill using the smokeball and getting flu. She was therefore entitled to the £100.

A more recent illustration is provided by the Court of Appeal in **Bowerman v Association of British Travel Agents Ltd** (1995). A school had booked a skiing holiday with a tour operator which was a member of the Association of British Travel Agents (ABTA). All members of this association display a notice provided by ABTA which states:

> *'Where holidays or other travel arrangements have not yet commenced at the time of failure [of the tour operator], ABTA arranges for you to be reimbursed the money you have paid in respect of your holiday arrangements.'*

The tour operator became insolvent and cancelled the skiing holiday. The school was refunded the money they had paid for the holiday, but not the cost of the wasted travel insurance. The plaintiff brought an action against ABTA to seek reimbursement of the cost of this insurance. He argued, and the Court of Appeal agreed, that the ABTA notice constituted an offer which the customer accepted by contracting with an ABTA member.

A contract arising from an offer to the public at large, like that in **Carlill**, is usually a unilateral contract.

Invitations to treat

Some kinds of transaction involve a preliminary stage in which one party invites the other to make an offer. This stage is called an invitation to treat. In **Gibson v Manchester City Council** (1979) a council tenant was interested in buying his house. He completed an application form and received a letter from the council stating that it 'may be prepared to sell the house to you' for £2,180. Mr Gibson initially queried the purchase price, pointing out that the path to the house was in a bad condition. The council refused to change the price, saying that the price had been fixed taking into account the condition of the property. Mr Gibson then wrote on 18 March 1971 asking the council to 'carry on with the purchase as per my application'. Following a change in political control of the council in May 1971, it decided to stop selling council houses to tenants, and Mr Gibson was informed that the council would not proceed with the sale of the house. Mr Gibson brought legal proceedings, claiming that the letter he had received stating the purchase price was an offer which he had accepted on 18 March 1971. The House of Lords, however, ruled that the council had not made an offer; the

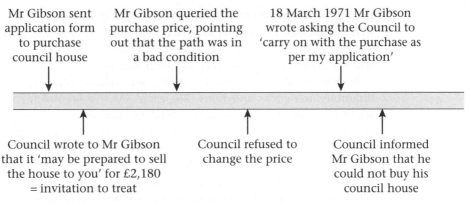

| Mr Gibson sent application form to purchase council house | Mr Gibson queried the purchase price, pointing out that the path was in a bad condition | 18 March 1971 Mr Gibson wrote asking the Council to 'carry on with the purchase as per my application' |

| Council wrote to Mr Gibson that it 'may be prepared to sell the house to you' for £2,180 = invitation to treat | Council refused to change the price | Council informed Mr Gibson that he could not buy his council house |

Figure 23.3 **Gibson v Manchester City Council** (1979)

letter giving the purchase price was merely one step in the negotiations for a contract and amounted only to an invitation to treat. Its purpose was simply to invite the making of a 'formal application', amounting to an offer, from the tenant.

Confusion can sometimes arise when what would appear, in the everyday sense of the word, to be an offer, is held by the law to be only an invitation to treat. This issue arises particularly in the following areas.

Quick quiz 23.2

1 Does a contract have to be in writing in order to be binding?

2 Was the case of **Great Northern Railway Co.** v **Witham** (1873) concerned with a bilateral or a unilateral contract?

3 Which is the leading case on offers to the public at large?

4 Is an invitation to treat equivalent to an offer?

Advertisements

A distinction is generally made between advertisements for a unilateral contract, and those for a bilateral contract.

Advertisements for unilateral contracts

These include advertisements such as the one in **Carlill** v **Carbolic Smoke Ball Co.**, or those offering rewards for the return of lost property, or for information leading to the arrest or conviction of a criminal. They are usually treated as offers, on the basis that the contract can normally be accepted without any need for further negotiations between the parties, and the person making the advertisement intends to be bound by it.

Advertisements for a bilateral contract

These are the type of advertisements which advertise specified goods at a certain price, such as those found at the back of newspapers and magazines. They are usually considered invitations to treat, on the grounds that they may lead to further bargaining – potential buyers might want to negotiate about the price, for example – and that since stocks could run out, it would be unreasonable to expect the advertisers to sell to everybody who applied.

In **Partridge** *v* **Crittenden** (1968), an advertisement in a magazine stated 'Bramblefinch cocks and hens, 25s each'. As the Bramblefinch was a protected species, the person who placed the advertisement was charged with unlawfully offering for sale a wild bird contrary to the Protection of Birds Act 1954, but his conviction was quashed on the grounds that the advertisement was not an offer but an invitation to treat.

It was held in **Grainger & Sons** *v* **Gough** (1896) that the circulation of a price-list by a wine merchant was not an offer to sell at those prices but merely an invitation to treat.

Shopping

Price-marked goods on display on the shelves or in the windows of shops are generally regarded as invitations to treat, rather than offers to sell goods at that price. In **Fisher** *v* **Bell** (1961) the defendant had displayed flick knives in his shop window, and was convicted of the criminal offence of offering such knives for sale. On appeal, Lord Parker CJ stated that the display of an article with a price on it in a shop window was only an invitation to treat and not an offer, and the conviction was overturned.

Where goods are sold on a self-service basis, the customer makes an offer to buy when presenting the goods at the cash desk, and the shopkeeper may accept or reject that offer. In **Pharmaceutical Society of Great Britain** *v* **Boots Cash Chemists (Southern) Ltd** (1953) Boots were charged with an offence concerning the sale of certain medicines which could only be sold by or under the supervision of a qualified pharmacist. Two customers in a self-service shop selected the medicines, which were price-marked, from the open shelves, and placed them in the shop's wire baskets. The shelves were not supervised by a pharmacist, but a pharmacist had been instructed to supervise the transaction at the cash desk. The issue was therefore whether the sale had taken place at the shelves or at the cash desk.

The Court of Appeal decided the shelf display was like an advertisement for a bilateral contract, and was therefore merely an invitation to treat. The offer was made by the customer when medicines were placed in the basket, and was only accepted when the goods were presented at the cash desk. Since a pharmacist was supervising at that point, no offence had been committed.

There are two main practical consequences of this principle. First, shops do not have to sell goods at the marked price – so if a shop assistant wrongly marks a CD at £2.99 rather than £12.99, for example, you cannot insist on buying it at that price. Secondly, a customer cannot insist on buying a particular item on display – so you cannot make a shopkeeper sell you the sweater in the window even if there are none left inside the shop. Displaying the goods is not an offer, so a customer cannot accept it and thereby make a binding contract.

Quick quiz 23.3

1 In the case of **Gibson** v **Manchester City Council** (1979) was there a binding contract between the council and Mr Gibson to sell the council house to Mr Gibson?

2 Is an advertisement for a bilateral contract an invitation to treat or an offer?

3 Are chocolates displayed in a sweet shop an invitation to treat or an offer?

4 What was the *ratio decidendi* of **Pharmaceutical Society of Great Britain** v **Boots Cash Chemists (Southern) Ltd** (1953).

Timetables and tickets for transport

The legal position here is rather unclear. Is a bus timetable an offer to run services at those times, or just an invitation to treat? Does the bus pulling up at a stop constitute an offer to carry you, which you accept by boarding the bus? Or, again, is even this stage just an invitation to treat, so that the offer is actually made by you getting on the bus or by handing over money for the ticket? These points may seem academic, but they become important when something goes wrong. If, for example, the bus crashes and you are injured, your ability to sue for breach of contract will depend on whether the contract had actually been completed when the accident occurred.

Although there have been many cases in this area, no single reliable rule has emerged, and it seems that the exact point at which a contract is made depends in each case on the particular facts. For example, in **Denton** v **GN Railway** (1856) it was said that railway company advertisements detailing the times at and conditions under which trains would run were offers. But in **Wilkie** v **London Passenger Transport Board** (1947) Lord Greene thought that a contract between bus company and passenger was made when a person intending to travel 'puts himself either on the platform or inside the bus'. The opinion was *obiter* but, if correct, it implies that the company makes an offer of carriage by running the bus or train and the passenger accepts when he or she gets properly on board, completing the contract. Therefore, if the bus crashed, an injured passenger could have a claim against the bus company for breach of contract despite not having yet paid the fare or been given a ticket.

However, in **Thornton** v **Shoe Lane Parking Ltd** (1971) it was suggested that the contract may be formed rather later. If the legal principles laid down in **Thornton** are applied to this factual situation, it would appear that passengers asking for a ticket to their destination are making an invitation to treat. The bus company makes an offer by issuing the tickets, and the passengers accept the offer by keeping the tickets without objection. Fortunately, these questions are not governed solely by the law of contract as some legislation relevant to the field of public transport has since been passed.

There are other less common situations in which the courts will have to decide whether a communication is an offer or merely an invitation to treat. The test used is whether a person watching the proceedings would have thought the party concerned was making an offer or not.

How long does an offer last?

An offer may cease to exist under any of the following circumstances.

Specified time

Where an offeror states that an offer will remain open for a specific length of time, it lapses when that time is up (though it can be revoked before that – see p. 488 below).

Reasonable length of time

Where the offeror has not specified how long the offer will remain open, it will lapse after a reasonable length of time has passed. Exactly how long this is will depend upon whether the means of communicating the offer were fast or slow and on its subject matter – for example, offers to buy perishable goods, or a commodity whose price fluctuates daily, will lapse quite quickly. Offers to buy shares on the stock market may last only seconds.

In **Ramsgate Victoria Hotel** *v* **Montefiore** (1866) the defendant applied for shares in the plaintiff company, paying a deposit into their bank. After hearing nothing from them for five months, he was then informed that the shares had been allotted to him, and asked to pay the balance due on them. He refused to do so, and the court upheld his argument that five months was not a reasonable length of time for acceptance of an offer to buy shares, which are a commodity with a rapidly fluctuating price. Therefore, the offer had lapsed before the company tried to accept it, and there was no contract between them.

Failure of a precondition

Some offers are made subject to certain conditions, and if such conditions are not in place, the offer may lapse. For example, a person might offer to sell their bike for £50 if they manage to buy a car at the weekend. In **Financings Ltd** *v* **Stimson** (1962) the defendant saw a car for sale at £350 by a second-hand car dealer on 16 March. He decided to buy it on hire-purchase terms. The way that hire-purchase works in such cases is that the finance company buys the car outright from the dealer, and then sells it to the buyer, who pays in instalments. The defendant would therefore be buying the car from the finance company (the plaintiffs), rather than from the dealer. The defendant signed the plaintiffs' form, which stated that the agreement would be binding on the finance company only when signed on their behalf. The car dealer did not have the authority to do this, so it had to be sent to the plaintiffs for signing. On 18 March the defendant paid the first instalment of £70. On 24 March the car was stolen from the dealer's premises. It was later found, badly damaged and the defendant no longer wanted to buy it. Not knowing this, on 25 March the plaintiffs signed the written 'agreement'. They subsequently sued the defendant for failure to pay the instalments. The Court of Appeal ruled in favour of the defendant, as the so-called 'agreement' was really an offer to make a contract with the plaintiffs, which was subject to the implied condition that the car remained in much the same state as it was in when the offer was made, until that offer was accepted. The plaintiffs were claiming that they had accepted the offer by signing the document on 24 March. As the implied condition had been broken by then, the offer was no longer open so no contract had been concluded.

Rejection

An offer lapses when the offeree rejects it. If Ann offers to sell Ben her car on Tuesday, and Ben says no, Ben cannot come back on Wednesday and insist on accepting the offer.

Counter-offer

A counter-offer terminates the original offer. In **Hyde** *v* **Wrench** (1840) the defendant offered to sell his farm for £1,000, and the plaintiff responded by offering to buy it at £950 – this is called making a counter-offer. The farm owner refused to sell at that price, and when the plaintiff later tried to accept the offer to buy at £1,000, it was held that this offer was no longer available; it had been terminated by the counter-offer. In this situation the offeror can make a new offer on exactly the same terms, but is not obliged to do so.

Requests for information

A request for information about an offer (such as whether delivery could be earlier than suggested) does not amount to a counter-offer, so the original offer remains open. In **Stevenson Jaques & Co.** *v* **McLean** (1880) the defendant made an offer on a Saturday to sell iron to the plaintiffs at a cash on delivery price of 40 shillings, and stated that the offer would remain available until the following Monday. The plaintiffs replied by asking if they could buy the goods on credit. They received no answer. On Monday afternoon they contacted the defendant to accept the offer, but the iron had already been sold to someone else.

When the plaintiffs sued for breach of contract, it was held that their reply to the offer had been merely a request for information, not a counter-offer, so the original offer still stood and there was a binding contract.

Death of the offeror

The position is not entirely clear, but it appears that if the offeree knows that the offeror has died, the offer will lapse; if the offeree is unaware of the offeror's death, it probably will not (**Bradbury** *v* **Morgan** (1862)). So if, for example, A promises to sell her video recorder to B, then dies soon after, and B writes to accept the offer not knowing that A is dead, it seems that the people responsible for A's affairs after death would be obliged to sell the video recorder to B and B would be obliged to pay the price to the executors.

However, where an offer requires personal performance by the offeror (such as painting a picture, or appearing in a film) it will usually lapse on the offeror's death.

Death of the offeree

There is no English case on this point, but it seems probable that the offer lapses and cannot be accepted after the offeree's death by the offeree's representatives.

Withdrawal of offer

The withdrawal of an offer is sometimes described as the revocation of an offer. The old case of **Payne v Cave** (1789) establishes the principle that an offer may be withdrawn at any time up until it is accepted. In **Routledge v Grant** (1828) the defendant made a provisional offer to buy the plaintiff's house at a specified price, 'a definite answer to be given within six weeks from date'. It was held that, regardless of this provision, the defendant still had the right to withdraw the offer at any moment before acceptance, even though the time limit had not expired.

A number of rules apply in relation to the withdrawal of offers.

Withdrawal must be communicated

It is not enough for offerors simply to change their mind about an offer; they must notify the offeree that it is being revoked. In **Byrne & Co. v Leon Van Tienhoven** (1880) the defendants were a company based in Cardiff. On 1 October they posted a letter to New York offering to sell the plaintiffs 1,000 boxes of tinplates. Having received the letter on 11 October, the plaintiffs immediately accepted by telegram. Acceptances sent by telegram take effect as soon as they are sent (see p. 497 for details of the postal rule).

In the meantime, on 8 October, the defendants had written to revoke their offer, and this letter reached the plaintiffs on 20 October. It was held that there was a binding contract, because revocation could only take effect on communication, but the acceptance by telegram took effect as soon as it was sent – in this case nine days before the revocation was received. By the time the second letter reached the plaintiffs, a contract had already been made.

The revocation of an offer does not have to be communicated by the offeror; the communication can be made by some other reliable source. In **Dickinson v Dodds** (1876) the defendant offered to sell a house to the plaintiff, the offer 'to be left open until Friday, June 12, 9 a.m.'. On 11 June the defendant sold the house to a third party, Allan, and the plaintiff heard about the sale through a fourth man. Before 9 a.m. on 12 June, the plaintiff handed the defendant a letter in which he said he was accepting the offer. It was held by the Court of Appeal that the offer had already been revoked by the communication from the fourth man, so there was no contract. By hearing the news from the fourth man, Dickinson 'knew that Dodds was no longer minded to sell the property to him as plainly and clearly as if Dodds had told him in so many words'.

An offeror who promises to keep an offer open for a specified period may still revoke that offer at any time before it is accepted, unless the promise to keep it open is supported by some consideration from the other party (by providing consideration the parties make a separate contract called an option).

An exception to the rule that the withdrawal must be communicated to the offeree exists where an offeree moves to a new address without notifying the

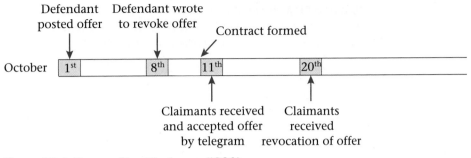

Figure 23.4 **Byrne** *v* **Van Tienhoven** (1880)

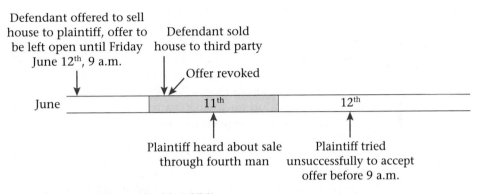

Figure 23.5 **Dickinson** *v* **Dodds** (1876)

offeror. In these circumstances, a withdrawal which is delivered to the offeree's last known address will be effective on delivery to that address. In the same way, where a withdrawal reaches the offeree, but the offeree simply fails to read it, the withdrawal probably still takes effect on reaching the offeree (see **The Brimnes** (1975), p. 497). This would be the position where a withdrawal by telex or fax reached the offeror's office during normal business hours, but was not actually seen or read by the offeree or by any of their staff until some time afterwards.

Many offices receive a lot of post every day. This post may not go directly to the person whose name is on the envelope, but is received, opened and sorted by clerical staff and then distributed to the relevant people. In these situations there may be some difficulty in pinpointing when the information in the letter is communicated for these purposes. Is it when the letter is received within the company, when it is opened, or when it is actually read by the relevant member of staff? There is no authority on the point but the approach of the courts would probably be that communication occurs when the letter is opened, even though there may in those circumstances be no true communication.

In **Pickfords Ltd** *v* **Celestica Ltd** (2003) two offers were made by Pickfords and the court had to decide whether the second offer had effectively withdrawn the first offer. Pickfords, the claimant, is a well-known furniture removal company. Celestica, the defendant, is an IT company which wished to use Pickfords services to move premises. The court observed:

'It is as if the facts of this case have been devised for an examination question on the law of contract for first year law students. They raise some basic questions in relation to offer and acceptance in the law of formation of contract.'

The litigation turned on the meaning and effect of three documents. The first document was a fax that was dated 13 September 2001 and which estimated the cost of the removal as being £100,000, though the final cost would depend on how many vehicle loads would be required. The second document was more detailed and was sent to the defendant on 27 September 2001. This contained a fixed quote for the removal of £98,760. The third document was a fax entitled 'Confirmation', which was sent by the defendant to the claimant and was dated 15 October 2001. This expressly referred to the fax dated 13 September 2001 and stated that the amount to be paid was 'not to exceed 100K'. The question for the court was whether the first offer on 13 September was capable of being accepted, or whether the second offer had withdrawn the first offer. The Court of Appeal concluded: 'In such a case, in my judgment, something more than the mere submission of the second quotation is required to indicate that A has withdrawn the first offer.' The question was whether the making of the second offer clearly indicated an intention on the part of the offeror to withdraw the first offer. The substantial differences between the two offers in this case went far beyond a mere difference in price which could have been explained as consistent with two alternative offers both being on the table for the defendant to choose which to accept. In the absence of any findings of fact as to the circumstances which gave rise to the second offer, the second offer superseded and revoked the first offer.

The fax was intended to be an acceptance of the first offer. Since the first offer had been revoked, the purported acceptance could not give rise to a contract. It was in law a counter-offer to accept the services offered by the claimant on the terms of the first offer, subject to the cap of £100,000. Since the work was carried out, this counter-offer must have been accepted by the claimant's conduct in carrying out the work.

Withdrawal of an offer to enter into a unilateral contract

There are a number of special rules that apply in relation to the revocation of an offer to enter into a unilateral contract. An offer to enter into a unilateral contract cannot be revoked once the offeree has commenced performance. Thus, in **Errington** *v* **Errington and Woods** (1952) a father bought a house in his own name for £750, borrowing £500 of the price by means of a mortgage from a building society. He bought the house for his son and daughter-in-law to live in, and told them that, if they met the mortgage repayments, the house would be signed over to them once the mortgage was paid off. The couple moved in, and began to pay the mortgage instalments, but they never in fact made a promise to continue with the payments until the mortgage was paid off, which meant that the contract was unilateral.

When the father later died, the people in charge of his financial affairs sought to withdraw the offer. The Court of Appeal held that it was too late to do so. The part performance by the son and daughter-in-law prevented the offer from being withdrawn. The offer could only be withdrawn if the son and daughter-in-law ceased to make the payments.

In **Daulia Ltd** *v* **Four Millbank Nominees Ltd** (1978) the Court of Appeal stated that, once an offeree had started to perform on a unilateral contract, it was too late for the offeror to revoke the offer. It should be noted that this statement was *obiter*, since the court found that the offeree in the case had in fact completed his performance before the supposed revocation.

There is an exception to this rule that part performance following an offer to enter into a unilateral contract prevents revocation of the offer. This exception applies in the context of unilateral offers to enter into a contract with an estate agent to pay commission for the sale of a property. In **Luxor (Eastborne) Ltd** *v* **Cooper** (1941) an owner of land had promised to pay an estate agent £10,000 in commission if the agent was able to find a buyer willing to pay £175,000 for the land. The arrangement was on the terms that are usual between estate agents and their clients, whereby the agent is paid commission if a buyer is found, and nothing if not. The House of Lords held that the owner in the case could revoke his promise at any time before the sale was completed, even after the estate agents had made extensive efforts to find a buyer or to stop trying to do so.

Where a unilateral offer is made to the world at large, to be accepted by conduct, it can probably be revoked without the need for communication if the revocation takes place before performance has begun. For example, if you place a newspaper advertisement offering a reward for the return of something you have lost, and then decide you might actually be better off spending that money on replacing the item, it would probably be impossible for you to make sure that everyone who knew about the offer knows you are withdrawing it – even if you place a notice of withdrawal in the newspaper, you cannot guarantee that everyone concerned will see it. It seems to be enough for an offeror to take reasonable steps to bring the withdrawal to the attention of such persons, even though it may not be possible to ensure that they all know about it. Thus, in the American case of **Shuey** *v* **United States** (1875) it was held that an offer made by advertisement in a newspaper could be revoked by a similar advertisement, even though the second advertisement was not read by all the offerees.

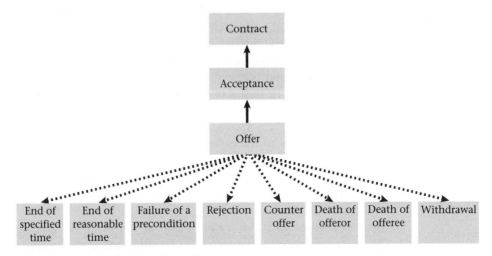

Figure 23.6 Termination of an offer

Acceptance

Acceptance of an offer means unconditional agreement to all the terms of that offer. Acceptance will often be oral or in writing, but in some cases an offeree may accept an offer by doing something, such as delivering goods in response to an offer to buy. The courts will only interpret conduct as indicating acceptance if it seems reasonable to infer that the offeree acted with the intention of accepting the offer.

In **Brogden** *v* **Metropolitan Rail Co** (1877) Brogden had supplied the railway company with coal for several years without any formal agreement. The parties then decided to make things official, so the rail company sent Brogden a draft agreement, which left a blank space for Brogden to insert the name of an arbitrator. After doing so and signing the document, Brogden returned it, marked 'approved'.

The company's employee put the draft away in a desk drawer, where it stayed for the next two years, without any further steps being taken regarding it. Brogden continued to supply coal under the terms of the contract, and the railway company to pay for it. Eventually, a dispute arose between them, and Brogden denied that any binding contract existed.

The courts held that by inserting the arbitrator's name, Brogden added a new term to the potential contract, and therefore, in returning it to the railway company, he was offering (in fact counter-offering) to supply coal under the contract. But when was that offer accepted? The House of Lords decided that an acceptance by conduct could be inferred from the parties' behaviour, and a valid contract was completed either when the company first ordered coal after receiving the draft agreement from Brogden, or at the latest when he supplied the first lot of coal.

Merely remaining silent cannot amount to an acceptance, unless it is absolutely clear that acceptance was intended. In **Felthouse** *v* **Bindley** (1862) an uncle and his nephew had talked about the possible sale of the nephew's horse to the uncle, but there had been some confusion about the price. The uncle subsequently wrote to the nephew, offering to pay £30 and 15 shillings and saying: 'If I hear no more about him, I consider the horse mine at that price.' The nephew was on the point of selling off some of his property in an auction. He did not reply to the uncle's letter, but did tell the auctioneer to keep the horse out of the sale. The auctioneer forgot to do this, and the horse was sold. It was held that there was no contract between the uncle and the nephew. The court felt that the nephew's conduct in trying to keep the horse out of the sale did not necessarily imply that he intended to accept his uncle's offer – even though the nephew actually wrote afterwards to apologise for the mistake – and so it was not clear that his silence in response to the offer was intended to constitute acceptance. This can be criticised in that it is hard to see how there could have been clearer evidence that the nephew did actually intend to sell, but, on the other hand, there are many situations in which it would be undesirable and confusing for silence to amount to acceptance.

It has been pointed out by the Court of Appeal in **Re Selectmove Ltd** (1995) that an acceptance by silence could be sufficient if it was the offeree who suggested that their silence would be sufficient. Thus, in **Felthouse**, if the nephew had been the one to say that if his uncle heard nothing more he could treat the offer as accepted, there would have been a contract.

Quick quiz 23.4

1 If an offeree makes a counter-offer, what impact does this have on the original offer?

2 If a man offers to sell a woman a second-hand television for £50 and the woman telephones the man to check how old the television is, what impact will this request for information have on the original offer to sell the television for £50?

3 If a woman offers to sell a man a book for £10 and the man agrees to buy it provided the woman delivers it to him within 24 hours, has the man accepted the woman's offer?

4 Can silence amount to an acceptance?

Acceptance of an offer to enter into a unilateral contract

Unilateral contracts are usually accepted by conduct. If I offer £100 to anyone who finds my lost dog, finding the dog will be an acceptance of the offer, making my promise binding – it is not necessary for anyone to contact me and say that they intend to take up my offer and find the dog.

There is no acceptance until the relevant act has been completely performed – so if Ann says to Ben that she will give Ben £5 if Ben washes her car, Ben would not be entitled to the money until the job is finished, and could not wash half the car and ask for £2.50.

Acceptance must be unconditional

An acceptance must accept the precise terms of an offer. In **Tinn** v **Hoffman** (1873) one party offered to sell the other 1,200 tons of iron. It was held that the other party's order for 800 tons was not an acceptance.

Negotiation and the 'battle of the forms'

Where parties carry on a long process of negotiation, it may be difficult to pinpoint exactly when an offer has been made and accepted. In such cases the courts will look at the whole course of negotiations to decide whether the parties have in fact reached agreement at all and, if so, when.

This process can be particularly difficult where the so-called 'battle of the forms' arises. Rather than negotiating terms each time a contract is made, many businesses try to save time and money by contracting on standard terms, which will be printed on company stationery such as order forms and delivery notes. The 'battle of the forms' occurs where one party sends a form stating that the contract is on their standard terms of business, and the other party responds by returning their own form and stating that the contract is on **their** terms.

The general rule in such cases is that the 'last shot' wins the battle. Each new form issued is treated as a counter-offer, so that when one party performs its obligation under the contract (by delivering goods, for example), that action will be seen as acceptance by conduct of the offer in the last form. In **British Road Services** *v* **Arthur V. Crutchley & Co. Ltd** (1968) the plaintiffs delivered some whisky to the defendants for storage. The BRS driver handed the defendants a delivery note, which listed his company's 'conditions of carriage'. Crutchley's employee stamped the note 'Received under [our] conditions' and handed it back to the driver. The court held that stamping the delivery note in this way amounted to a counter-offer, which BRS accepted by handing over the goods. The contract therefore incorporated Crutchley's conditions, rather than those of BRS.

However, a more recent case shows that the 'last shot' will not always succeed. In **Butler Machine Tool Ltd** *v* **Ex-Cell-O Corp (England) Ltd** (1979) the defendants wanted to buy a machine from the plaintiffs, to be delivered ten months after the order. The plaintiffs supplied a quotation (which was taken to be an offer), and on this document were printed their standard terms, including a clause allowing them to increase the price of the goods if the costs had risen by the date of delivery (known as a price-variation clause). The document also stated that their terms would prevail over any terms and conditions in the buyers' order. The buyers responded by placing an order, which was stated to be on their own terms and conditions, and these were listed on the order form. These terms did not contain a price-variation clause. The order form included a tear-off acknowledgement slip, which contained the words: 'we accept your order on the terms and conditions thereon' (referring to the order form). The sellers duly returned the acknowledgement slip to the buyers, with a letter stating that the order was being accepted in accordance with the earlier quotation. The acknowledgement slip and accompanying letter were the last forms issued before delivery.

When the ten months were up, the machine was delivered and the sellers claimed an extra £2,892, under the provisions of the price-variation clause. The buyers refused to pay the extra amount, so the sellers sued them for it. The Court of Appeal held that the buyers' reply to the quotation was not an unconditional acceptance, and therefore constituted a counter-offer. The sellers had accepted that counter-offer by returning the acknowledgement slip, which referred back to the buyers' conditions. The sellers pointed out that they had stated in their accompanying letter that the order was booked in accordance with the earlier quotation, but this was interpreted by the Court of Appeal as referring back to the type and price of the machine tool, rather than to the terms listed on the back of the sellers' document. It merely confirmed that the machine in question was the one originally quoted for, and did not modify the conditions of the contract. The contract was therefore made under the buyers' conditions.

The Court of Appeal also contemplated what the legal position would have been if the slip had not been returned by the sellers. The majority thought that the usual rules of offer and counter-offer would have to be applied, which in many cases would mean that there was no contract until the goods were delivered and accepted by the buyer, with either party being free to withdraw before that. Lord Denning MR, on the other hand, suggested that the courts should take a much less rigid approach and decide whether the parties thought they had made a binding contract, and if it

> ✓ **Know your terms 23.5**
>
> Define the following terms:
> 1 Invitation to treat.
> 2 Counter-offer.
> 3 The 'battle of the forms'.

appeared that they did, the court should go on to examine the documents as a whole to find out what the content of their agreement might be. This approach has not been adopted by the courts.

Specified methods of acceptance

If an offeror states that his or her offer must be accepted in a particular way, then only acceptance by that method or an equally effective one will be binding. To be considered equally effective, a mode of acceptance should not be slower than the method specified in the offer, nor have any disadvantages for the offeror. It was stated in **Tinn v Hoffman** (1873) that where the offeree was asked to reply 'by return of post', any method which would arrive before return of post would be sufficient.

Where a specified method of acceptance has been included for the offeree's own benefit, however, the offeree is not obliged to accept in that way. In **Yates Building Co. Ltd v R. J. Pulleyn & Sons (York) Ltd** (1975) the sellers stated that the option they were offering should be accepted by 'notice in writing . . . to be sent registered or recorded delivery'. The purchaser sent his acceptance by ordinary letter post, but the court held that the acceptance was still effective. The requirement of registered or recorded delivery was for the benefit of the offeree rather than the offeror (as it ensured that their acceptance was received and that they had proof of their acceptance) and was not therefore mandatory.

The case of **Felthouse v Bindley** (see p. 492 above) shows that, although the offeror can stipulate how the acceptance is to be made, he or she cannot stipulate that silence shall amount to acceptance. In the same way, if the offeror states that the performance of certain acts by the offeree will amount to an acceptance, and the offeree performs those acts, there will only be an acceptance if the offeree was aware of the terms of the offer and objectively intended their acts to amount to an acceptance. In **Inland Revenue Commissioners v Fry** (2001) the Inland Revenue claimed over £100,000 of unpaid tax from Mrs Fry. Following negotiations, Mrs Fry wrote to the Inland Revenue enclosing a cheque for £10,000. In her letter she said that if the Inland Revenue accepted her offer of £10,000 in full and final settlement, it should present the cheque for payment. The Inland Revenue cashed the cheque but subsequently informed Mrs Fry that her offer was unacceptable. The High Court held that the Inland Revenue was entitled to the full amount of tax which it had claimed. The court explained that it was fundamental to the existence of a binding contract that there was a meeting of minds. An offer prescribing a mode of acceptance could be accepted by an offeree acting in accordance with that mode of acceptance. However, the Inland Revenue received thousands of cheques each day and there was no evidence that, when it cashed the cheque from Mrs Fry, it knew of the offer. The cashing of the cheque gave rise to no more than a rebuttable presumption of acceptance of the terms of the offer in the accompanying letter. On the evidence, that presumption had been rebutted, as a reasonable observer would not have assumed that the cheque was banked with the intention of accepting the offer in the letter.

An offeror who has requested the offeree to use a particular method of acceptance can always waive the right to insist on that method.

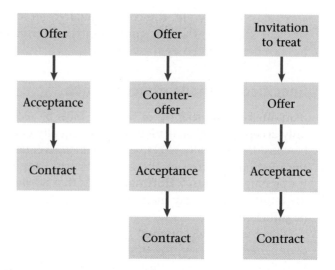

Figure 23.7 Three examples of how a contract can be made

Acceptance must be communicated

An acceptance does not usually take effect until it is communicated to the offeror. As Lord Denning explained in **Entores Ltd v Miles Far East Corporation** (1955), if A shouts an offer to B across a river but, just as B yells back an acceptance, a noisy aircraft flies over, preventing A from hearing B's reply, no contract has been made. A must be able to hear B's acceptance before it can take effect. The same would apply if the contract was made by telephone, and A failed to catch what B said because of interference on the line; there is no contract until A knows that B is accepting the offer. The principal reason for this rule is that, without it, people might be bound by a contract without knowing that their offers had been accepted, which could obviously create difficulties in all kinds of situations.

Where parties negotiate face to face, communication of the acceptance is unlikely to be a problem; any difficulties tend to arise where the parties are communicating at a distance, for example by post, telephone, telegram, telex, fax or messenger.

Exceptions to the communication rule

There are some circumstances in which an acceptance may take effect without being communicated to the offeror.

Terms of the offer

An offer may state or imply that acceptance need not be communicated to the offeror, although, as **Felthouse v Bindley** shows, it is not possible to state that the offeree will be bound unless he or she indicates that the offer is not accepted (in other words, that silence will be taken as acceptance). This means that offerors are free to expose themselves to the risk of unknowingly incurring an obligation, but may not impose that risk on someone else. It seems to follow from this that if the horse in **Felthouse** *v* **Bindley** had been kept out of the sale for the uncle, and the uncle had then refused to buy it, the nephew could have sued his uncle, who would have been unable to rely on the fact that acceptance was not communicated to him.

Unilateral contracts do not usually require acceptance to be communicated to the offeror. In **Carlill** *v* **Carbolic Smoke Ball Co** (1893) the defendants argued that the plaintiff should have notified them that she was accepting their offer, but the court held that such a unilateral offer implied that performance of the terms of the offer would be enough to amount to acceptance.

Conduct of the offeror

An offeror who fails to receive an acceptance through their own fault may be prevented from claiming that the non-communication means they should not be bound by the contract. In the **Entores** case (1955) it was suggested that this principle could apply where an offer was accepted by telephone, and the offeror did not catch the words of acceptance, but failed to ask for them to be repeated; and in **The Brimnes** (1975), where the acceptance is sent by telex during business hours, but is simply not read by anyone in the offeror's office.

The postal rule

The general rule for acceptances by post is that they take effect when they are posted, rather than when they are communicated. The main reason for this rule is historical, since it dates from a time when communication through the post was even slower and less reliable than it is today. Even now, there is some practical purpose for the rule, in that it is easier to prove that a letter has been posted than to prove that it has been received or brought to the attention of the offeror.

The postal rule was laid down in **Adams** *v* **Lindsell** (1818). On 2 September 1817, the defendants wrote to the plaintiffs, who processed wool, offering to sell them a quantity of sheep fleeces, and stating that they required an answer 'in course of post'. Unfortunately, the defendants did not address the letter correctly, and as a result it did not reach the plaintiffs until the evening of 5 September. The plaintiffs posted their acceptance the same evening, and it reached the defendants on 9 September. It appeared that if the original letter had been correctly addressed, the plaintiffs could have expected a reply 'in course of post' by 7 September. That date came and went, and they had heard nothing from the plaintiffs, so on 8 September they sold the wool to a third party. The issue in the case was whether a contract had been made before the sale to the third party on 8 September. The court held that a contract was concluded as soon as the acceptance was posted, so that the defendants were bound from the evening of 5 September, and had therefore breached the contract by selling the wool to the third party. (Under current law there would have been a contract even without the postal rule, because the revocation of the offer could only take effect if it was communicated to the offeree

– selling the wool to a third party without notifying the plaintiffs would not amount to revocation. However, in 1818 the rules on revocation were not fully developed, so the court may well have considered that the sale was sufficient to revoke the offer, which was why an effective acceptance would have to take place before 8 September.)

Application of the postal rule

The traditional title 'postal rule' has become slightly misleading because the rule does not only apply to the post but could also potentially apply to certain other non-instantaneous modes of communication. The postal rule was applied to acceptance by telegram in **Cowan *v* O'Connor** (1888), where it was held that an acceptance came into effect when the telegram was placed with the Post Office. These days the Post Office in England no longer offers a telegram service, but the same rule will apply to the telemessage service which replaced it.

It is not yet clear whether the postal rule applies to faxes, e-mails and text messages. Professor Treitel suggests that the rule's application should depend on the circumstances of each case. He considers that the postal rule should only apply where the person accepting the offer is not in a position to know that their communication has been ineffective:

> 'Fax messages seem to occupy an intermediate position. The sender will know at once if his message has not been received at all, and where this is the position the message should not amount to an effective acceptance. But if the message is received in such a form that it is wholly or partly illegible, the sender is unlikely to know this at once, and it is suggested an acceptance sent by fax might well be effective in such circumstances. The same principles should apply to other forms of electronic communication such as e-mail or website trading . . .'

Use of the postal service must be reasonable. Only when it is reasonable to use the post to indicate acceptance can the postal rule apply. If the offer does not dictate a method of acceptance, appropriate methods can be inferred from the means used to make the offer. An offer made by post may generally be accepted by post, but it may be reasonable to accept by post even though the offer was delivered in some other way. In **Henthorn *v* Fraser** (1892) the defendant was based in Liverpool and the plaintiff lived in Birkenhead. The defendant gave the plaintiff in Liverpool a document containing an offer in Liverpool, and the plaintiff accepted it by posting a letter from Birkenhead. It was held that, despite the offer having been handed over in person, acceptance by post was reasonable because the parties were based in different towns.

Where an offer is made by an instant method of communication, such as telex, fax or telephone, an acceptance by post would not usually be reasonable.

Exceptions to the postal rule

Offers requiring communication of acceptance

An offeror may avoid the postal rule by making it a term of their offer that acceptance will only take effect when it is communicated to them. In **Holwell**

Securities Ltd *v* **Hughes** (1974) the defendants offered to sell some freehold property to the plaintiffs but the offer stated that the acceptance had to be 'by notice in writing'. The plaintiffs posted their acceptance, but it never reached the defendants, despite being properly addressed. The court held that 'notice' meant communication, and therefore it would not be appropriate to apply the postal rule.

Instant methods of communication

When an acceptance is made by an instant mode of communication, such as telephone or telex, the postal rule does not apply. In such cases the acceptor will usually know at once that they have not managed to communicate with the offeror, and will need to try again.

In **Entores** *v* **Miles Far East Corporation** (1955) the plaintiffs were a London company and the defendants were an American corporation with agents in Amsterdam. Both the London company and the defendants' agents in Amsterdam had telex machines, which allow users to type in a message, and have it almost immediately received and printed out by the recipient's machine. The plaintiffs in London telexed the defendants' Amsterdam agents offering to buy goods from them, and the agents accepted, again by telex. The court case arose when the plaintiffs alleged that the defendants had broken their contract and wanted to bring an action against them. The rules of civil litigation stated that they could only bring this action in England if the contract had been made in England. The Court of Appeal held that because telex allows almost instant communication, the parties were in the same position as if they had negotiated in each other's presence or over the telephone, so the postal rule did not apply and an acceptance did not take effect until it had been received by the plaintiffs. Because the acceptance had been received in London, the contract was deemed to have been made there, and so the legal action could go ahead.

This approach was approved by the House of Lords in **Brinkibon** *v* **Stahag Stahl GmbH** (1983). The facts here were similar, except that the offer was made by telex from Vienna to London, and accepted by a telex from London to Vienna. The House of Lords held that the contract was therefore made in Vienna.

In both cases the telex machines were in the offices of the parties, and the messages were received inside normal working hours. In **Brinkibon** the House of Lords said that a telex message sent outside working hours would not be considered instantaneous, so the time and place in which the contract was completed would be determined by the intentions of the parties, standard business practice and, if possible, by analysing where the risk should most fairly lie.

Misdirected acceptance

Where a letter of acceptance is lost or delayed because the offeree has wrongly or incompletely addressed it through their own carelessness, it seems reasonable that the postal rule should not apply, although there is no precise authority to this effect. Treitel, a leading contract law academic, suggests that a better rule might be that if a badly addressed acceptance takes effect at all, it should do so at the time which is least advantageous to the party responsible for the misdirection.

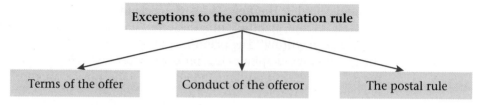

Figure 23.8 **Exceptions to the communication rule**

Effect of the postal rule

The postal rule has three main practical consequences:

■ A postal acceptance can take effect when it is posted, even if it gets lost in the post and never reaches the offeror. In **Household Fire Insurance *v* Grant** (1879) Grant had applied for (and therefore offered to buy) shares in the plaintiff company. The shares were allotted to him and his name was put on the register of shareholders. The company did write to say that the shares had been allotted to Grant, but the letter was lost in the post and he never received it. Some time later the company went into liquidation, and the liquidator claimed from Grant the balance owing on the price of his shares. It was held that Grant was bound to pay the balance, because the contract had been completed when the company's letter was posted.

It is likely that the same rule applies where the letter eventually arrives, but is delayed by postal problems.

■ Where an acceptance is posted after the offeror posts a revocation of the offer, but before that revocation has been received, the acceptance will be binding (posted acceptances take effect on posting, posted revocations on communication). This point is illustrated by the cases of **Byrne *v* Van Tienhoven** (1880) and **Henthorn *v* Fraser** (1892).

■ Where the postal rule applies, it seems unlikely that an offeree could revoke a postal acceptance by phone (or some other instant means of communication) before it arrives, though there is no English case on the point. A Scottish case, **Dunmore *v* Alexander** (1830), does appear to allow such a revocation, but the court's views were only *obiter* on this point.

Ignorance of the offer

It is generally thought that a person cannot accept an offer of which they are unaware, because in order to create a binding contract, the parties must reach agreement. If their wishes merely happen to coincide, that may be very convenient for both, but it does not constitute a contract and cannot legally bind them. Thus, if Ann advertises a reward for the return of a lost cat and Ben, not having seen or heard of the advertisement, comes across the cat, reads Ann's address on its collar and takes it back to Ann, is Ann bound to pay Ben the reward? No English case has clearly decided this point, and the cases abroad conflict with the main English case. On general principles Ben is probably unable to claim the reward.

In the American case of **Williams** *v* **Carwardine** (1833) the defendant offered a $20 reward for information leading to the discovery of the murderer of Walter Carwardine, and leaflets concerning the reward were distributed in the area where the plaintiff lived. The plaintiff apparently knew about the reward, but when she gave the information it was not in order to receive the money. She believed she had only a short time to live, and thought that giving the information might ease her conscience. The court held that she was entitled to the reward: she was aware of the offer and had complied with its terms, and her motive for doing so was irrelevant. A second US case, **Fitch** *v* **Snedaker** (1868), stated that a person who gives information without knowledge of the offer of a reward cannot claim the reward.

The main English case on this topic is **Gibbons** *v* **Proctor** (1891). A reward had been advertised for information leading to the arrest or conviction of the perpetrator of a particular crime and the plaintiff attempted to claim the reward, even though he had not originally known of the offer. He was allowed to receive the money, but the result does not shed much light on the problem because the plaintiff did know of the offer of reward by the time the information was given on his behalf to the person named in the advertisement.

Following the Australian case of **R** *v* **Clarke** (1927), it would appear that if the offeree knew of the offer in the past but has completely forgotten about it, they are treated as never having known about it. In that case a reward was offered by the Australian government for information leading to the conviction of the murderers of two policemen. The government also promised that an accomplice giving such information would receive a free pardon. Clarke was such an accomplice, who panicked and provided the information required in order to obtain the pardon, forgetting, at the time, about the reward. He remembered it later, but it was held that he was not entitled to the money.

Cross-offers

These present a similar problem. If Ann writes to Ben offering to sell her television for £50, and by coincidence Ben happens to write offering to buy the television for £50, the two letters crossing in the post, do the letters create a contract between them? On the principles of offer and acceptance it appears not, since the offeree does not know about the offer at the time of the potential acceptance. The point has never been decided in a case but there are *obiter dicta* in **Tinn** *v* **Hoffman** (1873) which suggest there would be no contract.

Quick quiz 23.6

1 What do we mean by the 'postal rule'?

2 Give two exceptions to the postal rule.

3 If Ben puts a sign in his car window saying 'For sale £500 ONO' and Ann, knowing that Ben wants to buy a new car but not having seen the advert in his car window, sends him an e-mail saying she will buy his car for £600, is there a binding contract between them?

4 If Ben puts a notice in his car that he would pay £500 to the first person who found his missing cat, and Ann had not seen the notice but found the missing cat and returned it to him, is Ben bound to pay Ann £500?

Time of the formation of the contract

Normally, a contract is formed when an effective acceptance has been communicated to the offeree. An exception to this is the postal rule, where the contract is formed at the time the acceptance is posted and there is no need for communication. A further exception to the general rule has been created by s. 11 of the Electronic Communications Act 2000. This establishes the precise time at which an electronic contract is made. Electronic contracts are concluded when the customer has both:

■ received an acknowledgement that their acceptance has been received; and
■ confirmed their receipt of that acknowledgement.

These communications are taken to be effective when the receiving party is able to access them. Section 11 applies unless the parties agree otherwise. Thus electronic contracts will normally be formed at a later stage than other contracts.

Offer and acceptance implied by the court

Sometimes the parties may be in dispute as to whether a contract existed between them. They may never have signed any written agreement but one party may argue that the offer and acceptance had been made orally or through their conduct. Thus, in **Baird Textile Holdings Ltd** *v* **Marks & Spencer plc** (2001) Marks & Spencer had been in a business relationship with Baird Textile Holdings (BTH) for 30 years. BTH were based in the United Kingdom and had been a major supplier of clothes to Marks & Spencer over the years. In October 1999, Marks & Spencer advised BTH that it was ending all supply arrangements between them with effect from the end of the current production season. BTH brought a legal action against Marks & Spencer, alleging that they had a contract with the company, and that a term of this contract had been breached by Marks & Spencer's terminating their supply arrangements in this way. The Court of Appeal held that there was no contract governing the relationship between the two litigants and that therefore Marks & Spencer were not in breach of a contract. It held that a contract should only be implied if it was necessary to do so 'to give business reality to a transaction and to create enforceable obligations between parties who are dealing with one another in circumstances in which one would expect that business reality and those enforceable obligations to exist'. It would not be necessary to imply such a contract if the parties might have acted in just the same way as they did without a contract. Marks & Spencer had preferred not to be bound by a contract so that they had maximum flexibility. For business reasons BTH had accepted this state of affairs.

How important are offer and acceptance?

Although offer and acceptance can provide the courts with a useful technique for assessing at what point an agreement should be binding, what the courts are really looking to judge is whether the parties have come to an agreement, and there are some cases in which the rules on offer and acceptance give little help.

An example of this type of situation is **Clarke v Earl of Dunraven** (1897), which concerned two yacht owners who had entered for a yacht race. The paper-work they completed in order to enter included an undertaking to obey the club rules, and these rules contained an obligation to pay for 'all damages' caused by fouling. During the manoeuvring at the start of the race, one yacht, the *Satanita*, fouled another, the *Valkyrie*, which sank as a result. The owner of the *Valkyrie* sued the owner of the *Satanita* for the cost of the lost yacht, but the defendant claimed that he was under no obligation to pay the whole cost, and was only liable to pay the lesser damages laid down by a statute which limited liability to £8 for every ton of the yacht. The plaintiff claimed that entering the competition in accordance with the rules had created a contract between the competitors, and this contract obliged the defendant to pay 'all damages'.

Clearly, it was difficult to see how there could be an offer by one competitor and acceptance by the other, since their relations had been with the yacht club and not with each other. There was obviously an offer and an acceptance between each competitor and the club, but was there a contract between the competitors? The House of Lords held that there was, on the basis that 'a contract is concluded when one party has communicated to another an offer and that other has accepted it or when the parties have united in a concurrent expression of intention to create a legal obligation'. Therefore, responsibility for accidents was governed by the race rules, and the defendant had to pay the full cost of the yacht.

There are problems in analysing the contract between the entrants to the race in terms of offer and acceptance. It seems rather far-fetched to imagine that, on starting the race, each competitor was making an offer to all the other competitors and simultaneously accepting their offers – and in any case, since the offers and acceptances would all occur at the same moment, they would be cross-offers and would technically not create a contract.

As we have seen, contracts for the sale of land are also examples of agreements that do not usually fall neatly into concepts of offer and acceptance. We will also see later that the problems arising from the offer and acceptance analysis are sometimes avoided by the courts using the device of collateral contracts.

Problems with offer and acceptance

Artificiality

Clearly there are situations in which the concepts of offer and acceptance have to be stretched, and interpreted rather artificially, even though it is obvious that the parties have reached an agreement. In **Gibson v Manchester City Council** (1979)

Lord Denning made it clear that he was in favour of looking at negotiations as a whole, in order to determine whether there was a contract, rather than trying to impose offer and acceptance on the facts, but his method has largely been rejected by the courts as being too uncertain and allowing too wide a discretion.

Revocation of unilateral offers

The problem of whether a unilateral offer can be accepted by part-performance has caused difficulties for the courts. It can be argued that, since the offeree has not promised to complete performance, they are free to stop at any time, so the offeror should be equally free to revoke the offer at any time. But this would mean, for example, that if A says to B, 'I'll pay you £100 if you paint my living room', A could withdraw the offer even though B had painted all but one square foot of the room, and pay nothing.

This is generally considered unjust, and various academics have expressed the view that, in fact, an offer cannot be withdrawn once there has been substantial performance. American academics have contended that the offeror can be seen as making two offers: the main offer that the price will be paid when the act is performed, and an implied accompanying offer that the main offer will not be revoked once performance has begun. On this assumption, the act of starting performance is both acceptance of the implied offer, and consideration for the secondary promise that the offer will not be withdrawn once performance begins. An offeror who does attempt to revoke the offer after performance has started may be sued for the breach of the secondary promise.

In England this approach has been considered rather artificial. Sir Frederick Pollock has reasoned that it might be more realistic to say that the main offer itself is accepted by beginning rather than completing performance, on the basis that acceptance simply means agreement to the terms of the offer, and there are many circumstances in which beginning performance will mean just that. Whether an act counts as beginning performance, and therefore accepting the offer, or whether it is just preparation for performing will depend on the facts of the case – so, for example, an offer of a reward for the return of lost property could still be revoked after someone had spent time looking for the property without success, but not after they had actually found it and taken steps towards returning it to the owner. This principle was adopted in 1937 by the Law Revision Committee.

Revocation of offers for specific periods

The rule that an offer can be revoked at any time before acceptance even if the offeror has said it will remain open for a specified time could be considered unfairly biased in favour of the offeror, and makes it difficult for the offeree to plan their affairs with certainty.

In a Working Paper published in 1975, the Law Commission recommended that where an offeror promises not to revoke the offer for a specified time, that promise should be binding, without the need for consideration, and if it is broken the offeree should be able to sue for damages.

An 'all or nothing' approach

The 'all or nothing' approach of offer and acceptance is not helpful in cases where there is clearly not a binding contract under that approach, and yet going back on agreements made would cause great hardship or inconvenience to one party. The problems associated with house-buying are well known – the buyer may go to all the expense of a survey and solicitor's fees, and may even have sold their own house, only to find that the seller withdraws the house from sale, sells it to someone else, or demands a higher price – generally known as 'gazumping'. So long as all this takes place before contracts are exchanged, the buyer has no remedy at all (though the government is proposing to legislate to deal with some of these specific problems). Similarly, in a commercial situation, pressure of time may mean that a company starts work on a potential project before a contract is drawn up and signed. They will be at a disadvantage if in the end the other party decides not to contract.

Objectivity

The courts claim that they are concerned with following the intention of the parties in deciding whether there is a contract, yet they make it quite clear that they are not actually seeking to discover what was intended, but what, looking at the parties' behaviour, an 'officious bystander' might assume they intended. This can mean that even though the parties were actually in agreement, no contract results, as was the case in **Felthouse** *v* **Bindley** – the nephew had asked for the horse to be kept out of the sale because he was going to sell it to his uncle, but because he did not actually communicate his acceptance, there was no contract.

Reading on the web

The Consumer Protection (Distance Selling) Regulations 2000 are available on the website of the Office of Public Sector Information at:

www.opsi.gov.uk/si/si2000/20002334.htm

The Office of Fair Trading provides a helpful guide to the distance selling regulations on its website at:

www.oft.gov.uk/Business/Legal/DSR/default.htm

Chapter summary

Introduction

For a contract to exist, usually one party must have made an offer, and the other must have accepted it. Once acceptance takes effect, a contract will usually be binding on both parties.

Unilateral and bilateral contracts

Most contracts are bilateral. This means that each party takes on an obligation, usually by promising the other something. By contrast, a unilateral contract arises where only one party assumes an obligation under the contract.

Offer

The person making an offer is called the offeror, and the person to whom the offer is made is called the offeree. A communication will be treated as an offer if it indicates the terms on which the offeror is prepared to make a contract and gives a clear indication that the offeror intends to be bound by those terms if they are accepted by the offeree. An offer may be express or implied.

Offers to the public at large

In most cases, an offer will be made to a specified person, though offers can be addressed to a group of people, or even to the general public. A contract arising from an offer to the public at large, like that in **Carlill** *v* **Carbolic Smoke Ball Co.** (1893), is usually a unilateral contract.

Invitations to treat

Some kinds of transaction involve a preliminary stage in which one party invites the other to make an offer. This stage is called an invitation to treat. Confusion can sometimes arise when what would appear, in the everyday sense of the word, to be an offer, is held by the law to be only an invitation to treat. This issue arises particularly in the following areas.

Advertisements

Advertisements for unilateral contracts are usually treated as offers. Advertisements for a bilateral contract are generally considered invitations to treat.

Shopping

Price-marked goods displayed on the shelves or in the windows of shops are generally regarded as invitations to treat, rather than offers to sell goods at that price: **Pharmaceutical Society of Great Britain** *v* **Boots Cash Chemists (Southern) Ltd** (1953).

Timetables and tickets for transport

The legal position here is rather unclear, no single reliable rule has emerged, and it seems that the exact point at which a contract is made depends in each case on the particular facts.

How long does an offer last?

An offer may cease to exist under any of the following circumstances:

Specified time

Where an offeror states that an offer will remain open for a specific length of time, it lapses when that time is up.

Reasonable length of time

Where the offeror has not specified how long the offer will remain open, it will lapse after a reasonable length of time has passed.

Failure of a precondition

Some offers are made subject to certain conditions, and if such conditions are not in place, the offer may lapse.

Rejection

An offer lapses when the offeree rejects it.

Counter-offer

A counter-offer terminates the original offer: **Hyde** v **Wrench** (1840).

Requests for information

A request for information about an offer (such as whether delivery could be earlier than suggested) does not amount to a counter-offer, so the original offer remains open.

Death of the offeror

The position is not entirely clear, but it appears that if the offeree knows that the offeror has died, the offer will lapse; if the offeree is unaware of the offeror's death, it probably will not.

Death of the offeree

There is no English case on this point, but it seems probable that the offer lapses and cannot be accepted after the offeree's death by the offeree's representatives.

Withdrawal of offer

The withdrawal of an offer is sometimes described as the revocation of an offer. The old case of **Payne** v **Cave** (1789) establishes the principle that an offer may be withdrawn at any time up until it is accepted. A number of rules apply in relation to the withdrawal of offers.

Withdrawal must be communicated

It is not enough for offerors simply to change their mind about an offer; they must notify the offeree that it is being revoked: **Byrne** *v* **Van Tienhoven** (1880). The revocation of an offer does not have to be communicated by the offeror; the communication can be made by some other reliable source: **Dickinson** *v* **Dodds** (1876).

Withdrawal of an offer to enter into a unilateral contract

There are a number of special rules that apply in relation to the revocation of an offer to enter into a unilateral contract. An offer to enter into such a contract cannot be revoked once the offeree has commenced performance: **Errington** *v* **Errington** (1952).

Acceptance

Acceptance of an offer means unconditional agreement to all the terms of that offer. Merely remaining silent cannot amount to an acceptance, unless it is absolutely clear that acceptance was intended: **Felthouse** *v* **Bindley** (1862).

Acceptance of an offer to enter into a unilateral contract

Unilateral contracts are usually accepted by conduct. There is no acceptance until the relevant act has been completely performed.

Acceptance must be unconditional

An acceptance must accept the precise terms of an offer.

Negotiation and the 'battle of the forms'

Where parties carry on a long process of negotiation, it may be difficult to pinpoint exactly when an offer has been made and accepted. In such cases the courts will look at the whole course of negotiations to decide whether the parties have in fact reached agreement at all and, if so, when. This process can be particularly difficult where the so-called 'battle of the forms' arises. The general rule in such cases is that the 'last shot' wins the battle. Each new form issued is treated as a counter-offer, so that when one party performs its obligation under the contract (by delivering goods, for example), that action will be seen as acceptance by conduct of the offer in the last form.

Specified methods of acceptance

If an offeror states that his or her offer must be accepted in a particular way, then only acceptance by that method or an equally effective one will be binding. Where a specified method of acceptance has been included for the offeree's own benefit, however, the offeree is not obliged to accept in that way.

Acceptance must be communicated

An acceptance does not usually take effect until it is communicated to the offeror.

Exceptions to the communication rule

There are some circumstances in which an acceptance may take effect without being communicated to the offeror.

Terms of the offer

An offer may state or imply that acceptance need not be communicated to the offeror.

Conduct of the offeror

An offeror who fails to receive an acceptance through their own fault may be prevented from claiming that the non-communication means they should not be bound by the contract.

The postal rule

The general rule for acceptances by post is that they take effect when they are posted, rather than when they are communicated: **Adams *v* Lindsell** (1818). The traditional title 'postal rule' has become slightly misleading because the rule does not only apply to the post but could also potentially apply to certain other non-instantaneous modes of communication. There are certain exceptions to the postal rule:

- offers requiring communication of acceptance;
- instant methods of communication;
- misdirected acceptance.

Ignorance of the offer

It is generally thought that a person cannot accept an offer of which they are unaware, because in order to create a binding contract, the parties must reach agreement. If their wishes merely happen to coincide, that may be very convenient for both, but it does not constitute a contract and cannot legally bind them.

Time of the formation of the contract

Normally, a contract is formed when an effective acceptance has been communicated to the offeree.

Question and answer guide

For exam questions covering the material in this chapter, please see the Question and answer guides section of Chapter 27: Compensatory damages.

mylawchamber

Visit **www.mylawchamber.co.uk/elliottqa** to access interactive questions, quizzes and activities to test yourself on this chapter.

Chapter 24 Intention to create legal relations

This chapter discusses:

- how an agreement will only be legally binding if the parties intend it to be so;
- where an agreement is domestic or social, there is a rebuttable presumption that the parties do not intend to create legal relations;
- for commercial agreements there is a presumption that the parties do intend the agreement to be legally binding;
- certain exceptions to these presumptions.

Introduction

If two or more parties make an agreement without any intention of being legally bound by it, that agreement will not be regarded by the courts as a contract. It is important to remember with regard to this issue that the courts assess the parties' intentions objectively – so, if to onlookers their behaviour or words would suggest they intended to be bound, the fact that one secretly had reservations is irrelevant.

As far as intent to be legally bound is concerned, contracts can be divided into domestic and social agreements on the one hand and commercial transactions on the other. Where an agreement falls into the domestic and social category, there is a rebuttable presumption that the parties do not intend to create legal relations. The reverse applies in commercial agreements, where it is presumed that the parties do intend such agreements to be legally binding. Again, this principle can be rebutted if there is evidence that the parties did not intend their agreement to be legally enforceable.

Social and domestic agreements

Agreements between husband and wife

Where a husband and wife who are living together as one household make an agreement, courts will assume that they do not intend to be legally bound, unless there is evidence to the contrary. In **Balfour** *v* **Balfour** (1919) the defendant was a civil servant stationed in Ceylon (now Sri Lanka). While the couple were on leave in England, Mrs Balfour was taken ill, and it eventually became clear that her husband would have to return by himself. He promised to pay her a monthly maintenance allowance of £30. They later decided to separate, upon which the husband refused to make any more payments. The Court of Appeal decided he was not bound to pay the allowance because at the time when the agreement was made there was no intention to create legal relations. When this type of agreement was made between husband and wife, said Atkin LJ, it was a family matter in which the courts really had no place to interfere.

On its facts, **Balfour** might well be decided differently if it arose today; while the courts still seem reluctant to give effect to agreements made while spouses are still cohabiting, there have been a string of cases in which those who are separating or divorcing are treated as intending to create legal relations. In **Merritt v Merritt** (1970) Mr Merritt had left his wife to go and live with another woman, and subsequently met his spouse to resolve various financial arrangements. Sitting in Mr Merritt's car, they decided that he would pay his wife £40 a month, out of which she was to pay the outstanding mortgage payments on their house; he would transfer the house to her sole ownership when the mortgage was paid off. Mrs Merritt then refused to get out of the car until her husband put the agreement in writing. Eventually, he signed a piece of paper stating what they had agreed. The wife duly paid off the mortgage, but the husband then refused to transfer ownership of the house to her. The Court of Appeal upheld the wife's claim. Lord Denning pointed out that the presumption applied in **Balfour v Balfour**, that an agreement between husband and wife was 'a family arrangement', and was not valid where the parties had separated or were about to do so. In such circumstances the parties 'do not rely on honourable understandings', but 'bargain keenly', and it could be safely presumed that any agreement between them was intended to be legally binding.

The US courts have shown themselves increasingly willing to give effect to domestic agreements, as shown by the case of **Morone v Morone** (1980), where an agreement between a cohabiting couple that the man would financially support the woman in return for her help in running their home and helping in his business was held to be binding.

Agreements between parent and child

Agreements of a domestic nature between parents and children are also presumed not to be intended to be binding, though again the presumption can be rebutted. In **Jones v Padavatton** (1969) the plaintiff was a resident of Trinidad. Her daughter had a secretarial job in Washington, but her mother wanted her to give it up and train to be a barrister in England. The mother therefore volunteered to give her daughter a monthly allowance for the duration of her Bar studies. The daughter accepted the offer and went to England. Later on, the pair made a second agreement, under which the mother bought a house for the daughter to live in, and in which she could rent out rooms in order to support herself, instead of receiving the allowance. Neither agreement was ever put in writing. The daughter persistently failed to pass her Bar examinations and, five years after the original bargain was made, they quarrelled, and her mother sought possession of the house. On the facts of the case, the majority of the Court of Appeal considered that neither agreement was intended to create legal relations: they were merely family arrangements in which both parties, who had been close at the time, were happy to trust each other to keep the bargain. The mother was therefore entitled to possession of the house.

Social agreements

The presumption that an agreement is not intended to be legally binding is also applied to social relationships between people who are not related. Again, it can be rebutted. In **Simpkins v Pays** (1955) the plaintiff enjoyed entering competitions run in Sunday newspapers. When he took lodgings in the defendant's house, she and her granddaughter began to do the competitions with him, sharing the cost of entry. The plaintiff filled in the forms in the name of the defendant, and she promised to share any winnings. Eventually, one of the entries was successful, and the defendant won £750. The plaintiff claimed a third of the sum as his share of the prize, but the defendant refused, claiming that she had not intended to be legally bound by the agreement. The court upheld the plaintiff's claim, considering that they had all contributed to the competition with the expectation that any prize would be shared.

Similarly, in **Peck v Lateu** (1973) the court found an intention to create legal relations where two women had agreed to share any money won by either of them at bingo.

Commercial agreements

There is a strong presumption in commercial agreements that the parties intend to be legally bound, and, unless there is very clear contrary evidence, this presumption will not be rebutted. In **Esso Petroleum Ltd v Customs and Excise Commissioners** (1976) Esso ran a sales promotion in which 'coins' showing members of the England football squad for the 1970 World Cup were to be given away free, one with every four gallons of petrol. The scheme was advertised on television and by posters at filling stations. The case arose when, for tax purposes, it became necessary to decide whether or not there was a contract of sale – did a motorist who bought four gallons of petrol have a contractual right to one of the coins? The House of Lords held, by a majority, that the coins were not being sold, and so were not liable for tax, but that there was intent to create legal relations. Lord Simon pointed out that 'the whole transaction took place in a setting of business relations', that it was undesirable to allow companies to make promises in advertisements that they were not bound to keep, and that Esso knew that, despite the coins' negligible monetary value, they would be attractive to motorists and Esso would therefore derive considerable commercial benefit from the scheme.

In **J Evans & Son (Portsmouth) Ltd v Andrea Merzario Ltd** (1976) the plaintiffs were machinery importers, who had regularly used the defendants, a firm of forwarding agents, to arrange transport of their goods. The machinery was prone to rust if stored on deck, and so it had always been agreed that it would be carried below decks. In 1967, in the course of a 'courtesy call' to the plaintiffs, the defendants' representative put forward the idea of carrying the goods by container transport, assuring them that their containers would always be kept below decks because of the rust problem (many container ships are designed to have the containers stacked on deck). The plaintiffs agreed to the change. About a year later, a container with one of the plaintiffs' machines inside was carried on deck instead of below, and, not being properly secured, fell overboard as the ship left port and was lost. The plaintiffs sued, and the defendants argued that the promise to store the containers below decks was not intended to be legally binding, since it was made in the course of a courtesy call, was not related to any particular transaction, and its future duration was not specified. The Court of Appeal rejected this argument, saying that the background to the promise meant that an intent to be contractually bound could be inferred: the parties had previously done business together, in which goods were always transported below decks, and the plaintiffs would not have agreed to the change in method if the promise had not been made.

The presumption that parties to a commercial agreement intend to create legal relations may be rebutted where the words of a contract, or an offer, suggest that legal relations were not intended. There are three main situations where this will occur.

'Mere puffs'

Where an offer is extremely vague, or clearly not intended to be taken seriously, the law will not give its acceptance contractual effect. In **Weeks** *v* **Tybald** (1604) the defendant announced that he would give £100 to any suitable man who would marry his daughter, but it was held that his words were not intended to be taken seriously, and his promise was not legally binding.

This principle is sometimes applied to the extravagant language used in advertising and sales promotions, but only if there is no evidence of contractual intent. In **Carlill** *v* **Carbolic Smoke Ball Co.** (1893) (discussed at p. 482, above), the defendants argued that their statement was 'a mere puff', an advertising gimmick which was never intended to be taken seriously. This contention was rejected by the court, pointing out that the advertisement stated that the company had deposited £1,000 with their bankers 'to show their sincerity', which was strong evidence that they had intended to be legally bound.

Honour clauses

In **Rose & Frank Co.** *v* **J. R. Crompton & Bros Ltd** (1923) the plaintiffs had been buying goods from the defendants for some time, and in 1913, the parties signed an agreement that this arrangement should continue for a specified period, with prices set for six months at a time. Though otherwise ordinary, the agreement contained one unusual term, the 'honourable pledge clause'. It stated: 'This agreement is not entered into . . . as a formal or legal agreement, and shall not be subject to legal jurisdiction in the law courts . . . but it is only a definite expression and record of the purpose and intention of the parties concerned, to which they each honourably pledge themselves.' In 1919, the defendants terminated the agreement without giving the specified notice. The plaintiffs sued, making two separate claims. The first was for breach of the agreement contained in the written document of July 1913, that the buying and selling arrangement would continue for the specified period. This claim was rejected by the court, which held that the wording of the agreement placed neither side under any obligation to go on giving or accepting orders. Scrutton LJ commented: 'I can see no reason why, even in business matters, the parties should not intend to rely on each other's good faith and honour, and to exclude all idea of settling disputes by an outside intervention . . .'

The second claim concerned non-delivery of goods, which the plaintiffs had ordered in accordance with the agreement, before it was terminated. This claim was upheld, on the basis that when each individual order was placed and accepted, it constituted a new and separate contract, which was enforceable in its own right, without reference to the original document.

Similarly, where a football pools coupon states that it is 'binding in honour only', the pools company cannot be sued for payment by a winner: **Jones v Vernon's Pools** (1938).

Agreement 'subject to contract'

Use of these words on an agreement is usually (though not always) taken to mean that the parties do not intend to be legally bound until formal contracts are exchanged. If the parties subsequently act upon the agreement, their conduct may be interpreted as amounting to an intention to create the final contract. In **Confetti Records v Warner Music UK Ltd** (2003) the claimants owned the copyright in a music track that the defendant wished to use on a compilation album. Terms were discussed between the parties and the defendant sent a fax to the claimants containing deal terms, but marked 'subject to contract'. The claimant signed this and faxed it back. The court held that this did not amount to a contract. However, shortly afterwards, the claimants sent the defendant a copy of the track and an invoice stating that it was licensed for 'three years non-exclusive'. The court held that this amounted to an offer which was accepted when the defendant started to record the album. It was therefore too late for the claimant subsequently to withdraw the track, as there was already a binding contract.

 Quick quiz 24.1

1 When does a presumption apply that the parties to an agreement intended to create legal relations?

2 If an estate agent tells you that a house is sold 'subject to contract', what does this mean?

3 If a car salesman tells you that a car is the best car in the world and you could not find a better car if you visited every car salesroom in England, could you sue the salesman for breach of contract if you subsequently saw a car that you preferred?

4 If two businessmen reach an agreement for the sale of some butter to be imported from France, but the terms of agreement are ambiguous as to whether they intended at this stage to be legally bound by this agreement, what approach will the courts take?

Ambiguity

Where the words of a business agreement are ambiguous, the courts will favour the interpretation which suggests that the parties did intend to create legal relations, and therefore find that there is a contract. In **Edwards *v* Skyways Ltd** (1964) the plaintiff was a pilot employed by the defendants. As part of a redundancy agreement, Skyways promised to make an *ex gratia* payment of a specified amount in return for Mr Edwards not claiming his full pension rights. Later, the company refused to make the payment, claiming that the words '*ex gratia*' showed that there was no intention to create legal relations. The Court of Appeal rejected this argument, stating that this was a commercial agreement and there was therefore a strong presumption in favour of creating legal relations. The words '*ex gratia*' merely signified that the employers were not admitting any pre-existing liability to make the payment; it did not mean that they were not bound by the agreement.

Collective bargaining agreements

There is one exception to the rule that the parties to a commercial agreement are presumed to intend to be legally bound. Under a collective bargaining agreement, an employer negotiates pay and conditions with the workforce as a whole (usually represented by a trade union), rather than on an individual basis. Such agreements are binding in most countries, but in **Ford Motor Co. Ltd *v* Amalgamated Union of Engineering and Foundry Workers** (1969) it was held that in English law such an agreement was not intended to be legally binding. A carefully worded written agreement had been drawn up between Ford and various trade unions, including a clause stating that the unions should not call a strike unless specified negotiating procedures had been carried out first. The union breached this clause, and the plaintiffs sought to prevent them calling the strike. The court, basing its decision on public policy, held that there was evidence that at the time, it was the general opinion in the industrial world that such agreements were not legally enforceable, and that both sides would have known this. Therefore, they could not be said to have intended to be legally bound.

This approach is now contained in the Trade Union and Labour Relations (Consolidation) Act 1992, which states that collective agreements are conclusively presumed not to be intended to be legally binding unless they expressly state otherwise in writing. This presumption is rarely, if ever, displaced, and in the past few years has been relied upon by employers seeking to break agreements to negotiate with unions.

> ✓ **Know your terms 24.2**
>
> Define the following terms:
> 1 Presumption.
> 2 Honour clause.
> 3 Ambiguity.
> 4 Collective bargaining agreement.

Domestic and social agreements	Commercial agreements
Presumption that parties *do not intend* to create legal relations	Presumption that parties do intend to create legal relations

Figure 24.1 **Creating legal relations**

How important is intention to create legal relations?

In practice, it is rare for contract cases to involve problems with the requirement of intention to create legal relations. This is largely because, in many of the situations in which the issue might be raised, particularly domestic and social ones, there is no consideration. The courts will only consider intent to create legal relations if offer and acceptance and consideration have already been established.

The US academic Professor Williston has suggested that in fact the common law does not demand any positive intention to create a legal obligation as an element of contract. In his view, the separate element of intention serves no purpose in our system, and is useful only in legal systems which do not have the test of consideration to help them to determine the boundaries of contract. He suggests that mere social arrangements will be enforced as contracts if the other requirements – offer and acceptance and consideration, for example – are present, and the issue of intention to be legally bound adds nothing to the decision of the court. But the case of **Balfour v Balfour** is an example of offer, acceptance and consideration existing but there still being no contract, and the only explanation for this lack of contract seems to be that there was no intention to be legally bound.

Feminists argue that the presumption against contractual intention in domestic agreements is in fact the law's way of saying that the work usually done by women is not to be regarded as important – it is seen as something done out of love for the family, rather than an economic contribution which ought to be paid for.

Chapter summary

An agreement will only be legally binding if the parties intend it to be so. The courts assess the parties' intentions objectively. As far as intent to be legally bound is concerned, contracts can be divided into domestic and social agreements on the one hand and commercial transactions on the other. Where an agreement falls into the domestic and social category, there is a rebuttable presumption that the parties do not intend to create legal relations. The reverse applies in commercial agreements, where it is presumed that the parties do intend such agreements to be legally binding.

Social and domestic agreements

Agreements between husband and wife

Where a husband and wife who are living together as one household make an agreement, courts will assume that they do not intend to be legally bound, unless there is evidence to the contrary: **Balfour v Balfour** (1919).

Agreements between parent and child

Agreements of a domestic nature between parents and children are also presumed not to be intended to be binding, though again the presumption can be rebutted: **Jones** *v* **Padavatton** (1969).

Social agreements

The presumption that an agreement is not intended to be legally binding is also applied to social relationships between people who are not related.

Commercial agreements

There is a strong presumption in commercial agreements that the parties intend to be legally bound, and, unless there is very clear contrary evidence, this presumption will not be rebutted.

Exceptions to the commercial agreements presumption

There are three main situations where this presumption will be rebutted.

'Mere puffs'

Where an offer is extremely vague, or clearly not intended to be taken seriously, the law will not give its acceptance contractual effect.

Honour clauses

In **Rose & Frank Co.** *v* **Crompton & Bros** (1923) Scrutton LJ commented: 'I can see no reason why, even in business matters, the parties should not intend to rely on each other's good faith and honour, and to exclude all idea of settling disputes by an outside intervention . . .'

Agreement 'subject to contract'

Use of these words on an agreement is usually (though not always) taken to mean that the parties do not intend to be legally bound until formal contracts are exchanged.

Ambiguity

Where the words of a business agreement are ambiguous, the courts will favour the interpretation which suggests that the parties did intend to create legal relations, and therefore find that there is a contract.

Collective bargaining agreements

In English law, collective bargaining agreements are not intended to be legally binding.

Question and answer guide

For exam questions covering the material in this chapter, please see the Question and answer guide section of Chapter 27: Compensatory damages.

Chapter 25

Consideration

This chapter discusses:

- the requirement of consideration, whereby each party must give something in return for what is gained under the agreement;
- consideration must not be past;
- consideration must be sufficient;
- consideration must be of economic value;
- consideration can be a promise not to sue.

Introduction

In English law, an agreement is not usually binding unless it is supported by what is called consideration. Put simply, this means that each party must give something in return for what is gained from the other party, so if you wish to enforce someone's promise to you, you must prove that you gave something in return for that promise.

Consideration may be a thing or a service – I give you my car and you give me £1,000, or you clean my windows and I pay you £5. It may also take the form of promises – I promise to work for you and you promise to pay me a salary. A promise not supported by consideration is called a gratuitous promise; for example, if I simply say I will give you my car, without requiring anything in return. This type of promise is not usually enforceable in law.

Although up to now we have been talking about the requirements for making a contract in the first place, it is important to note that many of the problems concerning consideration arise not when a contract is made, but when one or other party seeks to modify it – such as by paying a lower price than that agreed. A promise to accept such a modification was traditionally not binding unless supported by new consideration, but recent cases have changed the rules in such situations.

What is consideration?

Consideration is usually described as being something which represents either some benefit to the person making a promise (the promisor) or some detriment to the person to whom the promise is made (the promisee), or both.

In **Dunlop** *v* **Selfridge** (1915) the House of Lords explained consideration in terms of purchase and sale – the plaintiff must show that he or she has bought the defendant's promise, by doing, giving or promising something in return for it.

Atiyah has suggested that consideration can simply be seen as 'a reason for the enforcement of promises', with that reason being 'the justice of the case'.

Promisor and promisee

In most contracts, two promises will be exchanged, so each party is both a promisor and a promisee. In a contract case, the claimant will often be arguing that the defendant has broken the promise made to the claimant, and therefore the claimant will usually be the promisee, and the defendant will be the promisor. So if Ann contracts to paint Ben's bathroom and Ben promises to pay her £200 for doing it, there are two promises in this contract: Ann's promise to do the painting and Ben's promise to pay Ann £200. If Ann fails to paint the bathroom, Ben can sue her, and if the issue of consideration arises, Ben will seek to prove that his promise to pay £200 was consideration for Ann's promise to paint the bathroom. In that action, Ann will be the promisor, and Ben the promisee.

On the other hand, if Ann does the work but Ben does not pay the price, Ben can be sued by Ann, and if consideration is at issue, Ann will have to prove that her promise to paint the bathroom was consideration for Ben's promise to pay. In that action, Ann will be the promisee and Ben the promisor.

Ann's promise to paint the bathroom can be portrayed by the following diagram:

Paint the bathroom ⟶

Ann	Ben
promisor	promisee

Ben's promise to pay £200 can be portrayed by the following diagram:

⟵ £200

Ann	Ben
promisee	promisor

The contract between Ann and Ben can be portrayed by the following diagram:

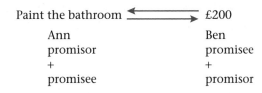

Paint the bathroom ⇄ £200

Ann	Ben
promisor	promisee
+	+
promisee	promisor

Consideration need not benefit the promisor

Consideration need not benefit the promisor – so there can be consideration where the promisee suffers some detriment at the promisor's request, but this gives no particular benefit to the promisor. For example, in **Jones** *v* **Padavatton** (see p. 511 above), the daughter's giving up her job would be consideration for the mother providing an allowance, even though it did not directly benefit the mother (though as we have seen, the mother's promise was not binding because there was no intention to create legal relations).

Another way in which consideration can be given by the promisee without benefiting the promisor is where contracts are made for the benefit of a third party – if, for example, Ann promises to pay Ben to give Ann's daughter driving lessons, Ben will be able to enforce this promise; although he has given no direct benefit to Ann, he has suffered some detriment in that he has provided the lessons.

'Executory' and 'executed' consideration

Consideration is often divided into two categories: executory and executed. Executory consideration is where something is to be done in the future after the contract has been formed. Executory consideration exists when the contracting parties make promises to each other because they are promising something for the future, after the contract has been made – on making the contract you promise to deliver some goods to me and I promise to pay for them when they arrive, for example. A bilateral contract usually involves executory consideration.

Executed consideration is where at the time of the formation of the contract the consideration has already been performed. If I promise to give £20 to anyone who finds my lost handbag, returning the bag is both acceptance of my offer (and thus the time when the contract is formed) and executed consideration for my promise. Executed consideration usually occurs in unilateral contracts.

Consideration must not be past

Lawyers often say that consideration must not be past, but this is slightly confusing because the emphasis is not really about the time that the consideration was given, but more about whether the consideration was given in exchange for the other party's consideration. Consideration must be given **in return** for the promise or act of the other party; something done, given or promised for another reason will not count as consideration. If one party has completed performance before the other offered consideration, then as a matter of fact it is unlikely that the earlier performance was done in return for that consideration. So, if Ann looks after Ben's dog while Ben is on holiday, and when Ben returns he promises to give Ann some money, Ann cannot enforce that promise because she did not look after the dog in return for it – she had already looked after the dog.

This issue arose in **Roscorla v Thomas** (1842). The defendant sold the plaintiff a horse. After the sale was completed, the defendant told the plaintiff that the animal was 'sound and free from any vice'. This turned out to be rather far from the truth, and the plaintiff sued. The court held that the defendant's promise was unenforceable, because it was made after the sale. If the promise about the horse's condition had been made before, the plaintiff would have provided consideration for it by buying the horse. As it was made after the sale, the consideration was past, for it had not been given in return for the promise.

Whether or not consideration is past is a question of fact, and the wording of an agreement will not necessarily be conclusive. In **Re McArdle** (1951) a widow had been left the family home in her husband's will. The will allowed her to live in it for the rest of her life, and on her death it was to be inherited by their five children equally. During the mother's lifetime, one of her sons and his wife lived with her in the house and the daughter-in-law paid for some home improvements. When these were finished, the other four children signed a document which promised to pay her £488 for the work, 'in consideration of [her] carrying out certain alterations and improvements to the property'.

After the mother died, the daughter-in-law tried to claim the money, but her husband's brothers and sisters refused to pay. The Court of Appeal held that although the wording of the document suggested that the payment related to work to be done in the future, the facts of the case made it clear that the promise was given in return for something already done; it was therefore past consideration, and the promise was not binding.

There are two exceptions to the rule that past consideration is no consideration. The first is where the past consideration was provided at the promisor's request, and it was understood that payment would be made. This exception can be traced back to the old case of **Lampleigh v Brathwait** (1615). Thomas Brathwait had been convicted of killing a man, and he asked Anthony Lampleigh to obtain a pardon for him from the King. After considerable trouble and expense, Lampleigh managed to do so. In the excitement of getting his pardon, Brathwait promised to pay Lampleigh £100, but later refused to hand over the money, so Lampleigh sued.

It might appear that Lampleigh's consideration was past, since he had secured the pardon before the promise to pay was made. In fact, the court upheld Lampleigh's claim. It reasoned that Lampleigh had obtained the pardon at Brathwait's own request, and this request carried with it the unspoken understanding that the service would be paid for. Lampleigh obtained the pardon after, and in return for, this implied promise to pay, and so obtaining the pardon was good consideration for the promise to pay. The later promise, specifying that £100 would be paid, was said to be merely confirmation of the original, unspoken one.

This reasoning seems less odd when we consider that today there are many requests which carry with them unsaid promises to pay – when we ask a taxi driver to take us somewhere, or ask the milkman to leave an extra pint, we do not actually say that we will pay for those goods and services, but clearly it is understood by both parties that we will. It may well be that requests to secure royal pardons had the same well-understood effect in 1615.

A (slightly) more recent case on this principle is **Re Casey's Patents** (1892). The defendants owned some patent rights, and the plaintiff worked for them. They wrote to him, saying that in consideration of his services as manager in relation to the patents, they were going to give him a one-third interest in them. They later claimed that, as their promise was made in relation to services which the plaintiff had already given, it was past consideration and therefore the promise was not

> ✓ **Know your terms 25.1**
>
> Define the following terms:
>
> 1 Consideration.
> 2 Past consideration.
> 3 Promisee.
> 4 Executory consideration.

binding. The court held, however, that the plaintiff's services were clearly always meant to be paid for, and the promise was merely putting this expectation into the form of a specified amount.

The second exception to the rule on past consideration is the bill of exchange. Under s. 27 of the Bills of Exchange Act 1882 an 'antecedent debt or liability' may be consideration for receipt of a bill of exchange.

Consideration must be sufficient

Although consideration must provide some benefit to the promisor or detriment to the promisee, these do not have to amount to a great deal. This principle is usually described in the rather confusing phrase 'consideration must be sufficient but need not be adequate', which effectively means that the courts will not inquire into the adequacy of consideration, so long as there is some. Providing something is given in return for a promise, it does not matter that it is not much, or not what the promise would usually be considered to be worth. So if, for example, A promises to sell B her state-of-the-art CD player for £5, the consideration paid by B clearly provides very little benefit to A, and amounts to only a small loss to B, but nevertheless, the transaction will be binding because some consideration has been provided by both sides. It is often said that just one peppercorn can be good consideration – even if the promisee does not like pepper!

The reason for this rule is the old idea of freedom of contract, which required that the parties themselves should be allowed to make the bargains that suit them, without interference from the courts.

In **Thomas** *v* **Thomas** (1842) the plaintiff was a widow whose husband had stated that, if he died before his wife, she should be allowed to live in his house for the rest of her life, after which it was to pass to his sons. When the man died, the defendant, who was his executor, agreed that the widow could continue to occupy the house in return for a promise that she would pay £1 a year and keep the house in good repair. Despite this, some time later, the defendants tried to evict the widow, so she sued them for breach of contract. The defendants claimed that their promise was not binding due to lack of consideration. However, the court held that the widow's promise to pay £1 and keep up the repairs was sufficient consideration to make the owners' promise binding.

The same principle was applied in **Chappell** *v* **Nestlé** (1960). Nestlé ran a special offer involving a record of a song called 'Rockin' Shoes' – customers could get a copy of the record by sending in 1s 6d (about 7.5p) and three wrappers from Nestlé's bars of chocolate. The copyright holders for the record brought an action against Nestlé, which among other things claimed that royalties should be paid on the price of the record.

To calculate the royalties due, it was necessary to establish what price Nestlé were charging for the record, and the copyright holder alleged that this price (which was the consideration for the promise to send the record) included the three wrappers. Nestlé, on the other hand, contended that the consideration was only the 1s 6d, and that they threw away the wrappers they received. The House of Lords held that the wrappers did form part of the consideration – the fact that they were of no real worth to Nestlé was irrelevant.

The interesting implication of this case is that, if the fact that the wrappers were useless to Nestlé was irrelevant, presumably wrappers alone could have amounted to consideration – if, for example, Nestlé had just asked for three wrappers, and not requested money in addition.

Consideration must be of economic value

It is sometimes said that consideration must have some 'economic' value, though, as the Nestlé case shows, this economic value may be negligible. What this principle basically seems to mean is that there must be some physical value, rather than just an emotional or sentimental one. In **Thomas** *v* **Thomas** (discussed above), for example, the plaintiff suggested that following her husband's wishes was part of the consideration, but the court rejected this argument because they said the husband's wishes had no economic value (though in the event this did not alter the outcome of the case, as the widow's own promise was consideration).

Similarly, in **White** *v* **Bluett** (1853), a father promised not to make his son repay money he had borrowed, if the son promised not to keep boring him with complaints. The court held that the son's promise was not sufficient consideration to make his father's promise binding, because it had no economic value.

Quick quiz 25.2

1 If I promise to love you forever if you give me a diamond ring, have I given consideration for the ring?

2 If I promise to love you forever and to bake your favourite chocolate brownies if you give me a diamond ring, have I given consideration for the ring?

3 If I promise to pay you £300 if you paint my mother's bathroom, is there consideration for a binding contract?

4 What is the *ratio decidendi* of **Lampleigh** *v* **Brathwait** (1615)?

Consideration can be a promise not to sue

If one party has a possible civil claim against the other, a promise not to enforce that claim is good consideration for a promise given in return. If, for example, Ann crashes into Ben's car, Ben might agree that he will not sue Ann if Ann pays for the damage, and Ben's promise not to sue will be consideration for Ann's promise to pay.

In **Alliance Bank Ltd** *v* **Broom** (1864) Broom had an overdraft of £22,000 with the bank, and they asked him to provide some security. Mr Broom promised to do so, but never did, and as a result the bank sued him. Mr Broom argued that there was no consideration for his promise to provide security, but the court held that the consideration was provided by the bank's implied promise not to sue for a while, giving Mr Broom time to provide security, even though they did sue fairly shortly afterwards.

Where forbearing to enforce a legal claim is offered as consideration, there must have been some intention actually to bring proceedings. In **Miles *v* New Zealand Alford Estate Co.** (1886) a company had bought some land which it was dissatisfied with. The seller later promised to make certain payments to the company, and the company alleged that it had provided consideration for this promise by not taking legal proceedings to rescind the contract when they found the problems with the land. This argument was rejected by the Court of Appeal, which held that there was no consideration for the vendor's promise, because there was no evidence that the buyers ever really intended to bring proceedings to rescind.

In the same case, it was pointed out that if the party who has the claim believes it to be legally valid, but it turns out not to be, the promise will still be good consideration if that party had honestly believed they had a valid claim – so in the car accident example above, even if it subsequently transpires that for some reason B could not have successfully sued A anyway, B's promise not to sue is still valid consideration, providing B honestly believes he has a claim against A.

One party's promise not to enforce an existing claim can only provide consideration if the promise given in return was actually induced by the promise not to enforce the claim. In **Combe *v* Combe** (1951) a husband and his wife were involved in divorce proceedings, during which he promised to pay her an annual allowance. She later brought an action to enforce this promise and argued, among other things, that she had given consideration for it by not exercising her right to apply to the court for a maintenance order. It was held that this could not be consideration because her husband had not asked her not to apply to the court, and therefore his promise had not been made in return for her promising not to do so.

This principle can be a difficult one to apply. In **Alliance Bank *v* Broom** the defendant did not ask the bank not to sue, yet the bank's forbearance to do so was held to constitute consideration. However, the decision has been explained on the basis that by promising to supply security, the debtor was by implication asking the bank not to sue.

Reading on the web

The Privy Council decision **R *v* Attorney-General for England and Wales** (2003) is available on its website (judgment No. 22) at:

> **www.privy-council.org.uk/output/Page331.asp**

Chapter summary

An agreement is not usually binding unless it is supported by consideration. This means that each party must give something in return for what is gained from the other party. Consideration may be a thing or a service. It is usually described as being something which represents either some benefit to the person making a promise (the promisor) or some detriment to the person to whom the promise is made (the promisee), or both.

Promisor and promisee

In most contracts, two promises will be exchanged, so each party is both a promisor and a promisee.

Consideration need not benefit the promisor

Consideration need not benefit the promisor – so there can be consideration where the promisee suffers some detriment at the promisor's request, but this gives no particular benefit to the promisor.

'Executory' and 'executed' consideration

Executory consideration is where something is to be done in the future after the contract has been formed. Executed consideration is where, at the time of the formation of the contract, the consideration has already been performed. Executed consideration usually occurs in unilateral contracts.

Consideration must not be past

Lawyers often say that consideration must not be past, but this is slightly confusing because the emphasis is not really about the time that the consideration was given, but rather about whether the consideration was given in exchange for the other party's consideration. Consideration must be given *in return* for the promise or act of the other party: **Roscorla** *v* **Thomas** (1842).

There are two exceptions to the rule that past consideration is no consideration. The first is where the past consideration was provided at the promisor's request, and it was understood that payment would be made: **Lampleigh** *v* **Brathwait** (1615). The second exception to the rule on past consideration is the bill of exchange under s. 27 of the Bills of Exchange Act 1882.

Consideration must be sufficient

Consideration must be sufficient but need not be adequate, the courts will not inquire into the adequacy of consideration, so long as there is some: **Thomas** *v* **Thomas** (1842).

Consideration must be of economic value

Consideration must have some physical value, rather than just an emotional or sentimental one: **White** *v* **Bluett** (1853).

Consideration can be a promise not to sue

If one party has a possible civil claim against the other, a promise not to enforce that claim is good consideration for a promise given in return: **Alliance Bank Ltd** *v* **Broom** (1864).

Question and answer guide

For exam questions covering the material in this chapter, please see the Question and answer guides section of Chapter 27: Compensatory damages.

mylawchamber

Visit **www.mylawchamber.co.uk/elliottaqa** to access interactive questions, quizzes and activities to test yourself on this chapter.

Chapter 26

Breach of contract

> This chapter discusses:
> - the two ways that a contract can be breached – actual breach and anticipatory breach;
> - the effect of a breach of contract.

Introduction

A contract is discharged when the rights and obligations agreed in it come to an end. There are four ways in which this can happen: performance, agreement, frustration and breach. In this chapter we will consider when a contract is breached. Where a contract is breached the innocent party will have a right to a remedy. This will in most cases be limited to financial compensation for loss suffered as a result of the breach.

Breach

A contract is said to be breached when one party performs defectively, differently from the agreement, or not at all (actual breach), or indicates in advance that they will not be performing as agreed (anticipatory breach).

Actual breach

An illustration of an actual breach of contract is **Pilbrow v Pearless de Rougemont & Co.** (1999). The appellant had telephoned a firm of solicitors and asked to make an appointment with a solicitor. The appointment was arranged with an employee

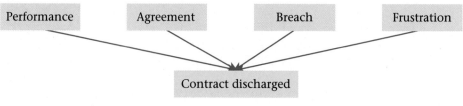

Figure 26.1 **Discharge of contract**

who was not a qualified solicitor. He was not informed that the employee was not a solicitor. The appellant was dissatisfied with the quality of the legal services he had received and refused to pay the outstanding fees. The firm sued for their fees. The Court of Appeal accepted that, as a matter of fact, the standard of legal services provided had been that of a competent solicitor. But it ruled that there had been a contract not just to provide legal services, but to provide legal services by a solicitor. The firm did not perform that contract at all. No legal services were provided by any solicitor; they therefore had no right to any payment. To avoid this problem in future, professionals should always make clear to the client whether their services are being provided by a qualified professional or not.

A case where breach of contract was not proven was **Modahl** *v* **British Athletic Federation Ltd** (1999). The claimant was a well-known British international athlete who was suspended from competition by the British Athletic Federation (BAF) because of an allegation that she had taken prohibited drugs to improve her performance. She successfully appealed against the doping allegation and brought an action for breach of contract and damages against BAF. She alleged that her suspension and the initiation of disciplinary proceedings were in breach of her contract with the defendant. She claimed damages for the financial loss suffered because she was unable to compete in international athletics for nearly a year. BAF was a member of the International Amateur Athletic Federation (IAAF). The IAAF had adopted its system of instant suspension followed by disciplinary proceedings in the belief that, although it might sometimes cause injustice in an individual case, it was necessary in the wider interests of the sport. The contract between Modahl and BAF was therefore interpreted as allowing the same procedures and no damages were awarded.

Anticipatory breach

Where an anticipatory breach occurs, the other party can sue for breach straight away; it is not necessary to wait until performance falls due. This was what happened in **Frost** *v* **Knight** (1872). The defendant had promised to marry the plaintiff once his father had died. He later broke off the engagement while his father was still alive, and when his ex-fiancée sued him for breach of promise (which was a valid claim in those days, though not any longer), he argued that she had no claim as the time for performance had not yet arrived. This argument was rejected and the plaintiff's claim succeeded.

In **Hochster** *v* **De la Tour** (1853) the parties had made a contract in April under which the plaintiff would be a tour leader in Europe for the defendant beginning on 1 June. In May the defendant informed the plaintiff that his services were no longer required. The plaintiff started his action for breach of contract on 22 May. The defendants argued that he should be required to wait until the date performance was due, which was 1 June, as there was no breach of contract until that date. The court rejected this argument. The plaintiff could commence proceedings immediately for damages, even though the date of performance had not yet arrived.

In some cases, the innocent party elects to wait until performance falls due, but this can mean they end up worse off than if they had sued immediately the anticipatory breach was known. In **Avery** *v* **Bowden** (1856) Bowden chartered Avery's ship and agreed to load up his cargo at Odessa within 45 days. However, Bowden later told Avery that he had no cargo and advised him to take the ship away. This was an anticipatory breach, and Avery could have sued for breach of contract immediately. Instead, he kept the ship available at the port, in the hope that Bowden would eventually fulfil his promise. Before the 45 days were up, the Crimean War broke out between England and Russia, so that performance became illegal and the contract was frustrated. The frustration then prevented Avery from suing for breach.

??? Quick quiz 26.1

1 If I am due to deliver some books to your house on Wednesday and I telephone you on Monday and tell you that I am not going to be able to deliver the books, is this an actual breach or an anticipatory breach of the contract?

2 If some books were due to be delivered on Wednesday and I tell you on Monday that I will not be able to deliver the books, can I start legal proceedings for breach of contract on Monday or do I need to wait until Wednesday?

3 If I am due to deliver some books to your house on Wednesday and by Thursday the books have still not arrived, is this an actual breach or an anticipatory breach of the contract.

4 In **Modahl** *v* **British Athletic Federation Ltd** (1999) was Modahl's application for damages successful?

Effect of breach

Any breach of contract will entitle the innocent party to sue for damages, but not every breach allows the wronged party to choose to discharge the contract. If the contract is not discharged, it will still need to be performed.

Chapter summary

There are four ways in which a contract can come to an end: performance, agreement, frustration and breach.

Actual breach

A contract is said to be breached when one party performs defectively, differently from the agreement, or not at all.

Anticipatory breach

An anticipatory breach occurs when one party indicates in advance that they will not be performing as agreed. Where an anticipatory breach occurs, the other party can sue for breach straight away; it is not necessary to wait until performance falls due.

Effect of breach

Any breach of contract will entitle the innocent party to sue for damages, but not every breach allows the wronged party to choose to discharge the contract.

Question and answer guide

For exam questions covering the material in this chapter, please see the Question and answer guides section of Chapter 27: Compensatory damages.

mylawchamber

Visit **www.mylawchamber.co.uk/elliottqa** to access interactive questions, quizzes and activities to test yourself on this chapter.

Part 15
THE CIVIL COURTS, PROCEDURE AND DAMAGES

** Please note that if you are studying *Section C: Introduction to Contract* of the AQA specifications, you will also need to study Chapter 20: Civil Court Procedure, above, which is also part of the 'Introduction to Contract' specifications.

Compensatory damages

> **This chapter discusses:**
> - the award of compensatory damages for breach of contract;
> - innocent parties are generally entitled to such damages as will put them in the position they would have been in if the contract had been performed;
> - damages aim to compensate the innocent party for their pecuniary loss and damages are generally not recoverable for non-pecuniary loss;
> - the three main limitations to the award of damages – causation, remoteness and mitigation;
> - how compensatory damages are calculated;
> - when calculating damages, the relevance of any profit made by the defendant through breaching the contract.

Introduction

This chapter is concerned with the compensatory damages that can be paid to the innocent party in the event of a breach of contract. An award of damages is the usual remedy for a breach of contract. It is an award of money that aims to compensate the innocent party for the financial losses they have suffered as a result of the breach. Damages for breach of contract are available as of right where the contract has been breached. The general rule is that innocent parties are entitled to such damages as will put them in the position they would have been in if the contract had been performed. When a contract is breached, a party may suffer pecuniary loss (that is to say financial loss) or non-pecuniary loss.

Pecuniary loss

Damages aim to compensate the innocent party for their financial losses that result from not receiving the performance bargained for. In general, such losses include physical harm to the claimants or their property and any other injury to their economic position.

Non-pecuniary loss

As we have seen, contract damages usually aim to compensate for financial (pecuniary) loss. They have traditionally not been available to compensate non-pecuniary loss, such as mental distress. This has been a key distinction between the law of contract and tort for, while in contract law damages for mental distress have not been available, such damages are available in tort law. In reality, following a breach of contract, a claimant might suffer not only financial loss but also mental distress, such as disappointment, hurt feelings or humiliation, but damages for such non-pecuniary losses are generally not recoverable in contract. The main policy consideration for this seems to be a concern to keep contractual awards down, to provide fair compensation without encouraging unnecessary litigation by offering excessive compensation. In **Hayes v Dodd** (1990) Staughton LJ stated:

> '. . . the English courts should be wary of adopting . . . the United States practice of huge awards. Damages awarded for negligence or want of skill, whether against professional men or anyone else, must provide fair compensation, but no more than that. And I would not view with enthusiasm the prospect that every shipowner in the Commercial Court, having successfully claimed for unpaid freight or demurrage, would be able to add a claim for mental distress suffered while he was waiting for his money.'

Damages for mental distress are not awarded in commercial contracts. The leading authority for this is **Addis v Gramophone Co. Ltd** (1909). The plaintiff had been employed as a manager of a company in India. He was wrongfully sacked for alleged dishonesty. He brought an action claiming that the manner of his dismissal had been harsh and humiliating. He had been ostracised by the British community in Calcutta. As a result he had suffered mental pain and anguish. The House of Lords held that he could recover the usual damages for loss of salary and commission, but not for the injury to his feelings caused by the way in which he was sacked.

However, recent cases have developed the principle that, in a limited number of situations, injury to feelings (generally called mental distress) and loss of amenity will be compensated. Initially, such compensation was limited to cases involving contracts whose whole purpose was the provision of pleasure, relaxation and peace of mind. More recently, the House of Lords has allowed damages for non-pecuniary loss where a major object (though not the whole purpose) of the contract was to provide pleasure, relaxation and peace of mind. Mental suffering can be compensated if it is related to physical inconvenience and discomfort caused by the breach of the contract. In addition, in contracts of employment, breach of the implied duty of mutual trust and confidence can give rise to an award of damages for financial loss resulting from the psychiatric harm caused.

Contracts where the whole purpose is pleasure, relaxation and peace of mind

The leading case on the provision of damages for non-pecuniary loss where a contract for recreation has been breached is **Jarvis v Swans Tours Ltd** (1973). The plaintiff was a solicitor who had booked a two-week winter sports holiday that was described in the brochure as a 'house party'. The brochure stated that there would be a welcoming party, afternoon tea and cakes and a yodelling evening. In the event, there was no welcoming party, the afternoon teas consisted largely of crisps and the yodeller turned out to be a local man who arrived in his working clothes, sang a couple of songs and then left. The 'house party' also left something to be desired, consisting of 13 holidaymakers in the house in the first week, but in the second week Mr Jarvis was the sole member of the 'house party'.

The holiday had cost £63. The holiday company was clearly in breach of contract and the judge at first instance awarded Mr Jarvis half the contract price, on the basis that Mr Jarvis had received some benefit, in the shape of transport and accommodation, and the sum awarded was the difference in value between what he expected and what he got. Not surprisingly, Mr Jarvis appealed. The Court of Appeal raised the damages to £125 on the basis that merely giving him back the cost of the holiday would not adequately compensate his loss, and instead the damages should take account of his disappointment and distress. Lord Denning explained:

> 'It is true he was conveyed to Switzerland and back and had meals and bed in the hotel. But that is not what he went for. He went to enjoy himself with all those facilities which the defendants said he would have. He is entitled to compensation for the loss of those facilities, and for his loss of enjoyment.'

The case was compared with where a man plans to go to an evening opera performance in Glyndebourne. He arranges to hire a car for the night, but the car fails to turn up and he misses the performance. He would be entitled to claim from the car hire company, not just the cost of his ticket, but also for his disappointment at missing the concert.

This case was affirmed in **Jackson v Horizon Holidays Ltd** (1975). In the Scottish case of **Diesen v Samson** (1971) the defendant had been booked to take photographs at the claimant's wedding. He failed to attend and damages were awarded to the bride for the distress of having no wedding photographs. This was not a purely commercial contract that fell within the rule in **Addis v Gramophone Co**. Instead, it was a contract under which the bride would get pleasure looking at the photographs in the years ahead.

In **Heywood v Wellers** (1976) the plaintiff, Sheila Heywood, was a single parent living in Penge who met a married man with whom she had an affair. Later, they split up, but he began stalking her. The plaintiff went to the defendants, a firm of solicitors, to seek an injunction against her former companion. The defendants negligently failed to do so, with the result that the plaintiff had to suffer further harassment. The Court of Appeal held that she could recover for the mental distress caused by the breach of contract.

Where a contract is for the provision of a product for leisure activities and this contract is breached, damages for loss of pleasure and amenity may be awarded. In **Ruxley Electronics and Construction Ltd v Forsyth** (1996) a contract had been entered into for the construction of a swimming pool for £70,000. The plaintiff made it clear that one end of the pool had to be 7 ft 6 in deep, as he needed this depth to feel safe when diving. In fact, on completion, it was only 6 ft 9 in deep. Mr Forsyth had contracted for a swimming pool for reasons of pleasure, and in this sense his expectation had not been fulfilled. The trial judge awarded the defendant £2,500 for loss of amenity and pleasure, an award that was approved by the House of Lords. This was to compensate the pleasure lost by the defendant by not feeling safe when he dived into the swimming pool.

Contracts where a major object is pleasure, relaxation and peace of mind

The House of Lords further considered the issue of the award of damages for loss of amenity in **Farley** *v* **Skinner** (No. 2) (2001). Mr Farley was thinking of buying a house in the Sussex countryside, where he would spend his retirement. He paid a chartered surveyor, Mr Skinner, to look at the property, and specifically instructed him to assess the impact of aircraft noise on the property. The house was 15 miles from Gatwick airport. The surveyor was negligent in carrying out this work and advised Mr Farley that it was 'unlikely that the property will suffer greatly from such noise'. After Mr Farley had spent a considerable amount of money renovating the house and had moved into the property, he discovered that the house was in fact badly affected by aircraft noise, particularly at weekends. It seems that the house was positioned near a navigation beacon and at busy times aircraft flew around this beacon while they waited for a slot to land. Mr Farley's enjoyment of the house was badly affected. He brought an action against the surveyor for the difference in the value of the house between what he paid and what it was worth with the aircraft noise. This part of his claim was unsuccessful because it was found that the price he paid was the market value for the house taking into account the aircraft noise. In addition, he included a claim for non-pecuniary damages for the loss of amenity caused by the aircraft noise. At first instance, the claimant was awarded £10,000 for distress and inconvenience. The House of Lords upheld this award. The House held that it did not matter that the object of the contract with the surveyor was not entirely to give pleasure, relaxation or peace of mind, since this was nonetheless a major and important object of the contract. The surveyor had been specifically asked to report on aircraft noise. It would be perverse to allow someone to recover damages if they had just asked a surveyor to report on aircraft noise, but not where the client (like Mr Farley) had specifically asked the surveyor about that issue as well as some other matter. That would be a distinction of form and not substance. From now on, 'it is sufficient if a major or important object of the contract is to give pleasure, relaxation or peace of mind'. The House emphasised that awards of damages in this area should be modest. While they allowed the trial judge's award of £10,000 to stand, it was noted that this was at the very highest end of the scale. They did not want the award to encourage a litigation culture.

Mental suffering caused by physical inconvenience

Mental suffering can be compensated if it is caused by physical inconvenience and discomfort resulting from the breach of contract. In **Perry** *v* **Sidney Phillips & Son** (1982) the plaintiff bought a house relying on a survey prepared by the defendants. Their report stated that the house was in good order, but it was found to have many faults, including a leaking roof and a septic tank that gave off an offensive odour. These problems with the property caused the plaintiff distress, worry and inconvenience. As well as awarding damages for the reduced value of the property, the Court of Appeal awarded damages for the physical inconvenience and discomfort caused by having to live in the house while the builders were doing repairs and for mental distress.

In **Bailey v Bullock** (1950) the plaintiff brought an action against his solicitor for failing to act to recover possession of a house which had been leased to a third party. As a result of the delay, the plaintiff was required to live in a small house with his parents-in-law. Damages for discomfort were awarded.

The House of Lords noted in **Farley v Skinner** that the concept of physical inconvenience should not be narrowly interpreted, and could include the harmful effects of aircraft noise. The House stated that 'aircraft noise was something which affects the plaintiff through his hearing and can be regarded as having a physical effect on him'.

Breach of implied duty of mutual trust and confidence

Contracts of employment include an implied duty of mutual trust and confidence. The House of Lords ruled in **Eastwood v Magnox Electric plc** (2004) that breach of this implied term can give rise to an award of damages for the financial losses incurred as a result of illness, including psychiatric illness, caused by unfair treatment by an employer in breach of the contract.

Limitations on awards of damages

The general rule is that innocent parties are entitled to such damages as will put them in the position they would have been in if the contract had been performed, but there are three limitations, which will be considered under the headings of causation, remoteness and mitigation.

Causation

A person will only be liable for losses caused by their breach of contract. The defendant's breach need not be the sole cause of the claimant's losses, but it must be an effective cause of their loss. It is not enough if the breach merely provided the claimant with the opportunity to sustain loss. Intervening acts between the breach of contract and the loss incurred may break the chain of causation. Those events which were reasonably foreseeable will not break the chain of causation. Sometimes a loss can be caused partly by a breach of contract and partly by some other factor. The general rule is that where breach can be shown to be an actual cause of the loss, the fact that there is another contributing cause will not prevent the existence of causation.

In **County Ltd v Girozentrale Securities** (1996) the plaintiffs' bank agreed to underwrite the issue of 26 million shares in a publicly quoted company. The defendants were stockbrokers who were engaged by the plaintiffs to approach potential investors in the shares. The brokers breached the terms of their contract and, in due course, the plaintiffs found themselves with some 4.5 million shares on their hands which, the price of the shares having fallen, represented a loss of nearly £7 million. They sued the stockbrokers and the main issue in the case was whether the plaintiffs' loss was caused by the defendants' breach of contract. In effect, the plaintiffs would not have suffered their loss if there had not been a concurrence of a number of events, of which the defendants' breach of contract was but one. The Court of Appeal held that the brokers' breach of contract remained the effective cause of the plaintiffs' loss; the breach did not need to be the only cause. The defendants were therefore liable to pay damages.

In **Quinn v Burch Bros (Builders) Ltd** (1966) the plaintiff was an independent sub-contractor carrying out such building work as plastering on a building project. In breach of their contractual undertaking to supply equipment 'reasonably necessary' for the work, the defendant failed to supply a step-ladder. The plaintiff found a folded trestle, and stood on it to do the work. He slipped and broke his hand. The Court of Appeal held that the cause of the plaintiff's injury was his own choice to use unsuitable equipment. The defendant's breach of contract was only the occasion for the accident, not its legal cause.

Remoteness

There are some losses which clearly result from the defendant's breach of contract, but are considered too remote from the breach for it to be fair to expect the defendant to compensate the claimant for them. Take, for example, the situation where a taxi driver is booked to take a passenger to the airport in time for a certain flight to New York, where the passenger expects to complete a deal worth £1 million. If the taxi driver breaches the contract by arriving late and makes the passenger miss the flight, the taxi firm may be liable for expenses such as any extra cost for getting the next flight, but is unlikely to be expected to compensate the passenger for the lost £1 million.

The rules concerning remoteness were originally laid down in **Hadley v Baxendale** (1854). The case concerned a contract for delivery of an important piece of mill equipment, which had been sent away for repair. The equipment, an iron shaft, was not delivered until some days after the agreed date. This meant that the mill, which could not work without it, had stood idle for that period. The mill owners attempted to sue for loss of the profits they would have made in the time between the agreed delivery date and the actual delivery. The court laid down two situations where the defendant should be liable for loss caused by a breach of contract:

1 Loss which would arise naturally, 'according to the usual course of things', from their breach.
2 Loss 'as may reasonably be supposed to have been in the contemplation of the parties at the time when they made the contract, as the probable result of the breach of it'.

In practice, it is the second 'reasonable contemplation' test which has proved the most important in subsequent cases. In this case, they did not consider the lost profit to fall within either category. The fact that the mill could not work without the equipment was not considered to be a loss that arose in the usual course of things, because there could well have been a spare; nor could such a loss be said to be within the contemplation of the defendants, because the mill owners had failed to make it clear that the mill could not work without the shaft. It is therefore important to inform the other contracting party at the time of contracting of circumstances which affect performance, to prevent a subsequent loss being found to be too remote.

The approach in **Hadley v Baxendale** was reaffirmed in **Victoria Laundry (Windsor) Ltd v Newman Industries Ltd** (1949) and then discussed again by the House of Lords in *The Heron II* (1969). These two cases addressed particularly the problem of abnormal losses – those which could not be said to occur 'in the normal course of things', but which, on the other hand, the defendant might well have been able to contemplate when making the contract.

In **Victoria Laundry** the plaintiffs were launderers and dyers, who needed to buy a large boiler in order to expand their existing business and take on a very well-paid government contract. They contracted to buy such a boiler, second-hand, from the defendants, making it clear that it was needed for immediate use. As the defendants dismantled the boiler in preparation for delivery, it was damaged, and so the delivery was considerably later than agreed. The launderers claimed loss of profits under two heads: £16 per week for the loss of 'normal' profits, which represented the additional ordinary work they could have taken on with the extra boiler; and £262 per week for the loss of a lucrative dyeing contract with the government.

Evidence was given that although the defendants knew the plaintiffs wanted the boiler working as soon as possible, they did not know about the government contract, or the fact that it was so much more lucrative than the laundry's other work. As a result, the Court of Appeal held that they were liable for the £16 per week, but not for the £262. The court stated that a defendant should only be liable for such losses as were 'reasonably foreseeable' as arising from the breach.

In *The Heron II* (1969) the plaintiff chartered a ship, the *Heron II*, to carry sugar to Basrah, where the cargo was to be sold. The journey was to take 20 days, but the shipowner strayed from the normal route and took 29 days. During the period between the agreed delivery date and the actual delivery, the market price of sugar at Basrah fell significantly. The late delivery put the shipowner in breach of contract, and the plaintiff claimed the difference between the price he would have got for the sugar had the delivery been made on time and the going price when the delivery was actually made. The shipowner had not been told that the plaintiff intended to sell the sugar as soon as it arrived in Basrah, but he did know that there was a market for sugar at Basrah. From this the court held that 'if he had thought about the matter he must have realised that at least it was not unlikely that the sugar would be sold in the market at market price on arrival'. In view of this, the House of Lords held that the plaintiff's intention to sell the sugar at Basrah when the ship arrived was so probable that it should be regarded as arising in the normal course of events, and would therefore be within the contemplation of the parties at the time the contract was made.

In **Jackson v Royal Bank of Scotland** (2005) the House of Lords emphasised that the time to determine what was reasonably foreseeable was the time at which the contract was made, not the time at which it was broken. This is because at the time the contract is made the parties can make provision for the distribution of risk in their negotiations if they wished to do so. The parties have the opportunity to limit their liability in damages when they are making their contract. They can at that stage draw attention to any special circumstances outside the ordinary course of things which they ought to have in contemplation when entering into the contract. In **Jackson**, the claimant imported cheap dog biscuits from Thailand and sold them on to its customer, known as Economy Bag, at a considerable profit. Economy Bag did not realise how cheap the biscuits were in Thailand until the defendant bank revealed this information to Economy Bag in breach of its contract with the claimants. Following this revelation, Economy Bag ceased to buy the biscuits from the claimants and bought them directly from Thailand. The claimant sued the bank for the loss of the repeat business with Economy Bag. The bank argued that the losses alleged to have been suffered by the claimant were too remote a consequence of the bank's breach of contract, stating that it had no reason to think that its breach of contract would lead Economy Bag to stop trading with the claimant. The bank argued that when the contract was made the parties' reasonable contemplation would have been that, as Economy Bag knew the identity of the supplier and where it could be contacted, no loss would flow from the disclosure to it of the amount of the claimant's mark-up.

The House of Lords held that the lost business was not too remote. As soon as the confidential information was released, there was no repeat business. All that the claimant had to show was that, at the time of the contract, the contract-breaker should have contemplated that damage of the kind suffered would have occurred as a result of his breach. Once it had decided, correctly, that it was a natural and probable consequence of the bank's breach that the claimant would suffer a loss of repeat business, there was no cut-off point. The claimants are entitled to an award of damages to put them in the same position as they would have been if there had been no breach of contract. The question that remains is one of assessment. The bank did not include any provision in the letter of credit limiting its liability for the loss of repeat business to any particular period. So the only limit on the period of its liability is that which the trial judge identified. This is when, on the facts, the question whether any loss has been sustained has become too speculative to permit the making of any award. The bank's liability was open-ended, as it had not limited its liability by the contract to any particular period. There was no evidence that the parties contemplated at the time of the contract that knowledge of the supplier's identity and its contact details would lead inevitably to knowledge of the prices which were being charged by it. It was only a matter of time before the harsh reality of doing business persuaded Economy Bag that it should take a closer interest in what its arrangements with the claimant were costing and reduce or eliminate those costs. In determining the amount of damages available, the House of Lords stated that the court had to consider how long it was or should have been in the reasonable contemplation of the parties at the time that the contract was made (and not at the time that it was broken) that the trading relationship would continue. On the facts this was four years. After this time the damages were too speculative to be recoverable.

In **The Heron II** the House of Lords discussed the level of probability required for an event to be considered to be within the contemplation of the parties. They disapproved of the phrase 'reasonably foreseeable', as used in **Victoria Laundry**, on the grounds that it suggested a very low degree of probability (similar to the remoteness test used in tort law). They stated that in order for a plaintiff to be held responsible for a loss, that loss must be such that both parties would, at the time the contract was made, have regarded it as 'liable to result' from the breach; the fact that they knew there was a very remote chance that the loss might occur would not be enough.

The above two cases make it clear that where a loss only results from a breach because of special circumstances (such as the unusually lucrative contracts in **Victoria Laundry**), the defendant will only be liable for that loss if they knew about the special circumstances at the time the contract was made, and contracted on the basis that such circumstances existed.

One way of looking at the two tests laid down in **Hadley** v **Baxendale** is that the first applied to normal losses (where the loss arose in the usual course of things) and the second applied to abnormal losses (where they were within the reasonable contemplation of the parties). In practice, the courts have not favoured this distinction and have preferred to see **Hadley** v **Baxendale** as laying down a single principle. Under this single principle, as the likelihood of the loss occurring diminishes, the degree of knowledge on the part of the defendant must increase for the loss to be recoverable in damages. The House of Lords explained in **Jackson** v **Royal Bank of Scotland** (2005) that the two rules in **Hadley** v **Baxendale** were not actually mutually exclusive. To determine whether a loss arose naturally and in the ordinary course of things, for the purposes of the first rule one needed to consider the terms of the contract, its business context, and the reasonable contemplation of the parties, though the latter issue was laid down in the second rule. Thus, if one contracting party told the other contracting party at the time of making the contract about special circumstances effecting the contract, losses resulting from those special circumstances would actually become the natural consequences of the breach. Lord Reid stated in the House of Lords in **Koufos** v **Czarnikow Ltd** (1969): 'I do not think that it was intended that there were to be two rules or that two different standards or tests were to be applied.' The important issue is what the contract-breaker knew or must be taken to have known, so as to bring the loss within the reasonable contemplation of the parties. When that is established, it may often be the case that the first and second parts of the rule overlap, or at least that it seems unnecessary to draw a clear line of demarcation between them.

In **Satef-Huttenes Albertus SpA** v **Paloma Tercera Shipping Co. SA**, *The Pegase* (1981) Goff J discussed the two rules laid down in **Hadley** v **Baxendale**. He stated that, in the light of the subsequent cases, the case should now be seen as laying down a single principle, whereby remoteness depended on 'the degree of relevant knowledge held by the defendant at the time of the contract in the particular case'. The test was now whether:

> '. . . the facts in question come to the defendant's knowledge in such circumstances that a reasonable person in the shoes of the defendant would, if he had considered the matter at the time of making the contract, have contemplated that, in the event of a breach by him, such facts were to be taken into account when considering his responsibility for loss suffered by the plaintiff as a result of such breach.'

A claimant does not have to contemplate the breach of contract in question; it is only the type of damage that must be contemplated. So long as the loss is of a type that could reasonably have been contemplated, the fact that the loss may turn out to be much greater than could be foreseen does not prevent the defendant from incurring liability for it. In **Vacwell Engineering Co. Ltd** v **BDH Chemicals Ltd** (1971) a scientist dropped an ampoule of chemicals into a bin which caused an explosion, killing both the scientist and a colleague, and causing extensive damage to property. Rees J stated that: 'the explosion and the type of damage being foreseeable it matters not in the law that the magnitude of the former and the extent of the latter were not.'

In **Wroth** v **Tyler** (1974) the defendant had contracted to sell his house to the plaintiffs for £6,000, but wrongfully repudiated the contract before the sale could take place. By the time the case came to court, house prices had begun to rise very quickly, and the house had gone up in value to £11,500. The plaintiffs claimed the difference between the contract price and the market price, as is usual in such a case. The defendant claimed that he was not liable for the full amount, because although he could have foreseen some increase in value, he could not have contemplated that prices would rise so sharply. His argument was rejected: Megarry J said that the defendant could escape liability if he could not have contemplated that a particular type of loss could result from his breach, but not simply because he could not have contemplated its extent.

The same point was made in **Brown** v **KMR Services Ltd** (1995). The case arose from the losses made by the 'Lloyd's names' (who had provided financial security for certain insurance policies). They had incurred substantial losses when large claims were made under the insurance policies. The action was brought against those who had encouraged the Lloyd's names to take on excessive liabilities. The losses were financial and therefore of a type which it could readily be foreseen might be incurred as a result of the breach of contract, but their extent went well beyond that which might in any year arise 'in the usual course of things'. The Court of Appeal said that such losses were recoverable. Only the type of loss needs to be foreseeable. The test was whether, at the time of making the contract, damage of the kind for which the plaintiff claims compensation was a reasonably foreseeable consequence of the breach of contract. If the kind of damage was reasonably foreseeable, it does not matter that the extent of the damage is not. The difficulty with this reasoning is that in the case of financial loss, it will not be easy to differentiate kinds of loss.

A recent case on remoteness is **Balfour Beatty Construction (Scotland)** v **Scottish Power plc** (1994). Balfour Beattie were building a section of motorway near Edinburgh. They needed a continuous supply of electricity to make concrete. The defendants agreed to set up a temporary electricity supply for the concrete plant. When this supply failed, a bridge under construction could not be completed and later had to be rebuilt. Balfour Beattie claimed the cost of rebuilding the bridge. The House of Lords held that the loss incurred was too remote. There was no evidence that Scottish Power knew that the concrete plant needed a continuous supply of electricity. The parties had to have reasonable knowledge of the other's business, but not every technical fact particularly of something as vast and complicated as major motorway construction.

Mitigation

Claimants cannot simply sit back and allow losses to pile up and expect the defendant to pay compensation for the whole amount if there is something they could reasonably do to reduce the loss. Claimants are under a duty to mitigate their loss, and cannot recover damages for losses which could have been avoided by taking reasonable steps. For example, if Jane has a contract with David to repair the machines in his factory, and fails to carry out her duties as agreed, David cannot simply keep the factory idle for years and submit a claim for lost profits; he will only be able to claim for such losses as he could not reasonably avoid by taking steps such as finding a replacement machine, or an alternative source of repairs.

The claimant does not have to prove that reasonable steps have been taken; it is up to the defendant to prove that the loss could have been mitigated, or better mitigated. Nor are claimants expected to make enormous efforts to mitigate the loss; they need only do what is reasonable.

In **Pilkington v Wood** (1953) the defendant, a solicitor, was in breach of contract for wrongly advising that the title to the plaintiff's house was good. The defendant argued that the plaintiff should have mitigated his loss by taking proceedings against the seller of the house for having conveyed a defective title. However, this would have involved complicated litigation, which would not necessarily have succeeded, and the court held that the purchaser was not required to take such onerous and uncertain steps in mitigation.

In the leading case of **Brace v Calder** (1895) the defendants, a partnership consisting of four members, had agreed to employ the plaintiff for two years as manager of a branch of their business. Five months later, two of the members retired and the partnership was dissolved, with the business being transferred to the remaining two. Legally, the dissolution of the partnership constituted wrongful dismissal of the plaintiff, but the two remaining partners offered to re-employ him, on the same terms as before. He rejected the offer and brought an action for breach of contract, seeking to recover the salary that he would have received had he served the whole period of two years. The claim was refused and only nominal damages awarded, on the grounds that it was unreasonable to have rejected the offer of continued employment.

Another illustration of the requirement of mitigation is **British Westinghouse Electric Co. Ltd v Underground Electric Rys Co. of London Ltd (No. 2)** (1912). The appellants had contracted to supply electricity turbines to the respondents' specification. The turbines delivered did not match these specifications, and the respondents replaced them with some other turbines made by a different manufacturer. These turbines were much more efficient, so that the replacement machines paid for themselves in a short time. The respondents claimed damages for the cost of replacing the original turbines, but the House of Lords rejected the claim. The respondents had rightly mitigated their loss, and had been so successful that most of the losses had been eliminated. They were therefore only entitled to compensation for the period of time when the original turbines were running inefficiently.

✓ **Know your terms 27.1**

Define the following terms:

1 Compensatory damages.
2 Non-pecuniary loss.
3 Causation.
4 Mitigation.

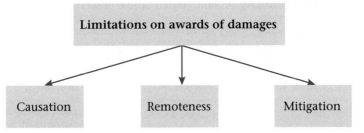

Figure 27.1 **Limitations on awards of damages**

Calculating loss

Once it has been established that a loss is one for which the defendant is liable, the court must calculate the sum of damages – what amount will compensate the claimant for the loss? There are two main ways in which the losses of a claimant in a contract action can be calculated: the loss of expectation and the reliance loss.

Loss of expectation

Where loss of expectation is the basis for calculating damages, the courts aim to put claimants in the position they would have been in if the contract had been performed. Thus the parties would have expected a certain result from the performance of the contract and the damages will compensate for the loss of this expectation. This can be described as the difference in value measure, that is the difference in value between the promised performance and the actual performance. If, for example, a claimant was buying goods with the intention of selling them and the supplier failed to supply the goods, the claimant can claim the profit that would have been made on that sale. A claimant who is forced to sell goods at a lower price when the original buyer pulls out can claim the difference between the contract price and the price at which the goods were eventually sold. Expectation losses provide an incentive to perform a contract: if the party contemplating a breach of contract knows that by failing to perform they will be liable for the full loss of profits, they are discouraged from breaking the agreement.

Reliance loss

Where reliance loss is the basis for calculating damages, the damages seek to put claimants in the position they were in before the contract was made. The damages will therefore compensate for the actual wasted expenditure and other losses incurred because of the contract which has been breached. Reliance loss is the normal test in tort law.

The case of **Anglia Television Ltd *v* Reed** (1972) established that reliance loss compensation can include money spent before the contract was made. The television company had planned to make a film for television, and had signed up an actor called Robert Reed to star in it. Reed signed the contract to perform in the film and then later pulled out in breach of contract. As a result, the film was not made. Clearly, the potential profits on a project such as a film are extremely difficult to predict; it could be a huge success, or sink without trace. Consequently, Anglia sought instead to claim back the money they had spent on making the film.

The amount they had spent after contracting with Reed was clearly recoverable, since it had been spent in reliance on him performing as agreed, but the film company also wished to claim money spent in the preparatory stages, before Reed was signed. It could not be said that this was spent in reliance on Reed, but the court said that there was, nevertheless, no reason why such expenditure should not be recovered, so long as it satisfied the rules on remoteness; if Reed could have been expected to realise that such losses were likely to result from his breach, he was liable for them. As Lord Denning MR pointed out, Reed would have known that money had been spent on the film before he signed up, and that that money would be wasted if the film was not made. Therefore, Anglia were allowed to recover all they had spent on the film before and after the contract was made with Reed.

Choosing between the expectation and reliance principles

As a rule, a claimant can choose whether to base a claim on loss of expectation or on reliance. In **Anglia Television** *v* **Reed** (1972) Lord Denning stated that a claimant could not claim for both expectation loss and reliance loss due to the risk of being compensated twice for the same loss. This is because wasted expenditure is normally included within a claim for lost performance, as the innocent party's expenditure would be taken into account when calculating how much profit they would have made from the performance of the contract. However, provided the claimant avoided such overlapping claims, there is no reason why they should not claim for both.

In practice, loss of expectation is the usual basis for calculating contract damages. Reliance loss is generally less generous than the loss of expectation measure. However, it may be seen as fairer in that it compensates for actual losses, rather than relying on guesses as to what the future gains from the performance of the contract would have been.

Limits on the claimant's choice

There are two main restrictions on the claimant's choice between the expectation and the reliance principles. These are the bad bargain rule and the speculative damages rule.

The bad bargain rule

If the claimant would have made a loss from the contract, then he or she will only be entitled to nominal damages, and will not be entitled to claim their expenses on the basis of reliance loss. To compensate on a reliance basis would mean that the injured party would be placed in a better position as a result of the breach than they would have been in if the contract had been performed. In **C & P Haulage** *v* **Middleton** (1983) the plaintiff had a licence to use premises in

Watford for six months, with the possibility that the contract could be renewed. He spent money on fixtures and fittings knowing that the contract stated that these could not be removed when the licence expired. When the contract was breached, the court held that the plaintiff could not recover for his expenditure and was entitled to nominal damages only. He could not claim for his wasted expenditure on the fixtures and fittings, because this would have been wasted even if the contract had been performed as agreed. If Robert Reed in the **Anglia Television** case could have shown that Anglia Television would not have made any money from the film anyway, the television company could not have claimed back the money they spent.

Expectation losses are 'too speculative'

The reliance basis for calculating damages must be used where it is virtually impossible to calculate what profit the claimant would have made if the contract had been performed correctly. In practice, the courts are reluctant to conclude that damages are too speculative and are prepared to base their awards on a certain amount of guesswork.

McRae *v* **Commonwealth Disposals Commission** (1951) was an Australian case heard by the Australian High Court. The plaintiff had successfully tendered for the salvage rights to an oil tanker, said to be wrecked on a reef approximately 100 miles north of Samarai. Despite being given an exact map reference for the location of the tanker, the plaintiff's salvage expedition failed to find the tanker, and it was eventually agreed that it was not in fact there at all. The plaintiff attempted to claim for loss of the profit he expected to make on salvaging the ship, but the court refused to allow this, on the grounds that it was impossible to calculate the value of a ship that did not exist. However, McRae was allowed to recover the wasted costs of the salvage trip – in other words, his reliance loss.

Damages were considered too speculative in **Sapwell** *v* **Bass** (1910). The plaintiff was a breeder of racehorses and the defendant the owner of a stallion who was paid £315 so that his stallion could 'serve' the plaintiff's mares. The defendant sold the stallion to a third party in South America, making it impossible to carry out the contract. The plaintiff claimed damages for the foals which he had lost, including the possibility he had lost a valuable prize-winning animal. The court held that these damages were too uncertain and instead made a nominal award.

Quantifying the expectation loss

Contract damages based on expectation loss aim to put the non-breaching party in the position they would have been in had the contract been performed as agreed. In calculating damages, the focus is on the claimant's loss. Claimants cannot recover more than their actual loss. If the claimant suffers no loss, they will only receive nominal damages. An award of damages can include compensation for a loss of profit which would have been made but for the breach of contract. The damages are essentially seeking to compensate the difference in value between the promised performance and the actual performance.

The market price rule

Where a contract has been breached, the law assumes that the wronged party will immediately mitigate their loss by buying similar goods which they had contracted for from another source or selling the goods which they had contracted to sell to another source. The wronged party will then suffer a loss only if they had to pay more for the substitute goods on the open market than they had originally contracted to pay, or had to sell the goods at a lower price. The buyer's damages will therefore be assessed by subtracting the contract price from the market price at the time of breach. A market price exists when goods can be bought and sold at a price fixed by supply and demand. This mode of calculating loss is expressly laid down for certain breaches of contracts for the sale of goods in ss. 50 and 51 of the Sale of Goods Act 1979, but the principle applies more generally.

As a result of the market price rule, the wronged party will often suffer no loss, as there is often no difference between the market price and the contract price. Take the example where Ann has two bags of flour and contracts to sell them to Ben at the market price of £10 per bag. If Ben later wrongfully refuses to accept the flour, Ann will almost certainly be able to sell them to Claire at the same price. Only nominal damages will be awarded. Ann may argue that she has lost profit because she would have been able to sell another two bags of flour to Claire. This argument may succeed if supply is greater than demand, that is to say that Ann had access to more sacks of flour which could have been sold to Claire, so that there is one lost sale.

An illustration of how the law applies in practice is **Thompson Ltd** *v* **Robinson (Gunmakers) Ltd** (1955). The buyers of a car were in breach of contract for refusing to accept delivery of the car from the sellers, who were car dealers. The dealers had to sell the car at the manufacturer's list price, which meant the market and contract prices were effectively the same. At the time, there was little demand for the type of car in question and supply was exceeding demand. Realising that they were unlikely to find another buyer, the dealers persuaded their suppliers to take the car back. The buyers admitted that they were in breach, but argued that the plaintiffs had in fact suffered no loss, as there was no difference between market and contract price at the time when they refused to accept delivery. The court disagreed, pointing out that s. 50 of the Sale of Goods Act was merely a *prima facie* rule which did not apply in this situation. The sellers were awarded £61, the profit they would have made on the sale. On the facts the dealers had lost a sale, which could not be mitigated. A contrasting case is **Charter** *v* **Sullivan** (1957). Here the facts were similar, except that the car was of a type which was in such demand at the time that the sellers admitted that they were easily able to sell every example they could get their hands on. As a result, it was easy to find another buyer, and the sellers were only awarded nominal damages.

Exclusion of the market price rule

The market price rule will not be used as the measure of loss either where there is no available market or where, in the circumstances, the non-breaching party is no expected to avail itself of the market to mitigate its loss. Where there is no market, the loss has to be quantified by the court estimating the actual value of the goods. There is no market for unique goods because alternative substitute goods cannot be obtained. In **Lazenby Garages Ltd** *v* **Wright** (1976) the sale of a second-hand car was treated as a sale of a unique item, but it is unlikely that every second-hand car would be treated as unique. There will be no market for goods where they have been specially manufactured to the exact specifications of the buyer, so that it is very unlikely that a different buyer would have ordered precisely the same goods.

Quick quiz 27.2

1 If I employ some builders to build a loft extension, but they make so much mess in my house and are so noisy that I have a nervous breakdown, can I sue them for my mental suffering?

2 As a general rule should the award of damages for breach of contract put the innocent party in the position they would have been in if the contract had never been made, or as if the contract had been performed?

3 What are the two main ways of calculating the losses of a claimant in a contract action?

4 What is meant by the 'market price rule'?

Cost of cure

Cost of cure is the other possible way of calculating expectation loss. In some cases, claimants may have wanted the performance of a contract for personal ('subjective') reasons. These subjective reasons are the value to the consumer of contractual performance which is over and above the market value of that performance. They can be described as the consumer surplus. Thus, an award of damages based on an objective difference in value between the contractual performance and the market value of the performance received will not compensate them for their loss.

The cost of cure may be significantly greater than the difference in value from that contracted for. The question, therefore, is whether the courts should take account of the consumer surplus and award higher cost of cure damages. Cost of cure damages will be awarded only where this would be reasonable. They will not be awarded where they would be out of all proportion to the consequences of the breach and there is a risk of unjust enrichment where the claimant is awarded cost of cure damages but then does not use the money to remedy the breach.

In a US case, **Jacobs & Young** *v* **Kent** (1921), the plaintiffs had specified in the contract for the construction of a house that a particular brand of piping had to be used for the plumbing work. A different make of piping of identical quality was in fact used. The court refused to allow damages on the basis of cost of cure, and allowed only the difference in value between the two types of pipe, which was purely nominal.

A leading case on the issue is **Ruxley Electronics and Construction Ltd** *v* **Forsyth** (1995). This case was discussed on p. 536. The plaintiff had contracted for the construction of a swimming pool in his garden. He had specified that the pool needed to be 7 ft 6 in deep so that he would feel safe when diving. The completed pool was only 6 ft 9 in deep. The cost of rebuilding the pool (the cost of cure) was out of proportion to the loss suffered and so the House of Lords held that the cost of cure was not recoverable. The House of Lords gave an example of the construction of a house where the owner specifies that some of the lower bricks should be blue. Instead of using blue bricks, yellow bricks are used. To conform with the contractual requirements, the house would have to be knocked down and rebuilt, but this would be disproportionately expensive. It would therefore be unreasonable to award cost of cure damages. By contrast, if a house was built so defectively that it is not inhabitable, it would be reasonable to award cost of cure damages.

The High Court concluded in **Birse Construction Ltd *v* Eastern Telegraph Co. Ltd** (2004) that an award of damages calculated on the basis of cost of cure would not be appropriate on the facts of the case. The claimants, Eastern Telegraph Company Ltd (ET) had entered into a contract with Birse Construction Ltd (BCL). Under this contract BCL agreed to build a residential training college for ET. The latter alleged that there were a number of defects with the building, but chose not to put most of them right because it had decided instead to try to sell the building. Whilst there were explanations for not dealing with some of the items (such as inaccessibility), the court was not convinced that there were any items which truly affected the general appearance, comfort and amenity of the college. If there were any such items, then any reasonable owner with resources (and ET had them) would have put them right promptly either at the same time as the main works or soon thereafter. The sale was close to completion and no discount had been required by the buyers to take into account the defects. BCL therefore argued that ET had suffered no loss and should be awarded only nominal damages. The court accepted that, following **Ruxley**, the normal measure of damages for defective works is the cost of putting the defects right (the remedial work). But this was not the measure for damages if this would be unreasonable on the facts of the case. Where the cost of the remedial works would, as a matter of common sense, be out of proportion to the claimant's real loss, then some other measure should be used. This is the case where there has been a modest effect on the utility of the works and where it would be reasonable to assess the loss on the basis of diminution in value. To award ET the cost of putting the defects right would be unreasonable and out of all proportion to ET's loss which appeared to be minimal. There was no evidence that ET's business had suffered or even that the work of any of its students had been affected. Moreover, if the college was sold, which was probable at the date of trial, ET's supposed loss would have been avoided and would not therefore be recoverable. ET was only entitled to nominal damages for the unremedied defects. It was unreasonable to award cost of cure damages as there was no intention to repair the defects and no financial loss had been suffered because the price to be obtained on the sale had not been reduced to take into account the defects. There appeared to be no real loss of amenity as no steps had been taken to rectify the defects.

Loss of opportunity damages

The loss of an opportunity is recoverable in damages if the lost chance is quantifiable in monetary terms and there was a substantial chance that the opportunity might have come to fruition. Otherwise, the loss of opportunity will be treated as too speculative. The leading case is **Chaplin *v* Hicks** (1911), in which the defendant, Sir Edward Seymour Hicks, was a theatre producer. He advertised a competition in the *Daily Express* for young women to send photographs to the newspaper to be shortlisted by readers for a prize. The winner of the competition would be offered a part in one of the defendant's plays. Six thousand photographs were sent in, each woman paying one shilling to take part in the competition. For the purposes of the competition, the country was divided into four areas, and the winners from each area were to attend the final round. The plaintiff, Eva Chaplin, came top in her area but was informed of this only at a very late stage, and was then unable to attend the final round. She sued for the loss of the chance to win the competition. The Court of Appeal held that she was entitled to damages for breach of contract. The mere fact that such damages were difficult to assess did not in itself mean that the plaintiff could not succeed. The court stated that, in calculating the damages, the jury 'must of course give effect to the consideration that the plaintiff's chance is only one out of four and that they cannot tell whether she would have ultimately proved to be the winner. But having considered all this they may well think that it is of considerable pecuniary value to have got into so small a class, and they must assess the damages accordingly.'

Lord Reid in **Davies *v* Taylor** (1974) put forward the requirement that there must have been a substantial chance that the opportunity would have come to fruition:

> 'The issues and the sole issue is whether that chance or probability was substantial. If it was it must be evaluated. If it was a mere possibility it must be ignored. Many different words could be and have been used to indicate the dividing line. I can think of none better than substantial on the one hand, or "speculative" on the other.'

The distinction between loss of a chance and speculative loss was discussed in **Allied Maples Group Ltd *v* Simmons & Simmons** (1995), in which the plaintiff sued a firm of solicitors for negligence in failing to pursue a claim. The court stated that the plaintiff could only succeed if the chance was substantial rather than speculative.

Tax

As we have seen, the aim of contract damages is to put the claimant in the position that they would have been in had the contract been performed. This means that, as a rule, the claimant should not make a profit from the defendant's breach if the profit would not have been made had the contract been performed as agreed. Therefore, where a claimant's claim includes money on which they would have had to pay income tax if it were earned by performing the contract, the amount of tax payable can be deducted from the damages.

This principle was established in **British Transport Commission *v* Gourley** (1956). This was actually a tort case, but the same principle applies to contract damages. The plaintiff had been seriously injured as a result of negligence by the defendants and was claiming for lost earnings of £37,000. The court awarded him the sum that he would have earned after paying tax, since that was what he would have received had the injury not occurred.

If the damages will themselves be subjected to tax, then the courts do not have to deduct tax themselves when calculating the damages, because this would lead to tax being deducted twice.

Profit made by the defendant

Contract damages are not intended to be a means of punishing the party in breach; they are intended to compensate the innocent party for any loss they have suffered as a result of the non-performance of the contract. For this reason, with minor exceptions, when calculating damages, the courts have traditionally not taken into account any profit the party in breach has made by breaking the contract, only the loss caused to the innocent party. So if, for example, Bill, a greengrocer, fails to make a delivery to Jill because a top chef has just come in and bought all his stock at a vastly inflated price, Bill will be liable to compensate Jill for any extra cost she incurred in buying elsewhere, but does not have to hand over the extra profit he made on the sale to the chef.

An award of damages calculated on the basis of a defendant's profit could be described as restitutionary rather than compensatory. Restitution is the remedy available where there has been unjust enrichment, and is not traditionally available for breach of contract. There are circumstances in which a claimant has not suffered any direct financial loss from the defendant's wrongdoing. Under the traditional basis of calculation, they could not be compensated. If compensation is calculated to take into account the defendant's profit, then the innocent party, who has suffered no direct loss in the traditional sense, can still receive compensation. It seems that some form of restitutionary damages will be available where compensatory damages do not provide a satisfactory remedy. In the most recent cases the courts now appear to be willing to compensate for a loss of profit in exceptional cases. It is in many ways unsatisfactory to have the two different principles of expectation and restitution simultaneously at work for the calculation of damages. Clear rules will have to be developed to determine when each principle should be relied upon.

In deciding whether to compensate for a loss of profit, the courts have drawn a distinction between where defendants are ordered to hand over part of their profits, and where they are ordered to hand over all their profit (known as 'an account of profits'). The court will now sometimes order the former, but only in very exceptional circumstances order the latter.

Defendants to hand over part of their profits

Until recently, the courts were not prepared to take into account a defendant's profit when calculating an award of damages. The position has now changed and the courts are prepared to make an award of damages that is calculated on the basis of the guilty party being required to return part of their profits.

A case that had originally rejected profit-based damages is **Surrey County Council v Bredero Homes Ltd** (1993). The Council sold land to the defendant property developer, who covenanted not to build more than 72 houses on it.

Without seeking a variation of the covenant, the developer built an additional five houses. The developer deliberately breached the covenant in order to make more profit. The council claimed damages, based on its estimate of what the defendant would have had to pay as the 'price' for variation of the covenant. While the developer had been 'unjustly enriched', the council had not suffered any loss. Normal contract damages were not recoverable, because the plaintiff was already in the position it would have been in had the contract not been breached. The question for the Court of Appeal was whether the deliberate breach of the contract should in some way be sanctioned by making the defendant hand over part of its profit. The court did not think it should.

A different approach was taken in **Wrotham Park Estate Co. Ltd *v* Parkside Homes Ltd** (1974). The defendant had built houses on his land which was in breach of a restrictive covenant in favour of a neighbouring property. The neighbour sought an injunction which would effectively have required the houses to be demolished. The courts refused to issue an injunction because this would have been an 'unpardonable waste of much needed houses'. Instead, they were awarded damages. If the usual measure of damages had been used, only nominal damages could have been awarded, because the construction of the houses had not caused any financial loss to the claimant – the construction of the houses had not affected the value of the neighbouring property. The court considered as the 'just substitute for a mandatory injunction . . . such sum as might reasonably have been demanded by the plaintiffs from Parkside as a *quid pro quo* for relaxing the covenant'. This was calculated on the basis of 5 per cent of the profit which the defendant made from the breach of covenant. This measure was used because it reflected the sum the neighbour might reasonably have required for the plaintiff's consent to the development.

The award could therefore be described as compensation rather than restitution, as it was compensation for the lost opportunity to negotiate a release from the covenant. This opportunity had been lost when the covenant was breached unilaterally.

The decision was approved by the House of Lords in **Attorney-General *v* Blake** (2001). The House preferred this case over the case of **Surrey County Council *v* Bredero Homes**. It viewed **Wrotham Park** as 'a solitary beacon'. It showed that 'in contract as well as tort damages are not always narrowly confined to recoupment of financial loss', and that in 'a suitable case damages for breach of contract may be measured by the benefit gained by the wrongdoer from the breach. The wrongdoer must make a reasonable payment in respect of the benefit he has gained'.

The House thought that these damages amounted to compensation and not restitution. Compensation seeks to compensate someone for their loss. The House thought that a broad view needed to be taken as to a party's loss – on the facts of the case the claimant's loss did not have to be limited to a loss in value to their property (which had not occurred). The House did not think that the award of damages came within the concept of restitution because it did not amount to the defendant handing back an unjust enrichment. The damages were calculated on the basis of the amount the defendant could have been required to pay for the plaintiff's consent to the development. The House considered this to be a form of compensation. In **Blake** the House commented that the law was giving effect to the instinctive reaction that, whether or not the appellant would have been better off if the wrong had not been committed, the wrongdoer ought not to gain an advantage for free, and should make some reasonable recompense. In such a context it is natural to pay regard to any profit made by the wrongdoer.

A recent case on the issue is **Experience Hendrix v PPX Enterprises** (2003). This case concerned the estate of the musician Jimi Hendrix, who died in 1970 at the age of 27. The claimant was a company that was effectively owned by Jimi Hendrix's father, who had inherited Hendrix's estate and held most of the rights to Hendrix's music. Under an agreement that had been signed in 1973, PPX had rights over some recordings of Hendrix's music, which were listed in the agreement. In breach of this agreement, PPX released some unlicensed recordings of Hendrix's music. The claimants therefore brought this action for an injunction requiring the defendant to deliver up the relevant master tapes and provide an account of profits.

The claimants were unable to prove or quantify any loss they had suffered as a result of these breaches. Thus, if the traditional approach to the calculation of damages was taken, they would only have received nominal damages. But, if the defendant had obtained permission for the issuing of licences, then they would have been required to pay the claimant royalties. It would therefore be illogical, when the courts had found a breach of the 1973 agreement, that the defendant should pay nothing for the use of these master tapes. The Court of Appeal decided that, as a matter of practical justice, the defendant was required to make reasonable payment for its use of the master tapes. But it was not appropriate to order a full account of all profits that had been made by the defendant. An award of damages calculated on the basis of part of the defendant's profits was appropriate because:

- there had been a deliberate breach by the defendant of its contractual obligations for its own reward;
- the claimants would have difficulty in establishing that they had suffered a financial loss as a result;
- the claimants had a legitimate interest in preventing the defendant from making a profit from its breach of contract.

An injunction was issued to prevent future breaches. For the past breaches, the defendant was ordered to pay a reasonable sum for its use of material in breach of the settlement agreement. These damages would be calculated by setting a royalty rate. That sum was the amount that could reasonably have been demanded by Jimi Hendrix's estate for the use of the material. This was the same approach that was adopted to the calculation of damages in **Wrotham Park**. The Court of Appeal acknowledged that there was an element of artificiality in this process, as the claimant might never have given permission for the material to be used. But the court still favoured taking this approach, because it 'directed the court's attention to the commercial value of the right infringed and of enabling it to assess the sum payable by reference to the fees that might in other contexts be demanded and paid between willing parties'. This remedy of requiring defendants to pay part of their profits to the innocent party is available for ordinary commercial contracts.

In **Lane _v_ O'Brien Homes** (2004), a case with similar facts to those in **Wrotham Park**, the High Court ordered the defendant to pay over 50 per cent of their profits to the claimant.

An account of profits

In exceptional circumstances, the courts will now order a party in breach of a contract to hand over all of the profit they have made from the breach of contract. Such an order will be made only where the other possible contractual remedies are not adequate. This change in the law was made by the House of Lords in **Attorney-General _v_ Blake** (2001). In that case Blake had been a member of the Secret Intelligence Service. In 1951 he became an agent for the Soviet Union. From that time until his arrest in 1960, he worked as a spy, disclosing valuable secret information. In 1961 he was convicted of committing offences under the Official Secrets Act 1911 and was sentenced to 42 years' imprisonment. Five years later he escaped from Wormwood Scrubs and made his way to the Soviet Union, where he now lives as a fugitive from justice.

The publishers, Jonathan Cape Ltd, agreed to pay the defendant £50,000 on signing a contract to write a book of his experiences, £50,000 on delivery of the manuscript and a further £50,000 on publication of the autobiography. In 1990 the book was published. The information in the book was no longer confidential and nor was its disclosure damaging to the public interest.

By the time the government knew about the book, Blake had already received £60,000, which could not in practice be recovered. Approximately £90,000 remained payable by the publisher and the present action was brought to prevent its payment to Blake.

In 1944, Blake had signed a declaration under the Official Secrets Act 1911 which included an undertaking not to divulge any official information gained as a result of his employment. The House of Lords held that this undertaking was contractually binding and had been breached by Blake.

The House accepted that following a breach of contract an account of profits could, in exceptional circumstances, be ordered. Under this order the defendant would have to hand over to the claimant any profits received from the breach of contract. This order could be made when the claimant's interest in performance made it just and equitable that the defendant should retain no benefit from the breach of contract. The House of Lords said that such an order would only be made in 'exceptional circumstances':

> 'Normally the remedies of damages, specific performance and injunction . . . will provide an adequate response to a breach of contract. It will be only in exceptional cases, where those remedies are inadequate, that any question of accounting for profits will arise. No fixed rules can be prescribed. The court will have regard to all the circumstances, including the subject matter of the contract, the purpose of the contractual provision which has been breached, the circumstances in which the breach occurred, the consequences of the breach and the circumstances in which relief is being sought. A useful general guide, although not exhaustive, is whether the plaintiff had a legitimate interest in preventing the defendant's profit-making activity and, hence, in depriving him of his profit.'

555

Lord Steyn stated that four conditions would need to be satisfied before there could be an order for an account of profits for a breach of contract:

- There must be a breach of a negative stipulation (in this case not to disclose official secrets).
- The contract breaker has obtained a profit by doing the precise opposite of what he promised not to do.
- The claimant has a special interest greater than the financial one of having the contract performed.
- Specific performance or an injunction (both discussed below) would be ineffective remedies.

The House considered that three facts would not in themselves be sufficient grounds for departing from the normal basis on which damages are awarded:

> 'the fact that the breach was cynical and deliberate; the fact that the breach enabled the defendant to enter into a more profitable contract elsewhere; and the fact that by entering into a new and more profitable contract the defendant put it out of his power to perform his contract with the plaintiff.'

The requirement of exceptional circumstances to order an account of profits was emphasised by the Court of Appeal in **Experience Hendrix v PPX Enterprises** (2003):

> 'The exceptional nature of Blake's case lay, first of all, in its context – employment in the security and intelligence service, of which secret information was the lifeblood, its disclosure being a criminal offence . . . Blake had furthermore committed deliberate and repeated breaches causing untold damage, from which breaches most of the profits indirectly derived in the sense that his notoriety as a spy explained his ability to command the sums for publication which he had done . . . Thirdly, although the argument that Blake was a fiduciary was not pursued beyond first instance, the contractual undertaking he had given was "closely akin to a fiduciary obligation, where an account of profits is a standard remedy in the event of breach".'

The claim in **Experience Hendrix** was not sufficiently exceptional to justify an account of profits. While the claimant had a legitimate interest in preventing the breach of the licences, the case raised no issues of national security and there was no fiduciary relationship.

The Court of Appeal distinguished the High Court judgment of **Esso Petroleum Co. Ltd v Niad** (2001). The High Court had given a much broader interpretation to the application of **Blake**, applying it to an ordinary commercial contract, an approach which is unlikely to be taken in future in the light of **Experience Hendrix**. In the latter case, the Court of Appeal pointed with approval to a case decided by an arbitration panel: **AB Corporation v CD Company (*The Sine Nomine*)** (2002). The tribunal refused an account of profits to charterers in circumstances where owners had wrongfully withdrawn the vessel from a charter after its market value had risen. The tribunal held that an award of wrongful profits was inappropriate where both parties were dealing with a marketable commodity (the services of a ship in that case) for which a substitute can be found on the market.

The Court of Appeal in **Experience Hendrix** stated that it did not regard the facts of the appeal as exceptional to the point where the court should order a full account of all PPX's profits which had been or might in the future be made by its breaches. Here, the breaches, though deliberate, took place in a commercial context. In **Esso Petroleum _v_ Niad**, the High Court had ordered an account of profits for breach of a commercial contract, but this case was distinguished, and is unlikely to be followed in the future.

Problems with damages

The interests protected

The law focuses mainly on one type of loss: financial loss to the party concerned. It generally ignores the mental distress, anxiety and sheer inconvenience which a breach of contract may cause. For example, the directors of large businesses may not lose any sleep over a supplier's failure to deliver, but the situation is very different for a small business, where such a breach may involve the proprietor in extra work finding alternative stock or, if this cannot be done, customers may be disappointed and shop elsewhere. The injured party may be able to claim for the cost of buying goods at a higher price, or the loss of the profit from the goods that should have been supplied, but will not be able to claim for the stress caused by extra work, or for the incalculable long-term damage caused by disappointing customers.

There are kinds of interest which contract law is simply not equipped to consider. Take, for example, a situation where a rich environmentalist, Sue, makes a contract with a farmer, Giles, under which she pays him not to tear up the hedgerows around the farm. What if Giles pulls up the hedges anyway? Sue could probably get her money back, but she has made the contract in order to protect the environment; not only will no damages be payable, as she has suffered no financial loss, but no damages could restore the position that would have existed had the contract been performed.

The law of contract needs to recognise that consumers tend to contract for reasons other than financial profit, so that remedies which focus entirely on their loss of economic bargain are inadequate.

Practicalities

Even where the damages that could be awarded would provide an adequate solution, there are many situations in which it is completely impractical for the claimant to make a claim, because the costs and/or time and effort involved in litigation are out of proportion to the amount that could be claimed. Because of this, it will frequently be obvious to a party considering breaching a contract that no action will be taken against them if they do, especially where they are the stronger party.

An additional problem is that, in many cases, the injured party does not know they have a right to claim. Even the considerable amount of consumer protection legislation enacted in recent years cannot protect a consumer who does not know what they are entitled to when buying goods or paying for a service.

Damages and profit

The decision of **Attorney-General v Blake** has been criticised as working against the creation of wealth. There is a theory, developed by the academic Posner, which is known as the 'economic theory of efficient breach'. Under this theory, contracts are made to generate wealth. Parties contract on terms that give them a benefit over and above the cost of their performance. Occasionally, there will be a change of circumstances, so that more wealth will be generated if the contract is not performed. This could be because one party might find someone else who is willing to pay considerably more for the goods that were to be sold under the contract, so that even after compensating the innocent contracting party they are left with a bigger profit. Under the theory of efficient breach, the defendant should only be required to compensate the innocent party for their loss, and should not be punished for non-performance by, for example, confiscating any profit made from their breach of contract. Such punishment would discourage the parties from generating further wealth. The traditional approach of contract law is therefore to give much greater weight to compensation and mitigation than to ensuring performance. The decision of **Attorney-General v Blake** is considered to conflict with a healthy market economy. A counter-argument to this is that if the courts are prepared to calculate damages to take into account the wrongdoer's profit, the parties would be encouraged to reach a negotiated agreement for their mutual release from the contract, which would be on favourable terms for both parties.

In its report, *Aggravated, Exemplary and Restitutionary Damages* (1997), the Law Commission considered the question of damages when the contract breaker has profited from their breach. It came to the conclusion that the law in this area should be left to the courts rather than being developed by statute. They pointed out that it would be difficult to draw the distinction between 'innocent' breaches of contract and 'cynical' breaches which were based on the parties' own commercial reasons. Thus any legislative provisions based on this distinction would lead to greater uncertainty in the assessment of damages in commercial and consumer disputes. It would also be difficult to show which profits were a direct result of the breach of contract.

Reading on the web

The Law Commission report *Aggravated, Exemplary and Restitutionary Damages* (1997) is available on its website at:

  www.lawcom.gov.uk/docs/lc247.pdf

The Law Commission report *Compound Interest* (2004) is available on its website at:

  www.lawcom.gov.uk/docs/lc287.pdf

The House of Lords' judgment **Farley v Skinner (No. 2)** (2001) is available at:

  www.publications.parliament.uk/pa/ld200102/ldjudgmt/jd011011/farley-1.htm

The House of Lords' judgment **Attorney-General v Blake** (1999) is available at:

  www.publications.parliament.uk/pa/ld199900/ldjudgmt/jd000727/blake-1.htm

The Law Commission report *Limitation of Actions* (2001) is available on its website at:

  www.lawcom.gov.uk/docs/lc270(2).pdf

Chapter summary

Compensatory damages

An award of damages is the usual remedy for a breach of contract. It is an award of money that aims to compensate the innocent party for the financial losses they have suffered as a result of the breach. The general rule is that innocent parties are entitled to such damages as will put them in the position they would have been in if the contract had been performed. When a contract is breached, a party may suffer pecuniary loss or non-pecuniary loss.

Pecuniary loss

Damages aim to compensate the innocent party for their financial losses that result from not receiving the performance bargained for.

Non-pecuniary loss

Damages for non-pecuniary losses are generally not recoverable in contract. Thus, damages for mental distress are not awarded in commercial contracts: **Addis v Gramophone Co. Ltd** (1909). Recent cases have developed the principle that, in a limited number of situations, injury to feelings (generally called mental distress) and loss of amenity will be compensated. Such compensation is available where the contract's whole purpose was the provision of pleasure, relaxation and peace of mind (**Jarvis v Swans Tours Ltd** (1973)); where a major object of the contract was to provide pleasure, relaxation and peace of mind (**Farley v Skinner (No. 2)** (2001)); and if the mental suffering is related to physical inconvenience and discomfort caused by the breach of the contract.

Limitations on awards of damages

The general rule is that innocent parties are entitled to such damages as will put them in the position they would have been in if the contract had been performed, but there are three limitations, which will be considered under the headings of causation, remoteness and mitigation.

Causation

A person will only be liable for losses caused by their breach of contract. The defendant's breach need not be the sole cause of the claimant's losses, but it must be an effective cause of their loss.

Remoteness

There are some losses which clearly result from the defendant's breach of contract, but are considered too remote from the breach for it to be fair to expect the defendant to compensate the claimant for them. The rules concerning remoteness were originally laid down in **Hadley v Baxendale** (1854). The court laid down two situations where the defendant should be liable for loss caused by a breach of contract:

1 Loss which would arise naturally, 'according to the usual course of things', from their breach.
2 Loss 'as may reasonably be supposed to have been in the contemplation of the parties at the time when they made the contract, as the probable result of the breach of it'.

The approach in **Hadley** *v* **Baxendale** was reaffirmed in **Victoria Laundry (Windsor) Ltd** *v* **Newman Industries Ltd** (1949) and then discussed again by the House of Lords in *The Heron II* (1969).

Mitigation

Claimants are under a duty to mitigate their loss, and cannot recover damages for losses which could have been avoided by taking reasonable steps.

Calculating loss

There are two main ways in which the losses of a claimant in a contract action can be calculated: the loss of expectation, and the reliance loss.

Loss of expectation

Where loss of expectation is the basis for calculating damages, the courts aim to put claimants in the position they would have been in if the contract had been performed. Thus, the parties would have expected a certain result from the performance of the contract and the damages will compensate for the loss of this expectation.

Reliance loss

Where reliance loss is the basis for calculating damages, the damages seek to put claimants in the position they were in before the contract was made. The damages will therefore compensate for the actual wasted expenditure and other losses incurred because of the contract which has been breached.

Choosing between the expectation and reliance principles

As a rule, a claimant can choose whether to base a claim on loss of expectation or on reliance. In practice, loss of expectation is the usual basis for calculating contract damages. There are two main restrictions on the claimant's choice between the expectation and the reliance principles. These are the bad bargain rule and the speculative damages rule.

■ *Bad bargain rule*: if the claimant would have made a loss from the contract, then he or she will only be entitled to nominal damages, and will not be entitled to claim their expenses on the basis of reliance loss.
■ *Expectation losses are 'too speculative'*: the reliance basis for calculating damages must be used where it is virtually impossible to calculate what profit the claimant would have made if the contract had been performed correctly.

Quantifying the expectation loss

Contract damages based on expectation loss are essentially seeking to compensate the difference in value between the promised performance and the actual performance.

The market price rule

Where a contract has been breached, the law assumes that the wronged party will immediately mitigate their loss by buying similar goods which they had contracted for from another source or selling the goods which they had contracted to sell to another source. The buyer's damages will therefore be assessed by subtracting the contract price from the market price at the time of breach. The market price rule will not be used as the measure of loss either where there is no available market or where, in the circumstances, the non-breaching party is not expected to avail itself of the market to mitigate its loss.

Cost of cure

Cost of cure damages will only be awarded where this would be reasonable. They will not be awarded where they would be out of all proportion to the consequences of the breach and there is a risk of unjust enrichment if the claimant is awarded cost of cure damages but then does not use the money to remedy the breach: **Ruxley Electronics and Construction Ltd *v* Forsyth** (1995).

Loss of opportunity damages

The loss of an opportunity is recoverable in damages if the lost chance is quantifiable in monetary terms and there was a substantial chance that the opportunity might have come to fruition. Otherwise, the loss of opportunity will be treated as too speculative.

Tax

Where a claimant's claim includes money on which they would have had to pay income tax if it were earned by performing the contract, the amount of tax payable can be deducted from the damages.

Profit made by the defendant

When calculating damages, the courts have traditionally not taken into account any profit the party in breach has made by breaking the contract, only the loss caused to the innocent party. In the most recent cases, the courts now appear to be willing to compensate for a loss of profit in exceptional cases. In deciding whether to compensate for a loss of profit, the courts have drawn a distinction between where defendants are ordered to hand over part of their profits, and where they are ordered to hand over all their profit (**Attorney-General *v* Blake** (2000)). The court will now sometimes order the former, but only in very exceptional circumstances order the latter.

** Please note that if you are studying *Section C: Introduction to Contract* of the AQA specifications, you will also need to study Chapter 20: Civil Court Procedure, above, which is also part of the 'Introduction to Contract' specifications.

Question and answer guide

1

Jim needed to buy a new photocopier for his business. He telephoned Techno Ltd., who agreed to sell him a photocopier for £55,000. Immediately after the telephone conversation, Techno Ltd. discovered they had given the price for the wrong photocopier and tried to telephone Jim back but could not get hold of him. Techno Ltd. then sent a letter in the post stating that they would sell the photocopier to Jim for £65,000. Jim received the letter the following day. Techno Ltd. refused to supply the photocopier at £55,000 and Jim refused to pay £65,000. Techno Ltd.'s prices were the standard prices for photocopiers at this time.

(a) (i) Explain the legal concept of an offer, giving examples.   *(7 marks)*
    (ii) Explain the legal concept of an acceptance, giving examples.   *(7 marks)*
(b) Explain whether Jim has entered into a contract with Techno Ltd.

(10 marks)

(c) If there is a contract between Jim and Techno Ltd., discuss whether are in breach of that contract.   *(7 marks)*
(d) If the parties enter into legal proceedings:
    (i) which court would hear the case and describe the pre-trial procedures that would be followed;   *(7 marks)*
    (ii) describe how the court would calculate any award of damages to Jim.

(7 marks)

(a) (i) An offer is any communication which indicates the terms on which one person is prepared to make a contract, and which clearly indicates his intention to be bound by those terms if they are accepted by the person to whom the offer is made.

An offer must be distinguished from an invitation to treat, i.e. an invitation to make an offer. Advertisements are usually considered invitations to treat (**Partridge v Crittenden**), unless they are for unilateral contracts, in which case they are usually treated as offers (**Carlill v Carbolic Smoke Ball Co.**). A display of price-marked goods on the shelves or in the windows of shops is generally regarded as an invitation to treat, rather than as an offer: **Pharmaceutical Society v Boots; Fisher v Bell**.

An offer may be revoked at any time up until it is accepted: **Payne v Cave**. However, the revocation is not effective until communicated to the offeree: **Byrne v Van Tienhoven**.

(a) (ii) An acceptance of an offer is an unconditional agreement to all the terms of that offer. Acceptance will often be oral or in writing, but in some cases an offeree may accept an offer by doing something, such as delivering goods in response to an offer to buy. Merely remaining silent cannot amount to an acceptance, unless it is absolutely clear that acceptance was intended: **Felthouse v Bindley**.

An acceptance does not usually take effect until it is communicated to the offeror. However, there are a number of exceptions to this rule, including the postal rule, which states that acceptances by post take effect when they are posted, rather than when they are communicated: **Adams v Lindsell**. The postal rule applies not only to postal acceptances but also to acceptances by certain other non-instantaneous modes of communication, e.g. telegrams: **Cowan** *v* **O'Connor**. The postal rule does not apply to revocations of offers: **Henthorn** *v* **Fraser**.

(b) For something to be an offer, it must indicate the terms on which the offeror is prepared to make a contract with the offeree. In Jim's case, one of those terms would have been the price. The question does not tell us what Jim said when he phoned Techno Ltd., but it is quite possible that he made no mention of any specific price. It is possible that what he said amounted to merely an inquiry as to price, which would not be an offer but an invitation to treat.

If this analysis is correct then Techno Ltd.'s 'agreement' to supply Jim with a photocopier for £55,000 in law was not an acceptance but merely an offer. Techno Ltd. were free to revoke this offer at any time up until it had been accepted. They did purport to revoke it when they tried to contact Jim on the phone. But a revocation is not effective until communicated. So this first purported revocation was ineffective. They made a second attempt at revocation when they posted Jim the price list. The postal rule does not apply to revocations, so this letter was not effective until Jim received it. But he did receive it, and apparently before he had accepted Techno Ltd.'s first offer. Accordingly, Techno Ltd.'s letter took effect as a revocation of their first offer and its replacement with a new offer. Since Jim clearly did not accept that new offer, there is now no contract between Jim and Techno Ltd.

If what passed between Jim and Techno Ltd. during their telephone conversation was an offer from Jim to buy a photocopier at a given price and Techno Ltd.'s acceptance of that offer, then a contract came into existence at that point.

(c) Breach of contract is when one party to a contract performs his obligations defectively, differently from the agreement, or not at all.

A breach can be either actual or anticipatory. An actual breach is when the defective performance occurs on or after the date for performance. An anticipatory breach is when one party indicates, before the date for performance, that he will not be performing his obligations when the date for performing them falls due.

Where an anticipatory breach occurs, the other party can sue for breach straight away; he does not have to wait until performance falls due: **Hochster** *v* **De la Tour**. If he elects to wait until performance falls due, he runs the risk that he will end up worse off than if he had sued immediately the anticipatory breach was known: **Avery** *v* **Bowden**.

Applying this principle to the facts, if, as stated in (b), the telephone conversation between Jim and Techno Ltd. brought a contract into existence, it was a contract under which Techno Ltd. agreed to supply a specified number of phones to Jim at £60,000. Since Techno Ltd. are now refusing to supply the copier at that price they are in breach of their contract with Jim.

(d) (i) Civil cases are only heard in the High Court if the claimant expects to recover more than £15,000 (or £50,000 if it is a personal injury case). Given that the amount of damage that Jim has suffered appears to be less than £15,000 (see answer to (d)(ii)), his case would be heard in a county court.

The proceedings start with Jim completing a claim form. This informs Techno Ltd. that an action is being brought against them, and provides a statement as to the value of Jim's claim. The claim form is then served on Techno Ltd., by the court using first class post, unless Jim elects to serve it himself. Techno Ltd. will need to acknowledge service.

Jim must then serve on Techno Ltd. his particulars of claim. Techno Ltd. must respond by filing either an acknowledgement of service or a defence. If they fail to do either within 14 days, Jim can enter judgment in default. If Techno Ltd. file a defence, the court will serve an allocation questionnaire on both parties. This is designed to enable the court to decide to which track it should assign the claim.

The disclosure procedures are then followed, under which the parties are required to disclose the documents on which they intend to rely and also the documents which go against their case.

If the case is not settled out of court or by alternative dispute resolution (which the court will actively promote), it proceeds to trial. The fast track is the one to which actions with a value of between £5,000 and £15,000 are assigned, so this is how Jim's claim will be dealt with.

(d) (ii) The general rule is that the innocent victim of a breach of contract is entitled to such damages as will put him in the position he would have been in if the contract had been performed. But the law assumes that the wronged party will mitigate his loss. This means that, in a case such as the present – i.e., a sale of goods contract where the seller fails to deliver – the buyer (Jim) is expected to buy the goods he wants from another source. Therefore, his damages will be assessed by subtracting the contract price from the market price at the time of breach: Sale of Goods Act 1979, s. 51. The contract price in Jim's case is £55,000, while it is reasonable to assume that the market price is £65,000, this being the price which, says the question, other suppliers are charging. Accordingly, the court would assess Jim's damages as £10,000.

Jim will not be entitled to damages for any disappointment or hurt feelings that Techno Ltd.'s breach might have caused him; damages for such non-pecuniary losses are generally not recoverable in contract: **Addis *v* Gramophone Co. Ltd**.

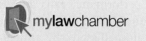 mylawchamber

Visit **www.mylawchamber.co.uk/elliottaqa** to access interactive questions, quizzes and activities to test yourself on this chapter.

Answering examination questions

At the end of each chapter in this book, you will find detailed guidelines for answering exam questions on the topics covered. Many of the questions are taken from actual A-level past papers, but they are equally relevant for candidates of all law examinations, as these questions are typical of the type of questions that examiners ask in this field.

In this section, we aim to give some general guidelines for answering questions on the English legal system.

Citation of authorities

One of the most important requirements for answering questions on the law is that you must be able to back the points you make with authority, usually either a case or a statute. It is not good enough to state that the law is such and such, without stating the case or statute which says that that is the law. Some examiners are starting to suggest that the case name is not essential as long as you can re-member and understand the general principle that the case laid down. However, such examiners remain in the minority and the reality is that even they are likely to give higher marks where the candidate has cited authorities; quite simply, it helps give the impression that you know your material thoroughly, rather than half-remembering something you heard once in class.

This means that you must be prepared to learn fairly long lists of cases by heart, which can be a daunting prospect. What you need to memorise is the name of the case, a brief description of the facts, and the legal principle which the case estab-lished. Once you have revised a topic well, you should find that a surprisingly high number of cases on that topic begin to stick in your mind anyway, but there will probably be some that you have trouble recalling. A good way to memorise these is to try to create a picture in your mind which links the facts, the name and the legal principle. For example, if you wanted to remember the contract law case of **Redgrave v Hurd**, you might picture the actress Vanessa Redgrave and the politician Douglas Hurd, in the situation described in the facts of the case, and imagine one of them telling the other the principle established in the case.

Knowing the names of cases makes you look more knowledgeable, and saves writing time in the exam, but if you do forget a name, referring briefly to the facts will identify it. It is not necessary to learn the dates of cases, though it is useful if you know whether it is a recent or an old case. Dates are usually required for statutes. Unless you are making a detailed comparison of the facts of a case and the facts of a problem question, in order to argue that the case should or could be distinguished, you should generally make only brief reference to facts, if at all – long descriptions of facts waste time and earn few marks.

When reading the 'Question and answer guides' sections at the end of each chapter in this book, bear in mind that for reasons of space, we have not highlighted every case which you should cite. The skeleton arguments outlined in those sections **must** be backed up with authority from cases and statute law.

When discussing the English legal system, as well as citing relevant cases and statutes, it is particularly important to cite relevant research and reports in the field being discussed. If there are important statistics in an area, being able to quote some of them will give your answers authority.

There is no right answer

In law exams, there is not usually a right or a wrong answer. What matters is that you show you know what type of issues you are being asked about. Essay questions are likely to ask you to 'discuss', 'criticise' or 'evaluate', and you simply need to produce a good range of factual and critical material in order to do this. The answer you produce might look completely different from your friend's but both answers could be worth 'A' grades.

Breadth and depth of content

Where a question seems to raise a number of different issues – as most do – you will achieve better marks by addressing all or most of these issues than by writing at great length on just one or two. By all means spend more time on issues which you know well, but be sure to at least mention other issues which you can see are relevant, even if you can only produce a paragraph or so about them.

Civil or criminal

In some cases, a question on the English legal system will require you to confine your answer to either the civil or criminal system. This may be stated in the question – for example, 'Discuss the system of civil appeals'. Alternatively, it may be something you are required to work out for yourself, as is often the case with problem questions. For example, a question might state:

'Jane has been charged with criminal damage.
(a) How may she obtain legal aid and advice? and
(b) If convicted, to which courts may she appeal?'

This question only requires you to discuss the legal aid and advice available in criminal cases, and the criminal appeals system; giving details of civil legal aid and the civil appeals system will waste time and gain you no marks, as would bringing the criminal appeals system into the previous question. Equally, where a question does not limit itself to either civil or criminal legal systems, you will lose marks if you only discuss one.

Because of this danger, it is a good idea to make a point of asking yourself before you answer any legal system question whether it covers just the civil legal system, just the criminal, or both.

The structure of the question

If a question is specifically divided into parts, for example (a), (b) and (c), then stick to those divisions and do not merge your answer into one long piece of writing.

Law examinations tend to contain a mixture of essay questions and what are known as 'problem questions'. Tackling each of these questions involves slightly different skills, so we consider each in turn.

Essay questions

Answer the question asked

Over and over again, examiners complain that candidates do not answer the question they are asked – so if you can develop this skill, you will stand out from the crowd. You will get very few marks for simply writing all you know about a topic, with no attempt to address the issues raised in the question, but if you can adapt the material that you have learnt on the subject to take into account the particular emphasis given to it by the question, you will do well.

Even if you have memorised an essay which does raise the issues in the question (perhaps because those issues tend to be raised year after year), you must fit your material to the words of the question you are actually being asked. For example, suppose during your course you wrote an essay on the advantages and disadvantages of the jury system, and then in the exam you find yourself faced with the question 'Should juries be abolished?' The material in your coursework essay is ideally suited for the exam question, but if you begin the main part of your answer with the words 'The advantages of juries include . . .', or something similar, this is a dead giveaway to the examiner that you are merely writing down an essay you have memorised. It takes very little effort to change the words to 'Abolition of the jury system would ignore certain advantages that the current system has . . .', but it will create a much better impression, especially if you finish with a conclusion which, based on points you have made, states that abolition is a good or bad idea, the choice depending on the arguments you have made during your answer.

During your essay, you should keep referring to the words used in the question – if this seems to become repetitive, use synonyms for those words. This makes it clear to the examiner that you are keeping the question in mind as you work.

Plan your answer

Under pressure of time, it is tempting to start writing immediately, but five minutes spent planning each essay question is well worth spending – it may mean that you write less overall, but the quality of your answer will almost certainly be better. The plan need not be elaborate: just jot down everything you feel is relevant to the answer, including case names, and then organise the material into a logical order appropriate to the question asked. To put it in order, rather than wasting time copying it all out again, simply put a number next to each point according to which ones you intend to make first, second and so forth.

Provide analysis and fact

Very few essay questions require merely factual descriptions of what the law is; you will almost always be required to analyse the factual content in some way, usually highlighting any problems or gaps in the law, and suggesting possible reforms. If a question asks you to analyse whether lay magistrates should be replaced by professional judges, you should not write everything you know about magistrates and judges and finish with one sentence saying that magistrates should/should not be kept. Instead, you should select your relevant material and your whole answer should be targeted at answering whether or not magistrates should be kept.

Where a question uses the word 'critically', as in 'critically describe' or 'critically evaluate', the examiners are merely drawing your attention to the fact that your approach should be analytical and not merely descriptive; you are not obliged to criticise every provision you describe. Having said that, even if you do not agree with particular criticisms which you have read, you should still discuss them and say why you do not think they are valid; there is very little mileage in an essay that simply describes the law and says it is perfectly satisfactory.

Structure

However good your material, you will only gain really good marks if you structure it well. Making a plan for each answer will help in this, and you should also try to learn your material in a logical order – this will make it easier to remember as well. The exact construction of your essay will obviously depend on the question, but you should aim to have an introduction, then the main discussion, and a conclusion. Where a question is divided into two or more parts, you should reflect that structure in your answer.

A word about conclusions: it is not good enough just to repeat the question, turning it into a statement, for the conclusion. So, for example, if the question is 'Is the criminal justice system satisfactory?', a conclusion which simply states that the system is or is not satisfactory will gain you very little credit. Your conclusion will often summarise the arguments that you have developed during the course of your essay.

Problem questions

In problem questions, the exam paper will describe an imaginary situation, and then ask what the legal implications of the facts are – for example:

> *'Jane had suffered physical violence at the hands of her husband for many years. One day she lashes out and kills him. She is arrested by the police and later charged with murder. In which court will Jane be tried? If she is convicted, to what court may she appeal?'*

Read the question thoroughly

The first priority is to read the question thoroughly, at least a couple of times. Never start writing until you have done this, as you may well get halfway through and discover that what is said at the end makes half of what you have written irrelevant – or at worst, that the question raises issues you have no knowledge of at all.

Answer the question asked

This means paying close attention to the words printed immediately after the situation is described. In the example given above, you are asked to advise about the courts and appeal procedure, so do not start discussing sentencing powers as this is not relevant to the particular question asked. Similarly, if a question asks you to advise one or other of the parties, make sure that you advise the right one – the realisation as you discuss the exam with your friends afterwards that you have advised the wrong party and thus rendered most of your answer irrelevant is not an experience you will enjoy.

Spot the issues

In answering a problem question in an examination you will often be short of time. One of the skills of doing well is spotting which issues are particularly relevant to the facts of the problem and spending most time on those, while skimming over more quickly those matters which are not really an issue on the facts, but which you clearly need to mention.

Apply the law to the facts

What a problem question requires you to do is to spot the issues raised by the situation, and to consider the law as it applies to those facts. It is not enough simply to describe the law without applying it to the facts. So in the example given above it is not enough to write about the appeal procedure in general for civil and criminal cases; you must apply the rules of criminal appeal to the particular case of Jane. She has committed an indictable offence that would have been tried by the Crown Court, so you are primarily concerned with appeals from the Crown Court to the Court of Appeal. Nor should you start your answer by copying out all the facts. This is a complete waste of time, and will gain you no marks.

Unlike essay questions, problem questions are not usually seeking a critical analysis of the law. If you have time, it may be worth making the point that a particular area of the law you are discussing is problematic, and briefly stating why, but if you are addressing all the issues raised in the problem you are unlikely to have much time for this. What the examiner is looking for is essentially an understanding of the law and an ability to apply it to the particular facts given.

Use authority

As always, you must back up your points with authority from case or statute law.

Structure

The introduction and conclusion are much less important for problem questions than for essay questions. Your introduction can be limited to pointing out the issues raised by the question, or, where you are asked to 'advise' a person mentioned in the problem, what outcome that person will be looking for. You can also say in what order you intend to deal with the issues. Your conclusion might simply summarise the conclusions reached during the main part of the answer, for example that Jane will be tried in the Crown Court and her main route of appeal will be to the Court of Appeal.

There is no set order in which the main part of the answer must be discussed. Sometimes it will be appropriate to deal with the problem chronologically, in which case it will usually be a matter of looking at the question line by line, while in other cases it may be appropriate to group particular issues together. Problem questions on the English legal system are often broken down into clear parts – a, b, c and so on – so the answer can be broken down into the same parts. Thus with the example about Jane, the question was clearly broken into two parts, and so your question should deal with first the trial court and then with the issue of appeal.

Whichever order you choose, try to deal with one issue at a time – for example, finish talking about the trial court before looking at the issue of appeal. Jumping backwards and forwards gives the impression that you have not thought about your answer. If you work through your material in a structured way, you are also less likely to leave anything out.

<table>
<tr><td>Appendix
2</td><td># A guide to law reports and case references</td></tr>
</table>

We have seen that much of the law is contained in cases decided before the courts. It is therefore important that a written record is kept of the decisions of the courts. Lawyers and students of law need to be able to find these written records.

The law reports

Over 2,000 cases are published in law reports each year. The most respected series of law reports is called *The Law Reports*, because before publication the report of each case included in the series is checked for accuracy by the judge who tried it. It is this series that should be cited before a court in preference to any other. The series is divided into several sub-series depending on the court which heard the case, as follows:

- **Appeal Cases** (decisions of the Court of Appeal, the House of Lords and the Privy Council).
- **Chancery Division** (decisions of the Chancery Division of the High Court and their appeals to the Court of Appeal).
- **Family Division** (decisions of the Family Division of the High Court and their appeals to the Court of Appeal).
- **Queen's Bench** (decisions of the Queen's Bench Division of the High Court and their appeals to the Court of Appeal).

Neutral citation

In 2001 a form of neutral citation was introduced in the Court of Appeal and Administrative Court. This form of citation was introduced to facilitate reference to cases reported on the internet and in CD-ROMs. Unlike reports in books, these reports do not have fixed page numbers and volumes. A unique number is now given to each approved judgment and the paragraphs in each judgment are numbered. The three forms of the neutral citation are as follows:

- Civil Division of the Court of Appeal: [2000] EWCA Civ 1, 2, 3, etc.
- Criminal Division of the Court of Appeal: [2000] EWCA Crim 1, 2, 3, etc.
- Administrative Court: [2000] EWHC Admin 1, 2, 3, etc.

The letters 'EW' stand for England and Wales. For example, if **Brown** *v* **Smith** is the fifth numbered judgment of 2002 in the Civil Division of the Court of

Appeal, it would be cited: **Brown** v **Smith** [2002] EWCA Civ 5. If you wished to refer to the fourth paragraph of the judgment, the correct citation is: [2002] EWCA Civ 5 at [4].

Case reference

Each case is given a reference(s) to explain exactly where it can be found in a law report(s). Such a reference can be used to go and find and read the case in a law library which stocks the relevant law report. This is important, as a textbook can only provide a summary of the case and has no legal status in itself; it is the actual case which contains the law.

The reference consists of a series of letters and numbers that follow the case name. The pattern of this reference varies depending on the law report being referred to. The usual format is to follow the name of the case by:

- **A year**. Where the date reference tells you the year in which the case was decided, the date is normally enclosed in round brackets. If the date is the year in which the case is reported, it is given in square brackets. The most common law reports tend to use square brackets.
- **A volume number**. Not all law reports have a volume number, sometimes they simply identify their volumes by year.
- **The law report abbreviation**. Each series of law reports has an abbreviation for their title so that the whole name does not need to be written out in full.

The main law reports and their abbreviations are as follows:

All England Law Reports	All ER
Appeal Cases	AC
Chancery Division	Ch D
Criminal Appeal Reports	Cr App R
Family Division	Fam
King's Bench	KB
Queen's Bench Division	QB
Weekly Law Reports	WLR

- **A page number**. This is the page at which the report of the case commences.
- **Neutral citation**. Where a case has been decided after 2001, the neutral citation for decisions of the Court of Appeal and Administrative Court will appear in front of the law report citation.

Examples of case references

Cozens v **Brutus** [1973] AC 854
The case was reported in the Appeal Cases law report in 1973 at p. 854.

DPP v **Hawkins** [1988] 1 WLR 1166
The case was reported in the first volume of the Weekly Law Report of 1988 at p. 1166.

R *v* **Angel** (1968) 52 Cr App R 280
The case was reported in the fifty-second volume of the Criminal Appeal Reports at p. 280.

Brown *v* **Smith** [2002] EWCA Civ 5, [2002] QB 432, [2002] 3 All ER 21
The case was the fifth decision to be decided in 2002 by the Civil Division of the Court of Appeal. It was reported in the Queen's Bench law report in 2002 at p. 432 and in the third volume of the All England Law Report in 2002 at p. 21.

Select bibliography

Abel, R. (1988) *The Legal Profession in England and Wales*, Oxford: Basil Blackwell.

Abel-Smith, B., Zander, M. and Brooke, R. (1973) *Legal Problems and the Citizen*, London: Heinemann-Educational.

Advice Services Alliance (2004) *The Independent Review of the Community Legal Service. The Advice Service's response to the Department of Constitutional Affairs consultation on the recommendations made by Matrix Research and Consultancy*, London: ASA.

Alternative Dispute Resolution – A Discussion Paper (1999), London: Lord Chancellor's Department.

Anti-Social Behaviour Orders – Analysis of the first six years (2004), London: National Association of Probation Officers.

Aquinas, St T. (1942) *Summa Theologica*, London: Burns Oates & Washbourne.

Atiyah, P. S. (1979) *The Rise and Fall of Freedom of Contract*, Oxford: Clarendon Press.

Audit Commission (1996) *Streetwise: Effective Police Patrol*, London: HMSO.

—— (1997) *Misspent Youth: Young People and Crime*, London: Audit Commission Publications.

—— (2003) *Victims and Witnesses*, London: Audit Commission Publications.

—— (2004) *Youth Justice*, London: Audit Commission Publications.

Auld, Sir R. (2001) *Review of the Criminal Courts*, London: HMSO.

Austin, J. (1954) *The Province of Jurisprudence Determined*, London: Weidenfeld & Nicolson.

Bailey, S. and Gunn, M. (2000) *Smith and Bailey on the Modern English Legal System* (4th edn), London: Sweet & Maxwell.

Baldwin, J. (1992) *The Role of Legal Representatives at the Police Station* (Royal Commission on Criminal Justice Research Study No. 2), London: HMSO.

—— (1997) *Small Claims in County Courts in England and Wales: The Bargain Basement of Civil Justice?* Oxford: Clarendon Press.

—— (1992) *Video Taping Police Interviews with Suspects: An Evaluation*, London: Home Office.

—— (2002) *Lay and Judicial Perspectives on the Expansion of the Small Claims Regime*, London: Lord Chancellor's Department.

—— (2003) *Evaluating the Effectiveness of Enforcement Procedures in Undefended Claims in the Civil Courts*, London: Lord Chancellor's Department.

Baldwin, J. and McConville, M. (1979) *Jury Trials*, Oxford: Clarendon Press.

Baldwin, J. and Moloney, T. (1992) *Supervision of police investigations in serious criminal cases* (Royal Commission on Criminal Justice Research Study No. 4), London: HMSO.

Barton, A. (2001) 'Medical litigation: who benefits?', 322 *British Medical Journal* 1189.

Bell, J. and Engle, Sir G. (eds.) (1995) *Statutory Interpretation*, London: Butterworths.

Bennion, F. A. R. (1999) 'A naked usurpation?', 149 *NLJ* 421.

Bennion, F. A. R. (2007) 'Executive estoppel: *Pepper v Hart* revisited', *Public Law* 1.

—— (1990) *Statutory Interpretation*, London: Butterworths.

Bird, S. and Brown, A. (2001) 'Criminalisation of HIV transmission: implications for public health in Scotland', *British Medical Journal* 323, 1174.

Blom-Cooper, L. (1972) *Final Appeal: A Study of the House of Lords in its Judicial Capacity*, Oxford: Clarendon Press.

Bond, R. A. and Lemon, N. F. (1979) 'Changes in Magistrates: Attitudes During the First Year on the Bench', in Farrington, D. P. *et al.* (eds.) (1979) *Psychology, Law and Legal Processes*, London: Macmillan.

Booth, A. (2002) 'Direct effect' *Solicitors Journal* 924.

Bottoms, A. E. and Preston, R. H. (eds.) (1980) *The Coming Penal Crisis: A Criminological and Theoretical Exploration*, Edinburgh: Scottish Academic Press.

Bowling, B. and Ross, J. (2006) 'The serious organised crime agency – should we be afraid', *Criminal Law Review* 1019.

Bowman, Sir J. (1997) *Review of the Court of Appeal (Civil Division)*, London: Lord Chancellor's Department.

Boyron, S. (2006) 'The rise of mediation in administrative law disputes: Experiences from England, France and Germany', *Public Law* 230.

Brazier, R. (1998) *Constitutional Reform*, Oxford: Oxford University Press.

Bridges, L. and Choongh, S. (1998) *Improving Police Station Legal Advice: The Impact of the Accreditation Scheme for Police Station Legal Advisers*, London: Law Society's Research and Planning Unit: Legal Aid Board.

Bridges, L. and others (2007) *Evaluation of the Public Defender Service in England and Wales*, London: TSO.

Brown, D. (1998) *Offending While on Bail*, Home Office, Report No. 72, London: Home Office.

Brown, D. and Neal, D. (1988) 'Show Trials: The Media and the Gang of Twelve', in Findlay, M. and Duff, P. (eds.) (1988) *The Jury under Attack*, London: Butterworths.

Brown, D. *et al.* (1992) *Changing the Code: Police Detention Under the Revised PACE Codes of Practice*, Home Office Research Study No. 129, London: HMSO.

Brownlee, I. (2004) 'The statutory charging scheme in England and Wales: towards a unified prosecution system', *Criminal Law Review* 896.

Burney, E. (1979) *Magistrates, Court and Community*, London: Hutchinson.

Campbell, S. (2002) *A review of anti-social behaviour orders*, Home Office Research Study No. 236, London: Home Office.

Carlen, P. (1983) *Women's Imprisonment: A Study in Social Control*, London: Routledge.

Carter, L. (2006) *Legal Aid: A Market-based Approach to Reform*, London: Department for Constitutional Affairs.

Carter, P. (2003) *Managing Offenders, Reducing Crime*, London: Strategy Unit, Home Office.

Chalmers, J., Duff, P. and Leverick, F. (2007) 'Victim impact statements: can work, do work (for those who bother to make them)', *Criminal Law Review* 360.

Citizens' Advice Bureau (2004) *Geography of Advice*, London: Citizens' Advice Bureau.

—— (2005) *No win, no fee, no chance*, London: Citizens' Advice Bureau.

Consumer Council (1970) *Justice Out of Reach: A Case for Small Claims Courts: A Consumer Council Study*, London: HMSO.

Cotton, J. and Povey, D. (2004) *Police Complaints and Discipline, April 2002–March 2003*, London: Home Office.

Cretney, S. (1998) *Law, Law Reform and the Family*, Oxford: Clarendon Press.

Criminal Justice: the Way Ahead (2001) Cm 5074, London: Home Office.

Criminal Statistics, England and Wales (2000), London: HMSO.

Cross, Sir R. (1995) *Statutory Interpretation*, London: Butterworths.

Cutting Crime – Delivering Justice: Strategic Plan for Criminal Justice 2004–08 (2004) Cm 6288, London: Home Office.

Darbyshire, P. (1991) 'The lamp that shows that freedom lives – is it worth the candle?', *Criminal Law Review* 740.

—— (1999) 'A comment on the powers of magistrates' clerks', *Criminal Law Review* 377.

De Tocqueville, A. (2000) *Democracy in America* (G. Lawrence, translator; J.P. Mayer, editor), New York: Perennial Classics.

Denning, A. (1952) 'The need for a new equity', 5 *Current Legal Problems* 1. Department for Constitutional Affairs (2004) *Broadcasting Courts*, Cp 28104, London: DCA.

Denning, A. (1982) *What Next in the Law?* London: Butterworths.

Dennis, I. (2006) 'Convicting the guilty: outcomes, process and the Court of Appeal', *Criminal Law Review* 955.

Department for Constitutional Affairs (2004) *Transforming Public Services: Complaints, Redress and Tribunals*, London: Stationery Office.

Department for Constitutional Affairs (2004) *The Independent Review of the Community Legal Service*, London: DCA.

Department for Constitutional Affairs (2005) *Supporting Magistrates Courts to Provide Justice*, Cm 6681, London: TSO.

Department for Constitutional Affairs (2006) *Delivery Simple, Speedy, Summary Justice*, 37/06 London: DCA.

Department for Trade and Industry (2004) *Fairness for All: A New Commission for Equality and Human Rights*, Cm 6185, London: Stationery Office.

Devlin, P. (1956) *Trial by Jury*, London: Stevens.

—— (1965) *The Enforcement of Morals*, Oxford: Oxford University Press.

—— (1979) *The Judge*, Oxford: Oxford University Press.

Dicey, A. (1982) *Introduction to the Study of the Law of the Constitution*, Indianapolis: Liberty Classics.

Dickens, L. (1985) *Dismissed: A Study of Unfair Dismissal and the Industrial System*, Oxford: Blackwell.

Director General of Fair Trading (2001) *Competition in the Professions*, OFT 328, London: OFT.

Dodgson, K. *et al.* (2001) *Electronic monitoring of released prisoners: an Evaluation of the Home Detention Curfew Scheme*, London: Home Office.

Dow, J. and Lapuerta, C. (2005) *The Benefits of Multiple Ownership Models*, available on the website of the former Department for Constitutional Affairs (www.dca.gov.uk/legalsys/ dow-lapuerta.pdf).

Durkheim, E. (1983) *Durkheim and the Law*, Oxford: Robertson.

Duster, T. (1970) *The Legislation of Morality*, New York: Free Press.

Dworkin, R. (1977) *Taking Rights Seriously*, London: Duckworth.

—— (1978) *Political Judges and the Rule of Law*, Proceedings of the British Academy.

—— (1986) *Law's Empire*, London: Fontana Press.

Edwards, I. (2002) 'The Place of Victims' Preferences in the Sentencing of "Their" Offenders', *Criminal Law Review* 689.

Ellis, T. and Hedderman, C. (1996) *Enforcing Community Sentences: Supervisors' Perspectives on Ensuring Compliance and Dealing with Breach*, London: Home Office.

Enright, S. (1993) 'Cost effective criminal justice', 143 *New Law Journal* 1023.

Epstein, H. (2003) 'The liberalisation of claim financing', 153 *New Law Journal* 153.

Evans, Sir A. (2003) 'Forget ADR – think A or D', *Civil Justice Quarterly* 230.

Evans, R. (1993) *The Conduct of Police Interviews with Juveniles*, London: HMSO.

Fenton, A. and Dabell, F. (2007) 'Time for change (1)', 157 *New Law Journal* 848.

Fenton, A. and Dabell, F. (2007) 'Time for change (2)', 157 *New Law Journal* 964.

Findlay, M. (2001) 'Juror Comprehension and complexity: strategies to enhance under-standing', 41 *British Journal of Criminalogy* 56.

Flood-Page, C. and Mackie, A. (1998) *Sentencing During the Nineties*, London: Home Office Research and Statistics Directorate.

Flood-Page, C. and Taylor, J. (eds) (2003) *Crime in England and Wales 2001/2002: Supplementary Volume*, p. 57, Table 3g and Figure 3.8.

Freeman, M. D. A. (1981) 'The Jury on Trial', 34 *Current Legal Problems* 65.

Fuller, L. (1969) *The Morality of Law*, London: Yale University Press.

Galanter, M. (1984) *The emergence of the judge as a mediator in civil cases*, Madison: University of Wisconsin.

Genn, H. (1982) *Meeting Legal Needs?: An Evaluation of a Scheme for Personal Injury Victims*, Oxford: S. S. R. C. Centre for Socio-Legal Studies.

—— (1987) *Hard Bargaining: Out of Court Settlement in Personal Injury Actions*, Oxford: Clarendon Press.

—— (1998) *The Central London County Court Pilot Mediation Scheme: Evaluation Report*, London: Lord Chancellor's Department.

—— (2002) *Court-based ADR Initiatives for Non-Family civil disputes: the Commercial Court and the Court of Appeal*, London: Lord Chancellor's Department.

Genn, H. and Genn, Y. (1989) *The Effect of Representation at Tribunals*, London: Lord Chancellor's Department.

Goriely, T. and Gysta, P. (2001) *Breaking the Code: The Impact of Legal Aid Reforms on General Civil Litigation*, London: Institute of Advanced Legal Studies.

Green, P. (ed.) (1996) *Drug Couriers: A New Perspective*, London: Quartet.

Griffith, J. A. G. (1997) *The Politics of the Judiciary*, London: Fontana Press.

Grout, Paul A. (2005) *The Clementi Report: Potential Risks of External Ownership and Regulatory Responses – A Report to the Department of Constitutional Affairs*, London: Department for Constitutional Affairs.

Gudjonsson, G. H. (1992) *The Psychology of Interrogations, Confessions and Testimony*, Chichester: Wiley.

Hale, Sir M. (1979) *The History of the Common Law of England*, Chicago: University of Chicago Press.

Halliday, J. (2001) *Making Punishment Work, Report of the Review of the Sentencing Framework for England and Wales*, London: Home Office.

Hart, H. L. A. (1963) *Law, Liberty and Morality*, Oxford: Oxford University Press.

—— (1994) *The Concept of Law*, Oxford: Clarendon Press.

Hayek, F. (1982) *Law, Legislation and Liberty: A New Statement of the Liberal Principles of Justice and Political Economy*, London: Routledge.

Hedderman, C. and Hough, M. (1994) *Does the Criminal Justice System Treat Men and Women Differently?* London: Home Office Research and Planning Unit.

Hedderman, C. and Moxon, D. (1992) *Magistrates' Court or Crown Court? Mode of Trial Decisions and Sentencing*, London: HMSO.

Herbert, A. (2003) 'Mode of trial and magistrates' sentencing powers: will increased powers inevitably lead to a reduction in the committal rate?', *Criminal Law Review* 314.

HM Chief Inspector of Prisons (1997) *Women in Prison: A Thematic Review*, London: Home Office.

HM Inspectorate (1999) *Police Integrity: Securing and Maintaining Public Confidence*, London: Home Office Communication Directorate.

Hohfeld, W. N. and Cook, W. W. (1919) *Fundamental Legal Concepts as Applied in Judicial Reasoning*, London: Greenwood Press.

Holland, L. and Spencer, L. (1992) *Without Prejudice? Sex Equality at the Bar and in the Judiciary*, London: Bar Council.

Home Office (1996) *Crime, Justice and protecting the Public*, Cm 965, London: Home Office.

—— (2000) *Making Sentencing Clearer*, London: Home Office.

—— (2003) *Statistics on Race and the Criminal Justice System*, London: Home Office.

—— (2003) *Statistics on Women and the Criminal Justice System*, London: Home Office.

—— (2004) *Are Special Measures Working? Evidence from surveys of vulnerable and intimidated witnesses*, Home Office Research Study 283, London: Home Office.

—— (2004) *Modernizing Police Powers to Meet Community Needs*, London: Home Office.

—— (2004) *One Step Ahead: A 21st Century Strategy to Defeat Organised Crime*, London: Stationery Office.

—— (2005) *Exclusion or Deportation from the UK on Non-conclusive Grounds*, London: Home Office.

—— (2007) Asset Recovery Action Plan, London: Home Office.

—— (2007) *Modernizing Police Powers: review of the Police and Criminal Evidence Act 1984*, London: Home Office.

Home Office Research Development and Statistics Directorate (2000) *Jury Excusal and Deferral* (Research Findings No. 102).

Honen, T., Charman, E. and levi, M. (2005) 'Factual and effective recall of pretorial publicity: their relative influence on juror reasoning and verdict in a simulated fraud trial', *Journal of Applied Social Applied Social Psychology*, 33(7): 1404.

Hood, R., Shute, S. and Seemungal, F. (2003) *Ethnic Minorities in the Criminal Courts: perceptions of fairness and equality of treatment*, London: Lord Chancellor's Department.

Horowitz, I. and Fosterlee, L. (2001) 'The effects of note-taking and trial transcript access on mock jury decisions in a complex civil trial', 25 *Law and Human Behaviour* 373.

Hucklesby, A. (2004) 'Not necessarily a trip to the police station: the introduction of street bail', *Criminal Law Review* 803.

Hutton, Lord J. B. (2004) *Report of the Inquiry into the Circumstances Surrounding the Death of Dr David Kelly C. M. G.*, London: Stationery Office.

Idriss, M. (2004) 'Police perceptions of race relations in the West Midlands', *Criminal Law Review* 814.

Ingman, T. (1987) *English Legal Process*, London: Blackstone Press.

Jackson, R. M. (1989) *The Machinery of Justice in England*, Cambridge: Cambridge University Press.

Johnson, N. (2005) 'The training framework review – what's all the fuss about?', 155 *New Law Journal* 357.

Joseph, M. (1981) *The Conveyancing Fraud*, London: Woolwich.

—— (1985) *Lawyers Can Seriously Damage Your Health*, London: Michael Joseph.

Kairys, D. (1998) *The Politics of Law: A Progressive Critique*, New York: Basic Books.

Kakalik, J. and others (1996) *An Evaluation of Judicial Case Management Under the Civil Justice Reform Act*, California Rand Corporation.

Kelsen, H. (1949) *General Theory of Law and State*, Cambridge, Mass: Harvard University Press.

Kennedy, H. (1992) *Eve was Framed: Women and British Justice*, London: Chatto.

King, M. and May, C. (1985) *Black Magistrates: A Study of Selection and Appointment*, London: Cobden Trust.

Law Commission (1976) *Criminal Law: Report on Conspiracy and Criminal Law Forum*, London: HMSO.

—— (1982) *Offences Against Public Order*, London: HMSO.

—— (1999) *Bail and the Human Rights Act 1998* (Report No. 157), London: HMSO.

Laws, J. (1998) 'The limitations of human rights', *Public Law* 254.

Lee, S. (1986) *Law and Morals*, Oxford: Oxford University Press.

Leigh, L. and Zedner, L. (1992) *A Report on the Administration of Criminal Justice in the Pretrial Phase in London, France and Germany*, London: HMSO.

Leighton Williams, J. (2006) 'What compensation?', *Solicitors Journal* July.

Leng, R. (1993) *The Right to Silence in Police Interrogation* (Royal Commission on Criminal Justice Research Study No. 10), London: HMSO.

Lester, A. (1984) 'Fundamental rights: the United Kingdom isolated?', Pub. L. 46.

Levi, M. (1988) 'The Role of the Jury in Complex Cases' in Findlay, M. and Duff, P. (eds.) (1988) *The Jury under Attack*, London: Butterworths.

—— (1992) *The Investigation, Prosecution and Trial of Serious Fraud*, London: HMSO.

Lidstone, K. (1984) *Magisterial Review of the Pre-Trial Criminal Process: A Research Report*, Sheffield: University of Sheffield Centre for Criminological and Socio-Legal Studies.

Lightman, J. (2003) 'The Civil Justice System and legal profession – the challenges ahead', *Civil Justice Quarterly* 235.

Llewellyn, K. (1962) *Jurisprudence: Realism in Theory and Practice*, Chicago: University of Chicago Press.

Lloyd-Bostock, S. (2007) 'The Jubilee line jurors: does their experience strengthen the argument for judge-only trial in long and complex fraud cases', *Criminal Law Review* 255.

Locke, J. (1967) *Two Treatises of Government*, London: Cambridge University Press.

Lord Chancellor's Department (1998) *Determining Mode of Trial in Either Way Cases*, London: Lord Chancellor's Department.

—— (2002) *Further Findings: A Continuing Evaluation of the Civil Justice Reforms*, London: Lord Chancellor's Department.

—— (2003) *Delivering Value for Money in the Criminal Defence Service*, Consultation Paper, London: Lord Chancellor's Department.

Macpherson Report (1999) Cm 4262-I, London: HMSO.

Mahar, F. and Duffy, M.J. (2002) *AQA General Certificate of Education Law Teachers' Guide 2001/2*.

Maine, Sir H. (1917) *Ancient Law*, London: Dent.

Mair, G. and May, C. (1997) *Offenders on Probation* (Home Office Research Study No. 167), London: HMSO.

Making Simple CFAs a Reality (2004), London: Department for Constitutional Affairs.

Malleson, K. (1993) *A Review of the Appeal Process* (Royal Commission on Criminal Justice Research Series No. 17), London: HMSO.

Malleson, K. and Roberts, S. (2002) 'Streamlining and Clarifying the Appellate Process', *Criminal Law Review* 272.

Mansfield, M. (1993) *Presumed Guilty: The British Legal System Exposed*, London: Heinemann.

Markus, K. (1992) 'The Politics of Legal Aid' in *The Critical Lawyer's Handbook*, London: Pluto Press.

Marsh, N. (1971) 'Law reform in the United Kingdom: A new institutional approach', 13 *William and Mary Law Review* 263.

Martinson, R. (1974) 'What work? questions and answers about prison reform', *The Public Interest*, 35: 22–54.

Marx, K. (1933) *Capital*, London: Dent.

Matthews, R., Hancock, L. and Briggs, D. (2004) *Jurors' Perceptions, Understanding Confidence and Satisfaction in the Jury Systems: A Study in Six Courts*, London: Home Office.

Mayhew, L. and Reiss, A. (1969) 'The social organization of legal contracts', 34 *American Soc. Rev.* 309.

McCabe, S. and Purves, R. (1972) *The Jury at Work: A Study of a Series of Jury Trials in which the Defendant was Acquitted*, Oxford: Blackwell.

McConville, M. (1992) 'Videotaping Interrogations: Police Behaviour On and Off Camera', *Criminal Law Review* 532.

McConville, M. and Baldwin, J. (1977) *Negotiated Justice: Pressures to Plead Guilty*, Oxford: Martin Robertson.

—— (1981) *Courts, Prosecution and Conviction*, Oxford: Oxford University Press.

McConville, M. and Hodgson, J. (1993) *Custodial Legal Advice and the Right to Silence* (Royal Commission on Criminal Justice Research Study No. 16), London: HMSO.

McConville, M., Sanders, A. and Leng, P. (1993) *The Case for the Prosecution: Police Suspects and the Construction of Criminality*, London: Routledge.

Mendelle, P. (2005) 'No detention please, we're British?', 155 *New Law Journal* 77.

Mill, J. S. (1859) *On Liberty*, London: J. W. Parker.

Millar, J., Bland, N. and Quinton, P. (2000) *The Impact of Stop and Search on Crime and the Community*, Police Research Series Paper 127, London: Home Office.

—— (2000) *Upping the PACE? An Evaluation of the Recommendations of the Stephen Lawrence Inquiry on Stop and Search*, Police Research Series Paper 128, London: Home Office.

Mirlees-Black, C. (1999) *Domestic violence: Findings from a New British Crime Survey Self-completion Questionnaire*, Home Office Research Study No. 191, London: Home Office.

Modernising Justice (1997) Cm 4155, London: Home Office.

Montesquieu, C. (1989) *The Spirit of the Laws*, Cambridge: Cambridge University Press.

Moore, R. (2003) 'The use of financial penalties and the amounts imposed: The need for a new approach', *Criminal Law Review* 13.

—— (2004) 'The methods for enforcing financial penalties: the need for a multi-dimensional approach', *Criminal Law Review* 728.

Moorhead, R. and others (2001) *Quality and Cost: Final Report on the Contracting of Civil, Non-Family Advice and Assistance*, London: TSO.

Morgan, R. and Russell, N. (2000) *The Judiciary in the Magistrates' Courts* (Home Office RDS Occasional Paper No. 66), London: Home Office.

Moxon, D. (1985) *Managing Criminal Justice: A Collection of Papers*, London: HMSO.

Moxon, D. and Crisp, D. (1994) *Case Screening by the Crown Prosecution Service: How and Why Cases are Terminated*, London: HMSO.

Mullins, C. (1990) *Error of Judgement: The Truth About the Birmingham Bombings*, Dublin: Poolbeg Press.

Narey, M. (1997) *Review of Delay in the Criminal Justice System*, London: Home Office.

National Association of Citizens Advice Bureau (1995) *Barriers to Justice: A Client's Experience of Legal Services*, London: NACAB.

—— (1999) *A Balancing Act: Surviving the Risk Society*, London: NACAB.

National Audit Office (1999) *Criminal Justice Working Together*, London: Stationery Office.

—— (2003) *Community Legal Service: The Introduction of Contracting*, HC 89, 2002–03, London: HMSO.

—— (2005) *Facing Justice: Tackling Defendants Non-attendance at Court* (HCL162), London: TSO.

New Zealand Law Commission (2001) *Juries in Criminal Trials*, Report 69, Wellington.

Nicholas, S., Povey, D., Walker, A. and Kershaw, C. (2005) 'Adults most at risk of violence, 2004/05', *British Crime Survey Interviews, Crime in England and Wales 2004/2005*, p. 84, Figure 5.7.

—— (2006) *CPS: effective use of magistrates' court hearings*: London: Stationery Office.

Nobles, R. (2005) 'The Criminal Cases Review Commission: establishing a workable relationship with the Court of Appeal', *Criminal Law Review* 173.

No More Excuses – A New Approach to Tackling Youth Crime in England and Wales (1998), London: Home Office.

Norwich Union (2004) *A Modern Compensation System: Moving from Concept to Reality*, Norwich: Norwich Union.

Nozick, R. (1975) *Anarchy, State, and Utopia*, Oxford: Blackwell.

Nuttall, C., Goldblatt, P. and Lewis, C. (1998) *Reducing Offending: An Assessment of Research Evidence on Ways of Dealing with Offending Behaviour* (Home Office Research Study No. 187), London: Home Office.

Olivercrona, K. (1971) *Law as Fact*, London: Stevens.

Ormerod, D. (2003) 'ECHR and the Exclusion of Evidence: Trial Remedies for Article 8 Breaches?', *Criminal Law Review* 61.

—— (2005) *Smith and Hogan Criminal Law*, Oxford: Oxford University Press.

Ormerod, D. and Roberts, A. (2003) 'The Police Reform Act 2002 – Increasing Centralisation, Maintaining Confidence and Contracting Out Crime Control', *Criminal Law Review* 141.

Owers, A. (1995) 'Not Completely Appealing', 145 *New Law Journal* 353.

Packer, H. (1968) *The Limits of the Criminal Sanction*, Stanford, California: Stanford University Press.

Pannick, D. (1987) *Judges*, Oxford: Oxford University Press.

Parliamentary Penal Affairs Group (1999) *Changing Offending Behaviours – Some Things Work*, London: Parliament.

Partington, M. (2004) 'Alternative Dispute Resolution: Recent Developments, Future Challenges', (2004) *Civil Justice Quarterly* 99.

Paterson, A. (1982) *The Law Lords*, London: Macmillan.

Peach, Sir L. (1999) *Appointment Processes of Judges and Queen's Counsel in England and Wales*, London: HMSO.

Philips C. (1981) *The Royal Commission on Criminal Procedure*, Cmnd 8092, London: HMSO.

Pickles, J. (1988) *Straight from the Bench*, London: Coronet.

Pleasence, P. (2004) *Causes of action: civil law and social justice*, London: HMSO.

Plotnikoff, J. and Wilson, R. (1993) *Information and Advice for Prisoners about Grounds for Appeal and the Appeal Process* (Royal Commission on Criminal Justice Research Study No. 18), London: HMSO.

Pound, R. (1968) *Social Control Through Law*, Hamden: Archon Books.

Quinton P., Bland, N. and Miller, J. (2000) *Police Stops, Decision-making and Practice*, Police Research Series Paper 130, London: Home Office.

Quirk, H. (2006) 'The significance of culture in criminal procedure reform: why the revised disclosure scheme cannot work', 10 *International Journal of Evidence and Proof* 42.

Race and the Criminal Justice System: an overview to the complete statistics 2003–2004 (2005) London: Criminal Justice System Race Unit.

Raine, J. and Walker, C. (2002) *The Impact of the Courts and the Administration of Justice of the Human Rights Act 1998*, London: Lord Chancellor's Department, Research Secretariat.

Ramsbotham, Sir D. (1997) *Women in Prison*, London: Home Office.

Rawls, J. (1971) *A Theory of Justice*, Oxford: Oxford University Press.

—— (1972) *Political Liberalism, John Dewey Essays in Philosophy*, New York: Columbia University Press.

Renton, D. (1975) *The Preparation of Legislation*, London: HMSO.

Restorative justice: helping to meet local need (2004), London: Office for Criminal Justice Reform.

Review of the Crown Prosecution Service (The Glidewell Report) (1998) Cm 3960, London: HMSO.

Robertson, G. (1993) *Freedom, The Individual and The Law*, London: Penguin.

Royal Commission on Criminal Justice Report (1993), Cm 2263, London: HMSO.

Royal Commission for the Reform of the House of Lords, Report of the (2000) *A House for the Future*, Cm 4534, London: HMSO.

Runciman, G. (1993) *Report of the Royal Commission on Criminal Justice*, London: HMSO.

Ryan, E. (2007) 'The unmet need: focus on the future', 157 *New Law Journal* 134.

Sanders, A., Hoyle C., Morgan, R. and Cape, E. (2001) 'Victim Impact Statements: Don't Work, Can't Work', *Criminal Law Review* 447.

Sanders, A. (1993) 'Controlling the Discretion of the Individual Officer', in Reiner, R. and Spencer, S. (eds.) *Accountable Policing*, London: Institute for Public Policy Research.

Sanders, A. and Bridge, L. (1982) 'Access to Legal Advice', in Walker, C. and Starmer, K. (eds.) *Justice in Error*, London: Blackstone Press.

Sanders, A. *et al.* (1989) *Advice and Assistance at Police Stations and the 24 hour Duty Solicitor Scheme*, London: Lord Chancellor's Department.

Scarman, L. (1982) *The Scarman Report: The Brixton Disorders, 10–12 April 1981*, London: Penguin Books.

Schur, E. (1965) *Crimes Without Victims: Deviant Behaviour and Public Policy, Abortion, Homosexuality, Drug Addiction*, New York: Prentice-Hall.

Sherman, L. and Strang, H. (2007) *Restorative Justice: The Evidence*, London: The Smith Institute.

Skryme, Sir T. (1979) *The Changing Image of the Magistracy* (2nd edn, 1983), London: Macmillan.

Smith and Bailey: see Bailey, S. and Gunn, M. (2002) *Smith and Bailey on the Modern English Legal System* (2nd edn), London: Sweet & Maxwell.

Smith and Hogan Criminal Law, Oxford: Oxford University Press, 2005.

Smith, D. and Gray, J. (1983) *Police and People in London* (The Policy Studies Institute), Aldershot: Gower.

Smith, J. C. and Hogan, B. (2002) *Criminal Law*, London: Butterworths.

Smith, R. and others (2007) *Poverty and Disadvantage Among Prisoners' Families*, London: Joseph Rowntree Foundation.

Spencer, J. R. (2006) 'Does our present criminal appeal system make sense?' [2006] Crim LR 677.

Stanko, E. (2000) 'The day to count: a snapshot of the impact of domestic violence in the UK', *Criminal Justice* 1, p. 2.

Stark E. and Flitcraft A. (1995) 'Killing the beast within: woman battering and female suicidality', *International Journal of Health Services* 25(1): 43–64.

Stern, V. (1987) *Bricks of Shame: Britain's Prisons*, London: Penguin.

Steyn, J. (2001) 'Pepper v Hart: A Re-examination', *Oxford Journal of Legal Studies* 59.

Summers, R. (1992) *Essays on the Nature of Law and Legal Reasoning*, Berlin: Duncker & Humblot.

Supperstone, M., Stilitz, D. and Sheldon, C. (2006) 'ADR and Public Law', *Public Law* 299.

Tain, P. (2003) 'Master of the game?', *Solicitors Journal* 192.

Tata, C. *et al.* (2004) 'Does mode of delivery make a difference to criminal case outcomes and clients' satisfaction? The public defence solicitor experiment', *Criminal Law Review* 120.

Taylor, R. (1997) *Cautions, Court Proceedings and Sentencing in England and Wales 1996*, London: Home Office.

Thomas, D. (1970) *Principles of Sentencing: The Sentencing Policy of the Court of Appeal Criminal Division*, London: Heinemann.

—— (2004) 'The Criminal Justice Act 2003: Custodial sentences', *Criminal Law Review* 702.

Tonry, M. (1996) *Sentencing Matters*, Oxford: Oxford University Press.

Twining, W. and Miers, D. (1991) *How To Do Things With Rules*, London: Weidenfeld & Nicolson.

Vennard, J. (1985) 'The Outcome of Contested Trials' in Moxon, D. (ed.) *Managing Criminal Justice*, London: HMSO.

Vennard, J. and Riley, D. (1988a) 'The use of peremptory challenge and stand by of jurors and their relationships with trial outcome', *Criminal Law Review* 723.

—— (1988b) *Triable Either Way Cases: Crown Court or Magistrates' Court?* London: HMSO.

Vogt, G. and Wadham, J. (2003) *Deaths in custody: redress and remedies*, London: Liberty.

Wade, Sir W. (2000) 'Horizons of horizontability', 116 *Law Quarterly Review* 217.

Wakeham, Lord (2000) *A House for the Future*, Cm 4534, London: HMSO.

Walby, S. (2004) *The Cost of Domestic Violence*. London: Office for National Statistics, Women & Equality Unit.

Waldron, J. (1989) *The Law*, London: Routledge.

Warnock, M. (1986) *Morality and the Law*, Cardiff: University College Cardiff.

Weber, M. (1979) *Economy and Society*, Berkeley: University of California Press.

White, P. and Power, I. (1998) *Revised Projections of Long Term Trends in the Prison Population to 2005*, London: Home Office.

White, P. and Woodbridge, J. (1998) *The Prison Population in 1997*, London: Home Office.

White, R. (1973) 'Lawyers and the Enforcement of Rights', in Morris, P., White, R. and Lewis, P. (eds.) *Social Needs and Legal Action*, Oxford: Martin Robertson.

Whittaker, C. and Mackie, A. (1997) *Enforcing Financial Penalties*, London: Home Office.

Williams, G. (1983) *Textbook of Criminal Law*, London: Stevens and Sons.

Willis, J. (1938) 'Statutory interpretation in a nutshell', 16 *Canadian Bar Review* 13.

Wilson, W. (2003) *Criminal Law Doctrine and Theory*, London: Pearson Education.

Windlesham, Lord (2005) 'The Constitutional Reform Act 2005: Ministers, judges and constitutional change, Part 1', *Public Law* 806.

Wolfenden, J. (1957) 'Report of the Committee on Homosexual Offences and Prostitution', Cmnd 2471, London: HMSO.

Women in Prison: A Thematic Review (1997), London: Home Office.

Woodhead, Sir P. (1998) *The Prison Ombudsman's Annual Report*, London: Home Office.

Woodhouse, D. (2007) 'The Constitutional Reform Act 2005 – defending judicial independence the English way', 5(1) *International Journal of Constitutional Law* 153.

Wooler, S. (2007) *Review of the Investigation and Criminal Proceedings Relating to the Jubilee Line Cases*, London: HM Crown Prosecution Service Inspectorate.

Woolf, Lord Justice H. (1995) *Access to Justice: Interim Report to the Lord Chancellor on the Civil Justice System in England and Wales*, London: Lord Chancellor's Department.

—— (1996) *Access to Justice*, London: Lord Chancellor's Department.

Wootton, B. (1981) *Crime and the Criminal Law: Reflections of a Magistrate and Social Scientist*, Oxford: Clarendon Press.

Yarrow, S. (1997) *The Price of Success: Lawyers, Clients and Conditional Fees*, London: Policy Studies Institute.

Yearnshire, S. (1997) 'Anyalysis of Cohort', in Bewley, S., Friend, J. and Mezey, G. (eds) *Violence Against Women*, London: Royal College of Obstetricians and Gynaecologists.

Young, J. (1971) *The Drugtakers: The Social Meaning of Drug Use*, London: Paladin.

Young, S. (2005) 'Clementi: in practice', 155 *New Law Journal* 45.

Your Right to Know (1997) Cm 3818, London: HMSO.

Zander, M. (1988) *A Matter of Justice*, Oxford: Oxford University Press.

—— (1998) 'The Government's plans on civil justice', 61 *Modern Law Review* 382.

—— (1999) *The Law-Making Process*, London: Butterworths.

—— (2000) 'The complaining juror', 150 *New Law Journal* 723.

—— (2001a) 'Should the legal profession be shaking in its boots?' 151 *New Law Journal* 369.

—— (2001b) 'A question of trust' *Solicitors Journal* 1100.

—— (2005) 'The Prevention of Terrorism Act 2005', 155 *New Law Journal* 438.

—— (2006) 'Mission Impossible', 156 *New Law Journal* 618.

—— (2007) 'Carter's wake (1)', 157 *New Law Journal* 872.

—— (2007) 'Carter's wake (2)', 157 *New Law Journal* 912.

—— (2007) 'Full speed ahead?', 157 *New Law Journal* 992.

—— (2007) 'Change of PACE', 157 *New Law Journal* 504.

Zander, M. and Henderson, P. (1993) *Crown Court Study*, London: HMSO.

Glossary

Absolute discharge   When a court has found a person guilty it can order an *absolute discharge*. This will be done where the court believes that in the circumstances it is unnecessary to punish the person. It effectively means that no action is taken at all against the individual.

Actus reus   Comprises all the elements of a criminal offence other than the state of mind of the defendant.

Administrative law   The body of law which deals with the rights and duties of the state and the limits of its powers over individuals.

ADR   An abbreviation for 'alternative dispute resolution'. It refers to methods of resolving disputes outside the traditional court forum.

Adversarial system   A legal system which puts considerable emphasis on a public trial where the parties are able to present evidence orally and the judge merely plays the role of an arbiter. The adversarial system is frequently contrasted with an inquisitorial system.

Advisory, Conciliation and Arbitration Service (ACAS)   This body mediates in many industrial disputes and unfair dismissal cases.

Advocates General   These assist the judges in the European Court of Justice. They produce opinions on the cases assigned to them, indicating the issues raised and suggesting conclusions. Their opinions do not bind the judges but are frequently followed in practice.

Alternative dispute resolution (ADR)   Methods of resolving disputes outside the traditional court forum.

Anti-social behaviour order   Section 1 of the Crime and Disorder Act 1998 provides that an anti-social behaviour order (ASBO) can be made against a person aged 10 or over who has acted in an anti-social manner and is likely to do so again. Anti-social behaviour is behaviour that is likely to cause harassment, alarm or distress to someone not in the same household. While the ASBO is obtained using civil procedures, breach of the ASBO can give rise to the criminal sanctions of a fine or imprisonment.

Appropriate adult   An adult who accompanies the young offender in the police station. They may be any responsible adult, including the young person's parent or a social worker.

Arbitrators   Individuals who hear arbitration cases. They may be lawyers or experts in the subject of the dispute.

Arraignment   The process whereby the accused is called to the Bar of the court to plead guilty or not guilty to the charges against him or her.

Bail   Bail may be granted to a person accused of an offence, convicted or under arrest. When a person is granted bail it means that they are released under a duty to attend a court or police station at a given time.

Bar Council   The governing body for barristers. It acts as a kind of trade union, safeguarding the interests of barristers, and also as a watchdog, regulating barristers' training and activities.

BarDIRECT   A scheme under which individuals and organisations, such as police forces and insurers, may be approved by the Bar Council to instruct barristers directly.

Bench   A term used to describe the judge or judges (including magistrates) who sit and hear a case.

Bill of Rights   A statement of the basic rights which a citizen can expect to enjoy.

Binding over to be of good behaviour   This order can be made against any person who has breached the peace. People who are bound over have to put up a sum of money and/or find someone else to do so; this sum will be forfeited if the undertaking is broken. The order usually lasts for a year.

Bye-laws   A form of delegated legislation made by local authorities, public and nationalised bodies.

Cab rank rule   Under the cab rank rule, barristers must accept any case which falls within their claimed area of specialisation and for which a reasonable fee is offered, unless they have a prior engagement.

Case management   The court, and in particular the judge, is the active manager of the litigation.

Case stated   Under this procedure, a person who was a party to a case before the magistrates (or the Crown Court when it is hearing an appeal from the magistrates) may question the decision of the court on the ground that there was an error of law or the court had acted outside its jurisdiction. The party asks the court to state a case for the opinion of the High Court on the question of law or jurisdiction.

Caution   1. A warning to an accused person administered on arrest or before police questioning. Since the abolition, by the Criminal Justice and Public Order Act 1994, of the right to silence, the correct wording is: 'You do not have to say anything. But it may harm your defence if you do not mention when questioned something which you later rely on in court. Anything you do say may be given in evidence.'
    2. A formal warning given to an offender about what he or she has done, designed to make him or her see that he or she has done wrong and deter him or her from further offending. This process is used instead of proceeding with the prosecution.

Caution-plus   Sir Robin Auld has recommended that a system of *caution-plus* should be introduced. This would allow the prosecutor, with the consent of the offender, to impose a caution combined with a condition as to their future conduct where a minor offence is alleged to have been committed. Offenders would be brought before the court if they breached one of the conditions.

Certiorari   An order quashing an *ultra vires* decision.

Chambers   The offices of a barrister.

Claimant   The party who issues legal proceedings.

Class action   A claimant or small group of claimants bring an action for damages on behalf of a whole class of claimants.

Committal proceedings   An initial hearing in the magistrates' courts for triable either-way offences. They are designed to allow the magistrates to check that there is sufficient evidence to proceed to a full Crown Court trial and to filter weak cases.

Community sentence   This means a sentence of one or more community orders.

Conditional fee agreement   A lawyer agrees to take no fee or a reduced fee if he or she loses a case, and raises the fee by an agreed percentage if it is won, up to a maximum of double the usual fee.

Constitution   A set of rules and customs which detail a country's system of government; in most cases it will be a written document but in some countries, including Britain, the constitution cannot be found written down in one document and is known as an unwritten constitution.

Contingency fee   A fee payable to a lawyer (who has taken on a case on a 'no win, no fee' basis) in the event of him or her winning the case.

Convention   1. A long-established tradition which tends to be followed, although it does not have the force of law.
   2. A treaty with a foreign power.

Conveyancing   The legal process of transferring an interest in land.

Corporation aggregate   This term covers groups of people with a single legal personality (e.g. a company, university or local authority).

Corporation sole   This is a device which makes it possible to continue the official capacity of an individual beyond their lifetime or tenure of office; e.g. the Crown is a corporation sole; its legal personality continues while individual monarchs come and go.

Council on Tribunals   A body that was established following the 1957 Franks Report. It exercises an advisory role over the tribunal system. It has 10 to 15 members appointed by the Lord Chancellor.

Counsel's opinion   A barrister's advice.

CPS   An abbreviation for 'Crown Prosecution Service'. This institution brings criminal prosecutions on behalf of the state.

Cracked trial   A case in which public money and administration is wasted because, once the court room is booked and the parties ready to proceed with a full trial, the defendant pleads guilty, leaving no time to arrange for another case to slot into the court timetable.

Criminal Defence Service   This has replaced the old system of criminal legal aid. Through the Legal Services Commission, the Criminal Defence Service provides direct funding for the provision of criminal legal services, employs public defenders and pays for duty solicitor schemes.

Crown Prosecution Service (CPS)   This institution brings criminal prosecutions on behalf of the state.

Curfew   Home detention curfews were introduced by the Crime and Disorder Act 1998. Released prisoners under a curfew are required to remain at a certain address at set times, during which period they will be subjected to electronic monitoring.

Custody officer   The police officer who has responsibility for the welfare of any individual being held in detention in the police station. One of the ways he or she does this is by maintaining a custody record.

Custody plus   Under a system of custody plus, an offender spends a maximum of three months in custody, and is then released and subjected to a minimum six months' post-release supervision in the community. A court can attach specific requirements to the sentence, based upon those available under a community sentence.

Custom   'Such usage as has obtained the force of law' (**Tanistry Case**, 1608).

Deferred sentence   A court is allowed to delay passing a sentence for up to six months after conviction.

Delay defeats equities   Where a claimant takes an unreasonably long time to bring an action, equitable remedies will not be available.

Directives   A form of European legislation.

Disclosure of documents   The procedure whereby one party to an action provides the other party with a list of documents relating to the action which are or have been in his or her possession. The other party can then ask to see some or all of the documents.

Divisional Court   This is also known as the Queen's Bench Division and is a Division of the High Court. The major part of its work is handling those contract and tort cases which are unsuitable for the county courts. Its judges also hear certain criminal appeals and applications for judicial review.

Double jeopardy   In the past once a person had been tried and acquitted they could not be retried for the same offence, under the principle of double jeopardy. The application of this principle has been significantly reduced by the Criminal Justice Act 2003.

Draft Bill   A proposed piece of legislation.

Duty solicitors   Solicitors working under the duty solicitor schemes. They are available to give free legal advice at police stations and magistrates' courts.

Either-way cases   Criminal cases that can be tried either in the magistrates' court or in the Crown Court.

Ejusdem generis rule   General words which follow specific ones are taken to include only things of the same kind.

Enabling Act   An Act of Parliament which grants the power to make delegated legislation.

Equity   In law it is a term which applies to a specific set of legal principles which were developed by the Chancery Court and add to those provided in the common law.

Executive   The administrative arm of the state.

Expert witness   A person who is not a party to legal proceedings, but who provides expert evidence to the court.

Expressio unius est exclusio alterius   Express mention of one thing implies the exclusion of another.

Freemasonry   A secret society with an all-male membership. Among its stated aims is the mutual advancement of its members.

Habeas corpus   This is an ancient remedy which allows people detained to challenge the legality of their detention and, if successful, to get themselves quickly released.

Hereditary peers   These are members of the British aristocracy who inherit their title.

He who comes to equity must come with clean hands   This means that a claimant who has been in the wrong in some way will not be granted an equitable remedy.

He who seeks equity must do equity   Anyone who seeks equitable relief must be prepared to act fairly towards his or her opponent.

Indictable offences   These are the more serious offences, such as rape and murder. They can only be heard by the Crown Court. The indictment is a formal document containing the alleged offences against the accused, supported by brief facts.

Inquisitorial system   A legal system where the judge plays a dominant role in collecting evidence before the trial. The final trial is often just to rubber-stamp the investigating judge's findings.

Intermediate recidivist   An offender in his or her late twenties or early thirties with a criminal record dating back to childhood.

Judicial review   The courts undertake a review of the process that has been followed in making a decision and can make sure that the public authority had the power to make this decision.

Jury vetting   This consists of checking that the potential juror does not hold 'extremist' views which some feel would make them unsuitable for hearing a case. It is done by checking police, Special Branch and security service records.

Justice of the peace   An alternative name for lay magistrates.

Law centres   Offices which offer a free, non-means-tested legal service to people who live or work in their area.

Law Commission   A government body that considers possible reforms of the law.

Law Officers   They are the Attorney-General and the Solicitor-General.

Law Society   The solicitors' professional body.

Lawyer   This is a general term which covers both branches of the legal profession, namely barristers and solicitors, as well as many people with a legal qualification.

Leap-frog procedure   This is the procedure provided for in the Administration of Justice Act 1969, whereby an appeal can go directly from the High Court to the House of Lords, missing out the Court of Appeal.

Legal executive   A member of the Institute of Legal Executives, who frequently carries out legal work within a firm of solicitors or as an in-house lawyer.

Limited liability partnerships   These were created in 2001. Solicitors can choose to form a limited liability partnership. Under this type of partnership a partner's liability is limited to negligence for which he or she was personally responsible.

Lord Chancellor   A government minister who used to be responsible for the Lord Chancellor's Department.

Lord Chief Justice   He or she presides over the Criminal Division of the Court of Appeal.

Mandamus   An order requiring a particular thing to be done.

Master of the Rolls   He or she presides over the Civil Division of the Court of Appeal.

McKenzie friend   A litigant in person may take with him to the court or tribunal someone to advise him (a McKenzie friend), but that person may not usually address the court.

Means test   This looks at the financial position of the applicant for state funding.

Mediation   This is an alternative method of dispute resolution. A mediator is appointed to help the parties to a dispute reach an agreement which each considers acceptable.

Mens rea   Traditionally refers to the state of mind of the person committing the crime.

Natural law   A kind of higher law, to which we can turn for a basic moral code. Some, such as St Thomas Aquinas, see this higher law as coming from God, others see it simply as the basis of human society.

Obiter dicta   This is Latin and can be translated as 'things said by the way'. All the parts of the judgment which do not form part of the *ratio decidendi* of the case are called *obiter dicta*. This part of the judgment is merely persuasive and not binding.

Orders in Council   A form of delegated legislation made by government in times of emergency. They are approved by the Privy Council and signed by the Queen.

Parenting order   A court order designed to help and support parents (or guardians) in addressing their child's anti-social behaviour.

Parliament   Consists of the House of Commons, the House of Lords and the monarch.

Per incuriam   Where a previous decision has been made in ignorance of a relevant law it is said to have been made *per incuriam*.

Pilot schemes   These are established to test in selected areas the impact of reforms that could subsequently be introduced more widely.

Plaintiff   This is the old term used to describe the person who issued legal proceedings. Following reforms introduced to civil litigation in 1999, the plaintiff is now known as the claimant.

Plea bargaining   This is the name given to negotiations between the prosecution and defence lawyers over the outcome of a case; e.g. where a defendant is choosing to plead not guilty, the prosecution may offer to reduce the charge to a similar offence with a smaller maximum sentence in return for the defendant pleading guilty to that offence.

Practice direction   An official announcement by the court laying down rules as to how it should function.

Pre-action protocol   A code of conduct for pre-trial proceedings.

Prohibition   An order prohibiting a body from acting unlawfully in the future; e.g. it can prohibit an inferior court or tribunal from starting or continuing proceedings which are, or threaten to be, outside their jurisdiction, or in breach of natural justice.

Public Bills   Proposals for a piece of legislation that have been prepared by the Cabinet.

Public defenders   Defence lawyers who are employed by the Legal Services Commission. They are based in regional offices, can provide the same services as lawyers in private practice and have to compete for work.

Puisne judges   High Court judges are also known as puisne judges (pronounced puny) meaning junior judges.

Pupillage   A one-year apprenticeship in which pupils assist a qualified barrister, who is known as their pupil master.

Queen's Bench Division   A Division of the High Court. The major part of its work is handling those contract and tort cases which are unsuitable for the county courts. Its judges also hear certain criminal appeals and applications for judicial review.

Queen's Counsel   Senior members of the barrister profession.

Ratio decidendi   This is Latin and can be translated as the 'reason for deciding'. The *ratio decidendi* of a judgment is the legal reasons on which the decision is based.

Remand   Detention prior to a conviction or sentencing where bail has been refused.

Restorative justice   Offenders are required to provide a remedy to their victims or the community at large.

Retribution   Retribution is concerned with recognising that the criminal has done something wrong and with taking revenge on behalf of both the victim and society as a whole.

Rights of audience   The rights to carry out advocacy in front of a court.

Royal Assent   A procedure under which the monarch consents to the passing of legislation. It transforms a Bill into an Act of Parliament.

Royal Commission   These are established to study a particular area of law reform, usually as a result of criticism and concern about the area concerned.

Secret soundings   A process which involves civil servants in the Lord Chancellor's Department gathering information about potential candidates for judicial office over a period of time by making informal inquiries from leading barristers and judges.

Small claims track   This is a procedure used by the county courts to deal with claims under £5,000.

Solicitor advocates   Solicitors who have successfully completed the additional training required in order to exercise their rights of audience before the higher courts.

Sovereignty of Parliament   This has traditionally meant that the law which Parliament makes takes precedence over that from any other source, but this principle has been qualified by membership of the European Union.

Stand by   As members of the jury panel are called and before they are sworn in, the prosecution may ask for them to *stand by*, without giving any reasons for this. They will then not be able to sit on the jury.

Stare decisis   This is Latin and can be translated as 'let the decision stand'. Under this principle, once a decision has been made on how the law applies to a particular set of facts, similar facts in later cases should be treated in the same way.

Statutory charge   Where a person has received state funding for civil proceedings, if the costs recovered from the other party and the contributions made by the state-funded party do not cover the amount paid by the state, the difference can be recovered from the damages awarded by the court (subject to certain restrictions in matrimonial cases). Where the statutory charge applies, the state funding is more like a loan.

Stereotype   A presumption as to the characteristics of a group of people.

Stipendiary magistrates   These judges are now known as 'district judges (magistrates' court)'. They are professional judges who sit in the magistrates' court.

Summary offences   These are most minor crimes and are only triable summarily in the magistrates' courts. 'Summary' refers to the process of ordering the defendant to attend court by summons, a written order usually delivered by post, which is the most frequent procedure adopted in the magistrates' court.

Tariff system   The tariff sentencing system is based on treating like cases alike: people with similar backgrounds who commit similar offences in similar circumstances should receive similar sentences.

Ultra vires   This is Latin and can be translated as 'beyond the powers'. It refers to the situation where a public authority has overstepped their powers.

Veto   A power to block a decision.

Wednesbury principle   This principle, which was laid down in **Associated Provincial Picture Houses Ltd *v* Wednesbury Corporation**, is that a decision will be held to be outside a public body's power if it is so unreasonable that no reasonable public body could have reached it.

Woolf Report   The official name of the Woolf Report is *Access to Justice*, which was published in 1996. It is the report of the review of the civil courts which was chaired by Lord Woolf and was the basis for the reforms to the civil justice system that were introduced in 1999.

Youth court   Young offenders are usually tried in youth courts (formerly called juvenile courts), which are a branch of the magistrates' court. Youth courts must sit in a separate court room, where no ordinary court proceedings have been held for at least one hour. Strict restrictions are imposed as to who may attend the sittings of the court.

Zero tolerance   A concept that was developed in the US during Ronald Reagan's time in office; it has come to mean that the law will be strictly enforced in order to reduce crime.

Answers to exercises

Chapter 1 Parliamentary law-making

Quick quiz 1.4

1 There are various pressure groups which you could have given as examples. Some examples are given in the text at p. 7.
2 There is no right or wrong answer here. One of the reasons the government was opposed to the campaign was that known paedophiles were likely to move and hide their new addresses, making them a greater danger to children as their movements could not be monitored by the police and social services.
3 1965.
4 No.

Task 1.6

A prohibition order prohibits a person from entering a place specified in the order for a maximum period of two years.

The explanatory notes state at para. 26 that: 'This Part of the Act provides for the extension of electronic monitoring. It creates a new disposal – an exclusion order – which can be used as a free-standing sentence or as a requirement of a community penalty. This order will require an offender to stay away from a certain place or places at certain times. Such monitoring is aimed at offenders who present a particular danger or nuisance to a particular victim or particular victims.'

Quick quiz 1.7

1 Green Paper.
2 Public Bill drafted.
3 First reading in the House of Commons.
4 Second reading in the House of Commons.
5 Committee stage in the House of Commons.
6 Report stage.
7 Third reading.
8 House of Lords considers the Public Bill.
9 Royal Assent.

Know your terms 1.8

1 *Hereditary peers* are members of the British aristocracy who inherit their title.
2 *Royal Assent* is when the monarch consents to the passing of legislation, transforming a Bill into an Act of Parliament.
3 *Public Bills* are proposals for a piece of legislation that have been prepared by the Cabinet.

Task 1.9

1 It prohibits the use of torture by the state.
2 The former leader of the Conservative Party.
3 They do not have the power to strike down Acts of Parliament, but can only declare an Act to be incompatible with the European Convention.

Chapter 2 Delegated legislation

Task 2.1

1 The Data Protection Act 1998 (Commencement) Order 2000 brought the 1998 Act into force. The power to make the Order was granted by ss. 67(2) and 75(3) of the Data Protection Act 1998.
2 The main provisions of the Data Protection Act 1998 came into force on 1 March 2000.

Know your terms 2.2

1 In a *judicial review* hearing the courts undertake a review of the process that has been followed in making a decision and can make sure that the public authority had the power to make this decision.
2 The term *ultra vires* is Latin and can be translated as 'beyond the powers'. It refers to the situation where a public authority has overstepped its powers.
3 *Bye-laws* are a form of delegated legislation made by local authorities, public and nationalised bodies.
4 *Orders in Council* are a form of delegated legislation made by government in times of emergency. They are approved by the Privy Council and signed by the Queen.
5 An *enabling Act* is an Act of Parliament which grants the power to make delegated legislation.

Quick quiz 2.3

1 Statutory instruments, bye-laws and Orders in Council.
2 You could mention any of the following: insufficient parliamentary time, speed, technicality of the subject matter, need for local knowledge, flexibility and future needs.
3 Under the affirmative resolution procedure delegated legislation is laid before one or both Houses of Parliament and becomes law only if a motion approving it is passed within a specified time.
4 Procedural *ultra vires*, substantive *ultra vires* and unreasonableness.

Chapter 3 Statutory interpretation

Quick quiz 3.1

Any of the following cases could have been mentioned:

Literal rule	See **Whitely v Chapell** (1868) and **Fisher v Bell** (1961) on p. 42.
Golden rule	See **R v Allen** (1872), **Adler v George** (1964) and **Inco Europe Ltd v First Choice Distribution** (2000) on p. 44.
Mischief rule	See **Smith v Hughes** (1960) and **Elliott v Grey** (1960) on p. 44.

Quick quiz 3.2

1 The literal rule, the golden rule and the mischief rule.
2 The statute itself, rules of language and presumptions.
3 You could mention any of the following: the historical setting, dictionaries and text-books, explanatory notes, reports that preceded the legislation, the Human Rights Act 1998 and *Hansard*.
4 The House of Lords ruled that *Hansard* could be consulted in order to determine the intention of Parliament when interpreting statutes.

Chapter 4 Judicial precedent

Know your terms 4.1

1 *Stare decisis*: this is Latin and can be translated as 'let the decision stand'. Under this principle, once a decision has been made on how the law applies to a particular set of facts, similar facts in later cases should be treated in the same way.
2 *Ratio decidendi*: this is Latin and can be translated as the 'reason for deciding'. The *ratio decidendi* of a judgment is the legal reasons on which the decision is based.
3 *Obiter dicta*: this is Latin and can be translated as 'things said by the way'. All the parts of the judgment which do not form part of the *ratio decidendi* of the case are called *obiter dicta*.

Task 4.2

The judges in **Re Pinochet** were Lord Browne-Wilkinson, Lord Goff, Lord Nolan, Lord Hope and Lord Hutton.

Quick quiz 4.3

1 Case law, Acts of Parliament and delegated legislation.
2 1966.
3 Where the previous decision was made in ignorance of a relevant law; there are two previous conflicting decisions; there is a later, conflicting, House of Lords decision; and a proposition of law was assumed to exist by an earlier court and was not subject to argument or consideration by that court.
4 The High Court.
5 When a decision of a lower court is overruled, the outcome of the decision remains the same. When it is reversed, the decision of the lower court is changed.
6 William Blackstone.

Task 4.4

1 In this context 'retrospectively' refers to the fact that judgments can have an effect on matters that occurred prior to the date that the decision was given.
2 See the first paragraph of the Practice Statement.
3 See the second paragraph of the Practice Statement.
4 See the third paragraph of the Practice Statement.

Chapter 5 The civil courts

Quick quiz 5.1

1 Queen's Bench Division, Family Division, Chancery Division.
2 Either the court that made the disputed decision, or the appellate court itself.
3 Three.
4 The Civil Division of the Court of Appeal.

Chapter 6 Tribunals

Task 6.1

1 The Human Rights Act 1998 has incorporated the European Convention into national law. See p. 14.
2 The appeal courts.
3 A tribunal called the 'School Admissions Appeal Panel' exists to consider these disputes.
4 The Review concluded that the system was not coherent and recommended the establishment of a single Tribunal Service.

Quick quiz 6.2

1 The Tribunals, Courts and Enforcement Act 2007.
2 The Administrative Justice and Tribunals Council.
3 Most tribunals consist of a legally trained chairperson, and two lay people who have some particular expertise in the relevant subject area.
4 No.

Chapter 7 Alternative methods of dispute resolution

Know your terms 7.1

1 An *adversarial process* places an emphasis on a public trial where the parties are able to present evidence and question the evidence of the other parties. The judge plays only a limited role in the trial proceedings. This type of procedure is frequently contrasted with an inquisitorial system.
2 *Arbitrators* hear arbitration cases. They may be lawyers or experts in the subject of the dispute.
3 *ADR* stands for 'alternative methods of dispute resolution'.
4 *ACAS* stands for 'Advisory, Conciliation and Arbitration Service'. This body mediates in many industrial disputes and unfair dismissal cases.

Quick quiz 7.2

1 The Advisory, Conciliation and Arbitration Service (ACAS).
2 The Family Law Act 1996.
3 The Association of British Travel Agents (ABTA).
4 The Arbitration Act 1996.

Chapter 8 Criminal courts

Task 8.1

Type of offence	Trial court
Summary	Magistrates' court
Triable either way	Magistrates' court or Crown Court
Indictable offence	Crown Court

Task 8.2

1 A motoring offence.
2 There is no fixed answer to this question.
3 46 per cent.
4 There is no fixed answer to this question.

Task 8.3

1 The House of Lords.
2 The Criminal Division.
3 Decrease.
4 The House of Lords' workload had remained the same until 2001, when it increased slightly. This increase has levelled out in recent years.

Know your terms 8.4

1 See p. 84.
2 The *Divisional Court* is also known as the Queen's Bench Division and is discussed at p. 82.
3 See p. 128.
4 See p. 125.

Quick quiz 8.5

1 The High Court.
2 The House of Lords.
3 1 per cent.
4 New evidence can be admitted if the Court of Appeal thinks it 'necessary or expedient in the interests of justice': Criminal Appeal Act 1968, s. 23(1).

Task 8.6

1 A stakeholder in this context is anyone with an interest in the service provided by the CCRC, which includes lawyers and convicts, and ultimately includes all members of the public.
2 The backlog in undecided cases.
3 An increase in the number of cases being referred to it and problems with recruiting staff.

Quick quiz 8.7

1 1995.
2 Where the court thinks the conviction is unsafe.
3 See p. 126.
4 The High Court.

Chapter 9 Magistrates

Quick quiz 9.1

1 The Lord Chancellor appoints lay magistrates in the name of the Crown.
2 The Local Advisory Committees interview candidates for the lay magistracy and make recommendations to the Lord Chancellor as to who should be appointed.
3 An applicant must be under 65 and live within 15 miles of the commission area for which he or she is appointed.
4 The Judicial Appointments Commission.

Know your terms 9.2

1 *Stipendiary magistrates* are now known as 'district judges (magistrates' court)'. They are professional judges who sit in the magistrates' court.
2 The term *Justice of the Peace* is an alternative name for lay magistrates.
3 *The Bench* is the term used to describe the judge or judges (including magistrates) who sit and hear a case.
4 *Royal Commissions* are established by the government to study a particular area of law reform, usually as a result of criticism and concern about the area concerned.

Quick quiz 9.4

1 See p. 140.
2 Three.
3 The primary function of the justices' clerk is to advise the lay magistrates on law and procedure. They are not supposed to take any part in the actual decision of the Bench.
4 See p. 144.

Chapter 10 The jury system

Quick quiz 10.1

1 No.
2 18–70.
3 Yes – see the case of **R** *v* **Abdroikov** (2005).
4 No, a majority verdict is now possible.

Quick quiz 10.2

1 See p. 154.
2 Where a jury has been reduced to ten, then a majority of nine votes is required. For a full jury a majority of ten is required.
3 You could have cited **R** *v* **Kronlid** (1996) or **R** *v* **Ponting** (1985).

Task 10.3

1 Yes.
2 No.

Quick quiz 10.4

1 On the ground that the jury's decision had been perverse.
2 The matter has not yet been considered by the European Court of Human Rights, but Sir Robin Auld thought that the Convention right was probably not violated.
3 A trial in a magistrates' court.
4 No.

Know your terms 10.5

1 *Jury vetting* consists of checking that the potential juror does not hold 'extremist' views which some feel would make him/her unsuitable for hearing a case. It is done by checking police, Special Branch and security service records.
2 As members of the jury panel are called and before they are sworn in, the prosecution may ask for them to *stand by*, without giving any reasons for this. They will then not be able to sit on the jury.
3 A *summary offence* is an offence that can only be tried in the magistrates' court.
4 *Jury nobbling* occurs when inappropriate pressure is put on a juror to reach a verdict regardless of the evidence.

Chapter 11 The legal profession

Know your terms 11.1

1 The *Law Society* is the governing body of the solicitor profession.
2 *Conveyancing* is the legal process of transferring an interest in land.
3 *Rights of audience* are the rights to carry out advocacy in front of a court.
4 *Solicitor advocates* are solicitors who have successfully completed the additional training required in order to exercise their rights of audience before the higher courts.

Quick quiz 11.2

1 98,000.
2 They automatically acquire full rights of audience on becoming qualified, though they are only able to exercise these rights on completion of the necessary additional training.
3 98 per cent.
4 The Legal Practice Course, the one year course required to quality as a solicitor.

Task 11.3

1 The Office of Fair Trading has suggested that the rank of QC inflates the prices of barristers' services. The Bar Council argue that it is an important quality mark which directs the clients to experienced, specialist lawyers as required.

Know your terms 11.4

1 *Limited liability partnerships* were created in 2001. Solicitors can choose to form a limited liability partnership. Under this type of partnership a partner's liability is limited to negligence for which he or she was personally responsible.

2 The *Bar Council* is the governing body for barristers. It acts as a kind of trade union, safeguarding the interests of barristers.
3 *Pupillage* is a one-year apprenticeship in which pupils assist a qualified barrister, who is known as their pupil master.
4 *Queen's Counsel* are senior members of the barrister profession.

Task 11.6

1 The person who uses the legal services.
2 Competition can ensure that professional fees are not higher than they need to be and that the professional rules do not unnecessarily inhibit efficiency.
3 Standards, integrity and concern for the client.
4 In trying to achieve a minor goal, something very valuable may be lost.

Chapter 12 Paying for legal services

Quick quiz 12.1

1 1 April 2000.
2 The Legal Services Commission.
3 The Funding Code sets out the criteria and procedures to be used when deciding whether a particular case should be funded.
4 The five categories are:
  ■ Legal Help.
  ■ Legal Representation.
  ■ Help at Court.
  ■ Approved Family Help.
  ■ Family Mediation.

Know your terms 12.2

1 See p. 205.
2 A *means test* looks at the financial position of the applicant for state funding.
3 The *Criminal Defence Service* has replaced the old system of criminal legal aid. Through the Legal Services Commission, the Criminal Defence Service provides direct funding for the provision of criminal legal services, employs public defenders and pays for duty solicitor schemes.
4 *Public defenders* are defence lawyers who are employed by the Legal Services Commission. They are based in regional offices, can provide the same services as lawyers in private practice and have to compete for work.

Task 12.4

1 A person being detained in a police station is in a very vulnerable position and access to a free lawyer aims to prevent miscarriages of justice. However, a minority of people detained in the police station are rich enough to pay for the services of a lawyer.
2 There might, for example, be cases which are particularly serious or where the detainee is particularly vulnerable (perhaps due to their age or disability) that make it particularly important that they see a lawyer.
3 Some defendants who turned up at court without a lawyer would have to represent themselves. They might not be able to express themselves clearly.
4 It may cause delay. Hearings may need to be postponed until a defendant has found a lawyer.
5 The number is likely to increase.

Quick quiz 12.5

1 See p. 213.
2 See p. 213.
3 The research found that many people felt that the legal system had given them a second-rate service. The research criticised the apparent lack of commitment and poor communication of some solicitors. There were still not enough solicitors and advisers specialising in areas like social security, housing, disability, discrimination, employment and immigration law.
4 An area where appropriate state funded legal advice services are not available.

Know your terms 12.6

1 *Duty solicitors* work under the duty solicitor schemes. They are solicitors who are available to give free legal advice at police stations and magistrates' courts.
2 *Pilot schemes* are established to test in selected areas the impact of reforms that could subsequently be introduced more widely.
3 *Law centres* offer a free, non-means-tested legal service to people who live or work in their area.
4 Under a *conditional fee agreement* a lawyer can agree to take no fee or a reduced fee if he or she loses a case and to raise the fee by an agreed percentage if he/she wins, up to a maximum of double the usual fee.

Chapter 13 The judiciary

Know your terms 13.1

1 The process of *secret soundings* involved civil servants in the Lord Chancellor's Department gathering information about potential candidates for judicial office over a period of time by making informal inquiries from leading barristers and judges.
2 A judge in the House of Lords.
3 The *Master of the Rolls* presides over the Civil Division of the Court of Appeal.
4 The *Lord Chief Justice* presides over the Criminal Division of the Court of Appeal.

Task 13.2

1 No.
2 Horse hair.
3 No.

Quick quiz 13.3

1 The Criminal Division of the Court of Appeal.
2 The body responsible for administering the judicial appointments process.
3 The Judicial Studies Board.
4 The doctrine of the separation of powers was first put forward by the eighteenth-century French political theorist, Montesquieu. This doctrine states that the only way to safeguard individual liberties is to ensure that the power of the state is divided between three separate and independent arms: the judiciary, the legislature and the executive. The idea is that each arm of the state should operate independently, so that each one is checked and balanced by the other two and none becomes all-powerful.

Quick quiz 13.4

1 Dismissal, discipline, resignation, retirement and removal.
2 The French political theorist, Montesquieu.
3 Sixty-six.
4 No.

Know your terms 13.5

1 The *executive* is the administrative arm of the state.
2 *Freemasonry* is a secret society with an all-male membership. Among its stated aims is the mutual advancement of its members.
3 The *Law Society* is the solicitors' professional body.
4 A *stereotype* is a presumption as to the characteristics of a group of people.

Chapter 14 Elements of a crime: *actus reus*

Quick quiz 14.1

1 To satisfy the 'but for' test it must be shown that but for the conduct of the accused the result of the offence would not have occurred as and when it did.
2 Under the 'thin skull' test, where the intervening cause is some existing weakness of the victim, the defendant must take the victim as he or she finds him.
3 The *ratio decidendi* of **R** *v* **Miller** was that people who are aware that they have done something which has endangered another's life or property, and do nothing to prevent the relevant harm from occurring, may be criminally liable, with the original act being treated as the *actus reus* of the crime.
4 Under a strict application of the law, a stranger might not owe a duty to a baby drowning in a puddle of water.

Chapter 15 Elements of a crime: *mens rea*

Know your terms 15.1

1 The *actus reus* comprises all the elements of the offence other than the state of mind of the defendant.
2 *Mens rea* traditionally refers to the state of mind of the person committing the crime.
3 *Cunningham* recklessness exists when a person foresees that the kind of harm that in fact occurred might occur, but goes ahead anyway and takes that risk.
4 Under the principle of *transferred malice*, if a person has the *mens rea* of a particular crime and does the *actus reus* of the crime, the person is guilty of the crime even though the *actus reus* may differ in some way from that intended. The *mens rea* is simply transferred to the new *actus reus*.

Quick quiz 15.2

1 A person who has direct intention wants to achieve a particular result. A person who has indirect intention does not want to achieve a particular result, but foresaw that result as a virtual certainty.
2 For **Cunningham** recklessness a person must simply have foreseen that a harm might occur. For indirect intention a person must have foreseen that a harm was virtually certain to occur.

3 **R** *v* **Woollin**.

4 No, motive is irrelevant to the *mens rea* issue.

Chapter 16 Non-fatal offences against the person

Know your terms 16.1

1 An *assault* consists of any act which makes the victim fear that unlawful force is about to be used against him or her.

2 A *battery* consists of the application of unlawful force on another.

3 In the case of **Miller** it was stated that '*actual bodily harm* includes hurt or injury calculated to interfere with health or comfort'.

4 In **Cunningham** it was stated that for the purpose of the 1861 Act *maliciously* means 'intentionally or recklessly' and 'reckless' is used in the **Cunningham** sense.

Quick quiz 16.2

1 Yes, words alone can constitute an assault.

2 The *mens rea* of assault is either intention or **Cunningham** recklessness. The defendant either must have intended to cause the victim to fear the infliction of immediate and unlawful force, or must have seen the risk that such fear would be created.

3 The *mens rea* of an assault occasioning actual bodily harm is the *mens rea* of an assault or battery.

4 The difference is that a higher level of *mens rea* is required for a s. 18 than for a s. 20 offence. The *actus reus* is identical.

Task 16.3

1 Violence that takes place in the home and the victim knows their aggressor well.

2 Yes.

3 People who are under 25.

Task 16.4

Intention is defined in Art. 14 of the Bill as:

'(1) A person acts intentionally with respect to a result if –

(a) it is his purpose to cause it, or

(b) although it is not his purpose to cause it, he knows that it would occur in the ordinary course of events if he were to succeed in his purpose of causing some other result.'

Task 16.5

1 'Court reports' are the reports on court cases in newspapers. 'Drama' is a reference to television programmes, such as *Ally McBeal* and *The Bill*.

2 'Unrepealed' means that the relevant parts of the Act have not been repealed and are still in force.

3 The law contained in a range of different sources is brought together in a single new Act.

4 The government wants to introduce law that is robust, clear and well understood. The government's aim is that the proposed new offences should enable violence to be dealt with effectively by the courts and that the law should be set out in clear terms and in plain, modern language.

Chapter 17 Strict liability

Quick quiz 17.1

1 Strict liability offences are those offences which can be committed without *mens rea* regarding at least one aspect of the *actus reus*.
2 There is a presumption that *mens rea* is required.
3 Cause, possession and knowingly.
4 If strict liability applies, an accused cannot use the defence of mistake, even if the mistake was reasonable.

Know your terms 17.3

1 A *regulatory offence* is one in which no real moral issue is involved, and usually (though not always) one for which the maximum penalty is small.
2 A *stigma* is damage to a person's reputation.
3 A *draft Bill* is a proposed piece of legislation. For further information see p. 10.
4 The *Law Commission* is a government body that considers possible reforms of the law. For further information see p. 8.

Chapter 18 Criminal procedure

Task 18.1

Type of offence	Trial court
Summary	Magistrates' court
Triable either way	Magistrates' court or Crown Court
Indictable offence	Crown Court

Chapter 19 Sentencing

Quick quiz 19.1

1 Punishment, reduction of crime, reform and rehabilitation, protection of the public and reparation.
2 Criminals often act on impulse.
3 See p. 336.
4 Cheaper.

Task 19.2

1 Some parents felt that they had been forced to become unpaid jailers.
2 No.
3 The aim should be to make a real impact on crime figures and reoffending rates.

Quick quiz 19.3

1 The judge.
2 Life imprisonment.
3 See p. 342.
4 Dr David Thomas.

Quick quiz 19.4

1 See pp. 347–349.
2 £36,000.
3 75,000.
4 Four per cent.

Know your terms 19.5

1 *Retribution* is concerned with recognising that the criminal has done something wrong and with taking revenge on behalf of both the victim and society as a whole.
2 *Reparation* occurs when offenders provide a remedy to their victims or the community at large.
3 When a court has found a person guilty, it can order an *absolute discharge*. This will be done where the court believes that in the circumstances it is unnecessary to punish the person. It effectively means that no action is taken at all against the individual.
4 Under a *curfew* a person's movements are restricted.

Chapter 20 Negligence

Task 20.1

1 The House of Lords.
2 The case is also reported in the 1932 volume of the Appeal Cases Reports at p. 562.
3 Five judges heard the case. Their names were Lord Buckmaster, Lord Atkin, Lord Tomlin, Lord Thankerton and Lord Macmillan.
4 'Per LORD ATKIN' means 'Lord Atkin said that'.
5 Lord Buckmaster and Lord Tomlin gave dissenting judgments.
6 Lord Atkin's judgment.
7 In the Bible.
8 The appellant's action was successful and he was entitled to an award of damages.

Quick quiz 20.2

1 **Donoghue** *v* **Stevenson** (1932).
2 A duty of care, breach of that duty and damage resulting from the breach.
3 The neighbour principle lays down a basic test to determine whether a duty of care is owed. Lord Atkin stated in **Donoghue** *v* **Stevenson** that: 'You must take reasonable care to avoid acts or omissions which you can reasonably foresee would be likely to injure your neighbour.' For these purposes, my neighbours are 'persons who are so closely and directly affected by my act that I ought to have them in contemplation as being so affected when I am directing my mind to the acts or omissions which are called in question'.
4 **Murphy** *v* **Brentwood District Council** is likely to be followed as this case overruled **Anns** *v* **Merton London Borough**.

Quick quiz 20.3

1 A duty of care is breached when the defendant has fallen below the standard of behaviour expected in someone undertaking the activity concerned. The duty is breached if a person has not done what a reasonable person would have done in the circumstances to prevent harm.

2 You could have listed any of the following:
   - the special characteristics of the defendant;
   - the special characteristics of the claimant;
   - the magnitude of the risk;
   - how far it was practicable to prevent the risk;
   - any benefits that might be gained from taking the risk.

3 Yes. Thus, where the defendant is a child, the standard of care is that of an ordinarily careful and reasonable child of the same age: **Mullin v Richards**.

4 Following **Bolitho v City and Hackney Health Authority** the doctor must have behaved in a reasonable way, in that he or she had weighed up the risks and benefits of a course of treatment and had a logical basis for their choice of treatment.

Quick quiz 20.4

1 The 'but for' test asks whether the damage would not have occurred but for the breach of duty.

2 **The Wagon Mound (No. 1)**.

3 The current test for remoteness is whether the kind of damage suffered by the claimant was reasonably foreseeable at the time of the breach of duty.

4 Yes, liability will be imposed because so long as the type of damage sustained is reasonably foreseeable, it does not matter that it is in fact more serious than could reasonably have been foreseen.

Know your terms 20.5

1 A *novus actus interveniens* is Latin for a 'new intervening event'. It is the term used to describe intervening events which break the chain of causation.

2 *Res ipsa loquitur* is Latin for 'the facts speak for themselves'. This maxim can apply where the facts of the case are such that an injury could only have been caused by negligence. When the maxim applies, the claimant does not have the burden of proving the existence of negligence.

3 An *objective test* is one which imposes the standards of the reasonable person, rather than the standards of the actual defendant.

4 *Contributory negligence* is a defence contained in the Law Reform (Contributory Negligence) Act 1945. Where the defence applies, damages can be reduced to take account of the fact that the fault was not entirely the defendant's.

Chapter 21 Civil procedure

Quick quiz 21.1

1 The burden of proof is usually on the claimant who must prove his/her case on the balance of probabilities.

2 The Courts and Legal Services Act 1990.

3 *Access to Justice*.

4 Queen's Bench Division, Family Division, Chancery Division.

Quick quiz 21.2

1 Preparation for a settlement.

2 26 April 1999.

3 The overriding objective is that the Civil Procedure Rules should enable the courts to deal with cases justly.

4 A claimant.

Task 21.3

1 Cases for a claim worth between £3,000 and £5,000.

2 Cases for a claim worth more than £50,000.

Quick quiz 21.4

1 A claim form.

2 The county court.

3 Compliance with a pre-action protocol is not compulsory, but if a party unreasonably refuses to comply, then this can be taken into account when the court makes orders for costs.

4 The judge in court.

Know your terms 21.5

1 The *Queen's Bench Division* is a Division of the High Court. The major part of its work is handling those contract and tort cases which are unsuitable for the county courts. Its judges also hear certain criminal appeals and applications for judicial review.

2 The official name of the Woolf Report is *Access to Justice*, which was published in 1996. It is the report of the review of the civil courts which was chaired by Lord Woolf and was the basis for the reforms to the civil justice system that were introduced in 1999.

3 See p. 431.

4 See p. 433.

Know your terms 21.6

1 See p. 436.

2 See p. 434.

3 See p. 437.

4 *MCOL* stands for Money Claim Online, discussed on p. 438.

Task 21.7

1 Access to justice.

2 An interim report is a report which is published before the final report, and contains the provisional proposals which, following consultation, may be changed in the final report.

3 No, the government has adopted most of Lord Woolf's proposals.

Quick quiz 21.9

1 Small claims track, fast track and multi-track.

2 The small claims track.

3 See p. 443.

4 Case management tended to increase costs.

Chapter 22 Compensatory damages

Quick quiz 22.1

1 The court seeks to put claimants in the position they would have been in if the tort had not been committed.
2 Examples include loss of earnings, medical expenses, damage to clothing and expenses incurred by a carer.
3 Damages for loss of amenity compensate a person where an injury has caused him/her to be unable to enjoy life to the same extent as before. It may include an inability to enjoy sport or any other pastime the claimant enjoyed before the injury, impairment of sight, hearing, touch, taste or smell, reduction in the chance of finding a marriage partner, and impairment of sexual activity or enjoyment.
4 Yes.

Quick quiz 22.2

1 Under the Supreme Court Act 1981, provisional damages can be awarded where there is a possibility that the injured person will, as a result of the tort, develop a serious disease, or serious physical or mental deterioration in the future.
2 Under the Supreme Court Act 1981, interim damages can be awarded before trial, where the defendant admits liability, and is only contesting the amount of damages claimed. The defendant must also be insured, or be a public body, or have the resources to make an interim payment.
3 No, it is a matter for the parties to agree between themselves.
4 Set-offs include the tax that a person would have paid on an award for loss of earnings, sick pay and social security benefits.

Chapter 23 Offer and acceptance

Know your terms 23.1 answers

1 A *unilateral contract* exists when only one party assumes an obligation under the contract.
2 A *bilateral contract* exists when all the parties assume an obligation under the contract.
3 An *offeror* is the person who makes an offer to contract.
4 An *offeree* is the person who receives an offer to contract.

Quick quiz 23.2 answers

1 No.
2 A unilateral contract.
3 **Carlill** *v* **Carbolic Smoke Ball Co.** (1893).
4 No. An invitation to treat is part of the preliminary negotiations before an offer is made.

Quick quiz 23.3 answers

1 No.
2 An invitation to treat.
3 An invitation to treat.
4 The shelf display in a shop is merely an invitation to treat, an offer to contract is made when a customer puts goods in their shopping basket. This offer is accepted at the cash till.

Quick quiz 23.4 answers

1 The original offer will cease to exist.
2 The offer will still stand.
3 No, the acceptance is not unconditional and amounts in fact to a new offer which the woman can choose to accept or not.
4 Only if it is absolutely clear that an acceptance is intended.

Know your terms 23.5 answers

1 An *invitation to treat* is part of the preliminary stages of the contracting process, when one party invites another to make an offer.
2 If one person makes an offer and the receiver of that offer chooses to make an alternative offer, this is called a *counter-offer*.
3 The *'battle of the forms'* arises when one party presents a form stating that the contract is on their standard terms of business and the other party responds by returning their own form and stating that the contact is on their own terms.

Quick quiz 23.6 answers

1 Under the postal rule, an acceptance by a non-instantaneous mode of communication, including the post, takes effect when it is posted rather than when it is communicated.
2 You could have discussed two of the following:
   ■ offers requiring communication of acceptance;
   ■ when an acceptance is made by an instant mode of communication;
   ■ where a letter of acceptance is lost or delayed because the offeree has wrongly or incompletely addressed it through their own carelessness.
3 No. The advert was only an invitation to treat (see p. 000). Ann's e-mail was an offer.
4 No. The advert was an offer to enter into a unilateral contract, but Ann was not aware of this offer when she returned the cat, so her actions could not amount to an acceptance (see p. 483).

Chapter 24 Intention to create legal relations

Quick quiz 24.1

1 When there is a commercial agreement.
2 The parties do not intend to be legally bound until formal contracts are exchanged.
3 No, these statements amount to a 'mere puff'.
4 This is a commercial agreement, so the courts will presume that the parties intended to be legally bound by the agreement.

Know your terms 24.2

1 A *presumption* is where certain facts are assumed to exist in the absence of counter evidence.
2 An *honour clause* is a term of an agreement that the parties intend to rely on each other's good faith and honour rather than relying on the courts to enforce the agreement.
3 An *ambiguity* is where something is unclear.
4 A *collective bargaining agreement* arises where an employer negotiates terms of employment with the workforce as a whole (usually represented by a trade union), rather than on an individual basis.

Chapter 25 Consideration

Know your terms 25.1

1 *Consideration* is usually described as being something which represents either some benefit to the person making a promise or some detriment to the person to whom the promise is made, or both.
2 *Past consideration* has not been given in return for the promise or act of the other party.
3 The person to whom a promise is made is the *promisee*.
4 *Executory consideration* is where something is to be done in the future after the contract has been formed.

Quick quiz 25.2

1 No, because love is of no economic value.
2 Yes, because the chocolate brownies have some economic value.
3 Yes, it does not matter that the mother is not providing the £300, the two parties to the contract are providing consideration, consideration need not benefit the promisor.
4 If past consideration was provided at the promisor's request and it was understood that consideration would be provided, then there will be sufficient consideration for a binding contract.

Chapter 26 Breach of contract

Quick quiz 26.1

1 An anticipatory breach.
2 You can start legal proceedings on Monday.
3 An actual breach of the contract.
4 No.

Chapter 27 Compensatory damages

Know your terms 27.1

1 *Compensatory damages* are the award of money to compensate an innocent party for a loss they have suffered.
2 *A non-pecuniary loss* is a loss which is not of a financial nature, such as mental distress.
3 *Causation* is the existence of a causal link. In the context of contract law, causation arises where one contracting party has breached the contract causing a loss to be suffered by another contracting party.
4 *Mitigation* involves reducing one's loss. In the context of contract law, a contracting party is required to take reasonable steps to reduce the loss they have suffered from a breach of contract.

Quick quiz 27.2

1 No, as there does not appear to have been any breach of contract.
2 The award of damages should put the innocent part in the position they would have been in if the contract had been performed.
3 The loss of expectation and the reliance loss.
4 Under the market price rule, the buyer's damages will be assessed by subtracting the contract price from the market price of the relevant goods at the time of breach.

Index

Note: Items in bold denote Glossary terms.